P9-BAT-888

THE OXFORD
DICTIONARY OF
POPES

KEL ODOP
24.95

R
262.13
KEL

The
Oxford Dictionary
of
Popes

J. N. D. KELLY

Oxford   New York
OXFORD UNIVERSITY PRESS
1986

HUNTINGTON BEACH PUBLIC LIBRARY
7111 Talbert Avenue
Huntington Beach, CA 92648

M12314369

Oxford University Press, Walton Street, Oxford OX2 6DP
Oxford New York Toronto
Delhi Bombay Calcutta Madras Karachi
Kuala Lumpur Singapore Hong Kong Tokyo
Nairobi Dar es Salaam Cape Town
Melbourne Auckland
and associated companies in
Beirut Berlin Ibadan Nicosia

Oxford is a trade mark of Oxford University Press

© J. N. D. Kelly 1986

First published 1986

All rights reserved. No part of this publication may be reproduced,
stored in a retrieval system, or transmitted, in any form or by any means,
electronic, mechanical, photocopying, recording, or otherwise, without
the prior permission of Oxford University Press

British Library Cataloguing in Publication Data
Kelly, J. N. D.
The Oxford dictionary of popes.
1. Papacy—History
I. Title
262'.13'09   BX955.2
ISBN 0–19–213964–9

Library of Congress Cataloging in Publication Data
Kelly, J. N. D. (John Norman Davidson)
The Oxford dictionary of Popes.
Includes index.
1. Popes—Biography—Dictionaries. I. Title.
BX955.2.K45 1986   282'.092'2 [B]   85–15599
ISBN 0–19–213964–9

Set by Wyvern Typesetting Ltd, Bristol
Printed in Great Britain by
Richard Clay (The Chaucer Press) Ltd,
Bungay, Suffolk

To
Queen's College, Oxford, St Edmund Hall, Oxford,
and Chichester Cathedral,
with gratitude and affection

PREFACE

This book has been written to fill a gap of which I have been increasingly conscious for a great many years. My interest in the papacy came alive in the mid-thirties when, as part of my first piece of academic research, I began exploring the obscure emergence of one-man episcopacy at Rome. It steadily grew as the years went by, reaching a personal high point in March 1966, when I accompanied the archbishop of Canterbury (Michael Ramsey) on his historic visit to Pope Paul VI. Throughout this whole span I have been disconcerted by the fact that, while there are full-dress biographies of a number of popes (fewer in fact than one would expect) and massive surveys of the papacy at particular epochs, it is almost impossible to come across a one-volume handbook in English containing systematic, concise accounts of all those who have been, or claimed to be, popes. There seems to be a real need for such a papal Who's Who, not least in view of the extraordinary popular attention the papacy has increasingly attracted since at any rate the election of Pope John XXIII; and I therefore decided, perhaps rashly, to attempt to supply one.

My aim has been to provide summary biographies not only of the officially recognized popes but also (a novel feature, I believe) of those who have been classified, rightly or wrongly, as antipopes. The list of pontiffs and, with minor discrepancies, the dating of their reigns are in general agreement with the 1984 edition of *Annuario Pontificio*. I have endeavoured, where information is available, to include details of each pope's family background and pre-papal career as well as of his activities in office. Each entry is furnished with a bibliography which, while necessarily cut to the minimum, normally includes references to primary sources as well as to specialized and more general studies. My original plan was to arrange the popes, as is the habit of dictionary-makers, alphabetically, but the arguments of friends persuaded me that a chronological order would be more helpful, enabling readers to view each pope in his historical context; at the same time, the alphabetical list of popes and antipopes at the beginning makes quick reference to an individual just as easy.

I should like to think that the work, despite the high degree of compression inevitable, may prove useful to scholars as well as general readers. Covering such a vast field, it cannot lay claim to much originality, although I hope I have thrown fresh light on a few popes and presented some others in perhaps novel perspectives; my consistent object has been to portray them all with cool but not unsympathetic detachment. My reading over the past few years has been voluminous, multifarious, and exhilarating; while I could not mention all the scholars to whom I have been indebted, I must make an exception of Franz

Xaver Seppelt, whose five-volume *Geschichte der Päpste* is surely the best informed and most balanced of papal histories. I owe heartfelt thanks to many friends, in Oxford and elsewhere, who have helped me (often unwittingly) either with encouragement or with the solution of problems which puzzled me. I have enjoyed working with the Oxford University Press for the first time, and am particularly grateful to my sympathetic and cooperative editor, Nicholas Wilson, and to my eagle-eyed and healthily sceptical copy-editor, Ena Sheen. The book is dedicated to three corporate institutions to which I have belonged for most of my life and which have contributed greatly to my happiness.

All Saints, 1985. J. N. D. K.

CONTENTS

ABBREVIATIONS

AAB	*Abhandlungen der deutschen (preussischen* to 1944) *Akademie der Wissenschaften* (Berlin)
AAM	*Abhandlungen der Bayerischen Akademie der Wissenschaften* (Munich)
AAS	*Acta apostolicae sedis* (Rome, 1909–)
AASS	*Acta Sanctorum* (Antwerp, 1643 ff.; Venice, 1734 ff.; Paris, 1863 ff.)
ACO	*Acta conciliorum oecumenicorum* (ed. E. Schwartz, Berlin, 1914 ff.)
ADRomana	*Archivio della Deputazione Romana di Storia Patria* (Rome)
AFrH	*Archivum Franciscanum Historicum* (Florence)
ALKGMA	*Archiv für Literatur- und Kirchengeschichte des Mittelalters* (Freiburg i.Br.)
AnB	*Analecta Bollandiana* (Paris and Brussels)
AnGreg	*Analecta Gregoriana* (Rome)
ASRomana	*Archivio della Reale Società Romana di Storia Patria* (Rome)
ASS	*Acta sanctae sedis* (Rome, 1865–1908)
AstIt	*Archivio storico Italiano* (Florence)
Baluze-Mollat	S. Baluzius, *Vitae paparum Avenionensium* (ed. G. Mollat, Paris, 1914)
Bertolini	O. Bertolini, *Roma di fronte a Bisanzio e ai Langobardi* (Bologna, 1943)
Brezzi	P. Brezzi, *Roma e l'impero medioevale 774–1252* (Bologna, 1947)
BSS	*Bibliotheca Sanctorum* (Rome, 1961–70)
BullCang	*Bulletin du Cange* (Brussels)
BullInstHistRes	*Bulletin of the Institute of Historical Research* (Malta)
BullJRL	*Bulletin of the John Rylands Library* (Manchester)
Bullliteccl	*Bulletin de littérature ecclésiastique* (Toulouse)
BullRom	*Magnum bullarium Romanum*: Leo X to Benedict XIII (Rome, 1733–62)
BullRomCon	*Bullarii Romani continuatio* (Rome, 1835–57; Prato, 1840–56)
BVM	Blessed Virgin Mary
BZ	*Byzantinische Zeitschrift* (Leipzig)
Caspar	E. Caspar, *Geschichte des Papstums von den Anfängen bis zur Höhe der Weltherrschaft* (Tübingen, 1930–3)
CCL	*Corpus Christianorum*, series Latina (Turnhout, 1953–)
CE	*Catholic Encyclopedia* (New York, 1907–14)
ChHist	*Church History* (Philadelphia)
CHJ	*Cambridge Historical Journal* (Cambridge)
CHR	*Catholic Historical Review* (Washington)
CSEL	*Corpus scriptorum ecclesiasticorum Latinorum* (Vienna, 1866–)
DA	*Deutsches Archiv für Erforschung des Mittelalters* (Cologne and Graz)
DACL	*Dictionnaire d'archéologie chrétienne et de liturgie* (Paris)
DBI	*Dizionario biografico degli Italiani* (Rome, 1960–)
DCB	*Dictionary of Christian Biography* (London, 1877–87)
DHGE	*Dictionnaire d'histoire et de géographie ecclésiastiques* (Paris, 1912–)
DNB	*Dictionary of National Biography* (London, 1865–1900)
DSp	*Dictionnaire de spiritualité* (Paris, 1937–)
DTC	*Dictionnaire de théologie catholique* (Paris, 1903–50)
EB	*Encyclopaedia Britannica*

EC	*Enciclopedia cattolica* (Vatican City, 1949–54)
EHR	*English Historical Review* (London)
ELit	*Ephemerides liturgicae* (Rome)
ET	English translation
FD	F. Dölger, *Regesten der Kaiserurkunden des oströmischen Reiches von 565–1453* (Munich and Berlin, 1924–65)
FM	A. Fliche and V. Martin, *Histoire de l'église depuis les origines jusqu'à nos jours* (Paris, 1935 ff.)
Grumel	V. Grumel, *Les regestes des actes du patriarcat de Constantinople* (Kadikoi and Bucharest, 1932 ff.)
Haller	J. Haller, *Das Papstum* (Stuttgart, 1948–54)
HJ	*Historisches Jahrbuch* (Cologne and Munich)
HTR	*Harvard Theological Review* (Cambridge, Mass.)
HZ	*Historische Zeitschrift* (Munich)
JEH	*Journal of Ecclesiastical History* (London)
JR	J. Richards, *The Popes and the Papacy in the Early Middle Ages* (London, 1979)
JRS	*Journal of Roman Studies* (London)
JTS	*Journal of Theological Studies* (Oxford)
JW	P. Jaffé, *Regesta pontificum Romanorum ab condita ecclesia ad annum post Christum natum MCXCVIII*, 2nd edn. by G. Wattenbach (Leipzig, 1885–8; photo-repr. Graz, 1956)
Löwenfeld	S. Löwenfeld, *Epistolae pontificum Romanorum ineditae* (Leipzig, 1885)
LP	*Liber Pontificalis* (ed. L. Duchesne, Paris, 1886–92). A collection of papal biographies from St Peter to Pius II (d. 1464), compiled in its first redaction in the middle of the 6th cent. and extended by later hands. While much of the material embodied, especially in the earlier section, is apocryphal, the work is in the main based on valuable sources, and while it is often biased it is indispensable for the history of the papacy.
LPDert	J. P. March, *Liber Pontificalis completus ex codice Dertusensi* (Barcelona, 1925)
LThK	*Lexikon für Theologie und Kirche* (2nd edn., Freiburg, 1957–65)
MA	*Le Moyen-âge* (Paris and Brussels)
Mann	H. K. Mann, *The Lives of the Popes in the Early Middle Ages* (London, 1902–32)
Mansi	J. D. Mansi, *Sacrorum conciliorum nova et amplissima collectio* (Florence and Venice, 1759–98)
MC	M. Creighton, *A History of the Papacy from the Great Schism to the Sack of Rome* (London, 1897)
MelArchHist	*Mélanges d'archéologie et d'histoire* (Paris)
MG	*Monumenta Germaniae historica* (Berlin, 1826–)
AA	Auctores antiquissimi
Cap	Capitularia
Const	Constitutiones
Ep	Epistolae
Epsaec XIII	Epistolae saeculi XIII
Epsel	Epistolae selectae
Leges	Leges

Liblit	Libelli de lite
SS	Scriptores
MIÖG	*Mitteilungen des Instituts für österreichische Geschichtsforschung* (Graz and Cologne)
MiscHistPont	*Miscellanea historiae pontificiae* (Rome)
MS	*Medieval Studies* (Toronto)
Muratori; Muratori²	L. A. Muratori, *Rerum Italicarum scriptores ab anno 500 ad 1500* (Milan, 1723–71; 2nd ser. Città di Castello, 1900–)
NA	*Neues Archiv der Gesellschaft für ältere deutsche Geschichtskunde* (Hanover)
NCE	*New Catholic Encyclopedia* (New York, 1967)
NDB	*Neue Deutsche Biographie* (Berlin, 1953–)
NRT	*Nouvelle revue théologique* (Tournai, Louvain, Paris)
NS	New series
NT	New Testament
OChP	*Orientalia Christiana Periodica* (Rome)
ODCC	F. L. Cross and E. A. Livingstone (eds.), *The Oxford Dictionary of the Christian Church* (2nd edn. Oxford, 1974)
OT	Old Testament
P	L. Pastor, *The History of the Popes from the Close of the Middle Ages* (ET, London, 1891–1953)
PG	Migne's *Patrologia Graeca* (Paris, 1857–66)
PL	Migne's *Patrologia Latina* (Paris, 1844–64)
PLSupp	*Supplementum* to Migne's *Patrologia Latina* (Paris, 1958–74)
Potthast	A. Potthast, *Regesta pontificum Romanorum 1198–1304* (Berlin and Paris)
PRE	*Realencyklopädie für protestantische Theologie und Kirche* (Leipzig, 1898–1908)
ProceedBritAcad	*Proceedings of the British Academy* (London)
PW	A. Pauly, *Real-Encyklopädie der classischen Altertumswissenschaft*, ed. G. Wissowa *et al.* (Stuttgart, 1893–)
QFGG	*Quellen und Forschungen aus dem Gebiet der Geschichte* (Paderborn)
QFIAB	*Quellen und Forschungen aus Italienischen Archiven und Bibliotheken* (Rome)
RAC	*Reallexikon für Antike und Christentum* (Stuttgart, 1950–)
RaccCon	A. Mercati, *Raccolta di Concordati* (Rome, 1954)
RBén	*Revue Bénédictine* (Maredsous)
Revbelge	*Revue belge de philologie et d'histoire* (Brussels)
RevIntTheol	*Revue internationale de théologie* (Berne)
RevQuestHist	*Revue des questions historiques* (Paris)
RevSR	*Revue des sciences religieuses* (Paris and Strasbourg)
RH	*Revue historique* (Paris)
RHE	*Revue d'histoire ecclésiastique* (Louvain)
RQ	*Römische Quartalschrift für christliche Altertumskunde und für Kirchengeschichte* (Freiburg i.B.)
RSR	*Recherches de science religieuse* (Paris)
RSTI	*Rivista di storia della chiesa in Italia* (Rome)
RTAM	*Recherches de théologie ancienne et médiévale* (Louvain)
SAB	*Sitzungsberichte der deutschen (preussischen to 1944) Akademie der Wissenschaften zu Berlin*

SAM	*Sitzungsberichte der Bayerischen Akademie der Wissenschaften* (Munich)
SBHeid	*Sitzungsberichte der Heidelberger Akademie der Wissenschaften*
SC	*Sources chrétiennes* (Paris, 1940–)
Schmidlin	J. Schmidlin, *Papstgeschichte der neuesten Zeit* (Munich, 1933–9)
Seppelt	F. X. Seppelt, *Geschichte der Päpste* (Munich, 1954–9)
ST	*Studi e Testi* (Rome)
StGreg	*Studia Gregoriana* (Rome)
Thiel	A. Thiel, *Epistolae Romanorum pontificum genuinae a S. Hilaro usque ad Pelagium II* (Brunswick, 1858)
TRE	*Theologische Realenzyklopädie* (Berlin and New York, 1976–)
TU	*Texte und Untersuchungen zur Geschichte der altchristlichen Literatur* (Leipzig and Berlin)
VC	*Vigiliae Christianae* (Amsterdam)
Watterich	I. M. Watterich, *Pontificum Romanorum . . . ab exeunte saeculo ix usque ad finem saeculi xiii Vitae ab aequalibus conscriptae* (Leipzig, 1862)
Z1	H. Zimmermann, *Papstabsetzungen des Mittelalters* (Graz, Vienna, Cologne, 1968)
Z2	H. Zimmermann, *Das dunkle Jahrhundert* (Graz, Vienna, Cologne, 1971)
ZKG	*Zeitschrift für Kirchengeschichte* (Stuttgart)
ZKTh	*Zeitschrift für Katholische Theologie* (Vienna)
ZNTW	*Zeitschrift für die neutestamentliche Wissenschaft* (Giessen and Berlin)
ZPR	H. Zimmermann, *Papstregesten 911–1024* (in J. F. Böhmer's *Regesta Imperii*: Vienna, Cologne, Graz, 1969)
*ZSavRG*Kan	*Zeitschrift der Savigny-Stiftung für Rechtsgeschichte*, Kanonische Abteilung (Weimar)

NOTE TO THE READER

The dates given in brackets after the names of prelates, monarchs, or other personages generally refer to their tenure of office, but sometimes to their life-span, or to the year of their death; the context should make it clear which is intended.

The feast-days of popes considered saints are generally the traditional ones, but they have been adjusted where appropriate to conform to the changes introduced into the church's general calendar in 1969.

Cross-references to another entry within the text are indicated by the use of small capitals. Asterisks refer the reader to the index; an explanation of the word or phrase asterisked will be found on the page whose number is printed there in italics.

As they have their separate entries, popes and antipopes appear only exceptionally in the index, although their original names, or family names where these are known, are listed there as a general rule.

The enumeration of general or ecumenical councils is that accepted in the Roman Catholic church; in the view of most other Christian communions there has been no general council since the schism between east and west, the Second Council of Nicaea (787) being the last.

ALPHABETICAL LIST OF POPES
AND ANTIPOPES

(names of antipopes in italics; page numbers in bold)

Siricius (384–99)	35	Urban I (222–30)	15
Sisinnius (708)	85	Urban II (1088–99)	158
Sixtus I (c.116–c.125)	9	Urban III (1185–7)	181
Sixtus II (257–8)	21	Urban IV (1261–4)	194
Sixtus (or Xystus) III (432–40)	42	Urban V (1362–70)	223
Sixtus IV (1471–84)	250	Urban VI (1378–89)	227
Sixtus V (1585–90)	271	Urban VII (1590)	273
Soter (c.166–c.174)	11	Urban VIII (1623–44)	280
Stephen I (254–7)	20	*Ursinus* (366–7)	34
Stephen (II) (752)	90		
Stephen II (III) (752–7)	91		
Stephen III (IV) (768–72)	95	Valentine (827)	102
Stephen IV (V) (816–17)	99	Victor I (189–98)	12
Stephen V (VI) (885–91)	113	Victor II (1055–7)	148
Stephen VI (VII) (896–7)	115	Victor III (1086–7)	157
Stephen VII (VIII) (928–31)	122	*Victor IV* (1138)	170
Stephen VIII (IX) (939–42)	124	*Victor IV*[1] (1159–64)	177
Stephen IX (X) (1057–8)	149	Vigilius (537–55)	60
Symmachus (498–514)	50	Vitalian (657–72)	75
Telesphorus (c.125–c.136)	9	Xystus, *see* Sixtus	
Theodore I (642–9)	73		
Theodore (687)	81	Zacharias (741–52)	89
Theodore II (897)	116	Zephyrinus (198/9–217)	12
Theoderic (1100–1)	161	Zosimus (417–18)	38

[1] As *Annuario Pontificio* (1984) notes, he should have been *Victor V*, but no account was taken of the previous antipope so styled, perhaps because his resistance was short-lived and he spontaneously submitted.

THE POPES

PETER, ST, APOSTLE (d. *c.*64). The papacy, through successive popes and councils, has always traced its origins and title-deeds to the unique commission reported to have been given by Jesus Christ to Peter, the chief of his Apostles, later to be martyred when organizing the earliest group of Christians at Rome. Information about Peter's career, personality, and standing in the primitive Christian community is provided by the NT, supplemented by ancient, reliable tradition. The NT accounts come from a variety of sources, originating at widely differing dates and coloured by the often divergent viewpoints of their authors, but the picture of the Apostle which emerges from them is consistent and lifelike.

Originally named Symeon, or Simon in Greek, he was a native of Bethsaida, a village on the Sea of Galilee, son of Jonas (Matt. 16: 17), and with his brother Andrew was a fisherman. When Jesus began his mission Simon was married and living at Capernaum with his mother-in-law and Andrew (Mark 1: 29 f.). According to the Synoptic Gospels, it was by the Sea of Galilee that Jesus summoned the two brothers, with James and John, to follow him. St John's Gospel, which places the call in Judaea (1: 37 ff.), represents the earliest disciples, including Simon, as having previously been disciples of John the Baptist. All four Gospels agree, with minor differences of emphasis, that from now onwards Simon was leader and spokesman of the group, recognized as such by the Lord. He is mentioned with conspicuous frequency, appears first in all lists of the Twelve, and belonged to the inner group present at such significant events as the raising of Jairus's daughter (Matt. 9: 18–26), the Transfiguration (Matt. 17: 1–8), and the Agony in the Garden (Matt. 26: 37). According to Matt. 16: 13–20, when Jesus asked the disciples whom they took him to be, Simon answered for them all that he was the Messiah, the Son of the living God; in reply Jesus pronounced him blessed because of this inspired insight, bestowed on him the Aramaic name Cephas (= 'rock'), rendered Peter in Greek, and declared that he would build his indestructible church on 'this rock', and would give him 'the keys of the kingdom of heaven' and the powers of 'binding and loosing'. At the Last Supper Jesus charged him to strengthen his brothers (Luke 22: 32). Warm-hearted and impetuous, he was rebuked by Jesus because, after confessing his messiahship, he refused to accept the necessity of his rejection and death (Mark 8: 31–3, etc.); when Jesus was arrested his courage failed, and he thrice denied knowing him (Matt. 26: 69–75, etc.). Nevertheless he was the first disciple to enter the empty tomb (Luke 24: 12), and the first to whom the risen Lord showed himself (Luke 24: 34; 1 Cor. 15: 5). In a later appearance, recorded only by St John (21: 15–17), Peter three times received from the Lord the pastoral charge to feed, i.e. be shepherd of, his sheep.

The first half of Acts discloses that after the Ascension, though his relationship to James, the Lord's brother, remains unclear, Peter was the undisputed leader of the youthful church. It was he who presided over the choice of a successor to Judas (1: 15–26), who explained to the crowd the meaning of Pentecost (2: 14–40), who healed the lame beggar at the Temple (3: 1–10), who pronounced sentence on Ananias and Sapphira (5: 1–11), and who opened the church to Gentiles by having Cornelius baptized without undergoing circumcision (10: 9–48). He was to the fore in preaching, defending the new movement, working miracles of healing, and visiting newly established Christian communities. Arrested by Herod Agrippa I, he was mir-

5

aculously released from prison (12: 1–17); at the council of Jerusalem he successfully championed a liberal policy towards Gentiles (15: 7–11). It was from Peter that Paul sought information about Jesus after his conversion (Gal. 1: 18); and although he felt obliged to rebuke Peter at Antioch (Gal. 2: 11–14), the context suggests the respect in which Paul held him. Although Paul describes his ministry as directed to Jews (Gal. 2: 7 f.), Peter was also prominent as a missionary in largely Gentile areas like Corinth (1 Cor. 1: 12) and Asia Minor (1 Pet. 1: 1). Early tradition, perhaps relying on the visit mentioned in Gal. 2: 11–14, connected him with Antioch, claiming him as its first bishop.

It seems certain that Peter spent his closing years in Rome. Although the NT appears silent about such a stay, it is supported by 1 Pet. 5: 13, where 'Babylon' is a code-name for Rome, and by the strong case for linking the Gospel of Mark, who as Peter's companion (1 Pet. 5: 13) is said to have derived its substance from him, with Rome. To early writers like Clement of Rome (c.95), Ignatius of Antioch (d. c.107), and Irenaeus (c.180) it was common knowledge that he worked and died in Rome. Nothing is known of the length of his residence: the story that it lasted twenty-five years is a 3rd-cent. legend. Ignatius assumed that Peter and Paul wielded special authority over the Roman church, while Irenaeus claimed that they jointly founded it and inaugurated its succession of bishops. Nothing, however, is known of their constitutional roles, least of all of Peter's as presumed leader of the community. They were both executed, according to the historian Eusebius (c.260–c.340), in Nero's reign (54–68), probably in the persecution of 64. Tertullian (c.160–c.225) reports that Peter was crucified, a fact already known to the fourth Gospel (John 21: 18 f.). In the 2nd and 3rd cents. two sites competed for his burial place, the 'Memorial of the Apostles' beneath S. Sebastiano on the Appian Way, and the tomb on the Vatican Hill referred to c.200 by the Roman presbyter

Gaius. The latter finally prevailed, and extensive excavations carried out in 1939–49 resulted in the discovery, not of the Apostle's actual bones (as claimed by PAUL VI on 26 June 1965), but of the spot believed in the 2nd cent. to be his resting place.

In the late 2nd or early 3rd cent. the tradition identified Peter as the first bishop of Rome. This was a natural development once the monarchical episcopate, i.e. government of the local church by a single bishop as distinct from a group of presbyter-bishops, finally emerged in Rome in the mid-2nd cent. The earlier tradition, however, which placed Peter and Paul in a class apart as the pioneers who together established the Roman church and its ministry, was never lost sight of. Two epistles are attributed to Peter in the NT; the first has a strong claim to derive from him, directly or indirectly, but the second is pseudonymous. In addition a mass of literature connected with his name, notably the Apocalypse of St Peter, the Acts of St Peter, and the Gospel of St Peter, sprang up in the 2nd cent., but while full of interest and attesting the Apostle's prestige in the early church, it is all entirely apocryphal. Feast with St Paul 29 June.

1 Clement 5 f.; Ignatius, Rom. 4, 2; Irenaeus, Adv. haer. 3, 1, 2 f.; 3, 3, 3; Tertullian, De praescr. 36; Scorpiace 15; Eusebius, Hist. eccl. 2, 25, 5–8; 3, 39, 15; C. H. Turner, 'St Peter in the New Testament', Catholic and Apostolic (London, 1931); O. Cullmann, Peter, Disciple, Apostle, Martyr (ET, 2nd edn., London, 1962); R. E. Brown and others, Peter in the New Testament (New York, 1973); R. Pesch, Simon-Petrus: Geschichte und geschichtliche Bedeutung (Stuttgart, 1980); Seppelt 1, 11–16; D. W. O'Connor, Peter in Rome (New York and London, 1969); J. Toynbee and J. Ward Perkins, The Shrine of St Peter and the Vatican Excavations (2nd edn., London, 1958).

LINUS, ST (c.66–c.78). According to the earliest succession lists of bishops of Rome, passed down by Irenaeus of Lyons (c.180) and Hegesippus (c.160) and attested by the historian Eusebius (c.260–c.340), he was entrusted with his office by the Apostles

PETER and Paul after they had established the Christian church in Rome. By this primitive reckoning he was therefore the first pope, but from the late 2nd or early 3rd cent. the convention began of regarding St Peter as first bishop. What Linus's actual functions and responsibilities were can only be guessed, for the *monarchical, or one-man, episcopate had not yet emerged in Rome. Irenaeus and Eusebius identified him with the Linus who, as a companion of St Paul, sent greetings from Rome to Timothy in Ephesus (2 Tim. 4: 21). The early sources agree that he held office for about twelve years, but differ about dates, which must remain approximate. His name occurs after those of the two Apostles in the ancient canon of the mass. The tradition that he died a martyr and was buried close to St Peter is legendary. While his existence and leading position in the Roman church need not be doubted, it is impossible, in view of the late development of the monarchical episcopate at Rome, to form any clear idea of his role and functions.

Irenaeus, *Adv. haer.* 3, 3, 2; Eusebius, *Hist. eccl.* 3, 2; 3, 4, 8; 3, 21; 5, 6, 1; *LP* 1, xc f., cii; 121; Caspar 1, 11–14; *DCB* 3, 726–9 (J. Barmby and G. Salmon); *DTC* 9, 772 (É. Amann); *BSS* 8, 56 f. (A. Amore); E. Caspar, *Die älteste römische Bischofsliste* (Berlin, 1926).

ANACLETUS, ST (c. 79–c. 91). In the earliest *succession lists of bishops of Rome he follows LINUS, second in the line inaugurated by the Apostles PETER and Paul. Later convention reckons him the third pope from St Peter. His actual functions and responsibilities can only be surmised, for the *monarchical, or one-man, episcopate had not yet emerged in Rome. His name, correctly given as Anencletus, is a Greek adjective meaning 'blameless'; the fact that St Paul required a bishop to be 'blameless' (Tit. 1: 7) has needlessly caused some to doubt his existence. The term was a not uncommon name for a slave, and this may give a clue to his social origins. Later lists, such as the 4th-cent. Liberian Catalogue and *LP*, mistakenly distinguish two

popes, Cletus and Anacletus, but Cletus was merely a shortened form of the full name. He is commemorated, as Cletus, in the ancient canon of the mass. Eusebius states that he died in the twelfth year of Emperor Domitian's reign (81–96). In view of his name there may be substance in *LP*'s report that he was a Greek in origin; but the tradition that he appointed twenty-five presbyters for Rome, erected a monument over St Peter's burial place, and himself died a martyr is without foundation. While his existence and leading position need not be doubted, the fact that the monarchical episcopate had not yet emerged at Rome makes it impossible to form any clear conception of his role.

Irenaeus, *Adv. haer.* 3, 3, 2; Eusebius, *Hist. eccl.* 3, 13; 3, 15; 3, 21; 5, 6, 2; *LP* 1, xix f., 52 f.; 125; E. Caspar, *Die älteste römische Bischofsliste* (Berlin, 1926); Caspar 1, 8–15; *DHGE* 2, 1407 f. (J. P. Kirsch); *EC* 1, 1126 (P. Goggi); *BSS* 1, 1032–6 (F. Cavatta); *NCE* 1, 460 (E. G. Weltin).

CLEMENT I, ST (c. 91–c. 101). In the 2nd-cent. *succession lists of bishops of Rome he follows ANACLETUS, being therefore third in the line inaugurated by the Apostles PETER and Paul; later convention reckoned him fourth pope in the line beginning with St Peter. Another tradition, attested by Tertullian (c. 160–c. 225) and Jerome (331–420), regarded him as having been consecrated by St Peter and as his immediate successor. Irenaeus (c. 180) states that, having seen and conversed with the Apostles, Clement was a repository of their teaching and tradition. Writers of the 3rd and 4th cents., like Origen, Eusebius, and Jerome, equate him, perhaps correctly, with the Clement whom St Paul mentions (Phil. 4: 3) as a fellow-worker. It is also possible, notwithstanding apparent difficulties of dates, that he was the Clement described by the 2nd-cent. writer Hermas as official correspondent of the Roman church. On the other hand, there is no reason for identifying him, as later legends do, with the consul Titus Flavius Clemens, a cousin of Emperor Domitian (81–96), who was executed in 95/96 for atheism, i.e. for adopting Jewish customs, although he may conceivably have been a freedman in Clemens's household. The claim that he died a martyr, supported by *LP* and the canon of the mass, should be rejected in view of the silence of the earliest authorities; the story, too, that he was banished to the Crimea, successfully preached the gospel there, and was killed by being drowned with an anchor round his neck, is without foundation. Almost the only reliable information that survives about him is that he was responsible for, probably author of, the so-called *First Epistle of Clement*, the most important 1st-cent. Christian document outside the NT. It was a letter of remonstrance addressed c.96 to the church at Corinth (where fierce dissensions had broken out and some presbyters had been deposed) which Clement probably drafted as the leading presbyter–bishop. After setting out the principle on which the orderly succession of bishops and deacons rests and tracing it back to Jesus Christ, it called for the reinstatement of the extruded presbyters. The letter is the earliest example of the intervention, fraternal but authoritative, of the Roman church, though not of the pope personally, in the affairs of another church. Widely read in Christian antiquity, it was sometimes treated as part of the NT canon.

While Clement's position as a leading presbyter and spokesman of the Christian community at Rome is assured, his letter suggests that the *monarchical episcopate had not yet emerged there, and it is therefore impossible to form any precise conception of his constitutional role. He enjoyed, however, such prestige in the early church that he was credited with the authorship of numerous spurious writings. Chief among these were the *Second Epistle of Clement*, a 2nd-cent. homily by an unknown hand, and the legendary 3rd-cent. *Clementine Homilies* and *Recognitions*. He was also believed to have been responsible for the *Apostolic Constitutions*, a late 4th-cent. collection of ecclesiastical law. The tradition, however, that the church of S. Clemente, Rome,

stands on the site of his house should not be lightly dismissed. Feast 23 Nov. in the west, 24 or 25 Nov. in the east.

W. K. Lowther Clarke, *The First Epistle of Clement* (London, 1937); K. Bihlmeyer, *Die Apostolische Väter* I (crit. edn., Tübingen, 1956); Eusebius, *Hist. eccl.* 3, 4, 9; 3, 15; 3, 21; 5, 6, 2 f.; 6, 25, 14; *LP* 1, xci; 123 f.; Jerome, *De vir. ill.* 15; Caspar 1, 2–7; *DHGE* 12, 1089–93 (G. Bardy); *RAC* 3, 188–97 (A. Stuiber); *NCE* 3, 926–8 (H. Dressler); Seppelt 1, 22–4.

EVARISTUS, ST (*c.*100–*c.*109). In the earliest *succession lists of bishops of Rome he is placed after ANACLETUS and CLEMENT I, fourth in the line inaugurated by the Apostles PETER and Paul. Another tradition, attested by *LP*, assigned him the same position but arranged his predecessors in the order Clement and Anacletus. The early sources differ about the length of his reign, Eusebius giving it as either eight or nine years, *LP* just under ten, and the 4th-cent. Liberian Catalogue (which names him Aristus) thirteen years and ten months; all these figures are guesses. His name suggests Greek origin, as *LP* states, but the other information it provides (that his father was a Jew from Bethlehem, that he divided the Roman parishes among his presbyters, and that he instituted seven deacons to escort the bishop) is historically valueless. In particular, its claims that he died a martyr and was buried near St Peter should be rejected. Two letters and two fragments of decretals circulating under his name are apocryphal. While there is no reason to doubt that he held a leading position in the Roman church, nothing is in fact reliably known about him, and in view of the late development of the *monarchical episcopate at Rome his role as a church leader there can only be surmised. Feast 26 Oct.

Irenaeus, *Adv. haer.* 3, 3, 3; Eusebius, *Hist. eccl.* 3, 34; 4, 1; 5, 6, 4; *Chron.* (Helm, p. 193); *LP* 1, xc–xci; 126; Caspar 1, 8; 13; 53; *DCB* 2, 426 (J. Bryce); *DHGE* 16, 111 (B. Botte); *LThK* 3, 1260 (J. P. Kirsch); *NCE* 5, 655 (E. G. Weltin).

ALEXANDER I, ST (*c.*109–*c.*116). In the earliest *succession lists of bishops of Rome he stands fifth in the line inaugurated by the Apostles PETER and Paul; later convention reckoned him the sixth pope from St Peter. The early sources differ about the length of his reign; the figures they give, which vary from seven to ten years, are clearly guesses. *LP* reports that he was a Roman, the son of a man also called Alexander. It attributes to him, with transparent anachronism, the insertion of the narrative of the institution of the Last Supper into the mass and the introduction of the practice of blessing houses with water mixed with salt. The Roman tradition, which it reproduces, that he died a martyr, being beheaded on the Via Nomentana leading north-east out of Rome, resulted from confusing him with an actual martyr bearing the same name whose tomb was discovered on the Via in 1855. In view of the silence of early authorities it is highly improbable that he was martyred. Virtually nothing is reliably known about him except that he held a leading position in the Roman church, and in view of the late emergence of the *monarchical episcopate at Rome his constitutional position as leader of the community remains obscure. Feast 3 May.

Irenaeus, *Adv. haer.* 3, 3, 3; Eusebius, *Hist. eccl.* 4, 1; 4, 4; 5, 6, 4; *LP* 1, lxxxix–xcii; 54 f.; 127; Caspar 1, 8–16; *DHGE* 2, 204–6 (A. Dufourcq); *EC* 1, 787 (P. Goggi); *BSS* 1, 792–8 (E. Josi); *NCE* 1, 288 (E. G. Weltin).

SIXTUS I, ST (*c.*116–*c.*125). In the earliest *succession lists Sixtus or (more correctly) Xystus was sixth bishop of Rome in the line inaugurated by the Apostles PETER and Paul. The later convention which reckoned St Peter the first pope counted him the seventh. The dates of his reign are quite uncertain, but the early sources agree that it lasted about ten years. *LP* states that he was a Roman, the son of one Pastor; his name in its original form suggests Greek extraction. Nothing is known of his activities, the details supplied by *LP* about his supposed disciplinary and liturgical innovations being transparently anachronistic. Later tradition represented him as a martyr, and he is

commemorated with the apostles and martyrs in the ancient canon of the mass; but the fact that Irenaeus, in his list of early Roman bishops, singles out only TELESPHORUS as having been one implies that Sixtus was not. *LP*'s further report that he was buried near St Peter on the Vatican Hill has no foundation, and, as with other leaders of the Roman church in this period, no clear conception can be formed of his role in its government. Feast 3 Apr.

Irenaeus, *Adv. haer.* 3, 3, 3; Eusebius, *Hist. eccl.* 4, 4, 1; 4, 5, 1; 5, 6, 4; *LP* 1, ccviii; 54–7; 128; Caspar 1, 8–16; *DCB* 4 (J. Barmby); *DTC* 14, 2193 f. (É. Amann); *BSS* 11, 1254–6 (M. da Alatri); *NCE* 13, 271 (E. G. Weltin).

TELESPHORUS, ST (*c.*125–*c.*136). In the earliest *succession lists of bishops of Rome he was seventh in the line inaugurated by the Apostles PETER and Paul. The later convention which reckoned St Peter the first pope counted him the eighth. While the dates of his reign are uncertain, the early sources agree that it lasted eleven years. *LP* states that he was a Greek, as his name confirms; it anachronistically adds that he had previously been an anchorite. It further represents him as instituting practices (e.g. a seven-week fast before Easter, and the use of *Gloria in excelsis* in the Christmas midnight mass) which were introduced some centuries later. More reliance can be placed on the report of Irenaeus (*c.*180) that he 'bore witness gloriously', i.e. suffered martyrdom. Eusebius (*c.*260–*c.*340) states that he was put to death in the first year of Emperor Antoninus Pius (138/9), but the closing years of Emperor Hadrian (117–38) offer a more probable date. In any case, he is the only 2nd-cent. pope whose martyrdom is reliably attested. As with other popes of this period when the *monarchical episcopate was slowly emerging at Rome, it is impossible to form any clear picture of his constitutional role. Feast 5 Jan.

Irenaeus, *Adv. haer.* 3, 3, 3; Eusebius, *Hist. eccl.* 4, 5, 5; 4, 10; 5, 6, 4; 5, 24, 14; *LP* 1, 56; 129 f.; Caspar 1, 21; 34; 48; *DCB* 4, 816 (J. Barmby); *DTC* 15, 82 (É. Amann); *LThK* 9, 1347 (A. Amore); *NCE* 13, 982 (E. G. Weltin).

HYGINUS, ST (c.138–c.142). In the earliest *succession lists of bishops of Rome he was eighth in the line inaugurated by the Apostles PETER and Paul. The later convention which reckoned St Peter the first pope counted him the ninth. Estimates vary of the length of his reign, the 4th-cent. Liberian Catalogue giving it as twelve years, but Eusebius (c.260–c.340) and *LP* more plausibly as four. According to *LP* he was a Greek from Athens who had previously been a philosopher; the career of his contemporary Justin Martyr (c.100–c.165), who came to Rome from the east and was a philosopher and Christian apologist, suggests that the latter detail should not be dismissed lightly. On the other hand, *LP*'s further claims that he reorganized his clergy on a hierarchical basis and was buried near St Peter are worthless. More significant, as indicative of the intellectual climate of the Roman church when he was bishop, is the report of Irenaeus (c.180) that during his reign the Gnostic teachers Valentinus and Cerdo came to Rome from Egypt and Syria respectively. Although he came to be venerated as a martyr, there is no evidence that he was one. While the *monarchical episcopate was beginning to emerge at Rome at this time, it is nevertheless difficult to picture his role in the government of the community. Feast 11 Jan.

Irenaeus, *Adv. haer.* 3, 3, 3; 3, 4, 2; Eusebius, *Hist. eccl.* 4, 10; 4, 11, 1 f.; 4, 11, 6; 5, 6, 4; *LP* 1, 131; Caspar 1, 8; 13; 21; 48; *DCB* 3, 184 (J. Barmby); *DTC* 7, 356 f. (É. Amann); *LThK* 5, 555 f. (R. H. Haacke); *BSS* 7, 652 (A. Amore); *NCE* 7, 282 (E. G. Weltin).

PIUS I, ST (c.142–c.155). Ninth in the earliest *succession lists of bishops of Rome, he was reckoned the tenth pope by the later convention which counted St PETER the first. The early sources are confused about his dates, some mistakenly placing him after his successor ANICETUS. *LP* reports that he was an Italian from Aquileia, son of Rufinus. The later 2nd-cent. Muratorian Canon, the oldest extant canon of NT writings and itself of Roman origin, states that he was the brother of Hermas, a former slave, author of the widely popular visionary summons to repentance known as *The Shepherd*. This latter work contains hints of disputes about rank among church leaders which suggest that the *monarchical episcopate was now a reality at Rome. Nothing is known directly of Pius's activities, but during his reign the leading Gnostics Valentinus and Cerdo, as well as Marcion of Pontus, who had arrived c.140 and rejected the OT, contrasting its God unfavourably with the God revealed by Jesus, were working out and disseminating their systems at Rome. Pius must have presided over the synod of presbyters which expelled Marcion from the orthodox community in July 144. He must also have known the Christian philosopher and apologist Justin (d. c.165), who was teaching in a house in Rome at this time. Pius is first mentioned as a martyr in the martyrology of Ado of Vienne (compiled 858), but there is no reason to suppose that he was one. Feast 11 July.

Muratorian Fragment, ll.74–7; Irenaeus, *Adv. haer.* 3, 3, 3; 3, 4, 3; Eusebius, *Hist. eccl.* 4, 11, 1 and 6 f.; 5, 6, 4; *LP* 1, lxxiii; 132 f.; Caspar 1, 8; 13; 21; *DCB* 4, 416 f. (J. Barmby); *DTC* 12, 1612 f. (É. Amann); *LThK* 8, 528 (G. Schwaiger); *NCE* 11, 393 (E. G. Weltin).

ANICETUS, ST (c.155–c.166). Tenth in the earliest *succession lists of bishops of Rome, he was reckoned the eleventh pope by the later convention which counted St PETER as the first. *LP* reports that he was a Syrian from Emesa (Homs), and Eusebius (c.260–c.340) that he reigned eleven years. Soon after his accession he received a visit from Polycarp, the octogenarian bishop of Smyrna, who, after they had reached agreement on other issues, tried to persuade him to adopt the practice of the churches of Asia Minor of observing Easter on the 14th of the Jewish month Nisan (the day of the Passover)—the so-called Quartodeciman date. At this time the Roman church did not have a special Easter festival, and Anicetus was able to plead that he felt obliged to abide by his predecessors' custom of celebrating the Lord's resurrection every Sunday. The two bishops remained in amicable fellowship, and Anicetus invited Polycarp to preside at mass. Although nothing else is known directly of his activities, he must have had contact with the scholar Hegesippus, author of anti-Gnostic works, who came to Rome about this time, and with the apologist Justin, who was martyred at Rome c. 165. It was probably Anicetus, not ANACLETUS as *LP* states, who erected the memorial shrine for St Peter on the Vatican Hill which was familiar to visitors c. 200 and which was revealed by the 1939–49 excavations. The tradition that he died a martyr lacks confirmation. Feast 17 Apr.

Irenaeus, *Adv. haer.* 3, 3, 3 f.; 3, 4, 2; Eusebius, *Hist. eccl.* 4, 11, 7; 4, 19; 5, 24, 14–17; *LP* 1, lxxi; 134; Caspar 1, 8 f.; 13; 21; 35; 47 f.; 52; M. Richard, 'La question pascale au iie siècle', *L'Orient Syrien* 6 (1961), 179–212; 'La lettre de s. Irénée au pape Victor', *ZNTW* 56 (1965), 260–82; *DHGE* 3, 280 f. (J. P. Kirsch); *LThK* 1, 562 (G. Schwaiger); *NCE* 1, 544 (E. G. Weltin).

SOTER, ST (c. 166–c. 174). Eleventh in the earliest *succession lists of bishops of Rome, he was reckoned the twelfth pope by the later convention which counted St PETER as the first. *LP* reports that he was an Italian, from Campania; the early authorities vary about his exact dates. At some stage he dispatched a letter, with charitable gifts, to the Corinthian church, and Eusebius (c. 260–c. 340) has preserved fragments of an effusive acknowledgement from Dionysius, bishop of Corinth, promising that Soter's letter would be regularly read at service at Corinth. Other letters of Dionysius have led scholars to suspect that Soter may have expressed disapproval of his lax attitude both to the ideal of sexual continence and to the restoration of penitent sinners to communion irrespective of the kind of sins they had committed, and that his obsequious reply may be an attempt to soothe the pope without yielding any point of principle. An event of great importance which seems to have occurred at Rome under Soter was the

introduction of Easter as an annual festival. It had not existed there previously, and the date now accepted, in contrast to the *Quartodeciman practice of the churches of Asia Minor, was the Sunday following the 14th of the Jewish month Nisan (the day of the Passover). Reports were circulating in the 5th cent. that Soter wrote critically of Montanism, the apocalyptic and ascetic movement started in Phrygia by the prophet Montanus, but they should be rejected. Although he came to be venerated as a martyr, there is no evidence that he was one. Feast 22 Apr.

Irenaeus, 3, 3, 3; Eusebius, *Hist. eccl.* 4, 19; 4, 23, 9–11; 4, 30, 3; 5, 24, 14–17; *LP* 1, 4 f.; 58 f.; 135; Caspar 1, 3; 8 f.; 13; 18; 21; 48; P. Nautin, *Lettres et écrivains chrétiens au iie et iiie siècles* (Paris, 1961), chap. 1; K. Holl, *Gesammelte Aufsätze* (Tübingen, 1927–8) 2, 214–19; M. Richard, 'La question pascale au iie siècle', *L'Orient Syrien* 6 (1961), 179–212; 'La lettre de s. Irénée au pape Victor', *ZNTW* 56 (1965), 260–82; *DTC* 14, 2422 f. (É. Amann); *NCE* 13, 444 (E. G. Weltin).

ELEUTHERIUS, or ELEUTHERUS, ST (c. 174 89). Last in the *succession list of bishops of Rome transmitted by Irenaeus (c. 180), he was twelfth in the line inaugurated by the Apostles PETER and Paul, thirteenth pope by the convention which reckoned St Peter the first. According to *LP* he was a Greek from Nicopolis, in Epirus, and reigned fifteen years and three months; Hegesippus, who was in Rome in the 160s, records that he was deacon to Pope ANICETUS. *LP* adds that a British king, Lucius, wrote to him asking to be made a Christian. This enigmatic story, which was taken up by Bede and later chroniclers, has been shown to rest on a confusion with Agbar IX, also named Lucius, king of Edessa (Urfa in Turkey) in northern Mesopotamia, who was later converted and may have sent enquiries to the pope. In 177/8 Eleutherius received a visit from Irenaeus of Lyons, bringing a letter from the church there, then suffering grievous persecution, setting out its views on *Montanism, the 'New Prophecy' recently started in Phrygia and now the subject of intense discussion. The pope's attitude to it remains unclear, but he evidently did not regard it as a danger and passed no judgement on its prophetic claims. His reign was a peaceful one, and while the sources differ about the date of his accession, it seems that he died in the tenth year of Emperor Commodus (180–92), i.e. 189. He is first mentioned as a martyr in the Martyrology of Ado of Vienne (compiled in 858). Feast 26 May.

Irenaeus, *Adv. haer.* 3, 3, 3; Eusebius, *Hist. eccl.* 4, 22, 3 (Hegesippus); 5, 3, 4; 5, 22; *LP* 1, cii–civ; 136; A. Harnack, 'Der Brief des britischen Königs Lucius an den Papst Eleutherus', *SAB* 1904, 909–16; *DHGE* 15, 147 f. (B. Botte); *LThK* 3, 802 (J. P. Kirsch); *NCE* 5, 265 (E. G. Weltin).

VICTOR I, ST (189–98). An African by birth and the first Latin pope, he may have advanced the Latinization of the Roman church, hitherto overshadowed by Graeco-Oriental influences. He was certainly the most forceful of the 2nd-cent. popes. Early in his reign, in the interests of uniformity but also probably provoked by the propaganda of an easterner named Blastus in favour of the *Quartodeciman date for keeping Easter, he exerted himself to bring other churches into line with the Roman practice of celebrating it on the Sunday following the 14th of the Jewish month Nisan (Passover day). At his instigation synods were held both at Rome and at other centres from Gaul to Mesopotamia, and majority opinion sided with him. The churches of Asia Minor, however, refused to abandon the age-old Quartodeciman custom of observing Easter on the 14th Nisan, whatever the day of the week on which it fell. Victor thereupon proclaimed their exclusion from communion, not simply with Rome but with the church generally. His action provoked a storm of protest, and Irenaeus of Lyons, whose church accepted his ruling, sharply reminded him that all previous popes down to SOTER had shown indulgence to the Quartodeciman practice at a time when Rome itself did not celebrate an Easter festival and the discrepancy was therefore all the more glaring. It is not clear how Victor reacted, but his *démarche* was a striking example, going beyond the impersonal action of CLEMENT I at Corinth, of a pope claiming the right to interfere in other churches. With similar vigour he excommunicated the leather-seller Theodotus of Byzantium—leader of an adoptionist group which taught that Jesus had been an ordinary, but supremely upright, man until the Spirit, or Christ, descended on him at his baptism—and deposed the Gnostic writer Florinus from the priesthood.

Victor is the first pope known to have had dealings with the imperial household. He supplied Marcia, mistress of Emperor Commodus (180–92) and herself a Christian, with a list of Christians condemned to the mines of Sardinia, and thus secured their release; they included a future pope, CALLISTUS I, whose name he had deliberately withheld. According to St Jerome, he was the author of Latin works of moderate quality. Reports that he was a martyr and was buried near St Peter are routine and should be rejected. Feast 28 July.

Hippolytus, *Ref.* 9, 12, 10–13; Eusebius, *Hist. eccl.* 5, 23–24; 5, 28, 3–6; Ps.Tertullian, *Adv. omn. haer.* 8 (*CSEL* 47, 225); Jerome, *De vir. ill.* 34; *LP* 1, 137; M. Richard, 'La lettre de s. Irénée au pape Victor', *ZNTW* 56 (1965), 260–82; Ch. Mohrmann, *VC* 16 (1962), 154–71; Caspar 1, 19–22; *DTC* 15, 2862 f. (É. Amann); *LThK* 10, 768 f. (G. Schwaiger); *NCE* 14, 646 (E. G. Weltin); Seppelt 1, 29–31.

ZEPHYRINUS, ST (198/9–217). Nothing is known of his background apart from the report of *LP* (for what it is worth) that he was a Roman, the son of Habundius. His caustic critic HIPPOLYTUS, later antipope, represented him as simple, uneducated, inexperienced in church decisions, and also avaricious. He was certainly a weak man and leaned heavily on his abler, more practical-minded archdeacon CALLISTUS, whom he had virtually rehabilitated. He directed his lower clergy through him, and appointed him administrator of the official cemetery the church now possessed.

Zephyrinus was probably the pope whom Tertullian (d. *c.*225), now turned *Montanist, reproached with having initially issued letters recognizing the Montanist movement and then revoking them at the instigation of one Praxeas. But the most bitter debates at Rome during his pontificate were Christological. *Adoptionism, or the view that Jesus had been an ordinary man until his baptism, still flourished despite its condemnation by VICTOR I, with the banker Theodotus and Asclepiodotus as its leaders, and for a time an adoptionist named Natalius set up as a salaried schismatic bishop. He came to his senses, however, and Zephyrinus readmitted him to communion after rigorous penance. More important was the modalism taught by Noetus, Praxeas, and Sabellius, which virtually obliterated the distinctions between the persons of the Trinity. Hippolytus criticized Zephyrinus for not condemning—even seeming to favour—it. In fact, analysis of a credal formula he published makes it clear that Zephyrinus was not a modalist, but was concerned to maintain at once the divinity of Christ and his personal distinction from the Father, although he lacked the necessary terminology to do so effectively. While Zephyrinus was pope the renowned Origen (d. *c.*254), the greatest of contemporary Christian intellectuals, visited Rome, 'being keenly desirous to set eyes on that most ancient church'. The tradition that he died a martyr is not supported by early sources and should be rejected. On the other hand, *LP*'s report that his burial-place was 'in his own cemetery near that of Callistus' on the Appian Way deserves credence. Feast 26 Aug.

Hippolytus, *Ref.* 9, 7–12; Eusebius, *Hist. eccl.* 2, 25, 6; 5, 28, 3–12; 6, 14, 10; 6, 20, 3; 6, 21, 2; *LP* 1, 139 f.; B. Capelle, 'Le cas du pape Zéphyrin', *RBén* 38 (1926), 321–30; J. N. D. Kelly, *Early Christian Doctrines* (5th edn., London 1977), 123–5; Caspar 1, 22–4; 38–40; *DTC* 15, 3690 f. (É. Amann); *LThK* 10, 1352 (K. Baus); *NCE* 14, 1118 f. (E. G. Weltin); Seppelt 1, 34–8.

CALLISTUS I (often **CALIXTUS**), **ST** (217–22). His career is chiefly known from the distorting but factually revealing account of his bitter critic, HIPPOLYTUS. In youth he was the slave of a Christian freedman, Carpophorus, who set him up in a bank. He panicked and fled when the business failed, with serious losses to Christian depositors, but his master brought him back and set him to work on a treadmill. His creditors, who hoped to recover their money, arranged his release, but he was charged with brawling in a synagogue on the sabbath and was sentenced by the city prefect to hard labour in the mines of Sardinia. When Marcia, mistress of Emperor Commodus (180–92), asked VICTOR I for the names of Christian convicts in the mines and obtained their release, Callistus prevailed on the governor to free him too, although Victor had deliberately withheld his name. When he got back to Rome, the pope sent him to live at Anzio on a monthly pension. Victor's successor, ZEPHYRINUS, however, recalled him, made him his principal deacon and adviser, gave him control of the lower clergy, and appointed him curator of the church's cemetery on the Appian Way (now the catacombs of S. Callisto). The hold he subsequently acquired over the pope, as well as his administrative skills, made him the real power in the Roman church, and on Zephyrinus's death he was elected pope. The presbyter Hippolytus refused to accept this decision, and (according to the accepted account) got himself elected bishop of a schismatic group.

Callistus's reign was marred by bickering with the aggressive antipope, who accused him of *modalism and of laxity in discipline, but whom he seems never to have formally censured. The former charge can be dismissed, for he excommunicated Sabellius, the intellectual leader of modalism, who maintained that Father, Son, and Holy Spirit do not represent real distinctions in the Godhead but successive modes of its self-revelation. This did not satisfy Hippolytus, who jeered that he had only passed the sentence out of fear of himself and was still a modalist. In fact Callistus was trying to steer a middle course between modalism, which he rejected, and Hippolytus's teaching that the Word is a distinct hypostasis or person, which he viewed as ditheistic. Hippolytus also complained that Callistus permitted a bishop guilty of grave offences to remain in office, was prepared to ordain men who had been married two or even three times, refused to condemn clergy who married, recognized unions (condemned by Roman law) between upper-class women and men of inferior status, and readmitted to the church without preliminary penance converts from heretical or schismatic sects. The implication of this is not, as has sometimes been contended, that Callistus was a daring innovator in penitential practice; he was not the 'supreme pontiff' who published a 'peremptory edict' on penance derided by Tertullian (d. c.225). Rather, in contrast to old-fashioned rigorists like Hippolytus, he taught the increasingly accepted view that the church was (as the parable of the tares among the wheat suggested) a home for sinners as well as saints, and should therefore offer reconciliation to Christians who had fallen into any sin after baptism.

Although his name appears in a 4th-cent. calendar of martyrs, it is unlikely, in view of the absence of persecution in the reign of Alexander Severus (222–35), that Callistus was a martyr in the strict sense. A legendary Passion purporting to describe his end suggests that he died a violent death, possibly in a popular riot. He was buried in Trastevere on the Via Aurelia, not in the cemetery named after him where other 3rd-cent. popes were interred; and this agrees with the story in the Passion that his death took place in Trastevere. His actual tomb was discovered in 1960 in the cemetery of Calepodius on the Via Aurelia; the crypt is decorated with later frescos depicting his alleged martyrdom. Feast 14 Oct.

Hippolytus, *Ref.* 9, 11–13; 10, 27; Tertullian, *De pud.* 1, 6; Eusebius, *Hist. eccl.* 6, 26, 2; *LP* 1, xcii f.; 141 f.; *AASS* 6 Oct. (1794), 401–48; J. J. I. von Döllinger, *Hippolytus and Callistus* (ET, Edinburgh, 1876); J. Gaudemet, 'La décision de Calixte en matière de mariage', *Studi in onore di Mgr E. Paoli* (Rome, 1955); B. Altaner and C. B. Daly, 'The Edict of Callistus', *TU* 78 (1961), 176–82; Caspar 1, 22–8; *DHGE* 11, 421–4 (G. Bardy); *NCE* 2, 1080–3 (J. Chapin); Seppelt 1, 34–42.

HIPPOLYTUS, ST (antipope 217–35). Born before 170, almost certainly in the Greek-speaking east, he seems to have come to Rome and been ordained in the time of VICTOR I. A man of Greek philosophical culture, he had studied Irenaeus of Lyons (*fl.* 180) but also the 2nd-cent. apologists, and soon became a leading presbyter as well as the chief intellectual of the Roman church. Such of his voluminous works as have survived indicate that he had a range comparable in variety, though not in depth, with that of Origen, the most profound Greek theologian (d. c.254), before whom he preached a homily in 212. They include exegesis, e.g. a commentary on Daniel (202–4); polemical and dogmatic writings, e.g. a treatise *Antichrist* (c.200) and a *Refutation of all Heresies* (after 222); history, e.g. a *Chronicle* of world history from Adam to 234; numerous homilies; and liturgy (the important *Apostolic Tradition*, which describes the contemporary baptismal and eucharistic rites at Rome, may be by him). Intransigent, ambitious, and a strict rigorist in matters of discipline, he was furious when ZEPHYRINUS, Victor I's successor, chose the former slave CALLISTUS, whom he both despised and disapproved of, as his collaborator, and was quick to denounce them both as virtually *modalists in Christology. He himself was an effective exponent of the Logos theology, which treated the Word as a hypostasis or person distinct from the Father, and was in turn criticized by them as a ditheist. When Callistus was elected pope, Hippolytus set himself up (it is held) as bishop of a small schismatic group, thus becoming the first antipope. He treated Callistus as a mere sectarian leader who was as misguided in theology as he was lax on disciplinary issues.

His own ethical rigorism not only envisaged the church as a community of saints, but tended to make the functions of its ministers depend for their validity on their personal holiness.

The unhappy schism continued during the reigns of URBAN I and PONTIAN. When Maximinus Thrax, however, became emperor in March 235 and adopted the policy of striking at church leaders, Hippolytus and Pontian were both arrested and sentenced to deportation to Sardinia, the notorious 'island of death', where they soon succumbed to cruel conditions. It is conjectured that, either in prison at Rome or in Sardinia before their death, they became reconciled. Pontian abdicated, and Hippolytus renounced his claim to be bishop and advised his followers to abandon their schism; thus unity was at last restored to the Roman church. Pope FABIAN had the bodies of both men brought back to Rome, where they were solemnly interred on 13 Aug. 236 or 237, Hippolytus 'the presbyter' in the cemetery henceforth bearing his name on the Via Tiburtina. Because he wrote in Greek and the Roman church was now thoroughly Latinized, most of his writings disappeared and his memory faded or became hopelessly confused; both Eusebius (c.260–c.340) and St Jerome introduce him as a prolific author and a bishop, but are ignorant of his see. A marble statue, 3rd-cent. in style, depicting him in the conventional dress of a philosopher or teacher and inscribed with a list (incomplete) of his writings, was discovered near the Via Tiburtina in 1551; it was installed in the Vatican Library by JOHN XXIII in 1959. Feast 30 June in the east, 13 Aug. in the west.

Although accepted by most scholars, the reconstruction outlined above has been increasingly called in question. First, attempts have been made to detach from Hippolytus some of the writings commonly attributed to him and to assign them to another hand. Secondly, it has been argued that there is not sufficient evidence for the view that the presbyter Hippolytus, the bit-

ter critic of Callistus I, ever got himself consecrated as an antipope or was the person deported to Sardinia with Pontian. The debate continues.

B. Altaner and A. Stuiber, *Patrologie* (8th edn., Freiburg, Basel, Vienna, 1978: full list of H.'s works, with notes on crit. edns.); Hippolytus, *Ref.* 9; Eusebius, *Hist. eccl.* 6, 20, 2; 6, 22; Jerome, *De vir. ill.* 61; Liberian Catalogue (in *LP* 1, 4 f.); J. J. I. von Döllinger, *Hippolytus and Callistus* (ET, Edinburgh, 1876); A. d'Alès, *La théologie de s. Hippolyte* (Paris, 1929); J. N. D. Kelly, *Early Christian Doctrines* (5th edn., London, 1977), 110–15; P. Nautin, *Hippolyte et Josipe* (Paris, 1947); M. Richard in *DSp* 7 (1969), 531–71; K. Baus, *Handbook of Church History* (ed. H. Jedin: ET, London, 1965) 1, 244–7; *DTC* 6, 2487–511 (É. Amann); *LThK* 5, 378–80 (R. Gögler); *NCE* 6, 1139–41 (M. R. P. McGuire); Seppelt 1, 34–43.

URBAN I, ST (222–30). The historian Eusebius (c.260–c.340) and the 4th-cent. Liberian Catalogue report respectively that he reigned eight and just short of nine years. According to *LP* he was a Roman, the son of Pontianus (the name also of his successor); but the rest of the information it supplies, e.g. that he insisted on the sacred vessels being made of silver and was himself a confessor in the days of Emperor Diocletian (284–305), is anachronistic fantasy, some of it borrowed from the legend of St Cecilia, with which he had become confusedly associated. His pontificate fell wholly in the reign of Emperor Alexander Severus (222–35), which was free from persecution. The schism of antipope HIPPOLYTUS continued (possibly) to divide the Roman church, but nothing is known of relations between the two men. The story of his martyrdom is apocryphal. The statement in *LP* that he was buried in the cemetery of Praetextatus rests on a confusion between him and a confessor of the same name who is mentioned both by St Cyprian (in several letters) and Eusebius. He was in fact interred, as the Martyrology of St Jerome (5th-cent.) confirms, in the cemetery of CALLISTUS, where a grave-slab bearing his name in Greek capitals has been found. Feast 25 May.

Eusebius, *Hist. eccl.* 6, 21, 2; 6, 23, 3; *LP* 1, xciii–xciv; 4 f.; 62 f.; 143 f.; *DCB* 4, 1062–4 (J. Barmby); *DTC* 15, 2268 f. (É. Amann); *BSS* 12, 837–40 (A. Amore); *NCE* 14, 447 (E. G. Weltin).

PONTIAN, ST (21 July 230–28 Sept. 235). The historian Eusebius (*c.*260–*c.*340) simply records that he reigned six years, between URBAN I and ANTERUS; *LP* adds that he was a Roman, son of Calpurnius. Virtually nothing is known of his activities, except that he must have presided over the Roman synod which endorsed the sentence of expulsion from Egypt and his teaching post and of demotion from the priesthood passed on Origen, the outstanding Greek theologian, by Demetrius, bishop of Alexandria, at two synods in 230/1. For most of his reign the Roman church enjoyed freedom from persecution as a result of the tolerant policies of Emperor Alexander Severus (222–35), but the schism started by HIPPOLYTUS in CALLISTUS I's reign probably continued. Maximinus Thrax, however, acclaimed emperor in Mar. 235, abandoned toleration and singled out Christian leaders for attack. Among the first victims were Pontian and Hippolytus, who were both arrested and deported to Sardinia, the notorious 'island of death'. Since deportation was normally for life and few survived it, Pontian abdicated (the first pope to do so), presumably to allow a successor to assume the leadership as soon as possible. He did so, according to the 4th-cent. Liberian Catalogue, on 28 Sept. 235, the first precisely recorded date in papal history (other apparently secure dates are based on inference). It was not long before he and Hippolytus succumbed to their harsh treatment and conditions, but it is conjectured that, either in prison at Rome or when they arrived in Sardinia, they became reconciled. Pontian's body, with that of Hippolytus, was brought back to Rome by Pope FABIAN in 236 or 237, and was interred in the newly completed papal crypt in the catacombs of S. Callisto; fragments of his grave-slab, with his name in Greek and his title of bishop inscribed on it,

were discovered there in 1909. Feast formerly 19 Nov.; now with Hippolytus 13 Aug.

Eusebius, *Hist. eccl.* 6, 23, 3; 6, 29, 1; Jerome, *Ep.* 33, 4; *LP* 1, xciv–xcv; 6 (Liberian Cat.); 145 f.; Caspar 1, 43–6; 48; *DCB* 4, 438 (J. Barmby); *DTC* 12, 1253 f. (É. Amann); *BSS* 10, 1013–15 (G. D. Gordini); *PW* 22, 25 (W. Ensslin).

ANTERUS, ST (21 Nov. 235–3 Jan. 236). Successor to PONTIAN, who abdicated on 28 Sept. 235, he was, as his name suggests and *LP* confirms, of Greek extraction. Nothing is certainly known of his activities during his brief reign, which fell during the sharp persecution of Emperor Maximinus Thrax (235–8); *LP*'s report that he collected and preserved the records of martyrs is plainly a romantic anachronism. It adds that he died a martyr, and he has often been represented as such. It is improbable, however, that he was; his name does not appear in early official lists of martyrs, and the 4th-cent. Liberian Catalogue pointedly remarks that he 'fell asleep', an expression it uses of popes who died a natural death. He was the first pope to be buried in the new papal crypt in the cemetery of CALLISTUS, the body of his predecessor Pontian being placed there not long after. Large fragments of the inscription over his tomb, in Greek letters, have been found there. Feast 3 Jan.

Eusebius, *Hist. eccl.* 6, 29, 1; *LP* 1, xcv–xcvi; 4 (Liberian Cat.); 147; Caspar 1, 48 ff.; *DHGE* 3, 520 f. (J. P. Kirsch); *BSS* 2, 51 f. (M. V. Brandi).

FABIAN, ST (10 Jan. 236–20 Jan. 250). A Roman, his reign coincided, save for its opening and closing years, with a period of exceptional peace, prosperity, and growth for the church, Emperor Gordian III (238–44) dropping his predecessor Maximinus's persecution of Christianity and Philip the Arab (244–9) being sympathetic towards it. An energetic and far-seeing administrator, he reorganized the local clergy, dividing the city (according to the 4th-cent. Liberian Catalogue) into seven ecclesiastical districts, apparently not based on the fourteen civic regions of Augustus, and placing a deacon supported by a subdeacon and six junior assistants in charge of each. He thus gave the Roman church a close-knit structure adapted to its increasing numbers. The Liberian Catalogue adds that he was responsible for numerous building works in the cemeteries; these probably included extensions to that of CALLISTUS. He also arranged for the return of the bodies of Pope PONTIAN and the antipope HIPPOLYTUS from Sardinia, where they had perished in exile, to Rome and their seemly burial there. This action suggests that he had influence at court, for the bodies of men sentenced to deportation could not be brought home or interred without the emperor's express, but rarely granted, permission. Little else is known about him, except that, when Bishop Donatus of Carthage had Bishop Privatus of Lambaesis condemned at an African council, Fabian endorsed his action; and that the Greek theologian Origen wrote to him, as to other bishops, defending his orthodoxy, presumably against the censures of Demetrius of Alexandria, which Pontian had approved. He also ordained NOVATIAN, before long to face his successor as antipope.

Fabian was a remarkable pope of whom contemporaries like Cyprian of Carthage spoke with deep respect. The story related by Eusebius (c.260–c.340)—that, when the clergy were considering a successor to ANTERUS, a dove settled on Fabian's head, designating a man who was in no one's thoughts as the choice of the Holy Spirit—legend though it is, reflects the widespread conviction that he was a leader given by God to the church. With his advent enhanced emphasis began to be placed on the high position of the bishops of Rome, the days of their elevation being formally noted and lists of names giving precise dates being prepared. His activities were brought to an abrupt close with the outbreak of the persecution unleashed by Emperor Decius at the beginning of 250; he was arrested and was among the first to die, probably in prison as a result of brutal treatment, on 20 Jan. of that year. He was buried in the papal crypt in the cemetery of Callistus; the grave-

slab bearing his name, title, and the abbreviated word 'martyr' in Greek letters was discovered there in 1854. His remains were later removed to S. Sebastiano, where a sarcophagus inscribed with his name was identified in 1915. Feast (with St Sebastian) 20 Jan.

Eusebius, *Hist. eccl.* 6, 29, 1–4; 6, 36, 4; 6, 39, 1; Cyprian, *Epp.* 9, 1; 49, 10, 1; Jerome, *Ep.* 84, 10; *LP* 1, 4 (Liberian Cat.); 148 f.; Caspar 1, 43 ff.; 48–53; *DCB* 2, 440 f. (J. Barmby); *DHGE* 16, 316 f. (P. Nautin); *LThK* 3, 1331 f. (G. Schwaiger); *NCE* 5, 783 (E. G. Weltin); Seppelt 1, 43–5; P. Styger, 'Scavi a San Sebastiano', *RQ* 29 (1915), 100–5.

CORNELIUS, ST (Mar. 251–June 253). The clergy deliberately postponed electing a successor to FABIAN because of the violence of the persecution of Emperor Decius (249–51) and the fact that several of their number, including the priest Moses, the man most likely to be chosen, were in gaol. For fourteen months they governed the church collegiately, with the priest NOVATIAN acting as its spokesman. When the persecution slackened in spring 251, an election became practicable. Moses having died, the choice of the great majority fell, not on Novatian (who had been expecting it), but on Cornelius, a Roman, possibly of the patrician *gens Cornelia*, whom Cyprian, the contemporary bishop of Carthage, described as an unambitious priest who had served in all the lower grades of the ministry. His election was at once strongly contested by Novatian, who, frustrated in his hopes, had himself consecrated rival bishop and, with a small group of supporters, moved into schism. The clash between the two men was sharpened by, indeed may have had its roots in, their divergent attitudes to the question of what should be done with the large numbers of Christians who had lapsed in the persecution but now wished to resume communion. Cornelius favoured their readmission after suitable penance, Novatian their complete exclusion; it is probable that the pope owed his election to his known support for the more realistic and compassionate policy. Cornelius's position was therefore difficult for some time. Novatian was working energetically and skilfully to get his own title as bishop recognized by the leading Christian centres, while in Rome a rigorist group of clergy and laity refused to accept the overlenient (as they judged him) Cornelius. Cornelius was eventually able to overcome these obstacles, especially when Cyprian of Carthage and Dionysius of Alexandria came out on his side. It is significant, however, that Cyprian, to Cornelius's annoyance, felt obliged to make enquiries before reaching his decision. Cornelius was greatly helped by Cyprian in winning over the rigorist opposition in Rome, which included some African confessors, and he had Cyprian's full support when he finally excommunicated Novatian and his adherents. This he did in autumn 251 at a synod in Rome, attended by sixty bishops as well as other clergy, which also affirmed the policy, in line with Cyprian's decisions in north Africa, of readmitting apostate Christians after they had done appropriate penance.

It is ironical that, after complaining about Cyprian's hesitation in recognizing his election, Cornelius should, in summer 252, have given a hearing to the envoys of an opposition bishop, Fortunatus, by whom Cyprian was troubled at Carthage. Although Cornelius repulsed them, Cyprian was understandably irritated and sent the pope a sharp rebuke. Cornelius is known to have written a number of letters, in the main making his position about the schism clear to other churches; two of these, addressed to Cyprian, survive as nos. 49 and 50 in the Cyprianic correspondence. In addition Eusebius (c.260–c.340) has preserved portions of a letter he sent to Fabius, the rigorist bishop of Antioch, urging him to suspend support of Novatian and accept the fact that the consensus of the churches favoured a moderate policy towards the lapsed. This letter paints an unattractive, even libellous, portrait of Novatian which does Cornelius little credit, but it also provides detailed statistics, of

great historical value, of the clergy of different grades serving the Roman church at the time. When Emperor Gallus (251–3) restarted persecution in June 252, Cornelius was arrested and banished to Centumcellae (Civitavecchia, now the port of Rome), where he received a letter of warm congratulation from Cyprian; he died there in the following June. The 4th-cent. Liberian Catalogue reports that he 'died gloriously', but he was not at first regarded as a martyr in the strict sense and was not listed as such in the 4th-cent. *Depositio martyrum*. His supposed trial before Emperor Decius, recounted by *LP*, is borrowed from an apocryphal 5th-cent. passion and has no historical basis. His body was subsequently taken back to Rome and interred in the crypt of Lucina in the cemetery of CALLISTUS; the inscription on his tomb was the first papal epitaph to be in Latin. Feast (with St Cyprian) 16 Sept.

Cyprian, *Letters* (esp. 44–55); Eusebius, *Hist. eccl.* 6, 39, 1; 6, 46, 3; 7, 2; Jerome, *De vir. ill.* 66; *LP* 1, ccviii–ccix; 4–6 (Liberian Cat.); 150–2; P. F. de' Cavaliere, 'La persecuzione di Gallo in Roma', *ST* 33 (1920), 181–210; *DCB*, 689 f. (G. H. Moberley); *DHGE* 13, 891–4 (G. Bardy); *LThK* 3, 57 f. (G. Schwaiger); *NCE* 4, 333 f. (J. Chapin).

NOVATIAN (antipope Mar. 251–8). Born c.200, he was intellectually gifted and received, as his writings demonstrate, a first-rate literary and philosophical education. A late report that he was a Phrygian is a mistake arising from the resemblance between his moral rigorism and that of Phrygian *Montanism. When he first appears, in 250, he was a leading presbyter in the Roman church, author of a remarkable treatise on the Trinity which has earned him the title of founder of Roman theology. His contemporary, Pope COR-NELIUS, depicted him as a man of unattractive personal qualities, who had been uncanonically ordained despite the strong opposition of clergy and laity, but this was malicious gossip. Not only did Cornelius's predecessor, FABIAN, judge Novatian suitable for ordination, but during the fourteen-month vacancy following Fabian's death he was accepted as leader and spokesman of the Roman college of presbyters, entrusted with drafting important letters to other churches in its name. His crisis came in Mar. 251, when the clergy, taking advantage of the slackening of the persecution of Emperor Decius (249–51), proceeded at last to elect a successor to Fabian and chose, by an overwhelming majority, his fellow-presbyter Cornelius. Personally disappointed, and also disapproving of their choice, Novatian had himself consecrated bishop by three bishops from southern Italy and, with a small band of like-minded adherents, went into schism. Cornelius and he held sharply opposed views on the proper treatment of Christians who sought to resume communion after apostatizing under persecution, the new pope favouring their readmission after suitable penance and Novatian their permanent exclusion. His attitude seems to have hardened after the split, for letters drafted by him during the vacancy suggest that his stance was then a moderate one. He now took energetic and skilful steps to convince the great churches of the validity of his position and circulated letters to their bishops; but while he found support at Antioch, and while some, like the famed Cyprian of Carthage, showed initial hesitation, the recognition of Cornelius as rightful pope was not long delayed. Soon Cornelius was able to convene a synod of sixty bishops as well as other clergy at Rome which excommunicated Novatian and his adherents. Dionysius, bishop of Alexandria, wrote to him urging him to make his peace with the pope, but in vain. The Novatianist church spread apace, with an organization modelled on that of the official church. Orthodox in doctrine but teaching that there was no forgiveness for serious sins after baptism, it established itself as far as Spain in the west and Armenia and Mesopotamia in the east; it persisted into the 5th cent. and, in isolated communities, much later.

Meanwhile Novatian himself had to leave Rome because of renewed persecution; the historian Socrates (d. 450) reports that he died a martyr, or at any rate as a confessor, in 258 in the persecution of Emperor Valerian (253–60). The 5th-cent. Martyrology of St Jerome mentions a Novatian among Roman martyrs on 29 June, and a tombstone was discovered in 1932 on the Via Tiburtina in Rome with an inscription honouring 'the blessed martyr Novatian'; but the absence of the title 'bishop' makes it uncertain whether either refers to Novatian the schismatic and antipope. He was a prolific writer: St Jerome names nine of his works, adding that there were many others. Of these, in addition to two, or possibly three, letters addressed in the name of the Roman clergy to Cyprian of Carthage, only *On the Trinity*, *On Jewish Foods*, *On Shows*, and *On the Excellence of Modesty* survive. Internal evidence shows that the last three were written when he was absent from Rome for his community there. All are composed in elegant rhythmic prose, and reveal their author as an acute theologian and pastor who owed much to the great north African writer Tertullian (d. *c*.225).

Works in *CCL* 4 (crit. edn. by G. F. Diercks, 1972); Eusebius, *Hist. eccl.* 6, 43, 1–21; 6, 45; 6, 46, 3; 7, 4–5, 2; 7, 7, 618; Jerome, *De vir. ill.* 70; Cyprian, *Letters* (*passim*); Socrates, *Hist. eccl.* 4, 28; A. d'Alès, *Novatien* (Paris, 1924); J. N. D. Kelly, *Early Christian Doctrines* (5th edn., London, 1977), 125 f.; *DCB* 4, 58–60 (G. T. Stokes); *DTC* 11, 816–29 (É. Amann); *LThK* 7, 1062–4 (J. Quasten); *NCE* 10, 534 f. (P. H. Weyer); Seppelt 1, 48–51; 55–7.

LUCIUS I, ST (25 June 253–5 Mar. 254). A Roman by birth (according to *LP*), he was banished from the capital by the persecuting emperor Gallus (251–3) almost immediately after being elected. His place of exile is not known, but he was soon able to make his way back with numerous Christians exiled with him, since the newly proclaimed emperor, Valerian (253–60), was at first favourably disposed towards Christians. On his return he received an enthusiastic letter from Cyprian, the influential bishop of Carthage, congratulating him on his willing suffering for the faith, and suggesting that perhaps the Lord had recalled him so that he might undergo actual martyrdom in the midst of his flock. Virtually nothing is directly known about his activities, but one of Cyprian's letters implies that, in dealing with Christians who had apostatized during persecution, he maintained CORNELIUS's policy of restoring them to communion after suitable penance. He therefore made no concessions to Antipope NOVATIAN and his adherents, who were still active during his reign. It is further reported that he received a letter from Bishop Dionysius of Alexandria on the validity of *baptism by heretics, a subject which was to be much debated during his successor's reign. Despite *LP*'s report that he was martyred by beheading, the earlier tradition of the 4th-cent. Liberian Catalogue suggests that he died a natural death. He was interred in the papal crypt in the cemetery of CALLISTUS, where a portion of the epitaph on his tomb, in Greek letters, has been recovered. Feast 4 Mar.

Cyprian, *Epp.* 61 and 68; Eusebius, *Hist. eccl.* 7, 2; 7, 10, 3; *LP* 1, xcvi–xcviii; ccxlviii; 6 f. (Liberian Cat.); 66–9; 153; P. F. de' Cavaliere, 'La persecuzione di Gallo in Roma', *ST* 33 (1920), 181–210; Caspar 1, 70; *DTC* 9, 1056 f. (É. Amann); *LThK* 6, 1176 (G. Schwaiger); *NCE* 8, 1059 (E. G. Weltin).

STEPHEN I, ST (12 May 254–2 Aug. 257). A Roman by birth, of the *gens Julia*, he succeeded LUCIUS I after a vacancy of some sixty days. A pope of some importance in the development of the holy see, he is chiefly known from certain clashes he had with Cyprian, the influential bishop of Carthage. The first arose out of the deposition of two Spanish bishops who had apostatized under persecution. One of them went to Rome and persuaded Stephen to rehabilitate him and his colleague. The Spanish churches then appealed to Cyprian, and he, having convened a council of north African bishops, published a synodical letter confirming the deposition; it excused Stephen on the ground that he had been deceived about the facts. The second concerned Bishop Marcian of Arles, who had adopted

the rigorist views of Antipope NOVATIAN and was refusing even deathbed reconciliation to Christians who had lapsed in persecution. The local bishops had written to Stephen urging him to have Marcian deposed, but he had taken no action. They turned therefore to Cyprian, who took up the case and called on the pope to excommunicate Marcian, arrange for a new bishop to replace him, and inform the African episcopate of his name so that they might know with whom they were in communion. The third clash was more important theologically, being over the question whether baptism administered by heretics was valid. Cyprian, with the churches of north Africa (except for some doubters), Syria, and Asia Minor generally, was positive that it was not: baptism could only be bestowed within the church, and heretics seeking reconciliation therefore needed catholic baptism, i.e. needed to be rebaptized. Stephen, representing the tradition of Rome, Alexandria, and Palestine, was adamant that heretical baptism was valid: to be reconciled, heretics and schismatics needed, not to be baptized afresh (which he regarded as illegitimate), but only to receive absolution by the laying on of hands. The question was a burning one at the time in north Africa, and Cyprian held two synods in 255 and 256 which reaffirmed his position. Meanwhile Stephen, determined to impose the Roman view everywhere, wrote to the churches of Asia Minor declaring that he could no longer hold communion with them since they rebaptized heretics; and when Cyprian sought to apprise him of the decisions of his synods, he refused to receive his envoys or even offer them hospitality. Rebaptism, he argued, was an innovation which violated tradition, and could not be accepted. An open breach between Rome and large sections of Christendom now threatened; it is not surprising that Bishop Dionysius of Alexandria, while sharing his view of the impropriety of rebaptism, felt obliged to write to Stephen imploring him to adopt a more pacific line. The situation might have become desperate had not Stephen died on 2 Aug. 257 and Cyprian, as a martyr, a year later.

These incidents throw light on the growing recognition, in the middle of the 3rd cent., of the pre-eminent position of Rome, as a court of appeal at any rate for Gaul and Spain, and as the see with which other sees deemed it appropriate to be in communion. Stephen emerges as an imperious and uncompromising prelate, fully aware of his special prerogative; his rival bishops did not hesitate to put the blame for splitting the church on him. It is interesting that he was accused of 'glorying in his standing as bishop and of claiming to hold the succession from Peter, on whom the foundations of the church were laid'. He was in fact the first pope, so far as is known, to find a formal basis for the Roman primacy in the Lord's charge to the Apostle PETER cited in Matt. 16: 18. Later legend reflected in *LP* treated him as a martyr, but the *Roman calendar of 354 names him only in its list of deceased bishops (not in that of martyrs). He was buried in the papal crypt in the cemetery of CALLISTUS on the Appian Way. Feast 2 Aug.

Cyprian, *Letters* 67–75; Eusebius, *Hist. eccl.* 7, 2; 7, 3; 7, 4–5, 6; *LP* 1, 68 f.; 154; Caspar 1, 70 f.; 79–83; 86–92; and index; *DCB* 4, 727–30 (J. Barmby); *DHGE* 15, 1183 f. (B. Botte); *LThK* 9, 1038 (G. Schwaiger); *NCE* 13, 694 (E. G. Weltin); K. Baus, *Handbook of Church History* (ET, London, 1965) 1, 358–63; Seppelt 1, 51–3; 56–8.

SIXTUS II, ST (Aug. 257–6 Aug. 258). Of Greek extraction, as *LP* states and his name (more correctly Xystus) makes probable, he was elected at the moment when Emperor Valerian (253–60), abandoning his earlier tolerant attitude, began persecuting Christians, ordering them to take part in state religious ceremonies and forbidding them to assemble in the cemeteries. For a time he was able to escape police vigilance and devote himself to repairing the breach which STEPHEN I had created between Rome and the churches of north Africa and Asia Minor because of their refusal to give up the practice of *rebaptizing heretics and schismatics who wished to be reconciled to the church. He upheld as firmly as Stephen the Roman view that baptism properly administered by heretics was valid, but seems to have restored friendly relations with Cyprian, bishop of Carthage, with whom Stephen had sharply clashed, and with the Asiatic churches. How he did this remains unclear, but he probably drew back from Stephen's posture of confrontation and quietly accepted the coexistence of divergent practices. In adopting this policy he owed much to advice given to him, and to his presbyters DIONYSIUS and Philemon, by Dionysius, bishop of Alexandria, who had vainly tried to induce Stephen to be less intransigent, and who now continued to write as a mediator, setting out (although himself opposed to rebaptism) considerations which might reasonably be advanced in its defence. Sixtus owed even more, however, to his own irenic temperament, for he was (as Cyprian's biographer noted) 'a good and peace-loving priest'.

Some scholars used mistakenly to attribute to Sixtus a short treatise attacking Antipope NOVATIAN; while in the late 4th cent. he was credited by Rufinus, equally erroneously, with the authorship of the edifying collection of ethical and religious aphorisms known as *The Sentences of Sextus*. His presumed connection with this latter prompted *LP* to describe him as having previously been a philosopher. In fact his only surviving production is a minute fragment, in an Armenian translation, of a letter to Dionysius of Alexandria defending the validity of heretical baptism if administered in the name of the Trinity. His brief reign was brought to an abrupt close by the publication of Valerian's second, more drastic, edict ordering the summary execution of Christian bishops, priests, and deacons, as well as draconian penalties on Christian laymen. On 6 Aug. 258 the authorities surprised him at divine service, seated in his episcopal chair addressing the congregation, in the cemetery of Praetextatus, a private burial place in which he and his flock had probably hoped to escape detection because it was not watched by the police. Here he was beheaded, and with him four of his deacons who were in attendance. Two of the remaining three deacons were executed the same day, while the seventh, Lawrence, suffered four days later. Sixtus's body was later transferred to the papal crypt, in the cemetery of CALLISTUS, and the four deacons who had shared his martyrdom were interred near by. The bloodstained chair on which he had been sitting was placed behind the altar in the chapel. A century later DAMASUS I composed an epitaph in ponderous hexameters describing the drama of his execution, and this was set up over his tomb. Sixtus II became one of the church's most venerated martyrs, and his name was included in the canon of the mass. Feast 7 Aug.

AASS Aug. II (1735), 124–42, and Nov. II (pt. 2, 1931), 420 f.; Cyprian, *Letter* 80; Eusebius, *Hist. eccl.* 7, 5, 3–6; 7, 6; 7, 9, 1–6; 7, 14; 7, 27, 1; A. Ferrua, *Epigrammata Damasiana* (Vatican City, 1942), 123–6; *LP* 1, 6 f.; 11; 68 f; 155 f.; P. F. de' Cavaliere, 'Un recente studio sul luogo del martirio di S. Sisto II', *ST* 33 (1920), 145–78; Caspar 1, 43; 46; 48; 71 f.; 91; *DCB* 4, 1197–9 (J. Barmby); *DTC* 14, 2194–6 (É. Amann); *DACL* 15, 1501–15 (M. Combet-Farnoux); *LThK* 9, 809 (B. Kötting); *NCE* 13, 271 (E. G. Weltin).

DIONYSIUS, ST (22 July 260–26 Dec. 268). Because of the severity of the persecution of Valerian (253–60), which entailed the summary execution of the clergy, the Roman church did not elect a successor to SIXTUS II until news of the emperor's death in captivity reached Rome; for almost two years the church was governed by the presbyters alone, all seven deacons having perished with Sixtus. The man eventually elected, Dionysius, probably of Greek descent, had been a leading presbyter under Sixtus II, corresponding with Dionysius, bishop of Alexandria, on the contentious issue of the *rebaptism of heretics, on which the bishop was trying to mediate between Rome and the churches of north Africa and Asia Minor. He had originally shared the rigid stance of STEPHEN I, who had broken

off communion with churches which insisted on rebaptizing heretics and schismatics, but seems to have softened his attitude by Sixtus II's time; the bishop at any rate regarded him as 'erudite and remarkable'. Once pope himself, he received a further letter from Bishop Dionysius on the same subject, and before long became involved in another correspondence with him, this time about the relations of the Father and the Son in the Godhead. Some Christians in Alexandria had denounced their bishop to the pope, charging him with separating the Son from the Father, even speaking of him as a creature, and refusing to describe him as one in essence with the Father. Dionysius of Rome straightway convened a synod which condemned the expressions complained of, sent the Alexandrian community an impressive exposition of the Roman theology of the Trinity, and tactfully wrote privately to his brother bishop requesting an explanation of his position. The Alexandrian responded with a reasoned apologia which, while insisting on the distinction of the divine persons, made it clear that he was no tritheist; and this seems to have settled the matter.

Dionysius exerted himself no less actively in practical affairs. At his accession he was faced, first, with the disarray of the Roman church caused by Valerian's persecution, and then by the problems created by Emperor Gallienus's (260–8) reversal of his father's policies and restoration of the church's confiscated property and cemeteries. Dionysius seems to have carried through, or at any rate inaugurated, a thorough reorganization of the church, a glimpse of which may be obtained from the report of *LP* that he allocated the parishes and the cemeteries to the several priests, and delimited new episcopal units in his metropolitan area. In addition, he vigorously maintained the Roman church's long-standing tradition of helping distressed Christians wherever they might be; more than a century later Basil the Great (d. 379) was to recall with admiration his generosity in dispatching letters of encouragement to the afflicted church in Cappadocia (central Turkey), as well as funds for ransoming Christians in captivity. The last mention of him is at the head of the letter which the synod of Antioch, which deposed Paul of Samosata for his *adoptionist leanings, addressed to him and Maximus, the new bishop of Antioch, announcing its decision in 268/9. Whether he received it or not is not clear, for he was dead by the end of 268. One of the most important popes of the 3rd cent., he was not a martyr, as claimed by *LP*, for the *Roman calendar of 354 placed him in its list of episcopal burials, not in that of martyrs. He was buried in the papal crypt in the cemetery of CALLISTUS. Feast 26 Dec.

Eusebius, *Hist. eccl.* 7, 5, 6; 7, 7, 6; 7, 13; 7, 26, 1; 7, 30, 1–18; Athanasius, *De decret.* 25 f.; *De sent. Dion. passim*; Basil, *Ep.* 70; *LP* 1, 157; C. H. Turner, 'The Papal Chronology of the Third Century', *JTS* 17 (1916), 348 f.; J. N. D. Kelly, *Early Christian Doctrines* (5th edn., London, 1977), 133–6; Caspar 1, 54; 84; 90–3; 222; *DHGE* 14, 247 f. (B. Botte); *LThK* 3, 405 (G. Schwaiger); *NCE* 4, 876 (E. G. Weltin); Seppelt 1, 59–64.

FELIX I, ST (3 Jan. 269–30 Dec. 274). Described by *LP* as a Roman by birth, son of Constantius, he is one of the obscurest popes, even his dates being conjectural. He was the recipient, probably, of the letter announcing the deposition of the local bishop, Paul of Samosata, for Trinitarian error, and the election of Domnus I in his place, which the synod of Antioch sent in 268/9 to Pope DIONYSIUS, Bishop Maximus of Alexandria, and other bishops. As a result he seems to have entered formally into communion with Domnus and corresponded with Maximus. A creed-like fragment bearing his name, which circulated in Alexandria and was cited by Cyril of Alexandria (d. 444) in the 5th-cent. Christological debates, may possibly be a retouched extract from his letter to Maximus. Although deposed, Paul of Samosata refused to vacate the church building at Antioch until Emperor Aurelian (270–5), to whom the orthodox appealed, ordered it to

be handed over to 'those with whom the bishops of Italy and of Rome were in communication'. It must therefore have been Felix who gave the decision in favour of Timaeus, the successor of Domnus (d. 270/1), and secured the undignified expulsion of Paul. Apart from these surmises, nothing is known about Felix's activities. *LP*'s report that he died a martyr and was buried on the Via Aurelia is erroneous, the result of a confusion between him and actual Roman martyrs bearing the same name. The *Roman calendar of 354 includes him in its list of episcopal burials, not that of martyrs; and the 4th-cent. Liberian Catalogue states that he was interred in the papal crypt in the cemetery of CALLISTUS on the Appian Way. Feast 30 May.

Eusebius, *Hist. eccl.* 7, 30, 19–23; 7, 32, 1; *LP* 1, cxxv; 158; Caspar 1, 43; 84; 468; J. Quasten, *Patrology* (Utrecht and Antwerp, 1953) 2, 242; H. Lietzmann, *Apollinaris von Laodicea und seine Schule* (Tübingen, 1904), 91–4; 318–21; C. H. Turner, 'The Papal Chronology of the Third Century', *JTS* 17 (1916), 349; F. Millar, 'Paul of Samosata, Zenobia and Aurelian', *JRS* 61 (1971), 1–17; *DHGE* 16, 886 f. (P. Nautin); *LThK* 4, 67 (G. Schwaiger); *NCE* 5, 878 f. (E. G. Weltin).

EUTYCHIAN, ST (4 Jan. 275–7 Dec. 283). He was, according to *LP*, a native of Tuscany, son of Marinus. While his dates can be fixed within a year, no reliable information about his activities or personality survives; the remainder of *LP*'s account is either anachronistic conjecture, e.g. that he decreed that only beans and grapes should be blessed at mass (a usage attested in the much later Gelasian and Gregorian Sacramentaries), or pure fantasy, e.g. that he personally buried 342 martyrs. It is worth noting that his pontificate fell wholly within the period of peace between the persecutions of Emperors Valerian (253–60) and Diocletian (284–305), when the Roman church was able to develop and consolidate its position (as is evidenced by the extensions of the official cemeteries undertaken then). Such records of his reign as existed may have perished in the devastation caused by Diocletian's persecution. *LP*'s assertion (only in its 2nd edition) that he died a martyr should be rejected. The *Roman calendar of 354 included him in its list of episcopal burials, not in that of martyrs. He was the last pope to be interred in the papal crypt in the cemetery of CALLISTUS, where fragments of his epitaph, in ill-formed Greek letters, have been found. Feast 7 Dec.

Eusebius, *Hist. eccl.* 7, 32, 1; *LP* 1, cxxxi–clix; 6 f.; 10; 159 f.; Caspari 1, 43; 84; *DCB* 2, 412 (J. Barmby); *DHGE* 16, 91 f. (H. Marot); *LThK* 3, 1214 (G. Schwaiger); C. H. Turner, 'The Papal Chronology of the Third Century', *JTS* 17 (1916), 350; P. Styger, *Die römischen Katakomben* (Berlin, 1933), 49.

GAIUS, or CAIUS, ST (17 Dec. 283–22 Apr. 296).

Although he was described by *LP* as Dalmatian in origin, a relative of Emperor Diocletian (284–305), these particulars are suspect; they derive from the 6th-cent. Passion of St Susanna, whose uncle he was supposed to be and with whom he became linked through the fact that her cult was localized at the *titulus*, or *title church, of Gaius at Rome. He also figures in the Passion of St Sebastian, which represents him as encouraging the soldier saint and his companions to face their impending martyrdom. *LP*'s further reports about him should also be dismissed as anachronistic, especially its statement that he took refuge in the catacombs during Diocletian's persecution and (in its 2nd edition) died a martyr. While his dates can be determined with a reasonable degree of accuracy, nothing is known about him or his activities; all that is clear is that his reign fell in a period of peace and consolidation for the Roman church. The *Roman calendar of 354 did not include him in its list of martyrs. He was buried in the cemetery of CALLISTUS in a sector separate from the old papal crypt, which was probably full; fragments of his epitaph, in Greek letters with his initial distinctly given as a *gamma*, were found there in the nineteenth century. Feast 22 Apr.

Eusebius, *Hist. eccl.* 7, 32, 1; *LP* 1, xcviii–xcix; 6 f.; 71 f.; 161; Caspar 1, 43 f.; 50 f.; 50 f.; 84; 97; *DCB* 1, 386 f. (E. B. Birks); *DACL* 2, 1736 (H.

Leclercq); *DHGE* 11, 237 f. (G. Bardy); *LThK* 2, 877 (G. Schwaiger); *BSS* 3, 646–9 (A. Amore); *NCE* 6, 241 (E. G. Weltin); C. H. Turner, 'The Papal Chronology of the Third Century', *JTS* 17 (1916), 350 f.

MARCELLINUS, ST (30 June 296–?304; d. 25 Oct. 304).

While nothing is known of his background, much the greater part of his reign fell in a period when the church enjoyed external peace. His sole recorded action in these years was, according to an inscription, to authorize one of his deacons, Severus, to carry out certain structural modifications in the cemetery of CALLISTUS. On 23 Feb. 303, however, Emperor Diocletian (284–305) issued his first persecuting edict ordering the destruction of churches, the surrender of sacred books, and the offering of sacrifice by those attending law-courts. Marcellinus complied and, probably in May 303, handed over copies of the Scriptures; he also, apparently, offered incense to the gods. Several of his clergy, including the presbyters MARCELLUS, MILTIADES, and SILVESTER, all three to become popes, were later said to have acted with him. The *Donatists used these facts, of which they had documentary evidence, in their controversy early in the 5th cent. with St Augustine, who, while denying the allegations, did so in a perfunctory and embarrassed manner. Marcellinus's guilt is borne out by the facts that his name was omitted from the official list of popes and that DAMASUS I completely ignored him when composing verse tributes to previous popes. By the end of the 5th and the beginning of the 6th cents. it is evident that his apostasy was frankly acknowledged, and efforts were being made to present it in a favourable light. Thus *LP*, basing itself on a now lost Passion of St Marcellinus, relates how he was ordered to sacrifice and proceeded to do so, but a few days later was filled with remorse for his weakness; he was then beheaded with three others on Diocletian's orders. An independent account of his apostasy, and supposed avowal of it at the pseudo-council of Sinuessa (west of

Capua), appears in the apocryphal acts (early 6th cent.). There is in fact no evidence of his martyrdom; no one in the 4th cent. seems to have had any inkling of it, and St Augustine made no reference to it when dealing with the Donatists' charges. On the other hand, his surrender of sacred books disqualified him from the priesthood, and if he was not actually deposed (as some scholars argue) he must have left the Roman church without an acknowledged head. The date of his abdication or deposition is not known. He died on 25 Oct. 304, and was buried in the cemetery of Sta Priscilla on the Via Salaria; this was presumably chosen because it was private property of the powerful family of the Acilii Glabrioni, the church's official cemeteries having been confiscated by the government at the beginning of the persecution. Because of the story of his execution at the emperor's behest he came to be venerated as a martyr. Feast 2 June.

Eusebius, *Hist. eccl.* 7, 32, 1; Augustine, *C. litt. Petil.* 2, 202; 2, 208; *De unic. bapt.* 16, 27; *Brevic. coll. cum Donat.* 3, 34; *LP* 1, lxxi–lxxiv; xcix; 72 f.; 162 f.; *PL* 6, 20 (Sinuessa); E. H. Röttges, 'Marcellinus–Marcellus', *ZKTh* 78 (1956), 385–420; A. Amore, 'Il preteso "lapsus" di papa Marcellino', *Antonianum* 32 (1955), 411–26; W. H. Frend, *Martyrdom and Persecution in the Early Church* (London, 1965), 503 f.; T. D. Barnes, *Constantine and Eusebius* (Harvard, 1981), 38; 303 f.; Caspar 1, 97–9; *DCB* 3, 804–6 (J. Barmby); *EC* 8, 10 f. (V. Monachino); *DACL* 10, 1762–73 (H. Leclercq); *LThK* 7, 1 (A. Stuiber); *NCE* 9, 188 (E. G. Weltin); Seppelt 1, 65–7.

MARCELLUS I, ST (Nov./Dec. 306–16 Jan. 308). Because of internal divisions as well as the persecution, the Roman see remained vacant for just over three and a half years after MARCELLINUS's apostasy. With the accession of Emperor Maxentius (306–12) and his adoption of toleration, an election became practicable. The man chosen, Marcellus, had been a leading presbyter under Marcellinus, and had probably played the key role during the vacancy. It is very unlikely that the *Donatists' later allegations that he had sur-

rendered sacred books to the authorities along with Marcellinus were true, for he proved a merciless judge of such conduct and seems to have expunged Marcellinus's name from official lists of popes. His dates, it should be noted, are uncertain, many scholars, for instance, accepting a later, shorter reign from 27 May or 26 June 308 to 16 Jan. 309. An important task facing him must have been the reorganization of the church in the improved political climate, and this probably underlies the anachronistically expressed report of *LP* that he divided the city into twenty-five *tituli*, or parishes, each under its presbyter. But a no less pressing issue was the multitude who had compromised the faith under persecution. To judge by the verse tribute composed for him by DAMASUS I, Marcellus was a rigorist whose hard-line penitential demands soon aroused majority opinion in the community against him. The resulting public disorder and even bloodshed led Maxentius to intervene, and when Marcellus was denounced to him by an apostate he banished him from the city as a disturber of the peace. He died shortly after, but it is not known where; his body was subsequently brought back to Rome and interred in the cemetery of Sta Priscilla, a private property which had not been impounded during the persecution. Later legend, reproduced by *LP* in its 2nd edition, embellished his death with the story that Maxentius, infuriated by his refusal to sacrifice to the gods, converted the building which was to become his *title church into a stable for horses of the imperial post and made the pope tend them as a groom, in which menial role he died. In fact, the 5th-cent. Martyrology of St Jerome records that he died as a confessor. Feast 16 Jan.

Since the late 19th cent. a case has been argued, on the basis of the confusion between them in the sources, the absence of one or other name from key texts, and other puzzling facts, for the identification of Marcellus with Marcellinus (of whose existence there can be no doubt), or at any rate for regarding him as a presbyter who exercised quasi-papal functions during the long interregnum rather than as an actual pope. It continues to attract support, but has to meet formidable difficulties, notably the appearance of both as popes in the Liberian Catalogue, compiled some forty years later, and Damasus I's description of Marcellus as 'rector', a term he reserves for a bishop, in his verse epitaph for him.

A. Ferrua, *Epigrammata Damasiana* (Vatican City, 1942), 181; *LP* 1, lxxiii–lxxiv; lxxix; ccxlix; 6 f.; 72–4; 164–6; T. Mommsen, *Neues Archiv* 21 (1896), 335–57; E. H. Röttges, 'Marcellinus–Marcellus', *ZKTh* 78 (1956), 385–420; A. Amore, 'E esistito papa Marcello?', *Antonianum* 33 (1958), 57–75; T. D. Barnes, *Constantine and Eusebius* (Harvard, 1981), 38; 303 f.; Caspar 1, 43; 54; 97–101; PW 14, 1494; *EC* 8, 16 f. (V. Monachino); *BSS* 8, 672–6 (A. Amore); *NCE* 9, 190 (E. G. Weltin).

EUSEBIUS, ST (18 Apr.–21 Oct. 310). While there is uncertainty about the year (308 or 309 has also been proposed), the days and months of his accession and death are supplied by the 4th-cent. Liberian Catalogue. According to *LP* he was a Greek by extraction (as his name would suggest) who had been a physician; its further attribution of the finding of the Saviour's cross to his pontificate is a patent anachronism. The dissension and rioting in the Roman community over the terms on which Christians who had lapsed in the persecution of Emperor Diocletian (284–305) should be readmitted to communion, which had led to the exile of MARCELLUS I, continued in Eusebius's brief reign. From the verse tribute which DAMASUS I composed in his honour, it appears that he allowed those who had apostatized to be restored after due penance, while Heraclius, the leader of an opposing faction who seems to have been a sort of antipope, resisted their readmission. In spite of Eusebius's efforts to maintain peace, the split in the community caused government intervention, and Emperor Maxentius (306–12) had both him and Heraclius deported to Sicily. There he soon died. His body was subsequently brought back to Rome and interred in the cemetery of CALLISTUS. In his eulogy Damasus designated him a martyr, but neither the *Roman calendar of 354 nor *LP* itself suggests that he was one. Feast 17 Aug.

A. Ferrua, *Epigrammata Damasiana* (Vatican City, 1942), 129–36; *LP* 1, cvii–cix; 8–10; 74 f.; 167; I. Carini, *I lapsi e la deportazione in Sicilia del papa s. Eusebio* (Rome, 1886); E. Caspar, 'Die römische Bischöfe der diokletianischen Verfolgung', *ZKG* 46 (1927), 330–3; *DHGE* 15, 1433 (H. Marot); *EC* 5, 857 (A. Amore); Caspar 1, 99–101; 128 f.; *LThK* 3, 1198 f. (G. Schwaiger).

MILTIADES, or MELCHIADES, ST (2 July 311–10 Jan. 314). The first pope to see the church not only tolerated but beginning to enjoy the active favour of the Roman government, he was elected, after a vacancy of indeterminate length, depending on whether EUSEBIUS's accession was in 310 or, as scholars variously argue, in 308 or 309, at a moment when the political situation made a new appointment urgently desirable. Although described by *LP* as an African, it is more likely that he was a Roman in origin. He had been a presbyter under Pope MARCELLINUS, and a century later was to be accused by the *Donatists of implication in his apostasy; no such charge seems to have been advanced in his lifetime. Hardly had he assumed office when Emperor Maxentius (306–12), anticipating the policies which were to be laid down by the convention of Milan in Feb. 313, ordered the restoration of the properties of the church, including land and buildings, confiscated at the beginning of Diocletian's persecution (303). It fell to Miltiades to send his deacons, armed with the imperial rescript, to the city prefect to claim formal restitution. As a result the Roman church, with him presiding, was able to celebrate Easter on 13 Apr. 312 in full security and possession of its holy places for the first time since the outbreak of persecution. He must have met Constantine the Great (306–37) soon after his triumph over Maxentius at the Milvian Bridge (28 Oct. 312), and it was probably during the emperor's stay in Rome (or perhaps later) that he presented Miltiades with the Empress Fausta's palace (the Lateran) on Monte Celio, henceforth the papal residence. Less than a year later, when the rigorist party in north Africa objected to Bishop Caecilian of Carthage on the ground that one of his consecrators had been a *traditor* (i.e. had surrendered sacred books during the persecution), elected a rival bishop Majorinus (soon to be replaced by Donatus), and appealed to Constantine to arbitrate, the emperor commissioned Miltiades, sitting with three Gallic bishops nominated by himself, to adjudicate the affair in Rome and report to him; the imperial letter, the first of its kind received by a pope, survives in a Greek translation. Miltiades shrewdly transformed the government commission of inquiry into a regular church synod by himself adding fifteen Italian bishops. The synod met in Fausta's palace, with both Caecilian and his principal accuser, Donatus, now Majorinus's successor, present, but it did not in fact investigate the charge that the consecrator, Felix of Aptunga, had been a *traditor*, since from the Roman point of view the effectiveness of a sacrament did not depend on the worthiness of the officiant. On 3 Oct. 313 it gave its verdict in favour of Caecilian, pronouncing him lawful bishop of Carthage, and excommunicated Donatus for requiring the *rebaptism of laity and reordination of clergy who had lapsed under persecution. On the other hand, Miltiades sought to isolate Donatus by offering communion to other dissident African bishops on terms which allowed them to retain their episcopal status. These decisions deeply disappointed the Donatists, as they came to be called after their leader, and led them later in the century to spread scandalous rumours about Miltiades' conduct during the persecution. They appealed again to Constantine, and he, although irritated by their obstinacy, summoned a council representative of all the western provinces to meet at Arles on 1 Aug. 314; it is noteworthy that, although the pope had pronounced, the emperor did not consider his verdict final. Before the council met, however, Miltiades was long dead; he was

buried in an as yet unidentified spot in the cemetery of CALLISTUS on the Appian Way. Feast 10 Dec.

Eusebius, *Hist. eccl.* 10, 5, 18–20; Optatus Milev., *De schism. Donat.* 1, 23 f.; Augustine, *Brevic. coll. cum Donat.* 3, 18, 34; *De unic. bapt.* 16, 28 f.; *C. ep. Parm.* 1, 10; *C. part. Donat.* 17; *Ep.* 43; *LP* 1, 8 f.; 168 f.; H. U. Instinsky, *Bischofsstuhl und Kaiserthron* (Munich, 1955); 'Zwei Bischofsnamen Konstantinischer Zeit', *RQ* 55 (1960), 203–11; E. Caspar, 'Die römische Synode von 313', *ZKG* 46 (1927), 333–46; Caspar 1, 102; 109 ff.; 124; *DTC* 10, 1764 (É. Amann); *EC* 8, 1015 f. (V. Monachino); PW 15, 1706 f. (W. Ensslin); *NCE* 9, 857 f. (J. Chapin); Seppelt 1, 72–5.

SILVESTER I, ST (31 Jan. 314–31 Dec. 335). Although *LP* describes him as a Roman, son of Rufinus, his origins are hopelessly entangled with later legend. This pictured him as having suffered in the persecution of Diocletian (284–305), and the use of 'most glorious' in addressing him indicates that in this respect at least the legend was correct. The story also makes it likely that the *Donatists' later allegation that as a presbyter he had joined with Pope MARCELLINUS in surrendering sacred books to the authorities was a libel. Although pope for almost twenty-two years of the reign of Constantine the Great (306–37), an epoch of dramatic developments for the church, he seems to have played an insignificant part in the great events that were taking place, and only one or two glimpses of him, negative but instructive, survive. First, when Constantine summoned the first council of Arles (1 Aug. 314) in a further attempt to adjudicate the claims of Caecilian to be bishop of Carthage, still contested by the Donatists in spite of Pope MILTIADES' decision in his favour the previous year, he did not make the bishop of Rome its chairman but entrusted its general conduct to Chrestus, bishop of Syracuse, while the bishop of Arles, Marinus, presided. Silvester did not attend but sent two priests and two deacons to represent him; his absence was caused not by disapproval of Constantine's initiative in calling a church council but (probably) by the difficulty of leaving Rome so soon after his installation. When it broke up, the council communicated its decisions to him in a letter which eloquently expressed its sense of his primacy over the west, and requested him to circulate them to all the churches. Secondly, Silvester was also absent from the ecumenical council which, again summoned by Constantine, met at Nicaea (Iznik, in north-west Turkey) in summer 325 and agreed a creed declaring the Son 'one in being' with the Father and condemning the teaching of Arius that he was a creature, inferior to the Father. Like other bishops of the empire, Silvester was invited to attend, but although he had been kept informed of the controversy as it developed he declined to do so, this time pleading old age. He sent two priests to represent him, and although they were not accorded any precedence at the council, they affixed their signatures to the acts before all the bishops present except Ossius of Cordoba, who as president signed first. In the 5th and 6th cents. the idea was to gain credence that Ossius had been commissioned by the pope, and even that the council had been summoned by the pope and the emperor in concert; but these are legends without historical foundation. There were certainly bishops whom Constantine made his confidants, and with whom he concerted his ecclesiastical policies; but Silvester was not one of them. He had the satisfaction, however, of seeing the church over which he presided enriched and beautified by the emperor's princely benefactions, which included great churches like the Basilica Constantiniana (later S. Giovanni in Laterano), with its baptistery, and the basilicas of St Peter and St Paul. It was appropriate that the bulk of Silvester's notice in *LP* should be devoted to listing these gifts in detail, for it was during his pontificate that Rome, as a result of Constantine's generosity, began to wear the external trappings of a Christian city. He was buried in the cemetery of Sta Priscilla on the Via Salaria. Feast 31 Dec.

Later generations found it incredible that

the pope could have played such an insignificant role beside the first Christian emperor, or that Constantine could have deferred his baptism until his deathbed, receiving it then from an Arian bishop (Eusebius of Nicomedia). In the second half of the 5th cent. a romanticized version of Silvester's life (the *Acts of St Silvester*) gained currency, in which, among other fictions, he was alleged to have converted Constantine, previously a persecutor, baptized him, cured him of leprosy, and imposed on him the penance of closing the pagan temples and setting imprisoned Christians free. Deriving from this, there came to be accepted as authentic the so-called 'Donation of Constantine', a document in which the emperor was represented as conferring on Silvester and his successors the primacy over the great ecclesiastical patriarchates, and temporal dominion over Rome, Italy, and all provinces and states of the west generally. Constantine was also represented as offering the imperial crown to Silvester, who declined to wear it but agreed to the transfer of the imperial government from Rome to Constantinople. A fabrication of the 8th–9th cents., this document came to be treated as authoritative even by opponents of the papacy, and was only exposed as false in the 16th cent.

Eusebius, *Hist. eccl.* 10, 5, 21–4; Jaffé 1, 28–30; *CSEL* 21, 206–10; *LP* 1, cix–cxx; clii–cliv; 74–81; 170–201; H. U. Instinsky, *Bischofsstuhl und Kaiserthron* (Munich, 1955), 83–102; Caspar 1, 115–30; *DCB* 4, 673–7 (J. Barmby); *DTC* 14, 2068–75 (É. Amann); *NCE* 13, 857 f. (J. Chapin). For the Silvester legend see W. Levison, 'Konstantinische Schenkung und Silvester-Legende', *ST* 38 (1924), 159–247; H. Fuhrmann, 'Konstantinische Schenkung und Silvesterlegende in neuer Sicht', *DA* 15 (1959), 523–40; E. Ewig, 'Das Bild Constantins des Grossen im abendländischen Mittelalter', *HJ* 75 (1956), 10–46; *NCE* 4, 1000 f. (W. Ullmann).

MARK, ST (18 Jan.–7 Oct. 336). Although *LP* describes him as a Roman, son of Priscus, nothing is reliably known of his background. He should possibly be identified with the Mark mentioned by Constantine the Great (305–37) in his letter to Pope MILTIADES in 313 asking him to hold a synod to adjudicate the case of Caecilian of Carthage; if so, he must have then been prominent among the Roman clergy. His short reign fell in eventful times, with Athanasius (c. 296–373) banished from Alexandria to Trier, Marcellus of Ancyra (d. c. 374) and other leaders of Nicene orthodoxy deposed, and the arch-heretic Arius on his deathbed; but there is no evidence that Mark was in any way involved in the struggle arising out of the council of *Nicaea (325); an exchange of letters attributed to Athanasius and him in the 9th-cent. collection known as the False Decretals is spurious. *LP* claims that he granted the pallium (a band of white wool decorated with crosses, worn by the pope and bestowed by him on metropolitans) to the bishops of Ostia and decreed that they should always consecrate the bishop of Rome. The former statement is doubtful, since while popes began using the pallium in the 4th cent. there is no proof of their conferring it on other prelates so early; but the latter may well be correct since St Augustine, writing in 413, takes it as established custom for the Roman pontiff to have the bishop of Ostia as the first of his three consecrators. It seems that Mark founded two churches. One was the *title church of Mark, originally named after him but later placed under the patronage of the Second Evangelist; probably a simple house which he owned and converted into a church, it was long ago incorporated into what is now the Palazzo di Venezia. The other was a basilica in the cemetery of S. Balbina on the Via Ardeatina, the ruins of which survived until the 17th cent. There is evidence that it was during his reign that the compilation of the *Depositio episcoporum* and the *Depositio martyrum*, the precious ancient lists of anniversaries of the deaths of Roman bishops and martyrs, was begun. Feast 7 Oct.

JW 1, 30–2; *LP* 1, 80 f.; 202–4; Caspar 1, 18; 142; *DCB* 3, 825 (J. Barmby); *DTC* 9, 1959 f. (É. Amann); *EC* 8, 50 (V. Monachino); *BSS* 8, 699 f.

(G. D. Gordini); *NCE* 9, 232 f. (J. Chapin); A. Ferrua, 'La basilica di papa Marco', *Civiltà cattolica* 99 (1948), 503–13; V. Monachino, *La cura pastorale a Milano, Cartagine e Roma nel iv secolo* (Rome, 1947), 282; 300.

JULIUS I, ST (6 Feb. 337–12 Apr. 352). A Roman of forceful character, elected after a four-month vacancy, he is chiefly known for his vigorous support of *Nicene orthodoxy and of its eastern champions, *Athanasius of Alexandria (d. 373) and Marcellus of Ancyra (d. c. 376), whom the Arianizing party associated with Eusebius of Nicomedia (d. c. 342), now dominant in the east, had ejected from their bishoprics. When Constantine the Great died (22 May 337) they were allowed by the government to return to their sees, but the dismayed Eusebians sought to enlist Julius's help to prevent this. Not only did he decline to endorse the bishops' deposition and replacement by Arianizing nominees, but when they fled to Rome he took them under his protection; he admitted Marcellus, suspected of *Sabellianism, to communion on the basis of his subscription to the Roman baptismal creed. In autumn 340 he held a synod at Rome (the easterners had originally proposed it, but now refused to attend) which completely cleared the bishops of doctrinal error. He communicated these decisions to the easterners in a masterly letter in which he reproached them for condemning bishops of apostolic sees without reference to the episcopate as a whole and, more particularly, for ignoring, in the case of Athanasius, the customary prerogatives of Rome in relation to Alexandria. An impasse was reached when the Eusebians, at the Dedication Council of Antioch in summer 341, reaffirmed their condemnation of Athanasius and adopted a creed which, omitting the Nicene key-phrase 'one in being with the Father', attacked the theology of Marcellus. To find a way out the two emperors, Constans (337–50) and Constantius II (337–61), at the request of Julius, convened a general council of east and west at Serdica (Sofia) in

342 (or 343). When the western delegation, however, insisted on Athanasius and Marcellus taking part in the proceedings, the eastern one indignantly withdrew and issued an encyclical not only reiterating the anathema on them but excommunicating leading western bishops, including Julius, whom it branded as the cause of all the trouble. Meanwhile the western majority continued to meet as a council, and although Julius was not personally present his influence can be detected in its renewed vindication of Athanasius and his colleagues, its condemnation of many of the Eusebians and their supporters, and its canons, particularly those (3, 4, 5) giving a deposed bishop the right to appeal to the pope.

A curtain falls over the rest of Julius's reign, but when Athanasius was allowed in 345 to return to Alexandria, he called on his way at Rome, where the pope furnished him with an eloquent letter congratulating his church on receiving back their valiant pastor. Julius also had the satisfaction in 347, when the tide seemed to be turning against them, of accepting a cringing recantation from Bishops Ursacius and Valens, two of Athanasius's bitterest foes and leaders of Arianism in the west, and of restoring them temporarily to communion. Information about his activities on the domestic front is sparse, but *LP* credits him, possibly correctly, with reorganizing the papal chancery on the model of imperial practice; for the first time mention is made of the *primicerius notariorum*, or senior notary. His care for the growing Christian population of Rome inspired him to found several churches, notably Sta Maria in Trastevere and the Julian basilica (now SS. Apostoli). He was buried in the cemetery of Calepodius on the Via Aurelia, his name being immediately included in the *Roman calendar of 354. Feast 12 Apr.

Athanasius, *Apol. c. Ar.* 21–35; 52 f. (two letters); *PL* 8, 857–944; *PLSupp* 1, 191 f.; JW 1, 30–2; E. Schwartz, *Gesammelte Schriften* (Berlin, 1936–63), 4; H. Hess, *The Canons of the Council of Serdica a.d. 343* (Oxford, 1958); *LP* 1, 8 f.; 205 f.;

Caspar 1, 142–65; Haller 1, 65–71; *DCB* 3, 526–32 (J. Barmby); *DTC* 8, 1914–17 (É. Amann); *PRE* 9, 619–21 (H. Böhmer); *LThK* 5, 1203 f. (R. Bäumer); *NCE* 8, 51 f. (J. Chapin); Seppelt 1, 86–95.

LIBERIUS (17 May 352–24 Sept. 366). A Roman by birth, he was elected at a time when the pro-*Arian faction was in the ascendant in the east and Constantius II (337–61), now sole emperor, was taking steps to force the western episcopate to fall into line and join the east in anathematizing Athanasius of Alexandria (d. 373), always the symbol of Nicene orthodoxy. The eastern bishops had recently written to JULIUS I urging him to examine afresh the case of Athanasius, whose deposition by the council of Tyre (335) the west steadfastly refused to accept, but the new pope, although mild and impulsive, lacking his predecessor's strength of character, rejected their accusations and sent envoys to Constantius, then resident at Arles, requesting him to summon a council at Aquileia which would settle the issues disputed between east and west. Instead the emperor, influenced by his theological advisers, the pro-Arian bishops Ursacius and Valens, held a synod there and then at Arles which, bypassing theological questions, reaffirmed the condemnation of Athanasius; under pressure, even the pope's legates concurred. Deploring their weakness, Liberius demanded a new general council, stressing that the *Nicene faith and not just the position of Athanasius was at stake. When the council met at Milan in Oct. 355 there was no discussion of the Nicene creed; once again the emperor used bullying tactics to extract a condemnation of Athanasius from all the delegates except three convinced Nicenes, who were promptly exiled. Since Liberius still held out, resisting bribery and then threats, he was brought by force to Milan and then, proving unyielding, banished to Beroea in Thrace. Here, as the months slipped by and the local bishop worked on him, his morale collapsed and, in painful contrast to his previous resolute stand, he now acquiesced in Athanasius's excommunication, accepted the ambiguous First Creed of Sirmium (which omitted the Nicene 'one in being with the Father'), and made abject submission to the emperor. His capitulation is pathetically mirrored in four letters which he wrote from exile in spring 357 to Arianizing bishops, and which suggest that he was ready to pay almost any price to return home. Finally, brought to Sirmium (Mitrovica in Yugoslavia) in 358, he was content to sign a formula which, while rejecting the Nicene 'one in being with the Father', declared the Son to be like the Father in being and indeed in everything.

The emperor, satisfied that public order in Rome could only be restored by his return, now allowed Liberius to go back. In his absence his archdeacon FELIX had been elected bishop, but had proved extremely unpopular. The Roman church was now informed that Liberius could return on condition that he and Felix reigned jointly. He was welcomed enthusiastically by the populace, who spurned the suggestion of a joint episcopate with the acclamation 'one God, one Christ, one bishop'. Felix had to withdraw to the suburbs, but the two bishops seem to have reached a *modus vivendi*, with the great majority of clergy and laity attached to Liberius. Despite his personal triumph in Rome, however, he was gravely compromised in the church at large; for several years leadership of the west passed effectively into other hands. Perhaps because of this, but also because there were two bishops in Rome, Liberius was not invited, nor did he send delegates, to the synod of Rimini (359), at which the western bishops were eventually browbeaten into accepting an Arianizing creed. With the death of Constantius (3 Nov. 361), however, he was free to re-assume his role as champion of Nicene orthodoxy. First, he published a decree setting aside the Arianizing decisions at Rimini. Then in 362, associating himself with conciliatory measures taken earlier in the year at the synod of Alexandria, he instructed the

bishops of Italy to enter into communion with those who had compromised themselves at Rimini provided they adhered to the Nicene faith. Finally in 366, when eastern bishops were seeking western support, he granted them communion on the strict condition that they accepted the Nicene creed.

Thus in his closing years Liberius atoned in some degree for his temporary capitulation, and made a contribution to the unity of east and west. The violent disorders, however, which erupted in Rome after his death suggest that he was a weak pope who failed to maintain cohesion in the Roman community. He built the huge Liberian basilica on the Esquiline, transformed in the 5th cent. into Sta Maria Maggiore. A discourse on virginity he is said to have delivered at the veiling of Marcellina, St Ambrose's sister, is largely the work of St Ambrose himself. The almanac known as the Chronograph of 354, comprising lists of emperors, consuls, popes, martyrs, etc., derives from his reign. In the 5th-cent. Martyrology of St Jerome he was commemorated on 23 Sept., but his name does not occur in later calendars; as early as the 6th cent. hostile legend represented him as a traitor to the faith and persecutor of the faithful. This is the distorted picture of Liberius which appears in *LP*.

PL 8, 1348–1410 (letters, etc); *Pl. Supp* 1, 197–201; *CSEL* 65, 155–73 (letters from exile); 35, 1 f. (Liberius and Felix); Sozomen, *Hist. eccl.* 4, 15; JW 1, 32–6; *LP* 1, cxx–cxxiii; 82 f.; 207–10; Caspar 1, 166–95; Haller 1, 71–5; *DCB* 3, 717–24 (J. Barmby); *DTC* 9, 631–59 (É. Amann); *EC* 7, 1269–72 (V. Monachino); Seppelt 1, 95–102.

FELIX II, ST (antipope 355–22 Nov. 365). Nothing is known about his background except that he was archdeacon when LIBERIUS was banished to Beroea by Emperor Constantius II (337–61) in late 355. Led by Felix, the Roman clergy solemnly swore to recognize no one else as their bishop during Liberius's lifetime. In spite of this, yielding to the emperor's demands, they soon elected Felix pope. He

DAMASUS I (366–84)

was consecrated by three *Arianizing prelates, not in a church but, according to
Athanasius of Alexandria (d. 373), in the
imperial palace, presumably at Milan, and
entered into communion with the Arianizing party favoured by Constantius. As some
of the clergy and almost all the laity
remained devoted to Liberius, Felix's
installation at Rome provoked a violent
popular reaction; when Constantius visited
Rome in Apr. 357, he was met with
demonstrations in favour of Liberius and
lobbied by society ladies demanding the
exile's return. The government's continued
recognition of Felix is revealed by a constitution of the Theodosian Code addressed
to him as bishop by Constantius Augustus
and Julian Caesar on 6 Dec. 357, confirming the exemption of clergy, their families
and employees from taxes and other
charges. Constantius was satisfied,
however, that the restoration of Liberius
was essential to the preservation of public
order, and, having bent him to his will,
permitted him to return in 358 on the
understanding that Felix and he should be
co-bishops. The citizens, however, objected to this unprecedented arrangement,
shouting the slogan 'One God, one Christ,
one bishop', and expelled Felix from the
city. When he staged a comeback and
attempted to celebrate mass in the Julian
basilica, he was thrown out again. He had to
resign himself to settling in the suburbs, but
seems to have retained loyal supporters,
including some clergy. According to LP, he
bought a property on the Via Aurelia, built a
church there, and was eventually buried in
it. It appears that from 357 to 365 Rome had
two bishops, Liberius occupying the
Lateran palace from 358 and Felix
established in the suburbs, with the clergy
and people unequally divided between
them. Each could appeal to the imperial
letter recognizing them as joint bishops; and
the sole concern of the city prefect was to
prevent clashes between the two communities pending the death of one of them. Felix
in fact died first, the exact date of his death
(22 Nov. 365) being carefully preserved by

his partisans, and Liberius was wise enough
to seek to amalgamate Felix's clergy with his
own. By a strange irony, however, Felix was
to enjoy a posthumous triumph. Although
contemporary documents speak of him as
an Arianizing interloper intruded by Constantius, he not only came to be included in
the official list of Roman popes with the
incorrect but traditionally accepted style of
Felix II (LP assigns him a special section,
almost all pure fiction), but through being
confused with Roman martyrs bearing the
same name was eventually venerated as a
martyr himself, with his feast on 29 July. As
his legend developed, he was believed to
have been a courageous defender of the
*Nicene faith and to have laid down his life
for it, while Liberius was represented as a
traitor to orthodoxy and a persecutor of the
faithful.

Athanasius, Hist. Ar. 75; Jerome, Chron. (Helm,
237); De vir. ill. 98; Collectio Avellana, ep. 1 (CSEL
35, 1–4); Sozomen, Hist. eccl. 4, 15; 4, 33;
Theodoret, Hist. eccl. 2, 17; LP 1, cxx–cxxv; 207–
11; Caspar 1, 188 f.; DCB 2, 480–2 (J. Barmby);
EC 5, 1134 f. (A. Amore); DHGE 16, 887–9 (P.
Nautin); Th. Mommsen, Gesammelte Schriften
(Berlin, 1905–13) 6, 570–81.

DAMASUS I, ST (1 Oct. 366–11 Dec.
384). Born in Rome c.305, he was son of a
father who rose to be priest of the church
later known as S. Lorenzo and of a mother
Laurentia; he had a sister Irene. A deacon
under LIBERIUS, he accompanied him into
exile in 355 but soon found his way back to
Rome where, in defiance of the oath of the
Roman clergy not to recognize anyone else
as pope while Liberius was alive, he took
service with Antipope FELIX II. When
Liberius was allowed to return in 358,
Damasus became at some point reconciled
with him. On Liberius's death on 24 Sept.
366 violent disorders broke out over the
choice of a successor. A group who had
remained consistently loyal to Liberius
immediately elected his deacon URSINUS in
the Julian basilica and had him consecrated
bishop, but a rival faction of Felix's
adherents elected Damasus, who did not
hesitate to consolidate his claim by hiring a

32

gang of thugs, storming the Julian basilica and carrying out a three-day massacre of Ursinians. On Sunday 1 Oct. his partisans seized the Lateran basilica, and he was there consecrated. He then sought the help of the city prefect (the first occasion of a pope enlisting the civil power against his adversaries), and he promptly expelled Ursinus and his followers from Rome. Mob violence continued until 26 Oct., when Damasus's men attacked the Liberian basilica, where the Ursinians had sought refuge; the pagan historian Ammianus Marcellinus reports that they left 137 dead on the field. Damasus was now secure on his throne; but the bishops of Italy were shocked by the reports they received, and his moral authority was weakened for several years. The antipope and his adherents, though repeatedly banished by the government, kept up continuous attacks on him throughout his reign. In about 371, through a converted Jew named Isaac, they brought a 'disgraceful charge', probably of adultery, against him, and only the emperor's intervention secured his acquittal.

In spite of these embarrassments, Damasus enjoyed the favour of court and aristocracy, not least of wealthy ladies; gossips nicknamed him 'the matrons' ear-tickler'. His magnificent life-style and hospitality helped to break down the anti-Christian prejudices of upper-class pagan families. He was active in repressing heresies, including *Arianism, and did not scruple to call in the secular power; but he failed to dislodge Auxentius (d. 374), the Arianizing bishop of Milan. His measures against the intransigently Nicene disciples of Lucifer of Cagliari (d. 370/1) were particularly brutal. In 380 he counselled moderation in dealing with Priscillianism, an esoteric Spanish heresy with dualist and *Sabellian traits, but at successive synods he anathematized Apollinarianism (which claimed that the Logos took the place of the human mind in the God-man) and Macedonianism (which denied the divinity of the Holy Spirit). His relations with the eastern churches, however, where Basil the Great (d. 379) was striving to restore orthodoxy on the basis of a subtle restatement of *Nicene doctrine, were less than happy. Like the west generally, he failed to understand the new developments and, when Antioch was split between rival bishops, persisted in backing Paulinus, the unrepresentative leader of a reactionary group, instead of Meletius, on whom eastern hopes for unity were centred; when Meletius died in 381, he refused to enter into communion with his successor Flavian. In despair Basil described him as impossibly arrogant. He took no part in the ecumenical council (the second) held at Constantinople in 381, and made no contribution to the constructive *détente* between east and west which was now under way.

Damasus was indefatigable in promoting the Roman primacy, frequently referring to Rome as 'the apostolic see' and ruling that the test of a creed's orthodoxy was its endorsement by the pope. In 378 he persuaded the government to recognize the holy see as a court of first instance and also of appeal for the western episcopate, but it declined to admit any special immunity for the pope himself from the civil courts. In tune with his ideas, Theodosius I (379–95) declared (27 Feb. 380) Christianity the state religion in that form which the Romans had once received from St PETER and Damasus of Rome and Peter of Alexandria now professed; for Damasus this primacy was not based on decisions of synods, as were the claims of Constantinople, but exclusively on his being the direct successor of St Peter and so the rightful heir of the promises made to him by Christ (Matt. 16: 18). This succession gave him a unique juridical power to bind and loose, and the assurance of this infused all his rulings on church discipline. He was also a builder of churches (including S. Lorenzo in Damaso), advanced the cult of the martyrs, and restored the catacombs with the aim of demonstrating that the real glory of Rome was not pagan but Christian. A man of cultivated interests, he organized and

33

rehoused the papal archives. He made friends with St Jerome, employed him as his secretary for several years, corresponded with him on points of exegesis, and commissioned him to revise the existing Latin translations of the gospels on the basis of the original Greek. He himself composed epigrams in sonorous, if turgid, verse, mostly in honour of martyrs and previous popes, and had them inscribed on marble slabs in the elegant lettering of his friend Filocalus; and St Jerome attributes to him essays in prose and verse on virginity. He was buried in a church he had built on the Via Ardeatina, but his remains were later transferred to S. Lorenzo in Damaso. Feast 11 Dec.

JW 1, 37–40; *PL* 13, 347–424; A. Ferrua, *Epigrammata Damasiana* (Vatican City, 1942); *Collectio Avellana* (*CSEL* 35, 1–4; 28–30; 49; 56 f.); Jerome, *De vir. ill.* 103; *ep.* 22, 22; *LP* 1, 212–15; A. Lippold, 'Ursinus und Damasus', *Historia* 14 (1965), 105–28; Caspar 1, 196–256; *DHGE* 14, 48–53 (A. van Roey); *EC* 4, 1136–9 (A. Ferrua); *LThK* 3, 136 f. (O. Perler); *NCE* 4, 624 f. (M. R. P. McGuire); Seppelt 1, 109–30.

URSINUS (antipope Sept. 366–Nov. 367: d. 385?). Nothing is known of his earlier history except that he was one of LIBERIUS's deacons. On Liberius's death on 24 Sept. 366 the animosity between his supporters and those of Antipope FELIX II, dormant since the latter's death on 22 Nov. 365, erupted afresh. The dead pope's unwavering adherents, including priests and three deacons, immediately assembled in the Julian basilica (Sta Maria in Trastevere), elected Ursinus, and had him consecrated there and then by Bishop Paul of Tibur (Tivoli). They were probably opponents of the irenic policy of Liberius, who had done his best to heal the schism after Felix's death. The former partisans of Felix, however, who may have been more numerous, elected the deacon DAMASUS, who thereupon hired a mob, savagely attacked the Ursinians, and was himself consecrated pope on 1 Oct. The bloody street-fighting continued, but Damasus eventually got the upper hand, enlisting the help of the city prefect, Viventius, who sent Ursinus and his deacons, Amantius and Lupus, into exile. He also had his priests arrested, but the Ursinians rescued them and then established themselves in the Liberian basilica (Sta Maria Maggiore), which they used for a while for worship. In response to their appeal, Emperor Valentinian I (364–75) now ordered the new city prefect, Vettius Agorius Praetextatus, to permit the return of Ursinus and his colleagues on condition that they kept the peace. The antipope and his deacons reentered the city in triumph on 15 Sept. 367. There were renewed disorders, however, and Damasus (it was alleged) having bribed the court, Ursinus was again exiled on 16 Nov., this time to Gaul. His clergy and many of his supporters were also expelled, and their last remaining church was, on government orders, handed over to Damasus. The Ursinians, however, continued to meet without clergy in cemeteries and in the church of Sta Agnese on the Via Nomentana, although they were soon brutally dislodged by the pope's henchmen. The bishops of Italy were understandably upset by the reports they received, and at a Roman synod (autumn 368) to celebrate Damasus's birthday pointedly turned down his request that they should condemn Ursinus. The government nevertheless maintained active support for Damasus, and *c.*370 issued instructions that the Ursinians should not hold meetings nearer than the twentieth milestone from Rome. A precarious peace having been thus patched up, Ursinus and leading members of his faction were released from confinement on the understanding that they did not set foot in Rome or its outskirts. They now settled in north Italy, and in the early 370s used a converted Jew named Isaac to bring a 'disgraceful charge' (of adultery, according to *LP*) against the pope. The charge was dismissed but the civil power had no option but to intervene again, relegating Ursinus to Cologne and Isaac to Spain; the Ursinians were forbidden to come within a hundred miles of Rome. Even so, the sentence seems to have been relaxed, for in Sept. 381 the synod of Aquileia complained to the emperors that Ursinus was still fomenting mischief, and requested them to get rid once for all of so persistent a trouble-maker. Yet he never abandoned hope of attaining the papal throne, and put himself forward as a candidate on Damasus's death in Dec. 384. An imperial letter survives, dated 24 Feb. 385, expressing the court's relief that he had been howled down and that SIRICIUS had been decisively elected. The date of his death is not known.

Collectio Avellana, Epp. 1, 5–13 (CSEL 35, 2–4; 48–55); Ammianus Marcellinus, Rer. gest. 27, 3; Rufinus, Hist. eccl. 2, 10; Ambrose, Ep. 11; JW 1, 36; LP 1, 212; A. Lippold, 'Ursinus und Damasus', Historia 14 (1965), 105–28; Caspar 1, 196–201; 203 f.; 208; 257; DCB 4, 1068–70 (J. Barmby); DHGE 14, 48–50 (A. van Roey); PRE 20, 346–8 (A. Jülicher); PWSupp X, 1141–8 (A. Lippold).

SIRICIUS, ST (Dec. 384–26 Nov. 399). A Roman by birth, he had been one of DAMASUS I's deacons, having before that served LIBERIUS as reader and then deacon. Although Antipope URSINUS again put himself forward, Siricius's election was unanimous, and was confirmed with evident satisfaction by Emperor Valentinian II (375–92) in a rescript (25 Feb. 385) probably intended to cut short any intrigues in the Ursinian camp. The emperor gave further proof of his approval by presenting funds for the restoration and enlargement to something approaching its present size of St Paul's basilica, which the new pope consecrated in 390.

St Jerome, who had once fancied himself as pope and in whose expulsion from Rome Siricius must at least have concurred, described him as guileless and easily imposed upon, while Paulinus of Nola (d. 431) complained of his haughty reserve. In fact he was an experienced, forceful pontiff who, though inevitably overshadowed by St Ambrose, bishop of Milan 374–97, was as fully aware as Damasus I of Rome's primatial status and his own role as successor of St PETER. He was the first pope to issue decretals, i.e. directives couched in

the authoritative chancery style of imperial edicts and, like them, carrying the force of law. The earliest surviving (11 Feb. 385) is addressed to Himerius, bishop of Tarragona, who had submitted fifteen questions on church discipline to Damasus I. Opening with the claim that the pope, or rather the Apostle Peter present in him, bears the burdens of the heavily laden, it proceeds to give peremptory rulings on questions like the readmission of heretics, the proper seasons (Easter and Pentecost) for baptism, the age and qualifications for ordinations, clerical continence and celibacy, and the penitential discipline. Siricius requests that these decrees (decretalia), which are as binding as the canons of synods, be communicated to the neighbouring provinces of Africa, Spain, and Gaul. In Jan. 386 he dispatched to Africa and other churches nine canons adopted by a synod meeting 'by the relics of the Apostle Peter' which laid down, inter alia, that no bishop should be consecrated without the cognizance of 'the apostolic see' or by only a single consecrator. He similarly responded with a series of canons to queries submitted by the bishops of Gaul.

Only rare glimpses of Siricius's general activities are available. To maintain Roman influence in east Illyricum (the south-east Balkan peninsula), now incorporated in the eastern empire, he conferred on the bishop of Thessalonica in 385 the unprecedented privilege of authorizing all episcopal appointments in that region, thus laying the foundation of the later papal vicariate. Although disapproving of *Priscillianism, he rebuked (386) the usurper Maximus (383–8) for executing the heretic Priscillian, refused communion to the bishops responsible for the tragic innovation of sentencing a heretic to death, and in 397 joined with St Ambrose in recommending lenient treatment for penitent Priscillianists. No opponent of asceticism, as sometimes misrepresented, he used a Roman synod of 392/3 to excommunicate Jovinian, a monk who had turned critic of fasting and celibacy and who argued that the BVM had lost her virginity in bearing the Saviour. Later he condemned the view of Bonosus, bishop of Naissus (Niš), that Mary had borne children to St Joseph after the Lord's birth, while leaving it to the bishops of Illyricum to judge the man himself. He also intervened successfully in the schism dividing Antioch, for it was on his advice that the council of Caesarea (in Palestine) recognized that Flavian, and not Evagrius, was the legitimate bishop. In the mid-390s he incurred the wrath of St Jerome, then settled in Bethlehem, and of his friends at Rome because of his favourable attitude to John, bishop of Jerusalem (d. 417), and to Rufinus of Aquileia (d. 410), both at that time in Jerome's blackest books.

Siricius was buried in the basilica of S. Silvestro near the cemetery of Priscilla; a contemporary column outside the north porch of St Paul's commemorates his dedication of the basilica. Although honoured as a saint in earlier centuries, he was omitted from the first edition (1584) of the Roman Martyrology because of the criticisms of St Jerome and St Paulinus of Nola. His name was added to it in 1748 by BENEDICT XIV, who wrote a dissertation to prove his holiness. Feast 26 Nov.

Jerome, *Ep.* 127, 9; Paulinus of Nola, *Ep.* 5, 14; *Collectio Avellana, Ep.* 40 (*CSEL* 35, 90 f.); *PL* 13, 1131–96; *LP* 1, 86 f.; 216 f.; JW 1, 40–2; H. Getzeny, *Stil und Form der ältesten Papstbriefe* (diss., Tübingen, 1922); Caspar 1, 257–85; *DCB* 4, 696–702 (J. Barmby); *BSS* 11, 1234–7 (V. Monachino); *DTC* 14, 2171–4 (É. Amann); *NCE* 13, 258 f. (P. T. Camelot); Seppelt 1, 127–33.

ANASTASIUS I, ST (27 Nov. 399–19 Dec. 401). A Roman by birth, he had hardly become pope when he was plunged into the quarrel then raging over Origen, the outstanding but controversial 3rd-cent. Greek theologian. This had been sparked off by a whitewashing translation of Origen's *First Principles* by Rufinus of Aquileia (*c.*345–410) which had greatly offended Jerome (331–420), now settled in Bethlehem, and his influential circle of friends in Rome. These had welcomed Anastasius's election because they judged him better disposed

than SIRICIUS to the strict ascetic movement, and they put pressure on him to condemn Origen's writings. The pope must have been thoroughly confused, for Origen was a mere name to him and he had little or no grasp of the issues at stake; but when a letter reached him in spring 400 from Theophilus, the powerful patriarch of Alexandria (d. 412), dwelling on the evils caused by Origen's works and reporting their recent condemnation in Egypt, he convened a synod which anathematized the controversial theologian's errors, and then wrote to Simplician, bishop of Milan (d. 400), inviting his and other northern Italian bishops' adhesion to the anathema. Feeling himself threatened, Rufinus sent Anastasius a short but spirited defence both of his translation and of his own theological position. Still under the influence of Jerome's friends, the pope wrote in 401 to Bishop John of Jerusalem making it plain that, while he remained sceptical about Rufinus's motives in making his notorious translation, he left him to God's judgement.

Like Siricius, Anastasius maintained a special relationship with the bishop of Thessalonica to prevent eastern Illyricum from drifting into the ecclesiastical sphere of Constantinople. Unlike Siricius, however, he was immensely admired by Jerome, who claimed that his pontificate had been cut short because Rome did not deserve so noble a bishop. He also enjoyed cordial relations with Paulinus of Nola (d. 431), whom Siricius had snubbed, inviting him to attend the anniversary of his consecration. When the African bishops, worried by a shortage of clergy, sought a relaxation of the ban on *Donatist clergy returning to the church, he replied in autumn 401 in distinctly unhelpful terms, exhorting them to continue to struggle against Donatism—advice the Africans tactfully ignored. *LP* attributes to him (possibly correctly) a constitution requiring bishops, as well as priests and deacons, to stand with bowed heads during the gospel at mass, and also reports his erection of the Basilica Crescentiana, of unknown location.

He was buried in the cemetery of Pontian on the Via Portuensis. Feast 19 Dec.

PL 20, 51–80; *PLSupp* 1, 790–2; Jerome, *Epp.* 95; 127, 10; 130, 16; Paulinus of Nola, *Ep.* 20; JW 1, 42 f.; *LP* 1, 218 f.; Caspar 1, 285–7; 291 f.; *DHGE* 2, 1471–3 (J. P. Kirsch); *EC* 1, 1154 f. (N. Turchi); *NCE* 1, 478 (P. T. Camelot); Seppelt 1, 133–5.

INNOCENT I, ST (21 Dec. 401–12 Mar. 417). Son of ANASTASIUS I and probably his deacon, he was a man of great ability and commanding character. At a time when the western empire was crumbling under barbarian invasions, he seized every opportunity of asserting the primacy of the Roman see, making more substantial claims for the papacy than his predecessors. As a result he not only proved one of the outstanding popes of the early centuries, but has sometimes been saluted as 'the first pope'.

His activities are mirrored in his correspondence, of which some thirty-six letters survive. For example, in decretals to Victricius of Rouen (d. *c.*407), Spanish bishops who had met in council at Toledo in 400, Exuperius of Toulouse (d. *c.*411), and Decentius of Gubbio (*fl.* 410), he laid down the law on a range of disciplinary and liturgical matters, insisting that 'the Roman custom' should be the norm. The letter to Exuperius advised him on the canonical books of the Bible, while that to Decentius is important for the history of the canon of the mass; it also deals with penance and extreme unction, and restricts the administration of confirmation to bishops. Innocent's tone was peremptory; as the gospel had reached the western churches from Rome, they should look to it for leadership, and recognize that Rome was their court of appeal, to which also 'weightier causes' should be referred.

Innocent formalized the special relationship with the bishop of Thessalonica which his predecessors had established so as to prevent eastern Illyricum (the south-east Balkan peninsula), since 391 a prefecture of the eastern empire, from falling under the ecclesiastical sway of Constantinople; he

entrusted Bishop Rufus (17 June 415) with control 'in our stead' of the church in that region. He was thus the true founder of the papal vicariate of *Thessalonica. His determination to assert himself in east as well as west was also shown in his support of John Chrysostom (*c.*347–407) and Jerome (331–420) in their hours of need. When John was deposed as bishop of Constantinople and exiled in 404, he sent him letters of encouragement, refused to recognize the bishop appointed in his place, called for an impartial council, and organized a delegation of protest to the eastern emperor. When his envoys were insulted and sent back and John died in exile, he broke off communion with the eastern bishops who had persecuted John. When news reached him (416) that Jerome's monasteries at Bethlehem had been destroyed and their inmates assaulted by hooligans, he at once wrote to him offering to exert 'the whole authority of the apostolic see' against the offenders, and sharply rebuked Bishop John of Jerusalem (d. 417) for allowing such atrocities in his diocese.

The imperious pope had little influence with the government, and was not consulted over its measures to crush *Donatism in north Africa in 405 and 412. The controversy with Pelagius (*c.*354–*c.*419), however, who was accused of playing down divine grace and exalting the role of free will, gave Innocent a welcome chance of emphasizing Rome's doctrinal magisterium. Alarmed by the rehabilitation of Pelagius at Diospolis (Lydda, 415), two African councils reaffirmed his condemnation (411) in summer 416 and deferentially asked the pope to add the anathema of the apostolic see to theirs. St Augustine and four other African bishops also wrote, sending him a copy of Pelagius's treatise *On Nature*. In three letters dated 27 Jan. 417 Innocent, while tactfully professing uncertainty about what had happened at Diospolis, condemned perverse views on grace and pronounced Pelagius and his colleague Caelestius excommunicate unless they returned to orthodoxy. He also praised his correspondents for referring the matter to his judgement (they had in fact not done so), thus following the ancient tradition that bishops everywhere should submit disputed matters of faith to PETER, the founder of their name and office. No previous pope had so clearly enunciated the view that the apostolic see possesses supreme teaching authority. St Augustine rejoiced that two councils had sent their decisions to the holy see, definitive rulings had come back, and the case was settled.

When Alaric the Visigoth (d. 410) laid siege to Rome in 408, Innocent witnessed the famine and despair that afflicted the city. While rejecting the demand for public sacrifices (by now illegal) to appease the angry gods, he apparently turned a blind eye to clandestine offerings. In 410 he led a deputation to Emperor Honorius (393–423) at Ravenna to negotiate a truce, but the negotiations came to nothing, and Alaric stormed and plundered Rome (24 Aug. 410). The pope's absence was interpreted by pious historians as providential; God had spared him, as he had spared Lot, from being engulfed with the sinful capital. He returned to Rome only in 412. When he died, he was buried in the same cemetery on the Via Portuensis as his father Anastasius I. Feast 28 July.

PL 20, 463–636; Collectio Avellana, Epp. 41–4 (CSEL 35, 92–8); JW 1, 44–9; LP 1, 220–4; H. Gebhardt, Die Bedeutung Innocenz I für die Entwickelung der päpstlichen Gewalt (dissert., Leipzig, 1901); B. Capelle, 'Innocent I et le canon de la messe', RTAM 19 (1952), 5–16; É. Demougeot, 'A propos des interventions du pape Innocent I dans la politique séculière', RH 212 (1954), 23–38; Caspar 1, 296–343; DCB 3, 243–9 (J. Barmby); DTC 7, 1940–50 (É. Amann); NCE 7, 519 f. (P. T. Camelot); Seppelt 1, 135–44.

ZOSIMUS, ST (18 Mar. 417–26 Dec. 418). A Greek, possibly of Jewish descent (his father's name was Abraham), he was a presbyter who had been recommended to INNOCENT I by John Chrysostom (c.347–407). Although he tirelessly upheld the papal claims, his short and turbulent reign was marred by blunders springing as much from insufficient knowledge of the west as from his impulsive temperament and high-handed methods. As early as 22 Mar. 417 he issued a decretal making Patroclus, bishop of Arles (412–26), an adventurer in Rome at the time who may have manipulated the election, metropolitan of the provinces of Vienne (a rival see) and the two Narbonnes, with authority to consecrate all bishops and adjudicate all matters not requiring reference to Rome; clergy from Gaul wishing to visit Rome had to obtain letters of credence from him. These unprecedented measures aroused resentment in Gaul, but Zosimus, influenced by Patroclus, rejected protests, even deposing (5 Mar. 418) Bishop Proculus of Marseilles when he proved recalcitrant. A letter to Hesychius of Salona (d. c.429), metropolitan of Dalmatia, suggests that the pope had plans for establishing similar vicariates there and, probably, in the western church generally.

His intervention in the *Pelagian controversy was even more clumsy. Despite Innocent I's recent censure of Pelagius and his disciple Caelestius, Zosimus reopened the question and allowed himself to be taken in by Pelagius's skilful letters and Caelestius's astute self-defence at a meeting in S. Clemente; they both professed readiness to defer to the judgement of the holy see. In brusque letters he informed the African episcopate that both heretics had cleared themselves, criticizing the action taken against them as over-hasty and based on unscrupulous witnesses. The outraged reaction of the African bishops, who frankly told him (Nov. 417) that Innocent's sentence must stand, forced Zosimus to beat a retreat; after lecturing them on papal supremacy, he assured them (21 Mar. 418) that the situation remained as in Innocent's days. Meanwhile the Africans had appealed to Emperor Honorius (393–423) at Ravenna, procuring from him a rescript (30 Apr. 418) condemning Pelagius, Caelestius, and their followers as heretics and disturbers of the peace. The pope had no option but to make a complete climb-down, and addressed to the bishops of east and west a lengthy document, known as his *Tractoria*, in which, reversing his previous stand, he anathematized the Pelagians and their teachings.

Zosimus again clashed with the African church, always jealous of its autonomy, over a disgruntled African priest, Apiarius, who, excommunicated by Bishop Urbanus of Sicca, had appealed to him. Although African canon law forbade appeals overseas, the pope acquitted him and sent him back to Africa with three legates instructed to demand (*a*) that African bishops should have the right to appeal to Rome, and priests and deacons to neighbouring sees; (*b*) that the African bishops should not make a habit of resorting to the court at Ravenna (their *démarche* in the case of Pelagius and Caelestius rankled); and (*c*) that Urbanus should be excommunicated unless he withdrew his sentence on Apiarius. Zosimus justified his interference by appealing to two canons of the council of Nicaea (325), which were really canons of Serdica (342/3) not recognized in Africa. The Africans referred the case to the next African council; meanwhile they informed the pope that, pending investigation, they would observe the two supposed canons without prejudice.

Zosimus's heavy-handed tactlessness excited considerable opposition in Rome itself; in his last months an opposition group of clergy was intriguing against him at the imperial court at Ravenna. He was taking measures to excommunicate the malcontents when he fell ill and, after a protracted sickness, died. He was buried in S. Lorenzo on the road to Tivoli. The factions which erupted after his death suggest that his rule was divisive as well as misguided. Omitted from the 5th-cent. Martyrology of St Jerome, his name first appears in the 9th-cent. Martyrology of Ado. Feast 26 Dec.

PL 20, 639–86; *PLSupp* 1, 796–8; JW 1, 49–51; LP 1, ccci; 225 f.; Caspar 1, 344–60; *DCB* 4, 1221–5 (J. Barmby); *DTC* 15, 3708–16 (É. Amann); *BSS* 12, 1493–7 (V. Monachino); Seppelt 1, 145–54.

EULALIUS (antipope 27 Dec. 418–3 Apr. 419: d. 423). ZOSIMUS had hardly been buried when the deacons of the Roman church, with a handful of presbyters, barricaded themselves on 27 Dec. in the Lateran basilica and elected Eulalius, his archdeacon and probably, like him, a Greek, as his successor. On 28 Dec. the great majority of the presbyters elected their elderly colleague BONIFACE. On Sunday 29 Dec. both men were separately consecrated, Eulalius in the Lateran by the bishop of *Ostia, who customarily ordained the bishop of Rome. The prefect of the city, the pagan Symmachus, immediately dispatched a report favourable to Eulalius to Emperor Honorius (393–423) at Ravenna, who accepted him as pope. Having soon received, however, from the Roman presbyters a different account of the election from Symmachus's, Honorius summoned both contestants before a synod of bishops meeting at Ravenna. When this reached no conclusion, he deferred the case to a more representative council, including bishops from Gaul and Africa, which should meet at Spoleto on 13 June 419; in the meantime both bishops should withdraw from Rome and the bishop of Spoleto, Achilleus, should take charge of the Easter ceremonies there on 30 Mar. Boniface complied, but Eulalius, determined to establish his position by presiding at the Easter services, returned to Rome on 18 Mar. and occupied the Lateran basilica by force. This proved his undoing, for it sparked off civil disorders, and the prefect expelled him from the city. On 3 Apr. an imperial edict was published excluding him from the see and confirming the appointment of Boniface; the projected council of Spoleto was dropped. Eulalius accepted the decision, retiring at first to Antium (Anzio, 60 km. from Rome), but he and his supporters seem to have retained hopes that he might stage a comeback; falling ill shortly afterwards, Boniface warned the emperor that the schism might break out afresh in the event of his death. In fact, when the pope died in Sept. 422, Eulalius made no attempt to recover the see although pressed to do so by his partisans. *LP* reports that he was assigned a provincial see, although its editions differ as to whether it was in Tuscany or in Campania. He died in 423.

Collectio Avellana, Epp. 14–36 (*CSEL* 35, 59–84); JW 1, 51 f.; *LP* 1, lxii; 88 f.; 227–9; Caspar 1, 361–4; *DCB* 2, 277–9; *DHGE* 15, 1385 (H. Marot); Haller 1, 130 f.; Seppelt 1, 154 f.

BONIFACE I, ST (28 Dec. 418–4 Sept. 422). A Roman by birth, son of a priest, Iocundus, he was a leading presbyter whom INNOCENT I entrusted with important missions to Constantinople. On ZOSIMUS's death, while the deacons and a few presbyters elected the archdeacon EULALIUS on 27 Dec., the great majority of the presbyters, with many laity, assembled in the basilica of Theodora on 28 Dec. and elected Boniface. Both were consecrated separately on 29 Dec., Boniface in the church of S. Marcello in the presence of nine bishops. The prefect of the city, Symmachus, a pagan, came down in favour of Eulalius in his report to Emperor Honorius (393–423) at Ravenna, and Boniface was ordered to quit Rome; he did so under protest. He was popular with the people, however, and had powerful friends at court, including Honorius's sister, Galla Placidia; and on receiving a petition from the Roman presbyters strongly favouring Boniface, the emperor summoned both rivals to a synod at Ravenna. When this reached no conclusion, he referred a decision to a council to be held at Spoleto on 13 June 419 at which bishops from Gaul and Africa would be present; in the meantime the rival bishops should withdraw from Rome and Achilleus, bishop of Spoleto, should conduct the Easter services there on 30 Mar. Boniface complied, but Eulalius's defiance of the order infuriated the government, which banished him from Rome and recognized Boniface (3 Apr. 419) as its lawful bishop. In July 420, when seriously ill and worried that schism might break out afresh if he died, Boniface requested the emperor to ensure peace if there had to be a new election. In reply

Honorius banned election intrigues, and decreed that, if two candidates should be elected, both should be disqualified and the government would only recognize a bishop chosen unanimously. This first attempt to regulate papal election remained without effect.

Elderly, frail in health, Boniface took steps to annul Zosimus's scheme for making Arles a papal vicariate, and restored their metropolitan rights to Marseilles, Vienne, and Narbonne. He faced a threat to the papal vicariate of *Thessalonica, formalized by SIRICIUS, when the eastern Emperor Theodosius II (408–50), in response to complaints from the bishops of Thessaly, issued a constitution (14 July 421) transferring ecclesiastical jurisdiction in east Illyricum, now a prefecture of the eastern empire, to Constantinople. Boniface worked energetically to reassert his authority in the region, impressing on Rufus of Thessalonica and the other bishops that the care of all the churches, including the eastern, rested by divine appointment with Rome; through Honorius he managed to persuade Theodosius to suspend his legislation, although he could not prevent its inclusion in the imperial codes. In Africa he inherited the case of the deposed priest Apiarius, whose reinstatement Zosimus had peremptorily demanded, and received a letter (31 May 419) from the African bishops reporting that, having avowed his misconduct, Apiarius had been ordered to officiate in another diocese. In the meantime they asked the pope to check the canons, supposedly Nicene but in fact Serdican, by which Zosimus had justified his intervention; they did not conceal their disgust at the arrogance of Zosimus's legate. On the other hand, Boniface was himself guilty of indiscretion when he entertained an appeal from Antony, a deprived bishop of Fussala in north Africa whom St Augustine had ill-advisedly appointed, and without hearing the case against him sent him back to Africa with orders for his rehabilitation.

In the struggle against *Pelagianism Boniface was an unswerving supporter of orthodoxy, and persuaded Honorius to publish an edict requiring all bishops to sign Zosimus's *Tractoria* outlawing the heresy. Two letters by Pelagian leaders calumniating St Augustine having come into his hands, he had them transmitted to St Augustine, who prepared an exhaustive treatise in reply to them. This he dedicated to the pope in a letter which bore testimony to his kindness and humility of character. A true Roman, Boniface was indefatigable in promoting the claims of the papacy, and once wrote, 'It has never been lawful for what has once been decided by the apostolic see to be reconsidered.' He had a chapel built in the cemetery of St Felicity on the Via Salaria, near her tomb; and it was there that he himself was buried. Feast 4 Sept.

PL 20, 745–92; JW 1, 51–4; *Collectio Avellana*, *Epp.* 14–37 (*CSEL* 35, 59–84); Theodosian Code 16, 2, 45; *LP* 1, 227–9; Caspar 1, 359–64; *DCB* 1, 327 f. (T. R. Buchanan); *DHGE* 9, 895–7 (G. Bardy); *BSS* 3, 328–30 (F. Caraffa); *NCE* 2, 668 f. (J. Chapin); Seppelt 1, 155–8.

CELESTINE I, ST (10 Sept. 422–27 July 432). Archdeacon of Rome, he was born in the Campagna, was a deacon under INNO-CENT I, and in 418 corresponded with Augustine. Elected without opposition, he proved a vigorous bishop in Rome itself, crushing the large *Novatianist minority and confiscating their churches so that they had to worship in private houses. He also restored the Julian basilica (Sta Maria in Trastevere), severely damaged in the sack of the city in 410; and the new basilica of Sta Sabina was constructed during his reign.

His conviction that Rome could receive appeals from any province brought him into collision with the north African church. Although he yielded to Augustine's plea not to demand the reinstatement of Antony of Fussala, a deposed bishop who had appealed to BONIFACE I, he ordered the rehabilitation of Apiarius, a disgraced priest who had been restored at ZOSIMUS's request but had again lapsed and been excommunicated, and sent him back to Africa with a notoriously arrogant legate,

Faustinus. A plenary council was held at Carthage (c.426) at which Apiarius broke down and admitted his guilt; the African bishops seized the opportunity to remind the pope of their traditional autonomy, and pressed him not to enter into communion with persons they had excommunicated. Celestine was more successful in asserting, as St PETER's successor, his general oversight over east Illyricum, and directed (423/4) the bishops there to regard Rufus, bishop of *Thessalonica, as his vicar. In July 428 he reminded the bishops of southern Gaul that they were subject to his surveillance and sharply censured abuses (including the innovation of wearing a distinctive episcopal costume) of which he had heard. His vigorous action succeeded in getting the leaders of *Pelagianism expelled from the west, and in 429, influenced by his deacon Palladius, he sent a mission headed by Germanus of Auxerre (c.378–448) to Britain to root out the heresy there; in 431 he consecrated Palladius and sent him to Ireland as its first bishop. In the same year, to counter Semi-Pelagianism (which allowed a place to free will in the first turning to grace), he wrote to the bishops of southern Gaul urging them, in general terms, to remain loyal to the revered Augustine. The so-called 'Chapters of Celestine', summarizing decisions of the holy see on grace and appended to this letter, should probably be attributed to Prosper of Aquitaine (c.390–c.463).

Late in his reign Celestine was drawn into the Christological debate between Nestorius of Constantinople (428–31) and Cyril of Alexandria (412–44), the one representing the Antiochene school with its tendency to hold apart Christ's divine and human natures, the other the Alexandrine school which stressed their dynamic unity. Nestorius was creating a stir by attacking the popular description of the BVM as 'mother of God' (*Theotokos*), and when both he and Cyril submitted their positions to him Celestine treated it as an appeal from the east to Rome. Briefed by Cyril, who portrayed Nestorius's views as a denial of the divinity of Jesus, and by a critique of them prepared for him by the monk John Cassian (c.360–435), he condemned these views at a Roman synod on 10 Aug. 430, called on Nestorius to recant within ten days or stand excommunicate, and asked Cyril to execute the sentence 'in our stead'. Cyril took the further step of forwarding the ultimatum to Nestorius accompanied by the demand that he sign twelve anathemas which excluded the Antiochene 'two-natures' Christology. Meanwhile Theodosius II (408–50) summoned a general council (the third) to meet at Ephesus in June 431 to settle the affair. Although invited, Celestine did not attend, but sent three legates with instructions, while upholding the decisions of the holy see, to work closely with Cyril and follow his judgement; he also wrote to Cyril urging him to be generous if Nestorius should show a change of heart. It was Cyril who now made the running. Reaching Ephesus first, he opened the council on 22 June without awaiting the arrival of the papal legates or the Antiochene bishops, and with his supporters excommunicated Nestorius. When the legates arrived on 10 July they endorsed the decisions already taken. The acts of the council were not submitted to Celestine, but in letters dated 15 Mar. 432 he expressed his satisfaction with its achievements. He deplored only the fact that Nestorius had been allowed to retire to Antioch, where he could create more trouble, and dissociated himself from the excommunication the council had passed on John of Antioch (d. 441), leader of the moderate Antiochene wing, leaving the door open to him to return to communion provided he accepted the council and disavowed Nestorius.

In his correspondence and through his legates at the council Celestine repeatedly asserted, with an unprecedented insistence, the pope's claim, as successor and living representative of St Peter, to paternal oversight of the entire church, eastern no less than western. He was buried in the cemetery of Priscilla, near the little basilica of S. Silvestro, his mausoleum being apparently decorated with paintings recalling the council of Ephesus. Feast 6 Apr.

PL 50, 417–558; PLSupp 3, 18–21; ACO I, 1, 7, 125–37; I, 2, 5–101; LP I, ccxi; 230 f.; JW I, 55–7; Caspar I, 381–416; DCB I, 584–8 (W. Bright); DACL 2, 2794–802 (F. Cabrol); DHGE 12, 56–8 (G. Bardy); BSS 3, 1096–1100 (I. Daniele); NCE 3, 263 f. (J. Chapin); Seppelt I, 150 f.; 158–71.

SIXTUS, or XYSTUS, III, ST (31 July 432–19 Aug. 440). A Roman by birth, son of Xystus, he had earlier had the reputation of being sympathetic to Pelagius, and had been claimed by Pelagians as an ally; but when ZOSIMUS published (418) his *Tractoria, he publicly anathematized *Pelagianism and made his rejection of it clear to its arch-adversary, Augustine. Nothing is known of his activities during the reign of BONIFACE I, but references in his early letters to CELESTINE I's correspondence with the east after the council of Ephesus (431) suggest that he had a hand in drafting it.

Sixtus continued Celestine I's policies, working hard, in collaboration with Emperor Theodosius II (408–50), to heal the breach which had opened at Ephesus between Cyril of Alexandria and John of Antioch (d. 441), leading proponent of the moderate Antiochene Christology. Avoiding mention of Cyril's *anathemas, he insisted that John and others sharing his views only needed to accept the decisions of Ephesus and disavow *Nestorius to be restored to communion. The reconciliation reached in spring 433 on the basis of the Symbol of Union, drafted by the Antiochenes but accepted by Cyril, gave him great satisfaction; he attributed the success to the Apostle PETER, guarantor of true faith and present in himself. The excellent relations Rome now enjoyed with the east were temporarily clouded when Proclus, the new bishop of Constantinople (434–446/7), initiated moves in 434 to detach east Illyricum (south-east Balkan peninsula) from its traditional ecclesiastical subjection to Rome. He had to warn the Illyrian bishops, who were showing signs of insubordination, to pay no attention to oriental synods, and to remind them that the bishop of *Thessalonica was still his vicar in east Illyricum. At the same time he requested (Dec. 437) Proclus not to receive bishops from Illyricum who failed to produce letters of credence from his vicar, Anastasius of Thessalonica. To conciliate Proclus, he informed him that a bishop of Smyrna who had been sentenced at Constantinople had appealed to Rome, but that he had simply endorsed his sentence. In 439, stiffened by his deacon LEO, he resisted the pleas of the Pelagian leader Julian of Eclanum (d. 454), who had been deposed and exiled in 418, to be allowed to return to his see in Apulia.

Sixtus founded the earliest recorded monastery in Rome at S. Sebastiano on the Appian Way. Helped by funds provided by the imperial family, he also carried out a more noteworthy building programme than any one of his predecessors, one of his motives being to make good the destruction wrought by the Visigoths in 410. He deliberately used two of his most remarkable works, his new octagonal baptistery at the Lateran and his reconstruction of the Liberian basilica as Sta Maria Maggiore, to advertise the dogmatic achievements of his age; the inscriptions in the former extolled divine grace and the theology of baptism, thus underlining the defeat of Pelagianism, and the mosaics of the latter celebrated the church's triumph over Nestorianism. His cult was late in developing, his name first appearing in the 9th-cent. Martyrology of Ado. Feast 28 Mar.

PL 50, 581–619; PLSupp 3, 21 f.; JW 1, 57 f.; LP 1, cxxvi f.; 232–7; Caspar 1, 416–22; DACL 13, 1204–7 (H. Leclercq); DCB 4, 706–8 (J. Barmby); DTC 14, 2196–9 (É. Amann); BSS 11, 1262–4 (V. Monachino); NCE 13, 271 f. (J. Chapin); Seppelt 1, 171–4; R. Krautheimer, 'The Architecture of Sixtus III', Essays in Honor of E. Panofsky (ed. M. Meiss, New York, 1961).

LEO I, ST (Aug./Sept. 440–10 Nov. 461). One of only two popes (the other being GREGORY I) to be called 'the Great', he was born in the late 4th cent., probably in Rome of Tuscan parentage, and was elected when absent in Gaul on a diplomatic mission with which the imperial court had entrusted him. As a deacon he exercised great influence on his two predecessors, arranging for CELESTINE I to be briefed about the *Nestorian heresy in 430, and stiffening SIXTUS III's resistance to the rehabilitation of the Pelagian Julian of Eclanum in 436. In 430 Cyril of Alexandria (d. 444) personally enlisted his support in blocking plans for raising Jerusalem to a patriarchate. He was consecrated on his return to Rome on 29 Sept., a day he was to celebrate annually as his 'nativity'. An energetic and purposeful pontiff, Leo infused all his policies and pronouncements, especially his anniversary sermons, with his conviction that supreme and universal authority in the church, bestowed originally by Christ on PETER, had been transmitted to each subsequent bishop of Rome as the Apostle's heir. As such, he assumed Peter's functions, full authority, and privileges; and just as the Lord bestowed more power on Peter than on the other apostles, so the pope was 'the primate of all the bishops', the Apostle's mystical embodiment.

Leo confidently asserted his authority everywhere in the west. His sermons, covering the liturgical year, reveal him as a pastor concerned to guide and instruct, watchful for heresy. He was particularly severe with Manichaeans, persuading the government to revive (June 445) the old penal legislation against them; and he sharply attacked the *Pelagians. He kept firm control of the bishops of Italy, including Milan and the north, insisting on uniformity of practice, correcting abuses, and settling disputes. In Spain, dominated by Arian Visigoths, he answered (21 July 447) an appeal for help against a revival of *Priscillianism, supplying the bishops with instructions for action. In Africa, traditionally jealous of its autonomy, his rulings on irregularities in elections and other scandals were eagerly sought and accepted. When Hilary of Arles (403–49) seemed to be treating his see as a patriarchate independent of Rome, Leo confined him to his diocese and obtained from Valentinian III (425–55) a rescript recognizing his jurisdiction over all the western provinces. To prevent the emergence of a patriarchate, he later (450) divided the bishoprics of Gaul between Arles and Vienne. In east Illyricum (southeast Balkan peninsula) he confirmed the papal vicariate, but sternly ordered Anastasius of *Thessalonica, his often blundering representative, to respect the rights of his metropolitans; as papal vicar, he had been granted a share in the pope's oversight, not the fullness of power.

In his dealings with the east Leo encountered a disinclination to accept the papal claims at their face value. In 448 he received an appeal from the monk Eutyches (d. 454), who had been deposed by his bishop, Flavian of Constantinople, for teaching the monophysite doctrine that Christ incarnate had only one nature, the human nature having been absorbed by the divine nature. When Leo grasped the true drift of this teaching, he dispatched (13 June 449) an important letter to Flavian, his so-called *Tome*, condemning Eutyches and setting out the permanent distinction of Christ's two natures in his one person. Theodosius II (408–50) called a council at Ephesus in Aug. 449, and Leo was represented by three delegates with his *Tome*, which he expected to be read out and endorsed. In the event the council spurned it, condemned Flavian, and rehabilitated Eutyches. Leo refused to recognize its proceedings, branding it as a 'brigandage' (*latrocinium*), and placed himself at the head of the rapidly growing opposition to it. The outcome was the fourth general council, held in Oct. 451 at Chalcedon (Kadiköy) on the Bosphorus, which reversed the decisions of Ephesus (449) and affirmed the doctrine that Christ is one person in two natures. If Leo's hopes that it would be held in Italy and that his legates would preside were frustrated, his legates were at least assigned a position of honour, and his *Tome* was received with respectful approval; in Leo's doctrine the fathers recognized 'the voice of Peter'. Having settled the

Christological issue, however, the council passed a number of canons, the 28th of which granted Constantinople the same patriarchal status as Rome on the ground that both were imperial cities. Leo found this so unacceptable that he took the dangerous step of postponing his endorsement of the council's proceedings until 21 Mar. 453; even then he declared canon 28 invalid as contravening the canons of Nicaea (325). In the following years, however, his chief concern was to stiffen the government in its efforts to consolidate the doctrinal position agreed at Chalcedon; to ensure that he was kept informed of events, but also to promote his own policies there, he established Julian of Cos, a Greek-speaking Italian, as his nuncio or *apocrisiarius* in Constantinople.

Declared a doctor of the church by BENEDICT XIV, Leo was a lucid codifier of accepted orthodoxy rather than an original or profound theologian. Although concerned for and accomplished in liturgy, he was not responsible for the so-called Leonine Sacramentary (6th/7th cent.). His surviving sermons (96) and letters (143: the product in the main of his chancery) are marked by clarity, terseness, and rhythmic prose; content and form are admirably united in them. But Leo was a man whose personality and courage impressed more than churchmen. In 452 near Mantua he personally confronted Attila the Hun, then ravaging north Italy and pressing southwards, and persuaded him to withdraw; in 455 he met the Vandal Gaiseric outside the walls of Rome and, if he could not prevent him from seizing and looting the city, he at least induced him to spare it from fire, torture, and massacre. When he died he was buried in the porch of St Peter's, his remains being translated to the interior in 688. Feast 10 Nov. (formerly 11 Apr.) in the west, 18 Feb. in the east.

PL 54–6; *CCL* 138 and 138A; *ACO* II, 1–4; JW 1, 58–75; *LP* 1, 238–41; T. G. Jalland, *The Life and Times of St Leo the Great* (London, 1941); W. Ullmann, 'Leo I and the Theory of Papal Primacy', *JTS* 11 (1960), 25–51; E. Dekkers,

'Autour de l'œuvre liturgique de S. Léon le Grand', *Sacris erudiri* 10 (1958), 363–98; Caspar 1, 462–564; PW 12, 1962–73 (H. Lietzmann); *DTC* 9, 218–301 (P. Batiffol); *NCE* 8, 637–9 (F. X. Murphy); Seppelt 1, 175–210.

HILARUS, ST (19 Nov. 461–29 Feb. 468). Sardinian by birth, son of Crispinus, he was LEO I's archdeacon and one of his legates at the 'robber council' of Ephesus (Aug. 449), where he protested against the condemnation of Flavian, bishop of Constantinople (446–9), and with difficulty escaped alive to bring Leo an eyewitness account of the disorderly proceedings and an appeal from Flavian (now dead). He attributed his escape to John the Evangelist, in whose burial-chamber outside the walls of Ephesus he had hidden himself.

A man of character and energy, Hilarus took his predecessor as his model. All that is known of his dealings with the east is a decretal which he apparently circulated to eastern bishops confirming the councils of Nicaea (325), Ephesus (431), and Chalcedon (451), and Leo's *Tome*, and also condemning heresies and emphasizing the Roman primacy. If authentic, the object of the decretal was to counter growing *monophysite opposition to Chalcedon. Nearer home he struggled to prevent the spread of *Arianism in Italy, where it enjoyed the protection of Ricimer, barbarian master of the west till his death in 472. He even had to put up with an Arian church in Rome, established by Ricimer, and an Arian bishop; but in 467, hearing that the new emperor Anthemius (467–72) might sanction meeting-places for heretics in the city, he boldly confronted him in St Peter's and made him swear that he would never consent to such a thing.

Hilarus frequently intervened in Gaul and Spain to consolidate Rome's authority and prevent the breakdown of canonical order. In Gaul he strove, without actually saying so, to rally the bishops around Arles as their metropolis, so that he could use the bishop of Arles as his channel for information and instructions. If he did not succeed

in his aim, it was because Leontius of Arles, whom he supported when the rights of his see were violated by Mamertus of Vienne (d. *c.*475), could not rise to the role expected of him. At a synod held in Sta Maria Maggiore on 19 Nov. 465 (the first Roman synod of which detailed minutes have been preserved) he dealt with complaints brought by Ascanius, metropolitan of Tarragona, against Silvanus of Calahorra, upholding the rights of metropolitans and forbidding bishops to designate their successors. Several of his letters reveal how dependent the Spanish episcopate was on Rome, and how readily and decisively the holy see solved their problems.

Among his buildings at Rome were three chapels attached to the Lateran baptistery, one dedicated to John the Evangelist as a thank-offering for his escape at Ephesus in 449. *LP* lists his lavish gifts to Roman churches, intended as replacements for the precious metal looted during the Vandal occupation of 455, and records that he founded a monastery at S. Lorenzo fuori le Mura, where he was buried. Feast 28 Feb.

PL 58, 11–31; *PLSupp* 3, 379–81; 441–3; JW 1, 75–7; Thiel 1, 126–70; *LP* 1, xxxviii; 242–8; Caspar 1, 483–95; 2, 10–14; *DCB* 3, 72–4 (J. Barmby); *DTC* 6, 2385–8 (É. Amann); *LThK* 5, 339 (G. Schwaiger); *BSS* 7, 737–53 (B. Cignitti); *NCE* 6, 1113 (J. Chapin); Seppelt 1, 191–3; 211 f.

SIMPLICIUS, ST (3 Mar. 468–10 Mar. 483). Born at Tivoli, son of Castinus, he saw the deposition in Sept. 476 of the last western emperor, Romulus Augustulus, the accession of a German general, the Arian Odoacer, as king of Italy owing theoretical allegiance to the eastern emperor Zeno (474–91), and the establishment of barbarian kingdoms in the rest of the western empire. His relations were primarily with the east, but in difficult times he worked hard to maintain Rome's authority in the west, intervening to censure Italian bishops who exceeded their authority, and being the first to commission the bishop of Seville as papal vicar in Spain.

Early in his reign Simplicius, appealing to its rejection by LEO I, resisted a move by Acacius of Constantinople (472–89) to obtain recognition of *canon 28 of the council of Chalcedon (451), granting his see an equivalent status to Rome. But the significant and, in western eyes, disturbing development in the east was the triumph during Basiliscus's usurpation of the throne (Jan. 475–Aug. 476) of the *monophysite 'one-nature' opposition to the Chalcedonian 'two-natures' Christology, followed by official moves to unite Chalcedonians and monophysites by a formula of compromise. Needing monophysite support, Basiliscus publicly condemned the *Chalcedonian Christology and Leo's *Tome, and allowed monophysites to get control of the great sees. The restoration of Zeno, however, did not assure Chalcedonian orthodoxy, for he and Acacius were soon pursuing a policy of conciliation which found expression in the *Henoticon (482), a superficially innocuous statement which made concessions to monophysitism. News of these happenings reached Simplicius, often belatedly, and until 479 his correspondence shows him struggling unsuccessfully to exert an influence: encouraging (Jan. 476) Acacius and his clergy to withstand the monophysite reaction, impressing on Basiliscus the soundness of Leo's *Tome*, calling on (Apr. 477) Zeno, now restored, to uphold the Chalcedonian doctrine, reluctantly accepting (June 479) an uncanonical appointment to the see of Antioch. After 479, however, Acacius deliberately kept him in the dark about events, especially the plans for the *Henoticon*, and he became an increasingly helpless spectator, remonstrating ineffectually with Zeno and Acacius on the return of the monophysite Peter Mongos to Alexandria, maladroitly backing an unacceptable candidate, John Talaia, for the see, and repeatedly complaining to Acacius that he was not keeping him informed. Clearly the holy see did not count for much with either emperor or patriarch.

Simplicius was a noteworthy builder, among other works converting a hall on the Esquiline Hill into the church of S. Andrea in Catabarbara (the first example of a public building being so adapted), and erecting the architecturally interesting S. Stefano in Rotondo on the Caelian Hill. He is reported to have arranged for priests from certain of the Roman *titular churches to assist with the services at the major basilicas of St Peter, St Paul, and S. Lorenzo. He died after a long illness and was buried near Leo I in the porch of St Peter's. Feast 10 Mar.

PL 58, 35–62; *Collectio Avellana*, *Epp.* 56–69 (*CSEL* 35, 124–55); E. Schwartz, *Publizistische Sammlungen zum Acacianischen Schisma*, *AAM* 10 (1934), 119–22; JW 1, 77–80; *LP* 1, 249–51; Caspar 2, 10–25; *DCB* 4, 690–5 (J. Barmby); *DTC* 14, 2161–4 (É. Amann); *NCE* 13, 232 (J. Chapin); Seppelt 1, 212–15.

FELIX III (II), ST (13 Mar. 483–1 Mar. 492). A Roman of aristocratic family, he was son of a priest, himself a widower with at least two children (from one of whom GREGORY I was descended). A decisive part in his election was played, at the request of his predecessor, by Basilius, praetorian prefect of Odoacer, king of Italy (476–93), who also had an ecclesiastical law promulgated forbidding the alienation of church property by the popes on pain of anathema. Because of the posthumous inclusion of Antipope Felix in the list of legitimate popes as FELIX II, he was improperly given the style Felix III.

Felix, who relied heavily on his archdeacon (and successor) GELASIUS, was from the start closely involved with the east. News had just reached Rome of the *Henoticon*, a compromise doctrinal statement designed to appease the *monophysite opposition to the 'two natures' Christology approved at Chalcedon (451) which Emperor Zeno (474–91) had published in 482. A monophysite, Peter Mongos, had been installed as bishop of Alexandria, and his orthodox but extruded predecessor, John Talaia, was in Rome full of bitter complaints. Felix dispatched an embassy to Constantinople with letters to emperor and patriarch. To Zeno he announced his election (the first instance of a pope so doing), sought his aid for catholics in north Africa persecuted by the Arian Vandals, but chiefly demanded the deposition of Peter Mongos and the maintenance of the *Chalcedonian Christology. A first letter to Patriarch Acacius reproached him for supporting Mongos and the *Henoticon*, but a subsequent one summoned him to Rome to answer the charges of John Talaia. The embassy proved a fiasco: the legates let themselves be imposed upon and failed to protest when Acacius included Mongos in the diptychs, i.e. the names of living and departed publicly prayed for at mass, thus giving the impression that Rome approved of him and the *Henoticon*. On their return the infuriated pope excommunicated both his legates and Acacius at a synod held on 28 July 484. He angrily warned the emperor not to interfere in matters which belonged to the church's bishops, and sent his sentence of excommunication on Acacius to Constantinople by a special messenger. Some over-zealous orthodox monks in the city made it blatantly public by pinning it on to Acacius's vestments as he was celebrating mass.

Felix's sentence had no practical effect on Acacius, beyond provoking him to remove the pope's name from the diptychs, but it started the Acacian schism, which divided the churches of east and west for thirty-five years (484–519). Even some of Felix's supporters in Constantinople were dismayed, but reports of this, and of the replacement of the Chalcedonian bishop of Antioch by a monophysite, only stiffened his attitude. He held a fresh synod (5 Oct. 485) which approved a letter confirming, for the benefit of the people of Constantinople, his excommunication of Acacius; he also deposed, without effect, the monophysite bishop of Antioch. In 488/9 an opportunity for healing the rift occurred when Odoacer, threatened by Theodoric the Ostrogoth, king of Italy (493–526), was seeking a political *rapprochement* with Zeno, but Felix's terms were complete submission by Aca-

cius. Again, when Acacius died (28 Nov. 489) and hopes of reunion ran high in Constantinople, he refused to accept any overtures so long as Mongos occupied the see of Alexandria and his name and that of Acacius were recited in the diptychs. In 491, when Mongos (29 Oct. 490) and Zeno (9 Apr. 491) were both dead, the new patriarch Euphemius, an orthodox Chalcedonian alarmed at the accession of an emperor, Anastasius I (491–518), with monophysite leanings, wrote to Felix seeking the restoration of communion between the two churches; but while commending his orthodoxy the pope declined to make any move until Acacius's name was removed from the diptychs.

Few glimpses survive of Felix's activities in the west. When the Vandal persecution in north Africa died down under King Guntamond (484–96), he had to determine what was to be done with the numerous Catholics who had been forcibly submitted to Arian rebaptism. His decision (13 Mar. 487) was exceptionally severe: persons in holy orders could only be restored to communion on their deathbed, others after many years of penitential discipline. According to some scholars he was the real author of certain letters fulminating against a resurgence of *Pelagianism in Dalmatia, and of a treatise attacking the pagan festival of the Lupercalia (15 Feb.), which are traditionally attributed to GELASIUS I.

Authoritarian and harsh, he kept alive by his intransigence the first schism between east and west. He was buried in St Paul's basilica, close to his father (who had been ordered by LEO I to repair it), his wife, and his children. Feast 1 Mar.

JW 1, 80–3; Thiel 1, 221–84; *LP* 1, 252–4; E. Schwartz, *Publizistische Sammlungen zum Acacianischen Schisma, AAM* 10 (1934), 202–19; A. Grillmeier and H. Bacht, *Chalkedon* (Würzburg, 1953), 1, 43–51; Caspar 2, 25–44; *DHGE* 16, 889–95 (P. Nautin); *LThK* 4, 685 (G. Schwaiger); *NCE* 5, 879 (J. Chapin); Seppelt 1, 217–22.

GELASIUS I, ST (1 Mar. 492–21 Nov. 496). Born in Rome of African descent, he had been influential as archdeacon, shaping FELIX III's policies as well as his letters. He faced a difficult situation on his accession. Barbarian kings, all Arian, ruled what had been the western empire; the Ostrogoths under Theodoric had overrun Italy and were besieging King Odoacer in Ravenna. As a result of the wars there was a breakdown of supplies, a swarm of refugees, and an acute shortage of clergy. No less serious, the schism with the eastern church caused by the imposition there of the *Henoticon*, seen by the west as a betrayal of the Chalcedonian settlement (451), and sealed by Felix III's excommunication (484) of Patriarch Acacius of Constantinople, continued unresolved.

Gelasius established excellent relations with Theodoric when the latter, having eliminated Odoacer in 493, became ruler of Italy. An Arian, he was a tolerant one who did not interfere in church affairs, and Gelasius gained from his friendship with him. A vigorous administrator, Gelasius used his private fortune to help the poor, relieved famine by sending supplies from the papal estates and calling on Theodoric for aid, and temporarily relaxed the criteria for ordination in order to recruit more clergy. In dealing with the *Acacian schism, however, he proved even more intransigent than Felix III. Thus he rejected the overtures of Euphemius, the orthodox patriarch of Constantinople (489–95), who could not understand how Acacius had been condemned, and kept on insisting that no reconciliation was possible until the names of Acacius (dead since 489) and others tainted with the *Henoticon* were expunged from the *diptychs. In letter after letter he tried to justify Acacius's excommunication, which the east judged uncanonical. His unyielding attitude alienated Emperor Anastasius I (491–519), caused the eastern bishops to complain that he was endangering the whole church, and encouraged growing unease in influential circles at Rome. As a result of pressures from these he was obliged (13 May 495) to rehabilitate Bishop Misenus of Cumae, whom Felix III

had sent as a legate to Constantinople in 484 but had excommunicated for compromising the Roman position.

Gelasius seized every opportunity of inculcating his conviction of the supremacy of the Roman see, and was the first pope known to have been saluted as 'vicar of Christ' (at the Roman synod of 13 May 495 which restored Misenus). It was the pope's prerogative, he claimed, to ratify councils and protect their decisions. But his most original contribution, expounded in a letter to Emperor Anastasius as well as in other texts, was his theory of the two powers which govern the world, the 'consecrated authority of bishops' and the 'royal power', the one centred in the pope and the other in the emperor. Each was a trust from God, sovereign and independent in its own sphere, but the spiritual authority was inherently superior since it provided for the salvation of the temporal. This teaching was to be used by canonists and others for centuries to come in their treatment of the problem of church and state.

Holding views like these, Gelasius had no patience with the claim of Constantinople, ratified by the council of Chalcedon (451), to rank second only to Rome in Christendom. Since the schism persisted, however, his letters and writings were inevitably preoccupied with justifying the hard Roman line. Examples were the warnings he sent, more than once, to the bishops of the south-east Balkans against the propaganda of Constantinople, notably to Bishop Andrew of Thessalonica, who had refused to disown the memory of Acacius. He drew greater satisfaction from the loyalty to the holy see of the churches of Italy and the west. Even here, however, as a result of the breakdown caused by barbarian invasions, there were defects and abuses to be corrected. Thus he encouraged the bishops of eastern Italy (Picenum) and Dalmatia to root out the remains of *Pelagianism. In Rome itself he took a stand against the pagan festival of the Lupercalia (15 Feb.), which a leading senator and his friends wanted to revive as a harmless carnival; they retaliated by accusing him of laxity in disciplining delinquent clerics. At his spring synod of 494 he published decretals covering the recruitment and formation of the clergy, the active care of souls, and the division of church funds. A prolific writer, he left over a hundred letters or fragments of letters, as well as six theological treatises. It is agreed that neither the Gelasian Decree, containing a canon of scripture and other acceptable writings, nor the Gelasian Sacramentary, in any of its forms, has anything to do with him. On the other hand, eighteen mass formularies preserved in the Leonine Sacramentary (early 7th-cent. MS) go back to him.

Next to LEO I, Gelasius was the outstanding pope of the 5th cent., and he surpassed Leo in theological grasp. His writings leave the impression of an arrogant, narrow-minded, and harsh pontiff; but the extraordinary reverence in which he was held by contemporaries is reflected in a description left by the monk Dionysius Exiguus, who lived in Rome *c.*500–*c.*550 and consorted with his disciples. This stresses his humility, his determination to serve rather than rule, his delight in conversation with God's servants and in Bible meditation, his personal mortification and generosity to the poor, and the way in which, modelling himself on the Good Shepherd, he lived as well as taught the divine precepts. He was buried in St Peter's. Feast 21 Nov.

PL 59, 13–190; PLSupp 3, 739–88; JW 1, 83–95; Thiel 1, 285–613; Löwenfeld 1, 1–12; Collectio Avellana, Epp. 94–101 (CSEL 35, 357–468); E. Schwartz, Publizistische Sammlungen zum Acacianischen Schisma, AAM 10 (1934); LP 1, 255–7; DCB 2, 617–20 (J. Barmby); BSS 6, 90–3 (V. Monachino); NCE 6, 315 f. (J. Chapin); PRE 6, 315 f. (B. Moreton); JR, 62–8; A. K. Ziegler, 'Pope Gelasius I and his Teaching on the Relation of Church and State', CHR 27 (1942), 412–37; B. Capelle, 'L'œuvre liturgique de S. Gélase', JTS 2 (1951), 129–44; G. Pomarès, Gélase I: Lettre contre les Lupercales et dix-huit messes du sacramentaire léonien (SC 65, Paris, 1959).

ANASTASIUS II (24 Nov. 496–19 Nov. 498). A Roman, son of a priest named Peter, his election reflected dissatisfaction in influential circles with the hard-line attitude of FELIX III and GELASIUS I to the *Acacian schism (484–519) with the east. As a deacon he had been prominent at the synod of 495 which rehabilitated Bishop Misenus, whom Felix III had excommunicated for betraying the Roman position when legate to Constantinople in 483. Once installed, the pope dispatched two bishops to Constantinople bearing a conciliatory letter to Emperor Anastasius I (491–519) in which, after announcing his election, he made clear his yearning for the restoration of church unity. While maintaining Rome's insistence that Acacius (dead since 489) should not be named in the *diptychs, he did so in restrained terms, and unambiguously recognized the validity of ordinations and baptisms conferred by Acacius and his clergy. Formally his proposals did not differ from those of Felix III and Gelasius I; unlike them, however, he made it evident that he wanted peace and was prepared to make concessions. He made no mention of Rome's other *bête noire*, the monophysite Peter Mongos of Alexandria (d. 490), only begging the emperor to help in bringing the Alexandrian church back to Chalcedonian orthodoxy.

The pope's embassy was linked with a mission which Theodoric the Ostrogoth sent at the same time to Constantinople to negotiate the recognition of himself as king of Italy (493–526). This mission was led by Festus, the senior Roman senator, who worked closely with the papal legates. There were conversations with the representatives in the city of the Alexandrian church, and these submitted a memorandum on faith which reproduced the *Henoticon almost word for word. The emperor exploited the situation and, while forbidding his patriarch, Macedonius, to communicate formally with Anastasius II, revived a compromise proposal, mooted in Gelasius's time, to recognize Theodoric as king in return for the acceptance of the

*_Henoticon_ by Rome. The reaction of the papal legates to this plan is unknown, but Festus on his own initiative undertook to persuade the pope to fall in with it, and on the basis of this assurance Emperor Anastasius I granted Theodoric his title, probably in 498. Earlier (497) the pope had reopened relations with Andrew, bishop of Thessalonica, whom Gelasius had denounced as a partisan of Acacius, had received his deacon Photinus, had entered into communion with him without consulting his clergy, and had then sent him to Constantinople to assist with the discussions with the Alexandrian representatives. By now, however, his conciliatory policies were creating dismay at Rome, and his reception of Photinus was regarded as a final betrayal. A number of his clergy withdrew from communion with him, and a schism was under way. At the height of the crisis, before the return of Festus and the papal legates, Anastasius II suddenly died. His critics were quick to claim that his death was the result of divine judgement; it remains possible that with him there passed away the last hope of reunion between west and east on the basis of an orthodox interpretation of the _Henoticon_.

Nothing survives of Anastasius's dealings with the west except a letter (498) to the bishops of Gaul condemning traducianism, i.e. the view that human souls are not created directly by God but generated by their parents in the same way as bodies. A letter purporting to congratulate Clovis, king of the Franks (481–511), on his conversion and baptism is now recognized as a forgery. Anastasius's name is not found in any ancient martyrologies, and there is no evidence of devotion paid to him. The medieval tradition, reflected in the slanderous notice assigned to him in _LP_ and in Dante's description (_Inferno_ xi, 6–9) of his tomb in hell, was that he was a traitor to the holy see who wished to restore the heretic Acacius. He was in fact buried in the portico of St Peter's, and his epitaph in elegiacs survives.

JW 1, 95 f.; Thiel 1, 615–39; _LP_ 1, 44; 258 f.; E. Schwartz, _Publizistische Sammlungen zum Acacianischen Schisma, AAM_ 10 (1934), 226–30; A. Grillmeier and H. Bacht, _Chalkedon_ (Würzburg, 1953) 2, 66–70; Caspar 2, 82–7; Haller 1, 234 f.; _DHGE_ 2, 1473–5 (J. P. Kirsch); _DBI_ 3, 22–4 (P. Bertolini); Seppelt 1, 232–5; JR 67–9.

SYMMACHUS, ST (22 Nov. 498–19 July 514). A Sardinian, a convert from paganism and by the time of his accession a deacon, he was elected in the Lateran basilica by a majority of the clergy who were dissatisfied with ANASTASIUS II's policy of making concessions in the attempt to heal the *Acacian schism (482–519) with the east. A minority of the clergy, however, supported by most of the senate and its leader Festus, favoured the continuation of _détente_, and on the same day elected the archpriest LAWRENCE in Sta Maria Maggiore. The divided election resulted in such brawling that both factions asked Theodoric, Ostrogothic king of Italy (493–526), Arian though he was, to settle the matter. Ruling that the man ordained first, or with the larger backing, should occupy the apostolic see, he assigned it to Symmachus. Returning from Ravenna, the new pope, with characteristic energy, held a synod in St Peter's (1 Mar. 499) which agreed a statute banning all discussion of a pope's successor during his lifetime while allowing him to designate, if practicable, the man he wished; the clergy should choose if he died before doing so, but participation by the laity was excluded. Lawrence signed the statute, and was appointed bishop of Nuceria in Campania.

For a time Symmachus was secure; with the senate he received Theodoric when he paid a state visit to Rome in 500. The aristocratic partisans of Lawrence, however, headed by Festus, were determined to unseat him, and in 501 accused him before Theodoric of having celebrated Easter according to the old Roman calendar, not the Alexandrian one. The king summoned him to Ravenna, but when he reached Rimini he discovered that he was also being charged with unchastity and misuse of church property. In a panic he returned to Rome and took refuge in St Peter's, then outside the walls. This ill-judged move not only set Theodoric against him but seemed an admission of guilt; many clergy withdrew from communion with him. On the petition of the Lawrentians the king took the grave steps of appointing the bishop of Altinum as visitor to celebrate Easter 502 in Rome and administer the see pending a decision on the charges against Symmachus, and of convening a synod of Italian bishops to adjudicate the charges. After two abortive sessions (Symmachus refused to give evidence at the first until the visitor was removed, and was prevented from attending the second by attacks on himself and his escort), the synod held its final session on 23 Oct. 502. Its verdict was that, as Symmachus was pope, no human court could judge him and judgement must be left to God. He was therefore freed of all charges, and his clerical opponents were urged to be reconciled with him.

Flushed with victory, Symmachus immediately summoned the bishops, with a number of priests and deacons, to a synod of his own in St Peter's on 6 Nov. 502. This declared invalid, because promulgated by Basilius, praetorian prefect of King Odoa-cer (476–93), the law of Mar. 483 prohibit-ing the alienation of church property by popes, and then re-enacted it in virtually the same form but with the authority of the pope and bishops. Symmachus's aim was both to eliminate lay interference and to underline his repudiation of practices of which he had been accused. The king, however, was dis-pleased by his acquittal, and the Lawren-tians were resolved to overthrow it. Lawrence was allowed to return to Rome and for four years ruled as pope in the Lateran, taking over the churches of the city and the papal property, while Symmachus was confined by street violence to St Peter's. This stormy period saw the launching of the 'Symmachan Forgeries', which attempted to demonstrate by spurious precedents that the pope can be judged by no man. It was only in 506, after intense diplomatic activity by the deacon Ennodius (473/4–521: later

bishop of Pavia) and the Alexandrian dea-con DIOSCORUS, that Theodoric, now politically alienated from Byzantium and its allies in Rome, was induced to confirm the synodical acquittal of Symmachus, and order Festus to hand back the churches and papal property to him and thus 'allow only one pontiff in Rome'.

Thus the split in the Roman church ended, and Lawrence had to withdraw. But the legacy of bitterness continued for the rest of Symmachus's reign, fuelled accord-ing to his critics by his own misconduct. Many, including the saintly deacon Pas-chasius, never became reconciled to him. The pope exercised his ministry vigorously, expelling the Manichaeans from Rome, sending generous gifts to orthodox victims of Arian persecution, and ransoming prisoners captured in the wars in north Italy. He restored the primatial rights of Arles over Gaul in 514, extending them to Spain, and sent its bishop, the famous Caesarius (502–42), the *pallium (the first bestowal of it on a bishop outside Italy). He introduced *Gloria in excelsis* into masses celebrated by bishops, and was an extensive builder and embellisher of churches in Rome. He paid particular attention to St Peter's, equipping it with a residence for the pope, accom-modation for his staff, and facilities for pilgrims. His victory over the pro-Byzantine opposition stiffened his attitude to Con-stantinople and the *Acacian schism; Emperor Anastasius I (491–519) branded the 'illegally ordained' pope as a Manichaean, and Symmachus retaliated in stridently abusive terms. It was only in 514 that, faced with riots in Constantinople and a serious revolt in Thrace, Anastasius decided to seek a *rapprochement* with Rome and wrote to the pope inviting him to preside over a great council at Heraclea, in Thrace, which would settle the doctrinal issues underlying the schism. Symmachus was dead, however, when it reached Rome. He was buried in the portico of St Peter's. Feast 19 July.

JW 1, 96–100; Thiel 1, 639–738; *MGAA* 12, 399–455; *LP* 1, 44–6 ('Laurentian fragment');

260–8; Caspar 2, 87–129; *DCB* 4, 751–5 (J. Barmby); *DTC* 14, 2984–90 (É. Amann); *NCE* 13, 876 f. (J. Chapin); *EC* 11, 629–31 (A. Amore); JR, 69–99; Seppelt 1, 235–44.

LAWRENCE (antipope 22 Nov. 498–Feb. 499; 501–6: d. 507/8). Archpriest of the Roman church, he was elected in Sta Maria Maggiore on the same day as SYMMACHUS in the Lateran basilica after a contested election marked by bribery on both sides. He was the choice of a minority of the clergy but the bulk of the aristocracy and senate, including its influential leader Festus, who favoured the late pope's policy of making concessions to heal the protracted *Acacian schism (484–519) with Byzantium. Symmachus had the votes of the mass of the clergy, who repudiated ANASTASIUS II's conciliatory line. So violent were the resulting disturbances that both factions requested Theodoric, Arian king of Italy (493–526), to decide between them, and on the principle that the man ordained first or with the larger backing should occupy the apostolic see, he assigned it to Symmachus. Lawrence at first accepted the position, and his name, with the description 'archpresbyter of the *title of Sta Prassede', stands first among the priests signing the decrees of a synod held by the new pope on 1 Mar. 499. He was then appointed to the see of Nuceria, in Campania, as a consolation prize.

While obliged to accept the king's ruling, the Lawrentian faction, spurred on by Festus, were determined to unseat Symmachus, and by 502 were able to lay serious charges against him before Theodoric, and even to persuade the king to appoint a visitor to administer the see pending their investigation. Even when the synod convened by Theodoric to adjudicate the case freed the pope of all charges (23 Oct. 502), they did everything they could to have the verdict reversed. Meanwhile Lawrence was allowed by the king, who was also dissatisfied with the verdict, to return to Rome from Ravenna, where he had taken refuge from Symmachus's attacks; he had already resigned his bishopric. Since the Lawren-

tians now dominated the streets with their mobs, Symmachus found himself imprisoned in St Peter's, then outside the walls, while Lawrence installed himself in the Lateran palace, took over the city churches and much of the papal property, and for four years ruled as pope.

During these years the rival factions fought bloodily in the streets, the Lawrentians maintaining the upper hand. It was only in autumn 506 that, moved by the adroit diplomacy of the Symmachans but also by his growing political alienation from Byzantium, Theodoric came round to accept the synod's decision in the pope's favour and ordered Festus to restore the churches and papal property to him. Lawrence, many of whose adherents continued loyal to him, was expelled from the city by Symmachus, but settled on a farm belonging to his patron Festus. There he devoted himself to asceticism, and soon died.

LP 1, 46–8; Theodorus Lector, *Hist. eccl.* 2, 16 f. (*PG* 86a, 189–93); JW 1, 100; *MGAA* 9, 324; 12, 416–55; G. B. Picotti, 'I sinodi romani nello scismo laurenziano', *Studi storici in onore di G. Volpe* (Florence, 1958) 2, 741–876; Caspar 2, 87–118; *DCB* 3, 629 f. (J. Barmby); *LThK* 6, 829 (G. Schwaiger); Seppelt 1, 235–42; JR, 69–76.

HORMISDAS, ST (20 July 514–6 Aug. 523). Born at Frosinone, Italian despite a Persian name, aristocratic and rich, he had been the trusted collaborator of SYMMACHUS, who probably nominated him. Married before ordination, he had a son, SILVERIUS, later himself a pope.

A peacemaker, he first extinguished the last embers of the Lawrentian schism, receiving into communion the diehard adherents of Antipope LAWRENCE. But he is chiefly remembered for his part in ending the long *Acacian schism (484–519) between Rome and the east. For four years he made little headway, although the eastern emperor, Anastasius I (491–518), faced with revolts and a resurgence of Chalcedonian orthodoxy at home, invited him early in 515 to preside over a council at

Heraclea, in Thrace, which would restore church unity. Being cautious, Hormisdas consulted Theodoric, king of Italy (493–526), and dispatched a carefully prepared embassy to Constantinople in Aug. 515, and, when it came to nothing, another in 517. Both carried his detailed, hard-line conditions for reunion, including public acceptance of the council of Chalcedon (451) and LEO I's letters, the condemnation of Acacius and others deemed tainted with *monophysitism, and the re-trial by Rome of all deposed or exiled bishops (the aim was to get Rome's jurisdictional primacy recognized). He skilfully used the second mission to rally the forces of Chalcedonian orthodoxy in the east to put pressure on Anastasius, but it failed like the first. Now politically stronger, the emperor refused to yield to the pope's inflexible demands.

The deadlock was broken by Anastasius's sudden death on 9 July 518. The new emperor, Justin I (518–27), was a staunch Chalcedonian and lost no time in re-establishing, with the enthusiastic support of the people of Constantinople, the 'two-natures' Christology as the official faith of the empire. In response to his warm invitation (7 Sept. 518) Hormisdas, again after obtaining Theodoric's agreement, sent a third delegation to Constantinople bearing identical terms for a settlement. A key member was the gifted Alexandrian deacon DIOSCORUS, an accomplished speaker of Greek. Both parties being basically agreed, there was no question of this mission failing, and on 28 Mar. 519, Dioscorus having skilfully explained Rome's aversion to Acacius (d. 489), the 'Formula of Hormisdas' was, on the emperor's orders, solemnly signed in the imperial palace by John, patriarch of Constantinople, after much heart-searching, and by all bishops and heads of monasteries present. This comprised not only acceptance of the *Chalcedonian Christology, but a clear acknowledgement of Rome as the apostolic see in which the Catholic faith had always been preserved in its purity, and the condemnation of Acacius and his four suc-

cessors. The Formula was to be frequently appealed to in later history; the First Vatican Council incorporated it in the dogmatic constitution *Pastor aeternus* (18 July 1870).

Although the Acacian schism was ended and a noteworthy blow struck for the council of Chalcedon (451), Hormisdas's triumph was not as unqualified as many have represented it. Intransigent as he was, he could have achieved nothing had not Justin I and his nephew Justinian (emperor 527–65) been convinced Chalcedonians who also needed reunion with Rome for their long-term objective of recovering Italy for the empire. They also avoided conceding jurisdictional supremacy to Rome by restoring the exiled orthodox bishops before starting negotiations; while in signing the Formula Patriarch John added a gloss expressing joy that old and new Rome were now one, i.e. equal in honour. In the following months, when the government was trying to implement the settlement, it became evident that Hormisdas either could not or would not understand the widespread hostility to it in the east; he kept on insisting that its terms must be strictly applied, while the emperor and the patriarch, behind a façade of deference, quietly went their own way and did what was practicable. In Mar. 521, while exhorting Justin not to shrink from coercion in imposing the settlement, Hormisdas simultaneously authorized the new patriarch, Epiphanius, as his representative, to remove the remains of the schism in the east, thereby in effect recognizing *canon 28 of Chalcedon and the patriarchal status of Constantinople.

The divergent attitudes of Rome and the east were again shown when a group of Scythian monks proposed the so-called Theopaschite formula—'One of the Trinity suffered in the flesh'—as a means of protecting the Chalcedonian Christology from any suspicion of *Nestorianism. Correct in itself, it had monophysite associations, and both the papal legates in Constantinople and Hormisdas at Rome treated it with great reserve. Without condemning it, the pope warned the emperor against it, arguing that Leo I's *Tome* and the Chalcedonian definition were entirely adequate. Justinian, on the other hand, concerned to win over moderate monophysites, was already prepared to approve the formula. Arising out of the affair of the Scythian monks, Hormisdas was consulted (520) about the orthodoxy of Faustus of Riez (c.459–c.490), whom they had portrayed as a Pelagian (he was in fact a *Semi-Pelagian). His discreet reply was that the church's teaching had been settled by CELESTINE I and St Augustine; as for Faustus, his writings could be read provided one did not follow any obnoxious teaching they contained.

In harmony with his concern for the east, Hormisdas commissioned Dionysius Exiguus, a Scythian monk resident c.500–c.550 in Rome, to prepare a Latin translation of the canons of the Greek church. He also kept up an active correspondence with the leading bishops of Gaul, Caesarius of Arles (d. 542) and Avitus of Vienne (d. c.519), and appointed papal vicars in Spain. Shortly before his death he had the satisfaction of learning that the persecution of Catholics in Africa had ceased with the death of the Vandal king Thrasamond (28 May 523), and that the restoration of the Catholic hierarchy could at last be taken in hand. He was buried in St Peter's, his epitaph in elegiacs being composed by his son Silverius. Feast 6 Aug.

PL 63, 367–534; *Collectio Avellana, Epp.* 105–242 (*CSEL* 35, 495–742); Thiel 1, 741–990; JW 1, 101–7; *LP* 1, 269–74; A. Grillmeier and H. Bacht, *Chalkedon* (Würzburg, 1953) 2, 73–94; R. Haacke, 'Die Glaubensformel des Papstes Hormisdas', *AnGreg* 20 (Rome, 1939); Caspar 2, 129–92; *DCB* 3, 155–61 (J. Barmby); *DTC* 7, 161–76 (É. Amann); *LThK* 5, 483 f. (R. Haacke); *NCE* 7, 148 (J. Chapin); Seppelt 1, 244–52; JR, 100–9; 242.

JOHN I, ST (13 Aug. 523–18 May 526). Born in Tuscany, he was a senior deacon, elderly and infirm, when elected. Earlier he had supported the pro-eastern Antipope LAWRENCE, but made his submission to SYMMACHUS on 16 Sept. 506. He was a revered friend of Boethius, the philosopher and statesman (c.480–524), who consulted him on his writings and dedicated three theological tractates to him; his election reflected the enhanced strength of the pro-eastern party as a result of the reunion between east and west accomplished by HORMISDAS. It is significant that as pope he was responsible for introducing, on the advice of Dionysius Exiguus, the Alexandrian computation of the date of Easter, an issue disputed between Lawrence and Symmachus; it came to be accepted throughout the west.

Shortly before John's accession Emperor Justin I (518–27), who in his zeal for orthodoxy had revived the old laws against heretics, began persecuting the Arians, including great numbers of Goths, in his realms. Their churches were seized, they were excluded from public office, and many were compelled to abandon the Arian faith. These measures infuriated and alarmed Theodoric, king of Italy (493–526), himself a Goth and an Arian, who had hitherto cultivated good relations with Catholics but now felt increasingly isolated. He summoned the pope to Ravenna and ordered him to lead a high-powered delegation of bishops and senators to Constantinople to secure the suspension of the persecution, the return of confiscated churches, and freedom for forcibly converted Arians to revert to *Arianism. Fearing for the fate of Catholics in the west if he refused, John undertook to do his best to obtain all the concessions demanded except the last; he frankly told the king he would not ask the emperor to grant this. Theodoric's reaction is not known; some have conjectured that he relied on other members of the mission to transmit his request to Justin I.

Leaving Ravenna early in 526, the embassy reached Constantinople shortly before Easter (19 Apr.). John was the first pope to leave Italy for the east, and his mission was a humiliating one. His reception, however, was brilliant: the whole city came out to the twelfth milestone to greet him, the emperor prostrated himself before

St PETER's vicar, and on Easter Day he was given a throne in church higher than the patriarch's, celebrated mass according to the Latin rite, and instead of the patriarch placed the customary Easter crown on Justin's head. When they got down to business, the emperor agreed to comply with most of Theodoric's demands, but rejected the one to which he attached most importance, that forcibly converted Arians should be permitted to revert to their original belief.

Knowing the king's impatience and believing they had achieved all that was possible, the legates hastened back to Ravenna, only to be confronted with Theodoric's unbridled fury. In his eyes the mission had been a failure since it had not brought about reciprocal toleration. He was also deeply angered by reports of the pope's magnificent reception and his gratified reaction to it. Morbidly suspicious, he had already executed his once trusted minister Boethius and other leading personages on charges of treasonable correspondence with the emperor; the pope's conduct made him fear that he too was prepared to betray him. Reports that he flung John and his fellow-legates into gaol and would have executed them had he not dreaded the emperor's wrath are certainly false. What he did with the other legates is not known, but he ordered John to remain in Ravenna at his disposal, making clear to him that he had forfeited his favour, trust, and protection. Before the king had reached a final decision about him, the wretched man, ill, worn out by his travels, and shattered by the terrible prospect before him, collapsed and died. His body, which immediately became the focus of veneration and miracles, was transported back to Rome and buried on 27 May in the nave of St Peter's. His epitaph in elegiacs salutes him as 'a victim for Christ'. Feast 18 May.

Thiel 1, 697; MGAA 9, 328; 11, 37–105; 306–28; JW 1, 109 f.; LP 1, 275–8; P. Goubert, 'Autour du voyage à Byzance du pape S. Jean I', OChP 24 (1958), 339–52; H. Löwe, 'Theoderich der Grosse und Papst Johann I', HJ 72 (1952), 83– 100; W. Ensslin, Theoderich der Grosse (Munich, 1947), 316; Caspar 2, 182–92; DTC 8, 593–5 (É. Amann); NCE 7, 1006 f. (J. Chapin); Seppelt 1, 255–7; JR, 109–13; 118–20.

FELIX IV (III), ST (12 July 526–22 Sept. 530). A Samnite by birth who as a deacon had been a member of the delegation sent by HORMISDAS in 519 to Constantinople, he was elected after a vacancy of fifty-eight days; in view of the posthumous inclusion of Antipope FELIX in the list of legitimate popes, he was improperly styled Felix IV instead of Felix III. LP states that he was consecrated by order of Theodoric, Ostrogoth king of Italy (493–526). The evidence suggests that there was a long, indecisive struggle between the pro-Gothic and pro-Byzantine parties (the latter comprising most of the senate), and that Theodoric, who after JOHN I wanted a reliable friend of the Goths as pope, intervened to break the deadlock. The king died on 30 Aug. 526, but, as his choice, Felix enjoyed good relations with his grandson and successor Athalaric (526–34), still a minor, and his widow Queen Amalasuntha, who acted as regent. Proofs of royal favour can be seen in an edict confirming that civil or criminal charges brought against clergy should be judged by the pope, and in the claim in Felix's epitaph that he increased the wealth of the papacy. The abnormally large number (55) of priests he ordained suggests a deliberate attempt to pack the clerical establishment with men sharing his outlook.

Early in his reign Felix wrote to Caesarius, bishop of Arles (502–41), approving the testing of laymen before ordination and deploring the return of ordained men to secular life. More important was his support of Caesarius in his efforts to combat *Semi-Pelagianism, then widespread in Gaul. When his Augustinian views on grace met with opposition at a synod at Valence in 528, Caesarius turned for help to Felix, who in early 529 sent him twenty-five propositions defining the church's teaching on grace and free-will, consisting mainly of texts of St Augustine assembled by Prosper of Aquitaine (c.390–c.463). These were adopted by the second council of Orange (July 529), and when approved by BONIFACE II (25 Jan. 531) effectively put an end to the controversy over grace.

With Queen Amalasuntha's permission Felix converted several temples and public buildings in the Forum to Christian worship. The splendid mosaics in one of them, the church of SS. Cosma and Damiano, which feature a portrait of Felix himself (the earliest surviving papal likeness), are due to him. As his death approached, he gathered his supporters among the clergy and senate around his sickbed and delivered them a 'precept' nominating his archdeacon Boniface as his successor; he even handed him his *pallium (on condition that he returned it if he recovered). He had the precept published in Rome and sent to the court at Ravenna. The majority of the senate reacted against this strictly unconstitutional action by forbidding any discussion of a pope's successor during his lifetime, or any acceptance of a nomination. Feast (now) 22 Sept.

PL 65, 11–23; PLSupp 3, 1280 f.; MGAA 12, 246; 255; JW 1, 110 f.; L. Duchesne, 'La succession du pape Félix IV', MelArchHist 3 (1883), 239–66; Caspar 2, 151 f; 193–7; Haller 1, 255–8; DHGE 16, 895 f. (H. Marot); LThK 4, 68 f. (G. Schwaiger); NCE 5, 879 f. (J. Chapin); Seppelt 1, 257–60; JR, 120–5.

DIOSCORUS (antipope 22 Sept.–14 Oct. 530). Although FELIX IV on his deathbed had designated his archdeacon BONIFACE, a Gothic partisan like himself, as his successor, the majority of the clergy and senate were indignant at this unconstitutional procedure; many of them also preferred a pro-Byzantine pope. When therefore the election meeting was held in the Lateran basilica, the deacon Dioscorus was chosen by a large majority, and was forthwith consecrated; the minority withdrew to a hall of the palace and elected Boniface, who was consecrated on the same day. There was thus a schism in the church, but Dioscorus's sudden death brought it to an end after only twenty-two days. Although LP did not assign him an entry, there is no doubt that, by the canon law of the time, he was legitimate pope.

Originally a deacon at Alexandria, Dioscorus supported the *Chalcedonian 'two-natures' Christology and fled to Rome, in circumstances which are unknown, to escape persecution by the *monophysites who dominated Egypt. A man of eloquence and political skill, he soon became a leading figure in the Roman church. During the Lawrentian schism (501–6) he backed SYMMACHUS, and in 506 intervened successfully on his behalf, persuading Theodoric, king of Italy (493–526), to recognize him as pope. A close confidant of HORMISDAS, he was a key member of the mission which went to Constantinople in 519 to negotiate the settlement of the *Acacian schism (484–519) and, familiar as he was with Greek and the eastern world, he was able, at the decisive meeting in the imperial palace on 27 Mar., to argue convincingly before Patriarch John II and his clergy for the soundness of Rome's anathema on Patriarch *Acacius. Hormisdas so admired his abilities that he tried, unsuccessfully, to persuade Emperor Justin I (518–27) to appoint Dioscorus bishop of Alexandria. While in Constantinople he led the campaign against the Scythian monks who were calling for the acceptance of the *Theopaschite formula—'One of the Trinity suffered in the flesh'—and was able to show that it was susceptible of monophysite misuse. His undiminished influence and prestige made him the obvious candidate of the pro-eastern party at the death of Felix IV. When he died, the sixty presbyters who had come out in his favour, after some initial hesitation, accepted Boniface as pope, but the latter forced them to sign a humiliating retractation and to condemn Dioscorus's memory. It was to the credit of Pope AGAPITUS I that he had the document brought out of the papal archives and solemnly burned in St Peter's in 535. The officials of the papal chancery, however, saw to it that the name of Dioscorus did not appear in the official lists of popes.

CSEL 35, 146; 149; 167; etc. (see index); LP 1, 46; 100–3; 265; 270; 273 f.; 281–3; JW 1, 112; L. Duchesne, 'La succession du pape Félix IV', MelArchHist 3 (1883), 239–66; Caspar 2, 116; 151–8; 195 f.; DHGE 14, 507 f. (H. Marot); EC 4, 1681 f. (A. Amore); LThK 3, 410 (G. Schwaiger); NCE 4, 878 (J. Chapin); Seppelt 1, 241; 247; 260 f.; JR, 76; 104; 107 f.; 123 f.; 253 f.

BONIFACE II (22 Sept. 530–17 Oct. 532). The son of Sigibuld, he was the first pope of Germanic stock, although born in Rome. A rich man, he served the church from childhood and was archdeacon when on his deathbed FELIX IV, wanting the pro-Gothic party to retain the papacy, formally designated him as his successor, even handing him his *pallium. The senate, outraged by such unconstitutional behaviour, published an edict forbidding discussion of the succession during a reigning pope's lifetime and also, on pain of exile and confiscation of property, the acceptance of nomination by anyone. The mass of the clergy were in agreement, and on Felix's death the deacon DIOSCORUS was elected by a large majority in the Lateran basilica. The minority belonging to the pro-Gothic faction withdrew to an adjacent hall and elected Boniface. The resulting schism, however, was short-lived, for Dioscorus died (14 Oct.) after twenty-two days, and the clergy backing him, now leaderless, after initial hesitation acknowledged Boniface as pope. He proved vindictive in his triumph, and at a synod held on 27 Dec. forced the sixty priests who had opposed him to sign a declaration admitting their guilt in disregarding Felix's nomination, promising never to attempt anything similar again, and condemning Dioscorus's memory. This he deposited in the papal archives.

Having thus assured his position, Boniface became conciliatory and made strenuous efforts, as his epitaph records, to reunite his divided flock. LP lists his gifts of plate to priests, deacons, subdeacons, and

notaries, and the alms he expended on helping the clergy when famine threatened. Like Felix, however, he was resolved to secure a pro-Gothic successor. So in 531, at a synod in St Peter's, having taken appropriate powers, he proposed a constitution nominating the deacon VIGILIUS as the next pope, and obliged the clergy to subscribe it with an oath. In view of the indignation this created, and probably also of objections from the court at Ravenna, he soon retreated and at a subsequent synod, in the presence of the senate, confessed that he had exceeded his rights, revoked his nomination, and burned the signed document before the tomb of the Apostle.

Boniface thus extricated himself, at the cost of some loss of face, from an awkward situation. The little that is known of the rest of his reign suggests that he strove to uphold the prestige of the holy see. It fell to him to confirm authoritatively (25 Jan. 531) the acts of the second council of Orange (July 529), which ended the controversy over grace. When the patriarch of Constantinople, in response to complaints from two Greek bishops, deposed and excommunicated the bishop of Larissa (Greece), Boniface held in 532 a synod which forcibly asserted the special rights of Rome over *Illyricum, within which Larissa lay. He was buried in St Peter's, but there is no evidence of any cult being devoted to him.

JW 1, 111 f.; LP 1, 281–4; A. Harnack, 'Der erste deutsche Papst', SAB (1924), 24–42; Caspar 2, 193–8; DHGE 9, 897 f. (G. Bardy); LThK 2, 588 (G. Schwaiger); DBI 12, 133–6 (P. Bertolini); NCE 2, 669 f. (A. H. Skeabech); Seppelt 1, 259–62; JR, 122–5; 242.

JOHN II (2 Jan. 533–8 May 535). The death of BONIFACE II was followed by an exceptionally long vacancy of two and a half months. It was a period of intrigue and corruption, with aspirants to the papal throne and their partisans resorting to canvassing and bribery; even church plate and funds collected for poor relief were squandered to obtain votes. Eventually a compromise candidate was chosen,

Mercury, an elderly priest of S. Clemente; because his name was a pagan god's, he assumed that of the martyred JOHN I, being the first pope to make such an alteration. It is significant that, after his installation, Athalaric, the Ostrogothic king of Italy (526–34), confirmed and extended a decree of the senate, published under Boniface II (530), which prohibited on pain of severe penalties improper practices in papal elections, and ordered that, inscribed on marble, it should be posted in St Peter's for all to see. He added strict limits to the sums that could be expended at elections or, in the case of disputed elections referred to the court, on procuring the necessary documents from royal officials.

John was on good terms with both Athalaric and the eastern emperor, Justinian I (527–65), who sent him handsome presents. He received deputations from the latter and, after holding a synod, formally accepted a dogmatic decree which the emperor had published on 15 Mar. 533. While acknowledging the teaching of the first four general councils, this decree included the *Theopaschite formula, 'One of the Trinity suffered in the flesh', which HORMISDAS had rejected as unnecessary and open to misunderstanding. The emperor favoured it because, by excluding *Nestorian interpretations of the *Chalcedonian Christology and fully expressing the teaching of Cyril of Alexandria (d. 444), it seemed calculated to appeal to *monophysites in the empire, whom it was his policy to win over. The Acoemetae (i.e. sleepless) monks of Constantinople, fervent champions of Chalcedonian orthodoxy and traditionally Rome's staunchest allies, appealed against it to the pope. John, to whom Justinian had written in deferential terms acclaiming Rome as 'the head of all the churches', did his best to persuade them to abandon their opposition, but when they refused excommunicated them as Nestorians and wrote to the emperor pronouncing his decree orthodox. Justinian was overjoyed, and incorporated both his letter and the pope's reply in his

Code. John's action has often been cited as a glaring example of a pope contradicting a previous pope in a matter of doctrine.

The only glimpse which survives of John's dealings with the west concerns the case of Bishop Contumeliosus of Riez, in Provence, whom a council presided over by Caesarius of Arles (d. 542) had found guilty of misconduct and, being divided about the proper sentence, had confined to a monastery. On being informed, John ordered (533) his deposition and appointed Caesarius temporary visitor of the see. The affair dragged on into the reign of AGAPITUS I.

MGAA 12, 279–82; *Collectio Avellana, Ep.* 84 (*CSEL* 35, 320–8); *PL* 66, 17–32; JW 1, 113; *LP* 1, 285 f.; *DCB* 3, 390 f. (J. Barmby); *NCE* 7, 1007 f. (J. Chapin); Caspar 2, 217–19; Seppelt 1, 263–5; JR, 126 f.; 251.

AGAPITUS I, ST (13 May 535–22 Apr. 536). Of aristocratic birth, son of a priest, Gordianus, who had been killed by partisans of Antipope LAWRENCE in Sept. 502, he was archdeacon when elected. A man of culture, he kept a library of the fathers in his family mansion on the Caelian Hill, and with the statesman and writer Cassiodorus (*c.*490–*c.*580) planned a Christian university for Rome modelled on the academies at Alexandria and Nisibis (in Mesopotamia). As one of the clergy who opposed the designation by a pope of his successor, he opened his reign by having the anathema on DIOSCORUS, which BONIFACE II had extorted from the clergy, publicly burned.

Forceful and independent in character, Agapitus, when appealed to by Contumeliosus of Riez, who had been deposed for misconduct by JOHN II, appointed fresh judges to examine the case; the outcome is not known. On grounds of canonical propriety he refused (July 535) Caesarius of Arles (d. 542) permission to apply church property for the relief of the poor. When the African bishops, Catholicism having been restored in north Africa after its recovery from the Arian Vandals by Emperor

Justinian I (527–65), sought his ruling, he took the hard line that *Arians converted to orthodoxy could never hold clerical office. As regards African Catholic clergy who abandoned their charges to seek refuge in Italy, he accepted the bishops' plea that these should not be received at Rome unless furnished with proper letters of authorization. In congratulating him on his election Justinian asked him to deal leniently with converted Arians, but Agapitus again replied (Oct. 535) that the canons did not allow a converted Arian priest to continue in office.

Meanwhile Justinian was energetically preparing to invade Italy, a Germanic kingdom since 476, and reincorporate it with the empire; the murder (5 Apr. 535) of Amalasuntha, widow of King Theodoric, by Theodahad, the last Ostrogothic king (534–6), gave him a pretext, since she had appealed to him. Alarmed, Theodahad charged Agapitus to lead a mission to Constantinople to persuade the emperor to abandon his plans. Such was the poverty of the Roman church at the time that the pope was forced to pawn sacred vessels in order to finance the journey. Although he was given a triumphal reception in the capital (Feb. 536), his mission proved a failure; Justinian explained that the enterprise was too far advanced to be called off. He scored greater successes in the ecclesiastical field. Having been warned that Anthimus, the patriarch and a favourite of Empress Theodora, was a *monophysite, he refused to communicate with him on the specious ground that he had been uncanonically translated from Trebizond. In spite of threats, promises, and proffered bribes, he stood his ground and, after a public disputation with Anthimus, convinced Justinian that he was a heretic. Anthimus was removed from office, and Agapitus consecrated his successor Menas (536–52) after he had signed an expanded version of the *Formula of HORMISDAS. At Justinian's request he then endorsed John II's declaration confirming the orthodoxy of the *Theopaschite formula (which Hormisdas

disapproved), and pronounced the emperor's faith, as set out in the edict he had sent to John, conformable with the teaching of the fathers and the apostolic see; he added the pointed rider that laymen nevertheless did not possess authority to preach.

Agapitus died in Constantinople on 22 Apr. 536. But his resolute stand for the *Chalcedonian Christology gave new heart to its supporters in the east, and in May–June a synod was held in Constantinople at which the clerical members of his delegation took part. This confirmed the deposition and excommunication of Anthimus and anathematized other leading monophysites, such as Severus of Antioch (d. 538). The dead pope's body, sealed in a leaden coffin, was brought back to Rome and interred in St Peter's on 20 Sept. 536. Feast in the west (now) 22 Apr., in the east 17 Apr.

PL 66, 35–80; *Collectio Avellana, Epp.* 82; 86–91 (*CSEL* 35, 229 f.; 330–47); JW 1, 113–15; *LP* 1, 287–9; H. I. Marrou, 'Autour de la bibliothèque du pape Agapit', *MelArchHist* 48 (1931), 124–69; Caspar 2, 199–229; *DHGE* 1, 887–90 (J. P. Kirsch); *DBI* 1, 362–7 (O. Bertolini); *LThK* 1, 182 (G. Schwaiger); *NCE* 1, 194 f. (J. Chapin); Seppelt 1, 265–9; JR, 127 f.

SILVERIUS, ST (8 June 536–11 Nov. 537: d. 2 Dec. 537). Born at Frosinone, son of HORMISDAS, he was, unprecedentedly, only a subdeacon when, news of AGAPITUS I's death at Constantinople having reached Rome, Theodahad, last Ostrogothic king of Italy (534–6), terrorized the clergy into electing him pope. One source suggests that Theodahad had been bribed; what seems certain is that, knowing that Agapitus had failed to deflect Emperor Justinian I (527–65) from his plans for the conquest of Italy, he wanted a pro-Gothic pope whom he could trust. Once Silverius had been consecrated, the clergy hostile to his appointment accepted him for the sake of unity.

The new pope was now caught in a fatal web of intrigue. While in Constantinople, Agapitus I had, to the chagrin of Empress Theodora, brought about the deposition of the *monophysite patriarch Anthimus;

VIGILIUS (537–55)

when Agapitus died, Theodora, a monophysite herself, made a compact with the
Roman deacon VIGILIUS, apocrisiarius
(nuncio) of the holy see, that she would get
him appointed pope if he would secure the
rehabilitation of Anthimus. Vigilius
hastened to Rome, only to find Silverius
already installed. Attempts were first made,
through Justinian's general Belisarius, who
occupied Rome on 10 Dec. 536, to induce
Silverius to stand down in compliance with
the empress's wishes. When he refused, he
was called to Belisarius's headquarters and
accused, with the aid of forged letters, of
having treasonably plotted with the Goths,
who were now besieging Rome, to open its
gates to them. Although he had in fact, with
the object of avoiding bloodshed, joined
with the senate in persuading the citizens to
surrender the city peacefully to the imperial
army, he was bound to be suspect as a pro-
Goth, and Belisarius, swayed by his wife
Antonina, had him stripped of his *pallium,
degraded him to the rank of a monk, and
then deposed him (11 Mar. 537). A subdeacon announced to the clergy that he was no
longer pope.

Silverius was deported to Patara, a sea-
port in Lycia (south-west Anatolia). The
local bishop, however, went to Constantinople to protest on his behalf to Justinian;
there were many kings in the world, he
declared, but only one pope, and Silverius
had been unjustly extruded. Justinian
ordered Silverius to be sent back to Rome
and given a fair trial: if found guilty, he
should be assigned another see; if innocent,
restored to his throne. This was too much
for Vigilius, now pope, and when Silverius
reached Rome he arranged with Belisarius
for him to be delivered into his own hands.
Silverius was then dispatched, under guard
of two agents of Vigilius, to Palmaria, an
island in the Gulf of Gaeta. Here his abdication seems to have been extorted from
him (11 Nov. 537), and shortly afterwards
he died (probably on 2 Dec.), the victim of
starvation and the hardships he had suffered. He was buried on the island, his grave
becoming the centre of cures and miracles,

and from the 11th cent. he was venerated as
a martyr for the orthodox faith. Feast 20
June.

Liberatus of Carthage, *Brev.* 22 (*PL* 68, 1039–
42); Procopius, *De bello Gothico* 1, 25 f.; 3, 15;
Anecd. 1, 14; JW 1, 115 f.; *LP* 1, 270–3; P.
Hildebrand, 'Die Ansetzung des Papstes
Silverius (537)', *HJ* 42 (1922), 213–49; O.
Bertolini, 'La fine del pontificato di papa Silverio',
ASRomana 47 (1924), 325–43; Caspar 2, 230–3;
DCB 4, 670–3 (J. Barmby); *DTC* 14, 2065–7 (É.
Amann); *BSS* 11, 1069–71 (V. Monachino); *NCE*
13, 217 (J. Chapin); Seppelt 1, 270–3; JR,
128–33.

VIGILIUS (29 Mar. 537–7 June 555).
Nobly born, son and brother of consuls, he
was a deacon when BONIFACE II designated
him his successor in 531, only to revoke the
nomination in face of a storm of protest.
Sent then as apocrisiarius (nuncio) to Constantinople, he became a confidant of the
*monophysite empress Theodora. When
AGAPITUS I died there (22 Apr. 536), she
made a secret compact with him, reinforced
with enormous gifts, that she would secure
the papacy for him if he would disavow the
council of Chalcedon (451) and reinstate
Patriarch Anthimus, whom Agapitus had
had deposed as a monophysite. Ambitious
and avaricious, Vigilius agreed, but on
reaching Rome he found SILVERIUS already
installed. After Belisarius, victorious commander of Emperor Justinian (527–65), had
deposed Silverius, he forced through the
election of Vigilius, probably on Theodora's
orders. The new pope's complicity in blocking the fair trial of Silverius ordered by
Justinian, and in his second, fatal exile,
cannot be evaded.

Given the prestige of the *Chalcedonian
Christology in the west, Vigilius could not
openly fulfil his undertaking to the empress.
Privately, however, he assured Anthimus
and other monophysites in the east that he
shared their opinions, although it would be
helpful if they could keep quiet about it.
Meanwhile he was kept busy restoring the
churches and other buildings in Rome
devastated during its recent siege by the
Goths. He maintained his predecessors'

policies in Gaul, empowering successive bishops of Arles to act as papal vicars. A decretal he addressed (29 Mar. 538) to Profuturus of Braga on disciplinary matters is liturgically important, and several masses in the Leonine Sacramentary (7th cent.) belong to him. It was his relations with Byzantium, however, which revealed his deviousness and weakness of character. In Sept. 540 he wrote fulsomely to Justinian, avowing himself a true-blue Chalcedonian who rejoiced in the emperor's repudiation of Anthimus and other monophysites. This reflected his real attitude, but also his awareness of Justinian's theological stance at the moment. When in Jan. 543 the emperor anathematized the teaching and person of Origen, the Greek 3rd-cent. theologian, Vigilius dutifully subscribed the edict with other patriarchs. Later that year, however, Justinian published a further edict anathematizing the 'Three Chapters', i.e. the person and writings of Theodore of Mopsuestia (d. 428), and certain writings of Theodoret of Cyrrhus (d. c.458) and Ibas of Edessa (d. 457), supporters of the 'two-natures' Christology whose orthodoxy the council of Chalcedon (451) had not questioned. Justinian was convinced that the monophysites in the empire, who regarded these three as virtually *Nestorians, might be won over by their denunciation, and he required all patriarchs, the pope included, to endorse his judgement.

This was Vigilius's great and, as it proved, fatal test. Menas of Constantinople and the eastern bishops, with notable exceptions, signed the anathemas under protest; but there was a violent reaction in the west, which saw the Chalcedonian settlement imperilled. At first the pope resisted, but Justinian, to whom his support was vital, had him arrested by Byzantine police at mass (22 Nov. 545) and, after a lengthy stay in Sicily, brought to Constantinople (Jan. 547). Once there, he for a time maintained his bold front, excommunicating Patriarch Menas for subscribing and being excommunicated by him in return. Gradually, however, observing the emperor's

determination, he allowed his resistance to be worn down, in June 547 resumed communion with Menas, secretly promised Justinian and Theodora that he would condemn the Three Chapters, and on 11 Apr. 548 sent Menas his *Iudicatum* or 'verdict', viz. that the Three Chapters should be condemned, although without prejudice to Chalcedon.

This betrayal, as it was considered, provoked intense indignation in the west. A synod of African bishops excommunicated Vigilius (550), and he himself had to excommunicate members of his own entourage. The crisis was such that emperor and pope agreed that it would have to be resolved by a council. Vigilius was allowed to withdraw his *Iudicatum*, but was obliged to give Justinian a private but written assurance that he would do all in his power to bring about the condemnation of the Three Chapters. In July 551, however, exasperated by delays and worked on by his theological adviser Askidas, Justinian issued a fresh edict anathematizing the Three Chapters. This was too much for the pope, who called for the withdrawal of the edict, excommunicated Askidas, and then sought sanctuary with his clergy in a church. After Justinian's police had physically assaulted him at the altar, he returned with a safe conduct to his lodgings, but since he was treated like a prisoner he fled a second time (23 Dec. 551) across the Bosphorus and took refuge, appropriately, in the council church at Chalcedon. Here he published an encyclical attempting to justify his behaviour and deposing Askidas. By June 552 a reconciliation had been patched up, but in spite of Vigilius's demand that the planned council should be held in Sicily or Italy, the emperor convened it (the Fifth General Council) in Constantinople on 5 May 553.

In spite of strong pressure to attend, the pope refused, pleading the complete inadequacy of western representation. Instead, assisted by his deacon PELAGIUS, he issued on 14 May a compromise document, his First Constitution, condemning sixty propositions attributed to Theodore but not his person, and declining to anathematize Theodoret and Ibas. It was a skilful manifesto, but Justinian rejected it. In reprisal, at the seventh session of the council (26 May) he humiliated Vigilius by revealing his secret correspondence condemning or promising to condemn them. He then ordered the pope's name to be struck from the *diptychs, making it clear, however, that he was severing communion with him personally, not with the holy see. The council was to anathematize the Three Chapters at its eighth session.

The council having proved compliant, it only remained for Justinian to bring Vigilius himself into line with his policies. His close advisers, including the deacon Pelagius, were flung into gaol, recalcitrant Latin bishops were deposed and exiled, and the pope himself was placed under strict house arrest. Isolated and ill, his spirit broken, he capitulated after six months, and on 8 Dec. 553 wrote to the new patriarch, Eutychius, revoking (he appealed to St Augustine's *Retractations* as a precedent) his earlier defence of the Three Chapters and confessing that, God having opened his eyes, he now agreed they deserved full condemnation. This being deemed insufficient, he issued on 23 Feb. 554 his Second Constitution fully endorsing the decisions of the council. He was now set free and allowed to return to Rome, where his presence was demanded. He stayed in Constantinople, however, for a year, and obtained from Justinian, as a reward for his loyal services, the so-called Pragmatic Sanction (13 Aug. 554), intended to establish orderly imperial government in Italy, now wrested from the Goths, but also assuring the church of important rights and privileges. In spring he set off, but succumbed to gallstones (from which he had long suffered) and died at Syracuse, Sicily. His remains were brought back to Rome and, in view of his unpopularity, were buried, not in St Peter's, but in S. Marcello on the Via Salaria.

PL 69, 15–328; CSEL 35, 230–320; 348–56; MGEp 3, 57–68; JW 1, 117–24; LP 1, ccliii f.;

281; 291; 296–302; E. Schwartz, 'Vigiliusbriefe' and 'Zur Kirchenpolitik Iustinians', *SAM* 1940, Heft 2; L. Duchesne, 'Vigile et Pélage', *RevQuest-Hist* 36 (1884), 369–440; 37 (1885), 529–93; A. Chavasse, 'Messes du pape Vigile', *ELit* 64 (1950), 161–213; 66 (1952), 145–215; Caspar 2, 229–86; *DTC* 15, 2994–3005 (É. Amann); *LThK* 10, 787 f. (K. Baus); *NCE* 14, 664–7 (F. X. Murphy); *PWSupp* 14, 864–85 (A. Lippold); Seppelt 1, 270–90; JR, 129–33; 141–60.

PELAGIUS I (16 Apr. 556–3 Mar. 561). A Roman, nobly born and rich, he was widely experienced and elderly when appointed. As a deacon he had accompanied AGAPITUS I in 536 to Constantinople, after his death representing the holy see at the anti-*monophysite synod held there in May–August. When SILVERIUS was exiled in 537, Pelagius was alleged, in deference to Empress Theodora's wishes, to have worked to prevent his return in order to retain the papacy for VIGILIUS. He had stayed in Constantinople as Vigilius's apocrisiarius and become the confidant of Emperor Justinian (527–65), who had consulted him on church appointments, used him on delicate missions, and under his influence published (early 543) a denunciation of the Greek theologian Origen (d. c.254). In 544, when Justinian issued his edict condemning the *Three Chapters, Pelagius had been in Rome, but had sought theological ammunition against it from Ferrandus of Carthage (d. 546/7). In 546, when Rome was besieged by the Goths, he had played a noteworthy role as vicar of the absent pope, spending lavishly on famine relief and, when the city fell (17 Dec.), intervening with the Gothic king Totila to prevent a massacre. Totila had sent him (547) to Constantinople to negotiate peace, but without success.

For the rest of his diaconate he had been deeply involved with the controversy over the Three Chapters. Like the west generally, he had rejected Vigilius's *Iudicatum* (547) condemning them. Returning to Constantinople in 551, he had stiffened the vacillating Vigilius's opposition to their condemnation, sharing his ill treatment, backing his demand for a general council to reassure the west, and, when it met in a form unlikely to do so, supporting his refusal to take part. It was he who had drafted Vigilius's First *Constitution. When the pope weakened and issued a Second Constitution, he had broken with him and, imprisoned in monasteries, had written, with other pamphlets, a *Defence of the Three Chapters*, branding Vigilius in it as a turncoat. But now he made an abrupt change of stance, accepting both the condemnation of the Three Chapters and the Fifth General Council. The reasons for his volte-face are obscure. It is likely that he had realized that Vigilius's endorsement of the council created a new situation, but also likely that he was aware that Justinian, who despite differences had never ceased to admire him, wished him to be the next pope provided he fell into line with his religious policy.

On Vigilius's death he returned to Rome as the emperor's nominee for the papacy. There seems to have been no election, but *LP* suggests that Justinian may have obtained the grudging assent of the Roman clergy in Constantinople. Not surprisingly, Pelagius had a hostile reception, many religious and nobles withdrawing from communion with him. His consecration had to be postponed until 16 Apr. 556 since no bishop would officiate, and it was then carried out by only two bishops (of Perugia and Ferentino), while a presbyter represented the bishop of *Ostia, normally a papal consecrator. Rumour implicated him in Vigilius's death, and he was execrated for his betrayal, as the west regarded it, of the Three Chapters. It is significant that, after his ordination, he broke precedent by solemnly affirming his loyalty to the first four general councils, especially Chalcedon (451), and in St Peter's, supported by the governor Narses and holding aloft a cross and the book of the gospels, swore that he had done no harm to Vigilius.

Pelagius worked energetically, using the temporal powers granted by Justinian's *Pragmatic Sanction, to restore order and the juridical system in Rome and Italy after the devastation of war. He was exceptionally active in relieving poverty and starvation and ransoming prisoners of war. Helped by a lay banker, Anastasius, he overhauled the papal finances and reorganized the papal properties in Italy, Gaul, Dalmatia, and north Africa, earmarking their income for the poor. He made special efforts to recover church plate dispersed during the troubles, and took steps to improve the quality of monastic life and fill the depleted ranks of the clergy, campaigning against simony and insisting on high moral standards. By efficient administration and pastoral care he speedily conciliated opinion in Rome, but elsewhere in the west, with certain notable exceptions (e.g. suburbicarian Italy—i.e. the seven dioceses within 60 km. of Rome—and Ravenna), he had an uphill and largely unsuccessful struggle to secure recognition for his authority as pope. In Gaul, where bitter comparisons were made between his earlier and later attitudes, he continued to be distrusted and hated, in spite of repeated, humiliating assurances of his orthodoxy. Hostility to his condemnation of the Three Chapters was most obdurate in north Italy, where the great sees of Aquileia and Milan renounced communion with him. To bring the schismatics to heel he even put pressure on the exarch (imperial governor or viceroy) Narses to use his troops, arguing that such action was permitted by divine law; but the great general shrank from doing so. Thus the reign of this gifted and energetic pontiff, the outstanding churchman of the day, was dogged with bitter frustration.

As a deacon Pelagius made a Latin translation of selections of the 5th-cent. Greek *Sayings of the Elders*. Before he died he had made a start on the cruciform church of Sts Philip and James (now SS. Apostoli), modelled on Justinian's *Apostoleion* at Constantinople and intended to commemorate Narses's triumph over the Goths. It was a fitting symbol of his collaboration with both the emperor and his commander. He was buried in St Peter's with an optimistic epitaph attributing to him more success in winning back schismatics than in fact he had.

P. M. Gasso and C. A. Batlle, *Pelagii I papae epistulae quae supersunt* (Montserrat, 1956); R. Devreesse, 'Pelagii diaconi *In defensione trium capitulorum*', *ST* 57 (1932); JW 1, 114–36; 2, 695; 738; *LP* 1, 303 f.; 309 f.; Caspar 2, 274–305; *DCB* 4, 295–8 (J. Barmby); *DTC* 12, 660–9 (R. Devreesse); *LThK* 8, 249 f. (G. Schwaiger); *PWSupp* 7, 836–47 (A. Nagl); *NCE* 11, 55 f. (F. X. Murphy); Seppelt 1, 286–92; JR, 142–8; 151–3 (and see index).

JOHN III (17 July 561–13 July 574). Originally named Catelinus, he was the son of Anastasius, a Roman senator and provincial governor; he is probably to be identified with the subdeacon John who completed PELAGIUS I's translation of the Greek 5th-cent. *Sayings of the Elders* and compiled an *Exposition of the Heptateuch*. A pro-easterner acceptable to Emperor Justinian I (527–65) and to Narses, his exarch (viceroy) in Italy from 554, he had to wait only four months after election before the imperial authorization necessary at this time for his consecration arrived from Constantinople.

John's reign, about which hardly anything is known, saw the invasion (568) of large parts of Italy by the Lombards under King Alboin; they met with little resistance since Justinian's successor Justin II (565–78) had dismissed Narses in response to popular demand. The invasion assisted the ending of the schism between Rome and the great churches of the west caused by the endorsement by Pelagius I of the condemnation of the *Three Chapters. Relations with north Africa became easier after Justinian's death in 565, and in 573 the new bishop of Milan, Laurentius II, elected in Genoa because of the occupation of his city in 569, deemed it prudent to renew communion with Rome and signed a document (countersigned by the future GREGORY I, then prefect of Rome) acquiescing in the condemnation of the Three Chapters. Aquileia, however, continued obdurate. But John had more than church affairs to worry about. As the Lombards poured south, he went in desperation to Naples, where Narses had

settled, and persuaded him to return (571) to Rome, reside in the imperial palace, and take charge of the crisis. In spite of the help he was providing, this created such disturbances among the populace and made John so unpopular that he judged it wise, so as to escape being involved in the quarrel, to withdraw from the city and take up residence at the church of SS. Tiburtius and Valerian two miles outside on the Via Appia. There he carried out all his duties, including the consecration of bishops, until Narses's death in Rome in 573/4. He himself died soon after his octogenarian friend and was buried in St Peter's. He completed the church of Sts Philip and James (now SS. Apostoli) begun by his predecessor to commemorate Narses's victories.

JW 1, 136 f.; *LP* 1, 305–7; O. Bertolini, *Roma di fronte a Bisanzio e ai Langobardi* (Bologna, 1941), 220–2; Caspar 2, 350 f.; *DCB* 3, 391 (J. Barmby); *DACL* 13, 1221 f. (H. Leclercq); *NCE* 7, 1008 (J. Chapin); Seppelt 1, 292 f.; JR, 162–6; 241; 243.

BENEDICT I (2 June 575–30 July 579). A Roman by birth, son of Boniface (otherwise unknown), he had to wait almost eleven months after his election before the necessary imperial confirmation, delayed by the breakdown of communications, arrived from Constantinople and he could be consecrated. His reign, about which almost nothing is known, saw the most cruel phase of the Lombard conquest, with armed forces pushing south and in summer 579 investing Rome. A delegation he and the senate sent to Constantinople to ask for help had little success. The troops dispatched by Emperor Justin II (565–78) were too few, and while the grain ships he had sent from Egypt provided valuable relief, it was short-lived. As the siege intensified and famine spread in the city, Benedict died. But certain actions of his stand out from the darkness. For a time at any rate he seems to have had good relations with the Lombard duke of Spoleto, for he was able to order the restitution of landed properties to the monastery of S. Marco near the city. He was exceptionally active pastorally, ordaining no fewer than twenty-one bishops. One of them was a Roman, John III, whom he appointed archbishop of Ravenna in Nov. 578, thereby consolidating papal influence in the city that was now the residence of the imperial governors of Italy. Finally, it was probably he who removed the future GREGORY I from his monastery and ordained him deacon, thus strengthening his administrative staff. He was buried in the sacristry of St Peter's.

JW 1, 137; 2, 695 f.; LP 1, 308; Caspar 2, 350 f.; DCB 1, 311 (T. R. Buchanan); DHGE 8, 7–9 (F. Baix); DBI 8, 324 f. (O. Bertolini); NCE 2, 273 (J. Chapin); Seppelt 1, 293; JR, 165 f.

PELAGIUS II (26 Nov. 579–7 Feb. 590).
Born in Rome, son of a Goth named Unigild, he was elected when the siege of the city by the Lombards was at its height. Because of the crisis he was ordained immediately, probably in Aug. 579, without waiting for the imperial mandate indispensable since the Byzantine conquest of Italy; his reign was officially dated from its arrival in late November.

He at once dispatched his deacon GREGORY to Constantinople as apocrisiarius and to beg for military aid. Hard pressed by the Persian war, Emperor Tiberius II (578–82) could spare only a few troops, but advised the Roman delegation to bribe the Lombard dukes and seek help from the Frankish king. In Oct. 580, therefore, Pelagius appealed to Aunarius, bishop of Auxerre; as neighbours sharing the orthodox faith, he pleaded, Providence had singled out the Franks to be Rome's and Italy's protectors. His appeal fell on deaf ears, and four years later he had to write to Gregory in Constantinople describing Italy's plight and urging him to bestir the emperor. In 585, however, Smaragdus, imperial exarch in Ravenna, arranged an armistice with the Lombards which lasted until 589. Pelagius took advantage of the reopening of access to northern Italy to correspond with Elijah, bishop of Aquileia (now at Grado), and the bishops of Istria, whose sees had renounced communion

with Rome in disgust at its condemnation of the *Three Chapters, in an attempt to end the schism. Although he was assisted by Gregory, now back from Constantinople, his efforts were fruitless despite the irenical tone and impressive theological content of his letters. He then got Smaragdus to use force to bring about a reconciliation, but he too was unsuccessful.

Under Pelagius the conversion of the Visigoths in Spain, under King Reccared (586–601), was proclaimed at the third council of Toledo (589). His reign also saw the beginning of a long controversy over the title 'ecumenical patriarch', used by bishops of Constantinople from the late 5th cent., originally with the meaning 'supreme within his own patriarchate'. When Patriarch John IV assumed it at a synod held in 588, Pelagius refused to endorse the acts since the title seemed to infringe papal supremacy, and called on his nuncio Gregory to break off communion with John until he repudiated it. In Rome he was an active builder and restorer; it was probably he who raised the presbytery of St Peter's so that the high altar was directly above the shrine of the Apostle, and he reconstructed S. Lorenzo fuori le Mura, where his portrait can be seen in contemporary mosaic on the triumphal arch. When plague began ravaging Rome as a result of flooding caused by an overflow of the Tiber in Nov. 589, he was one of its first victims. He was buried in the portico of St Peter's.

PL 72, 703–60; ACO IV/2, 105–36; JW 1, 137–40; LP 1, 309–11; Caspar 2, 353–74; DCB 4, 298–301 (J. Barmby); DACL 13, 1222–4 (H. Leclercq); DTC 12, 669–75 (É. Amann); NCE 11, 56–8 (J. Chapin); Seppelt 1, 293–6; JR, 166–8; 225–30.

GREGORY I, ST (3 Sept. 590–12 Mar. 604).
Like LEO I called 'the Great', he was born c.540 of a wealthy patrician family which had already provided two popes, FELIX III and AGAPITUS I. His education, which probably included legal studies, was the best available. After gaining administrative experience as prefect of Rome c.572–4,

65

GREGORY I (590–604)

he became a monk on the death of his father Gordianus (two paternal aunts were nuns), converted the family mansion on the Caelian Hill into the monastery of St Andrew in 574/5, and there embarked on a rigorous monastic apprenticeship. He also founded six monasteries on family estates in Sicily. Although he ruined his health with fasting, this was the happiest period of his life; but he was soon called to more active service, being made deacon in 578 by BENE-DICT I (probably), and in late 579 sent as apocrisiarius to Constantinople by PELA-GIUS II. In this key post he became expert on eastern church affairs (but learned no Greek), enjoyed close relations with the court and leading personalities (although he clashed with Patriarch Eutychius on doctrine), and struggled, with little success, to obtain military and material help for Rome and Italy, since 568 subject to invasion by the Lombards. Meanwhile he lived in his official residence as a monk with other monks. Recalled to Rome in 585/6, he resided in his monastery, but was chiefly employed as confidential adviser to Pelagius II, helping him with his difficult negotiations to end the schism with Venetia–Istria caused by Rome's condemnation of the *Three Chapters. He was responsible for the third, theologically most important, of the pope's letters, but the schismatics proved unyielding.

Although a junior deacon, Gregory was elected with rare unanimity on Pelagius II's death. Genuinely recoiling from promotion, he did everything possible to avoid it, even writing to Emperor Maurice (582–602) to ask him to withhold his consent. In the meantime he devoted himself to the plague-stricken city, organizing penitential processions and preaching calls to repentance. When the imperial mandate arrived he still sought escape, but was consecrated under protest on 3 Sept. 590. His early letters as pope graphically portray his unhappiness at being dragged from the contemplative life to shoulder his heavy burden. In fact, habitually describing himself as 'servant of God's servants', he proved an exceptionally

vigorous and confident pontiff whose reign was decisive for the subsequent history of the church and for the medieval papacy.

From the outset, owing to the breakdown of civil government, he was involved as much in temporal as in spiritual affairs. Hardly enthroned, he took in hand the provision of food and other necessities for the starving population. To find the means, he carried out a thorough reorganization of 'the patrimony of Peter', i.e. the vast estates owned by the holy see not only in Italy but in Sicily, Dalmatia, Gaul, and north Africa, appointing rectors directly responsible to himself in the several domains and insisting on efficient and humane management. He thus not only relieved social distress but laid the foundations of the future papal state. He also dealt personally with the Lombard threats to Rome since the imperial exarch at Ravenna would do nothing. In 592 he made a truce with Ariulf, duke of Spoleto, and when the exarch broke it and King Agilulf descended on Rome, he rallied the garrison and saved the city (593) by bribing him and promising yearly tribute. In these years he became virtually civil ruler of Italy, negotiating treaties, paying troops, and appointing generals. His aim was a general peace and the conversion of the Lombards to Catholicism. When the emperor chided him for being so simple as to be duped by barbarians, Gregory sent him (June 595) a stinging rejoinder defending what he was doing on behalf of 'my country' (patria).

With his tireless energy and unerring eye for what was needed, he quickly established a more effective oversight of the west than his predecessors, working where possible through metropolitans. In Italy he imposed a detailed code for the election and conduct of bishops, enforced clerical celibacy, and deposed offending prelates. Even if his efforts to end the schism in Venetia–Istria failed because the emperor, for political reasons, bade him desist, he managed to obtain the submission of several individual bishops. In Africa he struggled to counter a revival of *Donatism and assert Rome's authority, although an unco-operative exarch and the tradition of African independence made it uphill work. He had greater success in forging links with Visigothic Spain, where he found friends in the Catholic King Reccared and Bishop Leander of Seville (d. 600), and with Gaul, where he restored (595) the papal vicariate at Arles and kept up a friendly correspondence with the ferocious Queen Brunhild (d. 613). Of his missionary enterprises the most successful was his dispatch to England of Augustine, prior of his Roman monastery, with forty monks in 596. In 601 he sent reinforcements led by Mellitus and Paulinus (later bishops of London and York), and conferred the *pallium on Augustine as archbishop of the English.

Gregory's relations were different with the east, where there was an emperor whose subject he readily acknowledged he was. He frequently had to bow to his wishes in ecclesiastical policy. He was indefatigable, however, in upholding the Roman primacy, and successfully maintained Rome's appellate jurisdiction in the east. A major cause of friction, however, was the use of the title *'ecumenical patriarch' by the bishop of Constantinople. Although accepting *canon 28 of Chalcedon, Gregory strongly objected to it as challenging the pope's unique supremacy. Emperor Maurice rebuked him for making a fuss over a mere title, but Gregory argued that St PETER's commission made all churches, Constantinople included, subject to Rome. The wrangle dragged on for Gregory's entire reign, with the eastern authorities refusing to budge. It was resentment arising from it which caused him to greet the murder of Maurice and the usurpation of the tyrant Phocas (602–10) with unworthy jubilation in 602.

Gregory's interests and influence were wide-ranging. An admirer of Benedict of Nursia (c.480–c.550) and the first pope to be a monk, he was the propagator of monasticism, granting important privileges to monks and choosing them for his immediate circle. Although the Gregorian Sacramentary is a later compilation, he introduced a number of changes in the liturgy and concerned himself with liturgical music, probably setting up a school of singers. He was also a voluminous writer, practical rather than theoretical, an unoriginal but effective summarizer of Augustine's teaching; his works were so widely studied that he was acclaimed, with Ambrose, Augustine, and Jerome, a doctor of the church. His Register contains more than 850 letters and illuminates every aspect of his activities. His Pastoral Care (c.591) sets out his view of the bishop as a shepherd of souls; translated into Greek in his lifetime and into Anglo-Saxon by King Alfred, it became the textbook of the medieval episcopate. Of his sermons and commentaries 40 short Homilies on the Gospels (590–1), 22 longer Homilies on Ezekiel (593), two Homilies on Song of Songs, and part of a Commentary on 1 Samuel survive, graphically written and allegorical in approach. His Dialogues (593/4), relating the lives and miracles of Benedict of Nursia and other Italian saints, reflect the simple credulity of the age. His Moralia, a mystical and allegorical exposition of Job, begun in Constantinople and finished in 595, became a treasury of moral and ascetical theology in later centuries.

Gregory was a man of immense ability, determination, and energy, over-deferential to the great, but always realistic and humble-minded; what gave urgency to his thinking and action was his conviction of the imminent end of the world. The victim of ill health throughout his pontificate, he was racked with gout and unable to walk when he died. Threatened with a fresh siege, Rome was again in the grip of famine, and the mob, ironically, turned in exasperation on the man who had lavished everything on them. He was buried in St Peter's, his epitaph acclaiming him as 'consul of God'. Feast now 3 Sept.

PL 75–9 (works, etc.); MGEp 1 and 2; CCL 140–140A (letters); 142–4 (commentaries and Moralia); JW 1, 143–219; LP 1, 312–14; F. H.

Dudden, Gregory the Great: His Place in History and Thought (London, 1905); H. Grisar, *Gregor der Grosse* (Rome, 1928); P. Batiffol, *St Gregory the Great* (ET, London, 1929); J. Richards, *Consul of God* (London, 1980); N. Sharkey, *St Gregory the Great's Concept of Papal Power* (Washington, 1956); Caspar 2, 306–514; *DCB* 1, 779–91 (J. Barmby); *BSS* 7, 222–78 (V. Monachino); *DSp* 6, 872–910 (R. Gillet); *NCE* 6, 766–70 (G. Rush); Seppelt 2, 9–42.

SABINIAN (13 Sept. 604–22 Feb. 606).

Born at Volterra in Tuscany, he was a career cleric who as deacon served as GREGORY I's nuncio in Constantinople from 593 to 595. This indicates that Gregory then had a high opinion of him, but he incurred the pope's anger in 595 for not being sufficiently firm with Emperor Maurice (582–602) and Patriarch John IV in opposing the latter's use of the title *'ecumenical patriarch'. He was recalled, and later that year was a member of a papal mission to Gaul. Elected probably in Mar. 604, he had to await the arrival of the imperial mandate from Constantinople before being ordained in mid-Sept. His election represented a reaction against Gregory, who was unpopular in Rome at the time of his death; it is significant that, reversing Gregory's policy of relying on monks, he preferred to promote secular clergy. Almost nothing is known of his short reign, which saw a renewal of hostilities with the Lombards and an intensification of the famine gripping Rome when Gregory died. *LP* seems to suggest that he was involved in negotiations for a truce between Smaragdus, imperial exarch at Ravenna, and the Lombard king. His policy for alleviating the famine again contrasted with Gregory's, who had given away grain from the papal granaries freely; Sabinian kept a tight control and sold it, only to be accused of profiteering. This made him so unpopular with the masses that, in order to avoid hostile demonstrations, his funeral procession had to make a detour outside the city walls to reach St Peter's.

JW 1, 220; *LP* 1, 315; Caspar 2, 515 f.; *DCB* 4, 574 (J. Barmby); *DTC* 14, 438 f. (É. Amann); *NCE* 12, 784 (P. J. Mullins); Seppelt 2, 43; JR, 244; 260 f.

BONIFACE III (19 Feb.–12 Nov. 607).

Born in Rome of Greek family, he had to wait almost a year before being consecrated. In contrast to SABINIAN, he was a favoured protégé of GREGORY I, who after he had been chief executive agent of the church (*primicerius defensorum*) had made him a deacon and sent him as nuncio to Constantinople in 603, commending him warmly to the new emperor Phocas (602–10). A skilful diplomat, he established friendly relations with Phocas, and when he became pope obtained from him a formal declaration that Rome, the see of St PETER, was head of all the churches. Emperor Justinian (527–65) had issued a similar pronouncement, but this time it put a stop, for the moment at any rate, to the claim of bishops of Constantinople, exasperating to PELAGIUS II and Gregory I, to the title *'ecumenical patriarch'. The occasion was marked by the erection in Rome of a gilded statue of the tyrannical Phocas with an adulatory inscription. A further proof of good relations between Boniface and the emperor was the latter's ending of his predecessors' policy of tolerance towards the schism in Venetia–Istria caused by the *Three Chapters controversy, and his instruction to exarch Smaragdus to take energetic measures against its adherents. The only other noteworthy event of Boniface's reign was his holding of a synod to regulate papal elections; this forbade, on pain of excommunication, all discussion of a successor to a pope or bishop during his lifetime and until three days after his death. It is possible that Boniface's own election had been marked by canvassing and rivalries between the pro- and anti-Gregorian factions; this would explain the long vacancy better than delay, of which there is no evidence, in obtaining the necessary imperial confirmation.

JW 1, 220; 2, 698; *LP* 1, 316; Caspar 2, 517 f.; *DCB* 1, 329 (T. R. Buchanan); *DHGE* 9, 898 (G. Bardy); *NCE* 2, 670 (P. J. Mullins); *DBI* 12, 136 f.

(P. Bertolini); Seppelt 2, 43 f.; JR, 177; 259; 261–3.

BONIFACE IV, ST (15 Sept. 608–8 May 615).

Born in what is now the province of L'Aquila, son of a doctor, he is first mentioned in 591 as a deacon and treasurer to GREGORY I. The ten-month vacancy before his consecration was caused by the need to await the imperial mandate from Constantinople. A disciple and imitator of Gregory, as his epitaph emphasizes, he turned his house in Rome into a monastery on becoming pope and encouraged monks and monasticism. His reign was disturbed by famine, plague, and natural disasters, but he enjoyed good relations with Emperors Phocas (602–10) and Heraclius (610–41). Phocas granted his request to turn (13 May 609) the Roman Pantheon into a church dedicated to the BVM and all the martyrs (the first such conversion of a pagan temple), and he filled it with relics from the catacombs. In 610 he held a synod to regulate life and discipline in monasteries, and among those present was Mellitus (d. 624), first bishop of London. The pope and he conferred about the needs of the English church, and Mellitus returned home armed with the synod's decrees and letters for Archbishop Lawrence of Canterbury, King Ethelbert of Kent, and the English people generally. In 613 Boniface received a letter, deferential but full of impassioned reproaches, from the Irish monk Columban (543–615), now at Bobbio (in the Apennines), who, at the instigation of the Arian Lombard king Agilulf and his Catholic wife Theodolinda, besought him to repudiate his predecessors' condemnation of the *Three Chapters and convene a council to demonstrate his own orthodoxy. No rejoinder from Boniface has survived. On his death he was buried in St Peter's; his cult can be traced only to the reign of BONIFACE VIII. Feast 25 May.

JW 1, 220–2; MGEp 3, 163 f.; 170–7; LP 1, 317 f.; J. Rivière, 'St Columban et le jugement du pape hérétique', RevSR 3 (1923), 277–82; Caspar 2, 517–22; DACL 10, 2062–8; 13, 1063–7 (H.

Leclercq); DHGE 9, 898 f. (G. Bardy); NCE 2, 670 (P. J. Mullins); DBI 12, 137–40 (P. Bertolini); Seppelt 2, 44–6; JR, 53; 177; 256; 262–5.

DEUSDEDIT (later ADEODATUS I), ST (19 Oct. 615–8 Nov. 618).

A Roman by birth, son of a subdeacon Stephen, he was already elderly when elected, having served as a priest for forty years, and was himself the first priest to be made pope since JOHN II. He was the choice of the party opposed to the pro-monastic policies of GREGORY I and BONIFACE IV; LP records with satisfaction that 'he greatly loved the clergy', promoting them rather than religious to offices. He also ordained fourteen priests (the first to be ordained since Gregory I's death), and instituted an evening office, parallel to mattins, for the clergy. Practically nothing is known of his reign, except that during it Rome was afflicted with an earthquake and an outbreak of scab disease, and that there was a serious mutiny of the Byzantine forces in Italy, disgruntled at the failure of their pay to arrive. The exarch John and other government officials at Ravenna were butchered. Deusdedit continued loyal to Emperor Heraclius (610–41) throughout the upheaval, and gave a warm welcome to the new exarch, Eleutherius, when he visited Rome before moving to crush the revolt. Eleutherius, too, soon raised the standard of rebellion, but was cut down by troops as he marched on Rome. Deusdedit's epitaph, composed by HONORIUS I, describes him as simple, devout, wise, and shrewd; on his deathbed he made the first recorded funerary bequest by a pope to his clergy, the equivalent (it is conjectured) of a year's stipend to each. Feast 8 Nov.

JW 1, 222; 2, 698; LP 1, 319 f.; Caspar 2, 517 f.; 520; 523; DACL 13, 1229 f. (H. Leclercq); DHGE 14, 356 f. (B. Botte); BSS 1, 250 f. (I. Daniele); NCE 4, 822 (C. E. Sheedy); Seppelt 2, 46; JR, 178; 262–4.

BONIFACE V (23 Dec. 619–25 Oct. 625).

A Neapolitan, son of John, he had to wait some thirteen months after election before the imperial sanction for his consecration arrived. The reason for the delay was the preoccupation of Emperor Heraclius (610–41) with his campaigns against the Persians; it is significant that the responsibility for confirming a papal election was now delegated to the exarch at Ravenna. Nothing is known about Boniface's earlier career, but like DEUSDEDIT he represented the reaction against GREGORY I's pro-monastic policy. The sources stress his regard for the secular clergy, and his legislation showed his keenness to preserve their prerogatives: for example, he insisted that only priests, not acolytes, should transfer the relics of martyrs, and that acolytes should not act for subdeacons at baptisms. A businesslike administrator, he formally confirmed the right of asylum in churches, and brought ecclesiastical practice in the matter of bequests into line with civil law. Like BONIFACE IV, he took a special interest in the English church, writing to Mellitus (d. 624), archbishop of Canterbury, and to Bishop Justus of Rochester (d. c.627), and conferring the *pallium and the status of metropolitan on Justus (one of the monks sent to England by Gregory I) when he became archbishop (624). He also wrote directly to Edwin, king of Northumbria (616–33), and to his consort Ethelburga, who was already a Christian, with the object of securing the conversion of the king and his subjects. A compassionate and kindly man, he was generous to the needy and distributed his personal fortune in alms. He completed the cemetery of S. Nicomedes on the Via Nomentana, and when he died left handsome bequests to his clergy.

PL 80, 429–40; JW 1, 222 f.; 2, 698; LP 1, 321 f.; Bede, Hist. eccl. 2, 7 f.; 2, 10 f.; Caspar 2, 517–22; DCB 1, 330 (T. R. Buchanan); DHGE 9, 899 (G. Bardy); NCE 2, 670 (P. J. Mullins); DBI 12, 140–2 (P. Bertolini); Seppelt 2, 46 f.; JR, 178 f.; 244; 263 f.

HONORIUS I (27 Oct. 625–12 Oct. 638). A wealthy aristocrat from Campania, son of the consul Petronius, he was consecrated after only two days' vacancy; the imperial mandate necessary at this time was probably obtained from the exarch Isaac, who was staying in Rome. Nothing is known of his previous career, but he shared the ideals of GREGORY I and in a pontificate filled with wide-ranging activities took him as his model. Like him, he turned his mansion near the Lateran into a monastery, and employed monks rather than secular clergy for his staff.

Honorius was immediately involved in Lombard politics in north Italy, and, after initially backing the deposed Catholic king Adaloald and requesting the exarch's help in punishing bishops opposed to him, established cordial relations with his victorious rival Arioald, an Arian with a Catholic wife. Although his epitaph erred in claiming that he finally ended the schism of Venetia–Istria over the condemnation of the *Three Chapters, he was able, with assistance from the exarch, to replace Fortunatus, a schismatic bishop who had seized the see of Aquileia–Grado, with his own subdeacon Primogenius. He took steps to abate the rivalry between Ravenna, residence of the exarch, and Rome by endowing in Rome a church dedicated to Ravenna's patron, St Apollinarius, and arranging services in honour of him and St PETER. He actively supported the struggling English mission, congratulating King Edwin of Northumbria on his conversion (627), granting (634) the *pallium to the archbishops of Canterbury and York with instructions that when one of them died the survivor should nominate his successor, and dispatching (634) Birinus to evangelize the West Saxons. He had less success in persuading the Celtic Christians in Britain to abandon their non-Roman method of calculating the date of Easter. His interventions in Sardinia, Illyricum, and Spain seem to have been purposeful; his envoy at the sixth council of Toledo (638) urged the bishops to press on with the conversion of the Jews. On 11 June 628 he exempted (the first such exemption on record) the abbey of Bobbio, in the Apennines, from all episcopal jurisdiction except the pope's.

In 634 Honorius received a fateful letter

from Sergius I, patriarch of Constantinople (610–38), proposing that all talk of one or two modes of operation in Christ should be banned; instead it should be asserted that one and the same Son was the subject of every operation, human and divine, of the God-man. The formula 'two distinct natures but one operation', he explained, had been found invaluable in the east in winning over disaffected monophysites, but had come under fire from Sophronius, the new bishop of Jerusalem (634–8), as *monophysitism in disguise. In a hasty reply Honorius not only expressed approval, but went on to argue that, since the Word acted through both natures, he had only one will; he developed the same thesis (technically 'monothelitism') in further letters to Sergius, Sophronius, and others. This view fitted well with the policies of Sergius and of Emperor Heraclius (610–41), who in 638 published his *Ecthesis*, a decree which forbade all mention of operations, one or two, in Christ, and ordered the confession of a single will in him. Honorius was dead when the *Ecthesis* appeared, but his successors agreed in rejecting monothelitism as heretical, and he himself was formally anathematized by the Sixth General Council (i.e. the third council of Constantinople, 680–1), which proclaimed the existence of two wills, human and divine, in the Redeemer. This anathema, ratified as it was by LEO II when he approved the acts of the council in 682, has caused embarrassment and considerable discussion since the 15th cent., especially when (as at the First Vatican Council) the question of papal infallibility has been debated. The usual defence of Honorius has been that he was not so much heretical as imprudent.

Apart from his unfortunate incursion into theological controversy, Honorius was a pontiff whose leadership infused fresh vigour into the papacy. Not only did he reform the education of the clergy but, like Gregory I, he successfully shouldered temporal responsibilities with which the civil authorities could no longer cope, such as the restoration of Roman aqueducts and

the maintenance of the corn supply, acting as paymaster for the imperial troops in Rome, and instructing government officials how to administer the city of Naples. His management of the *patrimony of Peter was so efficient that he never lacked funds and was able to carry out a remarkable programme of building, repairing, and embellishing churches in Rome. This included, most notably, the complete restoration of St Peter's and of S. Agnese fuori le Mura. When he was interred in St Peter's, his epitaph acclaimed him as 'leader of the common people'.

PL 80, 467 94; 601–7, Mansi 11, 537–44; 549–63; 578; JW 1, 223–6; LP 1, 323–7; J. Chapman, 'The Condemnation of Pope Honorius', *Dublin Review* 139 (1906), 42–54; P. Galtier, 'La première lettre du pape Honorius', *Gregorianum* 29 (1948), 42–61; R. Bäumer, 'Die Wiederentdeckung der Honoriusfrage im Abendland', *RQ* 56 (1961), 200–14; G. Kreutzer, *Die Honoriusfrage im Mittelalter und in der Neuzeit* (Stuttgart, 1975); Caspar 2, 523–619; LThK 5, 474 f. (R. Bäumer); NCE 7, 123–5 (H. G. J. Beck); Seppelt 2, 47–58; JR, 179–84.

SEVERINUS (28 May–2 Aug. 640). A Roman, son of Avienus (an upper-class name), he was already elderly when elected in mid-Oct. 638, but he had to wait almost twenty months before the imperial mandate necessary for his consecration arrived. The exarch Isaac could not issue it since he had been sent Emperor Heraclius's (610–41) *Ecthesis* declaring that Christ had only one will (the monothelite heresy) with instructions that the pope-elect should subscribe it. This Severinus refused to do; as a result of representations by eastern opponents of *monothelitism the Roman church now had a more realistic appreciation of the issues involved than in HONORIUS I's time. Envoys had to be sent to Constantinople, where they were told that ratification of his appointment would be conditional on his acceptance of the decree. Only after protracted negotiations and promising to do their best to obtain Severinus's signature were they allowed to return to Rome with the mandate. Meanwhile the pope-elect had been subjected to brutal treatment which may be explained by an attempt to put pressure on him in view of his reported objection to the *Ecthesis*. Persuaded by the military registrar (*chartularius*) Maurice that their arrears of pay were being held in the papal treasure accumulated by Honorius I, the troops in and around Rome besieged Severinus and other leading clergy in the Lateran for three days, and then placed seals on the treasure. When exarch Isaac arrived, ostensibly to sort things out, he temporarily expelled the vicegerents of the see from the city, plundered the vaults and confiscated their contents, dividing the booty between the soldiers and his officials, but prudently sending part to Emperor Heraclius.

Severinus survived his consecration by little more than two months. It is not known whether he ever officially defined his attitude to the *Ecthesis*. Later reports that he explicitly condemned it, declaring that Christ had two wills and energies corresponding to his two natures, should be treated with reserve; his early death probably saved him from having to make a definitive pronouncement. A good and charitable man (according to *LP*), he belonged to the pro-clerical faction which opposed the pro-monastic policies of GREGORY I and his disciples. He showed his regard for the secular clergy by raising their stipends and granting them a year's full pay when he died. He was buried in St Peter's, the mosaic in the apse of which he had restored.

PL 129, 583–6; Mansi 10, 675–80; JW 1, 227; *LP* 1, 328 f.; E. Caspar, 'Die Lateransynode von 649', *ZKG* 51 (1932), 114, n. 87; Caspar 2, 526 f.; 537 f.; *DCB* 4, 628 (J. Barmby); *DTC* 14, 2006–8 (E. Amann); *LThK* 9, 700 f. (G. Schwaiger); Bertolini, 317 f.; *NCE* 13, 143 (C. M. Aherne); Seppelt 2, 56 f.; JR, 245; 264.

JOHN IV (24 Dec. 640–12 Oct. 642). A Dalmatian, son of a Venantius who was legal adviser (*scholasticus*) to the exarch at Ravenna, he was archdeacon of Rome when elected in Aug. 640. During the five-month interval while he awaited the imperial mandate then considered necessary for his consecration, the Roman church sent an authoritative letter to certain Irish bishops and abbots censuring their custom of observing Easter on the day of the Jewish Passover and warning them against *Pelagianism. It is interesting that, while the pope-elect was the second signatory, the first was the archpriest Hilarus, and that Hilarus and the chief secretary (*primicerius*) John, also a signatory, described themselves as 'vicegerents of the apostolic see'.

The exarch may have hoped that his official's son would accept the government's line on doctrinal matters, but in Jan. 641 John held a synod which condemned *monothelitism, favoured by the *Ecthesis* of Emperor Heraclius (610–41), as heretical. In fact Heraclius, disappointed that the *Ecthesis* had resulted only in divisions, wrote to the pope shortly before his death (11 Feb. 641) disavowing monothelitism and making the previous patriarch Sergius I (610–38) responsible for the *Ecthesis*. When the new patriarch Pyrrhus I (638–41), in his propaganda to get the *Ecthesis* accepted in the west, appealed to HONORIUS I's endorsement of it, John wrote to Emperor Constantine III (Feb.–May 641) expressing disgust that attempts were being made to link Honorius with such heretical novelties; his predecessor, he argued tortuously, when he spoke of one will in Christ, had been thinking exclusively of his human will, which he held was free from the division to which human wills are normally subject as a result of the Fall (Rom. 7: 14–23). He also demanded that copies of the *Ecthesis* posted in public places in Constantinople should be pulled down.

Mindful of the plight of his homeland, John sent Abbot Martin to Dalmatia with substantial sums to ransom Christians enslaved by the Avar and Slav invaders. He also endowed a chapel next to the Lateran baptistery in honour of the saints of Dalmatia and filled it with relics of St Venantius (his own father's name) and other Dalmatian martyrs which Martin had brought to Rome. His portrait can still be seen there in the mosaic of the apse, which his successor THEODORE I presented. On his death he granted his clergy a year's stipend each.

PL 80, 601–8; Bede, *Hist. eccl.* 2, 19; JW 1, 227 f.; LP 1, 330; Caspar 2, 365–8; DCB 3, 391 f. (J. Barmby); DTC 8, 597–9 (É. Amann); Bertolini, 325 f.; NCE 7, 1008 (H. G. J. Beck); Seppelt 2, 57–9; JR, 182; 184.

THEODORE I (24 Nov. 642–14 May 649). A Greek, born at Jerusalem and son of a bishop, he had probably come to Rome as a refugee from the Arab invasions. The choice of an easterner with close links with the chief critics of *monothelitism, Patriarch Sophronius of Jerusalem (634–8) and Maximus the Confessor (c. 580–662), can be explained by the need to elect a pope who could effectively resist the heretical view, imposed by the Byzantine court, that Christ had only one will. The short interval between his election and ordination indicates that the imperial mandate necessary for his consecration was obtained from the exarch at Ravenna, not from Constantinople.

One of Theodore's first acts was to write to the boy-emperor, Constans II (641–68), enquiring why the *Ecthesis* of Emperor Heraclius (610–41) was still in force, despite its repudiation by JOHN IV and by Heraclius himself before his death. He wrote in similar terms to Paul II, the new patriarch of Constantinople (641–53), declining also to recognize him until his predecessor Pyrrhus I (638–41) had been canonically deposed by a synod at which the holy see must be represented, and demanding that Paul himself should repudiate the *Ecthesis* and have it removed from public places where it was posted. When Pyrrhus renounced monothelitism in 645 after being defeated in public debate by Maximus the Confessor and, having travelled to Rome, published a solemn recantation, Theodore received him with patriarchal honours and recognized him as rightful bishop of Constantinople. Pyrrhus's abjuration of

monothelitism was received in the west as a notable triumph for orthodoxy, and the pope, encouraged by support from all quarters, did not hesitate to excommunicate and depose Patriarch Paul, who had now come out in favour of the *Ecthesis*. In the event Pyrrhus, disappointed in his hopes of actually recovering his throne, went to Ravenna, withdrew his recantation, and made peace with the court. In his fury Theodore excommunicated him too, signing the decree (it was said) on the Apostle's tomb in consecrated eucharistic wine.

In 648, convinced that the *Ecthesis* had failed to reconcile *monophysites in the east and was so unpopular in the west as to threaten political stability, Constans II promulgated the edict known as the *Typos*, or 'Rule', which Paul had drafted. This abrogated the *Ecthesis*, prohibited all discussion on the number of wills and operations in Christ, and ordered that church teaching should be restricted to what had been defined by the five general councils. Subscription was obligatory, and when the papal apocrisiarius Anastasius refused to sign he was arrested and exiled to Trebizond; the Latin chapel in the Placidia Palace, official residence of the pope's nuncios, was shut down and its altar demolished. Theodore's attitude to the *Typos* would certainly have been hostile, but he died before being able to formulate it. Although chiefly known as the implacable foe of monothelitism, he was also generous to the poor of Rome and, among other modest building works, embellished S. Stefano Rotondo on the Caelian Hill on the occasion of the translation to it of the relics of SS. Primo and Feliciano (the first recorded translation of relics in the city).

PL 87, 71–102; JW 1, 228–30; 2, 698; LP 1, 331–5; Caspar 2, 529; 543–53; Haller 1, 317–20; 543 f.; DCB 4, 949–51 (J. Barmby); DTC 15, 224–6 (É. Amann); LThK 10, 27 (G. Schwaiger); NCE 14, 16 (P. J. Mullins); Bertolini, 329–33; Seppelt 2, 59–61; JR, 184–6; 265; 269 f.

MARTIN I, ST (5 July 649–17 June 653: d. 16 Sept. 655). An Umbrian from Todi, he served for a time when deacon as THEODORE I's apocrisiarius in Constantinople, becoming thoroughly familiar with the leading personalities there and with the prevailing *monothelite teaching that Christ had only one will. Resolute and courageous, he is chiefly known for his uncompromising opposition to this heresy and for the tragic retribution it brought on him. He showed his independent spirit from the outset by having himself consecrated without seeking the imperial ratification deemed necessary at the time. It was a gesture which infuriated Emperor Constans II (641-68), who refused to recognize him as legitimate pope.

Almost at once he held an impressive anti-monothelite synod in the Lateran; it was attended by 105 western bishops, reinforced by an intellectually able group of exiled Greek clerics. After an exhaustive study (5-31 Oct. 649) of all the issues, this affirmed belief in two wills in Christ and anathematized both monothelitism and, with remarkable boldness, Constans's recent edict (the *Typos) banning discussion of the number of wills and operations in the Lord. These decisions were circulated immediately in the east as well as the west for subscription; Martin excommunicated Bishop Paul of Thessalonica for rejecting them, and appointed an orthodox apostolic vicar for Palestine, then a stronghold of monothelitism. He sent a copy of the decisions to Constans with a courteous letter inviting him to repudiate the heresy, the blame for which he tactfully laid on the advice of successive patriarchs.

The emperor, already apprised of this attack on his religious policies, at once sent the chamberlain Olympius as exarch to Italy with orders to arrest Martin and bring him to Constantinople. This move failed, for Olympius soon found that the pope had widespread support; he then came to an understanding with him, and finally himself revolted, not without Martin's connivance, against the emperor. It was not until summer 653 that the new exarch, Theodore Calliopas, seized (17 June) the bedridden

pontiff in the Lateran basilica, where he had sought sanctuary, handed his clergy the imperial order declaring that he had made himself pope illegally and was therefore deposed, smuggled him out of Rome, and, though racked by painful illness, put him under guard on a ship sailing to the capital. After a stop at Naxos, prostrated with gout and dysentery and brutally humiliated, Martin arrived in Constantinople on 17 Sept. 653 (not 654, as often stated), and after three months' solitary confinement was brought to trial on 19 Dec. on a charge of treason, viz. of having aided and abetted Olympius in his attempt to seize the throne. When he raised the doctrinal issue, it was dismissed as irrelevant; throughout he was treated, not as pope, but as a rebellious deacon and former apocrisiarius. As arranged, he was found guilty, condemned to death, and publicly flogged, but on the pleading of the dying patriarch Paul II (641-27 Dec. 653) the sentence was commuted to banishment. After three more months in prison, in appalling conditions, he was taken by ship (26 Mar. 654) to Chersonesus in the Crimea (near Sevastopol), where he died on 16 Sept. 655 from the effects of cold, starvation, and harsh treatment. He was buried there in a church dedicated to the BVM.

The most distressing feature of Martin's ordeal, as he made clear in vivid letters from exile, was his abandonment by the Roman church, which not only neglected (as he bitterly complained) to send him any supplies to alleviate his plight, but, contrary to his expectation and express wishes, elected a successor while he was still alive. He nevertheless resigned himself to the position, and prayed that God would preserve his church in the true faith and shield its new pastor from heresy and enemies. Although the Sixth General Council (Constantinople III, 680-1), at which the teaching for which he had fought and suffered triumphed, could not rehabilitate him, being held under the aegis of Constans II's son Constantine IV (668-85), who must have regarded him as guilty of high treason, it was not long before the Roman church came to venerate him as a martyr (the last pope to be so honoured), originally on 12 Nov., supposedly the anniversary of the translation of his relics to S. Martino ai Monti, but since 1969 on 13 Apr., his feast day also in the Greek church.

PL 87, 105–212; 129, 591–604; JW 1, 230–4; LP 1, 336–40; P. Peeters, 'Une vie grecque du pape S. Martin I', AnB 51 (1933), 225–62; W. M. Peitz, 'Martin I und Maximus Confessor', HJ 38 (1917), 213–36; E. Caspar, 'Die Lateransynode von 649', ZKG 51 (1932), 73–137; Caspar 2, 553–78; DTC 10, 182–94 (E. Amann); NCE 9, 300 f. (C. M. Aherne); DCB 3, 848–57 (J. Barmby); Seppelt 2, 61–7; JR, 186–91.

EUGENE I, ST (10 Aug. 654–2 June 657). A Roman, son of Rufinianus, he had been brought up in the church's ministry from childhood and was an elderly presbyter when elected after the deposition and banishment of MARTIN I by Emperor Constans II (641–68). It had been Martin's hope that the Roman clergy would not elect a successor while he was still alive, but in view of pressure from the Byzantine court and its exarch in Italy they had little option. Since Eugene did not seem likely to cause trouble, the government found no difficulty in ratifying their choice. According to many he should not be considered legitimate pope until Martin's death in Sept. 655, but while disappointed by his election Martin himself seems to have acquiesced in it.

As in Martin's time, the burning issue was still whether Christ had two wills, as Roman orthodoxy affirmed, or one, the view (*monothelitism) favoured at Constantinople in spite of the banning of discussion of the subject by the *Typos. A mild and saintly man, Eugene was out to be conciliatory after the brutal treatment meted out to Martin, and dispatched envoys to Constantinople to restore relations between the holy see and the court. These were warmly received by the recently appointed patriarch Peter (654–66), who proposed to them a compromise formula which maintained that, while each of Christ's two natures had its own will, considered as a

person or hypostasis he possessed only one will. Although this logically entailed that he had three wills, they were talked into accepting it, and on this basis, at Pentecost 655, entered into communion with the new patriarch. Peter then handed the envoys his synodical letters, announcing his appointment and containing his profession of faith, for transmission to the pope, and they returned to Rome. But when the profession, which embodied an ambiguous theory of Christ's wills, was formally read out in Sta Maria Maggiore, the outraged clergy and people prevented Eugene, who was disposed to accept it, from proceeding with the mass until he had promised to reject it. Thus instead of the peace he was working for, there was again schism between Rome and Constantinople. In his exasperation Constans II threatened that, once his hands were freed from fighting the heathen, he would administer the same treatment to Eugene as to Martin. Before any steps could be taken, however, the pope was dead. He was revered for his unaffected goodness, and left bequests for both the clergy and the people of Rome. Buried in St Peter's, he was ignored by the ancient martyrologies, and his name was inserted in the Roman Martyrology by the famous church historian Cesare Baronius (1538–1607). Feast 2 June.

JW 1, 233 f.; 2, 699; 740; LP 1, 341 f.; D. Mallardo, Papa S. Eugenio I (Naples, 1943); Caspar 2, 580–7; DCB 2, 270 (J. Barmby); DHGE 15, 1346 f. (H. Marot); BSS 5, 194 f. (P. Burchi); NCE 5, 624 f. (C. M. Aherne); Seppelt 2, 580–7; JR, 191–4.

VITALIAN, ST (30 July 657–27 Jan. 672). Born at Segni, near Rome, son of Anastasius, he immediately took steps on his accession to restore good relations between the holy see and Constantinople, strained to breaking-point in recent pontificates by divergent attitudes to *monothelitism (the heresy that Christ had only one will). Writing to Emperor Constans II (641–68) and to Patriarch Peter (654–66), whose ambiguous creed EUGENE I had been forced to reject, he maintained the Roman position but was deliberately conciliatory, playing down the doctrinal issue and passing over the *Lateran synod of 649 in silence. Constans reciprocated by sending him sumptuous gifts and in a rescript formally confirmed the privileges of the Roman church, while the patriarch included his name—the first pope to be so honoured since HONORIUS I—in the *diptychs at Constantinople. When Constans for political reasons paid Rome a twelve-day visit in July 663, Vitalian and his clergy received him with magnificent ceremonies, discreetly ignoring his brutal treatment of MARTIN I and his publication of the *Typos, which the Lateran synod had declared blasphemous. This show of friendship, however, did not prevent Constans either from stripping the Pantheon and other buildings of bronze tiles and ornaments, or from publishing in Sicily, on 1 Mar. 666, a decree making Ravenna, the seat of his exarch in Italy, an autocephalous see independent of Rome with the power not only to elect its bishop, subject to imperial confirmation, but also to have him consecrated by three of his suffragans, just like the bishop of Rome.

Deeply concerned for the Anglo-Saxon church, Vitalian backed the efforts of Oswy, king of Northumbria (655–70), to establish in England the Roman, as opposed to the Celtic, date for Easter and other Roman practices, as agreed by the synod of Whitby (664). On 26 Mar. 668 he consecrated the accomplished Greek monk, Theodore of Tarsus, as archbishop of Canterbury (668–90) and sent him to England to reorganize the English church. He arranged for the African abbot Hadrian and Benedict Biscop (d. 689/90) to accompany him to ensure that he did not introduce alien Greek ideas or customs. Nearer home, building on foundations laid by GREGORY I, he developed the song-school at the Lateran so as to train singers for the new, more elaborate and Byzantine-style papal rites; its chanters were called 'Vitaliani'. When Constans II was murdered in Sicily on 15 Sept. 668 and

the army sought to raise the Armenian Mezezius to the purple, Vitalian gave strong backing to Constans's son and legitimate successor, who as Constantine IV (668–85) was to prove mindful of his debt to the Roman church. Since the new emperor had no wish to enforce the *Typos*, Vitalian now felt able to assert the orthodox teaching on Christ's two wills more openly, and even declined to accept the synodical letters of the new patriarch, John V (669–75), because they were unorthodox. Because of this, Patriarch Theodore I (677–9) wanted to erase Vitalian's name from the diptychs, but the emperor firmly resisted the move. Feast 27 Jan.

PL 87, 999–1010; JW 1, 235–7; 2, 699; 740; *LP* 1, 343–5; Bede, *Hist. eccl.* 3, 29; 4, 1; S. J. P. Van Dijk, 'Gregory the Great Founder of the Urban *Schola cantorum*', *ELit* 77 (1963), 345–56; Caspar 2, 580–7; 678–82; Mann 1/2, 1–16; *DCB* 4, 1161–3 (J. Barmby); *DTC* 15, 3115–17 (É. Amann); *BSS* 12, 1232–5 (V. Monachino); *NCE* 14, 724 (C. M. Aherne); Bertolini, 355–64; Seppelt 2, 68–71; JR, 193–7; 201; 206; 273; 280.

ADEODATUS II (11 Apr. 672–17 June 676). A Roman, son of Jovinianus, he was from youth a monk of the community of S. Erasmo on the Caelian Hill. He was elected pope in old age at a time when there was an emotional revival of interest in Rome (stimulated by knowledge of the *Hypomnesticon*, written c.668 by the Greek monk Theodosius) in MARTIN I and Maximus the Confessor (c.580–662), both martyrs for their resistance to the *monothelite teaching favoured by the Byzantine government. Hence it is not surprising that, although his appointment was ratified after only a few weeks by the exarch at Ravenna, he himself rejected the synodical letters and profession of faith sent him by Constantine I, the new monothelite patriarch of Constantinople (675–7). As a result, his name was excluded from the *diptychs in the imperial city. Apart from this, his reign is extremely obscure. Two letters are attributed to him, one addressed to Hadrian, abbot of St Peter's monastery, Canterbury, confirming its exemption from episcopal supervision, and the other to the bishops of Gaul informing them of privileges granted to the monastery of St Martin of Tours (its authenticity has been doubted). Nothing else is recorded of him, except that he was generous to all, compassionate to pilgrims, and kind to his clergy, raising their customary honoraria on the death of a pope, and also that he restored the basilica of S. Pietro at the eighth milestone of the Via Portuense and reconstructed the buildings of his former monastery, raising its status.

JW 1, 237; *LP* 1, 364 f.; *PL* 87, 1139–44; 129, 681–90 (text of *Hypomnesticon*); Caspar 2, 587; *DCB* 1, 44 (G. H. Moberley); *DHGE* 1, 542 (A. Noyon); *EC* 1, 304 (I. Daniele); *DBI* 1, 272 f. (G. Arnaldi); Bertolini, 364 f.; Seppelt 2, 71; JR, 198; 201; 244; 266.

DONUS (2 Nov. 676–11 Apr. 678). A Roman by birth, son of Maurice, he was already elderly when elected; he had only to wait a few months before receiving the imperial mandate necessary for his consecration. His reign is even more obscure than that of ADEODATUS II, but it is known that he reached an accommodation (although it remained for the moment a dead letter) with Reparatus, archbishop of Ravenna, which implied the abandonment by that see of its claim to autocephalous status and independence from Rome, granted by Emperor Constans II (641–68) in 666. In Rome itself he had the shock of discovering that the Syrian monks occupying a well-known monastery were in fact *Nestorians; he replaced them by orthodox Roman monks and dispersed them among other monasteries in the hope that they might be converted to the *Chalcedonian doctrine. Meanwhile there was a growing desire in Constantinople for the restoration of unity with the holy see, for decades interrupted by the *monothelite controversy, and Emperor Constantine IV (668–85) put pressure on Patriarch Theodore I (677–9), who as a monothelite was initially reluctant, to write to Donus, not enclosing the customary profession of faith but

expressing his desire for amicable relations. Constantine himself addressed (12 Aug. 678) a courteous and conciliatory letter to the pope inviting him to send delegates to a conference which would thrash out the disputed theological issues; his exarch would provide transport and pay expenses. Donus, however, was dead before the letter left Constantinople. Little else is known of his reign except that he was active in building, restoring, and embellishing churches; among other works, he adorned the atrium before St Peter's with a marble pavement. He was reportedly generous to his clergy.

JW 1, 238; *LP* 1, 348 f.; FD 1, n. 242; Mansi 11, 196–201; Caspar 2, 585–8; *DHGE* 14, 671 f. (H. Marot); *NCE* 4, 1010 (C. M. Aherne); Bertolini, 365–7; Seppelt 2, 71; JR, 198.

AGATHO, ST (27 June 678–10 Jan. 681). A Sicilian who had been a monk, proficient in Greek as well as Latin, he had his election speedily ratified by the imperial exarch at Ravenna. His short reign was important for the abandonment of *monothelitism by the Byzantine government and the resultant reopening of amicable relations between the holy see and Constantinople.

Soon after his consecration Agatho received the letter which Emperor Constantine IV (668–85) had addressed (12 Aug. 678) to DONUS, proposing a conference at which the question whether Christ had two wills or one should be discussed and unity between the churches restored. The emperor had decided that monothelitism, repugnant to the west, was no longer useful for reconciling *monophysites in the east. He therefore invited the pope to send accredited representatives, including four from the now important Greek monasteries in Rome, to Constantinople to debate the issues with eastern theologians, promising free transport and safe conduct. Agatho welcomed the initiative, but first arranged for preparatory synods to be held in the west (including one at Hatfield, presided over by Archbishop Theodore of Canterbury), to formulate a united western attitude to monothelitism; the largest and most important was held at Rome (27 Mar. 680) by Agatho himself. On 10 Sept. 680 the impressive papal delegation (it included two future popes, JOHN V and CONSTANTINE) reached Constantinople bearing two lengthy documents, a letter from Agatho to the emperor and the synodical decree of the Roman council signed by 150 bishops, both condemning monothelitism and the former stressing Rome's role as the custodian of the true faith. Constantine now decided that his conference should be a full-dress council of the church and, having already deposed the monothelite patriarch Theodore I (677–9), instructed his successor George I (679–86) to summon the metropolitans and bishops under his jurisdiction to attend. The council, to be known as the Sixth General Council, met in the imperial palace in a domed hall (*trullus*: hence first Trullan council) from 7 Nov. 680 to 16 Sept. 681 and, presided over by the emperor, asserted, in explicit agreement with the pope's letters, the orthodox doctrine of two wills and operations in Christ; at its thirteenth session it anathematized the monothelite leaders, including HONORIUS I, without the papal delegates raising any objection. Agatho was dead before its deliberations were completed, but his decisive contribution was recognized in the congratulatory address it presented to Constantine at its closing session; this acknowledged that the true faith, written with God's hand, had been given to the church by Old Rome, and that PETER had spoken through Agatho. At the same time it applauded the emperor as the source of the initiative for restoring religious peace, and described him as collaborating with God himself.

Agatho had scored a further success when he invited Archbishop Theodore of Ravenna (677–91) to the Roman synod of 27 Mar. 680. In spite of Donus's agreement with Archbishop Reparatus, Ravenna still retained in practice the independence granted it by Constans II (641–68) in 666, but Theodore's envoys agreed that since matters of faith were to be discussed he might

attend. Once in Rome, however, he began negotiations with the pope for ending the autonomy and agreed, in return for Agatho's support against hostile elements at Ravenna, that in future its archbishops should be consecrated by the pope and receive the *pallium from him. This agreement was to be constitutionally confirmed in LEO II's reign.

An experienced administrator, Agatho broke precedent by acting, in view of the stringency of the church's finances, as treasurer (*arcarius*) of the holy see until obliged by ill health to delegate the office. He succeeded in obtaining from Constantine the abolition of the tax customarily paid to the exarch at papal elections, but in return the emperor stipulated that the earlier, time-consuming practice of seeking imperial ratification from Constantinople rather than from Ravenna should be restored. Agatho's interest extended to the English church, and at the Lateran synod of 679 he upheld the appeal of Wilfrid (634–709), bishop of York, against his deposition by Theodore, archbishop of Canterbury (668–90). He also sent John, precentor of St Peter's, to England, partly to teach liturgical chant and practice, but also to report on conditions in the English church.

A kindly man, Agatho was loved by all for his cheerful good humour. Although desperately short of funds, he was generous to his clergy, leaving them all a substantial bequest on his death; he also made gifts to the churches of SS. Apostoli and Sta Maria Maggiore. Buried in St Peter's, he came to be venerated in east as well as west, his feast in the latter being 10 Jan.

PL 87, 1161–258; JW 1, 238–40; 2, 699; *LP* 1, 350–8; FD 1, n. 242; Mansi 11, 165–922; Bede, *Hist. eccl.* 4, 18; 5, 19; Caspar 2, 588–610; *DHGE* 1, 916–18 (J. P. Kirsch); *BSS* 1, 341 f. (I. Daniele); *DBI* 1, 373–6 (G. Arnaldi); Mann 1/2, 23–48; *NCE* 1, 197 (C. M. Aherne); Bertolini, 377–83; Seppelt 2, 71–5; JR, 197–9; 265; 280 f.

LEO II, ST (17 Aug. 682–3 July 683). A Sicilian, trained in the papal choir-school, admired for his eloquence, culture, and proficiency in Greek as well as Latin, he was probably elected in Jan. 681 but had to wait some eighteen months before receiving the imperial mandate necessary for his consecration. The letters from the guardians of the holy see announcing AGATHO's death and Leo's election reached Constantinople on 10 Mar. 681, while the *Sixth General Council was still in progress, but Emperor Constantine IV (668–85) deliberately held up ratification of the election until the council had formally anathematized HONORIUS I along with the other champions of *monothelitism and Rome's acceptance of its decisions, including the anathema, was assured. The reluctance of the Roman envoys to accept the condemnation of a pope had to be overcome, and for this long and delicate negotiations, extending many months after the closure of the council (16 Sept. 681), were necessary. Only in July 682 did the envoys return to Rome taking with them, along with the acts of the council, the mandate for Leo's consecration. Constantine, whose power to withhold this had been his trump card, showed his satisfaction by inviting the new pope to send a resident apocrisiarius to court, and by diminishing the tax burden on the papal patrimonies in Sicily and Calabria as well as the corn requisition for the army.

Leo was realist enough to accept the situation, which opened a period of peace and collaboration between Rome and Byzantium. He had the acts of the council, which condemned monothelitism, translated from Greek into Latin and, in implementation of imperial policy, took steps to circulate them to the church leaders and rulers of the west with letters calling for their subscription. His most important letter (7 May 683) was to Constantine, ratifying the council's decisions with the authority of PETER and anathematizing the monothelite leaders it had condemned, including Honorius I. In the original Latin text he spoke of him as having 'attempted to subvert the pure faith by his profane betrayal'; in the Greek version this was softened to 'by his betrayal he allowed the

pure teaching to be sullied'. It is significant that, in his letter to the Spanish and, probably, other western bishops, he merely accused the dead pope of having failed through negligence to stamp out the flame of heresy. He was lenient too when Macarius I, deposed by the council (7 Mar. 681) as patriarch of Antioch, and other intransigent monothelites appeared in Rome, remitted by the emperor to him for judgement and sentence; with the exception of two, who recanted and were admitted to communion, he dispersed the rest among various monasteries.

A token of the new spirit of co-operation between emperor and pope was the definitive ending of Ravenna's short-lived bid for autocephalous status independent of Rome. Following a *rapprochement* made in Agatho's reign, Constantine revoked (682/3) the decree of Constans II (1 Mar. 666) granting Ravenna autonomy, and it was agreed that henceforth archbishops of that see should be consecrated by, and receive the *pallium from, the pope. In return Leo exempted them from the fees traditionally incidental to consecration and from the obligation to come personally to Rome for the annual synod.

A competent singer, Leo concerned himself with church music. *LP* applauds his love for the poor and the efforts he made to alleviate their condition. Among other works he restored S. Bibiana on the Esquiline, transferring there the relics of martyrs previously buried on the Via Portuense, and reconstructed S. Giorgio in Velabro for the use of the now flourishing Greek community in Rome. Feast 3 July.

PL 96, 387–420; JW 1, 240 f.; LP 1, 359–62; FD 1, n. 250–1; Mansi 11, 713–922; 1046–58; Caspar 2, 610–19; 624 f.; DTC 9, 301–4 (É. Amann); BSS 7, 1280–2 (P. Rabikauskas); LThK 6, 947 (G. Schwaiger); NCE 8, 639 (H. G. J. Beck); Bertolini, 383–92; Mann 1/2, 49–53; Seppelt 2, 75 f.; JR, 182; 197; 265–7; 278.

BENEDICT II, ST (26 June 684–8 May 685). Elected in early July 683, he had to wait almost a year before the imperial mandate sanctioning his consecration arrived from Constantinople. Roman by birth, he had enrolled in the clergy as a boy, had studied in the papal choir-school and served in every order, and was a priest when appointed. The choice of a local man, of traditional background, in contrast to his Greek-speaking Sicilian predecessors, may indicate Rome's new confidence *vis-à-vis* Byzantium following the reconciliation cemented by AGATHO and Emperor Constantine IV (668-85). Further tokens of the fresh atmosphere of co-operation were the emperor's agreement, in response to Benedict's petition, that in future papal elections should be ratified by the exarch in Italy, not by Constantinople, thereby enabling the pope-elect to assume office with the minimum of delay, and his unprecedented act of presenting, at a solemn ceremony, locks of his infant sons' hair to the clergy, army, and people of Rome as a symbol of their adoption of the princes.

Only glimpses of Benedict's short reign survive. While still pope-elect he pressed on with the task of securing the adhesion of the west to the *Sixth General Council (third council of Constantinople, 680-1) and its condemnation of *monothelitism, instructing the notary Peter, delayed by LEO II's death, to proceed to Spain with the acts of the council and the letters with which Leo had furnished him. The mission was mishandled, for Rome did not reckon with the fierce independence of the Visigothic church in Spain; and while the fourteenth council of Toledo endorsed the acts in Nov. 684, it subjected them first to an exhaustive examination. Julian, metropolitan of Toledo, dispatched his own profession of faith to Benedict, and when he learned that the pope had verbally criticized passages in it he sent him an indignant riposte. Again, while pope-elect Benedict issued a directive ordering Wilfrid (634-709), deprived as bishop of York in 678, to be restored, but it remained without effect. He was equally unsuccessful in his patient efforts to persuade Macarius I, deposed monothelite

patriarch of Antioch, now confined in a monastery in Rome, to abandon his heretical views.

LP describes Benedict as humble-minded and gentle, a lover of the poor who at Easter 685 distributed honours and promotions among the clergy of various ranks, and on his death bequeathed thirty pounds of gold to the clergy, the diaconal monasteries (Greek-style foundations for charitable relief attached to churches), and the lay sacristans of churches. He carried out restorations in St Peter's and S. Lorenzo in Lucina, and beautified S. Valentino on the Flaminian Way and Sta Maria ad Martyres (the former Pantheon). Feast 7 May.

PL 96, 423 f.; JW 1, 241 f.; 2, 699; *LP* 1, 363-5; FD 1, n. 252; Caspar 2, 614-19; 674 f.; *DHGE* 8, 9-14 (F. Baix); *BSS* 2, 1193 f. (I. Daniele); *DBI* 8, 325-9 (O. Bertolini); *NCE* 2, 273 (H. G. J. Beck); Seppelt 2, 76 f.; JR, 202 f.; 265 f.; 301 f.

JOHN V (23 July 685-2 Aug. 686). A Syrian from Antioch, son of Cyriacus, he perhaps came to Rome as a refugee from the Arab invasions. As a deacon he was one of AGATHO's three representatives at the *Sixth General Council (third council of Constantinople, 680-1), took a leading part in its discussions, and personally brought back to Rome the documents containing the conciliar decisions and Emperor Constantine IV's ratification of LEO II's election. He was archdeacon and an eminent cleric when he was unanimously elected in the Lateran basilica and then, under the new procedure waiving direct reference to Byzantium decreed by Constantine, installed at once in the Lateran palace to await confirmation of his appointment by the exarch at Ravenna. Nothing is known of his reign except that he took strong and successful action to check aspirations to autonomy in Sardinia, where Citonatus of Cagliari, the metropolitan, had consecrated a provincial bishop without reference to Rome. He suspended the bishop and then, at a synod held in Rome, reinstated him after getting it established that the holy see's authority in the island was paramount. Well educated and energetic, he was nevertheless so ill for much of his reign that he could hardly officiate at ordinations. He left a substantial legacy to his clergy, the charitable monasteries of the city, and the lay sacristans of churches. He was buried in St Peter's.

JW 1, 242 f.; LP 1, 366 f.; FD 1, n. 252; Caspar 2, 620–31; DCB 3, 392 (J. Barmby); DTC 8, 599 (É. Amann); NCE 7, 1008 f. (H. G. J. Beck); Bertolini, 395 f.; Seppelt 2, 78–82; JR, 202; 206 f.

CONON (21 Oct. 686–21 Sept. 687). On the death of JOHN V on 2 Aug. 686 the succession was hotly disputed between the clergy, who favoured the archpriest Peter, and the local militia, who wanted the priest THEODORE. An impasse was reached when the soldiery, who had occupied S. Stefano Rotondo on the Caelian Hill, sent armed pickets to prevent the clergy from entering the Lateran basilica. Eventually, negotiations having come to nothing, the clergy abandoned Peter and put forward the elderly, uncommitted Conon, a priest, as a compromise candidate. As son of a general who had served with the Thracesian regiment stationed in Asia Minor, he was acceptable to the army; his election was thus carried through with the support of the civil and military authorities, and was duly ratified by Theodore, the imperial exarch at Ravenna.

Like several other popes of the period, Conon had been brought up in Sicily; on coming to Rome he had worked his way up the ranks of the ministry. Unworldly and of saintly appearance, he was simple-minded and continuously ill. The new emperor, Justinian II (685–95; 705–11), although reappointing the monothelite Theodore I (686–7) as patriarch, at first continued his father's policy of détente with Rome, and Conon received a letter (17 Feb. 687) from him announcing that all the high officers of the empire, civil and ecclesiastical, had solemnly endorsed the acts of the *Sixth General Council (third council of Constantinople: 680–1); Justinian nevertheless made it clear that God had appointed him

guardian of the church's immaculate faith. The emperor also gave notice of welcome reductions in the taxes levied on the papal patrimonies in Lucania and Calabria, and the release of peasants who had been sequestered by the government as security against arrears of tax. Nearer home, however, Conon got into trouble by nominating, on the advice of interested parties, a deacon of the Syracusan church, Constantine, as rector of the Sicilian patrimony, a lucrative responsibility normally assigned to a Roman cleric, and allowing him the use of the ceremonial saddle-cloths (mappuli) jealously reserved for the Roman clergy. The appointment proved doubly disastrous, for Constantine's extortionate regime soon provoked a revolt by the papal tenantry, and this led to the rector's arrest and deportation by the governor of Sicily. But the real mistake in the election of a weak and ailing pontiff, without the strength to carry out such routine functions as ordinations, was that (as became apparent even before his death) it left the tensions in the Roman church unresolved and festering dangerously.

JW 1, 243; LP 1, 368–70; FD 1, n. 254–6; Caspar 2, 620–3; EC 4, 362 (P. Goggi); NCE 4, 182 (C. M. Aherne); Bertolini, 396–9; Seppelt 2, 80; JR, 206–8.

THEODORE (antipope 687). A Roman presbyter, he was the Roman militia's candidate for the papacy at the disputed election following the death of JOHN V on 2 Aug. 686. His rival, backed by the clergy, was the archpriest Peter, and in the resulting impasse a compromise candidate, CONON, was proposed, elected, and consecrated. On Conon's death on 21 Sept. 687 there was again a dispute about the succession, two candidates being put forward and elected by separate factions, the archdeacon PASCHAL and Theodore, who in the meantime had become archpriest. With their partisans they hastened to the Lateran, Theodore arriving first and occupying the inner apartments, and Paschal following and taking over the outer ones. Again resort was had to a compromise candidate, this time SERGIUS, titular priest of Sta Susanna, who was elected and, his election having been ratified by the Byzantine exarch in Italy, duly consecrated. When Sergius I was installed in the Lateran, Theodore accepted defeat with good grace, came forward, and embraced him in token of submission. Nothing further is known about him, and as he was never consecrated and accepted Sergius as legitimate pontiff, he is doubtfully reckoned an antipope.

JW 1, 243 f.; *LP* 1, 368; 371 f.; Caspar 2, 621 f.; Bertolini, 396 f.; Seppelt 2, 80 f.; JR, 206–8.

PASCHAL (antipope 687: d. 692). His background is unknown, but he was archdeacon of Rome under CONON, and was ambitious to succeed him. Confident that the elderly, ailing pontiff had not long to live, he wrote to the new Byzantine exarch at Ravenna, John Platyn, promising him a hundred pounds of gold if he would ensure his election; he hoped to recoup himself from the bequests he knew the pope was planning to leave to the clergy and others. John agreed, and privately instructed the officials he had appointed to govern Rome to arrange for Paschal's election. On Conon's death, however, the succession was disputed, one faction (probably comprising the officials) electing Paschal, but another the archpriest THEODORE. The two rivals were barricaded with their supporters in separate parts of the Lateran palace. When it became clear that neither group would give way, a meeting of leading civic officials, army officers, and the majority of the clergy (particularly the priests), as well as citizens, was held in the imperial palace on the Palatine and elected a compromise candidate, SERGIUS, titular priest of Sta Susanna. With the people acclaiming him as pope, Sergius was conducted to the Lateran and, the gates having been stormed, was installed there to await the exarch's ratification. When Theodore saw how things stood, he made his submission to Sergius, but Paschal had to be forced against his will to do so; he wrote secretly to John Platyn,

urging him to come in person to Rome and making renewed promises if he would overturn the election. Without announcement John came, but when he discovered that Sergius's election had been regular and had massive support he decided he had no option but to ratify it. Paschal continued, nevertheless, to intrigue against the pope, and was canonically arraigned, deposed from the archidiaconate, and imprisoned in a monastery on the charge of magical practices. He died there five years later, obdurately impenitent.

JW 1, 243; *LP* 1, 369–72; Caspar 2, 622 ff.; *DCB* 4, 195 (J. Barmby); *LThK* 8, 127 f. (G. Schwaiger); Bertolini, 399–401; Seppelt 2, 80 f.; JR, 207 f.

SERGIUS I, ST (15 Dec. 687–9 Sept. 701). Born at Palermo, of a Syrian family from Antioch, he came to Rome under ADEODATUS II, was ordained, studied at the choir-school, and became titular priest of Sta Susanna on the Quirinal. On CONON's death there was an electoral split, one faction electing the archdeacon PASCHAL (who had obtained the support of John Platyn, Byzantine exarch, by promising him a substantial bribe), the other the archpriest THEODORE. In the resulting stalemate a meeting of leading civil officials, army officers, and the bulk of the clergy was held in the Palatine palace and unanimously chose Sergius, who was already a marked man. He was then installed in the Lateran, the gates having to be stormed since it was occupied by the rival groups and their candidates. Theodore accepted the new pope-elect with good grace, but Paschal grudgingly and under compulsion, secretly urging the exarch to come to Rome to overturn the election. To everyone's surprise John Platyn did come, unannounced, but soon decided, in view of the overwhelming support for Sergius, that his election must stand. He therefore issued the mandate necessary for his consecration, but only after obliging him to hand over the hundred pounds of gold which Paschal had promised him.

Sergius proved an able and energetic pontiff who successfully asserted the authority of Rome in the west. Thus Bishop Damian of Ravenna came to Rome to be consecrated, the first holder of that see to do so since the ending of its short-lived (666–82/3) autonomy. Deeply concerned for the English church, he baptized (10 Apr. 689) the young Caedwalla, king of the West Saxons, granted the *pallium to Beorht-weald of Canterbury (693), and ordered Wilfrid (634–709) to be restored to the see of York (c.700). In 693 he authorized the mission to Frisia of the Anglo-Saxon Willibrord (658–739), whom Pepin of Herstal had sent to Rome, and on 27 Nov. 695 consecrated him archbishop of the Frisians, bestowing on him the pallium. In 700, following a council convened at Pavia by the Lombard king Cunibert, he received Aquileia, in schism since the condemnation of the *Three Chapters by VIGILIUS in 553, back into communion with Rome.

Sergius was no less determined and successful in resisting Emperor Justinian II's (685–95; 705–11) demand that he should endorse the second Trullan or Quinisext council. Eager to emulate his famous namesake Justinian I (527–65) by presiding over a great council, the emperor, without inviting the west, convened this assembly of eastern bishops in 692 to complete the work of the Fifth (553) and Sixth (680) General Councils (hence the title Quinisext) by promulgating 102 disciplinary and ritual canons. Oriental in inspiration, these ignored western canon law, banned practices (e.g. clerical celibacy and the Saturday fast in Lent) established in the west, and expressly renewed the *28th canon of Chalcedon (451) granting Constantinople patriarchal status second only to Rome (to which Rome had consistently objected). The papal apocrisiarii in Constantinople were induced to sign the acts of the council; but when copies were delivered to Sergius with a blank space for his signature, he firmly refused to insert it, or even to allow the canons to be publicly read out. Infuriated by his attitude, Justinian resorted to brute force and, after seizing and deporting the pope's principal advisers, sent Zacharias, commander of the imperial bodyguard, to Rome with orders either to obtain Sergius's signature or bring him as a captive to the capital. At this point, however, the limits to which the emperor's authority in Italy had been reduced were glaringly exposed. The imperial troops at Ravenna and elsewhere rallied to the pope, forced their way into Rome, and pursued Zacharias relentlessly until Sergius (under whose bed he had taken refuge) had to plead with them for his life. It was a humiliating defeat for Justinian which he could not avenge, for he himself was overthrown and exiled in late 695.

Sergius was an active restorer and embellisher of Roman churches, including St Peter's, St Paul's, and his own Sta Susanna. One of his first works (8 June 688) was to remove the remains of LEO the Great from their inconspicuous resting-place to an ornate tomb in full view of the public inside the basilica. An accomplished singer himself, he introduced the singing of Agnus Dei at mass, enriched the four great feasts of the BVM (Annunciation, Dormition, Nativity, and Presentation) with solemn processions, and seems to have inaugurated the feast of the Exaltation of the Cross. He was buried in St Peter's, and his mention in the primitive calendar of St Willibrord indicates that his cult started not long after his death. Feast 8 Sept.

JW 1, 244 f.; 2, 699; 741; *LP* 1, 371–82; FD 1, n. 259; Caspar 2, 620–36; *DCB* 4, 618–20 (J. Barmby); *DTC* 14, 1913–16 (É. Amann); *BSS* 11, 873–5 (N. Del Re); *NCE* 13, 112 (C. M. Aherne); Mann 1/2, 76–104; Bertolini, 398–409; Seppelt 2, 80–5; JR, 208–11; 266 f.; 274 f.; 278 f.; 280.

JOHN VI (30 Oct. 701–11 Jan. 705). Nothing is known of his background except that he was Greek by birth. The few glimpses that survive of his reign show him, at a time when Byzantium's hold on Italy was loosened in the confusion following the deposition of Emperor Justinian II in 695, accepted as a popular leader in Italy but careful himself to avoid any rupture with the empire. Thus when the Italian militias took up arms against the imperial exarch Theophylact, who had come to Rome from Sicily, John closed the city gates and saved his life, at the same time succeeding in pacifying the mutineers camped before the walls. It seems that Theophylact, acting on information received, was planning to exact retribution from citizens who had taken part in the humiliating rebuff administered to Zacharias, commander of the imperial bodyguard, when he came to Rome to arrest SERGIUS I on Justinian II's orders; in the event, having been rescued by the pope, it was the informers whom Theophylact was obliged to punish. John's difficulties, however, were illustrated when the Lombard duke Gisulf I of Benevento invaded Campania with his armies c.702, sacking towns and spreading devastation, and halted only at the fifth milestone on the Via Latina; John had to spend enormous sums on ransoming his prisoners and persuading him to withdraw, and even then behind greatly extended frontiers.

Three times driven from his see, Wilfrid of York (664-709) came to Rome in 703 (his third visit) to appeal to the pope. At a four-month-long synod held in Rome in 704 he was finally vindicated, and John wrote (his only extant letter) to the kings of Northumbria and Mercia directing that Beorhtweald, whom he had confirmed as archbishop of Canterbury (693-731), should endeavour to reach a satisfactory settlement of the affair at a synod; if he failed to do so, both parties should present themselves at Rome to thrash the matter out at a fuller council.

JW 1, 245 f.; 2, 700 f.; *LP* 1, 383 f.; Caspar 2, 624; 636; 688; 726; *DCB* 3, 392 f. (J. Barmby); *DTC* 8, 599 f. (É. Amann); *NCE* 7, 1009 (H. G. J. Beck); Bertolini, 408–10; Seppelt 2, 85; JR, 211.

JOHN VII (1 Mar. 705–18 Oct. 707). A Greek by birth, he was son of Plato and Blatta, his father being the highly placed official responsible for the maintenance of the imperial palace on the Palatine; he was the first pope to be son of a Byzantine official. A man of learning, eloquence, and artistic sensibility, he had earlier been the administrator (*rector*) of the papal patrimony on the Appian Way; as such he composed an epitaph in graceful verses for his father, and erected a memorial to both his parents with a touching, very human inscription.

As pope he enjoyed excellent relations with the Lombards, which were reflected in the return by King Aribert II (701–12) to the holy see of valuable estates in the Cottian Alps (Liguria) which it had lost when King Rotari (625–43) occupied the Ligurian coast. In 706 Emperor Justinian II, who had been overthrown in 695 but dramatically restored to the Byzantine throne in 705, dispatched two bishops to Rome with copies of the canons of the anti-Roman second Trullan or *Quinisext council (692), which SERGIUS I had flatly refused to endorse, and requested John to convene a synod and confirm such of them as he approved while rejecting the ones he found unacceptable. Terrified of offending the notoriously ruthless monarch, John did not dare take advantage of the apparently reasonable compromise proposed, but returned the canons to Constantinople without signifying assent or dissent, thereby earning a rebuke for cowardice from his biographer in *LP*. His readiness to comply with official Byzantine policy is borne out by the church decorations he had executed. Thus his artists' portraits of Christ tended to be modelled on the type favoured by Justinian's coinage, while in the Adoration of the Lamb they represented the Lamb in human form, as prescribed by canon 82 of the Quinisext council, and not as a lamb.

A devotee of the BVM who delighted to call himself her servant, John was a notable builder and patron of the arts. He began constructing a new papal residence (*episcopium*) at the foot of the Palatine, close to the Greek quarter and to the old imperial palace, now the residence of the deputy to the Byzantine exarch. His complaisance to Justinian was sharply criticized, and he perhaps felt the need for additional security.

In addition to building and restoring churches (Sta Maria Antiqua in the Forum, in particular), he liked adorning them with mosaics and frescos; not infrequently, as his biographer sardonically noted, he included representations of himself, and one such striking portrait in mosaic, originally designed for a chapel of the BVM which he added to St Peter's, is today preserved in the Vatican Grottoes. He died in his new palace, and was buried in his chapel of the BVM.

JW 1, 246 f.; *LP* 1, 385–7; P. J. Nordhagen, *The Frescoes of John VII in S. Maria Antiqua* (Rome, 1968); J. Breckenridge, 'Evidence for the Nature of Relations between Pope John VII and the Byzantine emperor Justinian II', *BZ* 65 (1972), 364–74; Caspar 2, 630–7; *DTC* 8, 600 f. (É. Amann); *DACL* 7, 2197–2212; 13, 1243 f. (H. Leclercq); *NCE* 7, 1009 (H. G. J. Beck); Mann 1/2, 109–23; Bertolini, 410–12; Seppelt 2, 85; JR, 211 f.; 226; 244; 267; 270.

SISINNIUS (15 Jan.–4 Feb. 708). Nothing is known of his background and earlier career, except that he was a Syrian by birth, his father's name being John. Elected probably in Oct. 707, he was already an old man, and so crippled with gout that he could not use his hands to feed himself. There was an interval of almost three months before he could be consecrated while ratification of his appointment by the Byzantine exarch was awaited. He was greatly respected and was considered a man of resolute character, with a genuine care for the inhabitants of Rome. Although pope-elect and pope for less than four months, he had the foresight and energy (no action was forthcoming from the civil authorities) to order the preparation of lime for the restoration of the walls of Rome, dangerously exposed to hostile attack as events in JOHN VI's reign had demonstrated. His sudden death prevented these orders from being carried out. His only recorded ecclesiastical act was the consecration of a bishop for Corsica.

JW 1, 247; *LP* 1, 388; Caspar 2, 620; 624; *DCB* 4, 705 (J. Barmby); *NCE* 13, 261 (M. A. Mulholland); Seppelt 2, 86.

CONSTANTINE (25 Mar. 708–9 Apr. 715). A Syrian like his predecessor and described by his biographer as 'exceedingly gentle', he should probably be identified with the subdeacon Constantine who was one of Pope AGATHO's representatives at the *Sixth General Council (third council of Constantinople, 680–1). His reign is reported to have witnessed the extremes of famine and abundance.

Early in 709 Constantine had a brush with Felix, newly elected archbishop of Ravenna, whom he consecrated but who, reasserting the autonomy from Rome that Ravenna had briefly (662–82/3) enjoyed, refused to provide the required oath of obedience and other tokens of submission in customary form. In 712, however, when Felix returned to his see from the exile to which Emperor Justinian II had sentenced him after putting out his eyes, he made his peace with the pope and died (723) in communion with Rome. But the centrepiece of Constantine's reign was the year-long journey (Oct. 710–Oct. 711) he made to the east on the express summons of the emperor. It was Justinian's wish to normalize relations with Rome by reaching a mutually satisfactory agreement about the disciplinary and ritual canons which the *Quinisext council (692), held at his instigation, had enacted but which SERGIUS I had refused to endorse because of the anti-western tone of many of them. The visit, which must have seemed ominous in prospect, proved a triumphant success. Accompanied by an impressive retinue, Constantine was royally received everywhere. The negotiations at Nicomedia (Izmit) were conducted with consummate skill by his deacon Gregory (soon to be GREGORY II), who in response to the emperor's enquiries convincingly explained the Roman objections to a number of the canons; and the pope seems to have finally approved, verbally at any rate, such of them as were not repugnant to western usage. Justinian, who had ceremonially kissed Constantine's feet on meeting him and received communion and absolution from him, was evidently well satisfied, and published a decree confirming the privileges of the Roman church, including probably its jurisdiction over Ravenna.

Constantine reached Rome, after a journey troubled by illness, on 24 Oct. 711. Soon after his departure in 710 the new exarch, John Rizocopus, for reasons which remain obscure, had brutally executed several of his senior, most valued officials; the news must have reached the pope at Constantinople, but he had not allowed it to interrupt the discussions. A fortnight later (4 Nov. 711) Justinian was murdered by mutinous troops. The new accord between Rome and Byzantium was at once shattered, for the new emperor, Philippicus Bardanes (711–13), was a fanatical *monothelite who, repudiating the Sixth General Council (680–1), sent the pope an official exposition of his belief in one will in Christ and demanded his adhesion. This Constantine refused, and in the resulting furious reaction in Rome Philippicus was rejected, his name omitted from public documents and from the prayers at mass, and his likeness removed from churches and the coinage. The exarch took steps to enforce the emperor's wishes, and there were bloody battles in the streets of Rome. The pope played a pacific role, sending out bands of priests armed with crosses and gospelbooks who prevailed on the anti-imperial mobs to withdraw. Fortunately Philippicus was soon overthrown (3 June 713), and his successor Anastasius II (713–15) promptly dispatched to Constantine formal assurances of his orthodoxy and adhesion to the Sixth General Council.

Visitors to Rome in Constantine's reign included Cenred, king of Mercia, Offa, the young and attractive son of the king of the East Saxons, and Benedict, archbishop of Milan. Both the former took the tonsure and became monks, dying shortly after. Benedict pressed on the pope the demand that bishops of Pavia should be consecrated at Milan, as they had been before the Lombard invasion. Constantine adopted the firm line that the right to consecrate bishops

of Pavia had belonged to the pope from ancient times, and should so continue.

JW 1, 247–9; LP 1, 389–95; 96; FD 1, nn. 266–9; 271; 273; Bede, Hist. eccl. 5, 19; Caspar 2, 638–43; DCB 1, 658 (G. H. Moberly); DHGE 13, 589–91 (G. Bardy); LThK 3, 48 (G. Schwaiger); Mann 1/2, 127–40; NCE 4, 223 f. (H. G. J. Beck); Bertolini, 413–23; Seppelt 2, 86–8; JR, 198 f.; 202; 213–15; 267; 274 f.

GREGORY II, ST (19 May 715–11 Feb. 731). Born 669 in Rome of wealthy stock, intellectually able, statesmanlike and resolute, he had been brought up in the Lateran, acting when subdeacon as keeper of the purse and then as librarian under SERGIUS I. As deacon he was a key member of the delegation Constantine led in 710–11 to Constantinople, and played a leading role in the negotiations with Emperor Justinian II (685–95; 705–11) over the canons of the *Quinisext council (692). He was the first Roman to be elected after seven popes of Greek or Syrian background, and proved the outstanding Roman pontiff of the 8th cent.

Gregory displayed political skill in handling the confused situation arising in Italy as Byzantine power waned. In 716 he persuaded Liutprand, the great Lombard king (712–44), to hand back valuable papal patrimonies that he retained in the Cottian Alps; later he secured the return to the empire by the Lombards of the key fortresses of Cumae and Sutri. Between 717 and 726, loyal subject of the empire though he was, he headed the angry resistance throughout Italy to crippling tax demands imposed by Emperor Leo III the Isaurian (717–41), with the result that the government made plans, frustrated in the event by his popularity, to have him either assassinated or deposed. During his reign he strove to contain the expansionist moves of the Lombards, but in 729 found Rome threatened by Liutprand and the exarch Eutychius, united in an unexpected and temporary alliance. Gregory made a dramatic appearance in the Lombard camp, making such an impression on the Catholic

Liutprand that he not only abandoned the siege but deposited his royal insignia at St Peter's tomb in token of submission. Although Eutychius installed himself in Rome, the pope patched up an agreement with him and, always loyal to the empire, helped him to crush Tiberius Petasius, a rebellious aspirant to the throne.

On the theological plane Gregory firmly resisted Leo the Isaurian's measures, motivated in part by the belief that they were an obstacle to the conversion of Jews and Muslims, to ban sacred images and their veneration. The new policy of iconoclasm, for which Leo began to campaign in 726 and which he promulgated in an edict signed by the eastern patriarch early in 730, was repugnant to Italy, and created consternation and revolts. Between these dates the emperor corresponded with Gregory requesting his approval, on pain of deposition, of the prohibition of images. Gregory's rejoinder (two letters, now accepted as broadly authentic, have been preserved) was uncompromising: he rejected iconoclasm as a heresy, warned Leo that dogma was not the business of princes but of priests (their two spheres were complementary but different), and countered his threats with the spirited reminder that, once three miles from Rome, the pope was safe since the entire west revered the successor of PETER. The news of Leo's ultimatum to Gregory gave the signal for uprisings in north Italy, and the emperor's hostility to devotion to images only served to detach his Italian subjects still further from the empire; yet Gregory himself never wavered in his loyalty.

Gregory's concern for the people of northern Europe was especially significant. He received both Duke Theodo of Bavaria (716) and Ine, abdicated king of Wessex (726), in Rome as pilgrims, and worked out with the former a tentative plan, to be implemented more than twenty years later, for the creation of an ecclesiastical province in his country. More far-reaching was his support of the missionary work of Wynfrith, whom he renamed Boniface (680-754), in Germany. Having come to Rome from England in spring 718, Boniface left the following year with a letter from Gregory, dated 15 May 719, commissioning him to evangelize the people of Frisia. On 30 Nov. 722, in view of the success of his work in Bavaria, Thuringia, and Hesse, the pope consecrated him bishop; he armed him with a letter of recommendation to Charles Martell, ruler of the Franks (716-41), whose protection would enable him to carry out his tasks successfully. Having imposed on Boniface an oath which bound him closely to the holy see, Gregory now gave him his full backing and was frequently in correspondence with him; as a result of his influence, Roman liturgical usage was everywhere adopted by the infant German church.

As a defensive measure Gregory started his reign by repairing the city walls; he also made good the ravages caused by the Tiber in flood. He carried out extensive restorations in many churches. He actively fostered monasticism, rebuilding and repopulating deserted and decaying monasteries, and turning his own family home into a monastery dedicated to St Agatha; he commissioned Abbot Petronax of Brescia to restore (720) Monte Cassino, which the Lombards had reduced to ruins. He was also a liturgical innovator who, among other things, introduced a mass for Thursdays in Lent. Before his death he was planning a visit to the north which he proved unable to carry out. Evidence of his cult appears first in the 9th-cent. Martyrology of Ado. Feast 11 Feb.

JW 1, 249–57; LP 1, 396–414; PL 89, 453–534; FD 1, nn. 279; 286 f.; 291; 298; MGEp 3, 698–702; Caspar 2, 643–64; 692–701; E. Caspar, 'Papst Gregor II und der Bilderstreit', ZKG 52 (1933), 29–89; G. Ostrogorsky, 'Les débuts de la querelle des images', Mélanges Ch. Diehl (Paris, 1930) 1, 244–54; DTC 6, 1781–6 (P. Moncelle); LThK 4, 1181 (L. Spätling); BSS 7, 287–90 (P. Rabikauskas); NCE 6, 770 (R. E. Sullivan); Bertolini, 435–52; Seppelt 2, 88–101; JR, 214; 218–23; 267.

GREGORY III, ST (18 Mar. 731–28 Nov. 741). Syrian by origin, an able and eloquent priest equally at home in Greek and Latin, he was seized by cheering crowds during the funeral of GREGORY II, rushed to the Lateran and elected pope by acclaim, and consecrated five weeks later after obtaining (he was the last pope to seek it) the Byzantine exarch's mandate.

The *iconoclastic controversy was now at its height, the prohibition of sacred images and of their veneration having been enacted by Emperor Leo III (717–41) in early Jan. 730. Eager for a *rapprochement* with the east, Gregory immediately appealed to Leo to abandon this policy, deeply offensive to western belief and practice. Receiving no response, he held a widely representative synod on 1 Nov. 731 which denounced iconoclasm and excommunicated anyone destroying images; the emperor and the eastern patriarch were by implication included. The successive envoys, however, carrying his original appeal and then the drastic synodal decrees, were intercepted by imperial officials in Sicily and gaoled. When eventually (733) one got through to Constantinople with letters from Gregory to Leo, his son, later Constantine V (741–75), and Patriarch Anastasius (730–54), the emperor decided to use force to bring the stubborn pontiff to heel. First, he dispatched an armed fleet to Italy, and then, when it was wrecked in the Adriatic, sequestered the papal patrimonies in Calabria and Sicily, and transferred the ecclesiastical provinces of Illyricum and Sicily from the pope's jurisdiction to that of the patriarch of Constantinople.

These were damaging blows, but did not alter Gregory's loyalty to the empire, still in his view the sole legitimate authority. Thus when Ravenna, the seat of Byzantine rule, fell to the Lombards in 733, his active support contributed greatly to its recapture by exarch Eutychius. Both Leo and Eutychius showed their gratitude, the one by making a tacit truce with the pope, the other by presenting him with six onyx columns which he placed before the *confessio*, or tomb, of the Apostle in St Peter's. Realizing, however, how vulnerable he was to the Lombards and their king Liutprand (712–44), Gregory rebuilt, at his own expense, the walls of Rome, restored those of Civitavecchia, and entered into defensive alliances with the dukes of Spoleto and Benevento, both enemies of Liutprand. These moves only added to the fury of the king, who after capturing Spoleto invaded the duchy of Rome, seizing four key fortresses, and threatened the city itself. In desperation, since no help could be expected from Byzantium, Gregory took the momentous step of seeking it from the Franks, and in 739 and again in 740 sent impressive embassies to Charles Martell, *mayor of the palace (716–41) and thus *de facto* ruler of the Merovingian Frankish kingdom, bearing sumptuous gifts and relics, and letters describing the pitiable plight of the holy city, and imploring him to defend 'the church of God and his peculiar people'; he also offered him the title of consul and the rank of patrician. Although courteously received, these appeals remained unanswered; Charles had no wish to march against Liutprand, who had recently (738) helped him against the Arab invaders of Provence. Left to himself, Gregory first appealed to Liutprand to give back the strongholds he had seized, and then, when his request fell on deaf ears, made the mistake of allying himself with the ineffective, treacherous Duke Trasamund of Spoleto, thereby inflaming the king's animosity.

In the strictly ecclesiastical field Gregory's actions revealed his awareness of the importance of the church in northern Europe. Thus he gave full backing to the missionary enterprises of Boniface (680–754) in Germany, granting him the *pallium and the rank of archbishop in 732, with authority to establish bishoprics; after Boniface's third stay in Rome (737–8) he commissioned him as 'legate of the apostolic see' to organize the church in Bavaria, Alemannia, Hesse, and Thuringia, urging bishops, abbots, and lay magnates to give him their fullest support. He also cemented relations between Rome and the English church, bestowing (735) the pallium on Egbert of York (d. 766); when Tatwine of Canterbury (d. 734) visited Rome, he not only gave him the pallium but appointed him his vicar for the whole of England.

Some political blunders apart, Gregory's pontificate was a decisive one; he foresaw, even if he could not bring about, a pact with the Franks which would help to maintain the independence of the holy see. He himself beautified Rome and its churches on an unprecedented scale; the numerous colourful and splendid images he set up had the additional purpose of proclaiming defiance of the iconoclastic heresy. A believer in the monastic life, he gave practical support to existing communities and founded new ones; and he carried out repairs in the cemeteries around Rome and reorganized the services held in them. One of his most significant constructions was an oratory in St Peter's dedicated to the Saviour and the BVM, for the reception of relics of saints, and it was here that he was buried. The first evidence of his cult is the appearance of his name in the 9th-cent. Martyrology of Ado. Feast 28 Nov.

JW 1, 257–62; LP 1, 415–25; PL 89, 557–98; MGEp 3, 290–4; 702–9; FD 1, nn. 301; 302; Caspar 2, 664–7; DCB 2, 796–8 (J. Barmby); DACL 13, 1245–50 (H. Leclercq); DTC 6, 1785–90 (P. Moncelle); LThK 4, 1181 f. (T. Schieffer); BSS 7, 290 4 (P. Rabikauskas); PRE 7, 91 f. (H. Böhmer); NCE 6, 770 f. (R. E. Sullivan); Bertolini, 453–77; Seppelt 2, 102–8; JR, 223–6; 268.

ZACHARIAS, ST (3 Dec. 741–15 Mar. 752).

Born in Calabria of Greek stock, he worked closely as a deacon with GREGORY III. The last of the Greek popes, he was a cultivated man who translated GREGORY the Great's *Dialogues* into Greek, and was admired for his gentle, compassionate bearing. He combined with this, however, political adroitness and great personal persuasiveness.

First, he reversed Gregory III's policy towards the Lombards, who had seized key fortresses in the Campagna and were threatening Rome itself. Abandoning the alliance with Duke Trasamund of Spoleto, he sent envoys to the Lombard king Liutprand (712–44), then met him personally in his camp at Terni (spring 742), and by promising the help of the Roman militia obtained not only the return of the fortresses and other towns, of confiscated papal estates, and of all prisoners, but a twenty-year truce between the Lombards and Rome. In 743, when the Lombards switched their attack to Ravenna and the remaining Byzantine possessions in Italy, and the distracted exarch Eutychius implored him to mediate, Zacharias again intervened, visited Liutprand at Pavia (June 743), and prevailed on the reluctant king to evacuate the occupied districts and consent to an armistice. Liutprand's successor Ratchis confirmed the twenty-year truce with Rome; but when he renewed the offensive against the exarchate, the pope induced (749) him too, by persuasion and gifts, to desist. But this was the last of his successes with the Lombards. Ratchis was obliged to abdicate and his brother Aistulf, who replaced him (July 749), revived the Lombard expansionist ambitions and, after capturing Ravenna (summer 751) and bringing the Byzantine exarchate to an end, was soon aiming his sights at Rome.

With Constantinople, relations with which had been stormy as a result of Emperor Leo III's (717–41) ban on images and their veneration (*iconoclasm), Zacharias was able to reach an at any rate temporary *modus vivendi*. Although his appointment had not needed imperial ratification, he was careful to send envoys to the capital to announce it and to convey synodical letters to the patriarch; he was the last pope to do so. While thus indicating that there was no break with the eastern church, he also made his objection to iconoclasm clear to Emperor Constantine V (741–75) and Patriarch Anastasius. When the envoys arrived, they found the usurper Artavasdus (741–2) on the throne, but while they had no option but to recognize him, both they and the pope seem to have behaved with diplomatic reserve. At any rate, when Constantine was restored in Nov. 743, he bore no grudge against Rome but made a grant to the holy see of the large and lucrative estates of Norma and Ninfa in south Lazio. In fact, while Constantine was a fanatical iconoclast and Zacharias an orthodox defender of images, they seem to have tacitly agreed to play the issue down. The emperor was aware of, and must have been grateful for, the help the pope had given his exarch to keep hold of Ravenna, and for the moment preferred to have him as a friend while he consolidated his position and dealt with the Arabs and Bulgars.

Zacharias's dealings with Boniface (680–754), Apostle of Germany, and with the Franks—since Charles Martell's death (29 Oct. 741) ruled by his sons Carloman and Pepin III (714/15–68) as mayors of the palace (originally supervisors of the royal household but now quasi-hereditary chief ministers)—were especially memorable. Like GREGORY II and GREGORY III, he gave full backing to Boniface, who continually referred matters to him, and both encouraged and directed his programme for the reform of the Frankish church, appointing him his legate. This was carried through, with the co-operation of Carloman and Pepin, by a series of important Frankish synods, the measures taken being ultimately approved by the pope. The result was the effective strengthening of the ties between the Frankish church and Rome, and the presentation to Zacharias of a remarkable expression of loyalty by a council of the entire Frankish episcopate early in 747. In the same year the pope confirmed the condemnation of two heretical impostors, Adalbert and Clement, by Boniface. In 750, in response to an embassy sent to Rome by Pepin, he delivered the momentous ruling that it was better for the royal title to belong to him who exercised effective power in the Frankish kingdom than to him who had none. The sequel was the deposition of King Childeric III, last of the feeble Merovingian line, the election of Pepin at Soissons (Nov. 751), and his anointing as

king by Boniface. Zacharias's part in the transference of the crown to the Carolingian dynasty was to prove of immense significance for future relations between pope and emperor.

Zacharias was an energetic and efficient administrator who, as well as controlling the militia and civil government of Rome, took an active interest in the papal patrimonies. To resettle abandoned land, but also to replace revenues lost through the confiscation of the Sicilian and Calabrian patrimonies by Emperor Leo III, he developed the system of *domus cultae*, estates held in perpetuity by the church and worked by tenant farmers settled around an oratory. Although he constructed no new church, he carried out a great deal of restoration and embellishment of churches in Rome, continuing JOHN VII's decorative work in Sta Maria Antiqua (where a contemporary fresco portrait of himself can be seen). He also brought the papal residence, moved by John VII to the Palatine, back to the Lateran, not only rebuilding the decaying palace but adorning it with painted murals and adding a sumptuous new dining-room for official purposes. Feast 15 Mar.

LP 1, 426–35; JW 1, 262–70; MGEp 3, 479–87; 709–11; Caspar 2, 710–40; 731–40; Seppelt 2, 108–19; DTC 15, 3671–5 (É. Amann); DACL 8, 1583; 1653 (H. Leclercq); BSS 12, 1446–8 (N. Del Re); NCE 14, 1106 f. (M. C. McCarthy); LThK 10, 1298 f. (L. Spätling); Mann 1/2, 225–88; Bertolini, 479–513; JR 226–31; 268; 278; 300 f.; O. Bertolini, 'I rapporti di Zaccaria con Constantino V e con Artavasado nel racconto del biografo e nella probabile realtà storica', ASRomana 78 (1955), 1–21.

STEPHEN (II) (22 or 23–25 or 26 Mar. 752). An elderly presbyter of whose previous career nothing is known, he was elected by the clergy and people of Rome a few days after the death of Zacharias on 15 Mar. 752. He was duly installed in the Lateran palace, but had a stroke three days later and died on the fourth day. As he was never consecrated, and consecration was deemed essential by the canon law of the time, he was not reckoned a pope by LP or any medieval document; only since the 16th cent. did the practice of considering him one, on the ground that valid election is all that is required for a man to be pope, become general in Catholic circles. Thus the *Annuario Pontificio* included him as 'Stefano II' in its official list until 1960, but editions since 1961 have suppressed his name and given subsequent popes called Stephen a dual numbering.

LP 1, 440; JW 1, 270; DCB 4, 730 (J. Barmby); DTC 5, 973 (A. Clerval); DHGE 15, 1184 (R. Aubert); NCE 13, 695 (P. J. Mullins); R. L. Poole, 'The Names and Numbers of Medieval Popes', EHR 32 (1917), 476 f.; R. Thibaut, 'Noms et chiffres pontificaux', NRT 72 (1950), 834–8.

STEPHEN II (III) (26 Mar. 752–26 Apr. 757). A Roman of aristocratic and wealthy family, he was orphaned in childhood and brought up with his younger brother Paul in the Lateran. ZACHARIAS made them deacons, and as such they signed the acts of the Roman synod of 743. When the priest STEPHEN, chosen to succeed Zacharias, died four days later, the elder brother was unanimously elected pope in Sta Maria Maggiore. His short reign witnessed not only the detachment of the papacy from Byzantium as it placed itself under the protection of the Frankish kingdom, but the formation of the papal state.

Shortly after his accession Stephen found Rome menaced by the Lombard king Aistulf (749–56) with his army, fresh from the conquest of Ravenna. Although initially promising a forty-year truce, it was soon apparent that Aistulf regarded the duchy of Rome as his fief, for he began exacting an annual tax from every inhabitant. At the same time he spurned the demands of a Byzantine envoy, accompanied by the pope's brother Paul, for the return of the imperial territories he had annexed. Further embassies to Aistulf, penitential litanies in Rome, and an appeal to Emperor Constantine V (741–75) for military aid having all proved fruitless, Stephen turned in desperation to Pepin III, king of the Franks (751–68) (as GREGORY III had

turned in 739 to Charles Martell), describing to him Rome's precarious situation and begging to be invited to visit him under a safe conduct.

Mindful of his debt to Zacharias, Pepin responded favourably, sending Bishop Chrodegang of Metz and his own brother-in-law Autcar as escorts, and Stephen set out on 14 Oct. 753. He stopped at Pavia, the Lombard capital, having been instructed by the Byzantine emperor to submit a fresh demand for the return of his confiscated possessions, but when this was rebuffed he moved north, with Aistulf's grudging consent, on 15 Nov. and crossed the Alps (the first pope to do so) by the Great St Bernard Pass. On 6 Jan. 754 he was obsequiously received by Pepin at Ponthion, south of Châlons-sur-Marne, while next day he and his clergy, in penitential garb, flung themselves at the king's feet and besought him, for the Apostles' sake, to deliver them and the Roman people from the Lombards. The outcome of this meeting, and of further deliberations culminating at Easter (14 Apr.) at Quierzy, near Laon, was that Pepin not only engaged himself and his sons in general terms to protect the Roman church and the prerogatives of St PETER (i.e. the pope), but also promised in writing (the 'donation of Pepin') to guarantee, as St Peter's rightful possessions, along with the duchy of Rome, Ravenna, the exarchate and other cities held by the Lombards, and probably also other extensive areas in northern and central Italy. According to many scholars Stephen produced as the legal basis of his claims the so-called *Donation of Constantine, a fictitious instrument drafted in the papal chancery under which Constantine the Great (d. 337) purported to confer on SILVESTER I, among other privileges, dominion over Rome, Italy, and 'the provinces, places and *civitates* of the western regions'. For his part Stephen, who had spent the winter gravely ill at the abbey of St Denis, near Paris, solemnly anointed (28 July 754) Pepin, his wife and sons, sealing thereby the legitimacy of their dynasty, and bestowed on Pepin and his sons, in token of their new role as protectors of the holy see, the title 'patrician of the Romans'.

In fulfilment of his promise Pepin first made several attempts to induce Aistulf to surrender the occupied territories peacefully. When diplomacy failed, he defeated the king in a swift campaign (Aug. 754) and made him swear (first Peace of Pavia) to hand over to the pope his conquests in the exarchate and the Pentapolis. Stephen, who had accompanied Pepin's army, was then conducted back to Rome and received a delirious welcome. Once the Franks had recrossed the Alps, however, Aistulf broke his oath and was soon (1 Jan. 756) besieging Rome and devastating its environs. In response to Stephen's repeated entreaties Pepin again invaded Italy, crushed Aistulf, and at the second Peace of Pavia (June 756) bound him to evacuate the territories previously agreed with the addition of Comacchio (south of the mouth of the Po). This time he left Fulrad, abbot of St Denis, behind with a small force to ensure that the terms of the peace treaty were carried out. When Byzantine officials protested that the territories legally belonged to the emperor, Pepin replied that he had taken up arms solely out of love for St Peter and for the forgiveness of his sins, and would not hand over his conquests to anyone but the Apostle. He then presented Ravenna and the cities of the exarchate, the Pentapolis (i.e. Rimini, Pesaro, Fano, Senigallia, and Ancona, with adjacent territories), and Emilia to St Peter and the Roman church in perpetuity, Fulrad depositing the keys of the cities and the instrument of donation upon the tomb of St Peter. Thus the papal state came into existence, although at first at any rate the emperor's suzerainty continued to be recognized in theory.

When Aistulf died without heir in Dec. 756, Stephen successfully backed Desiderius of Tuscany for the throne (757–74), receiving in return a promise to hand over several further cities, including Bologna. He also had a hand in getting the new dukes of Spoleto and Benevento to cut adrift from the Lombards and submit to

Pepin and the holy see. Stephen's letters to Pepin reveal his exultation at Aistulf's death and his joy at the way things were working out. But his own remarkable reign, which had given a new direction to papal policy, was nearing its end. As his biographer in *LP* remarked, he had worked hard, with God's blessing, 'to enlarge the republic', being effectively the founder of the papal state. Apart from these greater matters, he had been active in carrying out restorations and embellishments in Roman churches, had turned his family mansion into a monastery dedicated to St Denis, and had founded several hospices. Through his influence Pepin arranged that the Roman liturgy should replace the Gallican in his realms, while at Rome he insisted on the strict observance of the day and night offices.

LP 1, 440–62; JW 1, 271–7; *MGE*p 3, 487–507; *DCB* 4, 730–5 (J. Barmby); *DHGE* 15, 1184–90 (A. Dumas); *NCE* 13, 695 (P. J. Mullins); *LThK* 9, 1083 f. (Th. Schieffer); Bertolini, 515–82; E. Caspar, *Pippin und die Römische Kirche* (Berlin, 1914); L. P. Duchesne, *The Beginnings of the Temporal Sovereignty of the Popes* (ET, London, 1908); Mann 1/2, 289–330.

PAUL I, ST (29 May 757–28 June 767). A Roman of aristocratic and wealthy family, orphaned in childhood, brought up in the Lateran and ordained deacon by ZACHARIAS, he was elected immediately after the death of his elder brother STEPHEN II (III). He had been Stephen's right-hand man and trusted negotiator, but his consecration had to be put off for a month because a minority faction hostile to the Frankish alliance preferred Archdeacon Theophylact. While still awaiting consecration he announced his election to Pepin III, king of the Franks (751–68), using the formula earlier employed to notify the Byzantine exarch. While not asking for ratification, he pledged undying loyalty to the pact the king had made with Stephen II; and in his reply Pepin asked him to stand godfather to his infant daughter.

Paul's reign was a continuous struggle to defend and consolidate the young, still vulnerable papal state. It was threatened by

Desiderius, the new Lombard king (757–74), who not only refused to hand over several cities he had promised to Stephen II as the price for help in securing his throne, but invaded and devastated papal territories, subjugated (758) Spoleto and Benevento which had accepted Frankish and papal suzerainty, and negotiated with Byzantium for military aid to reconquer Ravenna and the exarchate. At a meeting with Paul in Rome Desiderius declared that any concessions he made would be conditional on the release of Lombard hostages still held by Pepin. As his correspondence was intercepted, the pope was reduced to begging Pepin in open letters to accede to these demands, while secretly urging him to resist them. All the time he was sending him anguished complaints about Desiderius's excesses and appeals for help, but with his preoccupations in Frankland and his anxiety to prevent a Lombard–Byzantine coalition Pepin had no wish to intervene militarily. By diplomacy, however, he brought about an uneasy *modus vivendi* between Desiderius and Paul in 760, but it meant that both had to yield points, the pope in particular abandoning parts of his grandiose vision of the papal state.

At this stage relations with Constantinople were becoming Paul's great concern. He was disturbed not only by Emperor Constantine V's (741–75) moves to establish relations with the Lombards and then with the Frankish court, but also by the denunciation of images and their worship ratified by the eastern council the emperor had held at Hieria in Feb.–Aug. 754. More than once he dispatched envoys to urge Constantine to restore the traditional veneration of images (hence *LP*'s salute to him as a 'courageous champion of the orthodox faith'), and when the persecution of image-worshippers intensified he welcomed crowds of eastern *émigrés* fleeing from it, and made the monastery of SS. Stefano and Silvestro, which he had founded in his home in 761, available for Greek monks. In 763 he joined forces with the patriarchs of Alexandria, Antioch, and

Jerusalem, who had protested against the persecution. In 765 Constantine sent envoys to the Frankish court seeking Pepin's support for *iconoclasm, and also to detach the Franks from Rome. Paul was filled with apprehension, but was overjoyed to learn not only that the king had rejected these overtures, but that when iconoclasm and Trinitarian doctrine were debated between Franks and Greeks at the synod of Gentilly in 767, the Roman acceptance of image veneration had prevailed.

Paul died shortly afterwards (28 June 767) at St Paul's basilica, where he had sought refuge from the excessive heat. He was temporarily buried there, his body being translated to St Peter's three months later. He had a high conception of the papal office, describing himself as 'mediator between God and men, the searcher of souls'. *LP* extols his compassionate nature and the zeal with which he visited paupers and prisoners, but he was criticized as a severe administrator who relied on oppressive subordinates. His reign was important for the history of the catacombs, for he transferred numerous bodies from them to churches and chapels in Rome, most notably that of Petronilla, whom (Paul's action had a political aim) the Frankish royal house revered as the supposed daughter of St Peter. There is no evidence of his cult before the 15th cent. Feast 28 June.

LP 1, 463–7; JW 1, 277–83; *MGEp* 3, 507–58; *DCB* 4, 263–6 (J. Barmby); *DACL* 13, 1252–4 (H. Leclercq); *BSS* 10, 283–5 (P. Rabikauskas); *NCE* 11, 12 (R. E. Sullivan); *LThK* 8, 197 f. (W. Ullmann); M. Baumont, 'Le pontificat de Paul I', *MelArchHist* 47 (1930), 7–24; Bertolini, 583–624; Seppelt 2, 139–47.

CONSTANTINE (antipope 5 July 767–6 Aug. 768: d. ?). A layman, brother of Duke Toto of Nepi, he irregularly succeeded PAUL I, whose harsh rule and reliance on the ecclesiastical bureaucracy had incensed the lay aristocracy. For them it was important to have a pope they could influence, not least because the papacy had become a temporal power with the foundation of the papal state. As Paul lay dying, Toto plotted his murder, but, along with other Roman leaders, was persuaded by Christopher, the chief notary, that the subsequent election must follow traditional form. On Paul's death (28 June 767), however, Toto broke his oath, had Constantine acclaimed pope by a mob of his soldiers and dependants, installed him in the Lateran, and forced Bishop George of Praeneste first to ordain him subdeacon and deacon, and then, with two other bishops, to consecrate him in St Peter's (5 July).

Constantine at once informed Pepin III, king of the Franks (751–68) and protector of the holy see, of his election, begging him to maintain the pact he had made with the two previous popes. Receiving no reply, he wrote again in Sept., using as a pretext an important letter which had arrived (12 Aug.) from Theodore, the new patriarch of Jerusalem; it was clear from his message that he was already encountering difficulties. In fact, the clerical party at Rome had regrouped and its leader, Christopher, had made contact with the duke of Spoleto and the Lombard king Desiderius (757–74). The Lombards were only too glad to exploit the situation, and with troops supplied by them Christopher's son Sergius carried out a coup in Rome on 30 July 768. Toto was killed in street fighting and Constantine fled to the Lateran oratory, where he was soon arrested. The Lombards momentarily sought to set up a pope of their own, the presbyter PHILIP, but he was almost at once ejected from the Lateran.

A new pope, STEPHEN III (IV), having been canonically elected, Constantine was dragged from his hiding-place, paraded ignominiously round the city, and at a synod on 6 Aug. stripped of the insignia of office and formally deposed. He was then imprisoned in a monastery where, attacked by a gang, he had his eyes gouged out. Finally, on 12 and 13 Apr. 769 he appeared before a synod held by Stephen III in the Lateran to settle the matter in proper form. At the first session he pleaded that the office of pope had been forced on him, but then

abjectly admitted his guilt. At the second session he altered his tune, invoking precedents for laymen and even married men being made bishops. This exasperated his judges, who manhandled him and threw him out. The acts of his election (signed by all the clergy, including Stephen) and of his administration were burned, his ordinations were declared invalid, and he himself was sentenced to lifelong penance in a monastery. From this point he disappears from history.

LP 1, 468–72; 475 f.; JW 1, 283 f.; MGEp 3, 649–53; Mansi 12, 717–20; Seppelt 2, 148–52; Z1, 13–25; DHGE 13, 591–3 (G. Bardy); Bertolini, 622–38; LThK 3, 48 (K. Baus).

PHILIP (antipope 31 July 768). When the chief notary Christopher and his son Sergius, with the help of Lombard troops, seized Rome during the night of 30/31 July 768 and imprisoned the usurping pope CONSTANTINE, the priest Waldipert, acting apparently on the instructions of the Lombard king Desiderius (757–74), went with a band of Romans to the monastery of S. Vito, on the Esquiline, brought out its chaplain, the priest Philip, and, shouting 'Holy Peter has chosen Philip for pope', conducted him to the Lateran basilica, where a bishop was found to pronounce the appropriate prayers. Waldipert's object was to exploit the confused situation to the advantage of the Lombards by appointing a pope who would be their king's creature. He succeeded in installing Philip in the *patriarchium*, where he gave a blessing from the papal throne and presided at the banquet customarily given by a new pope to local notables. When Christopher heard what had happened, however, he swore publicly that he would never set foot in Rome while Philip remained in the palace. A group of his followers took the hint, went to the Lateran, and escorted Philip back to his monastery. No harm was done to him, for it was recognized that he was merely the innocent tool of Waldipert and the Lombards. Nothing is known about his earlier or subsequent history, but he should in all fairness be reckoned as neither a pope nor an antipope.

LP 1, 470 f.; JW 1, 284; Seppelt 2, 149 f.; *DCB* 4, 357 (J. Barmby); Bertolini, 629 f.

STEPHEN III (IV) (7 Aug. 768–24 Jan. 772). A Sicilian who had been brought up in Rome, had served in the papal bureaucracy under ZACHARIAS and his successors, and was now priest of Sta Cecilia, he was elected to replace the usurper CONSTANTINE at the instance of Christopher, the powerful chief notary. Christopher planned to govern in his name, and his mastery was such that the new pope was helpless to prevent the barbaric vengeance which he and his partisans immediately wreaked on their opponents, including Waldipert, the agent in Rome of the Lombard king Desiderius (757–74).

Once installed, Stephen dispatched an embassy, led by Christopher's son Sergius, to the Frankish court to announce his election, but also to solicit the presence of Frankish bishops qualified in Scripture and canon law at a synod to be held the following year. King Pepin III having died (24 Sept. 768), the legates were received by his sons Charles (Charlemagne: 768–814) and Carloman, like him 'patricians of the Romans' and protectors of the holy see, who granted the pope's request. The main object of the synod, which met in the Lateran on 12 Apr. 769 with thirteen Frankish bishops attending, was to restore canonical order after Constantine's usurpation. This it did, after a dramatic avowal of guilt for having accepted his ministry, by sentencing him to lifelong penitence in a monastery, burning the decree of his election, declaring his acts and ordinations invalid, and prescribing that only deacons and cardinal priests should be eligible for election as pope and that the laity should have no vote in elections. The synod also anathematized the eastern *iconoclastic council of Hieria (754) and approved the traditional veneration of images.

For the rest of his reign Stephen vacillated ineffectually in face of Desiderius's intrigues and the new Frankish policy, promoted by the queen-mother Bertrada, of friendship with the Lombards. Flouting Rome's prerogatives, Desiderius sought to appoint (770/1) a creature of his own, whom Stephen declined to consecrate, to the see of Ravenna, and refused to hand over cities he had promised to the papal state for STEPHEN II's help in securing his accession. The pope was even more alarmed when he learned that, in furtherance of the new foreign policy, a marriage was being arranged (770) between Charles and Desiderius's daughter; he denounced it as devilish, a breach of the solemn pact between the Frankish royal house and St Peter, but the marriage went ahead. In fact Charles planned no diminution in his protection of the holy see, and it was Frankish pressure that induced Desiderius to give up meddling in Ravenna and to surrender substantial territory claimed by the pope in the duchy of Benevento. Feeling left in the lurch, however, and also chafing at the chief notary Christopher's dominance, Stephen reached an understanding with his natural enemy Desiderius, who had found a ruthless ally in the papal chamberlain Paul Afiarta. Taken in by the king's promise to hand over still more territory to the papal state, Stephen abandoned Christopher and Sergius to him and Afiarta, thereby conniving at their brutal murder and the resulting collapse of the Frankish party in Rome. To his shame he wrote to Charles and Bertrada alleging that the chief notary and his son, and Dodo, the envoy of Carloman (with whom Charles was then at odds), had plotted against his life, and that he had only been saved by timely help from his 'admirable son Desiderius' and the Apostle PETER. The outcome of his ill-judged policies was humiliating: Desiderius scornfully refused to yield an inch of territory, Stephen found himself as much subject to the king and Afiarta as he had been to Christopher, and the folly of *rapprochement* with the Lombards was exposed when Charles, sole ruler of the Franks from 771, repudiated his

Lombard wife and thus became Desiderius's mortal foe.

LP 1, 468–75; 89 f.; JW 1, 285–8; *MGE*p 3, 558–67; Mansi 12, 680–722; Seppelt 2, 150–8; *DCB* 4, 735–8 (J. Barmby); *DHGE* 15, 1190–3 (A. Dumas); *LThK* 9, 1039 (G. Schwaiger); *NCE* 13, 695 f. (C. M. Aherne); Bertolini, 628–64; Mann 1/2, 361–93.

HADRIAN I (1 Feb. 772–25 Dec. 795). Of noble Roman family, orphaned in childhood but brought up by his powerful uncle Theodotus, he was made subdeacon by PAUL I and deacon by STEPHEN III, whom he succeeded. The moment was a dangerous one, for Stephen had made an imprudent pact with the Lombard king Desiderius, whose agent, the chamberlain Paul Afiarta, now dominated Rome. Hadrian immediately amnestied Afiarta's numerous victims, sent him off as envoy to Desiderius and then had him arrested, and parried the king's request for an alliance by insisting that he must first make certain territorial restitutions he had promised to Stephen III. So far from complying, Desiderius, who was also intriguing to detach Hadrian from Charlemagne (768–814), since Dec. 771 sole king of the Franks, continued to occupy and threaten cities subject to the holy see. In winter 772/3 he moved on Rome itself, only retreating when the pope threatened excommunication. In the meantime, however, Hadrian secretly appealed to Charlemagne, invoking his help as protector of the holy see.

In autumn 773 Charlemagne, diplomatic approaches to Desiderius having come to nothing, descended on Italy and after a lengthy siege (Sept. 773–June 774) captured the Lombard capital Pavia and destroyed the Lombard kingdom, adding 'king of the Lombards' to his title. At Easter 774 he paid a surprise visit to Rome, and on 6 Apr. held a momentous meeting with the pope in St Peter's. In response to Hadrian's plea that he should implement the territorial promises made in 754 by Pepin III (741–68) to the Apostle PETER and Pope STEPHEN II, he drew up and personally signed a fresh

instrument of donation modelled on the earlier one and promising to St Peter approximately three-fourths of Italy. Although Hadrian began striking coins and dating documents by the years of his pontificate, it soon became clear that this instrument was more a recognition of claims than an actual transfer of sovereignty. Charlemagne restored the territories Desiderius had promised, and under almost continuous pressure from the pope added further areas on two later visits to Rome (781 and 787). Hadrian, however, had to relinquish important regions (Terracina, Tuscany, Spoleto), and while he has deservedly been called the second founder of the papal state, its extent fell far short of his earlier ambitious dreams. He also had the chagrin of discovering that Charlemagne, taking his title 'patrician of the Romans' seriously, did not hesitate as overlord of the papal state to interfere in its affairs, including those of Ravenna, as he thought fit. While often protesting, Hadrian proved in general a pliant partner, and was even prepared to back the king's secular policies (e.g. his measures to depose Duke Tassilo III of Bavaria) with spiritual anathemas.

In the ecclesiastical field Hadrian assisted Charlemagne's campaign to reform the Frankish church, supplying him with Roman disciplinary and liturgical precedents. More importantly, he gave his full support to the second council of Nicaea (the Seventh General Council) which, in Sept. 787, condemned *iconoclasm in the east and restored the veneration of images, sending to it not only two representatives but a dogmatic treatise, which was applauded at the council, defending the proper use of images; he only demanded—a demand tactfully ignored at the council—the return of papal patrimonies confiscated by Emperor Leo III (717–41) and the recognition of Rome as metropolitan of Illyricum. Charlemagne, however, who could not welcome the reconciliation of the pope with the Byzantine throne and had not himself been invited to the council, had a detailed refutation of its decisions (the *Libri Carolini*) composed by his theologians on the basis of a faulty translation of its acts supplied by Rome. Hadrian had the courage to defend the veneration of images to him, adding however that he would anathematize Empress Irene (780–802), widow of Emperor Leo IV the Khazar (775–80), and her son if the papal patrimonies and Rome's jurisdiction over Illyricum were not restored. When Charlemagne held his great synod of Frankfurt in June 794, the two papal legates and their master must have been relieved that only one proposition of Nicaea II, and that on the basis of faulty translation, was condemned, viz. that images might be *adored*. Hadrian, who had earlier condemned *adoptionism and dogmatically refuted it, had the satisfaction of seeing the heresy anathematized by the synod in terms borrowed from his own letter.

Profiting by the peaceful conditions ensured by Charlemagne, Hadrian not only built, restored, or beautified an extraordinary number of Roman churches, but renewed the city's walls, strengthened the embankments of the Tiber, and completely reconstructed four great aqueducts. He devoted care to the *diaconiae*, monastic foundations for the relief of the poor, and greatly developed the *domus cultae*, church-run farms near the city providing income for charitable objects or the support of churches. One of his great agricultural colonies was able to feed one hundred poor people daily. On the other hand, his tendency to advance his own relatives (e.g. his nephew Paschalis, whom he promoted chief notary) helped to sow the troubles which plagued his successor LEO III. Despite occasional tensions in their relationship, Charlemagne grieved at his death 'as if he had lost a brother or a child', caused masses to be said throughout his realms for his soul, and had a magnificent marble slab inscribed with memorial verses full of affection and respect sent to Rome; a masterpiece of Carolingian art, it can be seen in the portico of St Peter's.

LP 1, 486–523; JW 1, 289–306; *PL* 96, 1167–244; *MGE*p 3, 567–657; 5, 1–57; Seppelt 2, 158–84; *DCB* 2, 838–42 (J. Barmby); *DHGE* 1, 614–19 (M. Jugie); *DBI* 1, 312–23 (O. Bertolini); *NCE* 1, 144 f. (J. E. Bresnahan); *LThK* 4, 1306 (L. Spätling); DACL 13, 1255–64 (H. Leclercq); Mann 1/2, 394–497; E. Caspar, *Das Papstum unter fränkischen Herrschaft* (Darmstadt, 1956), 35–113; Bertolini, 663–719; 737–9; Brezzi, 3–31; R. Krautheimer, *Rome: Profile of a City* (New Jersey, 1980), esp. 109–14.

LEO III, ST (26 Dec. 795–12 June 816). A Roman, of modest, south Italian stock, he had served in the curia from boyhood and was cardinal priest of Sta Susanna when elected. He at once announced his election to Charles (Charlemagne), king of the Franks (768–814) and patrician of the Romans, sending him, in recognition of his suzerainty, the keys of St Peter's tomb and the banner of Rome, and requesting the presence of an envoy to receive the citizens' oath of loyalty. In his reply Charles stressed that, while his function was to defend the church and consolidate it by promoting the faith, the pope's was to pray like Moses for the realm and the victory of its army.

Although his election was unanimous, Leo's personality and methods aroused hostility in aristocratic circles led by HADRIAN I's relative Paschalis, chief notary, and Campulus, papal purse-keeper, and on 25 Apr. 799, as he was riding in procession to mass, a gang violently attacked him, attempting without success to cut out his eyes and tongue; after a formal ceremony of deposition he was shut up in a monastery. Helped by friends, however, he made his escape to Charles, at Paderborn, who received him with solemn courtesy, clearly not recognizing his deposition. Representatives of the rebels arrived too, and laid formal charges of perjury and adultery against him. The situation was delicate, for in Frankish circles these charges were held to be well founded. Charles's adviser Alcuin (c.735–804) reminded him that no power on earth could judge the apostolic see, and so, postponing a decision, the king had Leo escorted back to Rome, which he reached on 29 November. In December an investigation of the attack on the pope and of the accusations was carried out in the Lateran by Frankish agents, but though suspecting the latter to be true they had no power of decision and referred the affair to the king; meanwhile, to ensure peace in the city, the conspirators were temporarily sent to Frankland.

Charles took his time over the affair, reaching Rome in late Nov. 800, and was greeted with imperial-style ceremonial. On 1 Dec. he held a council of Frankish and Roman notables in St Peter's, explaining in his opening address that its purpose was to examine the charges against the pope, but the assembly replied that it did not wish to sit in judgement on him. Leo then declared his readiness to purge himself of 'the false charges ... following the example of his predecessors', and at a plenary session on 23 Dec. took an oath of purgation concerning them. His opponents were then condemned to death, but on his intercession the sentence was commuted to exile. Two days later, as the Christmas mass was beginning and Charles rose from praying before St Peter's tomb, the pope placed an imperial crown on his head; the assembled crowd acclaimed him emperor, and Leo knelt in homage (the first and last obeisance a pope was to offer a western emperor). In spite of the chronicler Einhard's report that the coronation came as an unwelcome surprise to Charles, everything indicates that the ceremony, of momentous significance for subsequent history, had been carefully prearranged.

Now fully rehabilitated, Leo continued to enjoy Charles's confidence, journeying (for example) to Aachen to spend Christmas 804 with him. As pope, however, he was overshadowed by the towering personality of the emperor, who paid little attention to papal rights and, despite repeated complaints, interfered through his agents in the affairs of Rome and the papal state. As his subject, Leo dated his coins by Charles's regnal years. It was Charles, too, who took the lead in organizing religious affairs in his realms.

Thus it was at his prompting that in 798 Leo raised Salzburg to metropolitan status and held a synod at Rome which confirmed the condemnation of the *adoptionism of Felix of Urgel in Spain (d. 818). It was Charles who instructed Leo, after the conquest of the Avars, to take in hand the organization of the church in their regions. All the more striking was Leo's resistance, in 810, to Charles's request that he should add the clause 'and from the Son', i.e. the *Filioque, already adopted by the Frankish church, to the article on the procession of the Holy Spirit in the creed; he approved the doctrine implied by the proposed addition, but disapproved alterations in the creed.

Leo maintained relations with the English church, helping to restore King Eardulf of Northumbria (d. 810) to his throne, withdrawing the *pallium from the bishop of Lichfield, and settling several other matters of dispute between the archbishops of Canterbury and York. On Charles's death (28 Jan. 814) he was able to act more independently, and when a fresh conspiracy to depose and assassinate him was discovered, he personally tried those involved (something Charles would never have permitted) on charges of treason, and ruthlessly condemned scores to death (815). His action alarmed the court at Aachen, but Leo was able to provide explanations which satisfied it.

Leo proved a highly efficient administrator of the papal patrimonies, worked hard and successfully to extend the church's system of social welfare, and continued Hadrian I's policy of reviving the splendour of Christian Rome by lavishly constructing, restoring, and embellishing churches. One of his most remarkable works was the new hall (*triclinium*) he added to the Lateran for holding banquets, receptions, synods, and legal proceedings. The two great mosaics he set up in it emphasized his ideal of the co-operation of pope and emperor, the one showing Christ himself commissioning both SILVESTER I and Constantine the Great, the other depicting the Apostle PETER handing the pallium to the kneeling

Leo and to Charles, also kneeling, a royal banner. Although a harsh and divisive pontiff, he was included in the catalogue of saints in 1673 because of the presumed miracle of the restoration of his eyes and tongue, although the sources in fact speak only of an attempt to remove them. Feast (now suppressed) 12 June.

JW 1, 307–16; LP 2, 1–48; PL 102, 1023–72; MGEp 5, 58–68; 85–104; E. Caspar, 'Das Papstum unter fränkischen Herrschaft', ZKG 54 (1935), 214–64; Z1, 26–36; R. Baker, 'The Oath of Purgation of Pope Leo III in 800', Traditio 8 (1952), 35–80; L. Wallach, 'The Roman Synod of December 800 and the Alleged Trial of Leo III', HTR 49 (1965), 123–42; W. Mohr, 'Karl der Grosse, Leo III, und der Römische Aufstand von 799', BullCang 30 (1960), 39–98; DTC 9, 304–12 (É. Amann); BSS 7, 1283–8 (P. Rabikauskas); NCE 8, 640 (R. E. Sullivan); Mann 2, 1–110; Seppelt 2, 184–200.

STEPHEN IV (V) (22 June 816–24 Jan. 817). A Roman of aristocratic family, brought up from childhood in the Lateran under HADRIAN I, he succeeded LEO III, who had ordained him subdeacon and deacon. Conciliatory and universally popular, he was probably chosen to heal the divisions at Rome opened up by his predecessor. He was also the first pope elected since the establishment of the Carolingian empire; the role of the Frankish emperor in papal elections and in relation to the papal state was still undefined.

After making the people of Rome swear allegiance to Charlemagne's successor, Louis the Pious (814–40), Stephen dispatched envoys to him to announce and give an account of his election, and to ask for a personal meeting. The meeting took place at Rheims in Oct. 816, the pope being welcomed with elaborate ceremonial, and at a festive mass in the cathedral Stephen anointed and crowned Louis and his consort Irmengard, using an alleged 'crown of Constantine' which he had brought from Rome for the purpose. This was the first anointing of an emperor by a pope; Louis, who had been crowned as co-emperor in 813, must have regarded the whole

ceremony as spiritually reinforcing his royal position, but it was historically important as suggesting that the intervention of the pope was necessary for the full exercise of the imperial power. The two held prolonged daily discussions, the detail of which can only be guessed; but it is certain that the emperor formally renewed the long-standing pact of friendship and protection between the Frankish crown and the holy see. Further, the guarantees for the autonomy of the papal state and the freedom of papal elections embodied in the 'privilege' which Louis was later to grant to Stephen's successor, PASCHAL I, must have been worked out at Rheims. A concession which Stephen obtained, important for peace at home, was a pardon for the aristocratic conspirators whom Charlemagne had banished to Gaul in 800 for their part in the rebellion against Leo III.

When Stephen set off for Rome with the amnestied exiles, Louis loaded him with sumptuous gifts and presented him with a royal villa near Troyes. Just three months after reaching the city the pope died.

LP 2, 49–51; JW 1, 316–18; MGSS 2, 466–516; 585–648; Seppelt 2, 201–3; DHGE 15, 1193 f. (A. Dumas); NCE 13, 696 (J. E. Bresnahan); LThK 9, 1039 f. (G. Schwaiger); Mann 2, 111–21.

PASCHAL I, ST (24 Jan. 817–11 Feb. 824). Born in Rome and educated in the Lateran school, he was ordained priest by LEO III and, after long service in the papal administration, was abbot of St Stephen's monastery, near St Peter's, when elected pope. He was consecrated the day following his election, the exceptional haste reflecting anxiety in Rome to anticipate interference from the Holy Roman emperor, now protector of the holy see; but Paschal was careful to announce his accession at once to Louis I the Pious (814–40), stressing that he had not sought office but that it had been thrust upon him. Not long afterwards, in response to his request for the renewal of Rome's long-standing relationship with the Frankish crown, Louis issued a statute (the *pactum Ludovicianum*), the terms of which he had worked out with STEPHEN IV. Under this he confirmed the pope in the possession of the papal states and of the patrimonies outside them, bound himself (in contrast to Charlemagne) not to interfere in the papal domains unless invited, or obliged by the claims of the oppressed, to do so, and guaranteed the freedom of papal elections, requiring only that after being consecrated the new pope should notify the emperor and renew the treaty of friendship.

The harmonious relationship presupposed by these concessions continued for most of Paschal's reign, and papal envoys frequently visited the court and imperial envoys Rome. Thus when Louis sent Archbishop Ebbo of Rheims (*c.*775-851), chosen to evangelize the Danes, to Rome in 822, Paschal not only commissioned him, along with Halitgar of Cambrai (d. 830), but appointed him papal legate for the northern regions. When Louis's son Lothair, crowned as co-emperor in 817, came to Italy in 823, Paschal invited him to Rome and, doubtless with Louis's agreement, solemnly anointed him again on Easter Sunday, presenting him also (this was the first occasion of the ceremony) with a sword as a symbol of the temporal power needed for the suppression of evil. From now onwards the pope's right to crown the emperor, and Rome's to be the place of his coronation, came to be increasingly recognized. While in Rome, however, Lothair seems to have decided that firmer control of the papal state than was presupposed in Louis's statute was desirable. Exercising his royal rights, he held a court and gave judgement for the abbey of Farfa (40 km. north of Rome), exempting it from tribute claimed by the holy see. His vigorous action kindled anti-Frankish feelings in Rome; at the same time upper-class opponents of Paschal's high-handed rule turned to the young monarch for support against the clerical party. After Lothair's departure two leaders of the pro-Frankish party, the chief notary Theodore and the nomenclator Leo, were blinded and then beheaded in the Lateran because of their loyalty to him; the culprits belonged to the papal household, and rumour linked Paschal himself with the foul deed. Although he dispatched disclaimers to Aachen, the emperor sent an investigating commission to Rome. Paschal deemed it prudent, like Leo III before him, to take an oath of purgation before a synod of thirty-four bishops; he added that the murdered men had been lawfully executed as traitors.

Paschal's reign saw the revival of *iconoclasm in the east by Emperor Leo V (813-20), and Theodore of Studios (759-826), the leading defender of image veneration, appealed for help to him. Paschal seems to have protested to the eastern emperor, but without success; but he gave hospitality to refugee Greek monks fleeing the persecution. As a builder and restorer of churches in Rome he was exceptionally active, his new churches including Sta Prassede on the Esquiline, Sta Maria in Domnica (or della Navicella) on the Caelian, and Sta Cecilia in Trastevere; all three contain splendid mosaics with lifelike portraits of himself. The style of his work suggests the deliberate aim of renewing Rome and her monuments in the spirit of the art and ideals of the age of Constantine the Great.

It is clear that, by his self-willed and harsh government, Paschal made many enemies and was widely detested in Rome. When he died popular uproar prevented his body from being interred, as had been intended, in St Peter's; it was left unburied until his successor, securely installed, arranged for it to be placed in Sta Prassede. His name was inserted in the calendar by the historian C. Baronius in the late 16th cent., but his feast (14 May) was dropped in 1963.

JW 1, 318-20; LP 2, 52-68; MGEp 5(1), 68-71; 528; 605; MGCap 1, 352-5, PL 106, 405-28; O. Bertolini, 'Osservazioni sulla *Constitutio Romana* ... dell'824', *Studi medievali in onore di A. de Stefano* (Palermo, 1956), 43-78; Seppelt 2, 203-6; Mann 2, 122-55; DTC 11, 2054-7 (É. Amann); LThK 8, 128, (G. Schwaiger); BSS 10,

353–6 (P. Rabikauskas); Brezzi, 43–61; R. Krautheimer, *Rome: Profile of a City 312–1308* (Princeton, 1980), 109–34.

EUGENE II (5(?) June 824–27(?) Aug. 827). Disturbances lasting several months followed the death of PASCHAL I, the nobility and the clerical bureaucracy making rival nominations, but after prolonged discussions the monk Wala (*c.*755–836), trusted adviser of Emperor Louis I the Pious (814–40) and his son Lothair I (840–55), pushed through the election of the candidate favoured by himself and the nobility, Eugene, then archpriest of Sta Sabina on the Aventine. Eugene at once not only notified the Frankish court but, going further than his predecessors, acknowledged the emperor's sovereignty in the papal state and swore an oath of loyalty to him.

In late August 824 Louis sent Lothair to Rome to restore order after the troubles of the previous reign and to establish a constitutional relationship between the empire and the papal state which would exclude arbitrary excesses like Paschal's. With the pope's co-operation he made proper provision for the widows and children of persons assassinated under Paschal and decreed the return of exiles. More far-reaching was the 'Roman constitution' which he published, again with Eugene's agreement, on 11 Nov. 824, which marked the high point of Frankish control of the papacy. This granted, first, immunity to all persons under either imperial or papal protection. Secondly, it provided that ordinary citizens should be judged by Roman, Frankish, or Lombard law according to their choice. Thirdly, with the object of keeping a tight rein on the pope's administration of Rome, it set up a supervisory commission consisting of one imperial and one papal delegate which would report annually to the emperor. Lastly, it restored the ancient tradition, suspended since STEPHEN III's synod of 769, by which the people of Rome as well as the clergy took part in papal elections,

stipulating that before being consecrated the pope-elect should take an oath of loyalty to the emperor before the imperial legate. The emperor's sovereignty over the papal state was emphasized by the oath of allegiance which all citizens were to take.

Eugene held an important synod in the Lateran in Nov. 826 at which these rules for elections were ratified. But if he had to show deference to the court in temporal matters, in the spiritual field he asserted an independence which his predecessors had lost under Charlemagne (768–814). Thus, while adopting the Frankish legislation for proprietary churches (i.e. churches with a secular or spiritual proprietor who claimed to control them), the synod published a collection of reforming disciplinary canons (dealing with simony, the qualifications and duties of bishops, clerical education, monastic arrangements, Sunday observance, marriage, etc.) which were extended to the Frankish church. Again, when Louis sent envoys to Rome in 824 to persuade the pope to accept a compromise on sacred images, Eugene firmly insisted that the question had been settled in favour of image veneration by the second council of *Nicaea (787). *Iconoclasm had flared up afresh at Constantinople under Emperor Leo V (813–20), and his successor Michael II (820–9), whose attitude was one of reserve, had enlisted the help of Louis in approaching Rome, knowing that the Frankish position was that, while images were permissible, they were not to be adored. On 1 Nov. 825, with Eugene's consent, Louis convened a commission of Frankish theologians at Paris to examine the issues, and this duly produced a report rejecting Nicaea II and censuring the pope for protecting error and superstition; but nothing could induce Eugene to budge. It is significant that Louis did not put pressure on him, but left the final decision to him.

Meanwhile Eugene had been in correspondence with Theodore of Studios (759–826), spiritual leader of the venerators of images in the east, who placed great reliance on Rome's support; he had also given hospitality to refugees fleeing from the ban on images. Among his concerns was the evangelization of the pagan world, and in 826 he commended the mission of Anskar (801–65), Apostle of the north, and his companions in Denmark to the whole Catholic church.

JW 1, 320–2; LP 2, 69 f.; MGCap 1, 322–4; O. Bertolini, 'Osservazioni sulla Constitutio Romana ... dell'824', Studi medievali in onore di A. de Stefano (Palermo, 1956), 43–78; DHGE 15, 1347–8 (A. Dumas); LThK 3, 1171 f. (G. Schwaiger); NCE 5, 625 (H. G. J. Beck); Brezzi, 46–8; Mann 2, 156–82; Seppelt 2, 208–14.

VALENTINE (Aug.–Sept. 827). A Roman of upper-class family, son of Leontius of the Via Lata, he early entered the service of the church, being ordained and brought into the papal palace by PASCHAL I and being eventually made archdeacon. On the death of EUGENE II he was unanimously elected pope by the clergy, nobility, and people of Rome; the participation of the laity indicates that the *constitution of 824 promulgated by Emperor Lothair I (840–55) and ratified by Eugene II was strictly observed. He was duly consecrated, but according to LP died forty days later; the Annals attributed to Einhard (c.770–840), Charlemagne's biographer and counsellor, give his reign as less than a month. LP applauds his piety and other virtues in conventional terms, but there is no record of any acts performed by him.

LP 2, 71 f.; JW 1, 322 f.; DTC 15, 2497 (É. Amann).

GREGORY IV (late 827–25 Jan. 844). A Roman of aristocratic family, cardinal priest of S. Marco, he owed his election to the votes of the lay nobility. In compliance with Lothair I's *constitution of 824, his consecration (29 Mar. 828) was deferred until an imperial legate had approved his election and he himself had sworn allegiance. The dependence of the papal state on the Holy Roman emperor remained effective in the early years of his reign; when in 829 imperial judges sitting in Rome decided against the Roman church in favour of the abbey of Farfa, which Lothair had exempted from tribute to the holy see in PASCHAL I's time, the Frankish court seems to have rejected his appeal.

This dependence was loosened as a result of the dynastic struggles between Emperor Louis I the Pious (814–40) and his sons Lothair I (840–55), Pepin (d. 838), and Louis the German (d. 876). When these three rebelled against their father, Gregory supported Lothair and accompanied him across the Alps to Frankland. He hoped that his mediation would be understood as intended to promote peace, but the mass of Frankish bishops were outraged by his partisanship, reminded him of his oath of fealty to Louis, and threatened excommunication if he persisted in disloyalty. He was at first shaken but, encouraged by leading churchmen like Agobard of Lyons (769–840) and Wala of Corbie (c.755–836), furiously rebuked his critics, insisting that the authority of St PETER's successor was supreme, that the peace and unity of the empire were his concern, and that the papacy, entrusted with the care of men's souls, was superior to the imperial power. When the armies faced each other at Rotfield, near Colmar, in summer 833, the brothers persuaded him to go to Louis's camp to negotiate, but when he returned with what seemed a reasonable basis for a reconciliation, he found that he had been duped by Lothair. On the night of the pope's return most of Louis's supporters deserted him, and on 30 June he had to surrender unconditionally, only to be deposed and humiliated. Gregory returned to Rome from 'the field of lies' bitterly regretting his intervention. Louis was restored in Mar. 834, and in 837 reopened relations with the pope, with the object ostensibly of making a pilgrimage to Rome but really to detach him from Lothair. Gregory was delighted and sent an embassy to Louis, but it was held up by Lothair at Bologna; he managed, however, to smuggle a letter through. After Louis's death (20 June 840), he made timid attempts to mediate in the bloody conflict which ensued between the brothers, but without success. Apart from these ineffective political manoeuvres, little is known of Gregory's pontificate. The Saracens, established in Sicily since 827, were now a constant threat to mainland Italy; to counter this he built a powerful fortress, named Gregoriopolis, at Ostia. In 831/2 he received Anskar, since 826 missionary in Denmark and recently consecrated bishop of Hamburg, gave him the *pallium, and named him legate for Scandinavia and the Slav missions. In 831 he also received the liturgist Amalarius of Metz (c.780–c.850) and assigned him an archdeacon to teach him Roman liturgical usage. At Gregory's suggestion, four years later, Louis I extended the observance of All Saints day throughout his dominions. In Rome the pope spent lavishly on building and decorating churches; his portrait in mosaic, commissioned by himself, can be seen in the apse of S. Marco. Among his other works was the reconstruction of a ruined aqueduct linked with the Janiculum, which provided not only water for domestic purposes but power to operate mills.

LP 2, 73–85; 3, 122 f.; JW 1, 323–7; MGEp 5, 228–32; Mann 2, 187–231; EC 6, 1128 (L. Spätling); PRE 7, 92 f. (H. Böhmer); NCE 6, 771 (H. G. J. Beck); Brezzi, 49 f.; Seppelt 2, 214–21.

JOHN (antipope Jan. 844) On the death of GREGORY IV (25 Jan. 844) the populace of Rome, with violent demonstrations, proclaimed a deacon named John as his successor, and seizing the Lateran palace enthroned him there. The lay aristocracy, however, elected the elderly, nobly born archpriest SERGIUS, ejected John from the Lateran, and swiftly crushed the opposition. Sergius's consecration was rushed through without waiting for imperial ratification. Although some of his supporters wanted John put to death for what they considered his presumption, his life was spared by Sergius and he was confined in a monastery. Nothing further is known about him.

LP 2, 86 f.; JW 1, 327; LThK 5, 988 (G. Schwaiger); EC 6, 582 (P. Brezzi).

SERGIUS II (Jan. 844–27 Jan. 847). A Roman aristocrat, he had been made acolyte by LEO III, subdeacon by STEPHEN IV (V) (a close kinsman), priest by PASCHAL I, and archpriest by GREGORY IV. On Gregory's death the Roman populace proclaimed the deacon JOHN pope, seized the Lateran palace, and enthroned him there. The nobility, meeting in the basilica of S. Martino, elected Sergius, elderly and gout-racked but a grandee of their own class, and swiftly crushed all opposition; at Sergius's request John's life was spared. Because of the tense situation, but also as a gesture of independence, Sergius's consecration was then rushed through without awaiting ratification by the Frankish court.

Emperor Lothair I (840–55) reacted angrily to this flouting of the Roman *constitution of 824. In June his son Louis, recently installed at Pavia as viceroy of Italy, with Archbishop Drogo of Metz (801–55), leading Frankish churchman, as his mentor, marched south with a punitive army which, as evidence of the royal displeasure, mercilessly pillaged the papal territories through which it passed. Although Sergius cooled the atmosphere by receiving Louis with ceremonial deference, he had to submit to a tough and protracted investigation of his title by a synod (in which some twenty Italian bishops participated) in St Peter's. Eventually his election was ratified; but in return he, with the citizens of Rome, had to swear allegiance to Lothair and accept that a pope-elect could not be consecrated save on the emperor's orders and in the presence of his representative. Sergius then (15 June 844) crowned young Louis king of the Lombards, anointing and girding him with a sword. Although declining to swear allegiance to him too (that would have implied that the papal state belonged to his kingdom), he felt obliged to gratify Lothair by nominating Drogo apostolic vicar for the countries north of the Alps. He would not accede, however, to Drogo's proposal that Ebbo and Bartholomew, deposed as archbishops of Rheims and Narbonne in 835 for their part in the humiliation of Louis I the

Pious (814–40), should be rehabilitated.

Sergius's general administration came in for sharp criticism. An ambitious builder (he enlarged St John Lateran and restored the Marcian aqueduct), he resorted to dubious methods of raising the necessary funds, and because of age and infirmity allowed himself to be dominated by his unscrupulous, power-hungry brother Benedict, whom he made bishop of Albano and who by bribery got himself appointed imperial representative in Rome. Under them simony flourished, and bishoprics and other church offices were sold to the highest bidder. These internal disorders were compounded in Aug. 846 when, in spite of advance warning, Muslim pirates landed in force at the mouth of the Tiber, stormed Porto and Ostia with its fortress *Gregoriopolis (the garrison fled), and plundered St Peter's and St Paul's (both outside the Aurelian walls), stripping them of all their treasures. Contemporaries were sure that this disaster had been unleashed by Providence as a punishment for the abuses rampant in Rome. Sergius himself died suddenly when trying to mediate in a dispute between Patriarchs Venerius of Grado and Andrew of Aquileia.

LP 2, 86–105; JW 1, 327–9; NCE 13, 112 (C. M. Aherne); DTC 14, 1916–18 (É. Amann); EC 11, 385 f. (G. Fasoli); Seppelt 2, 221–5; Mann 2, 232–57; Brezzi, 50–2.

LEO IV, ST (10 Apr. 847–17 July 855). A Roman, son of Radoald and probably of Lombard extraction, brought up as a Benedictine monk, he was made subdeacon to serve in the curia by GREGORY IV, then cardinal priest of SS. Quattro Coronati by SERGIUS II. Elected unanimously on the day of Sergius's death, he was consecrated six weeks later without awaiting the imperial consent as required by the Roman *constitution of 824. The excuse put forward was that the crisis of the recent Saracen raids made delay impracticable, but assurances had to be given of more orderly procedures in future.

In fact Leo's immediate task was the defence of Rome against the Saracens and the repair of the damage inflicted by them in 846. With extraordinary energy he strengthened the city walls and, reviving plans of LEO III, constructed new walls, with financial help from Emperor Lothair I (840–55), on the right bank of the Tiber, bringing St Peter's, hitherto exposed to enemy attack, within the defensive system and creating the 'Leonine city'. These new defences were solemnly dedicated on 27 June 852. In 849 he organized the fleets of Naples, Amalfi, and Gaeta and defeated the Muslims in a decisive sea-battle just outside Ostia. In 854 he rebuilt Centumcellae, destroyed by them, on a more secure site, naming it Leopolis (today Civitavecchia), while at Porto he settled Corsican refugees as a defensive garrison.

These and similar successful measures could not but enhance Leo's prestige, and his reign saw a notable reassertion of papal authority. Outwardly he seemed to defer to the Frankish emperors, often seeking their consent to episcopal appointments and other routine acts of administration. As Lothair was increasingly occupied elsewhere, Leo's dealings were mainly with his son Louis II (sole emperor 855–75), whom he crowned and anointed in Rome at Easter 850 and whose personal envoy resided there. Relations between pope and emperor were frequently strained, as when Leo had three imperial agents executed for murdering one of his legates, or when Louis, not without grounds, suspected circles close to the curia of harbouring treasonable ideas. Leo's authoritative style was seen in his denunciation of powerful prelates like Hincmar, archbishop of Rheims (845–82), and John, archbishop of Ravenna (850–61), his excommunication of ANASTASIUS, cardinal of S. Marcello (soon to be antipope), in spite of Louis's favour for him, his intervention on behalf of the Breton bishops against Duke Nomenoë of Brittany, and his stubborn refusal to accede to Lothair's requests that he appoint Hincmar apostolic vicar and grant the *pallium to the bishop of Autun. A high point of his assertion of Rome's authority was his annulment of the synod of Soissons (Apr. 853), which had declared void the ordinations carried out by Ebbo, deposed as bishop of Rheims but temporarily (840/1) reinstated, and his demand for another council presided over by papal legates. Towards Constantinople he adopted an imperious tone, rebuking Patriarch Ignatius for not consulting Rome when he deposed the bishop of Syracuse (in Sicily) and, instead of confirming the sentence as requested, summoning both parties to Rome.

Leo not only fiercely defended papal rights but was active in restoring church discipline and, when necessary, introducing reforms. Notable examples were the exhaustive reply he sent in 849 to a wide-ranging questionnaire submitted by the bishops of Britain, and the sharp reminder he gave in 853 to Galerius, bishop of Tripoli, that the old-fashioned penitential discipline must be maintained. The acts survive of an important synod he held in St Peter's in Dec. 853, at which he insisted on the renewal and strengthening of the reforming canons of EUGENE II. He keenly promoted church music and instituted the observance of the octave of the Assumption of the BVM. In 853 he is said to have hallowed Alfred (849–99), then a small boy staying in Rome, as future king of England. He restored or rebuilt many churches in Rome, including his original monastery of S. Martino near St Peter's, and his contemporary portrait in fresco can be seen in the lower basilica of S. Clemente. Feast (now suppressed) 17 July.

LP 2, 106–39; JW 1, 329–39; *MGE*p 5(2), 585–612; Mansi 14, 852–1030; Mann 2, 258–307; Haller 2, 31–3; 51–4; 62–6; *DTC* 9, 312–16 (É. Amann); *BSS* 7, 1289–93 (G. Boccanera); *NCE* 8, 640 f. (R. E. Sullivan); Brezzi, 53–60; Seppelt 2, 225–35.

BENEDICT III (29 Sept. 855–17 Apr. 858). A Roman, with a great reputation for piety and learning, he was educated in the Lateran school, ordained subdeacon by GREGORY IV, and made cardinal priest of S. Callisto by LEO IV. On Leo's death (17 July 855) the first choice of clergy and people was HADRIAN, cardinal priest of S. Marco, but on his refusal they elected Benedict. An influential imperialist group, however, preferred ANASTASIUS, the ambitious cardinal priest whom Leo IV had anathematized and deposed but who had found protection with Emperor Louis II (855–75). Exploiting the fact that Benedict could not be consecrated save with the emperor's consent and in the presence of his envoys, they had his election disallowed, put forward Anastasius as pope, and brought him to Rome, where he was installed in the Lateran while Benedict, dragged from the papal throne, was ejected and imprisoned. Only when the general support for Benedict and the revulsion for his rival became clear did the envoys and the imperial party give way and allow Benedict's consecration to go ahead. This was a notable reverse for Louis, but his agents obliged Benedict to treat Anastasius and his adherents leniently and to accept the surveillance of Bishop Arsenius, Anastasius's kinsman and leading partisan, in the role of imperial representative in Rome.

Only scattered glimpses survive of Benedict's brief reign, which seems in several respects to have foreshadowed that of his energetic successor NICHOLAS I, on whose counsel he in fact relied heavily. Emperor Lothair I (840–55) having died on the day of his consecration, he intervened, in ways which remain obscure, to ensure a peaceful settlement, at least temporarily, between his sons Lothair II (855–69), Louis II (855–75), and Charles the Bald (875–77). He did not hesitate to threaten Hubert, brother of Queen Theutberga of Lorraine, with excommunication for plundering monasteries, or to demand of Louis II that Ingeltrude, wife of Count Boso, who had fled with her lover to Lothair II's domains, should be fetched back to her husband. He took up vigorously, though unsuccessfully, the cause of four bishops in Brittany who had been uncanonically removed and replaced by the local prince; and although at the request of Hincmar, archbishop of Rheims (845–82), he endorsed the controversial council of Soissons (853) which Leo IV had repudiated, he added the cautious proviso that his endorsement was subject to the report he had received being correct. Towards Constantinople he firmly asserted Rome's primatial jurisdiction, and when invited by Patriarch Ignatius to confirm his deposition of Gregory of Syracuse and other Sicilian bishops, he declined to do so until both parties had come to Rome and he had examined the case himself.

Aethelwulf, king of Wessex (839–58), with his son Alfred resided in Rome as a pilgrim during the first year of Benedict's reign, and not only completed the repair of the Saxon compound (near S. Spirito in Sassia) but made sumptuous gifts to the Roman churches and people (at the pope's behest) and promised annual contributions of money from England in future. Benedict restored the baptistery of Sta Maria Maggiore and several other churches, including St Paul's, and completely reconstructed the cemetery of S. Marco. His reign witnessed repeated floodings of the Tiber, and it fell to him to make good the extensive damage.

LP 2, 140–50; 151; 173; JW 1, 235 f.; PL 115, 698–701; 129, 1001–12; MGEp 5, 612–14; Mann 2, 308–28; DHGE 8, 14–27 (F. Baix); LThK 2, 174 (G. Schwaiger); DBI 8, 330–7 (O. Bertolini); NCE 2, 273 (S. McKenna); Brezzi, 60 f.; Seppelt 2, 231–5.

ANASTASIUS BIBLIOTHECARIUS
(antipope Aug.–Sept. 855). Born some time between 800 and 817, nephew of Arsenius (d. 868), powerful bishop of Orte (south of Orvieto), he early acquired a thorough knowledge of Greek, probably from Greek monks in Rome, and in 847/8 was ordained cardinal priest of S. Marco by LEO IV. A man of exceptional abilities and culture, he almost at once found himself at bitter odds with the pope and sought refuge in Emperor Louis II's (855–75) dominions, residing mainly in the diocese of Aquileia. Leo, who

knew his ambition and saw him as a potential rival, repeatedly summoned him to Rome, and when he refused to return excommunicated, anathematized, and degraded him at synods in Dec. 850, and May, June, and Dec. 853. On Leo's death, after the election of BENEDICT III but before the imperial consent required for his consecration had been obtained, a determined attempt was made by Arsenius and the Frankish party, with Louis's full support, to get Anastasius appointed instead. The envoys carrying the decree announcing Benedict's election to the emperor were met by Arsenius at Gubbio and won over to the cause, Benedict's election was disallowed, and Anastasius was irregularly elected at Orte; accompanied by imperial messengers, he came to Rome, took possession of the Lateran by force, and rudely ejected and imprisoned Benedict. He caused uproar by violently pulling down, along with sacred images of the Saviour and the BVM, a painting over the portal of St Peter's depicting the synods which had condemned him. For three days anarchy reigned, but it soon became apparent not only that Anastasius lacked popular support, but that a man who had been formally excommunicated was totally unacceptable; the bishops of *Ostia and Albano, two of the three who traditionally consecrated the pope, could not be induced, even by threats of torture, to act. Even Louis's envoys were forced to accept that the clergy and people were united in wanting Benedict, and grudgingly allowed his consecration to go ahead. Anastasius was stripped of his papal insignia and ejected from the Lateran, but, under a bargain struck with Louis's envoys, Benedict refrained from reprisals and merely had him reduced to lay communion and confined to the monastery of Sta Maria in Trastevere.

After spending Benedict's reign in obscurity, Anastasius, by an amazing reversal of fortune, became the increasingly important counsellor of the following three popes. NICHOLAS I promoted him abbot of Sta Maria in Trastevere and drew on his advice in drafting letters, especially in connection with Byzantine affairs; in the meantime he did not hesitate to get rid of documents in the papal archives incriminating himself. On the day of HADRIAN II's consecration (14 Dec. 867) his suspension as priest was lifted, and he was immediately named Librarian (hence his sobriquet Bibliothecarius) of the Roman church. In 868, through alleged involvement in a scandal, he was dismissed, but was soon restored. He retained his position as Librarian, and a key role in the chancery, under JOHN VIII. In 869 he was sent to Constantinople on a diplomatic mission by Louis II, and took part in the last session of the Eighth General Council (869-70). His voluminous writings are in the main Latin translations, notably of the acts of the Seventh (second council of *Nicaea: 787) and Eighth General Councils. For centuries he was considered the compiler of *LP*, but it is probable that only the notices of Nicholas I and Hadrian II come from his pen. He must have died between 29 May 877, the last official mention of him, and 29 Mar. 879, when Zacharias of Anagni is first mentioned as Librarian.

LP 2, 141-4; 175; *PL* 129, 9-744 (translations, etc.); *MGEp* 7, 395-442; A. Lapôtre, *De Anastasio Bibliothecario sedis apostolicae* (Paris, 1885); E. Perels, *Papst Nikolaus I und Anastasius Bibliothecarius* (Berlin, 1920); P. Devos, 'Anastase le Bibliothécaire: sa contribution à la correspondance pontificale; la date de sa mort', *Byzantion* 32 (1962), 97-115; *DBI* 3, 25-37 (G. Arnaldi); *Z*1, 42-7; *NCE* 1, 480 f. (P. Devos); Seppelt 2, 229-33; 243; 278; 289 f. 303.

NICHOLAS I, ST (24 Apr. 858-13 Nov. 867). Born in Rome *c*.820, son of a leading city official named Theodore, he wielded increasing influence in the Lateran under SERGIUS II and LEO IV, and was the trusted counsellor of BENEDICT III. On Benedict's death, after the cardinal priest HADRIAN (to be his successor) had refused to stand, he was elected in the presence and with the approval of Emperor Louis II (855-75), who had hastened to Rome immediately he heard of the pope's death (17 Apr. 858). A

man of commanding personality and formidable energy, he held an exalted view of the papal office inherited from LEO I, GELASIUS I, and GREGORY I. For him the pope was God's representative on earth with authority over the whole church, synods serving merely as organs for carrying out his decisions; and while the spheres of church and state were distinct and any interference by princes in the former was to be condemned, the church had the right to watch over and influence the state, and to look to it for protection and support.

A determination to make the papacy thus conceived a reality animated all his actions. First, he asserted his authority over metropolitans who resented papal intervention. A notorious example was John, archbishop of Ravenna (850-61), who in the tradition of his see acted as if he enjoyed autonomy from Rome, interfering with his suffragans, abusing the pope's subjects and agents, and refusing to obey his summons. Nicholas excommunicated and deposed him (24 Feb. 861), only restoring him after he had sworn (Nov. 861) to be subject to Rome in future. Nicholas clashed even more sharply with Hincmar, archbishop of Rheims (845-82), the most powerful metropolitan in the empire, insisting on reviewing and revising the cases of deposed clergy who had appealed to Rome. Thus he ordered a re-examination of the deposition of Bishop Rothad of Soissons (d. 869) by Hincmar in 862, and in Jan. 865 rehabilitated and reinstated him. On this occasion he invoked the so-called False Decretals, attributed to Isidore of Seville (d. 636), which were in fact compiled *c*.850 in France, and which purported to defend the rights of diocesan bishops against their metropolitans and to assert the superiority of the pope over the authority of synods and metropolitans; it remains a question whether he was aware that they were forgeries.

An uncompromising defender of the sanctity of marriage, he did not hesitate to intervene when Theutberga, repudiated on a false charge of incest by her husband

Lothair II of Lorraine (855–69), appealed to him. A synod at Aachen (29 Apr. 862) had sanctioned the divorce, while another at Metz (June 863), attended by papal legates who yielded to bribes, ratified Lothair's new marriage to his mistress Waldrada. When Archbishops Gunthar of Cologne (d. 873) and Theutgaud of Trier (d. 868) brought the synodal decrees to Rome, Nicholas's fury knew no bounds; he not only quashed the decisions but, creating a precedent, deposed and excommunicated the two archbishops for conniving at bigamy. Emperor Louis II took up their cause and threatened Rome with troops, forcing Nicholas to seek refuge in St Peter's, but in the end Louis had to give way and constrain the archbishops to accept their sentence. Lothair was obliged to submit and be reconciled, at any rate temporarily, with his wife. The pope's moral victory was complete.

Nicholas was no less vigorous in asserting Rome's supremacy in the east. Not only did he seek to revive its long obsolete jurisdiction over Illyricum, but when Ignatius, patriarch of Constantinople (847–58; 867–77), was forced to abdicate (late 858) and was replaced by the brilliant layman Photius (858–67; 878–86), the pope complained to Emperor Michael III (846–67) and dispatched envoys to Constantinople to investigate the matter, meanwhile refusing to recognize Photius. When the envoys reported in Photius's favour he disavowed them, and after being one-sidedly informed by Ignatius's supporters, deposed and excommunicated Photius at a synod held in the Lateran in Aug. 863. When the emperor angrily protested, Nicholas sent him (28 Sept. 865) a stinging rebuke, defending his actions and expounding at vast length the inalienable rights of the holy see. Meanwhile relations were further exacerbated when Nicholas, responding to an appeal from its king Boris I (d. 907), dispatched missionary bishops (including Bishop FORMOSUS of Porto) to Bulgaria and supplied it with detailed advice, often anti-Byzantine in tone, on moral and canonical

issues; as Formosus was already bishop of Porto, Nicholas refused to name him archbishop in Bulgaria. As Bulgaria fell largely within the spiritual jurisdiction of Constantinople and had recently been evangelized by Byzantine missionaries, Photius was understandably indignant. After denouncing the Latin intervention to the patriarchs of the east, he held a synod at Constantinople (Aug.–Sept. 867) which pronounced Nicholas excommunicate and deposed. The pope was dead before the news reached Rome, but the sentence he had pronounced on Photius and the one Photius had pronounced on him inevitably contributed to the final separation of east and west.

Nicholas was extensively assisted, in his policies as well as his correspondence, by his able secretary, ANASTASIUS the Librarian, the disgraced antipope whom he had rehabilitated, but the responsibility for them remained his own. An outstanding and masterful pontiff, he was immensely respected by his contemporaries, and was able to strike awe into the most powerful princes and prelates. Through his efforts the papacy came to be recognized, for a brief moment, as the supreme authority in the void created in the west by the steady erosion of the imperial power since its partition (treaty of Verdun) in 843; while his assured claim to override the decisions of metropolitans anticipated the complete doctrine of papal theocracy. Shortly after his death his successor Hadrian II advised the bishops attending the synod of Troyes (8 May 868) to have his name included in the prayers at mass, but it was not formally inserted in the Roman Martyrology until 1630. Feast 13 Nov.

LP 2, 151–72; JW 1, 341–68; *PL* 119, 753–1212; *MGE*p 6, 257–690; *DTC* 11, 506–26 (E. Amann); *NCE* 10, 441 (H. G. J. Beck); *LThK* 7, 976 f. (T. Schieffer); *BSS* 9, 860–9 (P. Rabikauskas); *PRE* 14, 68–72 (H. Böhmer); Seppelt 2, 241–88; F. A. Norwood, 'The Political Pretensions of Pope Nicholas I', *ChHist*15 (1946), 271–85; F. Dvornik, 'The Patriarch Photius and the Roman Primacy', *Chicago Studies* 2 (1963), 94–107; *The*

Photian Schism (Cambridge 1948); Mann 3,
1–148.

HADRIAN II (14 Dec. 867–Nov. or Dec.
872). Born in Rome in 792, of the same
aristocratic family as STEPHEN IV and
SERGIUS II, he was married before ordination, was made subdeacon and in 842 cardinal priest of S. Marco by GREGORY IV,
and subsequently held such important positions in the Lateran and was so highly
regarded because of his charitableness that
he was twice, in 855 and 858, proposed as
pope but declined office. On NICHOLAS I's
death (13 Nov. 867), after violent disputes
between critics and supporters of the late
pope's forceful policies, he accepted election as a compromise candidate. Although
Emperor Louis II (855–75), then fighting
the Saracens in south Italy, readily gave his
consent, Hadrian's reign started disastrously with the pillaging of Rome, for
reasons not fully explained, by Duke Lambert of Spoleto. His own daughter, too, was
raped and then brutally murdered with her
mother by a brother of ANASTASIUS, the
former antipope whom he had made papal
archivist. As Anastasius was suspected of
complicity in the affair, Hadrian felt obliged
to dismiss and then (12 Oct. 868) formally
excommunicate him, but it was typical of
him that less than a year later he restored
him to his offices in his chancery.

Elderly and vacillating, Hadrian had
neither the strength of character nor the
personal impressiveness to maintain the
papacy at the glittering heights to which
Nicholas I had raised it. He showed weakness in dealing with the burning issue of the
broken marriage of King Lothair II (855–
69) of Lorraine, on which Nicholas had
taken a firm line, for while pressing the king
to take back his lawful wife Theutberga, he
accepted his assurances of compliance and
admitted him to communion pending a
council which would reach a final decision
on the affair. Again, in return for assurances
he lifted the excommunication Nicholas
had imposed on Lothair's mistress Waldrada. On Lothair's death (8 Aug. 869) he

struggled ineffectually to secure the succession for Louis II, only to see Lorraine
divided (treaty of Meerssen, 870) between
Louis's uncles Charles the Bald (823–77)
and Louis the German (c.806–76), and to
receive himself a sharp rebuke for interfering. Equally ineffectual were his attempts to
bring civil and ecclesiastical disputes in the
Carolingian realms before the papal court.
His imperious demands, drafted
intemperately by Anastasius, met with even
more imperious warnings from Archbishop
Hincmar of Rheims (845–82) against intervening where he had no title to do so. The
pope had to make a shameful climbdown,
privately disowning the letters his secretary
had written and even holding out to Charles
the prospect of the imperial crown on Louis
II's death.

Apprised of the sentence of deposition
and excommunication pronounced on
Nicholas I in 867 by Photius, then patriarch
of Constantinople but recently deposed,
Hadrian held a synod in June 869 which
anathematized him and his associates for
their unexampled impudence. On the invitation of Emperor Basil I (867–86) he sent
two personal representatives to the fourth
council of Constantinople (869–70: since
the 12th cent. recognized in the west as the
Eighth General Council), although they
were not allowed to preside as he had
requested; Anastasius represented Louis II.
This council fully upheld the Roman
synod's condemnation of Photius, but also
(canon 21) placed the great patriarchates in
the order of precedence accepted in the
east: Rome, Constantinople, Alexandria,
Antioch, Jerusalem. Rome had hitherto
objected to Constantinople being placed
ahead of Alexandria, but the success of the
council temporarily restored peace between
east and west. Three days after its closure,
however, the delegates of the eastern
patriarchates, summoned by Emperor
Basil, ruled, in the teeth of protests from the
papal envoys, that Bulgaria fell under the
ecclesiastical jurisdiction of Constantinople, not of Rome as Nicholas I had
claimed. A Byzantine metropolitan was

consecrated for it, the Latin priests working there were expelled, and a fresh source of conflict was opened up; Bulgaria was lost to the Roman church. As a compensation for this reverse Hadrian was able, by sanctioning the use of Old Slavonic in the liturgy when the missionary brothers Cyril (d. 869) and Methodius (d. 885), renowned as Apostles of the Slavs, visited Rome in 867/ 8, and later by consecrating Methodius as archbishop of Sirmium (Sremska Mitrovica in Yugoslavia) and legate to the Slavs, to retain Moravia for the western church.

Hadrian's last recorded act was to re-crown Louis II in St Peter's at Pentecost (18 May) 872, a gesture intended to show his continued confidence in the emperor after his humiliating imprisonment by Duke Adelgis of Benevento; at the same time he released him from his vow, extorted from him by force, to take no action to avenge his maltreatment. Hadrian died at an undetermined date between mid-Nov. and 13 Dec. 872.

LP 2, 173–90; JW 1, 368–75; PL 122, 1259–320; MGEp 6, 691–765; 7, 403–5; 499; DHGE 1, 619–24 (A. Noyon); DBI 1, 323–9 (O. Bertolini); EC 1, 341–4 (I. Daniele); PRE 7, 305–7 (R. Zoepfl and C. Mirbt); Seppelt 2, 302–6; Brezzi, 50; 65–70; NCE 1, 145 (A. J. Ennis); Mann 3, 149–230.

JOHN VIII (14 Dec. 872–16 Dec. 882).

A Roman, son of Gundo, for twenty years archdeacon, the close collaborator of NICHOLAS I, he was elected at an uncertain interval after HADRIAN II's death. Although elderly, he was energetic, resourceful, and highly experienced; in a crowded reign he struggled to uphold the papal leadership with GREGORY the Great and Nicholas I as his inspiration.

Externally the urgent need was to defend Italy and the papal state against the destructive raids of the Saracens, based in south Italy. Not content with appeals to others for help, John personally took charge of military operations, building a defensive wall around St Paul's basilica and commanding a small papal fleet which he founded. He worked tirelessly to unite the states of southern Italy against the Muslim menace, but when his efforts came to nothing through their collusion with the invaders, he too was reduced to buying them off with tribute. For a time he had an ally in Emperor Louis II (855–75), but on his death (12 Aug. 875) he got the clergy and senate of Rome to acclaim Louis's uncle Charles the Bald (823–77) as emperor, reckoning he would be more helpful to Rome than his half-brother Louis the German (c.806–76). He crowned him emperor at Christmas 875; Charles in return not only extended the boundaries of the papal state, but renounced the emperor's right to have resident envoys in the city and a guiding hand in papal elections. Soon after (Apr. 876), to secure his position in Rome against the intrigues and plots of power-hungry nobles, John excommunicated the most dangerous of them in their absence. They included FORMOSUS, bishop of Porto, successful missionary to Bulgaria and future pope, whom he also suspected of aspiring to the papacy and (although he had earlier trusted him) in 878 degraded and exiled.

Before long the failure of John's policies became evident. Not only did Charles's help prove inadequate, but when Carloman (828–80), Louis the German's son, marched into Italy to assert his dynastic claims, Charles retreated and died while crossing the Alps (6 Oct. 877). Carloman, now master of Italy, demanded the imperial crown, and John played for time. When Carloman fell ill and had to withdraw, his supporters, Dukes Lambert of Spoleto and Adalbert of Tuscia, accompanied by John's excommunicated enemies, occupied Rome, imprisoned him, and forced the citizens to vow allegiance to Carloman. John refused all concessions, however, and when he had secured his liberty made by ship for Provence and manoeuvred to find a suitable heir for the imperial crown. Disappointed first in Louis the Stammerer (846–79), whom he crowned on 7 Sept. 878 but who died on 10 Apr. 879, then in Louis II's brother-in-law Boso (d. 887), he finally settled, in spite of his repugnance for the German Franks, for Louis the German's second son Charles the Fat (839–88), recognizing him as king of Italy in 879 and crowning him as emperor in Feb. 881. As a result of these moves the pope emerged as effective arbiter of the imperial office.

The desperate need for help from whatever quarter against the Saracens encouraged John to seek a *rapprochement* with Constantinople. The difficulty here was that Photius, whom Hadrian II had anathematized in 869, had been restored as patriarch and Emperor Basil I (867–86) was requesting Rome to recognize him as such. John agreed to do so, and to send legates to the council that Basil wanted, on the strict condition that Photius publicly apologized for his past misdeeds and that Constantinople abandoned its claim to jurisdiction in Bulgaria. When the council met in Haghia Sophia in Nov. 879 with Photius presiding, these conditions had already been recognized as unrealistic, and the papal letters containing them were drastically modified in the Greek translations read out, although the passages stressing the papal primacy were left virtually intact. Skilfully managed, the council, recognized in the east as the Eighth General Council, pronounced the second council of *Nicaea (787) the Seventh General Council, annulled the synods which had anathematized Photius, reaffirmed the creed of Constantinople (381), and forbade any additions to it; the Romans could assent because there was no discussion of the doctrine of the double procession of the Holy Spirit, and the creed used in Rome did not yet include the *Filioque*. John was statesman enough to ratify its decisions with the saving postscript that he rejected everything his legates might have agreed contrary to his instructions. In fact, he had secured peace between the churches, and the Byzantine military aid he needed; and while the council had brushed aside the Bulgarian question, the compromise agreed in practice (though it proved ineffective because of the striving of the Bulgars for an auton-

omous church) was that Bulgaria should be subject to Roman jurisdiction but Greek missionaries working there should not be disturbed.

Often considered a largely political pope, John was not neglectful of his duties as a churchman. A striking initiative, frustrated by Hincmar, archbishop of Rheims (845–82), was his appointment of Anségise of Sens in Jan. 876 as his vicar for Gaul and Germany. He frequently intervened with authority in the nomination, or again condemnation, of bishops, and was in general a forceful promoter of the indissolubility of marriage and the freedom of episcopal elections. When Methodius (d. 885), the apostle of Moravia, clashed with the German clergy and was imprisoned, he obtained (873) his release, and although at first forbidding him to use Slavonic in the liturgy, he sanctioned it in June 880 when Methodius, summoned to Rome on a charge of heresy, completely vindicated himself.

The first pope to be assassinated, John was, according to the Annals of Fulda, poisoned by members of his entourage and then clubbed to death.

LP 2, 221–3; JW 1, 376–442; *MG*Ep 7, 1–133; *DTC* 8, 601–13 (É. Amann); *NCE* 7, 1009 f. (C. E. Sheedy); *LThK* 5, 988 f. (Th. Schieffer); *PRE* 9, 258–61 (H. Böhmer); F. Dvornik, *The Photian Schism* (Cambridge, 1948), 172–225; Seppelt 2, 305–29; D. Lohrmann, *Das Register Papst Johannes VIII* (Tübingen, 1968); A. Lapôtre, *L'Europe et le saint siège à l'époque carolingien: le pape Jean VIII* (Paris, 1895); F. E. Endgreen, 'Pope John VIII and the Arabs', *Speculum* 20 (1945), 318–30; Mann 3, 231–352; Brezzi, 69–80.

MARINUS I (16 Dec. 882–15 May 884). Sometimes mistakenly listed as Martin II, he was son of a priest and born at Gallese, in Tuscany, entered the service of the Roman church when twelve years old, was made deacon by NICHOLAS I, and as such proved the most effective of three legates representing HADRIAN II at the fourth council of Constantinople (869–70), which anathematized the recently deposed patriarch Photius (858–67; 878–86). On this occasion he had a sharp brush with Emperor Basil I (867–86) through refusing to depart from Hadrian's instructions. Later he became archdeacon and treasurer (*arcarius*) of the Roman church, and also bishop of Caere (now Cerveteri) in Etruria. JOHN VIII used him for difficult missions to the future Emperor Charles III (the Fat, 881–7) in Mar. 880, and in 882 to Athanasius of Naples, when he succeeded in breaking the bishop's alliance with the Saracens. When he succeeded John, he was the first bishop of another see to be elected pope in violation of the ancient canons (notably canon 15 of *Nicaea) prohibiting the translations of bishops from one see to another (a prohibition to which Nicholas I had appealed when refusing to appoint Bishop FORMOSUS of Porto, later to be pope, to the archbishopric of Bulgaria).

Marinus's election was carried through without consulting Charles III, but when the emperor visited Italy in June 883 Marinus met him at Nonantula, near Modena, secured his recognition, and held important discussions with him. One result of these was his decision to pardon Formosus of Porto and others accused of conspiring against John VIII, whom John had excommunicated and exiled, and to restore Formosus to his see and to release him from the vows he had sworn under duress to the pope. The belief that he refused to announce his election to Photius, reinstated as patriarch in 878, and that he and Photius excommunicated each other, is unfounded; Photius did his best to be reconciled to his former enemies, and Marinus went out of his way to retain Zacharias of Anagni, a friend of Photius and a supporter of pro-Greek policies at Rome, in the key position of papal librarian. A further result of his conversations with Charles III was that, exasperated by the pressure of Duke Guido III of Spoleto (crowned emperor in 891: d. 894) on the papal patrimony, he persuaded the emperor to pronounce a sentence of deposition on him.

Little else is known of Marinus's short reign, except that he had to settle a dispute between the archbishops of Rheims and Sens over a newly founded monastery, and that he entertained excellent relations with Alfred the Great of England (849–99), out of regard for whom he exempted the *Schola Saxonum*, or English quarter in Rome, from taxes.

JW 1, 425 f.; 2, 704; *LP* 2, 224; *PL* 126, 966–70; *DTC* 9, 2476 f. (E. Amann); *PRE* 12, 340 (H. Böhmer); *NCE* 9, 222 (V. Gellhaus); Brezzi, 83 f.; Mann 3, 353–60; Seppelt 2, 297 f.; 331 f.; J. Duhr, 'Le pape Martin I: était-il évêque ou archidiacre lors de son élection?', *RSR* 24 (1934), 200–6.

HADRIAN III, ST (17 May 884–mid-Sept. 885). Born in Rome, the son of one Benedict, he succeeded MARINUS I in circumstances which remain obscure. Almost nothing is known of his short reign, but he seems to have been sympathetic to the policies of JOHN VIII, for one of his few recorded acts was his blinding of a high official of the Lateran palace, George of the Aventine, one of John's sworn enemies whom Marinus had permitted to return from exile. The report of his having a noble lady, perhaps the widow of another dignitary who had been murdered at the accession of Marinus, whipped naked through the streets suggests the continuance of the bloody vendettas which prevailed at the time of John's assassination. Like John and Marinus, Hadrian adopted a conciliatory approach to the east, sending Patriarch Photius (878–86) the customary letter announcing his election. In summer 885 Emperor Charles the Fat (881–8), who had no legitimate male heir and wished to secure the succession for his bastard son Bernard, summoned him to attend the imperial diet at Worms to settle the matter, and Hadrian set out from Rome entrusting its protection and government during his absence to the imperial envoy, John, bishop of Pavia. This fact suggests that there was already an understanding that, in return for his help over the succession, the emperor would give him his full backing in his struggle with his internal enemies. Any such plans, however, were cut short by his death at S. Cesario sul Panaro, near Modena. Foul play has been suspected, and it is significant that his body was not brought back to Rome but was buried in the abbey of Nonantula. His cultus developed locally and was approved by the holy see on 2 June 1891. Feast 8 July.

LP 2, 225; JW 1, 426 f.; DBI 1, 329 f. (O. Bertolini); BSS 1, 271 f. (F. Carotta); DHGE 1, 624 (A. Noyon); NCE 1, 145 f. (A. J. Ennis); LThK 4, 1307 (G. Schwaiger); Mann 3, 360–6; Seppelt 2, 332.

STEPHEN V (VI) (Sept. 885–14 Sept. 891). A Roman of aristocratic family who entered the Lateran under HADRIAN II, he was cardinal priest of SS. Quattro Coronati when he was elected by acclamation by the clergy and leading laity. Emperor Charles the Fat (881–8), annoyed because he had not been consulted about the election and preferring a creature of his own, sent his chancellor Liutward to Rome to have him deposed. Stephen, however, was able to satisfy Liutward that he had been the unanimous choice of the electors and that the resident imperial envoy had even assisted him to take possession of the papal palace. The matter was dropped.

After carrying out a thorough purge and reorganization of the Lateran, Stephen invited Charles to come to Italy to fulfil his duties as protector of the church; he was threatened by party strife in Rome and by increasing Saracen raids. Charles made the journey in spring 886, but was almost at once obliged to recross the Alps to deal with trouble in France. The help which Stephen urgently needed never came. In Nov. next year Charles was deposed, and when he died on 13 Jan. 888 the empire of Charlemagne finally disintegrated. Desperate for a protector, Stephen first (890) summoned Arnulf (c.850–99), Charles's nephew, who had been proclaimed king of the East Franks in 887, to rescue Italy from the devastations of 'pagans and evil Christians'. As Arnulf, occupied with other tasks, could do nothing for the moment, Stephen made a drastic change of papal

policy and drew closer to Guido III, duke of Spoleto (d. 894), who had seized the throne of Italy in 889; he adopted him as son and eventually (21 Feb. 891) was induced, probably by fear, to crown him Holy Roman emperor in St Peter's. But while Guido entered into the customary pact guaranteeing the privileges of the Roman church, he had effectively secured the supremacy over the papal state for which he had striven.

Although his reign was a mainly political one, Stephen forcefully asserted his authority over bishops in France and Germany. Like his immediate predecessors, he maintained friendly relations with Constantinople, all the more closely as he needed military aid from it. Although he had to reprove Emperor Basil I (867–86) for hostile references to MARINUS I, he was on good terms with him personally, asking him to send warships to defend the coasts of the papal state against Saracen attacks and cooperating with Byzantium against the Muslim peril. When Basil was succeeded by Leo VI (886–912) and the great patriarch Photius (858–67; 878–86) had to abdicate, Stephen seems to have acknowledged the new patriarch, Stephen I (the emperor's brother).

The victim of intrigues he did not understand, Stephen missed a great opportunity in Moravia, where Archbishop Methodius, apostle of the Slavs and promoter of the Slavonic liturgy, had died on 6 Apr. 885. He had designated his disciple Goradz as his successor, but influenced by German clergy the pope summoned Goradz to Rome, forbade the Slavonic liturgy, and appointed Bishop Wiching of Nitra, Methodius's suffragan, as administrator of the metropolitan see. The Moravian church was to be organized according to the wishes of the German hierarchy. As a result the small group of Methodius's disciples were unable to maintain themselves and escaped to Bulgaria, where they reverted to the Byzantine rite in the Slavonic tongue. The foundations were thus laid for a Slav-speaking church which would eventually spread to include Russia, but which was alien from

Rome and maintained close ties with Orthodoxy.

LP 2, 191–8; JW 1, 427–35; 2, 705; NCE 13, 696 (P. J. Mullins); LThK 9, 1040 (G. Schwaiger); DHGE 15, 1194–6 (A. Dumas); F. Dvornik, Les Slaves, Byzance et Rome au ixe siècle (Paris, 1926); The Photian Schism (Cambridge, 1948), 219–37 and passim; G. Lahr, 'Das Schreiben Stephans V und Sventopulk von Mähren', NA 47, 1928, 159–73; Seppelt 2, 333–8; Mann 3, 367–401.

FORMOSUS (6 Oct. 891–4 Apr. 896). Born c.815, probably at Rome, gifted and well educated, named bishop of Porto in 864, he proved such a brilliant missionary in Bulgaria in 866–7 that King Boris I (852–89) pressed NICHOLAS I, and then HADRIAN II, to appoint him metropolitan of the country; both popes refused because of the canons prohibiting the translation of bishops. He served as papal legate in France and Germany under Nicholas I and Hadrian II, and played a leading role at the Roman synod of July 869 which anathematized the great Byzantine patriarch Photius (858–67; 878–86). JOHN VIII entrusted him in 875 with the task of offering the imperial crown to Charles II the Bald (875–7), but soon became suspicious and hostile for personal and political reasons. In Apr. 876 he had him excommunicated and deposed on charges of treason, deserting his see (he had fled Rome for safety), and aspiring to the papacy; but in Aug. 878 he admitted him to lay communion after he had abjectly avowed his guilt and sworn to remain in exile permanently and never to attempt to regain his see. In the reaction after John's death MARINUS I recalled him from exile in France, rehabilitated him, and restored him as bishop of Porto. As such he was a consecrator of STEPHEN V in 885, and on Stephen's death, though advanced in years, was himself elected pope. The fact that he was already bishop of another see was not held against him until after his death.

Formosus was active in strengthening and advancing Christianity in England and north Germany. In 893 he confirmed Adalgar in possession of the united see of Bremen–Hamburg against the protests of the archbishop of Cologne, and he defended the Carolingian Charles the Simple (879–929) against Eudes, count of Paris and then (888–98) king of France. He maintained amicable relations with Constantinople and in 892 attempted to heal the schism between the fanatical disciples of the former patriarch Ignatius (d. 877) and Patriarch Stephen I, whom they rejected as having been ordained by Photius; he proposed that the ordinations of Photius's first patriarchate should be treated as invalid, but those of his second patriarchate as valid. The compromise was well intended but unrealistic, and came to nothing. He faced difficult political problems in Italy, however, his predecessor having crowned Duke Guido III of Spoleto (d. 894) as emperor. In Apr. 892 he was forced to re-crown Guido at Ravenna and at the same time to crown his son Lambert (d. 898) as co-emperor. The dominance of the Spoletan dynasty, however, boded no good for the holy see, and as early as autumn 893 he was appealing to Arnulf, king of the East Franks (c.850–99), to rescue Rome from its tyranny. After repeated appeals Arnulf eventually invaded Italy and in Feb. 896 stormed Rome. Guido being now dead, Formosus crowned Arnulf in St Peter's in mid-Feb. 896. But the campaign they planned against Spoleto never materialized, for Arnulf was struck down by paralysis and had to abandon Rome and return to Germany; soon after his departure Formosus himself was dead.

A man of exceptional intelligence, exemplary life, and strict asceticism (the only fault alleged against him was ambition), Formosus had bitter and relentless foes who included Lambert, once more ruler of Rome, and his own successor STEPHEN VI, and who did not scruple to subject him to the most macabre humiliation. Nine months (Jan. 897) after his death they had his decaying corpse exhumed and, propped up on a throne in full pontifical vestments, solemnly arraigned at a mock trial presided over by Stephen VI himself; a deacon stood by answering the charges on his behalf. He was found guilty of perjury, of having coveted the papal throne, and of having violated the canons forbidding the translation of bishops. His acts and ordinations were pronounced null and void, and his body (the three fingers of his right hand which he had used to swear and bless having been hacked off) was first placed in a common grave and then flung into the Tiber. A hermit subsequently retrieved and reinterred it.

JW 1, 435–9; MGEp 7, 366–70; PL 129, 837–48; E. Dümmler, Auxilius und Vulgarius (Leipzig, 1866); J. Duhr, 'Le concile de Ravenne en 898; la réhabilitation du pape Formose', RSR 22 (1932), 541–79; 'Humble vestige d'un grand espoir deçu: épisode de la vie de Formose', ibid. 42 (1954), 361–87; G. Arnaldi, 'Papa Formoso e gli imperatori della casa di Spoleto', Annali della Facoltà di Lettere di Napoli 1 (1951), 84–104; Seppelt 2, 309 f.; 337–47; Mann 4, 42–72; DTC 6, 594–9 (F. Vernet); LThK 4, 214 f. (G. Schwaiger); Z1, 47–73; NCE 5, 1024 (S. P. Lindemans).

BONIFACE VI (Apr. 896). A Roman by birth, son of a bishop named Hadrian, he was elected almost immediately after the death of FORMOSUS, probably on 11 Apr. 896. His past had been murky, for he had been twice degraded by JOHN VIII, first as subdeacon and then, after rehabilitation, as priest, for immorality; after his second unfrocking he had not been restored. His election was forced through by the rioting populace, and may have represented hostility to the absent German emperor, Arnulf (896–9), and his resident governor Farold. The victim of severe gout, he died after fifteen days, and was buried in the portico of the popes in St Peter's. The Roman synod held by JOHN IX in 898 deplored, and prohibited the repetition of, such an uncanonical promotion.

LP 2, 228; JW 1, 439; Mansi 18, 223 f.; PL 135, 829 (Flodoard of Rheims); DBI 12, 142 f. (P. Bertolini); DHGE 9, 899 f. (F. Baix); EC 2, 1866 (P. Goggi); NCE 2, 670 (A. T. Ennis); Seppelt 2, 341.

STEPHEN VI (VII) (May 896–Aug. 897). Nothing is known of his background except that he was a Roman by birth, son of a

presbyter, and was consecrated bishop of Anagni by FORMOSUS, whose implacable foe he nevertheless became. Although originally loyal to the German emperor Arnulf (896–9), crowned by Formosus on 22 Feb. 896, he switched his allegiance to Lambert of Spoleto (d. 898), whom Formosus had crowned as co-emperor with his father Guido III (d. 894) in 892, when after Arnulf's paralysis and return to Germany Lambert emerged as ruler of Italy. The sole important event of his reign which has been recorded is the macabre 'cadaver synod' over which he presided in Jan. 897, and which was instigated in part by Lambert and his mother Ageltrude, resentful against Formosus for having crowned Arnulf, but also by the bitter personal animosity which he and a powerful faction of Romans nourished against the dead pontiff. At this mock trial Formosus's disinterred corpse, clad in full papal vestments and propped up on a throne, was solemnly arraigned on charges of perjury, violating the canons prohibiting the translation of bishops, and coveting the papacy. A deacon stood by and answered for him. Formosus was found guilty, and all his acts were declared null and void, including his ordinations; his body was finally flung into the Tiber. While Stephen's participation in this gruesome affair can only be explained by near-hysterical hatred, it is evident that he personally profited by the nullification of Formosus's acts since the resulting cancellation of his own consecration as bishop of Anagni swept away any objections that might be raised, under the canon law of the time, to his elevation to the papacy.

In the following months Stephen was active in requiring clergy ordained by Formosus to produce letters renouncing their orders as invalid. His appalling conduct, however, did not long remain unpunished. A few months later there was a popular reaction, and the outraged supporters of Formosus, encouraged by reports of miracles worked by his humiliated corpse, perhaps also interpreting the sudden collapse of the Lateran basilica as a divine judgement, rose in rebellion, deposed Stephen, stripped him of his papal insignia, and threw him into gaol, where he was shortly afterwards strangled.

JW 1, 439 f.; 2, 705; *LP* 2, 229; E. Dümmler, *Auxilius und Vulgarius* (Leipzig, 1866); J. Duhr, 'Le concile de Ravenne en 898', *RSR* 22 (1932), esp. 576–8; Seppelt 2, 341–3; 346; 349; *DHGE* 15, 1196 f. (A. Dumas); *NCE* 13, 696 (P. J. Mullins).

ROMANUS (Aug.–Nov. 897: d. ?). Nothing is known of his background except that he was born at Gallese, near Città Castellana, and became cardinal priest of S. Pietro in Vincoli. When the outraged partisans of the posthumously humiliated FORMOSUS had deposed, imprisoned, and murdered STEPHEN VI, he was elected as his successor at a date which cannot be precisely ascertained. Virtually nothing is known of his reign except that he was a pro-Formosan, and that he bestowed the *pallium on Vitalis, patriarch of Grado, and on the request of their bishops confirmed the sees of Elne, in Rousillon, and Gerona, in Spain, in the possession of their property. He was pope for only four months; according to one recension of *LP*, he 'was afterwards made a monk', i.e. confined in a monastery. If this report rests on reliable tradition, it suggests that he was deposed by the pro-Formosan faction, presumably to make way for a pope who would take more energetic steps to vindicate their hero. On any supposition the date of his death is not known.

JW 1, 441; *LP* 2, 230; Mansi 18, 186–8; E. Dümmler, *Auxilius und Vulgarius* (Leipzig, 1866); Seppelt 2, 342; *DTC* 13, 2847 (É. Amann); *NCE* 12, 641 (P. J. Mullins); Z1, 59.

THEODORE II (Nov. 897). Nothing is known of his background or earlier career except that he was a Roman by birth. In the violent reaction in favour of the posthumously humiliated FORMOSUS which overthrew STEPHEN VI, he was elected to replace the short-lived ROMANUS. Described as a man who loved peace, he reigned for only twenty days, the exact dates of his accession and death being unknown. Even so, he threw himself energetically into the task of restoring some kind of order into the confused situation in which the Roman church found itself. First, he held a synod which effectively annulled the *'cadaver synod' of Jan. 897 at which the corpse of Formosus had been subjected to a macabre mock trial, completely rehabilitating the dead pope, recognizing the validity of his ordinations, and ordering the burning of the letters of renunciation which the men it had ordained had been compelled by Stephen VI to sign. Secondly, he arranged for Formosus's body, cast up by the Tiber into which it had been flung and then clandestinely interred, to be exhumed afresh, reclothed in pontifical vestments, and reburied, with as much honour as possible, in its original grave in St Peter's. The cause of his early death is not known.

LP 2, 231; JW 1, 441; Mansi 18, 221; E. Dümmler, *Auxilius und Vulgarius* (Leipzig, 1866); *DTC* 15, 226 (É. Amann); *NCE* 14, 17 (C. M. Aherne); Seppelt 2, 342 f.; Z1, 59 f.

JOHN IX (Jan. 898–Jan. 900). On the death of THEODORE II the partisans of STEPHEN VI, sworn foes of his posthumously condemned victim FORMOSUS, seized the initiative and elected SERGIUS, bishop of Caere (Cerveteri), as pope. Although he took possession of the Lateran, the Formosan party, with help from Lambert of Spoleto, king of Italy since 891, whom Formosus had crowned emperor on 30 Apr. 892, forcibly expelled him and elected John, a Benedictine monk born at Tivoli, whom Formosus had ordained. The scanty records of this turbulent period have left the course of events and their dates obscure.

With co-operation from the emperor, who controlled Rome and most of Italy, John at once continued Theodore's policy of restoring order in the confused situation arising out of Stephen VI's trial of the dead Formosus and the ensuing violent clashes between Formosans and anti-Formosans. He convened a synod at Rome, attended also by bishops from north Italy, which annulled the *'cadaver synod's' sentence on Formosus and burned its acts; those who had taken part in it were pardoned after pleading that they had done so under duress; only Sergius and five close associates were deposed and placed under a ban. The trial of dead persons was prohibited in future. Formosus's ordinations were recognized as valid, as was his anointing of Lambert as emperor; but his anointing of Arnulf, king of the East Franks, as emperor was rejected as 'barbaric' and as having been extracted from him by force. The prohibition of the translation of bishops was confirmed, the case of Formosus being treated as exceptional. To prevent disorders at papal elections it was decreed (reviving the *constitution of Emperor Lothair I of 824) that in future, while the pope should be elected by bishops and clergy on the request of the senate and people, his consecration could only take place in the presence of imperial emissaries.

Shortly afterwards John held a second, more numerously attended, synod at Ravenna, in the presence and under the protection of Emperor Lambert, which confirmed these decisions and sought to ensure the support of the Spoletan royal house for the Roman church. In particular, the synod provided every Roman, clerical or lay, with the right to appeal to the emperor and restored his supreme jurisdiction. In return Lambert renewed the ancient privileges of the holy see and guaranteed its territorial possessions, his own position as overlord being ensured. The bright prospects which these agreements seemed to hold out were cruelly dashed when the young emperor was unexpectedly killed in a hunting accident on 15 Oct. 898.

An important letter of John's indicates that he either prepared or at any rate ratified the reconciliation in the Byzantine church of the schismatic followers of Patriarch Ignatius (d. 877) with Patriarch Antony Cauleas (893–901). In it the pope assured Metropolitan Stylianos, leader of the Ignatian faction, that Rome fully recognized

'Ignatius, Photius [i.e. at least his second patriarchate from 877–86], Stephen, and Antony', and exhorted him to live in communion with clergy ordained by them. In Moravia, where the arrangements made by STEPHEN V had collapsed, John tried to restore order by sending an archbishop and two legates, only to be reproached by the bishops of Bavaria for intruding. But in 906 the Moravian state was to fall in pieces before the Magyar invaders. In France he restored Argrinus of Langres, deposed by Stephen VI, to his see. He is recorded as having confirmed the privileges of the great abbey of Monte Cassino, province of Frosinone, founded by St Benedict (c.480–c.550) in 529.

LP 2, 232; JW 1, 442 f.; 445; 2, 705; PL 131, 27–46; MGLeges I, 562–5; E. Dümmler, Auxilius und Vulgarius (Leipzig, 1866); F. Dvornik, The Photian Schism (Cambridge, 1948), 262–71; J. Duhr, 'Le concile de Ravenne en 898', RSR 22 (1932), 541–79; DTC 8, 614–16 (É. Amann); LThK 5, 989 (G. Schwaiger); NCE 7, 1010 (P. J. Mullins); EC 6, 584 f. (G. B. Picotti); Seppelt 2, 343–5; Mann 4, 91–102.

BENEDICT IV (May/June 900–Aug. 903). An upper-class Roman, son of Mammolus, he succeeded JOHN IX at a time when Rome was still racked by internecine strife between devotees and haters of the posthumously condemned FORMOSUS. The paucity of records, the result mainly of the prevailing turbulence, makes the circumstances and date of his election uncertain. Apart from the fact that, like John IX, he had been ordained by Formosus and counted as a Formosan, only a handful of scraps of isolated information survive about his reign. Thus, following the line taken by his predecessor, he held a synod in the Lateran on 31 Aug. 900 at which he confirmed Argrinus as bishop of Langres (he had been deposed by STEPHEN VI but restored by John IX) and ratified the grant of the *pallium made to him by Formosus. Again, he formally excommunicated the murderers of Fulk, archbishop of Rheims (d. 17 June 900), and exhorted the French bishops to concur in this sentence. He intervened energetically to support the election of Stephen, formerly bishop of Sorrento, as archbishop of Naples on the death of the controversial Athanasius II (d. 898). He also generously took up the cause of Macla-cenus, bishop of Amasea (Amasya) in Cappadocia, who had been driven from his see by the Saracens (in fact, the Turks), furnishing him with letters recommending him to the care and protection of all Christians.

Benedict was inevitably conscious of the political void created by the death without male heir of Lambert of Spoleto on 15 Oct. 898; Formosus had crowned Lambert emperor, and John IX had made arrangements with him which seemed to secure the papacy. Berengar I of Friuli (c.850–924), king of Italy since 888, might have taken his place, but he was disastrously defeated by the Magyars in 899, and then found his supremacy in Italy disputed by the young king Louis 'the Blind' of Provence (887–928), grandson of Emperor Louis II (855–75). Encouraged by Louis's initial successes, Benedict crowned him emperor in Feb. 901. But fortune's wheel turned swiftly; Berengar recovered the upper hand, defeated Louis in Aug. 902, and forced him to recross the Alps after swearing never to set foot in Italy again. The result was that, without an imperial protector, Rome again lapsed into the anarchy of party strife.

Benedict was a moderate pope who was praised by the chronicler Flodoard of Rheims (d. 966) for his generosity to the destitute. It has been conjectured that he was murdered by agents of Berengar, but no contemporary evidence supports this.

PL 131, 39–44; LP 2, 233; JW 1, 306; Flodoard, De Chr. trium. 14, 7 (PL 135, 831); MGSS xiii, 624 f.; Auxilius, Lib. in defens. Steph. episcopi (ed. E. Dümmler, Leipzig, 1866); DHGE 8, 27–31 (F. Baix); NCE 2, 273 (S. McKenna); Brezzi, 98 f.; DBI 8, 337–42 (O. Bertolini); Mann 4, 103–10; Seppelt 2, 345 f.

LEO V (Aug.–Sept. 903: d. early 904). Parish priest at Priapi, near Ardea 37 km. south of Rome, he succeeded BENEDICT IV.

How a man who did not belong to the Roman clergy came to be elected in this period is not known; it has been conjectured that the clergy and nobility could not agree on a local candidate and therefore settled for a stranger of whose high repute they had heard. Nothing is known of his earlier career, but the fact that Auxilius (c.870–c.930), the champion of the posthumously arraigned and controversial FORMOSUS, describes him as an admirable and holy person suggests that, like his immediate predecessors, he was a pro-Formosan. After he had held office for only thirty days there was a palace revolution and one of his clergy, the priest CHRISTOPHER, overthrew him, flung him into gaol, and had himself made pope. As it seems likely that Christopher was a Formosan too, there must have been a split in the Formosan faction, perhaps prompted by resentment against someone who must have seemed to many an outsider. Christopher himself was soon displaced by SERGIUS III and sent to join Leo in prison, where after languishing several weeks in misery both were eventually murdered.

A legend which first appears in the 11th cent. identifies Leo V with Tutwal (also Tual, Tugdual), patron saint of Tréguier, on the north coast of Brittany. The legend, which seems of French rather than Breton origin, relates that the holy man, who in fact lived in the 6th cent. and founded a monastery at Tréguier, was visiting Rome in hopes of an audience with the pope, but when he arrived there found the apostolic throne vacant and the clergy and people busy with an election. As the result of a miracle the choice fell on him, and as pope he assumed the name Leo the Breton (Britigena). The story probably developed from a misunderstanding of the title Pabu or Papa which, like other Breton saints, Tutwal bore.

LP 2, 234; JW 1, 444; 2, 746; E. Dümmler, Auxilius und Vulgarius (Leipzig, 1866), 60 and 135; Flodoard, De Chr. triumph. 12, 7 (PL 135, 831); DTC 9, 316 (É. Amann); NCE 8, 641 (O. J.

Blum); *BSS* 12, 723 f. (H. Platelle: for the legend).

CHRISTOPHER (antipope Sept. 903– Jan. 904: d. early 904). A Roman by birth, priest of S. Damaso, one of the twenty-five ancient parish, or *'title', churches of Rome, he headed a coup which overthrew LEO V, flung him into gaol, and had himself proclaimed and consecrated pope. Nothing is known of his earlier career, but on the assumption that he, like Leo, was a supporter of the posthumously condemned FORMOSUS, there must have been a split in the Formosan faction, perhaps caused by resentment against Leo as an outsider foisted on the Roman church. Christopher's triumph lasted only four months; early in 904 SERGIUS, elected in 898 but supplanted by JOHN IX, moved on Rome with an armed force, seized power, and was acclaimed and consecrated pope. Christopher, of whom only one bull (confirming the privileges of the abbey of Corbie) survives, was rudely deposed, stripped of his insignia and robed as a monk, and sent to join his own victim Leo in gaol. A few months later Sergius, moved by pity (it was said) for their wretched plight, had them both executed. Although sometimes listed as a pope, Christopher is properly reckoned an antipope.

LP 2, lxix; 235; JW 1, 444 f.; E. Dümmler, *Auxilius und Vulgarius* (Leipzig, 1866), 60 and 135; Flodoard, *De Chr. trium.* 12, 7 (*PL* 135, 831); Herimannus Augiensis, *Chron.* a. 904 (*MGSS* 5, 111); Mariannus Scottus, *Chron.* (*MGSS* 5, 487); *DHGE* 12, 778 f. (G. Bardy).

SERGIUS III (29 Jan. 904–14 Apr. 911). A Roman of aristocratic birth, made deacon by STEPHEN V, he was consecrated bishop of Caere, i.e. Cerveteri (unwillingly, he was to allege), by FORMOSUS, took part in the *'cadaver synod' presided over by STEPHEN VI, and, when it posthumously condemned Formosus and annulled his ordinations, gladly regarded himself as reduced to the diaconate and accepted reordination as priest by Stephen VI; ambitious for the papacy, he did not wish the fact that he was a

bishop to exclude him. A virulent hater of Formosus, he was elected pope by the anti-Formosan faction on the death of THEODORE II (Dec. 897) and was even installed in the Lateran, but had to give way to the pro-Formosan JOHN IX, who had the support of Emperor Lambert of Spoleto (d. 898). Deposed, condemned, driven into exile, he had his chance seven years later when the Formosan party in Rome split and the priest CHRISTOPHER overthrew and imprisoned LEO V. Aided by Duke Alberic I of Spoleto (d. *c.*925), Sergius marched on Rome with an armed force, threw Christopher into gaol, was acclaimed pope, and was consecrated on 29 Jan. 904. Not long after, moved, it was said, by pity, he had Leo V and Christopher strangled in prison.

Sergius dated his reign from his original abortive election in Dec. 897, treating all his predecessors from John IX as intruders. In order to undo their work he immediately press-ganged the clergy by threats and violence to attend a synod which overturned John IX's Roman and Ravennate synods of 898, reaffirmed the 'cadaver synod's' condemnation of Formosus, and once again declared null and void the orders he had conferred during his 'usurpation'. As Formosus had created many bishops, who in turn had ordained numerous clergy, the resulting confusion was indescribable. Sergius insisted that those whose orders were annulled should be ordained afresh; his policies were carried out with such threats and violence that few had the courage to resist. One who did resist was the Frankish priest Auxilius (*c.*870–*c.*930), whose acute and hard-hitting pamphlets defending the ordinations of Formosus (also of Stephen of Naples, another bishop who had moved sees) provide invaluable information about the controversy. His protests found echoes elsewhere throughout Italy, but in Rome the scandalized opposition had to keep quiet. There Sergius had the support of the noble families, notably that of Theophylact (d. *c.*920), financial director of the holy see but also consul and commander of the militia, and his ambitious, determined wife, the senatrix Theodora (d. after 916). In the absence of an emperor this family effectively governed Rome, and Sergius enjoyed such intimacy with it that he was reputed to have had a son, the future pope JOHN XI, by Theodora's fifteen-year-old daughter Marozia. His and his immediate successors' dependence on the family was complete, and degrading, causing the following decades to be castigated as the pornocracy of the holy see.

Apart from his campaign against Formosus and his ordinations, little is known of Sergius's general activities. Only a few routine decisions survive in his meagre register. At some stage, however, he called upon the Frankish episcopate for help in refuting the case made by Patriarch Photius (858–67; 878–86) against the Latin doctrine of the *double procession of the Holy Spirit. Again, when the Byzantine emperor Leo VI (886–912), lacking a male heir, married for the fourth time (906) and found himself banned by Patriarch Nicholas I Mysticus (901–7; 912–25), he had recourse to Rome and the great oriental patriarchates. The envoys whom Sergius sent to Constantinople, disregarding the greater strictness of eastern canon law and its antipathy to tetragamy, gave a verdict approving Leo's fourth marriage, with the result that Nicholas was deposed and exiled and the eastern church entered on a period of confusion and controversy.

Sergius completed the restoration, begun by John IX, of St John Lateran, which had been heavily damaged by an earthquake during the holding of the 'cadaver synod' in 897. His own tomb in St Peter's bore a eulogistic epitaph recalling his election after the death of Theodore II, his seven-year exile from his rightful see, and his relentless war against the 'wolves' who had usurped office before his triumphant return. Like other popes, he minted his own coinage, but was the first since HADRIAN I to impress his own effigy, wearing a conical mitre, on his coins.

LP 2, 236–8; JW 1, 445–7; E. Dümmler, *Auxilius und Vulgarius* (Leipzig, 1866); Auxilius, *De ordin.*

a Formoso papa factis and *Infensor et Defensor (PL* 129); Flodoard, *De Chr. trium.* 12, 7 *(PL* 135, 831); *DTC* 14, 1918–21 (É. Amann); *EC* 11, 386 f. (A. P. Frutaz); Seppelt 2, 343 f.; 346–51; L. Duchesne, 'Serge III et Jean XI', *MelArchHist* 33 (1913), 25–55; *NCE* 13, 112 (V. Gellhaus); Mann 4, 119–42.

ANASTASIUS III (*c.* June 911–*c.* Aug. 913). A Roman by birth, son of Lucian, he was elected and died at dates which cannot be firmly determined. Nothing is known of his earlier career or of the circumstances of his election. At this troubled time Rome was dominated by Theophylact (d. *c.*920), consul and senator, financial director of the holy see, and his ambitious, energetic wife Theodora the Elder (d. after 916); the papacy itself was effectively controlled by this powerful, unscrupulous family. It is likely that Anastasius too, the mildness of whose rule is praised by the chronicler Flodoard (893/4–966), was subject to its influence and did not exercise much, if any, independent initiative. He did, however, bestow the *pallium on Ragimbert, bishop of Vercelli, and at the request of Berengar I, king of Italy (888–924), grant certain honours to the bishop of Pavia; as both were important cities in Berengar's dominions, these actions suggest that the king valued good relations with Rome, and was regarded in a friendly light there. In 912 Anastasius received a lengthy, forcefully expressed letter from Nicholas I Mysticus, now restored as patriarch of Constantinople (912–25), deploring both Rome's attitude in approving Emperor Leo VI's (886–912) fourth marriage in 906 and the behaviour of Sergius III's envoys, and demanding amends. His reply is not known, but Nicholas cannot have found it satisfactory, for he proceeded to remove the pope's name from the *diptychs, and a gulf yawned between Rome and Constantinople.

LP 2, 239; JW 1, 448; 706; Flodoard, *De Chr. trium.* 12, 7 *(PL* 135, 831); *PG* 111, 196–220 (Nicholas's letter: No. 32); *DBI* 3, 24 (P. Bertolini); *DHGE* 2, 1475 (A. Clerval); *NCE* 1, 479 (A. J. Ennis); Z2, 43.

LANDO (c. Aug. 913–c. Mar. 914). Born in Sabine territory north-east of Rome, son of a wealthy Lombard count named Taino, he reigned, according to a contemporary chronicler, six months and eleven days. Nothing is known of his earlier career or of the circumstances of his election, and nothing is recorded of his reign except a benefaction, in pious memory of his father, to the cathedral of Sabina, S. Salvatore in Fornovo. In all probability he was the candidate put forward, or at any rate approved, by the powerful family of Theophylact (d. c.920), consul and senator, financial director of the holy see, and his ambitious, energetic wife Theodora (d. after 916), which dominated Rome at this time and effectively controlled the papacy.

LP 2, 239; JW 1, 448; Flodoard, De Chr. trium. 12, 7 (PL 135, 831); EC 7, 887 (A. Ghinato); Z2, 43.

JOHN X (Mar./Apr. 914–deposed May 928: d. 929). Born at Tossignano in the Romagna, ordained at Bologna, a deacon at Ravenna frequently sent on missions to Rome, elected but not consecrated bishop of Bologna, he had been archbishop of Ravenna for nine years (905–14) when, on the demand of the Roman nobility, in effect of the all-powerful family of Theophylact (d. c.920) and Theodora (d. after 916), he was elected successor to LANDO (913–14). While at Ravenna, he had had close relations with Berengar I, king of Italy (888–924), a fact which also counted in his favour. Scandalous tongues alleged that Theodora wanted him in Rome because he had been her lover when visiting the city as a deacon, but the real reason for his choice was Rome's desperate need for a vigorous and experienced leader. His translation evoked protests among supporters of Pope FORMOSUS since it made nonsense of Formosus's posthumous condemnation for having moved from one see to another, but there is no evidence that his policies were anti-Formosan. With the growing recognition of the unique position of the holy see, the old canonical objections to a bishop's promotion to it were losing force.

John immediately set himself to deal finally with the Muslims, whose devastating raids were terrorizing and impoverishing central Italy. It was because he seemed capable of doing this that the Roman aristocracy, alarmed for their estates, had taken the unprecedented step of summoning him from Ravenna. With Theophylact and his son-in-law Alberic I, duke of Spoleto (d. c.925), he skilfully organized a coalition of Italian rulers, with Count Landulf of Capua negotiated naval assistance from Byzantium, and after a three-month siege of their stronghold at the mouth of the river Garigliano decisively defeated the Saracens (Aug. 915). He was later to recall proudly the part he had personally taken in fighting the dread enemies who had devastated Roman territory for sixty years. At the height of his political success he crowned (Dec. 915) Berengar I as emperor in St Peter's; in return Berengar took the traditional oath to guarantee the rights and patrimony of the holy see.

More than a politician and man of action, John carried out a wide range of ecclesiastical policies which enhanced the prestige of the papacy. In 915 and 920 he settled damaging splits over the succession to the sees of Narbonne and Louvain respectively, in the latter case favouring the candidate of King Charles III the Simple (879–929). In Sept. 916 his legate presided at the synod of Hohenaltheim, in Swabia, important not only for re-establishing church discipline but in buttressing the shaky throne of King Conrad I (911–18). Although his efforts were to prove unsuccessful, he struggled for years to bring Croatia and Dalmatia back to Roman obedience and to suppress the use of the Slav language in the liturgy. His decisions were sometimes motivated by expediency, as when he confirmed the election of a count's five-year-old son to an archbishopric. On the other hand, he gave the bishops of Rouen and Rheims wise pastoral advice on dealing with converted Normans who were relapsing into paganism. Towards the end of 923 his legates were able to restore unity with the eastern church, interrupted since 912 when Patriarch Nicholas I, furious that Rome had sanctioned Emperor Leo VI's (886–912) fourth marriage and refused to go back on that decision, struck the pope's name from the *diptychs. According to the patriarch, writing to Tsar Simeon of Bulgaria, they agreed to condemn tetragamy as an abomination, but this is an improbable simplification. It is likely that they recognized the eastern legislation of 920 forbidding fourth marriages as the local law of the Byzantine church. Early in 928 he intervened on behalf of the Benedictine abbey of Cluny, founded in 909, emphasizing that it was under the protection of the holy see.

In Rome itself John thoroughly reconstructed the Lateran, decorating it with splendid pictures, and promoted the singing school, important for the education of the clergy. His determination, however (unlike most popes of this period), to remain independent of the aristocracy which governed Rome inevitably led to his downfall. After Berengar's death in April 924, he tried to secure his position by making a pact in 926 with Hugh of Provence, now king of Italy (926–47), and by working closely with his own brother Peter, who was becoming an increasingly powerful figure. These moves alarmed the ruthless senatrix Marozia (d. after 932), Theophylact's daughter and since his death (c.920) omnipotent ruler of Rome, and her new husband Guido, marquis of Tuscany. Together they organized a revolt against John and his brother, the story having got about that Peter had brought the Magyars into Italy; towards the end of 927 Peter was struck down in the Lateran before John's eyes. In May next year John himself was deposed, allegedly by popular demand, and flung into gaol in Castel Sant'Angelo. He remained there several months, and in the middle of 929 he died, almost certainly suffocated by a pillow.

LP 2, 240 f.; JW 1, 449–53; 2, 706; NA 9 (1883), 513–40 (early letters); Grumel 1, 671; 675; 711; 712; P. Fedele, ASRomana 33 (1910), 177–247; T. Venni, 'Giovanni X', ADRomana 59 (1936), 1–136; Z1, 73 f.; Z2, 44–75; Seppelt 2, 350–5; Mann 4, 149–87.

LEO VI (May–Dec. 928). A Roman of upper-class origin, son of the notary Christopher, he was cardinal priest of Sta Susanna and already an old man when he succeeded JOHN X, recently deposed and still alive in prison. He owed his election to Marozia, now head of the house of Theophylact (d. c.920) and, with the titles 'senatrix' and 'patricia', all-powerful ruler of Rome along with her second husband Guido, marquis of Tuscany. Like his successor STEPHEN VII, he was a stopgap appointment pending the time when Marozia's own son JOHN was ready to succeed. Virtually nothing is known of Leo's short reign, his only surviving letter being one to the bishops of Dalmatia and Croatia requesting them to be obedient to their archbishop, John of Spalato, to whom he had granted the *pallium, and to be content with their territorial boundaries. It is likely, however, that he was entirely dependent on Marozia and the governing clique in Rome. He died well before his hapless predecessor was murdered in prison.

LP 2, 242; JW 1, 453; Z2, 66, 77; Watterich 1, 33.

STEPHEN VII (VIII) (Dec. 928–Feb. 931). A Roman by birth, he was priest of S. Anastasia when elected to succeed LEO VI, the deposed JOHN X being still alive in prison. Like Leo, he owed his appointment to the all-powerful Marozia, now head of the house of Theophylact (d. c.920) and effective ruler of Rome; like Leo, too, he was a stopgap appointment pending the time when Marozia's own son JOHN was ready to succeed. As pope under this dictatorial lady he had no power of independent initiative except in strictly ecclesiastical affairs. Through the absence of records the period is of exceptional obscurity, and his only recorded actions are the confirmation or extension of privileges to religious houses in Italy and France.

LP 2, 242; JW 1, 453 f.; ZPR, 37–9; Z2, 77; PL 132, 1049–56; DHGE 15, 1197 f. (R. Aubert); Mann 4, 189 f.

JOHN XI (Feb. or Mar. 931–Dec. 935 or Jan. 936). A Roman, in his early twenties but already cardinal priest of Sta Maria in Trastevere, he succeeded STEPHEN VII through the influence of his mother Marozia (d. after 932), patrician and senatrix, at this time the all-powerful ruler of Rome. He was almost certainly, according to Liutprand of Cremona (c.920–72), but also *LP*, her illegitimate son by Pope SERGIUS III; she expected him to be her tool, and her object in getting him appointed was to enhance her own authority and power.

One of his first acts was, on the petition of his abbot Odo (878/9–942), to confirm the privileges of protection by the holy see and free election of abbots enjoyed by the reforming abbey of Cluny, in Burgundy, since its foundation in 909, and to encourage it to become the model for other monasteries seeking reform. At the same time he granted similar privileges to Odo's monastery at Déols. When the eastern emperor Romanus I (920–44) invited him (early 932) to approve the appointment of his sixteen-year-old son Theophylact as patriarch of Constantinople, he readily gave his dispensation and dispatched two bishops as his legates to take part in the boy's consecration and enthronement (27 Feb. 933). Marozia may have had a hand in this decision, which understandably shocked the eastern church, for she was trying to arrange a marriage between her little daughter Bertha and one of the royal princes whom Romanus had raised to the dignity of associate Caesar.

In summer 932 Marozia, now a widow for the second time but insatiably ambitious, married Hugh of Provence, king of Italy (926–48), then at the height of his power. John must have officiated at the wedding, although it was uncanonical by the standards of the time since Hugh was his bride's brother-in-law. The union was unpopular with the Romans, suspicious of foreign rule, and provoked a revolt, incited by Alberic II (c.905–54), Marozia's son by her first marriage, whom Hugh had insulted

at the wedding-feast and who had his own reasons for viewing the marriage with dismay. In Dec. 932 the armed mob stormed Castel Sant'Angelo, where the royal couple were installed and from which Marozia dominated the city. Hugh was lucky to escape with his life, but Alberic imprisoned both his mother and his half-brother the pope, and then had himself proclaimed prince of Rome, senator of all the Romans, count and patrician. In fact, he was to govern Rome firmly and successfully until his death in 954. Nothing more is heard of Marozia, but John seems to have been released from prison though kept under house-arrest in the Lateran and limited to strictly ecclesiastical functions. Liutprand of Cremona remarked that Alberic treated John as his personal slave, while the chronicler Flodoard (d. 966) dismissed him in a contemptuous hexameter as 'powerless, lacking all distinction, administering only sacraments'.

LP 2, 243; JW 1, 454 f.; *ZPR*, 40–6; *PL* 132, 1055–62; Liutprand of Cremona, *Leg.* 62 (*PL* 136, 934); Flodoard, *De Chr. Irium.* 12, 7 (*PL* 135, 832); L. Duchesne, 'Serge III et Jean XI', *MelArchHist* 33 (1913), 25–64; P. Fedele, *ASRomana* 33 (1910), 211–40; Seppelt 2, 355 f.; Z2, 77–84; 88; 97; Mann 4, 191–204; *NCE* 7, 1011 (M. A. Mulholland).

LEO VII (3 Jan. 936–13 July 939). The successor of JOHN XI, he owed his elevation to Alberic II, prince of Rome, patrician and senator of all the Romans, who ruled the city with absolute control from 932 to 954. Nothing is known of his background except that he was a Roman by birth, cardinal priest of S. Sisto, and in all probability a Benedictine; this last fact may have recommended him to the prince, who was devout and deeply interested in monasticism and monastic reform. Although restricted by Alberic to ecclesiastical functions, he was active, with his full support, in fostering monastic revival. At the beginning of his reign the great reforming abbot Odo of Cluny (878/9–942) was invited to Rome, and at the pope's request negotiated a fragile settlement between Alberic and King

Hugh of Italy (926–48), who since his expulsion from Rome in 932 had been making persistent efforts to regain control of the city. While there, Odo was entrusted with the reform of religious houses in Rome and its neighbourhood, beginning with that of St Paul's basilica. In the same year Leo renewed the privileges of the restored abbey at Subiaco, 80 km. east of Rome, site of the grotto of St Benedict (*c.*480–*c.*550), and in Jan. 938 those granted by his predecessor to Cluny and Déols. Later he extended similar privileges to the revived abbey of Gorze (near Metz), the pioneer of a somewhat different reforming movement in Lorraine.

In 937 or thereabouts Leo sent the *pallium to Adaldag, archbishop of Bremen–Hamburg, and appointed Archbishop Frederick of Mainz apostolic vicar and legate for all Germany, entrusting him with a comprehensive programme for the much-needed reform of clergy of all grades, and encouraging him to expel Jews who refused to be baptized. The contemporary chronicler Flodoard of Rheims (d. 966), who visited and dined with him in 936, formed a highly favourable impression of his character, wisdom, and personal warmth.

LP 2, 244; JW 1, 455–7; 2, 706; ZPR, 46–60; PL 132, 1065–88; NA 10 (1885), 380–6 (letters); Flodoard, *De Chr. trium.* 12, 7 (PL 135, 832); DTC 9, 316 f. (É. Amann); Mann 4, 205–7; NCE 8, 641 (O. J. Blum); Z2, 88–90; 114.

STEPHEN VIII (IX) (14 July 939–late Oct. 942). Although later sources describe him as of German descent, imposed on the holy see by Otto I (962–73), king of Germany since 936 and later emperor, he was in fact a Roman by birth, born in the last quarter of the 9th cent., and was cardinal priest of SS. Silvestro and Martino when elected. Like his predecessor, he owed his elevation to Alberic II (*c.*905–54), prince of Rome, senator and patrician, who was absolute ruler of the city from 932 to 954 and, like his mother Marozia (d. after 932), appointed the popes of his choice. A learned man, Stephen was said to be blameless in

his private life and in his public relations devoted to peace. In Rome and the papal state, wholly subject to Alberic, he was allowed no independent role and confined himself to routine acts of administration; even when he supported the movement, radiating from Cluny in Burgundy, for the reform of monasteries in Rome and central Italy, he was collaborating with one of Alberic's deepest interests. In the wider political sphere, however, he intervened in early 942 in favour of Louis IV d'Outremer (936–54), son of Charles the Simple (879–929), who had been crowned king of France in 936 but was facing a formidable rebellion; he dispatched Bishop Damasus as papal legate to France to urge the nobility and people of France and Burgundy, on pain of excommunication, to recognize Louis as king and give up their hostility to him. Later in the year he sent the *pallium to Archbishop Hugh of Rheims, restored to his see after being displaced for several years, and this conciliatory gesture helped to quell the opposition to Louis.

In his last months Stephen seems to have fallen foul of Alberic and to have taken part in a conspiracy or uprising directed against him. Although the reports are late and differ in details, there is no reason to doubt their substance. It appears that the pope was imprisoned, brutally mutilated, and died of his injuries.

LP 2, 244; JW 1, 457 f.; ZPR, 60–4; Watterich 1, 34; 671; MGSS 22, 431; DHGE 15, 1198 (R. Aubert); Z2, 84; Mann 4, 212–17; NCE 13, 677 (M. A. Mulholland).

MARINUS II (30 Oct. 942–early May 946). Often mistakenly listed as Martin III, he was a Roman by birth and cardinal priest of S. Ciriaco when elected; nothing else is known of his origins and earlier career. Like his two predecessors, he owed his elevation entirely to Alberic II of Spoleto (*c.*905–54), prince of Rome, senator and patrician, who ruled the city from 932 to 954 and had his nominees appointed to the papacy. Indeed, Marinus is reported never to have dared to do anything without the prince's instructions; while his coins bore his monogram and that of St Peter on the obverse, they showed Alberic's name and his title on the reverse. A Vatican MS cited by C. Baronius (1538–1607) more flatteringly represents him as shunning warlike conflicts and devoting himself to the reform of both secular clergy and monks, the restoration of church buildings, and the care of the poor. His recorded acts in fact consist largely of routine administrative decisions. Among the more significant were bulls (1) rebuking Bishop Sico of Capua for alienating properties of the abbey of Monte Cassino; (2) confirming (21 Jan. 944) the abbey's possessions and privileges; and (3) placing (summer 945) Abbot Baldwin of Monte Cassino in charge of the monastery attached to St Paul's-without-the-Walls. A fourth bull (early 946) confirmed the appointment of Frederick, archbishop of Mainz (d. 954), as papal vicar and envoy to Germany with authority to hold synods and root out abuses among clergy and monks—an office and dignity granted two centuries earlier to St Boniface (680–754), apostle of Germany. The exact date of Marinus's death in early May 946 is uncertain.

LP 2, 245; JW 1, 458; *ZPR*, 64–72; *DTC* 9, 2477 (É. Amann); *EC* 8, 163 (A. Ghinato); Mann 4, 218–23; *NCE* 8, 223 (M. A. Mulholland).

AGAPITUS II (10 May 946–Dec. 955).

The successor of MARINUS II, he owed his promotion to Alberic II (*c.*905–54), prince of Rome and from 932 to 954 its all-powerful ruler. Except that he was a Roman by birth, nothing is known of his origins or previous career. While the other popes appointed by Alberic were largely restricted to ecclesiastical functions, he was able, at any rate at the beginning of his reign, to exercise considerable initiative in the political field outside Italy; his name in full appeared on coins in contrast to the simple monogram of Alberic's earlier nominees.

He co-operated fully with Alberic in fostering monastic reform, confirming the special status of Cluny, near Mâcon, and

arranging for monks to come from Gorze (diocese of Metz) to restore discipline in the abbey attached to St Paul's-without-the-Walls. Farther afield, his legate, Bishop Marinus, was dispatched in spring 948 to the court of King Otto I of Germany (936–73: in 962 emperor), and then presided with Otto and Louis IV d'Outremer of France (936–54) over the important synod of Ingelheim (7 June), which not only settled the contested succession to the see of Rheims in favour of Artaud, King Louis's candidate, but attempted to remedy the troubled situation in the kingdom of France by ordering Louis's rebellious vassal, Hugh the Great, to make his submission on pain of excommunication. Agapitus ratified these decisions at a Roman synod early in 949. In a bull dated 2 Jan. 948 he had extended the jurisdiction of the metropolitan of Hamburg over Denmark and other northern countries. He worked closely with, and admired, Otto, and when the Saxon king crossed the Alps in autumn 951, assumed the royal power at Pavia, and sent envoys to Rome (significantly to the pope and not the prince) to negotiate for the imperial crown, Agapitus would gladly have offered it to him had he been free to do so. He was obliged to refuse, however, since Alberic, who had no wish to see Rome dominated by a foreign emperor, was firmly opposed to the project. In spite of this Agapitus continued his active support for Otto, granting him broad jurisdiction over monasteries, in 954 permitting his brother Bruno, archbishop of Cologne (953–65), to wear the *pallium at will, endorsing the king's plan to transform the monastery of St Maurice he had founded at Magdeburg in 937 into a metropolitan see with oversight of the mission to the Slavs, and (as emerges from a letter of protest addressed to the pope in 955 by William, archbishop of Mainz) giving him authority to establish archbishoprics and bishoprics and define ecclesiastical boundaries as he thought fit. He thus played a definite role in the process which was to lead to the imperial restoration in 962.

Notwithstanding his energy and independence, the weakness of Agapitus's position was revealed when Alberic lay dying. Anxious that all power in Rome, spiritual as well as temporal, should be concentrated in his family, the prince assembled the nobility and clergy, with the pope, in St Peter's and made them swear that after Agapitus's death they would elect his bastard son Octavian, who was to succeed him as prince, as supreme pontiff as well. Agapitus was thus forced to be a party to this profoundly uncanonical undertaking. Alberic died on 31 Aug. 954, being succeeded by Octavian as temporal ruler, and Agapitus a little more than a year later; he was buried behind the apse of St John Lateran.

LP 2, 245; JW 1, 459–63; ZPR, 72–98; PL 133, 889–932; P. Jaffé, Bibliotheca rer. Germ. (Berlin, 1866) III, 345–50; MGLeges 2, 19–26; Rivista Ital. di numismatica 33 (1920), 225–7; DBI 1, 367 f. (G. Arnaldi); DHGE 1, 890–2 (J. P. Kirsch); Mann 4, 224–40; NCE 1, 195 (C. M. Aherne).

JOHN XII (16 Dec. 955–14 May 964). Originally named Octavian and born c.937, he was the bastard son of Alberic II (c.905–54), prince and all-powerful ruler of Rome from 932 to 954. On his deathbed Alberic obliged the leading Romans to swear that, when the reigning pope AGAPITUS II died, they would elect Octavian, who was to succeed him as prince, as supreme pontiff as well. Although this undertaking violated the decree of Pope SYMMACHUS (1 Mar. 499) forbidding agreements during a pope's lifetime about the choice of his successor, it was carried out, Octavian changing his name (the second pope known to do so; JOHN II in 533 was the first) to John. Already in orders, he was hardly eighteen, and contemporary reports agree about his disinterest in spiritual things, addiction to boorish pleasures, and uninhibitedly debauched life. Gossipy tongues accused him of turning the Lateran palace into a brothel.

However scandalous his conduct, John maintained a show of administrative activity, seizing every opportunity to assert the papal authority. His standing in the church at large was not apparently affected. The Spanish church, for example, subject to Muslim domination, sought his counsel, and noteworthy visitors to whom he presented the *pallium were the newly appointed archbishops Oskytel of York (957) and Dunstan of Canterbury (960). He shared his father's interest in monastic reform, materially assisting the abbeys of Farfa, 40 km. north of Rome, and Subiaco, 80 km. east of Rome, and going on pilgrimage to the latter in May 958. Meanwhile his political situation was deteriorating. An ill-judged attempt in 958 to enlarge the papal state by attacking Capua and Benevento failed miserably, while its northern territories were being plundered by Berengar II, king of Italy (950–63), who conquered the duchy of Spoleto in 959. Conscious of his weakness, John dispatched two envoys in late 960 to Otto I, since 936 king of Germany, demanding help and offering him the imperial crown. This was a complete reversal of Alberic's policies, but John was probably not a free agent and acted under pressure from the Roman opposition increasingly influenced by reforming ideals and outraged by his deplorable behaviour.

Otto, who had vainly sought the imperial crown in 951, welcomed the invitation. First, he made a compact with the envoys to protect the pope and the patrimony of Peter, which was to remain inviolate, and to refrain from interference in Rome's internal affairs. He then marched to Lombardy in late summer, quickly restored his sovereignty there, and was in Rome on 31 Jan. 962. On 2 Feb. John anointed and crowned him, with his queen Adelaide, in St Peter's, and with the leading Romans swore to be loyal to him and refuse support to Berengar. Thus was reinaugurated the Holy Roman Empire (to last until the abdication of Francis II in 1806). A synod was then held which, after admonishing John to improve his way of life, decided certain issues affecting the German church; in particular, John met the emperor's wishes by

LEO VIII (963–5)

raising Magdeburg to an archbishopric with oversight of missionary work among the Slavs. Finally, on 13 Feb. Otto published the 'Ottonian privilege', solemnly confirming the *donations of Pepin and Charlemagne, with significant additions which extended the papal state to about two-thirds of Italy, binding the emperor to defend the church's rights and possessions, and also restoring (this section may have been added in Dec. 963) the rules for free papal elections subject to imperial approval of the man elected, his obligation to swear fealty to the emperor, and the recognition of the emperor as overlord in the papal state, as laid down in the *constitution of Lothair I of 824.

Pope and emperor had been mutually mistrustful, and when Otto left Rome to fight Berengar, John, who had looked for a protector not a master, immediately began intriguing against him with Berengar's son Adalbert, and also with the Magyars. On 1 Nov. 963 an infuriated Otto returned; John, who at first thought of armed resistance, fled with the papal treasure to Tivoli. After making the Romans swear never in future to elect a pope without his consent, Otto presided over a synod in St Peter's at which, after the clergy had charged John with appalling misbehaviour, he accused him of perfidy and treachery. The synod thrice wrote to John asking him to appear before it and justify himself, but he refused and threatened excommunication. In his absence he was deposed on 4 Dec., and Otto, begged by the synod to replace the 'apostate' by a worthy successor, proposed a highly placed Lateran official (*protos-criniarius*), LEO, who was elected and consecrated as Leo VIII two days later. The validity of John's deposition, which violated the ancient principle that the holy see can be judged by no earthly power, has been called in question.

On 3 Jan. 964 a revolt in Rome, provoked by John, was repressed with bloodshed. As a result of his intrigues and the ill-judged actions of Leo VIII, John had so improved his standing in the city that, when Otto

departed later in Jan. to rejoin his army, he was able to re-establish himself in February. Leo had fled, but John inflicted savage reprisals on such of his opponents as he could find. At a synod held on 26 Feb. he quashed the acts of the imperial synod, deposed Leo as a usurper, and pronounced his ordinations invalid. But his triumph was short-lived. Otto marched on Rome, and John, who was hoping to patch up an agreement with him, prudently sought refuge in the Campagna in April. There, in early May, he suffered a stroke, allegedly while in bed with a married woman, and a week later he died, still in his middle twenties.

PL 133, 1013–41; *LP* 2, 246–9; JW 1, 463–7; *ZPR*, 98–139; *MG*Const 1, 23–7 (Ottonianum); 532–6; Watterich 1, 41–62; 672–9; K. Hampe, 'Die Berufung Ottos des Grossen zu Rom durch Papst Johannes XII', *Festschrift für K. Zeuner* (Weimar, 1910); P. Schramm, *Kaiser, Rom und Renovatio* (2nd edn., Darmstadt, 1957); W. Ullmann, 'The Origins of the Ottonianum', *CHJ* 11 (1953), 114–28; *DTC* 8, 619–26 (É. Amann); Z1, 77–92; Z2, 134–52; Mann 4, 241–72; *NCE* 7, 1011 (S. McKenna); Seppelt 2, 361–71

LEO VIII (4 Dec. 963–1 Mar. 965). When the Roman synod of 4 Dec. 963 presided over by Emperor Otto I (962–73) deposed JOHN XII (955–64) in his absence, the man elected by acclaim, with Otto's approval, was Leo, an experienced Lateran official of exemplary character, chief notary (*protos-criniarius*) of the church. A layman, he was at once installed in the Lateran, in spite of canonical impropriety rushed through the lower orders in a single day, and consecrated by the bishops of *Ostia, Porto, and Albano on 6 Dec., the rites used (for the first time in the case of a pope) being the revised ones introduced to Italy by Otto. It is likely that before consecration he swore fealty to the emperor, and it has been argued that the section of the *'Ottonian privilege' prescribing such an oath was inserted at this date. The legitimacy of Leo's pontificate, at least until John XII's death, has been contested; it depends on the validity, debated among canonists, of John's deposition.

Neither Otto's masterful rule nor, apparently, the choice of Leo was popular, and on 3 Jan. 964 a revolt threatening their lives, instigated by John XII at Tivoli, had to be crushed by the imperial troops. Anxious to halt the bloodshed, Leo unwisely persuaded Otto to release the hostages the Romans had given him and be content with a renewed oath of loyalty. So far from winning Leo support, this led, when the emperor and his forces left Rome in mid-Jan., to violent disturbances which eventually forced the pope to seek refuge in the imperial court and enabled John to resume the reins of authority. At a synod in St Peter's on 26 Feb. he deposed and excommunicated Leo as a usurper of the holy see, uncanonically ordained, and guilty of perfidy to his lawful pope. Anyone he had ordained was compelled to confess that his orders were void.

On John's death (14 May 964) the Romans, ignoring Leo, besought the emperor to be allowed to elect the cardinal deacon BENEDICT. For Otto the restoration of Leo involved his personal prestige, and he flatly refused. The Romans notwithstanding elected and enthroned Benedict as Benedict V, and only gave in and surrendered him when Otto's army besieged the hunger-stricken city. Otto re-entered it on 23 June and reinstated Leo, who a few days later held a synod which deposed and degraded Benedict.

Apart from a few routine decisions little else is known of Leo's reign. Three documents attributed to him (the *Cessatio donationum*, the *Privilegium maius*, and the *Privilegium minus*), which purport to restore to Otto and his successors a number of territories in the patrimony of St Peter, as well as granting them the right to nominate and install archbishops and bishops, have been shown to be 11th-cent. forgeries by Italian supporters of Emperor Henry IV in the *investiture struggle; they reflect the conviction that Leo was the mere creature of Otto.

LP 2, 246–50; JW 1, 466–70; 2, 706; MGConst 1, 532–6 (deposition); 663–78 (forged privileges);

ZPR, 129–50; DTC 9, 317–20 (É. Amann); Seppelt 2, 367–72; Z1 88–95; 235–51; Z2 150–4; Th. Klauser, HJ 53 (1936), 186–9; M. Andrieu, 'La carrière ecclésiastique des papes', RevSR 21 (1947), 109 f.; W. Ullmann, The Growth of Papal Government (3rd edn., London, 1970), esp. 352–8.

BENEDICT V (22 May–deposed 23 June 964: d. 4 July 966). A Roman by birth, described by contemporaries as devout, morally exemplary, and learned (*grammaticus*), he was a deacon who favoured the movement for reform in the church. Although he apparently took part in the election of LEO VIII on 6 Dec. 963 after the (temporary) deposition of JOHN XII, he did not play a prominent role in the bitter factional strife at the time; when John resumed control of the holy see in Feb. 964 and had Leo deposed, he left Benedict, who was in the city, undisturbed. On John's death on 14 May the Romans, instead of recalling Leo, sent envoys to Emperor Otto I (962–73), at Rieti, begging leave to elect Benedict; they wanted a reformer in place of a libertine, had no liking for Leo, and perhaps hoped that Otto would be prepared to drop him in favour of such an irreproachable candidate. Otto, however, angrily refused. In spite of this the clergy and people elected and enthroned Benedict, promising to defend him at all costs. Only when Otto laid siege to the city and looked like starving it out, notwithstanding the anathemas Benedict hurled at the besieging army from the walls, did the citizens yield and hand him over (23 June). A synod was immediately held in the Lateran, presided over by Leo and Otto, which condemned Benedict as a usurper (he was in fact one if Leo VIII was legitimate pope). Humbly refusing to defend himself, he was formally stripped of his pontifical robes and insignia, and had his pastoral staff (the first recorded mention of the papal sceptre) broken over his head by Leo himself as he lay prostrate; the story of the chronicler Liutprand (d. 972) that he removed his robes himself is a canard intended to suggest that he abdicated voluntarily. On the emperor's intervention he was allowed to retain the rank of deacon but was exiled to Hamburg, where the bishop, Adaldag, treated him with marked consideration. On Leo's death there was a call, which went unheeded, for his restoration. He died at Hamburg, deeply respected for his holy life, on 4 July 966. His remains were brought back to Rome by Emperor Otto III in 988.

LP 2, 251; JW 1, 469 f.; *ZPR*, 139–51; Mann 4, 273–81; *DBI* 8, 342–4 (P. Delogu); *DHGE* 8, 31–8 (F. Baix); Seppelt 2, 371; *NCE* 2, 273 f. (S. McKenna); Z1, 92–5; Z2, 151–3.

JOHN XIII (1 Oct. 965–6 Sept. 972). A Roman, son of John Episcopus (a surname) but not related, as is often supposed, to the powerful Crescentii, he was brought up in the papal court, held successive offices and was librarian under JOHN XII, and was then promoted bishop of Narnia in Umbria. Five months after LEO VIII's death (in the interval the Romans had vainly asked for the restoration of BENEDICT V) he was elected pope with the agreement of two bishops whom Emperor Otto I (962–73) sent to Rome to represent him. He was a compromise appointment; but if Otto reckoned that he could rule Rome better with an establishment figure as pope, his choice at first seemed disastrous, for John's dependence on a German sovereign combined with his high-handed rule made him hated in the faction-riven city. In Dec. 965 it revolted; John was assaulted, imprisoned, and banished to the Campagna, but he managed to escape, made contact with the emperor, and on 14 Nov. 966, the Romans having repented of their foolhardiness, returned in triumph. Otto reached Rome at Christmas, and the participants in the revolt were punished with gruesome brutality.

From now onwards John was protected by the emperor, who resided in Italy until summer 972. Although John was a mainly subservient partner, the two worked together to their mutual benefit. At a synod at Ravenna in Apr. 967 Otto confirmed the restoration to the papal state of large territories, including the former exarchate, which it had lost. Measures were taken, probably inspired by Otto, to promote clerical celibacy and continue favours to the monastery of Cluny, near Mâcon. For his part John definitively raised Magdeburg to an archbishopric, a project dear to the emperor's heart, agreed by John XII in 962 but hitherto obstructed by the bishops of Mainz and Halberstadt. Otto's original idea had been to make it the base for the conversion of all the Slavs east of the Saale and Elbe, but in his bulls (20 Apr. 967 and 18 Oct. 968) confirming its privileges and granting the *pallium to its first archbishop, Adalbert, John limited the see to 'the recently converted Slavs' and assigned the creation of new bishoprics not to the emperor but to the metropolitan: evidence, it has been claimed, that he retained some independence.

At Christmas 967 John crowned Otto's twelve-year-old son Otto II (955–83) as co-emperor. The urgency, in view of the restoration of the western empire in 962 and of Otto's efforts to extend his control in territories in southern Italy under Byzantine suzerainty, of putting relations with Constantinople on a constructive footing was now obvious. Otto formed the plan of achieving this by a diplomatic marriage, and on 14 Apr. 972 John married Otto II and the Greek princess Theophano, niece of Emperor John I Tzimisces (969–76), and crowned her. Even so, tension between the eastern and western churches could not be avoided; when John, in support of Otto's political designs, erected Capua and Benevento into metropolitan sees, the patriarch of Constantinople retaliated by making the bishop of Otranto an archbishop with five suffragans under him and attempting to check Roman influence in the Byzantine provinces of Apulia and Calabria.

Although it lasted only a year, John made Vich, in north-east Spain, a metropolitan see on its own. In 972 Oswald (d. 992), newly appointed archbishop of York, visited him, ostensibly to receive the *pallium but probably also to discuss the reorganization of monastic life in England on the reformed lines now becoming accepted on the Continent. John's patronage assisted the family of the Crescentii, a member of which had fought for him in the troubled days of 965, to enhance its power in Rome. He was buried in St Paul's-without-the-Walls.

LP 2, 253–4; JW 1, 470–7; 2, 706 f.; ZPR, 150–203; Watterich 1, 44; 684–6; Brezzi, 142–8; A. Brackman, 'Die Ostpolitik Ottos des Grossen', HZ 134 (1926), 242–56; DTC 8, 626–8 (É. Amann); Mann 4, 282–304; Seppelt 2, 372–8; Z1, 95–8; Z2, 153–85.

BENEDICT VI (19 Jan. 973–July 974). Nothing is known of his background except that he was a Roman, son of a Hildebrand who became a monk, and was cardinal priest of S. Teodoro when he was elected. The exact date and circumstances of his election are obscure, but the increasingly dominant Crescentii family strongly backed a candidate of its own, the deacon Franco. Benedict, however, had the support of both the imperial party and, in all probability, of reforming circles opposed to a purely political appointment. He must have been elected in Sept. or Oct. 972; the delay in proceeding to his consecration was caused by the necessity, under the *Ottonian privilege of 962, of obtaining the authorization of Emperor Otto I (962–73), then in Germany.

For the moment the Crescentii had to swallow their disappointment. Benedict embarked on policies characteristic of the Ottonian papacy, confirming the precedence of Trier as the oldest see in Germany, favouring reforming monasteries, and strictly forbidding bishops to charge fees for ordinations and consecrations. The death of Otto, however, on 7 May 973, fatally undermined his position in faction-riven Rome, and a year later, at a juncture when the new emperor, Otto II (973–83), was preoccupied with troubles in Germany, a nationalist party arose against him, led by the consul Crescentius I (d. 984), son of Theodora the Younger (d. c.950) and head of the Crescentian clan. Although concrete evidence is sparse, it is likely that the Byzan-

tines, anxious to exploit the crisis in the empire and to overthrow German sovereignty in Italy, had a hand in the revolt. In June 974 Benedict was seized by the rebels and imprisoned in Castel Sant'-Angelo to await trial. Nothing is known of the process or of the charges brought against him, but the deacon Franco was hastily elected and consecrated pope with the name BONIFACE VII. The imperial representative, Count Sicco of Spoleto, hurried to Rome in July and peremptorily demanded Benedict's release, but in vain. Boniface had him strangled by a priest named Stephen, probably judging that his own title to the holy see would look more credible if its legitimate tenant were out of the way.

Two privileges purporting to emanate from Benedict VI and to settle a dispute between Archbishop Frederick of Salzburg and Bishop Piligrim of Passau over jurisdiction in Hungary have been shown to be forgeries.

LP 2, 255–7; JW 1, 477–9; 2, 707; ZPR, 203–11; DHGE 8, 38–43 (F. Baix); DBI 8, 344–6 (P. Delogu); P. E. Schramm, 'Kaiser, Basileus und Papst in der Zeit der Ottonen', HZ 33 (1924), esp. 436 f.; Mann 4, 305–14; Z1, 99 f.; Z2, 202 f.; 209; Seppelt 2, 377–9.

BONIFACE VII (antipope June–July 974; Aug. 984–20 July 985). A Roman, son of Ferrucius and himself named Franco, he was a cardinal deacon in 972, and on the death of JOHN XIII on 6 Sept. seems to have been the candidate favoured by the Crescentii family, then dominant in Rome. The man chosen by the imperial party, however, and approved by Emperor Otto I (962–73), was BENEDICT VI, who had little following among the aristocracy and whose weakness was exposed on Otto's death in May 973. In June 974, when the new emperor Otto II (973–83) was preoccupied with difficulties in Germany, there was a rising against Benedict led by Crescentius I de Theodora; he was imprisoned in Castel Sant'Angelo, and Franco was consecrated pope with the title Boniface VII. The emperor's representative, Count Sicco, hastened from Spoleto and demanded Benedict's release; but Boniface, aware that Sicco was certain to restore the legal pope, had him strangled. Horror at the murder turned the populace against him, and soon he had to take refuge in Castel Sant'Angelo. Sicco stormed the fortress but Boniface escaped, taking part of the papal treasure with him, and made for Byzantine territory in south Italy.

Meanwhile BENEDICT VII (974–83) was elected pope in Oct. with the approval of Sicco and, apparently, the Crescentii. One of his first measures was to hold a synod at which Boniface was excommunicated, the sentence being circulated in the east as well as the west. The usurper was far from finished, however, and was even able, in summer 980, possibly during the pope's absence, to establish himself temporarily in Rome. Benedict sent an urgent appeal to Otto, and managed to return only in Mar. 981 accompanied by the emperor and armed soldiers. Boniface was driven out and fled to Constantinople.

Four years later, exploiting the confusion following Otto II's death on 7 Dec. 983 and the unpopularity of Benedict's successor JOHN XIV, Boniface made a second, successful if short-lived, comeback. Supplied by Byzantium with ample funds, he returned to Rome in Apr. 984, found powerful allies, had John imprisoned, deposed, and four months later (20 Aug. 984) murdered, and then re-ascended the papal throne. Almost nothing is known of his reign, but the fact that it lasted eleven months without imperial intervention is proof not only of the weakness of the government but of the support which, in spite of opposition (to quell which he had the cardinal deacon John blinded), he must have enjoyed.

On 20 July 985 he died suddenly. The conjecture that he was assassinated, the victim of a palace conspiracy, is plausible but not supported by the sources. There was certainly a revulsion of public opinion, for his death saw a furious outburst of detestation against him, and his corpse, stripped of its vestments, was dragged through the streets and exposed naked beneath Marcus Aurelius's statue, then in front of the Lateran, but now on the Capitol, where people trampled on it and stabbed it with their spears. In popular speech his name was twisted from 'Bonifatius' to 'Malefatius'.

Classified since 1904 as an antipope, he appears in the ancient official lists of popes, though usually described as an intruder; the next pope to assume the name Boniface was reckoned the eighth. Some have argued that he was legitimate pope at any rate from the date of John XIV's death in Aug. 984. He himself professed to regard Benedict VII and John XIV as intruders, and insisted on dating his reign from his consecration in 974.

LP 2, 255–9; JW 1, 485; 2, 707; 747; ZPR, 211 f.; 231–3; 253–6; Brezzi, 148–57; DHGE 9, 900–4 (F. Baix); LThK 2, 589 (G. Schwaiger); EC 2, 1866 (P. Goggi); DBI 12, 143–6 (P. Delogu); Seppelt 2, 378–83; Z1, 99–103; Z2, 202–4; 206; 213; 225–7.

BENEDICT VII (Oct. 974–10 July 983). A Roman aristocrat, son of David, kinsman of Prince Alberic II, who had ruled Rome 932–54, and connected with the powerful Crescentii family, he was bishop of Sutri, near Viterbo, when with the consent of Count Sicco, representative of Emperor Otto II (973–83), he succeeded BENEDICT VI, whom the intruder pope BONIFACE VII had had assassinated. Sicco refused to recognize Boniface, who escaped to south Italy, and a fresh election was held. The choice of Benedict was a useful compromise: though the candidate of the imperial party, he was also acceptable to the noble families. He immediately held a synod at which Boniface was excommunicated, but even so his position was not secure. Based on Byzantine territory in south Italy, Boniface carried out a coup in summer 980 which compelled the pope to leave Rome. Benedict appealed urgently to the emperor, and succeeded in returning only in Mar.

981 when Otto had established himself in Italy.

A deeply religious man, Benedict promoted monasticism and monastic reform; he also collaborated obediently with the emperor. Thus many of his enactments in his early years aimed at settling, in the confusion resulting from recent wars, the relative status of great German sees; for example, in 975 he granted the bishop of Mainz the right to crown German kings and confirmed his primacy as apostolic vicar, and permitted Dietrich of Trier singular ceremonial privileges and assigned him the cell of SS. Quattro Coronati on the Caelian (the first foreigner to possess a *title church in Rome). In early 976 he approved the appointment of Thietmar as bishop of the new see of Prague, originally planned to have oversight of Moravia as well as Bohemia. At the same time he gave active support to bishops who, especially in Germany (e.g. Dietrich of Trier), were restoring monasteries on reformed lines. He himself was in touch with Maiolus, the saintly fourth abbot of Cluny, near Mâcon in Burgundy, and placed the island of Lérins under Cluny. In Rome in 977 he refounded, under the refugee patriarch Sergius of Damascus (expelled by the Arabs), the monastery of SS. Bonifacio and Alexio on the Aventine, which maintained contact with eastern, and especially Slav, Christianity. He had a keen interest in Subiaco, east of Rome, site of St Benedict's grotto, where he consecrated the church of Sta Scholastica on 4 Dec. 980.

His relations with Otto became even closer after his return to Rome in spring 981. The emperor now resided in Italy, and was present with him at an important synod in St Peter's in Mar. 981 which prohibited simony, or the sale or purchase of any rank of holy orders; the decision was communicated to the entire Christian world. At the Lateran synod of 9 and 10 Sept. 981 Benedict, in compliance with the emperor's wishes, suppressed the see of Merseburg, dividing its territory among the dioceses of Halberstadt, Zeitz, and Meissen. Although

there were practical considerations in favour of this rearrangement, its real object was to gratify the ambition of Otto's favourite, Bishop Giseler of Merseburg, who was now translated to the grander see of Magdeburg. Benedict also co-operated with Otto's anti-Byzantine policies in south Italy, making Salerno an archbishopric and setting up Trani as a bishopric of Latin obedience independent of Byzantine-controlled Bari.

For all his subservience to the emperor, Benedict's reign witnessed an enhancement of the holy see in the consideration of the Christian west. Visits by leading prelates and layfolk *ad limina* (i.e. 'to the thresholds', or the tombs, of the Apostles Peter and Paul: a technical expression for formal visits to the holy see) became more frequent; the practice of referring issues to the pope increased: not only did Sergius of Damascus seek refuge in Rome, but James, elected bishop of Carthage in difficult circumstances, came to Rome to be consecrated. Benedict was buried in Sta Croce in Gerusalemme, one of the seven ancient patriarchal basilicas of Rome; at some date prior to his election he was reputed to have gone as a pilgrim to Jerusalem and to have brought back a fragment of the true cross.

LP 2, lxx; 256; 258; JW 1, 479-84; 2, 707; ZPR, 213-58; PL 137, 315-58; Brezzi, 152 f.; Mann 4, 315-27; DHGE 8, 46-61 (F. Baix); EC 2, 1271 f. (B. Pesci); DBI 8, 346-50 (P. Delogu); Z1, 101 f.; Z2, 204-7; Seppelt 2, 378-80.

JOHN XIV (Dec. 983–20 Aug. 984).

On the death of BENEDICT VII (10 July 983) Emperor Otto II (973-83) seems to have first offered the papal throne to Maiolus, saintly fourth abbot of Cluny (965-94), who declined it. He thereupon nominated his former arch-chancellor for Italy, Peter Canepanova, from 966 bishop of Pavia, his birthplace. The time-taking negotiations he had to conduct explain the length of the vacancy. Otto appears to have imposed Peter without consulting the Roman clergy and people; there is no evidence of a regular election. As a result the new pope, who took the name John so as to avoid that of the Prince of the Apostles, had no allies in any section of Roman society and depended wholly on his patron's protection.

No doubt Otto looked for loyal co-operation from his trusted former minister, and in fact John's only surviving bull is one bestowing the *pallium, in furtherance of the emperor's south Italian policies, on Archbishop Alo of Benevento. Unfortunately he had scarcely been installed in the Lateran when Otto, who had returned to Rome from the south stricken with malaria, died in his arms after receiving absolution (7 Dec. 983). Empress Theophano was obliged to return at once to Germany to defend the interests of her three-year-old son Otto III (980–1002). Without friends, regarded by the Romans as forced upon them, John was then defenceless and fell an easy prey to BONIFACE VII, raised up as antipope by the powerful Crescentii family in 974, excommunicated by Benedict VII, but now biding his time in Constantinople. In Apr. 984 he returned, and John was seized, brutally assaulted, formally deposed, and flung into gaol in Castel Sant'Angelo; no details of the charges or trial survive. Four months later he died in the fortress of starvation; according to some reports, he was poisoned. His epitaph in St Peter's, which records 20 Aug. as the date of his death, was engraved during Boniface's lifetime and, significantly, did not describe the circumstances of his end.

LP 2, 259; JW 1, 484 f.; *ZPR*, 250–5; *PL* 137, 357; Mann 4, 330–8; *DTC* 8, 628 (É. Amann); *NCE* 7, 1012 (S. McKenna); Z1, 102; Z2, 223 f.; Seppelt 2, 380 f.

JOHN XV (mid-Aug. 985–Mar. 996). A Roman, son of a priest Leo, a learned man and the author of books, he was cardinal priest of S. Vitale when he was elected, in the turbulent situation following Antipope BONIFACE VII's death (late July 985), as the agreed candidate of leading curial officials and John Crescentius (d. 988), head of the powerful Crescentii family. The regent Theophano, widow of Emperor Otto II

(973–83), being preoccupied in Germany, John Crescentius acted as political ruler of Rome and the papal state with the official title 'patrician'. Although restricted to ecclesiastical affairs, the new pope threw in his lot with the nobility, thereby alienating his clergy; his rapacity also set them against him. The imperial government, which had taken no part in the papal election, acquiesced in the arrangement, and when Theophano spent some months in Rome in winter 989/90 and asserted her youthful son's sovereignty, she maintained amicable relations with both pope and patrician.

However reduced his role at home, John acted vigorously in the church at large. When war seemed imminent between King Aethelred II of England (978–1016) and Duke Richard I of Normandy (946–96), he mediated and arranged a peaceful settlement (1 Mar. 991). In 992 Duke Mieszko I of Poland (c.960–92) presented his whole realm to St Peter and the pope, his object being to ensure more effective protection for it against Germany and Bohemia. In Germany John co-operated with the church policies of the imperial government, and on 31 Jan. 993, at a synod in the Lateran, solemnly canonized Ulrich, bishop of Augsburg (923–73), the first ritual canonization of a saint by a pope. In 992, spurred on by the German episcopate, he intervened in the affair of the deposition of Arnoul, archbishop of Rheims (988–1021), at the instigation of Hugh Capet, king of France (987–96), by the synod of Saint-Basle, Verzy (June 991), and his replacement by Gerbert of Aurillac (the future pope SILVESTER II). The French bishops had acted independently, convinced that they were within their rights and that the papacy had lost all moral authority; when John's legate, Abbot Leo, summoned them, with Hugh Capet and his brother Robert, to present themselves at Rome, they rejoindered, at the synod of Chelles (993 or 994), that a pope who transgressed the decrees of the fathers was no better than a heretic. Nevertheless John was able, through his legate, to have Gerbert suspended by the synod of Mouzon in the Ardennes (995). The incident has been described as one of the first and most serious manifestations of Gallicanism, i.e. the claim by the French church to more or less complete freedom from the authority of the papacy. After Theophano's death (15 June 991) John's position in Rome had deteriorated. John Crescentius died in 988, and his brother Crescentius II Nomentanus seized power in the papal state and ruled it as a tyrant. The French bishops at Saint-Basle complained that he had refused their envoys access to the pope, and had prevented him from dealing with their business unless lavish bribes were provided. Abbot Leo had to admit that he held John 'in such tribulation and oppression' that he could vouchsafe no answer to them or others. In Mar. 995, persecuted by Crescentius, hated by his clergy for his avariciousness and nepotism, John was forced to seek refuge in Sutri; in the summer he sent envoys to the German king Otto III, now fifteen and deemed of age, begging for help against his oppressors. The news of this *démarche*, and of Otto's decision to move south, obliged Crescentius and the Roman nobility to make their peace with the pope, invite him back to Rome, and reinstall him in the Lateran with every honour. Otto set out from Regensburg in Feb. 996, but before he reached Rome John had a violent attack of fever and died.

LP 2, 260; JW 1, 486–9; 2, 707 f.; ZPR, 256–96; Z1, 104 f.; Z2, 227–54; Seppelt 2, 381–7; W. Koelmel, 'Beiträge zur Verfassungsgeschichte Roms im 10 Jahrhundert', HJ 55 (1935), 527–44; K. G. von Žimgrod-Stadnicki, *Die Schenkung Polens an Papst Johannes XV* (Fribourg, 1911); F. Schneider, 'Johann XV, Papst, und Ottos III Romfahrt', MIÖG 39 (1923), 193–218; DTC 8, 628 f. (É. Amann); NCE 7, 1012 (W. M. Plöchl).

GREGORY V (3 May 996–18 Feb. 999). When Emperor Otto III (996–1002), moving from Germany in response to JOHN XV's appeal for help, reached Pavia at Easter 996, he learned that the pope was dead (March). Soon a delegation of the Roman nobility waited on him at Ravenna begging him to nominate a new pontiff; their attitude was a measure of their fear of his anger at their maltreatment of John XV. Otto chose a twenty-four-year-old relative born in 972, Bruno, son of his cousin Duke Otto of Carinthia, a priest of first-rate education who had gained experience of business in the royal chapel. Accompanied by Archbishop Willigis of Mainz and Bishop Hildibald of Worms, Otto's chancellor, Bruno went to Rome, was formally elected, and at his consecration as the first German pope took the name Gregory V, adopting GREGORY the Great (590–604) as his model.

On Ascension day (21 May) he crowned Otto as emperor and patrician in St Peter's, making him thus protector of the church. On 22 May Otto passed judgement on the dictator Crescentius II Nomentanus, who had persecuted John XV; he was sentenced to banishment, but was pardoned on the ill-advised intercession of Gregory, who was hoping to conciliate the powerful Roman families. Meanwhile, as the new pope asserted his independence and began adopting the curia's point of view as his own, relations quickly became clouded between him and the emperor. Otto refused both to renew the pact with the holy see which Emperor Otto I (962–73) had issued in his own and his son's names, and to restore the *Pentapolis (part of the *donation of Pepin) to the papal state, as Gregory demanded. For his part Gregory did not hesitate (May 996) to declare Gerbert (future pope SILVESTER II), whom John XV had suspended but who had become a close friend of Otto, an intruder on the see of Rheims and his deposed predecessor Arnoul its lawful bishop (988–1021).

In early June Otto left Rome, seeking a cooler climate. A month later Gregory, by now aware of the resentment aroused in Rome by the appointment of a foreign pope and feeling his position threatened, besought him to return, but he declined, pleaded ill-health, and referred him to the dukes of Tuscany and Spoleto for protec-

JOHN XVI (antipope 997-8)

tion. In early Oct., Otto being now in Germany, the Romans led by Crescentius II revolted and drove Gregory, stripped of everything, out of the city. He sought refuge in Spoleto, and although he made two armed attempts to recover Rome they both failed.

In Jan. 997 Gregory moved to Lombardy, where he held discussions with local bishops; probably also with John Philagathos, archbishop of Piacenza, recently returned from a diplomatic mission to Byzantium. In early Feb. he held a synod at Pavia at which Crescentius was excommunicated and the old rules (going back to SYMMACHUS, 1 Mar. 499) prohibiting agreements about his successor during a pope's lifetime and the purchase of clerical offices with money were re-enacted. Later in the month, on the pretext that the papal throne was vacant, Crescentius and his adherents, with active support from the Byzantine envoy Leo, had John Philagathos elected and installed with the title of JOHN XVI. The usurper was soon excommunicated by the western episcopate, but as the emperor had immediate preoccupations in Germany it was only in Feb. 998 that he could take possession of Rome. Here Gregory, finally restored, presided over a synod at which John Philagathos, already appallingly mutilated, was deposed and imprisoned in a monastery; Crescentius was beheaded on the battlements of Castel Sant'Angelo.

For the rest of his reign Gregory worked closely with Otto, although their different conceptions of their respective roles did not make for easy relations. Determined to uphold the papal point of view, he suspended the French bishops who had taken part in the deposition of Arnoul of Rheims and ratified his restoration as bishop (Pavia, Feb. 997); but when Otto made Gerbert archbishop of Ravenna, he had to accept his appointment and send him the *pallium. A keen reformer, he excommunicated King Robert II of France (996-1031) for refusing to give up his cousin Bertha, whom he had uncanonically mar-

ried; and against the emperor's will he took steps (early 999) to restore the see of Merseburg, suppressed in 981.

His unexpected death in Feb. 999 started the rumour that he had been poisoned, but in fact he fell a victim to malaria. He was still under thirty, a hard and determined man of restless energy; his epitaph celebrated his ability to preach in French and German as well as Latin.

LP 2, 261 f.; JW 1, 489–95; ZPR, 296–342; Z1, 104–13; Z2, chap. 10; Seppelt 2, 387–92; K. Guggenberger, Die deutschen Päpste (Cologne, 1916), 15–28; K. and M. Uhlirz, Jahrbücher des deutschen Reiches: Otto III (Berlin, 1954), passim; Mann 4, 389–446; LThK 4, 1182 (Th. Schieffer); NCE 6, 771 (F. Dressler).

JOHN XVI (antipope Feb. 997–May 998: d. 26 Aug. 1001). A Greek from Rossano in Calabria, John Philagathos was appointed chancellor for Italy (980) and then (982) abbot of Nonantola, near Modena, by Emperor Otto II (973–83). After Otto's death his widow Empress Theophano made him (987) tutor to her seven-year-old son, King Otto III (emperor 996–1002), and then bishop of Piacenza (988), Pope JOHN XV raising this see for his sake to an archbishopric and detaching it from Ravenna. In 991 he again became chancellor for Italy, and in 994 was sent as special envoy to Constantinople to find a Byzantine princess as bride for Otto III. He returned to Italy, accompanied by a Byzantine ambassador, Bishop Leo of Synada, in early November 996, shortly after the Roman rising against GREGORY V and his expulsion by Crescentius II Nomentanus, now dictator of Rome. While Leo went to Rome, John Philagathos spent some weeks in north Italy, where he was in touch with Emperor Otto III at Aachen as well as with Crescentius. In early Feb. 997, when Gregory, still exiled from Rome, held a synod at Pavia, there were rumours that a fresh papal election was pending, and shortly after John Philagathos, visiting Rome ostensibly as a pilgrim, allowed himself to be elected and installed as John XVI.

What prompted his decision, apart from vain ambition, was powerful pressure from Crescentius and the Greek envoy Leo; the former hoped that the emperor, alienated from Gregory V and aware of his unpopularity, would be content to see such a trusted friend on the papal throne, while the latter (as he boasted in letters home) could see only advantage for Constantinople in separating Rome from its German master. But the usurper was not allowed to enjoy his new role for long. In Mar., by order of emperor and pope, he was replaced as abbot of Nonantola and archbishop of Piacenza; either then or soon after his formal excommunication followed. In summer 997 he received a highly critical letter from his saintly compatriot, Abbot Nilus of Rossano (c. 910–1004), who sharply rebuked him for his unchristian ambition, and also severe remonstrances from his former pupil Otto, for the moment detained in Germany. It must by now have become clear to him that he was no more than Crescentius's creature, confined to purely spiritual functions. By early autumn he was promising to submit to all the emperor's demands, but Crescentius prevented any negotiation by putting the imperial messengers under lock and key.

In Dec. 997 Otto marched with his army into Italy; John abandoned his cause as lost and fled to the Campagna—a fact which explains the attribution to him, in most papal lists, of a reign of ten months. In Feb. 998 Otto, accompanied by Gregory, entered Rome, which opened its gates without resistance. A detachment of troops led by Count Berthold discovered the usurper in a fortified castle, seized him, and handed him over to a Roman monastery. Either at his capture or, more probably, later with the consent of emperor and pope, he was blinded and appallingly mutilated in his nose, tongue, lips, and hands; he was then paraded around the city, sitting back to front on an ass. Later, probably in May, a formal trial was held under the presidency of Gregory, and he was condemned, deposed, degraded from his priestly rank,

and ritually stripped of his pontifical robes. Abbot Nilus, who had interceded in vain for him, was furious and left the city on the same day, placing a curse on both Otto and Gregory. Finally, the broken and humiliated man was shut up in a Roman monastery, where he was allowed to receive occasional visits and where he lingered on until 26 Aug. 1001.

LP 2, 261 f.; JW 1, 495 f.; *ZPR*, 313–35; 378; Z1, 105–13; Z2, 259–64; Seppelt 2, 388 f.; M. Uhlirz, *Jahrbücher des deutschen Reiches: Otto III* (Berlin 1954) (index); T. De Luca, *Giovanni Filagato, Almanacco Calabrese* (Rome, 1955), 81–92; P. E. Schramm, 'Kaiser, Basileus und Papst in der Zeit der Ottonen', *HZ* 129 (1924), 424–75; 'Neun Briefe des Byzantinischen Gesandten Leos', *BZ* 25 (1925), 89–105.

SILVESTER II (2 Apr. 999–12 May 1003). On the death of GREGORY V Emperor Otto III (996–1002), advised by Abbot Odilo of Cluny (d. 1049), appointed his friend and tutor, Gerbert, then archbishop of Ravenna, to succeed Gregory. The first Frenchman to become pope, he named himself after SILVESTER I (314–35), traditionally regarded as the model of papal partnership with the emperor.

Born c.945 in Auvergne of humble parentage, he received a thorough education, first at Aurillac and then at Vich, where he became exceptionally proficient in mathematics and astronomy. Taken to Rome in 970, he impressed JOHN XIII by his brilliance and was introduced to Emperor Otto I (962–73). In 972 he went to study dialectic at Rheims, where the archbishop, Adalbero, soon appointed him head of his cathedral school. His renown as a wide-ranging, strikingly original teacher spread, and when visiting the court of Otto II (973–83) at Ravenna with Adalbero in 980 he debated in the emperor's presence with Otric, head of the cathedral school at Magdeburg. Otto was so delighted that he named him abbot of Bobbio, 60 km. northeast of Genoa; but in spite of the attractions of the great library he encountered, as a foreigner, such administrative and other practical difficulties that in 984 he resumed his teaching at Rheims.

Becoming involved in politics, he assisted Bishop Adalbero in getting Hugh Capet elected king of France (987–96). On Adalbero's death (23 Jan. 989) Gerbert hoped to succeed him at Rheims, but Hugh Capet nominated Arnoul, bastard son of the former Carolingian king Lothair (954–86). Only when he discovered that Arnoul, who had sworn fealty, was intriguing against him with his rival Charles, duke of Lorraine (d. *c.*994), did the king, after vainly awaiting the assent of JOHN XV, have him deposed and replaced by Gerbert at the synod of Saint-Basle, Verzy (17 June 991). Bishop Arnoul of Orléans, furnished with arguments by Gerbert, rejected the plea that papal approval for the deposition was necessary, claiming that synods could judge bishops when the case was clear and determined by law (an early manifestation of *Gallicanism), and that in any case the holy see had lost moral credibility. John XV, however, refused to recognize Arnoul's enforced resignation, and at the synod of Mouzon (June 995) his legate suspended Gerbert, who in the meantime had been openly attacking the papal pretensions. His position at Rheims now became untenable, and in spring 996 he betook himself to the court of Otto III, becoming his close friend and adviser, and ably defending himself at the coronation synod in May. His problems at Rheims were solved when in Apr. 998 Otto procured his appointment as archbishop of Ravenna.

Once installed as pope, Silvester showed himself an intransigent champion of the traditional rights of the papacy which he had earlier assailed. Thus he immediately authorized his old rival Arnoul to resume his functions as archbishop of Rheims on the ground that his deposition had not been sanctioned by the holy see, and proceeded to act with a high hand against metropolitans and bishops who incurred his disapproval. An active reformer, he denounced simony and nepotism, called for celibacy, and insisted on the free election of

abbots by monks. Throughout he worked in close concert with Otto, in whose imagination he helped to shape the vision of a renewed, Christian Roman empire. Otto esteemed him so highly that he handed over to him (Jan. 1001), as St PETER's representative, the eight counties of the *Pentapolis which Gregory V had demanded in vain, making it clear, however, that he did so of his own free will and not in fulfilment of the *Donation of Constantine, which he dismissed as a forgery. As Otto's conception of his role in the renewed Christian empire developed, Silvester was inevitably the junior partner, but among their successful joint achievements was the organization of the church in Poland and in Hungary, with archbishoprics at Gniezno and Esztergom respectively; in 1001 Silvester sent the royal crown to King Stephen I of Hungary.

In Feb. 1001, dissatisfied with foreign rule, the Romans revolted, and emperor and pope were forced to quit the city. Otto died of malaria on 23 Jan. 1002 before he could re-establish his authority. John II Crescentius (d. 1012) now ruled Rome with a firm hand as patrician (1003–12), but he allowed Silvester to return and function as a spiritual leader until his death less than a year later. Overshadowed politically by the emperor, but an astute statesman who kept in touch with most of the leading personalities of the day, Silvester dazzled contemporaries by the versatility and brilliance of his intellect. His reputation rests less on his work as a churchman than on his many-sided culture, especially in the fields of science, music, and mathematics, but also in literature (e.g. the collection and preservation of manuscripts of classical Latin authors). He was a pioneer of the abacus, terrestrial and celestial globes, and the organ. Later credulity invented the legend that he was a magician who had made a pact with the devil, to whom he owed his unprecedented promotion from Rheims to Ravenna, and then to Rome; the three initial Rs were deemed portentously significant.

PL 139, 57–338 (works); A. Olleris (ed.), *Œuvres de Gerbert* (Clermont-Ferrand, 1867); N. Bubnov (ed.), *Gerberti opera mathematica* (Berlin, 1899; repr. 1963); F. Weigle, *Die Briefsammlung Gerberts von Reims* (*MG, Briefe der deutschen Kaiserzeit* 2 (1966)); H. P. Lattin (ed.), *The Letters of Gerbert and his Papal Privileges* (New York, 1961); *LP* 2, 263 f.; JW 1, 496–501; *ZPR*, 343–86; K. and M. Uhlirz, *Jahrbücher der deutschen Geschichte: Otto III* (see index); *DTC* 14, 2075–83 (É. Amann); Z2, see index; J. Leflon, *Gerbert: Humanisme et chrétienté au Xe siècle* (St Wandrille, 1946); P. E. Schramm, *Kaiser, Rom und Renovatio* (Darmstadt, 1957); Seppelt 2, 384–6; 390–401; *NCE* 13, 858–60 (H. P. Lattin).

JOHN XVII (16 May–6 Nov. 1003).

SILVESTER II's successor was John Sicco, son of a father also named John and born in the Biberetica district of the city near Trajan's column. Nothing is known of his earlier career or of the circumstances of his election except that he must have been the nominee of John II Crescentius (d. 1012), son of the Crescentius executed in 998 for his part in the revolt against GREGORY V, who since the death of Emperor Otto III (996–1002) without heir held effective power—with the rank of patrician of the Romans (1003–12)—over Rome, the papal state, and the papacy itself. John was probably related to the family of the Crescentii, and he seems to have been the puppet of the patrician. A chronicler reports that he was keen (as he well might have been) to establish relations with the new German king, Henry II (1002–24), but was prevented from taking any steps by John Crescentius. His only recorded act of significance is his authorization of the Polish missionary Benedict, a disciple of Bruno of Querfurt, and his brethren to engage in evangelistic work among the Slavs. It is not known how he died or how old he was. Three of his kinsmen—a bishop, a deacon, and a high dignitary of the Lateran chancery (*secundicerius*)—are commemorated in an epitaph dated 1040; they evidently took pride in being related to a pope, even one so short-lived and obscure.

LP 2, 265; JW 1, 501; *ZPR*, 386–8; R. Poupardin, 'Note sur la chronologie du pontificat de Jean XVII', *MelArchHist* 21 (1901), 387–90; *DTC* 8, 629 (É. Amann).

JOHN XVIII (25 Dec. 1003–June or July 1009).

A Roman, John Fasanus ('Cock') by name, son of Ursus and Stephania, he was cardinal priest of St Peter's when he succeeded JOHN XVII. Like him, he owed his appointment to the patrician John II Crescentius, all-powerful ruler of Rome from 1003 to 1012, with whose family he also may have been connected.

Although Crescentius's nominee, John seems (from the sparse reports that survive) to have taken a vigorous initiative in church affairs. By putting pressure on the new German king, Henry II (1002–24), he brought about (1004) the restoration of the see of Merseburg, which BENEDICT VII had suppressed and GREGORY V had sought to revive. In 1007 he approved the foundation of the see of Bamberg (Bavaria) by Henry, who wanted to make it both a base for missionary work among immigrant Slavs and a political centre on the upper Main; he made it suffragan to Mainz rather than to Würzburg, as the latter's bishop desired, and placed it under papal protection. When he learned (late 1007) that the bishops of Sens and Orléans had threatened the privileges of the abbey of Fleury, ordering its abbot to burn the bulls granting it papal exemptions, he peremptorily summoned them to Rome on pain of excommunication, and even threatened King Robert II of France (996–1031) that he would place his entire kingdom under a ban if they failed to appear.

The chronicler Thietmar of Merseburg (975–1018) noted that John was eager for Henry II to visit Rome, presumably in May 1004 when he was crowned king of Italy at Pavia, but that Crescentius set his face against the idea. On the other hand, it may have been Crescentius, with his pro-Byzantine sympathies, who brought about the temporary suspension during this pontificate of the schism between Rome and the eastern church. At any rate there is evidence that the name of John XVIII was at some date restored to the *diptychs at Constantinople. Following the precedent set by JOHN XV, he solemnly canonized (mid-1004) the five Polish martyrs, Benedict, John, Isaac, Matthew, and Christian. He sent the *pallium to Archbishops Meingandus of Trier and Elphege (d. 1012) of Canterbury.

When he died, John is stated to have been a monk at St Paul's-without-the-Walls. The general view is that he retired there, possibly having abdicated, shortly before his death, but the circumstances are wrapped in obscurity; the possibility that his withdrawal was forced upon him rather than voluntary is a very real one.

LP 2, 266; JW 1, 501-3; 2, 708; *ZPR*, 388-409; *DTC* 8, 629 f. (É. Amann); Brezzi, 185; Z1, 114; *NCE* 7, 1012 (W. M. Plöchl); Seppelt 2, 401.

SERGIUS IV (31 July 1009-12 May 1012). A Roman, son of Peter, a shoemaker of the Ad Pinea district, and his wife Stephania, originally himself named Peter with the nickname *Os* or *Bucca Porci* ('Pig's Snout'), he had been bishop of Albano for five years when he succeeded JOHN XVIII. The circumstances of his appointment remain obscure, but like John he owed it to the patrician John II Crescentius, Rome's all-powerful dictator from 1003 to 1012. He altered his name out of respect for the Prince of the Apostles. Reliable information about his activities, apart from the routine granting or confirmation of privileges, is sparse, but it is noteworthy that he was in touch with Henry II of Germany (1002-24), sending envoys to the consecration of the cathedral of his beloved Bamberg (Apr. 1012) and ratifying the privileges granted it by John XVIII. It is probable that he took advantage of this occasion to sound the king on a visit to Rome, but any such project was frustrated not only by the political situation in Germany but by the unyielding opposition of Crescentius. At the request of its bishop (the chronicler Thietmar: 975-1018) he confirmed (1009) the possessions of the recently restored see of Merseburg. There is a tradition that the eastern

patriarch Sergius II (1001-19), after the temporary recognition of John XVIII, again struck the pope's name out of the *diptychs of Constantinople, but no credence should be given to the suggestion that Sergius IV was himself responsible for this by sending to Constantinople, along with the announcement of his election, a profession of faith containing the *Filioque* clause. An encyclical in which he purports to appeal to the faithful everywhere to prepare an armed expedition to avenge the destruction of the Holy Sepulchre in Jerusalem by Caliph al-Hakim on 18 Oct. 1009 is almost certainly spurious; the elements of truth in the story are the undoubted arrival in Rome in Sergius's reign of the news of the disaster, and his attempts (unrelated) to mobilize the Italian powers to drive the Arabs from Sicily.

The disappearance of both Sergius and Crescentius from the scene within less than a week of each other (12 and 18 May), the violent political upheaval which took place in Rome at the time, and the immediate election of a pope of the rival Tusculan family have given rise to the suspicion that neither man may have died a natural death. Sergius was buried in St John Lateran, where his eulogistic epitaph can still be read.

LP 2, 266 f.; JW 1, 504 f.; *ZPR*, 409-24; *PL* 139, 1499-528; A. Gieysztor, 'The Genesis of the Crusades: the Encyclical of Sergius IV', *Medievalia et Humanistica* 5 (1948), 3-34; Mann 5, 142-54; *DTC* 14, 1921 f. (É. Amann); J. Gay, *Les papes du XIᵉ siècle et le chrétienté* (Paris, 1926); Seppelt 2, 401 f.

BENEDICT VIII (17 May 1012-9 Apr. 1024). The almost simultaneous deaths (12 and 18 May) of SERGIUS IV and the patrician John II Crescentius coincided with a political upheaval in Rome in which the family of the counts of Tusculum, descended from the senator *Theophylact (d. probably 926), wrested power from the Crescentii, the ruling house since 1002. In bitter rivalry the Crescentians elected one GREGORY, while the Tusculans chose and installed Theophylact, second son of Count Gregory of Tusculum, born *c.*980, still a layman, who assumed the name Benedict. In June–July he used armed force to crush the Crescentians in their mountain strongholds, while his brother Romanus (later JOHN XIX) took over the civil government of Rome. His rival Gregory fled to Germany to plead his cause before Henry II (1002–24), but before the year's end the king effectively recognized Benedict, asking him to confirm the rights of his much loved see, Bamberg. He must have known that Benedict was in full possession of the holy see, authoritatively dealing with the church's business in ways that gratified him (e.g. granting the *pallium to archbishops of Mainz in Aug. and Oct.).

One of Benedict's achievements was to restore relations with the German royal house, and he not only confirmed the rights of Bamberg but proposed that Henry should visit Rome. The king agreed, and on Feb. 1014 was crowned emperor in St Peter's; he had first sworn to be the church's faithful protector, but had not insisted on the traditional suzerainty. Benedict had already authorized him, when at Ravenna in Jan., to restore his half-brother Arnold as archbishop there. At the synod following the coronation the pope not only consecrated Arnold, but yielded to Henry's request that the creed (with the addition of the *Filioque*) should be sung at mass, a northern practice previously not accepted at Rome. Pope and emperor then moved to Ravenna, where they held a reforming synod which settled the minimum ages for holy orders and legislated against simony and other abuses.

Henry now left for Germany, pressing the pope to visit him there, while on his instructions Benedict by force of arms restored to the abbey of Farfa, 40 km. north of Rome, certain possessions which the Crescentians had seized. An efficient administrator and soldier who has been likened to a feudal baron, he spent much of the next six years in campaigns aimed at making Rome the political centre of Italy.

By force of arms he restored papal authority in the Campagna and Roman Tuscany. Forming an alliance with Pisa and Genoa, he defeated Arab invaders in north Italy in a sea-battle in which he himself took part and liberated Sardinia (1016). At the same time, with an eye to the papal possessions and claims in south Italy, he supported revolts against Byzantine rule there, putting Norman knights at the disposal of the insurgents' leaders. When the Byzantines crushed the insurgents at Cannae in 1019 and advanced north, he betook himself to Germany, ostensibly in response to Henry's personal invitation but really to seek his help. The personal appearance of the pope on German soil created an immense impression. At Easter 1020 the two conferred at Bamberg, and Henry gave Benedict an imperial privilege which verbally reproduced the *Ottonian privilege granted by Otto I in 962, including the rights of sovereignty it conferred on the emperor; he also promised military aid. He fulfilled his promise in 1022 when, accompanied by the pope, he marched with a powerful army to south Italy, but although he scored some successes these were soon lost, and Benedict had to be satisfied that the advance of the Byzantines had at least been halted.

The Italian expedition enabled Henry and Benedict to extend the reforms on which they had embarked in 1014, and at the synod of Pavia (1 Aug. 1022) they promulgated drastic canons prohibiting marriage or concubinage for all clerics, including those of the rank of subdeacon, and reducing the children of such unions to serfdom; it was important that Henry at once embodied these canons in the imperial code. It was he who was the leading spirit in these reforms; while Benedict personally admired Odilo, fifth abbot of Cluny (d. 1049), and favoured reforming abbeys, his chief concern (as his address at the synod made clear) was for church property, liable to be dissipated when the clergy indulged in families.

A man of action and statecraft rather than spirituality, Benedict wielded more power, as a contemporary noted, than any of his immediate predecessors. Tenacious of the rights of the holy see, he did not hesitate to take the strongest measures against Aribo, archbishop of Mainz (1021–31), when at the synod of Seligenstadt (1023) he banned appeals to Rome, over the heads of metropolitans, on disciplinary matters. There is a report that Patriarch Sergius (1001–19) removed the pope's name from the *diptychs at Constantinople, to which it had been restored in JOHN XVIII's time; if true, the cause is likely to have been Benedict's enthusiastic support for revolts against Byzantine rule in south Italy. A man of energy, perspicacity, and decision, who perceived the importance of co-operation between the papacy and the German crown, prepared the alliance of the holy see with the Normans, and championed the independence of Italy against the Saracens, he enhanced the prestige of his office in an age of eclipse.

LP 2, 268; JW 1, 506–14; *ZPR*, 425–501; *PL* 139, 1579–638; K. J. Herrmann, *Das Tuskulaner Papstum (1012–1046)* (Stuttgart, 1973); E. Joranson, 'The Inception of the Career of the Normans in Italy', *Speculum* 23 (1948), 353–96; M. Fornasari, 'Enrico II e Benedetto VIII ed i canoni del presunto concilio di Ravenna del 1014', *RSTI* 18 (1964), 46–55; P. G. Wappler, *Papst Benedikt VIII* (Leipzig, 1897); *DHGE* 6, 61–92 (F. Baix); Mann 5, 155–211; *DBI* 8, 350–4 (G. Tellenbach); *NCE* 2, 274 (V. Gellhaus); Seppelt 2, 403–8.

GREGORY (VI) (antipope May–Dec. 1012). On the death of SERGIUS IV on 12 May 1012, followed almost immediately by that of the patrician John II Crescentius on 18 May, the Crescentian family, which had ruled Rome since Emperor Otto III's death in 1002 and had nominated the last three popes, found control of the city wrested from it by the rival family of the counts of Tusculum. In a bitter struggle for power the Tusculans elected and enthroned Theophylact as pope with the style BENEDICT VIII, while the Crescentians put forward and elected one Gregory (either his original name or the name he assumed), about whose antecedents and position at the

time nothing is known. It is not clear whether he was actually installed or not, but his subsequent actions make it certain that there was a *prima facie* legal basis to his appointment. With Benedict established in the Lateran, however, and waging war on the Crescentians, his position was hopeless from the start, and there is no record of any official acts attributed to him. At some date in the summer he was ejected from Rome, and in spite of the traditional hostility of the Crescentians to the German royal house made his way to the court of King Henry II (1002–24) to seek recognition. At Christmas 1012, robed in full pontificals and bitterly complaining of his expulsion, he appeared before the king at Pöhlde, in Saxony. According to the chronicler Thietmar (975–1018), Henry received him with cool courtesy, promised to settle the disputed election 'according to Roman custom' once he got to Rome, but took his ceremonial cross from him and bade him in the meantime desist from the exercise of his office. Gregory complied, doubtless expecting that the king would treat his rival similarly. In fact Henry was already in touch with Benedict, and his formal recognition of him was only a matter of weeks. From this moment the luckless Gregory disappears from history.

ZPR, 425 f.; 435; Thietmar, *Chron.* 6, 101 (*MGSS* NS 9, 394); K. J. Herrmann, *Das Tuskulaner Papstum (1012–1046)* (Stuttgart, 1973), 5; 7; 25–7; *EC* 6, 1129 (A. Frutaz); Z1, 115–17; Seppelt 2, 402 f.

JOHN XIX (19 Apr. 1024–20 Oct. 1032). On the death of BENEDICT VIII (1012–24) the Tusculan family, regarding the papacy as their private property, had his younger brother Romanus elected and enthroned, with the name John. A layman who held office as 'consul, dux, and senator', he was said to have obtained the succession by lavish bribery; his elevation from layman to pope in a single day also shocked many. Although generally reckoned an ineffectual pontiff, he was politically astute, and both strengthened his own position and ensured peace by conciliating other noble families, including the displaced Crescentii, and by transferring his brother Alberic from the city judiciary to the Lateran palace.

In the first year of his reign, if the chronicler Rudolf Glaber (c.990–1046/7) can be trusted, he received a delegation from the eastern patriarch and emperor Basil II (976–1025) seeking his agreement to the recognition of Constantinople as having universal jurisdiction in the east parallel to Rome's in the west; it was the old question of the title *'ecumenical patriarch'. The delegation brought rich gifts, and John was attracted; but when it got abroad that he was thinking of compromising Rome's universal primacy there was a storm of protest, especially from the monks of Cluny, near Mâcon (Burgundy), and Abbot William of Dijon (990–1031), and he had to climb down. As it stands, the story is suspect; it is inconceivable that the curia would have countenanced his making any such deal. It may recall, however, in garbled form a serious attempt by the Byzantine authorities, not least in view of Benedict VIII's anti-Byzantine policies in south Italy, to reach agreement with Rome about their respective zones of influence. It remains a fact that from this time the pope's name ceased to be mentioned in the *diptychs of Constantinople.

Early in 1027 Conrad II (1024–39), successor as German king to Henry II (1002–24), having received the Lombard crown at Pavia, came to Rome, and on 26 Mar. John crowned him emperor in St Peter's, in the presence of kings Rodolphe III of Burgundy (993–1032) and Cnut of England and Denmark (1016/17–1035). It is significant that the new emperor neither swore to protect the Roman church nor renewed the *Ottonian privilege granted by his predecessors. Indeed, far from establishing a relationship of co-operation with John such as Henry II had had with Benedict VIII, Conrad regarded him as a person of little consequence whom he could use, or even humiliate, as suited his whim. Thus, to gratify his loyal friend Poppo, German

archbishop of Aquileia, he obliged the compliant pope to decree not only that Grado, in defiance of an earlier decision of his own, was subject to Aquileia, but that Aquileia was 'metropolis of all the churches of Italy' (Apr. and Sept. 1027). Again, when Bishop Warmann of Constance complained that John had granted the abbot of Reichenau the right to wear pontifical vestments at mass, Conrad promptly ordered the abbot to hand the bull and the insignia to the bishop, who publicly burned them. In spite of these disagreements, however, his prestige stood high in the church at large. He made a great impression in 1027 on King Cnut, who obtained from him, in return for the regular payment of Peter's Pence, the remission in future of the exorbitant sums he was in the habit of charging for granting the *pallium, as well as the exemption of the English compound in Rome from the customary tribute. For most of his reign he enjoyed excellent relations with Abbot Odilo of Cluny, twice confirming the privileges of the abbey in the most absolute terms and taking effective action against Bishop Gouzlin of Mâcon when he attacked them. In France his decision in May 1031 that Martial, 3rd-cent. first bishop of Limoges, should rank as an apostle and be commemorated yearly on 30 June, was accepted by all parties as authoritative.

LP 2, 269; JW 1, 514–19; 2, 709; 748; Watterich 1, 70; 75; 708–11; Rudolfus Glaber, *Hist.* 1, 4 (ed. M. Prou, Paris, 1886: 93 f.); K. J. Herrmann, *Das Tuskulaner Papstum (1012–1046)* (Stuttgart, 1973), see index; *DTC* 8, 630–2 (É. Amann); A. Michel, 'Die Weltreichs—und Kirchenteilung bei Rudolf Glaber', *HJ* 70 (1950), 53–64; Mann 5, 212–37; Seppelt 2, 408–12.

BENEDICT IX (21 Oct. 1032–Sept. 1044; 10 Mar.–1 May 1045; 8 Nov. 1047–16 July 1048: d. 1055/6). On the death of JOHN XIX his brother Alberic III, now head of the ruling Tusculan family, bribed the electorate and had his son Theophylact, nephew of both John XIX and BENEDICT VIII, elected and enthroned, with the style Benedict IX. Still a layman, he was not, as later gossip alleged, a lad of ten or twelve but was probably in his late twenties; his personal life, even allowing for exaggerated reports, was scandalously violent and dissolute. If for twelve years he proved a competent pontiff, he owed this in part to native resourcefulness, but in part also to an able entourage and to the firm control which his father exercised over Rome. He was the only pope to hold office, at any rate *de facto*, for three separate spells.

In general his policies followed those of his predecessors. In 1037, however, he made important changes in the curia aimed at centralization, perhaps also at getting rid of German control. Emperor Conrad II (1024–39) found him less pliant than John XIX; when he invited him to Cremona in 1037, expecting him to ratify his deposition of Aribert, the rebellious archbishop of Milan (1018–45), the pope first sought to arrange a compromise. Only a year later did he excommunicate Aribert and recognize his imperial replacement. Meanwhile, as a result of his aunt's marriage to Pandulf, brother of Count Waimar of Salerno, he was able to play a helpful role in Conrad's expedition to south Italy. A beneficiary was the Benedictine abbey of Monte Cassino, midway between Rome and Naples, which on 1 July 1038 he placed under papal protection. With Conrad's successor, Henry III (1039–56), his relations were initially friendly. At the Roman synod of Apr. 1044, however, he asserted his independence, restoring to Grado the patriarchal status of which John XIX, in abject deference to Conrad, had deprived it in 1027.

In Sept. 1044 there was a sudden reversal of his fortunes. An insurrection at Rome, to which growing disgust at his loose life and, even more, resentment at the Tusculan domination contributed, forced him to abandon the city. Bloody fighting ensued, but on 20 Jan. 1045 the Stephanian branch of the Crescentian family succeeded in getting their local bishop, John of Sabina, installed as Pope SILVESTER III. Benedict, who had never been formally deposed and whose partisans were based in Trastevere,

promptly excommunicated Silvester, and on 10 Mar. expelled him from Rome and reassumed the papacy. His second term in the Lateran, however, lasted less than two months; on 1 May he made out a deed of abdication in favour of his godfather John Gratian, who was then elected and took the style GREGORY VI. A feeling of insecurity based on awareness of the hostility of the people, probably also pressure from friends, and according to some the desire to marry, seem to have impelled him to this surprising step. But John had to raise and hand over to him a huge sum of money; this has been implausibly represented as an inducement to stand down rather than as strict payment for the papal office, which it was almost certainly intended to be.

Benedict now withdrew to family properties near Tusculum (close to Frascati). In autumn 1046 Henry III reappeared in Italy, intent on church reform and on receiving the imperial crown from unsullied hands. Benedict was cited, with Silvester III and Gregory VI, to appear before a synod which he held at Sutri, near Rome, on 20 Dec. Having failed to do so, Benedict was formally deposed at the Roman synod of 24 Dec. Henry had already deposed Silvester and Gregory at Sutri, and now appointed Suidger of Bamberg as pope with the name CLEMENT II. Clement's sudden death after a reign of less than eight months was the signal, after a show of resistance by the imperial faction, for the restoration of Benedict, on a wave of popular enthusiasm assisted by bribery, on 8 Nov. 1047; the evidence sometimes adduced for a fresh election by the Roman clergy and people cannot hold water. From that date he was *de facto* pontiff until 16 July 1048, when Count Boniface of Tuscany, reluctantly yielding to Henry's orders, forcibly ejected him and installed Poppo of Brixen as DAMASUS II on the papal throne. Safe in his Tusculan homeland Benedict continued to regard himself as rightful pope and to breathe defiance at Damasus II and, after his death, at LEO IX. A synod meeting in the Lateran in Apr. 1049 summoned him to face the charge of simony, and when he declined to appear excommunicated him. Later Leo IX is said to have lifted this sentence, and on his deathbed to have prayed that the recalcitrant man would come to see the truth. Benedict was still alive on 18 Sept. 1055, when he is recorded as making a donation, along with his three brothers, to the monastery of SS. Cosma and Damiano in Rome; but he was dead by 9 Jan. 1056, when his brothers arranged for masses for his soul. He was buried, and probably died, at Grottaferrata, in the Alban hills; the story that he had settled for the contemplative life in the monastery there is difficult to assess.

LP 2, 270–2; 331; JW 1, 519–23; Watterich 1, 71–6; 711–17; R. Lane Poole, 'Benedict IX and Gregory VI', *Proceedings of the British Academy* 8 (1917–18), 199–235; K. J. Herrmann, *Das Tuskulaner Papstum (1012–1046)* (Stuttgart, 1973), index; *DHGE* 8, 93–105 (F. Baix and L. Jadin); Mann 5, 212–37; *DBI* 8, 354–66 (O. Capitani); Z1, 110–35; Seppelt 2, 412–18.

SILVESTER III (20 Jan.–10 Mar. 1045: d. 1063). When BENEDICT IX was violently ejected from Rome in Sept. 1044, the Romans, after bitter and protracted infighting, elected and installed Bishop John of Sabina (the homeland of the Crescentian family) in Jan. 1045. The Crescentians were behind the move; they were using him, probably as a reluctant instrument, to win back the supreme power the Tusculans had wrested from them in 1012. He was later charged, probably libellously, with having used bribery to get himself elected. He adopted the name Silvester, but on hearing of his appointment Benedict promptly sought to undermine any legitimacy he might have by excommunicating him. His reign was short, for on 10 Mar. Benedict staged a comeback and expelled him with ignominy. He returned to his original see, which he had not relinquished; here the protection of the Crescentians enabled him to ignore the papal ban and carry on with his episcopal duties. Some eighteen months later, when King Henry III of Germany (1039–56) intervened, he was cited before the synod of Sutri (20 Dec. 1046), con-

demned as an invader of the holy see, and sentenced to confinement in a monastery and deprivation of orders. The sentence must have been suspended, however, for he continued to function, and to be recognized, as bishop of Sabina until at least 1062; he must have died before Oct. 1063, when the name of a successor is recorded. Succeeding popes probably left him undisturbed because he was known to have no ambition for the papal throne. His right to be considered an authentic pope is open to question.

JW 1, 523 f.; 525; Watterich 1, 70; 72–6; 713–15; *DTC* 14, 2083 f. (É. Amann); Seppelt 2, 414–17; Z1, 121–34; J. Gay, *Les papes du XIe siècle et la chrétienté* (Paris, 1926).

GREGORY VI (1 May 1045–20 Dec. 1046: d. late 1047). An elderly man respected in reforming circles, possibly related to the wealthy banking family of the Pierleoni, John Gratian was archpriest of St John at the Latin Gate when his godson BENEDICT IX, recently restored to the papal throne, made out a deed of abdication in his favour on 1 May 1045. It is widely conjectured that John was among those who persuaded him to take this step. A huge sum of money apparently changed hands; according to most sources Benedict sold the papal office, according to others the Roman people had to be bribed. The whole transaction remains obscure, probably because it was deliberately kept dark at the time; but the most likely explanation is that John, eager to secure Benedict's resignation, paid over the money with trusting naïvety as compensation, either for him or his relatives or for both, for his relinquishing the papacy and its emoluments.

Although designated by Benedict as his successor (in itself a gross irregularity), there is some evidence that the forms of an election were observed; it is said that the new pope was given the name Gregory by popular acclaim. His accession was at first greeted with enthusiasm by friends of reform, and Peter Damiani, reformer and doctor of the church (1007–72), congratulated him fulsomely, claiming that his election had struck a blow at simony (news of the financial deal had not yet leaked out). A cleric who served him in the curia, and became a close friend, was Hildebrand (later GREGORY VII). But Gregory's position was far from assured. When King Henry III of Germany (1039–56) crossed the Alps in autumn 1046, his main object may have been to receive the imperial crown, but church reform and the restoration of order to the papacy, of the parlous condition of which he had been informed, were also in his mind. A synod over which he presided at Pavia prepared for what was to come by publishing a general prohibition of simony. Evidently ill at ease, Gregory went to meet him at Piacenza; he is said to have been courteously received, but nothing in fact is known of the meeting. On 20 Dec. he appeared before the synod of Sutri, near Rome, to which he had been cited along with Benedict IX and SILVESTER III. After the circumstances of his election had been investigated, the emperor and the synod pronounced him guilty of simony in obtaining the papal office, and deposed him. According to some accounts, he was brought to acknowledge his culpability and voluntarily laid down his office, judging himself unfit to hold it. But these, like the reports that it was Gregory and not Henry who summoned and presided over the synod, reflect later embarrassment that the emperor should have presumed to preside over a council and judge the supreme pontiff.

The synod had not determined what was to be done with Gregory. For the moment he was kept in custody, but eventually Henry decided, in view of the danger of allowing a deposed pope to remain in Rome, to take him back with him to exile in Germany. In the spring he set out, accompanied by Hildebrand, for 'the banks of the Rhine', where Bishop Hermann of Cologne, imperial chancellor for Italy, was commissioned to watch over him. When the emperor, on the sudden death of CLEMENT II (9 Oct. 1047), questioned the episcopate

about a successor, Bishop Wazo of Liège (1042–8) argued that Gregory should be restored since his deposition had been invalid, the pope being incapable of being judged by anyone. Henry was not persuaded, and in any case Gregory died at Cologne, of an illness which has not been identified, towards the end of the year.

JW 1, 524 f.; LP 2, 270 f.; Watterich 1, 72 f.; 75–8; 79–80; 712–16; Anselm, Gesta episcop. Leod. (MGSS VII, 228 f.); G. B. Borino, 'L'elezione e la deposizione di Gregorio VI', ASRomana 39 (1916), 142–252; 295–410; R. Lane Poole, 'Benedict IX and Gregory VI', ProceedBritAcad 8 (1917–18), 199–235; K. J. Herrmann, Das Tuskulaner Papstum (1012–1046) (Stuttgart, 1973), 154–60; Z1, 122–36; Seppelt 2, 415–18; D. Freymans, 'Grégoire VI était-il simoniaque?', Revbelge 11 (1932), 130–7; EC 6, 1129 f. (L. Spätling).

CLEMENT II (24 Dec. 1046–9 Oct. 1047). Originally named Suidger, as bishop of Bamberg, in Bavaria, he accompanied King Henry III of Germany (1039–56) to Italy in autumn 1046 and, after the deposition of SILVESTER III, GREGORY VI, and BENEDICT IX on 20 and 24 Dec., was elected pope on the nomination of the king, the first of four German popes he was to impose. Henry's first choice had been Adalbert, archbishop of Hamburg-Bremen, who declined. Suidger had long enjoyed the king's confidence. Of noble Saxon stock, he had been canon of Halberstadt, had become chaplain to his provost, Hermann, when he was appointed archbishop of Hamburg in 1032, and after Hermann's death in 1035 had entered the royal chapel. Still a deacon, he was consecrated, on Henry's nomination, bishop of Bamberg on 28 Dec. 1040.

Henry's initiative in rescuing the papacy from feuding Roman families was generally approved in reforming circles. Suidger shared his concern for reform in the church; his choice of the name Clement underlined his resolve to look for inspiration to primitive Christianity. Enthroned on 25 Dec. 1046, he crowned Henry and his queen Agnes as emperor and empress on the same day. Henry then had himself invested with the rank of patrician, which empowered him to take the lead in the appointment of a pope, and the Romans had to undertake afresh not to elect a pope in future without the approval of emperor and patrician. The constitutional issue settled, Clement started his reform programme, presiding on 5 Jan. 1047 over a synod which sharply condemned simony and decreed a forty days' penance for any who had knowingly been ordained by simoniacal bishops. After the synod he accompanied Henry (mid-Jan.) on his progress to south Italy, at Salerno (18 Feb.) confirming John of Paestum as archbishop after checking that he had obtained the see without simony, and placing Benevento under an anathema when it refused to open its gates to the emperor. At the end of Feb. he returned to Rome, conferring there in the spring or summer with the aged Odilo, fifth abbot of Cluny (d. 1049), and publishing a bull commending his abbey to leading personalities in France. The reformer Peter Damiani (1007–72) also wrote to him expressing disappointment at the slow progress of his reforming policies. In late summer he moved to the Marches (some think he had to leave Rome because of serious disturbances there), and on 24 Sept. he issued a bull, lyrical in tone, confirming the privileges of Bamberg, his 'most sweet spouse' from whom he could not bear to be separated; in fact he remained its bishop throughout his pontificate. On 1 Oct. he was at the abbey of S. Tommaso, near Pesaro; he was seriously ill and died there on 9 Oct. A rumour, soon in circulation, that he had been poisoned by Benedict IX is probably groundless. His body was taken to Bamberg and buried in his cathedral. When the tomb was opened on 22 Oct. 1731, he was found to have been a man well over six feet tall with yellow hair. It was again opened on 3 June 1942 and the remains subjected to an exhaustive examination which disclosed that he probably died of lead poisoning.

JW 1, 525–8; LP 2, 272; PL 142, 577–90; Watterich 1, 73 f.; 77–80; 714–17; Peter Damiani, Ep. 1, 3 (PL 144, 297 f.); E. von Guttenberg, Die Regesten der Bischöfe und des Domkapitels von Bamberg (Würzburg, 1932) 1, 99–108; DHGE 12, 1093–6 (F. Foreville); NCE 3, 928 f. (F. Dressler); Z1, 132 f.; Seppelt 3, 9–11; NDB 3, 281 f.; K. Guggenberger, Die deutschen Päpste (Cologne, 1916), 29–37; K. Hauch, 'Zum Tode Papst Clemens II', Jahrbuch für fränkische Landesforschung 19 (1959), 265–74; S. Müller-Christiansen, Das Grab des Papstes Clemens II im Dom zu Bamberg (Munich 1960).

DAMASUS II (17 July–9 Aug. 1048). Originally named Poppo, he was the second of the German popes nominated by Emperor Henry III (1039–56). Of Bavarian stock, he is first mentioned as bishop of Brixen, in Tyrol, on 16 Jan. 1040, when it is plain that he already stood high in the king's favour. He was in Henry's entourage when he travelled to Italy in autumn 1046, and took a prominent part in the Roman synod of 5 Jan. 1047; he probably returned to Germany with the emperor in mid-May. On the death of CLEMENT II on 9 Oct., the clergy and people dispatched an embassy to Henry at Pöhlde with the request to name a successor. Bishop Wazo of Liège had argued that GREGORY VI, now in exile at Cologne, whom he considered wrongfully deposed, should be restored, but on 25 Dec. the emperor, in his capacity as patrician of the Romans, nominated Poppo. Meanwhile, however, BENEDICT IX had re-emerged from his Tusculan retreat and seized the papal throne, bringing over Boniface, the powerful count of Tuscany, to his side. Poppo, who retained the see of Brixen until his death, set out for Rome, but was prevented from getting there by Boniface, who pleaded that Benedict had successfully re-established himself as pope. When Poppo returned and informed him, the emperor threatened Boniface that, unless he carried out his orders, he would come himself and give the Romans a new pope. Boniface judged it wise to obey, had Benedict expelled from Rome on 16 July, and on 17 July had Poppo consecrated and enthroned. To mark his devotion to the ancient and pure church, he adopted the style Damasus II, but within twenty-three days died at Palestrina, where he had gone to escape the heat. Although poison was hinted at in some quarters, the most likely cause of his death was malaria.

JW 1, 528 f.; *LP* 2, 274; 332 f. (*Annales Romani*); Watterich 1, 74; 78–80; 716 f.; *NDB* 3, 498 (R. Elze); *DHGE* 14, 53 f. (A. van Roey); Seppelt 3, 9–11; K. Guggenberger, *Die deutschen Päpste* (Cologne 1916), 38–40; Mann 5, 286–92.

LEO IX, ST (12 Feb. 1049–19 Apr. 1054). Born 21 June 1002 as Bruno, son of Count Hugh of Egisheim, Alsace, related to the imperial house, he was the third and greatest of the popes nominated by the German emperor Henry III (1039–56). Educated at Toul, a canon of its cathedral and already known at court, he served under his kinsman King Conrad II (1024–39) in Lombardy in 1025/6 at the head of troops supplied by his ailing bishop. On the bishop's death Conrad appointed him to the see (9 Sept. 1027). As bishop he was energetic in raising the moral standards of monasteries and clergy in his diocese, while his diplomatic skill was shown in negotiations he conducted in 1032 between Conrad and King Henry I of France (1031–60). On the death of DAMASUS II (9 Aug. 1048), brushing aside the preference expressed by a Roman delegation for Halinard of Lyons, Henry III nominated Bruno, whose reforming zeal he appreciated, at Worms in Dec. 1048. Bruno only accepted, it is reported, on the condition of the choice being ratified by the Roman clergy and people; he also retained the see of Toul until 1051. When he reached Rome, deliberately in the garb of a pilgrim, he was received with acclamation and crowned on 12 Feb. 1049, adopting a name intended to recall the ancient, still pure church.

The new pope demonstrated his reforming resolve at his first synod (at Rome, 9–15 Apr. 1049), fulminating against simony and clerical unchastity. Several simoniacal bishops were deposed, and the penance imposed by CLEMENT II on clergy knowingly ordained by simoniacal bishops was renewed; his first wish was to degrade them, but they were too numerous for this to be practicable. Meanwhile he enlisted able, like-minded personalities, mostly from Lorraine, to assist him—Hildebrand (later GREGORY VII), Hugh Candidus of Remiremont (*c.* 1020–*c.* 1098), Frederick of Liège (later STEPHEN IX), and, most notably, Humbert of Moyenmoutier (d. 1061), later cardinal bishop of Silva Candida, his closest confidant and virtual secretary of state. By using these as his advisory senate he started a radical transformation of the curia. He also relied on the counsel of leading reformers, such as Abbot Hugh of Cluny (d. 1109), Archbishop Halinard of Lyons (d. 1052), and Peter Damiani (1007–72).

To give the widest impact to his policies he adopted the revolutionary tactic of making impressive progresses throughout Europe and pressing home the need for renewal at synods in the principal centres—Pavia, Rheims, and Mainz (1049), Rome (1050, 1051, 1053), Siponto, Salerno, and Vercelli (1050), Mantua and Bari (1053). If his chief concern at these was with clerical unchastity and simony (such was his horror of the latter that he on occasion reordained men ordained by simoniacal bishops), at Rheims he insisted that bishops and abbots must be elected by clergy and people, and also seized the opportunity to publish a vigorous affirmation of the pope's unique primacy over the universal church; while at Rome (1050) and Vercelli he condemned the teaching of Berengar of Tours (*c.* 1010–88) that, while the bread and wine in the eucharist become Christ's body and blood, they do so figuratively, remaining substantially what they were.

Leo's last years were clouded with failure and disappointment. In May 1053, to protect the papal state and its population from the marauding raids of the Normans in south Italy, he personally led a small, ill-equipped force against them; he had failed, through opposition from imperial chancellor Gebhard of Eichstätt (destined to succeed him as VICTOR II), to get reinforcements from the emperor, but hoped to link up with the Byzantines led by Argyros, governor of south Italy. Before he could do so, his army was overwhelmed near Civitate and he himself was captured on 18 June. Although the Normans treated him respectfully, they kept him prisoner for nine months, though allowing him to maintain contact with the outside world, and only released him after he had, probably, made humiliating concessions. While he was sharply criticized in reforming circles for this military adventure, it led to what was to prove, historically, the most significant event of his reign, the breach with the eastern church. Angered by his interference in south Italy in areas claimed by Byzantium, not least by his holding of a synod at Siponto and his naming Humbert archbishop of Sicily, the fanatically anti-Latin patriarch Michael Cerularius (1043–58) shut down the Latin churches in Constantinople in 1053 and launched a violent attack on western religious practices, such as the use of unleavened bread in the eucharist. On Leo's behalf Humbert of Silva Candida prepared a ferocious riposte, arguing the case for the Roman primacy with extensive quotations from the (forged) *Donation of Constantine. A political alliance being urgently necessary, however, an attempt at conciliation was made by both emperor and pope, and in Jan. 1054, while still a prisoner, Leo sent an embassy, headed by Humbert, to Constantinople. Through the intransigent behaviour of the principals on both sides the mission proved a disastrous failure, and on 16 July 1054 Humbert, in full view of the congregation, placed on the altar of Haghia Sophia a bull excommunicating the patriarch and his supporters. Cerularius responded with counter-anathemas on 24 July. The schism between the eastern and western churches is conventionally dated from this event; although Leo was dead at the time, it must be attributed to his pontificate since the Roman legates were acting in his name.

Carried back to Rome from Benevento on 12 Mar. 1054, ill and broken in spirit, he

died a month later, breathing his last prayers in his native German. A real, if limited, precursor of the Gregorian reforms, who after decades of humiliation brilliantly restored the prestige of the papacy, he was soon saluted as a saint; in 1087 VICTOR III is said to have had his body disinterred and placed over an altar in St Peter's because of the miracles it had caused. Feast 19 Apr.

AASS Apr. 2 (1675), 648–727; JW 1, 529–49; *PL* 143, 457–800 (letters, decrees, etc.); Watterich 1, 93–177; 731–8; *AnB* 25 (1906), 258–96; *EB* (15th edn.) 10, 804 f. (W. Ullmann); *BSS* 7, 1293–301 (J. Choux); *DTC* 9, 320–9 (É. Amann); K. Guggenberger, *Die deutschen Päpste* (Cologne, 1916), 41–71; Seppelt 3, 12–31; L. Sittler and P. Stinzi, *S. Léon IX: le pape alsacien* (Colmar, 1950); P. P. Bruckner, *Leben Papstes Leos IX* (Strasbourg, 1902); D. M. Nicol, 'Byzantium and the Papacy in the 11th century', *JEH* 13 (1962), 1–20; Mann 6, 19–182.

VICTOR II (13 Apr. 1055–28 July 1057).

A Swabian, son of Count Hartwig and born *c*.1018, Gebhard of Dollnstein-Hirschberg was the last of the four German popes nominated by Henry III (1039–56). Promoted bishop of Eichstätt in 1042 when still in his twenties, his great administrative gifts enabled him to render important services to the emperor, whose indispensable counsellor he became in the early 1050s. An example of his influence was his blocking of military aid for LEO IX's campaign against the Normans in 1053. On Leo's death (19 Apr. 1054), after protracted discussions at Mainz with Roman legates headed by the deacon Hildebrand (later GREGORY VII), Henry named (Nov. 1054) Gebhard as pope. The legates would probably have preferred someone else, but Henry wanted to have an imperial pontiff loyal to himself in Rome, not least as a counterweight to his old enemy Duke Godfrey of Lorraine (*c*.1040–96), now married to the widow of Count Boniface of Tuscany (*c*.986–1052) and threateningly established in central and upper Italy. Gebhard hesitated for four or five months, only agreeing at Regensburg in Mar. 1055 when assured that certain territories and properties taken from the holy see would be restored to it. Enthroned almost a year after Leo's death, he took the name Victor, and while pope remained bishop of Eichstätt.

Primarily a powerful minister, Victor was also concerned for church reform: a great synod held by him and the emperor at Florence on 4 June 1055 anathematized not only simony and clerical unchastity but also the alienation of church property; several bishops were deposed. Similar decisions were published in France in 1056 by synods presided over by local bishops as his representatives and by Hildebrand as his legate. But Henry had political aims in coming to Italy in summer 1055. His vigorous action caused Godfrey of Lorraine to flee for safety, while his wife and stepdaughter Matilda (future countess of Tuscany) were seized as hostages; Godfrey's brother Frederick, chancellor of the Roman church, prudently retired to Monte Cassino as a monk. To strengthen Victor's position *vis-à-vis* Tuscany and the Normans in the south, Henry appointed him duke of Spoleto and count of Fermo. After the emperor's departure, Victor was increasingly preoccupied with the Norman expansion in south Italy, and in autumn 1056 went to Germany to seek (ironically, like Leo IX) reinforcements against them. On 5 Oct., however, Henry died after a short illness, entrusting the care of the empire and his five-year-old son to his trusted pope. With great political skill Victor was able to ensure at Aachen the succession of Henry IV (1056–1106) and the appointment of his mother Agnes as regent, with the right to designate a successor if her son should die. At Cologne in Dec., with skill and foresight, he negotiated a reconciliation between the imperial house and both Godfrey of Lorraine and Baldwin, count of Flanders (1036–67), its two most powerful vassals.

Returning to Italy in mid-Feb. 1057, Victor held a synod in the Lateran on 18 Apr. To gratify Godfrey of Lorraine, now a powerful support in central and north Italy to both papacy and empire, he pushed

through the election of his brother Frederick as abbot of Monte Cassino and on 14 June, before consecrating him abbot, made him cardinal priest of S. Crisogono. But he was already stricken, and after holding a local synod at Arezzo on 23 July died there of fever on 28 July. His German entourage wished to take his body back to Eichstätt for burial in his cathedral, but the citizens of Ravenna seized it; he was finally interred in Sta Maria Rotonda (the mausoleum of Theodoric the Great: d. 526) just outside the walls of the city.

LP 2, 277; 333 f. (*Annales Romani*); JW 1, 549–53; Watterich 1, 177–88; 738; Mansi 19, 833–62; F. Heidingsfelder, *Die Regesten der Bischöfe von Eichstätt* (Erlangen, 1915), 66–76; Anon. Haserensis, *Lib. de episc. Eichstet.* (*MGSS* 7, 263–6); *Chron. monast. Casin.* (*MGSS* 35, 1980: index); *DTC* 15, 2863–6 (É. Amann); Mann 6, 183–206; Seppelt 3, 32–5; K. Guggenberger, *Die deutschen Päpste* (Cologne, 1916), 72–8; *NCE* 14, 646 f. (O. J. Blum).

STEPHEN IX (X) (2 Aug. 1057–29 Mar. 1058). When the news of VICTOR II's unexpected death on 28 July 1057 reached Rome, the reform leaders there immediately consulted Frederick of Lorraine, abbot of Monte Cassino, about a successor. He proposed five names, including those of Hildebrand (later GREGORY VII) and Humbert of Silva Candida (*c.* 1000–61), but in the event was himself elected on 2 Aug. and consecrated next day; he took the name of Stephen I, whose feast fell on 2 Aug. No approach was made to the German imperial family, which had nominated the four previous popes, and this omission has been interpreted as an attempt to take advantage of the minority of Henry IV (1056–1106) and the weakness of Empress Agnes, the regent, to free the papacy from its control. A more likely explanation is that speedy action was deemed necessary to forestall any move by aristocratic Roman families to recover their influence in papal appointments; the fact that, if trouble arose, the pope chosen could rely on the support of his powerful brother Godfrey, duke of Lorraine and count of Tuscany (*c.* 1040–96), must have told in his favour. It is significant that a delegation led by Hildebrand reached the court at Pöhlde, in Saxony, in Dec., where it must have obtained retrospective approval of the choice that had been made.

Stephen's earlier career argued for a strong, progressive pontificate. Youngest son of Duke Gozelon I of Lorraine, educated at Liège, he had been a canon and then archdeacon there under bishops sympathetic to reform in the church. LEO IX, who probably met him at the reforming synod of Mainz in Oct. 1049, brought him to Rome as one of his close collaborators, making him chancellor and librarian of the Roman church on 12 Mar. 1051. He accompanied Leo on his campaign against the Normans, and was one of his legates to Constantinople in 1054. Although a leading member of the curia, he judged it prudent in 1055, in view of the forthcoming visit to Italy of Emperor Henry III (1039–56), his brother Godfrey's enemy, to retire as a monk to Monte Cassino. He enjoyed, however, the confidence of Victor II, who on Henry's death (3 Oct. 1056) reconciled Godfrey with the royal house, and next summer had Frederick elected (23 May) abbot of Monte Cassino (Humbert having forced the existing one to resign), and then (14 June) promoted him (an unprecedented appointment) cardinal priest of S. Crisogono.

In his brief reign Stephen gave an impetus to reform. At Monte Cassino, where he remained abbot, he tried to restore the rule of poverty. He opened up a wider role for Peter Damiani, propagandist of reform (1007–72), by making him, in spite of his protests, cardinal bishop of Ostia. Humbert of Silva Candida, whose view that episcopal appointments should be free of lay interference he probably shared, was his chancellor, and Hildebrand a close adviser. He frequently denounced clerical marriage and marriage within the forbidden degrees; and in summer 1057 he showed interest in the Patarenes (Pataria), a revolutionary reformist movement at Milan hostile to simony and clerical unchastity, sending

Hildebrand to investigate its adherents. In spring 1058, reviving Leo IX's policies, he was planning a campaign against the Normans in south Italy, to be financed out of the treasure of Monte Cassino, and seems to have considered crowning Duke Godfrey as emperor so as to enlist his support; he also proposed sending envoys to Constantinople to negotiate an alliance against the common foe. In Mar. he travelled to Florence to consult Godfrey about the enterprise, died there, and was buried in S. Reparata. Being already seriously ill, he had bound the clergy and people, before leaving Rome, by a solemn oath not to elect a successor, in the event of his death, until Hildebrand returned from his mission to the German court. He probably wished to ensure that a pope would be chosen who would continue the work of reform.

LP 2, 278; 334; 356; JW 1, 553–6; Watterich 1, 188–204; 738; 748 f.; *PL* 143, 865–84; V. Robert, *Un pape belge: Histoire du pape Étienne IX* (Brussels, 1892); G. Depsy, 'La carrière lotharingienne du pape Étienne IX', *Revbelge* 31 (1953), 955–72; *DHGE* 15, 1198–203 (F. J. Schmale); *LThK* 9, 1041 (K. Rendel); Seppelt 3, 34–8; *NCE* 13, 697 (J. Gilchrist).

BENEDICT X (antipope 5 Apr. 1058–Jan. 1059: d. after 1073). On the death of STEPHEN IX, while the leading Roman clergy, in obedience to their oath to him, deferred electing a successor until Hildebrand (later GREGORY VII) returned from a mission to Germany, a clique of nobles led by Gregory of Tusculum and Gerard of Galeria saw their chance to seize control of the papacy and, winning over the people by bribery, had John Mincius, cardinal bishop of Velletri, elected and enthroned with the style Benedict X. Their choice was astute, for although John, a Roman by birth, belonged to the Tusculan family, he was highly esteemed in reforming circles and had been one of the five proposed by Frederick of Lorraine (later Stephen IX) when consulted in July–Aug. 1057 about a successor to VICTOR II. But if his backers hoped that, taken by surprise, the reformers would accept the *fait accompli*, they were mistaken. They all fled from Rome, anathematizing Benedict, who had to be irregularly consecrated since Peter Damiani, who as bishop of *Ostia had the right to officiate, refused to do so.

Nevertheless for some nine months, while the reformers concerted their plans, Benedict managed to function as pope; one of his few recorded acts was to send the *pallium to Archbishop Stigand of Canterbury (d c. 1072). In Dec. 1058, however, the cardinals elected NICHOLAS II at Siena. Early in Jan. 1059 Nicholas held a synod at Sutri, with the imperial chancellor Guibert representing the regent Agnes, and excommunicated Benedict as an 'invader' of the holy see and as a perjuror for breaking his oath to the dying Stephen IX. When Nicholas took possession of Rome on 24 Jan., Benedict sought refuge in Gerard's castle at Galeria. When Gerard eventually surrendered it after two sieges in autumn 1059, Benedict renounced all claim to the holy see, removed his pontifical insignia in token of this, and retired to a family property near Sta Maria Maggiore; but a month later Hildebrand, now archdeacon, gaoled him. Finally, his voluntary abdication not being deemed sufficient, he was publicly tried, with Hildebrand as his accuser, in Apr. 1060 and, in spite of protesting that the papal office had been forced upon him against his will, was ceremonially deposed and degraded. Sentenced to confinement in the hospice of Sant'Agnese on the Via Nomentana, he lived on there at least until the accession of Hildebrand as Gregory VII (1073). When he died, his old adversary relented sufficiently to arrange for him to be honourably buried in that church.

LP 2, 279; 334–6 (Ann. Romani); JW 1, 556 f.; Watterich 1, 203–5; 738; Leo Ostiensis, Chron. II, 99 (MGSS 7, 695); Bonizo of Sutri, Ad amicum vi (MGLiblit 1, 592 f.); Peter Damiani, Ep. 3, 4 (PL 144, 291); DHGE 8, 105 f. (J. Gay); DBI 8, 366–70 (O. Capitani); Z1, 141–6.

NICHOLAS II (6 Dec. 1058–19 or 26 July 1061). Originally Gerard, born c. 1010 in Lorraine or French Burgundy, bishop of Florence from 1045, he was a leading figure in the 11th-cent. reform movement when elected. On STEPHEN IX's death (28 Mar. 1058) a powerful anti-reformist aristocratic clique on 5 Apr. elected Bishop John of Velletri as BENEDICT X, but the reform cardinals, loyal to their promise to the dying Stephen to take no action until Hildebrand (later GREGORY VII) returned from a mission to Germany, refused to recognize him, abandoned Rome, and eventually through Hildebrand's influence, after securing the agreement of Duke Godfrey of Lorraine and Tuscany (c. 1040–96) and then satisfying itself of the good will of the German court, elected Gerard at Siena in Dec. The new pope, who called himself after NICHOLAS I and retained the see of Florence, held a synod at Sutri, near Rome, in early Jan. 1059, in the presence of the imperial chancellor Guibert, and anathematized Benedict. Supported by Godfrey's troops, he then moved to Rome, from which Benedict had fled, and was there enthusiastically installed on 24 Jan. 1059, Hildebrand having swung over popular opinion by lavish largesse.

The friend of Desiderius of Monte Cassino (later VICTOR III), Nicholas was greatly influenced by reformers like Humbert of Silva Candida (c. 1000–61), Hildebrand (whom he created archdeacon), and Peter Damiani (1007–72), propagandist for reform. At the Lateran synod of 13 Apr. 1059 he promulgated a momentous electoral decree providing that papal elections should conform to the reformers' principles; it also had the immediate objects of stamping Benedict's election as uncanonical and legitimizing the irregular features in his own. This decree ruled that, to exclude simony, the cardinal bishops should effectively choose the pope, the cardinal clerks should then be brought in, and the remaining clergy and the people should finally give their assent; it also permitted, if circumstances warranted it, the choice of a non-Roman cleric and the holding of the election outside Rome. There was a vague clause about the emperor's right to approve, which was not envisaged as unconditional; it had to be granted to each successive ruler, and could be forfeited by misuse. The synod then legislated against clerical marriage and concubinage, for the first time issued a general prohibition of *lay investiture by forbidding clerics to acquire churches from lay persons, and required the clergy of one church to share a common life. *Berengar of Tours appeared before it and was forced to sign a crudely realistic statement, drafted by Humbert, of the real presence in the eucharistic bread.

Politically Nicholas now took the far-reaching decision, on the advice of Desiderius and Hildebrand, to reverse previous policies and make an alliance between the papacy and the Normans in southern Italy. He cemented this at the synod of Melfi (23 Aug. 1059), capital of Norman Apulia, at which, in addition to passing measures to enforce clerical celibacy, he invested Richard of Aversa with the principality of Capua and Robert Guiscard (c. 1015–85) with the duchies of Apulia and Calabria and the lordship of Sicily in return for fealty and the promise of military assistance. Thus at a stroke the Roman church gained feudal suzerainty over much of south Italy; an immediate dividend was that Richard stormed the stronghold of Galeria, where Antipope Benedict had sought refuge, and handed him over as a prisoner to Nicholas, who later formally deposed and degraded him.

Further synods were held in 1060 and 1061 dealing in the main with simony and the problems raised by simoniacal ordinations; and Nicholas used legates to strengthen the growing spirit of reform in western countries. In northern Italy he advanced the cause of reform, and reinforced the position of the holy see, by sending Peter Damiani and Anselm of Lucca (later ALEXANDER II) to Milan in 1059 to make contact with the populist movement of the *Pataria. A striking result was the (temporary) conversion of Archbishop Guido of Milan and his clergy to the ideals of celibacy and the repudiation of simony; Guido attended the Roman

synod of 1060, accepting his ring from the pope and thereby acknowledging that his previous investiture by the emperor had been simoniacal. Meanwhile Nicholas's alliance with the Normans on the one hand and his stiff disciplinary demands on the other had aroused the fierce resentment both of the German royal house and of the German episcopate, led by Archbishop Anno of Cologne (1056–75). When Cardinal Stephen appeared as a papal legate at the court in 1061 to justify the pope's policies, he was not received. Worse followed, for a synod of German bishops close to the court declared Nicholas's acts null and void and broke off communion with him. Before he could react he had died in Florence. Like Stephen IX, he was buried there in S. Reparata.

LP 2, 280; 335 f.; JW 1, 557–66; MGConst 1, 537–51; Watterich 1, 206–35; A. Clavel, Le Pape Nicholas II: son œuvre disciplinaire (Lyons, 1906); K. Guggenberger, Die deutschen Päpste (Cologne, 1916), 89–94; H. G. Krause, 'Das Papstwahldekret von 1059', StGreg 7 (1960); DTC 11, 526–32 (É. Amann); Mann 5, 226–60; LThK 7, 977 f. (Th. Schieffer); NCE 10, 441 f. (W. M. Plöchl); Seppelt 3, 37–50.

ALEXANDER II (30 Sept. 1061–21 Apr. 1073). Originally Anselm, born of a prominent family at Baggio, near Milan, a student at Lanfranc's (c. 1010–89) school at Bec, ordained at Milan c. 1055, a familiar figure at the court of Emperor Henry III (1039–56) and named bishop of Lucca in 1057, he was elected, at the instigation of Archdeacon Hildebrand (later GREGORY VII), to succeed NICHOLAS II, being installed by Norman troops because of disturbances in Rome. Earlier he had been involved sympathetically in the beginnings of the revolutionary *Pataria at Milan; now he proved a champion both of church reform and of the rescue of once Christian lands from Islam.

In the spirit of the *electoral decree of 1059 the cardinals did not consult the German court, with which a rift had opened in Nicholas II's last years. The court now nominated a rival pope, HONORIUS II

(Cadalus of Parma), with whom Alexander had to contend for several years. Although the court eventually dropped Honorius, Alexander had the humiliation of having to withdraw in May 1062 to Lucca, of which he had remained bishop, to await its decision, and of having to appear in May 1064 at a synod at Mantua, over which he presided but which the government had summoned, to clear himself of charges of having obtained the papacy by simony and force of arms. This he successfully did by taking an oath of purgation before Anno, archbishop of Cologne (1056-78) and now regent for Henry IV (1056-1106).

Even before the decision of Mantua, the main lines of Alexander's programme, in carrying out which he was firmly guided by Hildebrand, were made clear. At the Lateran synod of 1063 he renewed Nicholas II's decree against simony, forbade attendance at masses celebrated by married priests and the acceptance of *lay investiture without the diocesan's permission, and recommended the common life to the clergy. From 1063 onwards the pace quickened, and a series of reforming synods and inquisitions was held by his legates in France and Spain; in 1068 King Sancho V Ramirez of Aragon (1063-94) placed his country under the feudal protection of the pope, and in 1071 substituted the Roman for the Mozarabic liturgy. On Hildebrand's advice Alexander backed Duke William of Normandy (1028-87), an active promoter of reform, against Harold of England, and blessed his campaign by sending St Peter's banner; under it William fought and won the battle of Hastings (1066). In 1063 he sent banners and granted indulgences to Norman warriors and French knights fighting against the Muslims in Sicily and Spain respectively, and in 1072 blessed a similar expedition undertaken by the French Count Ebolus of Roucy. In Germany he took an inflexible line, only handing the *pallium to Udo of Trier when he had proved himself guiltless of simony, in 1070 citing powerful prelates to Rome to clear themselves of the same charge, and forcing the resignation of

a suspect bishop of Constance. Even King Henry IV, in face of the pope's objections voiced by the reformer Peter Damiani (1007-72) in 1068, deemed it prudent to abandon the project of divorcing his wife Bertha.

Relations between court and curia came to breaking-point on the death of Archbishop Guido of Milan (23 Aug. 1071). Henry tried to force his nominee Godfrey on the Milanese as his successor and got the Lombard bishops to consecrate him, but the outraged adherents of the Pataria, with the papal legate's full support, elected the priest Atto, who was sympathetic to their cause. Schism was the result; and since Henry stood by Godfrey, Alexander excommunicated five royal counsellors for simony at his last Lenten synod.

Early in his reign Alexander made contact with Byzantium, the first such move since the breach under LEO IX in 1054, and in 1071 he sent Peter of Anagni (d. 1105) as his representative to Emperor Michael VII Ducas (1071-8). Concrete negotiations for union must have been begun, but no settlement was reached.

LP 2, 281; 358-60; JW 1, 566-92; *PL* 146, 1271-430; Watterich 1, 235-90; C. Violante, *La pataria milanese e la riforma ecclesiastica* (Rome, 1955); V. Grumel, 'Le premier contact de Rome avec l'Orient après le schisme de Michel Cérulaire', *BullItteccl* 43 (1942), 21-9; *DBI* 2, 176-83 (C. Violante); Mann 5, 261-369; *NCE* 1, 288 (J. J. Ryan); Seppelt 3, 50-64.

HONORIUS (II) (antipope 28 Oct. 1061-31 May 1064: d. 1071/2). On NICHOLAS II's death in July 1061 Peter Cadalus, born 1009/1010 of wealthy German stock near Verona, by 1041 comptroller of the see of Verona, bishop of Parma by May 1046, was elected pope, on the nomination of Empress Agnes as regent for the youthful Henry IV (1056-1106), by a miscellaneous assembly at Basle; he took the style Honorius II. The Roman nobility, set on seizing the papacy for themselves, had sent an embassy to the German court bearing the insignia of the patrician of the Romans to request Henry, in virtue of that office, to name a new pope;

there had also arrived, led by Guibert, the royal chancellor, a delegation of Lombard bishops hostile to the reform movement. Because of his prominence, his close relations with the royal house, and his wealth, Cadalus was an obvious choice; he was also, although founder in 1046 of the monastery of S. Giorgio at Verona, an opponent of reform, in particular of the revolutionary reform movement known as the *Pataria.

One month earlier (30 Sept.) the reform party at Rome had elected Bishop Anselm of Lucca as Pope ALEXANDER II. In Apr. 1062, after defeating his rival's troops, Honorius installed himself in Rome, but failed to exploit his success. In May Duke Godfrey of Lorraine, arriving with superior forces, persuaded both popes to withdraw to their dioceses until the German court decided on their claims. This meant in effect that the decision lay with Anno, the reform-minded archbishop of Cologne (1056–78), who had now replaced Agnes as regent and who personally favoured Alexander. After investigations, first at Augsburg in Oct. 1062 and then at Rome at the end of the year, judgement was given in Alexander's favour. But Honorius was far from finished. Anathematized by Alexander (20 Apr. 1062), he anathematized him in turn from Parma, and in May 1063 attacked Rome, seizing Castel Sant'Angelo and holding it for several months. As the schism dragged on and Alexander's title continued to be disputed, Anno was persuaded by the reformer Peter Damiani (1007–72) to convene a synod of German and Italian bishops at Mantua in May 1064 to which both popes were invited. Honorius refused to attend since his request to preside was not granted, but Alexander attended, presided, and, after disclaiming simony on oath, was definitively acknowledged as pope. Honorius was then formally anathematized. He now returned to Parma, remaining its acknowledged bishop until his death towards the end of 1071 or the beginning of 1072. He never abandoned his claims to the papacy, and at least twice, in 1065 and 1068, had serious grounds for hoping that the attitude of the German court would again alter in his favour.

JW 1, 530; 566–94; *LP* 2, 281; 284; 336 f.; 358–60; Watterich 1, 235–90; *DHGE* 11, 53–99 (F. Baix: complete bibliography to 1949); *DBI* 2, 176–82 (C. Violante: on Alexander II); Z1, 148–58; Seppelt 3, 51–6; F. Herberhold, 'Die Angriffe des Cadalus von Parma . . . auf Rom in den Jahren 1062 und 1063', *StGreg* 2 (Rome, 1947), 477–503.

GREGORY VII, ST (22 Apr. 1073–25 May 1085). Originally Hildebrand, born *c.*1020 of humble parentage in Tuscany, he came to Rome as a child and was educated in Sta Maria all'Aventino and in the Lateran palace. Having received minor orders, he became chaplain to GREGORY VI and accompanied him in 1046 to exile at Cologne. On Gregory's death (1047) he probably entered Cluny, near Mâcon, or a Cluniac monastery, but LEO IX soon summoned him to Rome, ordained him subdeacon, and appointed him treasurer of the Roman church and prior of St Paul's monastery. He was now a marked man in reforming circles, being sent on missions to France in 1054 and 1056 and Germany in 1057. Archdeacon since 1059, he became the chief shaper of policy under NICHOLAS II and, still more, under ALEXANDER II. On Alexander's death he was elected pope by popular acclaim, naming himself after Gregory I the Great and deferring his consecration out of regard for the apostles Peter and Paul until after their feast on 29 June. He did not notify or seek the approval of King Henry IV (1056–1106), then under a cloud with the holy see for continuing to associate with advisers whom Alexander II had excommunicated.

A man of exceptional ability, determination, and experience, whose intellectual stature shines out in his letters, Gregory made reform the keynote of his programme. His exalted mystique of the papacy, set out in the twenty-seven propositions of his *Dictatus papae* (Mar. 1075), included not only the pope's personal sanctity inherited from St PETER, but his supremacy over, and right to depose, all princes, temporal as well as spiritual; all Christians were subject to the pope, who had supreme legislative and judicial power. With the object of rooting out moral abuses in the church and freeing it from lay control, he first reinforced, at his Lenten synods of 1074 and 1075, his predecessors' decrees against clerical marriage and simony. This provoked great resistance, especially in France and Germany, but special legates armed with overriding powers were able to overcome most of it. Secondly, however, his prohibition of *lay investiture —i.e. interference in church appointments through the right to install clerics in their offices—issued in general terms in 1075 but more precisely at later synods, created an even greater storm and brought him into collision with Henry IV; his programme envisaged the abolition of royal control of bishops. At first, involved in the Saxon revolt, the king seemed prepared to cooperate, but after defeating the Saxons (9 June 1075) he proceeded to nominate his own creatures, not only to Milan and sees in Germany but to Fermo and Spoleto. When Gregory sharply rebuked him (Dec. 1075), he convened a synod of German bishops at Worms (24 Jan. 1076) which deposed the pope, and himself called on him to abdicate; at Piacenza the Lombard bishops joined the German episcopate. Gregory's reaction, at his Lenten synod, was to excommunicate Henry, suspend him from exercising royal powers, and release his subjects from allegiance. Initially this gave Henry's opponents their chance, and in his imperilled situation he found it prudent to promise the pope obedience and seek absolution in penitential garb at Canossa, near Reggio in north Italy, in Jan. 1077. But Gregory's pastoral clemency was to prove a political mistake. For three years he tried to mediate between Henry and his rival Rudolf of Swabia (d. 1080), elected antiking in 1077, but in 1080, persuaded that the king was intransigent, he again excommunicated and also deposed him (his right to do so was much debated at the time), recognizing Rudolf as lawful king. Henry's reply to this sentence was the council of imperial

bishops at Brixen (25 June 1080), which declared Gregory deposed and elected Guibert of Ravenna as CLEMENT III to replace him. A political compromise was still possible, for Henry was eager to be crowned emperor, but Gregory was not the man for compromise; indeed, his inflexible attitude caused many of his supporters, including thirteen cardinals, to desert him. When Henry seized Rome in Mar. 1084, the Norman Robert Guiscard (c.1015–85) eventually rescued Gregory, but the populace was antagonized by the excesses of his troops and vented their wrath on the pope. He had to leave the city, first for Monte Cassino and then for Salerno, where he died, protesting that he had loved justice and hated iniquity. He was buried there.

Gregory's reign was remarkable apart from his dramatic conflict with the empire. His letters attest his keen concern for the church's fortunes in countries as distant as Norway and Denmark in the north, Spain in the west, Poland and Hungary in the east. He was forever striving, with varying degrees of success, to bind temporal rulers to the holy see by feudal ties; while with the aim of centralizing authority in the church he extended the use of legates, insisted that metropolitans should come to Rome to receive the *pallium, and made little use himself of the college of cardinals. His relative moderation towards Philip I of France (1060–1108), in spite of having uttered bitter complaints and vehement threats, as well as the good relations he enjoyed with William the Conqueror (1066–87) in England, in spite of the king's refusal to budge on lay investiture, provide evidence of his shrewd political realism when that was required. He achieved a signal success in Spain when Alfonso VI of Castile (1072–1109) established the Roman liturgy, already in use in Aragon, in his realms in 1080 in place of the old Mozarabic rites. In the early years of his reign he was much preoccupied with plans for a crusade, to be led by himself personally, which would free the Byzantine empire from the Turks and then restore

CLEMENT III (antipope 1080; 1084-1100)

union with the eastern church; his appeals envisaged the recovery of the Holy Sepulchre in Jerusalem as the goal of the enterprise. The distraction of other controversies caused the dream to come to nothing, although he maintained friendly contact with Emperor Michael VII Ducas (1071–8). Nor should his interest in sound doctrine be overlooked; in 1079, after long debates, he brought *Berengar of Tours to accept a eucharistic statement which admitted a substantial change in the consecrated bread and wine.

Acknowledged generally as one of the greatest popes and most impressive figures of the medieval world, he remains as much a subject of controversy today as he was among contemporaries. In general authoritative and unyielding, but with a profoundly religious passion for 'justice', he pursued his vision of a 'pure' and 'free' church with a single-minded fanaticism which dismayed some of his closest friends. Although his efforts seemed to end in failure, the ideas for which he struggled were to prevail through his successors and helped to shape western Christendom.

Beatified in 1584, he was canonized by PAUL V in 1606. Feast 25 May.

Life by anonymous monk of Whitby: see B. Colgrave (ed.), *The Earliest Life of Gregory the Great* (Lawrence, Kansas, 1967); Bede, *Hist. eccl.* 2, 1; JW 1, 594–649; *PL* 148, 283–645; E. Caspar (ed.), *Das Register Gregors* (MGEpsel 2: 1955); Watterich 1, 293–546; E. Caspar, 'Studien zum Register Gregors VII', *NA* 38 (1913), 145–226; P. Jaffé, *Monumenta Gregoriana* (Bibl.rer.Germ., 1865); H. E. J. Cowdrey, *Epistolae Vagantes* (with ET, Oxford, 1972); Mann 7, 1–217; H. X. Arquillière, *Saint Grégoire VII* (Paris, 1934); J. P. Whitney, *Hildebrandine Essays* (Cambridge, 1932); A. J. Macdonald, *Hildebrand* (London, 1932); A. Murray, 'Pope Gregory VII and his Letters', *Traditio* 22 (1966), 149–201; *LThK* 4, 1183–5 (Th. Schieffer); *BSS* 7, 294–379 (G. Miccoli); *NCE* 6, 772–5 (W. Ullmann); Seppelt 3, 65–120 (also index).

CLEMENT III (antipope 25 June 1080; Mar. 1084–8 Sept. 1100). Born at Parma c.1025 of a family related to the counts of Canossa, Guibert came to the German

court in 1054 and, on the nomination of Empress Agnes, was imperial chancellor for Italy 1058–63. As such he was present in Jan. 1059 at the synod of Sutri at which NICHOLAS II anathematized Antipope BENEDICT X; the claim that the reference to the king in the *electoral decree of that year was a compromise suggested by him is open to question. On Nicholas's death, when the reform party at Rome elected ALEXANDER II, Guibert was one of the moving spirits in the election of Cadalus as Antipope HONORIUS II at Basle in Oct. 1061. In 1072 he was nominated archbishop of Ravenna by King Henry IV (1056–1106); Alexander II was at first reluctant to consecrate the backer of his rival, but was persuaded to do so by his archdeacon, Hildebrand, after Guibert had taken the oath of allegiance. When Hildebrand became pope as GREGORY VII in 1073, Guibert at first co-operated with him, but soon moved into the camp of his enemies. In 1075 Gregory suspended him for failing to appear at his Lenten synod; in Feb. 1076 he was excommunicated for his part in the meeting of Lombard bishops which had purported to depose Gregory. When the final break between Henry IV and Gregory came, the king had Guibert elected pope at Brixen in June 1080. When Henry at last took possession of Rome four years later, the Roman clergy and people elected Guibert pope, and he was enthroned in the Lateran basilica on 24 Mar. 1084 with the style Clement III. On 31 Mar., while Gregory still held out in Castel Sant'Angelo, he crowned Henry as emperor in St Peter's. The approach of Robert Guiscard, duke of Apulia (c.1015–85), however, with a Norman army obliged Henry and Clement to abandon Rome. The antipope betook himself to Ravenna, of which he had remained archbishop and which from c.1080 onwards he organized as a centre of pamphlet war against Gregory and the Gregorian party.

Clement impressed friends and foes alike as a man of irreproachable character, first-rate ability and education, and remarkable eloquence. He was no tool, as has sometimes been supposed, of the emperor, but developed policies of his own, and was personally responsible for effective anti-Gregorian propaganda. Because of the support he enjoyed among the clergy (thirteen of the cardinals had come over to him) and the people, he was able to return to Rome and exercise his role as pope throughout VICTOR III's reign and most of URBAN II's.

He made strenuous efforts, with differing degrees of success, to have his legitimacy recognized not only in Germany and north Italy, but in England, Portugal, Denmark, Hungary, Croatia, and Serbia; and he negotiated with both Archbishop John II of Kiev and the eastern emperor and patriarch in the interest of union. No opponent of reform, he legislated at a Roman synod in 1089 against simony and clerical marriage and in favour of clergy living in common; he also condemned the uncanonical practice of the Gregorians of treating the sacraments of schismatic priests as invalid. He was indirectly responsible for the development of the college of cardinals, for he allowed so much influence to the cardinal priests who came over to his side that Urban II had to treat the ones who supported him with like consideration. In the mid-nineties his power and authority began to wane; he was driven out of Rome by the Pierleoni family in 1098, and Castel Sant'Angelo, the last Clementine stronghold in the city, fell to Urban II on 24 Aug. of that year. On the accession of PASCHAL II in 1099 he prepared to renew the struggle, but was ejected from Albano by Norman troops. He died at Civita Castellana, 57 km. north of Rome, in Sept. 1100.

JW 1, 649–55; Watterich 1, 293; MGLiblit 1, 621–6; 2, 169–72; MGConst 1, 541–6 n. 383; O. Köhncke, *Wibert von Ravenna* (Leipzig, 1888); P. Kehr, 'Zur Geschichte Wiberts von Ravenna', *SAB* (1921), 355–68; 973–88; K. Jordan, 'Die Stellung Wiberts in der Publistik des Investiturstreites', *MIÖG* 62 (1954), 155–64; Seppelt 3, 93–134; *NCE* 6, 836 f. (F. Dressler); *LThK* 10, 1087 f. (K. Reindel).

VICTOR III, BL. (24 May 1086; 9 May–16 Sept. 1087). The death of GREGORY VII

in exile at Salerno on 25 May 1085 threw the reform party in Rome, weakened by desertions to Antipope CLEMENT III, into confusion; almost a year elapsed before, under pressure from the Norman prince Jordan of Capua, the cardinals, much against his will, elected Desiderius, abbot of Monte Cassino. Although not one of the three recommended by the dying Gregory, he seemed the right choice because of his influence with the Normans, whose support was now more than ever necessary, and because his record suggested that he might effect a *rapprochement* with Emperor Henry IV (1056–1106). He adopted the name of Victor II, Henry III's (1039–56) nominee and guardian of Henry IV, as a token of conciliation.

Originally Daufer or Daufari, born *c.*1027 and related to the Lombard dukes of Benevento, he had early tried out the life of a hermit, then become a monk at Benevento (where he took the name Desiderius), and finally, after service with LEO IX, entered Monte Cassino in 1055, becoming abbot on 19 Apr. 1058. His rule marked a golden period, for he not only completely rebuilt the abbey, but expanded its property and library, and encouraged literature and the arts; he himself (1076–9) wrote a treatise on St Benedict's miracles. In Mar. 1059 NICHOLAS II named him cardinal priest and papal vicar of the monasteries of south Italy. That summer he negotiated the alliance between the papacy and the Normans, with whom he had cultivated good relations, and in June 1080 reconciled Gregory VII and the Norman Robert Guiscard, duke of Apulia (*c.*1015–85). In 1082 he incurred the pope's wrath, but probably not excommunication, by attempting to mediate between him and Henry IV and promising the latter to do what he honourably could to help him to obtain the imperial crown; but he sheltered Gregory, fleeing from Rome in spring 1084, at Monte Cassino, and was with him at his deathbed.

Four days after his election, before he could be consecrated, Victor was forced by rioting and other disturbances to leave

Rome. Disheartened, perhaps also aware of the indignation his elevation had caused among the more fanatical Gregorians, he laid aside the papal insignia, retired to Monte Cassino, and resumed his functions as abbot. In Mar. 1087, however, at the instigation of Jordan of Capua, he convened a synod at Capua, not as pope but as *ex officio* papal vicar in southern Italy. On this his election of the previous year was activated and he was persuaded, in the teeth of bitter opposition from a minority led by Archbishop Hugh of Lyons (*c.* 1040–1106), finally to accept office. On 9 May, after Norman troops had wrested the *Leonine city from Antipope Clement III, he was at last consecrated in St Peter's.

Despite the efforts of his powerful friends, Jordan of Capua and the Countess Matilda of Tuscany (1046–1115), he found it impossible to establish himself in Rome, largely occupied as it was by Clement III's troops, and after about a week returned to Monte Cassino. In early June, however, at the urgent pleading of the countess, he went back to Rome by sea in spite of ill health, and on 1 July succeeded in gaining full control of the city from the antipope's forces. In mid-July, faced with rumours of Henry IV's arrival in Italy, he returned to Monte Cassino, and in late Aug. held an important council at Benevento. Although seriously ill all the time, he seems to have continued unremittingly active both at Monte Cassino, of which he remained abbot until three days before his death, and in the wider church, where there is evidence that he made an impact not only in north Italy but in France and Germany. Although its decisions are hard to assess, the council of Benevento seems to have republished Gregory VII's prohibition of *lay investiture, declared simoniacal ordinations invalid, and anathematized not only Clement III but the Gregorian ultras, including Hugh of Lyons; the report that it renewed the ban on Henry IV should be rejected. His reign also saw a momentous Pisan and Genoese naval expedition against the Saracens at Mahdia (eastern Tunisia), which

sacked the city in Aug. 1087 and presented part of the spoils to St Peter's. A prudent and cautious pontiff, he evidently regarded himself as the trustee of the Gregorian cause, and as such was viewed by the antipope's party as an intruder on the holy see. During the council of Benevento his condition deteriorated, and he hastened to Monte Cassino and there died. His cult began soon after his death, and his beatification (feast 16 Sept.) was confirmed by LEO XIII in 1887.

Desiderius, *Dialogi de miraculis S. Benedicti* (*MGSS* 30/2, 1111–52); JW 1, 655; Watterich 1, 549–71; F. Hirsch, 'Desiderius von Monte Cassino als Papst Victor III', *Forschungen zur deutschen Geschichte* 7 (1867), 1–112; H. E. J. Cowdrey, *The Age of Abbot Desiderius* (Oxford, 1983); *DTC* 14, 2866–72 (É. Amann); *LThK* 10, 769 f. (K. Reindel); *NCE* 14, 667 (H. Bloch); Seppelt 3, 95–100; 115–18.

URBAN II, BL. (12 Mar. 1088–29 July 1099). Of noble parentage, born *c.* 1035 at Châtillon-sur-Marne, Odo (Eudes) studied under St Bruno, founder of the Carthusians (*c.* 1032–1101), at Rheims, was made canon and then archdeacon there, and *c.* 1068 became a monk at Cluny, near Mâcon, and rose to be prior. Joining the service of GREGORY VII, he was created cardinal bishop of Ostia *c.* 1080, and served as his legate in Germany in 1084–5. He loyally supported Gregory during his conflict with Henry IV (1056–1106), presiding over a synod at Quedlinburg, in Saxony, in 1085 which anathematized Antipope CLEMENT III. On VICTOR III's death at Monte Cassino, Rome being controlled by Clement III and the reform cardinals unable to gain access to it, he was elected after long delay at Terracina, south of Rome near Gaeta, and adopted the name Urban. Faced with a hostile emperor and a successful antipope, he judged it his immediate task to establish his position as legitimate pontiff and, although announcing his devotion to Gregory's reform programme, was prepared for a time to apply it with diplomatic circumspection.

Thus while renewing Gregory's legislation against clerical marriage, simony, and *lay investiture at Melfi in Sept. 1089, he laid down relatively moderate guide-lines for his legate in Germany. He himself preferred to dispense when it seemed reasonable to do so, recognizing, for example, a bishop who had been invested by his sovereign but canonically elected, and the validity of the masses of properly ordained priests who had gone over to the schism. Modifying Gregory's methods, he temporarily abandoned the use of standing legates to enforce reforms. This conciliatory approach brought him criticism in Gregorian circles, but led to a softening of the conflict and a gradual strengthening of his position. It did not, however, ease relations with Henry IV, whose successful Italian campaigns of 1090-2 forced him to surrender Rome to Clement III and seek refuge with the Normans in southern Italy. But by skilful diplomacy and by exploiting the emperor's misfortunes he was able to neutralize his domination. While Henry remained for several years bottled up in the region of Verona, Urban was able to return definitively to Rome in late 1093, and by astute bribery to get possession of the Lateran in 1094; it was probably by bribery too that he won Castel Sant'Angelo in 1098.

His realism and conciliatory approach brought him successes in other countries. He had special difficulties with England, where William II (1087-1100), at first neutral, only recognized him in 1095 in return for significant concessions, notably his agreement that legates needed the royal permission to enter the kingdom; and he never reached a final decision in the long-standing quarrel between the king and Anselm of Canterbury (1093-1109). But in France, where he took a cautious line with Philip I's (1060-1108) adulterous marriage, he found increasing backing for the reform papacy and its policies. In Spain he encouraged successfully the reconquest from the Moors, extended the feudal suzerainty of the holy see over states like Aragon and Catalonia, and reorganized the country ecclesiastically; in 1088 he restored Toledo as an archbishopric, and granted the new archbishop the *pallium as primate of the whole of Spain. The Normans in south Italy and Sicily were his especial allies, and to maintain his fruitful relations with Roger I, count of Sicily (1072-1101), he even conceded (5 July 1098) to him and his successor quasi-legatine powers of control over the church in the island (the so-called 'Sicilian monarchy', to be finally withdrawn only in Oct. 1867 by PIUS IX).

By 1095, in spite of the continuance of the schism, Urban's position was secure, and he embarked on a triumphant series of synods. At Piacenza in Mar. 1095 he declared the ordinations of Clement III and his adherents void, condemned afresh the eucharistic teaching of *Berengar of Tours (c. 1010-88), enacted reform legislation, and in response to an appeal from the Byzantine emperor Alexius I Comnenus (1081-1118) called on Christian warriors to defend the eastern church. Moving to France, he again renewed Gregory VII's reform legislation at Clermont in Nov. 1095, extending it by forbidding bishops and clerics to become vassals of their king or other laymen; he also decreed that the Truce of God, i.e. the suspension of hostilities on days ordained by the church, should be observed weekly throughout Christendom. This synod is chiefly famous, however, for his initiative in issuing a summons to the First Crusade (1095-9) on 27 Nov., calling on Christians to deliver Jerusalem from Muslim domination. At Bari, where he sought to reach an accommodation on doctrine and practice with the Greek bishops of south Italy, he was able, assisted by the subtle reasoning of Anselm of Canterbury, to convince the easterners of the propriety of the belief in the *double procession of the Holy Spirit, i.e. from the Son as well as the Father (the *Filioque).

Urban's launching of the crusade, which was his most memorable achievement, was the climax of a policy of *rapprochement* with Byzantium, with church union as the ultimate goal, on which he had embarked as early as 1088. If his success in preaching the crusade illustrated the remarkable recovery the papacy had made under him, his vision of closer relations with the eastern church was doomed to failure. His pontificate saw an increased centralization of church government, the reorganization of the papal finances, the emergence of the curia (the expression *curia Romana* first appears in a bull of 1089) as an institution analogous to the royal or imperial court, and a growth in the influence of the college of cardinals. A monk himself, he had special concern for monasticism, and fostered the position of canons regular, i.e. canons living under rule; he was also a learned canonist many of whose decisions were to be incorporated in the church's legal code.

Urban died two weeks after the taking of Jerusalem by the crusaders (15 July 1099). He was beatified by LEO XIII in 1881, his feast being 29 July.

LP 2, 293–5; JW 1, 657–701; PL 151, 9–582 (with Ruinart's life); Watterich 1, 571–620; L. Paulot, *Un pape français: Urban II* (Paris, 1903); A. Becker, *Papst Urban II*, Pt. 1 (Stuttgart, 1964); H. E. J. Cowdrey, 'Pope Urban II's Preaching of the First Crusade', *History* 55 (1970), 177–88; W. Holtzmann, 'Die Unionsverhandlungen zwischen Kaiser Alexios I und Papst Urban II im Jahre 1089', *BZ* 28 (1928), 38–66; Mann 7, 250–346; *EB* (15th edn.) 18, 1044 f. (A. Becker); *DTC* 15, 2269–85 (É. Amann); *NCE* 14, 477 f. (M. W. Baldwin); Seppelt 3, 118–34.

PASCHAL II (13 Aug. 1099–21 Jan. 1118). Born at Bieda di Galeata in the Romagna, of modest family background, Rainerius as a boy became a monk in a community which cannot now be identified. GREGORY VII appointed him abbot of S. Lorenzo fuori le Mura and c. 1078 cardinal priest of S. Clemente; URBAN II entrusted him with an important mission to Spain. Sixteen days after Urban's death (29 July 1099) he was elected pope with the style Paschal II. Timid and weak, but also inflexible, he inherited the *investiture controversy, and like Urban was initially faced with a hostile emperor (Henry IV: 1056–1106) and his antipope (CLEMENT III).

At first the omens seemed favourable. With the help of Norman gold he ejected Clement III from the neighbourhood of Rome; when Clement died (8 Sept. 1100) he soon disposed of the antipopes (THEODERIC, ALBERT, SILVESTER IV) who were successively set up. Henry IV had no hand in their elevation and, Clement being dead, wanted reconciliation, always provided that he could exercise his right to invest bishops and abbots with ring and crozier. This was the issue to which the struggle between the empire and the reform papacy over the control of church appointments had now been narrowed, and as Paschal made the abolition of *lay investiture the central article of his policy, conflict could not be delayed.

First, in Mar. 1102 Paschal reiterated Urban's prohibition of investiture and renewed the ban on Henry and his advisers imposed by Gregory VII. Then in 1105 he supported Henry V's (1106–25) successful revolt against his father, releasing him from his oath of loyalty; but he soon found that, after initial signs of compliance, the new king was no less tenacious than the old of the royal right of investiture. Finally, after the pope had banned investiture at synods at Guastalla (1106), Troyes (1107), Benevento (1108), and the Lateran (1110), Henry V set out for Rome, resolved to be crowned emperor and to settle the investiture dispute. At Sutri (9 Feb. 1111) Paschal, to avoid further conflict, proposed a radical solution: Henry should renounce investiture and allow free elections, and in return the German churches should surrender the *regalia*, i.e. all property and rights which had come to them from the empire, retaining only strictly ecclesiastical revenues like tithes. Henry accepted this concordat, unrealistic though it was; but when it was read out at the coronation service in St Peter's on 12 Feb., it was greeted with a tumult of protest, and the coronation had to be brought to a halt. Henry's reaction was to withdraw his acceptance and arrest Paschal and the cardinals. After two months' harsh imprisonment, and the threat to recognize Antipope Silvester IV in the event of refusal, he forced the pope, in the 'privilege of Ponte Mammolo' (near Tivoli, 12 Apr. 1111) to concede the king's right to invest bishops and abbots with ring and crozier after canonical election with royal consent and before consecration. Next day Paschal, who had also had to swear never to excommunicate Henry, crowned him as emperor in St Peter's.

Paschal's capitulation aroused a storm of criticism; it seemed the reversal of all the reform party had struggled for. He himself was abashed by what he had done, and in summer 1111 considered abdication. He acquiesced in the annulment of the *pravilegium* (i.e. mockery of a privilege, as the privilege of Ponte Mammolo was satirically described) at the Lateran synod of 1112, and expressly withdrew it in 1116, renewing the prohibition of investiture. Meanwhile, however, a practical solution of the vexed issue had been reached in England, where Henry I (1100–35) renounced investiture but retained the right to receive homage from bishops before consecration (council of London, Aug. 1107), and, less formally, in France, where the king also renounced investiture but was content with an oath of allegiance. These settlements, which reflected a distinction developed chiefly by Ivo of Chartres (c. 1040–1115) between the spiritual office and the temporalities attaching to it, were approved by Paschal although they had been reached without his direct participation.

The news of the capture of Jerusalem (15 July 1099) by the First Crusade reached Rome shortly after Paschal's enthronement, and he warmly encouraged the crusading movement. In 1105 he gave his blessing to Bohemond I's (c. 1052–1111) expedition against the eastern empire, having been deceived into thinking that it was really a crusade and not just a self-interested military adventure; his support was to sour the attitude of the Greek church to western Christendom. In 1112 Emperor Alexius I (1081–1118) entered into negotiations with

Paschal with a view to reunion (he had political objectives in mind too), but they foundered on the pope's insistence on recognition of the primacy of the holy see as a precondition.

Paschal's last years were troubled. Rioting in Rome caused him to leave the city in 1116, and he again left it for Benevento when Henry V arrived there for a few months in 1117; from Benevento he excommunicated Archbishop Maurice of Braga (Antipope GREGORY VIII), who without authority had crowned Henry and his wife Matilda at Easter. He had hardly returned to the strife-ridden city in early 1118 when he died in Castel Sant'Angelo, a pontiff under whom the papacy suffered a marked set-back.

JW 1, 702–72; LP 2, 296–310; 3, 143–56; MGConst 1, 134–52; 564–74; PL 163, 31–448; C. Servatius, *Paschalis II* (Stuttgart, 1979); J. G. Rowe, 'Paschal II and the Relation between the Spiritual and Temporal Powers in the Kingdom of Jerusalem', *Speculum* 32 (1957), 470–501; 'Paschal II, Bohemond of Antioch and the Byzantine Empire', *BullJRL* 49 (1967), 165–202; *PRE* 14, 717–24 (C. Mirbt); *LThK* 8, 128 f. (Th. Schieffer); *DTC* 11, 2057–74 (É. Amann); *NCE* 10, 1049 (J. Gilchrist); Seppelt 3, 134–52; Mann 8, 1–119.

THEODERIC (antipope Sept. 1100–Jan. 1101: d. 1102). On the death of Antipope CLEMENT III (8 Sept. 1100) his adherents in Rome, meeting secretly by night in St Peter's, elected, consecrated, and enthroned Theoderic, cardinal bishop of Albano (not S. Rufina, as mistakenly recorded), as his successor. Little is known about him except that he was cardinal deacon of Sta Maria in Via Lata in 1084, became one of Clement's leading supporters and served him as legate in Germany, and probably sheltered him in the Alban hills when he was driven out of Castel Sant'Angelo. As Pope PASCHAL II was absent from Rome in south Italy at the time, he was able to maintain his position for one hundred and five days, but on Paschal's return attempted to make his escape to Emperor Henry IV (1056–1106), who in fact had had no hand in his elevation and was not averse from an understanding with the new pope. He was quickly arrested by Paschal's supporters, brought before him and sentenced to confinement in Holy Trinity monastery at La Cava, near Salerno, where the Normans could be relied upon to ensure his custody. There he became a monk, dying in 1102. He was buried in the community cemetery; the gravestone recording his name and the date is preserved.

LP 2, 298; 345 (*Ann.Romani*); Watterich 2, 89–91; P. Kehr, 'Zur Geschichte Wiberts von Ravenna (Clemens III)', *SAB* 1921, 981–8; C. Servatius, *Paschalis II* (Stuttgart, 1979), 42 f.; 70–2; 339.

ALBERT or **ADALBERT** (antipope 1101: d. ?). Immediately after the arrest and imprisonment of Antipope THEODERIC in early 1101, the adherents of the earlier antipope CLEMENT III gathered in the church of SS. Apostoli and elected Albert, cardinal bishop of Silva Candida (S. Rufina), to succeed him. Little is known about him except that he must have been appointed and consecrated bishop by Clement by 1084, and that when the Clementine cardinals wrote in Aug. 1098 summoning their Gregorian opponents, with the promise of a safe conduct, to a synod to meet in Rome on 1 Nov., his name headed the list of signatories. When news of his election got abroad there was rioting in the city, and he sought refuge in the house of a Clementine sympathizer near S. Marcello (a Clementine centre). Before it came to a serious struggle, however, his protector succumbed to bribery and handed him over to PASCHAL II. After being stripped of his insignia, publicly humiliated, and briefly imprisoned in a tower at the Lateran, he was sentenced to lifelong confinement in the monastery of S. Lorenzo at Aversa, just north of Naples, where the Normans could be relied upon to ensure his safe custody. Nothing is known of his later history or the date of his death.

LP 2, 298; 345; JW 1, 773; *MGL*iblit 2, 405–7; P. Kehr, 'Zur Geschichte Wiberts von Ravenna (Clemens III)', *SAB* 1921, 980–8; C. Servatius, *Paschalis II* (Stuttgart, 1979), 42 f.; 71 f.; 339; *EC* 1, 687 (P. Brezzi).

SILVESTER IV (antipope 18 Nov. 1105–12 Apr. 1111: d. ?). In Nov. 1105 an attempt was made to set up another pope in place of PASCHAL II. Those involved were probably not, as commonly stated, adherents of the late antipope CLEMENT III but imperially minded malcontents belonging to the Roman aristocracy. Meeting in Sta Maria Rotonda (the Pantheon) and alleging that Paschal was guilty of simony and heresy, they elected Maginulf, archpriest of S. Angelo. Nothing reliable is known about him; Paschal stated that he was a stranger to Rome and that he had no idea who had ordained him, while his enemies accused him of dabbling in magic. Things cannot have gone according to plan, for his partisans had to appeal for help to Count Werner of Ancona. No doubt hoping to do Emperor Henry V (1106–25) a service, Werner came at once to Rome with a contingent of soldiers. Paschal being outside Rome itself in the *Leonine city, Maginulf went under Werner's protection to the Lateran and was there consecrated and enthroned on 18 Nov. as Silvester IV. On Paschal's return there was a period of bloody fighting in which the usurper's troops more than once soundly defeated the pope's. When Silvester's money ran out, however, his following crumbled away and he found himself obliged to leave the city. After a short stay at Tivoli, he settled under Werner's tutelage at Osimo (prov. of Ancona). Here he lived in obscurity until spring 1111 when Henry V, wishing to put pressure on Paschal, had him brought to his camp near Rome as a warning to the pope that, if he did not fall in with the king's wishes, there was a rival at hand to replace him. Once he had obtained what he wanted, Henry dropped him; on 12 Apr., on the king's orders, he renounced all claim to the papacy and promised obedience to Paschal. He passed the remainder of his life under the care of his patron Werner. It is not known when he died.

LP 2, 298; 348 f.; JW 1, 773 f.; MGConst 1, 146 nr. 98; MGSS 19, 281 f. (Ann. Ceccanenses); C. Servatius, *Paschalis II* (Stuttgart, 1979), 43; 71-4; 220; 232; 245; 251.

GELASIUS II (24 Jan. 1118-29 Jan. 1119). The successor of PASCHAL II, John of Gaeta came of a respected family, as a boy studied and became a monk at Monte Cassino, and there wrote three lives of saints which reflect the stylistic influence of his teacher Alberic, the noted Cassinese author. URBAN II appointed him cardinal deacon in 1088 and chancellor in 1089. He held this key office for three decades, being responsible both for enlarging the staff of the chancery and for reviving the fine rhythmic style of papal documents. As chancellor he collaborated loyally with Paschal II, shared his imprisonment by Emperor Henry V (1106-25) from Feb. to Apr. 1111, and at the Lateran synod of 1116 stoutly defended him against the critics of his capitulation on the *investiture issue.

Already elderly, he had an exceptionally harassed reign. Elected in Sta Maria in Pallara on the Palatine, he was at once brutally attacked and imprisoned by Cencius Frangipani, head of a patrician family which detested Paschal and his associates, and was only set free in response to the demands of the Romans led by the city prefect. On 1 Mar. fear of Henry V, who hastened from Lombardy to Rome on hearing of his election, forced him to flee with the cardinals to his native Gaeta, where he was ordained priest and consecrated bishop and pope on 9 and 10 Mar. Henry now demanded his return so that they could reach an amicable settlement of the investiture dispute, but he refused, explaining that he planned to hold a council for this purpose at Milan or Cremona in the autumn. In his exasperation Henry had Archbishop Maurice of Braga proclaimed pope as GREGORY VIII (8 Mar.). Gelasius retaliated by anathematizing both the emperor and his antipope at Capua on 9

Apr., and by sending letters denouncing him to all major centres he effectively crushed any hope Gregory may have had of obtaining recognition. When Henry left Rome Gelasius was able to return, but the city was controlled by the antipope and other hostile elements and he could not install himself in the Lateran or St Peter's; on 21 July he was again set upon by the Frangipani during mass in Sta Prassede. Although he managed to escape, he deemed it prudent to withdraw to France, and with several cardinals sailed from Genoa, reaching Marseilles on 23 Oct. At Saint-Gilles, near Nimes, Norbert of Xanten (c.1080-1134), to be founder of the austere, evangelistic Premonstratensians or White Canons, visited him and was given permission to preach the gospel wherever he thought fit. Gelasius held a synod at Vienne in early Jan. 1119 and then, falling seriously ill, retired to Cluny, near Mâcon, where he died at the end of the month without being able to organize the council which would settle the issues dividing church and empire. He was buried in the abbey there.

LP 2, 311-21; 347; PL 163, 473-514; JW 1, 775-80; Watterich 2, 91-114; R. Krohn, *Der päpstliche Kanzler Johannes von Gaeta* (diss., Marburg, 1918); Mann 8, 120-38; NCE 6, 316 f. (H. Bloch); Seppelt 3, 151-4.

GREGORY (VIII) (antipope 8 Mar. 1118-Apr. 1121: d. c.1140). Born in southern France of modest parentage, a Cluniac at Limoges, Maurice Burdinus (a nickname meaning 'ass') was taken to Spain and educated there by Archbishop Bernard of Toledo, became archdeacon of Toledo, and by 1099 was promoted bishop of Coimbra. When his metropolitan Gerald of Braga visited Rome in summer 1103, he placed Maurice in charge of the see. Between autumn 1104 and spring 1108 he was on pilgrimage in the Holy Land, and in Jan. 1109 himself became archbishop of Braga, receiving the *pallium in Rome from PASCHAL II. He was soon at loggerheads with Bernard of Toledo over the boundaries of their dioceses, but in Nov. 1114, after he had gone to Rome in person, Paschal settled the dispute decisively in his favour. After enjoying his triumph briefly at Braga, he was again at the papal court in autumn 1116, this time to protest against decisions favouring Santiago de Compostela to the detriment of Braga. Paschal, impressed perhaps by his eloquence and diplomatic skill, now dispatched him to Lombardy on a peace mission to Emperor Henry V (1106–25), who wanted a definitive clarification of his relation to the holy see. At this point Maurice defected to the emperor, and was in his entourage when he entered Rome in early 1117 (Paschal had moved to south Italy). At the Easter mass (25 Mar.), at which monarchs customarily donned crowns, it was Maurice who crowned Henry, notwithstanding the anathemas placed on him by several prelates. Paschal at once deposed and excommunicated him at a synod at Benevento, and instructed the Spanish authorities to elect a new archbishop of Braga.

When GELASIUS II succeeded Paschal II (24 Jan. 1118), Henry at once came to Rome and requested the new pope, who had retreated to Gaeta (his home town), to return so that the long-standing dispute between church and empire over the control of church appointments could be amicably settled. When Gelasius refused, the exasperated emperor, advised by his jurists (notably Irnerius of Bologna: d. c.1130), had Maurice proclaimed pope on 8 Mar. 1118. Taking the style Gregory VIII, he made peace between church and empire the theme of his early sermons, and when Henry returned to Germany in the summer remained in Rome, master of St Peter's, Castel Sant'Angelo, and the parts of the city dominated by the towers of the Frangipani family. But Gelasius, who had excommunicated him with his master on 8 Apr., had also denounced him in letters sent throughout Europe, effectively destroying any hopes he may have had of being recognized. Henry, too, had no further use for him; on Gelasius's death (29 Jan. 1119) he soon made *rapprochement* with CAL-

LISTUS II his objective. In 1119 Gregory withdrew to the stronghold of Sutri, but in Apr. 1121 Callistus besieged the town and the citizens surrendered him. To ruin his credibility once for all the pope made him traverse Rome in mock triumph, mounted backwards on a camel and exposed to the jeers and peltings of the populace. He was then gaoled for the rest of his life—first in Rome, then at Passerone, then at La Cava near Salerno, then at Rocca Iemolo near Monte Cassino, and in 1125 at Castel Fumone near Alatri and Frosinone. In Aug. 1137 he was still alive, back at La Cava.

JW 1, 821 f.; 2, 715; *LP* 2, 315; 347; 3, 162 f.; 169; Watterich 2, 15; 119 f.; C. Erdmann, 'Mauritius Burdinus', *QFIAB* 19 (1927), 205–61; P. David, 'L'énigme de Maurice Bourdin', *Études historiques sur la Galice et le Portugal* (Lisbon, 1947), 441–501.

CALLISTUS II (2 Feb. 1119–14 Dec. 1124). Son of Count William of Burgundy, born c.1050 and related to the German, French, and English royal houses, Guido became archbishop of Vienne in 1088. Although he did not scruple to use forged documents to promote the primatial claims of Vienne against Arles, he was an indefatigable champion of reform, leading the attack on PASCHAL II's enforced capitulation on investiture to Emperor Henry V (1106–25), and in Sept. 1112 presiding over a synod at Vienne which denounced *lay investiture as heresy and declared the 'king' (it did not recognize him as emperor) excommunicate. On the death of GELASIUS II at Cluny on 29 Jan. 1119, the handful of cardinals with him elected Guido, who was crowned as Callistus II at Vienne on 9 Feb.; in the difficult situation of the church majority of cardinals at Rome, with the clergy and people, had little choice but to ratify the election retrospectively (1 Mar. 1119).

Notwithstanding his previous intransigence, Callistus was alive to the importance of reaching an honourable settlement of the investiture issue between church and empire, and sent envoys to treat with Henry at Strasbourg. The emperor, too, was ready for *rapprochement*; the practice prevalent in France convinced him that abandoning the right of investiture did not entail losing the services, tribute, and allegiance of churchmen. The two sides agreed a draft treaty which was to be signed at Mouzon, on the Meuse, but its terms proved too vague for Callistus; through misunderstanding and mutual mistrust this first initiative foundered. Disillusioned, Callistus reiterated the prohibition of investiture and the anathema on Henry at Rheims (29 and 30 Oct. 1119). He then made a triumphal progress through Lombardy and Tuscany and was enthusiastically received at Rome on 3 June 1120. Antipope GREGORY VIII, whom Henry had by now dropped, had fled to Sutri, but after a siege its citizens surrendered him to Callistus, who publicly humiliated him and then had him shut up in a monastery.

The time was now ripe for the resumption of negotiations: Callistus's position was greatly strengthened, while at Würzburg in autumn 1121 the German princes agreed that Henry should recognize him, undertaking in return to mediate a settlement between him and the church which would not damage the honour of the empire. An embassy was sent to Rome in early 1122; Callistus received it favourably and sent Lamberto of Ostia (later HONORIUS II) and two other cardinals as plenipotentiaries to Germany. After three weeks' arduous negotiations the famous concordat of Worms was agreed there on 23 Sept. 1122. Under this the emperor renounced the right to invest with ring and crozier, symbols of spiritual authority, and guaranteed canonical election and free consecration. To Henry personally Callistus conceded that elections to bishoprics and abbeys in Germany should be held in his presence, and that he should invest the person elected with the temporalities by means of the sceptre, the symbol of temporal authority. In disputed elections the emperor was to decide in favour of 'the sounder party'. Outside Germany, the emperor's presence was not

required at elections, and investiture with the temporalities was to follow within six months after consecration.

The concordat of Worms ended the long struggle between church and empire over investiture. Although he had made concessions, Callistus had secured the freedom of the church in the central issue of investiture; his pride in his achievement was eloquently attested in frescos celebrating the settlement with which he embellished the Lateran. In Mar. 1123 he convened a great council (the first Lateran council; to be recognized in the west as the Ninth General) which solemnly ratified the concordat. At this he overcame the objections of strict Gregorians by arguing that the concessions he had made were to be tolerated for the sake of peace, not accepted in principle. The council also published twenty-two disciplinary canons, mostly repeating earlier legislation, renewed URBAN II's indulgence for crusaders, declared Antipope Gregory VIII's ordinations void, and provided protection for pilgrims and penalties for violators of the *Truce of God.

LP 2, 322–6; 376–9; JW 1, 780–821; U. Robert, *Bullaire du pape Calixte II* (2 vols., Paris, 1891); Watterich 2, 115–53; *MG*Const 1, 159–61 (Worms); *MG*Liblit 3, 21–8; *DBI* 16, 761–8 (G. Miccoli); *EC* 3, 391–3 (P. F. Palumbo); *NCE* 2, 1081 (D. D. McGarry); *DHGE* 11, 424–38 (E. Jordan); Seppelt 3, 153–64; S. A. Chodorow, 'Ecclesiastical Politics and the Ending of the Investiture Contest', *Speculum* 46 (1971), 613–40; Mann 8, 139–230.

HONORIUS II (21 Dec. 1124–13 Feb. 1130). The election following CALLISTUS II's death was a turbulent one. First, a majority of cardinals, with the Pierleoni family, put forward Cardinal Saxo of S. Stefano; they then dropped him, and the cardinal priest Teobaldo was unanimously proclaimed as CELESTINE II. While his installation was in progress, the Frangipani family, with the connivance of the chancellor Aimeric, broke into the assembly and at sword-point had Cardinal Lamberto of Ostia acclaimed pope. Celestine resigned, and after Aimeric and Leo Frangipani had squared the city prefect and the Pierleoni with substantial bribes Lamberto, who had laid down the papal insignia, was duly elected and enthroned as Honorius II.

Often explained in terms of the rivalries of patrician families, these proceedings in fact reflected a struggle among the cardinals themselves, with the old-school Gregorians who formed the majority being outmanoeuvred by a younger group led by Aimeric who, regarding the *investiture issue as settled, were now concentrating on the inner renewal of the church. Humbly born near Imola (prov. of Bologna), reputedly learned, Lamberto Scannabecchi was one of these. Made cardinal bishop of Ostia by PASCHAL II in 1117, he had accompanied GELASIUS II to France, been a trusted adviser of Callistus II, and taken a decisive part in negotiating the concordat of *Worms (1122). Like Aimeric, whom he confirmed as chancellor, he was a canon regular.

Honorius used the peace with the empire which the church had secured at Worms to strengthen its position and promote reform. In 1125 he backed Count Lothair III of Supplinburg for the German crown (1125–37); the new king unprecedentedly asked him to confirm his election. He maintained his support for Lothair by anathematizing (1128) not only his rival Conrad but Archbishop Anselm of Milan, who had crowned Conrad king of the Lombards. In France his diplomatic patience, which aroused the indignation of the increasingly influential Bernard of Clairvaux (1090–1153), eventually led King Louis VI (1108–37) to settle his conflicts with the hierarchy; while he was able to secure the admission of papal legates to England after 1125. His efforts to prevent the formation of à Norman kingdom in southern Italy were less successful, and in Apr. 1128 he was forced to recognize Roger II, count of Sicily (1095–1154), as duke of Apulia in return for his oath of fealty.

Honorius's internal church policies were guided by his increasingly powerful chancellor Aimeric. The majority both of the cardinals he created and of his legates shared their aspirations for moral and spiritual reform in the church; he also showed marked favour to the canons regular, believing them better qualified than the old orders to collaborate in the work. In the same spirit he sanctioned the Premonstratensian canons, recently founded by Norbert of Xanten (c. 1080–1134), in 1126; two years later, through his legate at the council of Troyes, he approved the rule of the Knights Templar, in preparing which Bernard of Clairvaux, Aimeric's close friend, had taken a large part. His interventions at Cluny, where he condemned and imprisoned the former abbot Pontius in 1126, and at Monte Cassino, where he forced the resignation of Abbot Oderisius shortly after, have been explained as illustrating the inevitable frictions between the older and younger generations of reformers.

Honorius fell gravely ill in Jan. 1130, and Aimeric, foreseeing the resurgence of party strife when he died and determined to ensure a congenial successor, had him removed to the monastery of S. Gregorio on the Caelian, protected by the strongholds of the sympathetic Frangipani family. When the pope died during the night of 13/14 Feb., he had him temporarily buried immediately in a makeshift grave in the monastery so that an election could proceed without any delay. His body was then moved to the Lateran once INNOCENT II had been elected.

JW 1, 823–39; 2, 755; PL 166, 1217–320; LP 2, 327 f.; 379; 3, 136 f.; 170 f.; LPDert, 203–17 (more reliable); Watterich 2, 157–73; DTC 7, 132–5 (É. Amann); NCE 7, 125 f. (J. M. Muldoon); Seppelt 3, 165–71; H. W. Klewitz, Reformpapstum und Kardinalkolleg (Darmstadt, 1957); 'Das Ende des Reformpapstums', DA 3 (1939), 372–412; F. J. Schmale, Studien zum Schisma des Jahres 1130 (Cologne, 1961); G. Tellenbach, 'Der Sturz des Abtes Pontius von Cluny und seine Geschichtliche Bedeutung', QFIAB 42 f. (1963), 13–55; H. E. J. Cowdrey, 'Two Studies in Cluniac History 1049–1126', StGreg 11; Mann 8, 228–305.

CELESTINE (II) (15/16 Dec. 1124: d. 1125/6). In the turbulent election following CALLISTUS II's death a majority of cardinals first supported the candidature of Cardinal Saxo of S. Stefano. They then dropped him, and on the motion of the cardinal deacon Jonathan, a close friend of the powerful Pierleoni family, the cardinal priest Teobaldo was unanimously elected with the style Celestine II. No sooner had he been clothed in the red mantle and the singing of the *Te Deum* been started than Robert, of the Frangipani family, broke into the assembly with armed troops and acclaimed Cardinal Lamberto of Ostia as pope. There was a violent struggle in which Teobaldo suffered blows and severe wounds, but the outcome was that he was either forced or persuaded to resign while Lamberto was elected and installed as HONORIUS II.

A Roman of the Boccapecorini family, Teobaldo Boccapecci had been promoted cardinal priest of Sta Anastasia by Callistus II in 1123. Previously he had been cardinal deacon of Sta Maria Nuova for at least twenty years, having been appointed by PASCHAL II. In spite of the appearance of family in-fighting, this disorderly election reflected a partisan struggle in the college of cardinals between older Gregorians who still thought in terms of conflict between church and empire and the younger reformers who wished now to concentrate on the deeper renewal of the church. It is probable that, in putting Teobaldo forward, the former group hoped that he would seem an acceptable compromise to the younger group because of the ties he had formed, when in charge of Sta Maria Nuova, with the neighbouring Frangipani, whom they were using to accomplish their plans. If so, their hopes were frustrated, and Teobaldo himself, already an elderly man, seems to have died soon after the election, a victim of the violent treatment he had received. Because he had not been consecrated or enthroned although he was canonically elected, he does not feature in the officially accepted list of popes but is classified, unfairly, as an antipope.

LPDert, 204 f.; 211; Watterich 2, 157–9; Peter, *Chron. mon. Cassin.* (*MGSS* 6, 804); H. W. Klewitz, 'Das Ende des Reformpapstums', *DA* 3 (1939), 400–2; *DHGE* 12, 58 f. (R. Mols).

INNOCENT II (14 Feb. 1130–24 Sept. 1143). A Roman of patrician family, Gregorio Papareschi was cardinal deacon of S. Angelo by 1116, in 1122 helped to negotiate the concordat of *Worms, and next year was legate in France with his later rival Pietro Pierleoni. When HONORIUS II died in S. Gregorio monastery in the night of 13/14 Feb. 1130, the powerful chancellor Aimeric, with a minority of cardinals sympathetic to the newer reform tendencies, mostly from north Italy and France, hastily buried the dead pope in a temporary grave and then clandestinely elected Gregorio as Innocent II, enthroning him at daybreak in the Lateran. When the news got abroad, the majority of cardinals, most of them old Gregorians from Rome and south Italy, refused to accept the coup and, meeting later in the morning in S. Marco, elected Cardinal Pietro Pierleoni as ANACLETUS II. Both elections were irregular, Innocent's glaringly so, but both popes were consecrated on 23 Feb., Innocent in Aimeric's titular church of Sta Maria Nuova by the bishop of *Ostia.

The result was an eight-year schism, with both claimants (they stood for different conceptions of reform) competing for recognition. Anacletus had an initial advantage through his mastery of Rome and his alliance with the Norman Roger II (1095–1154) to whom he granted the crown of Sicily, Apulia, and Calabria. Innocent had to flee to France, but very soon his title was acknowledged everywhere except in Scotland, Aquitaine, and south Italy. He owed this to the close ties which Aimeric and his other electors had with influential reform circles, notably the canons regular. His most effective advocates were Abbot Bernard of Clairvaux (1090–1153), who won Louis VI of France (1108–37) and Henry I of England (1100–35) for him, and Archbishop Norbert of Magdeburg (1126–

34), founder of the Premonstratensians, who swayed the German episcopate and King Lothair III (1125–37). By 1132 he felt secure enough to reject Anacletus's proposals for arbitration on the ground that Christendom had already pronounced in his favour.

In Mar. 1131 he met Lothair at Liège and induced him, with the promise of the imperial crown, to fight Anacletus and to escort him to Rome; Lothair in vain requested the restoration of the royal rights of *investiture surrendered at *Worms. After holding a synod at Rheims at which he anathematized Anacletus and crowned the French king's heir, Innocent joined Lothair at Piacenza in Aug. 1132. Lothair marched on Rome in spring 1133, but as the Anacletans firmly held St Peter's and the *Leonine city, the pope had to crown him on 3 June in the Lateran; Lothair renewed his demand for the restoration of the rights of investiture, but all Innocent would grant was an injunction that bishops and abbots in Germany should do homage before taking possession of the temporalities attaching to their offices. In addition he enfeoffed him with the vast estates of Countess Matilda of Tuscany (1046–1115), who in 1111 had appointed the emperor heir to her patrimonial possessions (originally intended for the holy see) while continuing to recognize the papal right to proprietorship. He could not maintain himself in Rome, however, when Lothair returned to Germany, and retreated to Pisa, where he held a synod which excommunicated Anacletus and Roger II. In 1136, after Bernard of Clairvaux had gained Milan for Innocent, Lothair again invaded Italy, but his campaign against Roger proved indecisive, he had differences with Innocent, and Rome could not be taken. He died on 4 Dec. 1137 on his way back to Germany, but Innocent and his supporters, including Bernard, had already entered into negotiations with Roger with the object of detaching him from Anacletus by demonstrating to him the superiority of Innocent's claims.

In effect it was the death of Anacletus on 25 Jan. 1138 that ended the schism; his adherents elected Antipope VICTOR IV as successor but he resigned on 29 May, and his electors and the Pierleoni family itself now made their submission to Innocent, who was back in the Lateran by 21 Mar. In Apr. 1139 he held the second Lateran council (later recognized in the west as the Tenth General) which finally settled all problems arising out of the schism, in particular annulling all decisions, acts, and ordinations of Anacletus and his adherents with a severity which shocked Bernard; it also republished and consolidated the reform legislation of previous decades. In 1140 Innocent confirmed the condemnation passed on the philosopher and theologian Peter Abelard (1079–1142) and his teaching by the council of Sens (June 1140). His last years, however, were beset with troubles. Militarily defeated and captured by Roger II in July 1139, he was forced to acknowledge his title as king of Sicily (treaty of Migniano, 25 July 1139); in 1141 he fell out with Louis VII of France (1137–79) over an appointment to the see of Bourges and laid an interdict on any place which sheltered him; and in 1143 he faced violence and rioting in Rome, where the citizens set up a commune with an independent senate.

Contrary to a widely held view, Innocent was no mediocre personality inferior in culture and leadership to Anacletus; in political skill as also in sureness of his position he was markedly his superior. His reign and his victory in the schism were significant in that, continuing the new course charted by CALLISTUS II, he steered the church once for all away from arid juridical conflicts with the secular authorities to concern with the deeper, wider-ranging reforms which GREGORY VII had called for at the Lateran synod of 1059 but which had been in danger of being overlooked.

JW 1, 840–911; LP 2, 379–85; PL 179, 55–686; Watterich 2, 174–275; DTC 7, 1950–61 (É. Amann); EC 7, 7–10 (P. F. Palumbo); NCE 7, 520

f. (J. R. Sommerfeldt); *LThK* 5, 686 (F. J. Schmale); F. J. Schmale, *Studien zum Schisma des Jahres 1130* (Cologne, 1961); H. W. Klewitz, 'Das Ende des Reformpapstums', *DA* 3 (1939), 372–412; Mann 9, 1–101; Seppelt 3, 171–87.

ANACLETUS II (antipope 14 Feb. 1130–25 Jan. 1138). On the death of HONORIUS II (13 Feb. 1130), while a minority of cardinals led by the chancellor Aimeric rushed through the clandestine election of INNOCENT II, the majority meeting in S. Marco later in the day, in the presence of the clergy and people, elected Cardinal Pietro of Sta Maria in Trastevere; he was enthroned as Anacletus II by the bishop of Porto in St Peter's. The disputed election reflected, not the rivalries of powerful families, but a deep-seated division among the cardinals between a younger group devoted, since the concordat of *Worms, to the inner renewal of the church, and an older group which still understood reform in terms of extracting further concessions from the empire.

Pietro, of the famous Pierleoni family, great-grandson of the converted Jew Baruch-Benedict, was the leading member of the latter group. Educated in Paris, later a monk at Cluny under Abbot Pontius, he was created cardinal deacon of SS. Cosma and Damiano, probably as a result of family pressure, by PASCHAL II in 1111 or 1112. He was one of the cardinals who accompanied GELASIUS II to France in 1118, and played a decisive part in the election of CALLISTUS II at Cluny in Feb. 1119. So far Callistus had shown himself one of Emperor Henry V's (1106–25) fiercest opponents, and Pietro himself was undoubtedly a hardliner on the *investiture issue. It was the money of Pietro's father that ensured the return of Callistus and the curia to Rome, and the pope's promotion of the son as cardinal priest of Sta Maria in Trastevere in 1120 can be seen as expressing his gratitude. In 1121 and 1122/3 he served as legate in England and France respectively, but from 1123 to 1130 he disappears almost entirely from view. There is nothing surprising in this, for almost all missions in this period were entrusted to friends of the chancellor Aimeric, the leader of the newer reform tendencies; but it is noteworthy that the power and prestige of the Pierleoni family were meanwhile increasing, and that it identified itself with attempts to restore the role of the people in papal elections.

Once elected, Anacletus was undisputed master of Rome through the wealth, influence, and weapons of his family. His immediate object (as was Innocent II's) was to obtain recognition throughout Christendom, and he dispatched a stream of letters seeking it to the kings of Germany and France and leading churchmen everywhere. In these he made much of the fact that, in contrast to the handful of cardinals who had chosen Innocent, the whole of Rome had participated in his election; what is even more striking is his evident insecurity and reliance on personal appeals. Very soon, however, he lost the war of propaganda; largely through the efforts of Bernard of Clairvaux (1090–1153) and Norbert of Xanten (c. 1080–1134) Europe came out in favour of Innocent, with the exceptions of Aquitaine, Scotland, Milan, and certain other cities of north Italy, and southern Italy. This last he won over by making (27 Sept. 1130) Roger II of Sicily king not only of Sicily but of Calabria and Apulia, as well as overlord of Capua, Naples, and Benevento.

When Lothair III of Germany (1125–37) came to Italy with Innocent in spring 1133, Anacletus in alarm proposed that the claims of himself and his rival should be submitted to arbitration, but the suggestion was rejected. Secure in the impregnable *Leonine city, he could do nothing to prevent the crowning of Lothair as emperor by Innocent in June; but when Lothair returned to Germany a few days later, he was able to make conditions in Rome too hot for Innocent, who speedily retreated to Pisa. But from now onwards Anacletus's influence was on the wane; when Bernard of Clairvaux gained Milan for Innocent in 1136, his support was reduced to Roger's kingdom.

VICTOR IV (antipope 1138)

The final blow came in Nov./Dec. 1137 when representatives of both popes debated their respective cases before Roger at Salerno; several of Anacletus's leading adherents, including the distinguished canonist Peter of Pisa, yielded to Bernard's eloquence and abandoned his cause. He himself continued to hold out, unassailable in Rome, until his death on 25 Jan. 1138. This effectively ended the schism, for although his followers elected a successor (Antipope VICTOR IV), he submitted to Innocent after two months.

There has been a tendency to represent Anacletus as outstanding in character, personality, and ability, and to discount the reports of his ambition, venality, and loose living as the gossip of enemies. Against this it seems clear that at every stage in his career he owed at least as much to family influence as to native brilliance, while his inordinate ambition at least and his readiness to exploit unscrupulously the wealth and arms at the disposal of the Pierleoni cannot be denied.

PL 179, 687–731 (letters, etc.); JW 1, 911–19; DHGE 2, 1408–19 (E. Vacandard); DBI 3, 17–19 (R. Manselli); P. F. Palumbo, 'La cancelleria d'Anacleto II', *Scritti di paleografia e diplomatica in onore di Vincenzo Federici* (Florence, 1945); H. W. Klewitz, 'Das Ende des Reformpapstums', DA 3 (1939), 371–412; F. J. Schmale, *Studien zum Schisma des Jahres 1130* (Cologne, 1961); EC 1, 1126–8 (P. Brezzi).

VICTOR IV (antipope mid-Mar.–29 May 1138: d. ?). Born at Ceccano (prov. of Frosinone), Gregorio Conti became cardinal priest of SS. Apostoli in the first decade of PASCHAL II's pontificate. In 1111 he was one of the sixteen cardinals who confirmed under oath the privilege extorted from Paschal by Emperor Henry V (1106–25) under the treaty of *Mammolo. In so doing he was acting under duress, for at the Lateran synod of Mar. 1112 he was among the pope's severest critics, collaborating with Gerard of Angoulême in preparing the formal condemnation of the privilege. This opposition seems to have cost him his title; but CALLISTUS II restored him in Dec. 1122. With his unbending views it was

inevitable that, at the double election of 1130, he should be among the cardinals opposing INNOCENT II and voting for Pietro Pierleoni (ANACLETUS II). When Roger II of Sicily (1095–1154) invited the rival popes to present their respective claims before him at Salerno in Nov. 1137, Gregory was one of three representing Anacletus. On the antipope's death on 25 Jan. 1138 his adherents, after seeking the permission of Roger II, elected Gregory as his successor with the style Victor IV. His reign, however, proved a meaningless interlude; no pontifical acts of his survive, and his already reduced following rapidly fell away, in part as a result of bribes offered by Innocent II. On 29 May 1138 he resigned owing to the intervention of Bernard of Clairvaux (1090–1153), who brought him and the other leading Anacletans to Innocent to make their submission. The pope pardoned them, promising to allow Victor and the other cardinals to retain their rank; but at the second Lateran council (Apr. 1139) he went back on his word and deposed Victor and the others, earning a severe rebuke from Bernard. Nothing is known of Gregory's subsequent life or of the date of his death.

LP 2, 383; 3, 138; Mansi XXI, 535; MGConst I, 143; 573; JW 1, 919; Watterich 2, 178; 248 ff.; Bernard of Clairvaux, *Epp.* 213, 317 (PL 182, 378; 523); H. W. Klewitz, 'Das Ende des Reformpapstums', DA 3 (1939), 376 f.; 397; F. J. Schmale, *Studien zum Schisma des Jahres 1130* (Cologne, 1961), 60 f.; 175 f.; EC 12, 1543 (A. P. Frutaz); Seppelt 3, 184.

CELESTINE II (26 Sept. 1143–8 Mar. 1144). Originally Guido of Città di Castello, in Umbria, son of aristocratic parents, pupil and life-long admirer of the philosopher and theologian Peter Abelard (1079–1142) and himself a learned scholar entitled to be addressed as 'master', he was brought to Rome by CALLISTUS II, was made cardinal deacon of Sta Maria in Via Lata by HONORIUS II in 1127, and in 1134 was promoted cardinal priest of S. Marco by INNOCENT II, whom he had supported at the double election of 1130. In 1131/2 he served as papal legate in Cologne and

Aachen, and was one of those who presented the case for Innocent II's legitimacy before Roger II of Sicily (1095–1154) at Salerno in Nov. 1137. He was legate in France in 1139/40. In 1140 or 1141 Bernard of Clairvaux (1090–1153), conscious of the resistance in the curia to the condemnation of Abelard at Sens in 1140, wrote to Guido warning him not to allow affection for his old teacher to make him sympathetic to his doctrines. Two days after Innocent II's death he was unanimously elected to succeed him, and adopted the name Celestine. He had been one of the five persons recommended by the late pontiff; his election is also said to have had the warm support of Empress Matilda, widow of Henry V (1106–25).

Already an old man, he had for years belonged to the circle of close friends of Aimeric, chancellor of the Roman church (1123–41), and shared their concern for the inner renewal of the church. His two most important acts reversed decisions of his predecessor. First, through the good offices of Abbot Suger of St Denis and Bernard of Clairvaux, he lifted the interdict which Innocent had laid in 1141 on all places sheltering Louis VII of France (1137–79); the king had agreed to accept the duly elected archbishop of Bourges whom he had previously opposed. Secondly, he refused to ratify the treaty of *Migniano (July 1139) under which Innocent, taken prisoner in battle, had been forced to recognize Roger II's sovereignty over southern Italy as well as Sicily. But the critical situation on the borders of the papal state, particularly at Benevento, soon obliged him to modify his intransigence and send envoys to Roger's court at Palermo.

'For the ransom of his soul' Celestine bequeathed fifty-six volumes from his personal library (including two by Abelard) to the church of S. Florido, Città di Castello; the silver altar-frontal which he also presented to it remains one of the treasures of the town.

JW 2, 1–7; 716; 758; LP 2, 385; 449; PL 179, 761–820; Watterich 2, 276–8; John of Salisbury,

Hist.pontif. 42 (ed. M. Chibnall, 85); DHGE 12, 59–62 (R. Mols); LThK 2, 1254 (H. Wolter); NCE 3, 364 f. (M. W. Baldwin); A. Wilmart, 'Les livres légués par Célestin II à Città de Castello', RBén 35 (1923), 98–102; Mann 9, 102–12.

LUCIUS II (12 Mar. 1144–15 Feb. 1145). The successor of CELESTINE II, Gherardo Caccianemici was born at Bologna, and before joining the curia was a canon of S. Frediano, Lucca, the most important Italian congregation of canons regular. CALLISTUS II appointed him cardinal priest of Sta Croce (which he renovated, attaching to it a body of canons regular), and from then on he was a leading member of the curia, distinguished for his exemplary character and energetic service to successive popes. As HONORIUS II's legate in Germany he worked in 1125 for the election of Lothair III as king (1125–37), and in 1126 for the nomination of Norbert of Xanten (c. 1080–1134) as archbishop of Magdeburg. Rector, i.e. governor, of Benevento in 1130, he collaborated with Chancellor Aimeric in 1138 in supporting INNOCENT II in a dispute with Lothair over Monte Cassino, and on Aimeric's death in 1141 Innocent appointed him chancellor and librarian. His friends included Bernard of Clairvaux (1090–1153), Walter of Ravenna, and Abbot Peter the Venerable of Cluny (c. 1092–1156).

Lucius restored to Tours (May 1144) its metropolitan jurisdiction over Brittany, temporarily usurped by the bishop of Dol (near Mont St Michel); he confirmed the primacy of Toledo over the Iberian peninsula, including Portugal; and he accepted Portugal as a fief of the holy see. But he faced political difficulties in Rome itself, where a popular commune had recently been proclaimed. It now set up a senate independent of the holy see and its rule, and appointed as its leader, with the title of patrician, none other than Giordano Pierleoni, brother of the late antipope ANACLETUS II.

To secure support Lucius sought to reach an understanding with Roger II of

Sicily (1095–1154), with whom he had enjoyed friendly relations since his time as rector at Benevento. A meeting at Ceprano, however, came to nothing, Roger's sons resumed their attacks on the papal states, and the pope had to content himself with a seven-year armistice under which Roger retained possession of the occupied territories but undertook to take no action against Benevento or other papal lands. In his need Lucius turned for help against the insurgent citizens, who were demanding independence from ecclesiastical control and the restriction of the clergy to spiritual functions and spiritual dues, to the new German king, the Hohenstaufen Conrad III (1138–52), but he was too deeply involved with trouble at home to provide it. Lucius then decided, in order to restore his authority in Rome, to take up arms himself at the head of such forces as remained at his disposal. Leading an unsuccessful assault on the Capitol, where the senate was installed, he was injured by heavy stones used as ammunition, and died shortly afterwards in the monastery of S. Gregorio.

PL 179, 819–938; *LP* 2, 385 f.; JW 2, 7–19; 717; 758; Watterich 2, 278–81; F. J. Schmale, *Studien zum Schisma des Jahres 1130* (Cologne, 1961), esp. 48–50; *DTC* 9, 1057 f. (É. Amann); *EC* 7, 1633 (S. Majarelli); Seppelt 3, 187–9; Mann 9, 113–26.

EUGENE III, BL. (15 Feb. 1145–8 July 1153). Hurriedly elected on the very day of Lucius II's death from wounds, Bernardo Pignatelli was at the time abbot of the Cistercian house of SS. Vincenzo and Anastasio outside Rome. Born at Pisa of unidentified but humble parentage, he was probably prior of S. Zeno, Pisa, in 1128 and was administrator of the see in the late 1130s when, meeting Abbot Bernard of Clairvaux (1090–1153), he fell under his spell and became a monk at Clairvaux. When Bernard heard of his election, he was dismayed that the cardinals should have chosen such an inexperienced, cloistered man; but the new pope, whom he pressed to take in hand the radical reform of the

church, was to prove more capable than he anticipated. The first Cistercian to be elected, Eugene never discarded the habit and life-style of a simple monk.

Since he refused to recognize the popular commune which, rejecting the pope's temporal powers, then held sway in Rome, Eugene had to be consecrated at Farfa (40 km. north of Rome), and took up residence at Viterbo. By putting pressure on the commune he forced it to accept his suzerainty and was able to keep Christmas 1145 in Rome; but the compromise soon broke down and he was back in Viterbo in Jan. 1146. While there in 1145 he had learned of the capture of the crusader outpost Edessa (Urfa in south-east Turkey) by the Turks (23 Dec. 1144); he had also received a delegation of Armenian bishops seeking support against Byzantium. Stirred to action, he sent a bull on 1 Dec. 1145 to Louis VII of France (1137–79) proclaiming the Second Crusade; on 6 Mar. 1146 he renewed the bull, commissioning Bernard of Clairvaux to preach the crusade. Meanwhile (Jan. 1146) he himself travelled via Pisa to France to forward its preparation. He had limited his appeal to France since he needed the help of Conrad III of Germany (1138–52) against the revolutionary Romans and Roger II of Sicily (1095–1154), but when Bernard's eloquence persuaded Conrad to take the cross he had no option but to give reluctant approval. The failure of the crusade, the most impressive of all the crusades in its scope, was a bitter disappointment, all the more so as he had hoped that it would assist reconciliation with the eastern church. Although reproached by Bernard, he remained cool towards plans for a crusade against Byzantium promoted by Roger of Sicily and Louis VII in 1150.

Following Bernard's advice, Eugene was an ardent reformer, always striving to raise clerical and monastic standards. At the height of his powers he held important synods at Paris (Apr.–June 1147), Trier (winter 1147/8), and Rheims (Mar. 1148) at which, in addition to the enactment of reforming canons, such doctrinal issues as the orthodoxy of the realist scholastic Gilbert de la Porrée (c. 1083–1154) and the visions of Hildegard of Bingen (1098–1179) were reviewed. He intervened forcefully in England, supporting Archbishop Theobald of Canterbury (1138–61) in his relations with King Stephen (1135–54) and deposing William Fitzherbert (St William of York: d. 1154) from the see of York. He strengthened the ties of the holy see with Ireland, which he provided with four metropolitan sees. In his invitation to the synod of Rheims he expounded the doctrine that through St PETER Christ had granted the pope supreme authority in temporal as well as spiritual affairs. It was at his instigation that Burgundio of Pisa produced Latin translations of certain homilies of John Chrysostom and of John of Damascus's treatise *De fide orthodoxa*.

He returned to Italy in June 1148, and at Cremona on 15 July excommunicated the radical reformer Arnold of Brescia (d. 1155), who, pardoned in 1146, had allied himself with the Roman commune and denounced the pope as a 'man of blood'. In Dec. 1149 he returned to Rome with military help from Roger of Sicily, but the hostile atmosphere soon obliged him to leave. He now began negotiations with Conrad III, whom the commune had independently approached, and it was arranged that the king should come to Rome to be crowned in autumn 1152. Although Conrad died on 15 Feb. 1152, his successor Frederick I Barbarossa (1152–90) sent envoys to the pope announcing his election and promising protection; he did not seek approval for his election, but in his reply Eugene granted it. In spite of initial friction, an expedition by Frederick to Italy was agreed at the diet of Würzburg in Oct. 1152; and through the mediation of the king's envoys Eugene reached an understanding with the Roman citizens which enabled him at last to install himself precariously in the city. On 23 Mar. 1153 he concluded with Frederick the treaty of Constance under which each undertook to

protect and guarantee the other's 'honour', i.e. sovereign rights, the pope promised the king the imperial crown and the king swore not to make peace with the Roman citizens or the Normans without the pope's consent, and each agreed to make no territorial concessions to Byzantium.

Eugene died at Tivoli long before Frederick could come to Rome. He had been fortunate in having Bernard of Clairvaux, who wrote for him a treatise (*De consideratione*) on the duties of a pontiff, as his constant counsellor, but the extent of that influence can be exaggerated: while often confessedly dependent on Bernard, he not infrequently acted independently, or even in disregard, of him. The last representative of the reform papacy, he was buried in St Peter's next to GREGORY III. Revered in his lifetime, he soon had miracles attributed to his intercession, and PIUS IX beatified him in 1872. Feast 8 July.

PL 180, 1013–642; JW 2, 20–89; 717–19; 759; *LP* 2, 386 f.; Watterich 2, 283–321; *BSS* 5, 196–200 (I. Daniele); *DHGE* 15, 1349–55 (M. A. Dimier); *NCE* 5, 625 f. (M. W. Baldwin), H. Gleber, *Papst Eugen III* (Jena, 1936); E. Caspar, 'Die Kreuzzugsbullen Eugens III', *NA* 45 (1924), 285–305; P. Rassow, *Honor Imperii* (Darmstadt, 1961: with text of treaty of Constance), Seppelt 3, 189–213; Mann 9, 127–220.

ANASTASIUS IV (8 July 1153–3 Dec. 1154). A Roman from the Suburra (a quarter between the Esquiline, Viminal, and Quirinal), he was originally named Corrado and probably came of bourgeois stock. Nothing is known of his career until PASCHAL II appointed him cardinal priest of Sta Pudenziana between 1111 and 1114. In 1125 he intervened on HONORIUS II's behalf in a controversial choice of abbot at Farfa, and in 1127 at Monte Cassino to settle the succession to a deposed abbot; in the second half of 1126 he was created cardinal bishop of Sta Sabina. After the divided election of 1130 he proved a determined partisan of INNOCENT II and opponent of ANACLETUS II. During Innocent's absence from Rome from 1130 to 1137, and again in 1339, he remained in the city, or near it, as his vicar. He also served as vicar for EUGENE III, possibly in summer 1145, certainly from the beginning of 1147 to Nov. 1149 and from summer 1150 to Dec. 1152. On the very day of Eugene's death he was himself elected pope, and was enthroned in the Lateran on 12 July as Anastasius IV.

A very old man, he had amassed great experience in curial business and had proved his abilities as vicar of the holy see in testing times. He was probably chosen because, a Roman born who had resided for long stretches in the city, he seemed uniquely qualified, through the contacts he had made with the citizens, to reach a working relationship with the popular commune (in general ill disposed to the curia) which had dominated Rome since 1143. He must have had the confidence of the people's senate, for he was not only consecrated in the Lateran but, in marked contrast to Eugene III and HADRIAN IV, was able to reside undisturbed in Rome; nor did the commune make any attempt during his reign, as it had done in the past and would do again, to play off the pope and the German king against each other. It is also evidence of the good relations he enjoyed with the civic authorities that he was able to build a new palace near the Pantheon.

A similarly conciliatory approach characterized other decisions of his which were to be criticized as showing weakness. Thus, whereas Eugene III had refused to ratify an appointment made by Frederick I Barbarossa (1152–90) to the see of Magdeburg, Anastasius did so after his envoy had failed to move the king, and gave the archbishop the *pallium when he came to Rome. Again, on the death of Henry Murdac, archbishop of York (1147–53), he closed the dispute which had raged through four pontificates over the appointment of William Fitzherbert (St William of York: d. 1154), deposed by Eugene as archbishop of York, by reinstating him and sending him the pallium. In his reign, through the efforts of Nicholas Breakspear (later HADRIAN IV) as legate in Scandinavia, the payment of Peter's Pence

by both Norway and Sweden was organized.

He was buried in the Lateran, which he had greatly loved and embellished, in the porphyry sarcophagus of St Helena.

PL 188, 989–1088; JW 2, 89–102; LP 2, 388; Watterich 2, 321 f.; F. J. Schmale, *Studien zum Schisma des Jahres 1130* (Cologne, 1961), index; P. Classen, 'Zur Geschichte Papst Anastasius IV', *QFIAB* 48 (1968), 36–63; *DBI* 3, 24 f. (R. Manselli); *DHGE* 2, 1475 f. (A. Clerval); *NCE* 1, 479 (M. W. Baldwin); Mann 9, 221–30.

HADRIAN IV (4 Dec. 1154–1 Sept. 1159). So far the only English pope, Nicholas Breakspear was born c.1100 at Abbot's Langley, near St Albans, son of a humble clerk who became a monk at the abbey. Leaving England as a lad, he studied in France, and eventually joined the canons regular of St Rufus, Avignon, rising to be prior and, in 1137, abbot. The community complained to Rome of his excessive strictness, and EUGENE III, discerning his abilities, removed him but in 1149 created him cardinal bishop of Albano. From 1150 to 1153 he proved a brilliant papal legate in Scandinavia, reorganizing the church on reforming principles, establishing Trondheim as the metropolitan see of Norway, and preparing the ground for the later elevation of Uppsala to an archbishopric. Returning in triumph, he was unanimously elected pope on ANASTASIUS IV's death.

Strong-willed and clear-sighted, determined to assert the full monarchical claims of the papacy, Hadrian at once (Jan. 1155) renewed the treaty of *Constance with the German king Frederick I Barbarossa (1152–90), whose help he needed against the hostile popular commune which controlled Rome, and against William I of Sicily (1154–66), who was attacking the papal state. He then took strong action himself against the commune, placing Rome under an interdict until it expelled the leading agitator, Arnold of Brescia. With Frederick's co-operation he later had Arnold arrested and executed (1155). Yet he could never bring the commune finally to heel: it made life hazardous for him in Rome, it independently offered Frederick the imperial crown, and it was negotiating with him for recognition shortly before Hadrian's death.

The establishment of an accord with the German king was vital, but doomed to failure because Hadrian's aspirations as pope were matched by Frederick's resolve to restore the empire as Charlemagne (800–14) and Otto I (962–73) had known it. Their first meeting, at Sutri on 8 June 1155, got off to a bad start when Frederick only reluctantly consented to pay the pope the customary deferential courtesies. Hadrian crowned him in St Peter's on 18 June, significantly altering the service so as to bring out the emperor's subordination to the pope. The Romans, whose offer of the crown Frederick had spurned, revolted, and although they were soon crushed he decided to return to Germany. Already there was friction between him and Hadrian because of his insistence on his imperial rights, and because he had not given the pope the looked-for help.

Disappointment, mistrust of Frederick, and his own difficult military situation now drove Hadrian to a momentous switch of papal policy which disturbed the majority of cardinals. By the treaty of Benevento (18 June 1156) he made peace with William I of Sicily, recognizing him as king with authority over most of south Italy and special rights over the church in Sicily; in return William acknowledged the pope's feudal suzerainty and agreed to pay an annual tribute. Hadrian was thus able to consolidate his position in the papal state and even to return to Rome in Nov. 1156; but to Frederick the arrangement seemed treason to the treaty of Constance. The resulting tension came to a head at the diet of Besançon (Oct. 1157), to which Hadrian sent envoys both to explain the situation and to voice certain grievances. His letter referred to the 'benefits' he had conferred on Frederick, and uproar broke out when the German chancellor translated this as implying, as it was probably intended to do,

that the emperor was the pope's vassal. The envoys were sent packing, and next June Hadrian deemed it prudent to send Frederick a letter explaining that there were no insulting implications in his use of the word 'benefits'.

Although peace was patched up, a final break seemed unavoidable when Frederick, at the diet of Roncaglia (Nov. 1158), asserted imperial claims over north Italy and Corsica which infringed papal prerogatives, and Hadrian refused to approve his nominee to the see of Ravenna. As exchanges between them became sharper, he withdrew for security to Anagni, where he discussed an alliance against Frederick with discontented Lombard cities and agreed to excommunicate him unless he annulled the Roncaglia decrees within forty days. Before the interval expired, Hadrian was dead.

A man who combined unyielding resolution with amiability and, as his friend John of Salisbury (c. 1115–80) noted, a willingness to listen to criticism, Hadrian used Cardinal Roland (later ALEXANDER III) as his closest counsellor, but left the curia divided over his policies of relying on a Sicilian alliance against the empire. During his reign the use of the title Vicar of Christ for the pope became current. His chief intervention in English affairs was his encouragement of King Henry II (1154–89) to incorporate Ireland in the English realm; but the authenticity of the bull Laudabiliter, purporting to authorize this, is still subject to discussion.

PL 188, 1361–640; JW 2, 102–45; 720 f.; 760 f.; LP 2, 388–97; Watterich 2, 323–74; John of Salisbury, Matalogicon IV, 42; Policraticus VI, 24; DNB 1, 143–6 (M. Creighton); Mann 9, 231–340; NCE 1, 146 (W. Ullmann); LThK 4, 1307 f. (G. Schwaiger); Seppelt 3, 213–34; FM 9, 5–49 (R. Foreville); E. M. Almedingen, The English Pope (London, 1925); W. Ullmann, 'The Pontificate of Adrian IV', CHJ 11 (1953–5), 233–52; R. W. Southern, Medieval Humanism and Other Studies (Oxford, 1970), 234–52; M. P. Sheehy, Pontificia Hibernica I (Dublin, 1962), 15 f. (text of Laudabiliter); W. L. Warren, Henry II (London, 1973), 194–8.

ALEXANDER III (7 Sept. 1159–30 Aug. 1181). Born at Siena c.1100, Orlando (Roland) Bandinelli, son of Ranuccio, was a celebrated professor of law at Bologna (1139–42) and then canon of Pisa, author of a commentary on the 12th-cent. canonist Gratian and of theological *Sentences* reflecting the influence of the philosopher and theologian Abelard (1079–1142). Created cardinal deacon in 1150, cardinal priest in 1151, and chancellor in 1153, he was HADRIAN IV's closest adviser, identified with his pro-Norman and anti-imperial policy and clashing with Frederick I Barbarossa (1152–90) at the diet of *Besançon (Oct. 1157). On Hadrian's death, while a handful of pro-imperial cardinals chose Cardinal Ottaviano, the great majority elected Orlando. There were violent scenes, for it had been agreed that the election should be unanimous, and Orlando had to seek refuge in the Vatican fortress next to St Peter's. On 20 Sept. he was consecrated as Alexander III at Ninfa, south-east of Velletri, by the bishop of *Ostia; Ottaviano was consecrated as VICTOR IV at the imperial abbey of Farfa north-east of Rome on 4 Oct.

The schism played into the emperor's hands; to resolve it he convened a council of mainly German and Italian bishops at Pavia in Feb. 1160 which endorsed Victor and excommunicated Alexander. The pope, who had already excommunicated Victor, replied (24 Mar.) by anathematizing Frederick; in Oct. the episcopates and monastic orders of most western countries, including Spain, met at Toulouse in the presence of Henry II of England (1154–89) and Louis VII of France (1137–79) and declared for Alexander. The schism was to last eighteen years, for when Victor died he was replaced by antipopes PASCHAL III (1164) and then CALLISTUS III (1168). Faced with imperial opposition in Italy, Alexander moved to France in Apr. 1162, settling with the curia at Sens from 1163 to 1165. Although he returned to Rome at the invitation of the citizens in Nov. 1165, he could not prevent its occupation by Frederick or his coronation by Paschal III in

summer 1167, and he eventually resided at Benevento. Here abortive negotiations were begun, in 1166 or 1167, with the eastern emperor, Manuel I Comnenus (1143–80), who held out the prospect of the reunion of the Greek and Latin churches if Alexander would crown him universal emperor. Meanwhile Alexander was steadily gaining ground in Burgundy and, after Victor's death in Apr. 1164, in Germany; in Italy, too, where his support of the league of Lombard cities formed to combat Frederick's harsh policies was acknowledged by the naming of the newly founded city of Alessandria (1168) after him. His patience finally bore fruit when, defeated by the Lombard league at Lagnano on 29 May 1176, Frederick embarked on negotiations. By the peace of Venice (24 July 1177), in return for the withdrawal of excommunication, the emperor acknowledged him as pope and agreed to armistices with the Lombards and with Sicily.

Although he was moral victor and emerged triumphant from the schism, Alexander had been outmanoeuvred by Frederick, who had driven a wedge between him and the Lombard league. The peace of Venice was no more than a truce, and the important issues at stake between church and empire had been shelved. Meanwhile Alexander had been asserting the authority of the holy see over other rulers within the limits of the politically possible. Thus he supported Thomas Becket, archbishop of Canterbury (1162–70), in his dispute (1164–70) with Henry II over the Constitutions of Clarendon (1164), which aimed at nullifying the growing independence of the English church from the crown, but he did so with a hesitancy and occasional duplicity which sprang from fear lest the king should join the antipope's camp; after Thomas's murder (29 Dec. 1170) he was able to impose the fullest sanctions on the king and eventually reach a working arrangement with him. In 1179, in return for an annual tribute, he confirmed the right of Alfonso I of Portugal (1139–85) to his crown, and in 1181 he placed William I of Scotland

(1165–1214) and his realm under an interdict for interfering in church appointments. Finally, from 5 to 19 Mar. 1179, he presided over the impressively attended third Lateran (Eleventh General) council, which not only definitively ended the schism but marked an important stage in the development of papal legislative authority. Among its more significant decrees were those requiring a two-thirds majority of cardinals at papal elections (still in force, hardly modified, today), encouraging universities and calling on cathedrals to maintain schools, and providing for the persecution of heretics, in particular the Cathari or Albigenses, a puritanical, dualist sectarian movement in Germany and southern France. Alexander himself was the first great lawyer pope, and many of his decisions were embodied in the later codes of canon law. He stood resolutely in the reforming tradition, one of his characteristic measures being the effective abolition of the right to hold *proprietary churches by reducing it to a right of patronage. As a man he had a clear vision of what was required, but preferred peaceful solutions so long as the essential interests of the church were safeguarded. If he could on occasion be indecisive and vacillating, he was unyielding in matters of principle, and deserves credit for preventing Frederick from reducing the church to a condition of dependence.

Soon after the Lateran council Alexander was forced by the popular commune to leave Rome; in Sept. 1179 a fourth antipope, INNOCENT III, was set up, but he had no difficulty in getting rid of him. He spent his last two years in various towns in the papal state, and was at Città Castellana, 55 km. north of Rome, when he died. His body was taken back to Rome to be buried in the Lateran basilica, but the citizens covered it with insults. He was in fact a great pope who left a lasting mark on the church.

WORKS: F. Thaner, *Die Summa Magistri Rolandi* (Innsbruck, 1874); A. Gietl, *Die Sentenzen Rolands* (Freiburg, 1891).

PL 200, 69–1320 (letters, etc.); *LP* 2, 397–446; JW 2, 145–431; Watterich 2, 377–649; W. Holtzmann, 'Die Register Papst Alexander III in den Händen der Kanonisten', *QFIAB* 30 (1940), 13–87; 'Quellen und Forschungen zur Geschichte Friederich Barbarossas', *NA* 48 (1930), 384–413; U. Stutz, 'Papst Alexander III gegen die Freiung langobardischer Eigenkirchen', *AAB* 1936, No. 6; M. Pacaut, *Alexandre III* (Paris, 1956); M. W. Baldwin, *Alexander III and the Twelfth Century* (London, 1968); Haller 3, 145–252; *DBI* 2, 183–9 (P. Brezzi); *NCE* 1, 288–90 (M. W. Baldwin); *EB* (1977) 1, 466 f. (J. M. Powell); *EC* 1, 790–2 (P. Paschini); Mann 10, 1–238.

VICTOR IV (antipope 7 Sept. 1159–20 Apr. 1164). The death of HADRIAN IV on 1 Sept. 1159 was followed by a disputed election in which, while a large majority elected Cardinal Orlando Bandinelli, an exponent of Hadrian's policy of resisting Emperor Frederick I Barbarossa (1152–90), a handful of imperialist cardinals voted for Cardinal Ottaviano of Monticelli. There were violent scenes in which Ottaviano, whose armed adherents broke into the meeting, tore the red mantle from Orlando's shoulders, and forced him to withdraw while he himself was enthroned. The result was an eighteen-year schism, for while Orlando was consecrated as ALEXANDER III on 20 Sept., Ottaviano was consecrated as Victor IV at the imperial abbey of Farfa on 4 Oct. (no account being taken of the short-lived antipope Victor IV of 1138). He managed to get so far, notwithstanding the sparseness of his backing, because of the moral and military assistance of Otto of Wittelsbach, Frederick's envoy, then resident in Rome, and because of the support of the senate and people of the city.

Nobly born in the Sabina, Ottaviano had had a distinguished career. Created cardinal of Sta Cecilia in 1138, he had been involved in peace negotiations with Roger II of Sicily (1095–1154) under CELESTINE II and LUCIUS II. He had been present at Frederick Barbarossa's election in May 1152, had close personal ties with him, and for some time had represented the interests of the empire in the curia. In an early encyclical he stressed his sincere love for the 'honour' of the empire.

Although his preference for Victor could not be doubted, Frederick affected neutrality after the double election; but it was no surprise when the synod of Pavia, attended by some fifty German and north Italian bishops, which he convened in Feb. 1160 to decide between the rivals, pronounced in favour of Victor. From now onwards the emperor treated him with the deference traditionally due to the pope and did whatever he could to promote his recognition. In Oct. 1160, however, the episcopates and monastic orders of the western countries met at Toulouse in the presence of Henry II of England (1154–89) and Louis VII of France (1137–79) and, after hearing arguments from representatives of both claimants, gave their verdict for Alexander and anathematized Victor, as Alexander had already done. The great abbey of Cluny, near Mâcon, for reasons of its own adhered to him, but in general support for him was confined to the emperor's dominions; even there it was not universal. His prospects looked brighter in 1162 when Frederick consolidated his hold on northern Italy and the papal states and rebel vassals in the Norman kingdom in southern Italy acclaimed him, and still more when the emperor and Louis VII agreed to arbitrate between the rival popes at Saint-Jean-de-Losne in Sept. of that year. But the project came to nothing, and although Victor was able to preside over a synod at Dôle on 7 Sept. and renew his ban on Alexander, it was plain that Frederick's efforts to win universal recognition for him had failed; he had not allowed for the widespread objection in the rest of Europe to a revival of imperial control over the papacy. From now onwards, with defections multiplying and Alexander gaining ground in Germany, Victor's star was on the wane. In spring 1164, while travelling with Rainald of Dassel, formerly Frederick's chancellor, now archbishop of Cologne (1159–67), in Lombardy, the Romagna and Tuscany, he suddenly fell ill at Lucca and after a short, painful illness died there on 20 Apr. Since the clergy of both the cathedral and S.

Frediano refused to offer a resting place to an excommunicate cardinal, he was buried in a poor monastery outside the walls. When he heard the news Alexander wept, and rebuked his cardinals when they gave way to unseemly exultation. It was left to GREGORY VIII, when visiting Lucca in Dec. 1187, to order the antipope's tomb to be broken open and his remains thrown out of the church.

JW 2, 418–26; Watterich 2, 377–537; P. Kehr, 'Zur Geschichte Viktors IV', *NA* 46 (1926), 58–85; H. Schwarzmaier, 'Zur Familie Viktors IV in der Sabina', *QFIAB* 48 (1968), 64–79; P. Brezzi, 'Lo "schisma inter regnum et sacerdotium"', *ADRomana* 63 (1940), 1–98; Seppelt 3, 232–48.

PASCHAL III (antipope 22 Apr. 1164–20 Sept. 1168). On the death of VICTOR IV, the first antipope set up against ALEXANDER III by the pro-imperial party, at Lucca on 20 Apr. 1164, Rainald of Dassel, Emperor Frederick Barbarossa's (1152–90) chancellor and vicar for Italy, on his own initiative had Guido of Crema, cardinal priest of S. Callisto, elected as his successor. The election was glaringly uncanonical, being carried out by two schismatic cardinals, two German bishops, and the prefect of Rome. Guido was consecrated as Paschal III at Lucca by the bishop of Liège on 26 Apr. Of aristocratic lineage, he had been in the service of the holy see since the time of INNOCENT II, and at the divided election of 7 Sept. 1159 was the most prominent of the cardinals supporting Cardinal Ottaviano (Antipope Victor IV).

The emperor had no hand in the election, but he soon ratified it. In Italy and Burgundy, however, the bishops declined to accept Paschal; in Germany the opposition to Alexander III began to crumble after Victor's death, and several leading prelates switched to him. To stem the tide Frederick took a solemn oath at the diet of Würzburg (22 May 1165) never to acknowledge Alexander but only Paschal. He was followed by all the prelates and princes present, including the ambassadors of Henry II of England (1154–89), and the same oath was demanded, under threat of dire penalties, of all clerical and lay persons. On 8 Jan. 1166, presumably with Paschal's approval, Frederick had Charlemagne (c.742–814), his 'admired exemplar', canonized in Aachen by Rainald of Dassel in his capacity as archbishop of Cologne (1159–67). He was now actively insisting on loyalty to Paschal in Burgundy and Italy, and in many places bishops favouring Alexander III were replaced by men prepared to conform. In July 1167 Paschal had the satisfaction of accompanying Frederick to Rome, where Alexander III had to go into hiding, while on 22 July he was himself at last enthroned in St Peter's, on 30 July consecrated some fifteen patriarchs and bishops, and on 1 Aug. crowned the emperor (his second coronation) and his consort Beatrix.

This was his last triumph; Frederick was already proposing that both Paschal and Alexander III should abdicate and leave the way clear for a fresh election. At this point, however, an epidemic of malaria in Rome decimated the imperial army. Frederick, himself seriously ill, returned to Germany with what was left of his forces, taking Paschal with him. Paschal did not return to Rome until the beginning of 1168, when he was escorted by Archbishop Christian of Mainz. Even then the Romans tolerated his presence only because they had to be on their best behaviour until those of their fellow-citizens who had been captured by the emperor's troops had been set free. There were rumours that the new senate to be elected on 1 Nov. would come out in favour of Alexander III, and Paschal shut himself for safety in the stronghold adjacent to St Peter's; but he was dead before the elections took place.

JW 2, 426–9; LP 2, 410–20; Watterich 2, 537–78; John of Salisbury, Letter 280 (ed. Millor and Brooke, vol. 2, 610 f.); PRE 14, 724 f. (H. Böhmer); EC 9, 904 f. (G. Mollat); Seppelt 3, 248 f.; 273–5; 278.

CALLISTUS (III) (antipope Sept. 1168–29 Aug. 1178: d. c.1183).

Originally named Giovanni, he was the third of the imperial antipopes set up during the struggle between ALEXANDER III and Emperor Frederick I Barbarossa (1152–90). He was abbot of Struma, a Vallambrosan monastery near Arezzo, when the imperialist party in Rome elected him to succeed Antipope PASCHAL III, who died there on 20 Sept. 1168. Almost nothing is known of his earlier life except that he entered the monastery as a monk when still a lad and later became its abbot. Already one of Frederick's keenest partisans in Tuscany, he came out in favour of Antipope VICTOR IV and against Alexander III after the divided election of 1159. Although Victor created him cardinal bishop of Albano, he was not immediately consecrated but continued as abbot.

The new antipope, who called himself Callistus III, made contact with Frederick through envoys at the diet of Bamberg in June 1169, but the emperor, who had had no direct hand in his election, did not recognize him unambiguously until the negotiations on which he was then engaged with Alexander broke down. Later in the year Callistus, who desperately wanted Frederick to come to Italy to his aid, sent a second embassy to Germany, but although the emperor supplied him with financial assistance he only used him as a means of putting pressure on Alexander. Callistus's following was in fact a modest one in comparison with his predecessors'; only Rome and some districts of the papal state and Tuscany in Italy, and in Germany parts of the Rhineland, acknowledged him as pope. He himself resided chiefly at Viterbo. In 1173 he sent his chancellor, Martin of Tusculum, to Germany to take part in the discussions for an alliance between Frederick and Louis VII of France (1137–79), but nothing is known of his activities in the following years.

When Frederick reached agreement with Alexander at Anagni in Nov. 1176 and, finally, at Venice in July 1177, he abandoned his pope, stipulating only that he should be granted an abbey and that the cardinals created by him should be restored to their previous positions. Notwithstanding the peace Callistus still held out, much to the emperor's annoyance; but when the imperial chancellor restored Alexander to Rome in spring 1178, he could no longer remain at Viterbo but took refuge at Monte Albano, a village near Mentana 23 km. from Rome. He finally submitted to Alexander, abjuring his schism, at Tusculum on 29 Aug. 1178. The pope magnanimously entertained him at his table and appointed him rector, i.e. governor, of Benevento, where he must have died at some date before 1184 when another rector is recorded as holding office.

PL 2, 429 f.; LP 2, 420 f.; Watterich 2, 411 f.; 577; 640–2; DBI 16, 768 f. (K. Jordan); EC 6, 610 (P. F. Palumbo); Seppelt 3, 259; 266 f.; 271 f.

INNOCENT (III) (antipope 29 Sept. 1179–Jan. 1180: d. ?). Originally Lando, he came of an old Lombard family and was born at Sezze, a hill town in Latina province overlooking the Pontine plain. Nothing is known of his earlier career except that he was created cardinal deacon of S. Angelo by VICTOR IV, first of the antipopes set up by the pro-imperial faction against ALEXANDER III. Just over a year after CALLISTUS III, the third of the antipopes, had made his submission, Lando was proclaimed pope by a small group of schismatic cardinals at Rome, which Alexander had been forced by the hostile attitude of the citizens to leave during the summer, and was consecrated as Innocent III. His adherents included relatives of Antipope Victor IV, and one of these, a knight who was a brother of Victor's, gave him hospitality in a fortified keep between Palombara and Rome. After consulting with his cardinals, Alexander dispatched Cardinal Ugo Pierleoni to treat with the knight, who in return for a substantial sum handed the stronghold over to him and with it Innocent and his modest entourage. The pope sentenced him to confinement in the Benedictine abbey of SS. Trinità of La Cava, in the province of Salerno, for the rest of his life. The date of his death is not known.

JW 2, 431; Watterich 2, 647 f.; F. Gregorovius, Geschichte der Stadt Rom (Stuttgart, 1877), IV, 563 f.; Brezzi, 367; PRE 9, 111 (R. O. Zöpffel/C. Mirbt); EC 7, 886 (A. Ghinato); LThK 5, 687 (G. Schwaiger).

LUCIUS III (1 Sept. 1181–25 Nov. 1185). Successor to ALEXANDER III, Ubaldo Allucingoli was born c.1110 at Lucca, received into the Cistercian order by Bernard of Clairvaux (1090–1153), made cardinal deacon by INNOCENT II, and then cardinal bishop of Ostia and Velletri by HADRIAN IV in 1159. He was a leading negotiator in 1156 of the treaty of *Benevento, and, as Alexander III's closest adviser, of the peace of *Venice in 1177. He also enjoyed the confidence of Frederick I Barbarossa (1152–90), who nominated him to the commission for settling issues left open by the peace. Although elected in Rome, he deemed it prudent, having infuriated the citizens by refusing them the largesse they expected and by attempting to save Tusculum from their depredations, to be crowned at Velletri (6 Sept.) and, apart from Nov. 1181–Mar. 1182, to reside outside Rome, mostly at Velletri and Anagni.

Elderly, honest (one of only two cardinals judged by Thomas Becket to be unamenable to bribery), well-meaning, but weak, Lucius wanted peace; Emperor Frederick, too, was eager for a settlement on matters dividing church and empire. Chief among these was the inheritance of Countess *Matilda of Tuscany (1046–1115), which the emperor had promised at Venice to restore to the church 'saving the rights of the empire'; but Lucius felt obliged to reject Frederick's compromise proposals that the holy see should either waive its title in return for an annual income (spring 1182) or accept an exchange of territories (summer 1184). Eventually, by mutual agreement, the two met at Verona in Oct.–Nov. 1184. Here they first formulated a programme, embodied in the decretal Ad abolendum (4 Nov.) and sometimes called the charter of the Inquisition, for the repression of heretics: if judged recalcitrant, they were to be excommunicated by the church and then handed over to the secular arm for punishment. Then, in response to pleas from the Latin patriarch of Jerusalem and the grand masters of the military orders, Lucius urged a new crusade on the emperor, who undertook that preparations would be in hand by Christmas. Lucius, however, received no assurance of imperial help against the rebellious Romans, and on other issues they reached a deadlock. Thus the question of the *Matildine estates had again to be postponed. On the matter of clergy schismatically ordained during Alexander III's reign, Lucius was at first disposed to grant Frederick's request for their restoration, but then ruled that this could only be decided by a general council. Thirdly, faced with a divided election to the see of Trier, he was initially inclined to consecrate the candidate whom the emperor favoured and had already invested, but then deferred a decision on the ground that the rival candidate had appealed to Rome. Lastly, after a show of willingness to grant it, he rejected Frederick's request that he should crown his son Henry (Emperor Henry VI: 1191-7), arguing that there could not be two emperors at the same time.

This vacillation and increasing reserve may have been due to the curia or to German bishops opposed to Frederick. A more likely explanation lies in the fears excited by the engagement of Frederick's son Henry to Constance, daughter of Roger II of Sicily (1130-54) and aunt of William II, reigning king of Sicily (1166-89). Lucius himself, with the interests of peace and a crusade in mind, probably favoured the union, but the curia must have foreseen the dangers to the holy see which an alliance between the empire and Sicily carried. At any rate the discussion at Verona, which had opened propitiously, ended abruptly, and Frederick, irritated by the pope's lack of cooperation, left the city a few days after announcing the engagement. Although talks continued, relations between the imperial and papal courts were strained, but

Lucius died before an open rupture could take place. His body lies in the Duomo at Verona.

PL 201, 1067-380; LP 2, 450; Watterich 2, 650-62; JW 2, 431-92; 725; 766-9; NCE 8, 1060 (M. W. Baldwin); Brezzi, 367-9; Seppelt 3, 291-8; K. Wenck, 'Die römischen Päpste zwischen Alexander III und Innocenz III', in A. Brackmann (ed.), Papstum und Kaisertum (Festschrift P. Kehr, Munich, 1926), 415-74; DTC 9, 1058-62 (É. Amann); Mann 10, 239-83.

URBAN III (25 Nov. 1185-19/20 Oct. 1187). On the very day of LUCIUS III's death Umberto Crivelli was unanimously elected in Verona to succeed him. Of an aristocratic Milanese family, he had been archdeacon of Bourges and then of Milan before being promoted cardinal of S. Lorenzo by Lucius in 1182, and then archbishop of Milan on 9 Jan. 1185. Their choice suggests that the cardinals wanted a pontiff less inclined than Lucius to appease Emperor Frederick I Barbarossa (1152-90); if so, they got more than they bargained for. Urban, as he styled himself, was an avowed opponent of the emperor; his family had suffered grievously in the sack of Milan in Mar. 1162. As pope he retained his see so as to prevent its revenues (the regalia), as was customary, from passing for a year to the imperial treasury.

In the letter announcing his election Urban, who resided at Verona because of the hostile atmosphere at Rome, assured Frederick of his eagerness to reach agreement on issues still unsettled affecting church and empire, and in fact negotiations already in progress continued. In the vexatious case of a double election to the see of Trier Urban swore that he would not consecrate the candidate opposed by the emperor; and he sent legates to Milan to represent him at the marriage (27 Jan. 1186) of Frederick's son Henry (Emperor Henry VI: 1191-7) and Constance of Sicily in spite of the ominous prospect of possible German domination of southern Italy. Like Lucius, however, he refused to crown Henry as co-emperor, but then took umbrage when Frederick had him crowned king of Italy by the patriarch of Aquileia; he at once suspended the patriarch, whose metropolitan he was as archbishop of Milan. He himself proceeded to enlarge the breach by protesting against the practice, accepted in France and England as well as the empire, whereby the revenues of a see or abbey accrued to the crown during a vacancy, and the so-called right to the spoils, by which the crown appropriated the movable property of a deceased prelate. The final break came when, in spite of his earlier oath, Urban rejected the emperor's candidate and on 1 June 1186 consecrated his rival Folmar as archbishop of Trier.

Frederick at once retorted by ordering Henry to invade and occupy the papal states and by bottling up the pope and curia in Verona without contact with the outside world. Matters had been made worse by Urban's folly in encouraging Cremona to revolt and seeking to frustrate the emperor's campaign against the city. He now tried to bring the German episcopate over to his side, and appointed Philip, the influential archbishop of Cologne and leader of the opposition to Frederick in Germany, as his legate. But at the diet of Gelnhausen, in Nov. 1186, the emperor succeeded in isolating Philip and uniting the bishops behind him. They wrote reproachfully to the pope and cardinals urging them to listen to Frederick's just complaints; he was always ready to respect the rights of the church.

Driven into a corner by Frederick's diplomacy, Urban in consternation made a complete climb-down, asking Archbishop Wichmann of Magdeburg (1152–92) to mediate, dropping Folmar, and accepting the emperor's project for a fresh election at Trier. Frederick was ready for fresh negotiations, declared himself satisfied with the draft proposals his envoys worked out with the curia, and sent them back to Verona. In the meantime, however, Urban's intransigence had reasserted itself, and he was planning to excommunicate Frederick. The civic authorities, loyal to the empire, refused to have him staying in their city, although he

had just consecrated its cathedral, and he set out on horseback for Ferrara. Falling ill on the road, he died when he reached the city, thus saving the church a fresh crisis. His body lies in the Duomo of Ferrara.

PL 202, 1331–534; *LP* 2, 451; JW 2, 492–528; 726; 769 f.; Watterich 2, 663–83; K. Wenck, 'Die römischen Päpste zwischen Alexander III und Innocenz III', in A. Brackmann (ed.), *Papstum und Kaisertum* (Festschrift P. Kehr, Munich, 1926), 415–74; Haller 3, 259–62; Mann 10, 284–311; *DTC* 15, 2285–8 (É. Amann); Seppelt 3, 297–301.

GREGORY VIII (21 Oct.–17 Dec. 1187). On the day following URBAN III's death the cardinals at Ferrara, after considering two other names, elected Alberto de Morra, chancellor of the Roman church since 1178, as his successor. An elderly man, born *c.*1110 at Benevento, he had earlier been a canon regular at Laon and then professor of law at Bologna. HADRIAN IV promoted him cardinal, and ALEXANDER III employed him on missions to England, Dalmatia, and Portugal; on the first (1171–3) he had the important responsibility of reconciling Henry II (1154–89) after the murder of Thomas Becket (29 Dec. 1170). As chancellor he wrote a *Forma dictandi* which was influential in shaping the rhythmic prose of papal documents.

His abilities and experience apart, what determined the curia's choice was its disenchantment with Urban's disastrous policy of confrontation with Frederick I Barbarossa (1152–90). Alberto was known to enjoy the emperor's confidence, and warmly received the embassy he had sent to Urban. Later he wrote to him and his son Henry (Emperor Henry VI: 1191–7) in conciliatory terms, addressing Henry as 'emperor elect' in spite of Urban's having declined to crown him. He also rebuked Folmar, whom Urban had consecrated to the see of Trier in spite of Frederick's having invested another candidate, for his severity towards his rival's supporters. These and similar moves swiftly created an atmosphere of *détente*; the emperor lifted the virtual house arrest he had imposed on Urban and the curia, and instructed the Roman consul Leone de Monumento and the governor of Tuscany that Gregory was to travel and be received wherever he wished, with a military escort provided; clearly the pope's return to Rome was envisaged.

Devout and humble-minded, Alberto founded a monastery at Benevento shortly before his election; its statutes reveal him as a reformer concerned for austerity and evangelical simplicity. As pope he declared that it was not for the clergy to take up arms but to devote themselves to alms-giving and praising God; he forbade their indulgence in extravagant clothes and gaming. He also tried to reform the curia by referring appeals brought to it on minor matters to bishops and archdeacons. But his chief preoccupation during his hectic 57-day pontificate was the preparation for a fresh crusade. The news of the Christian disaster at Hattin in Galilee (4 July 1187), soon followed by reports of Saladin's capture of Jerusalem (2 Oct.), shocked the entire west. Even before his coronation Gregory proclaimed a crusade, and soon dispatched legates to Germany, France, Denmark, even Poland, to preach it. In his eyes the catastrophes in the Holy Land were God's punishment for the sins of Christians, and he demanded penitential dress and deportment from all taking part in the crusade.

In mid-Nov. he left Ferrara, moving south via Modena and Parma. Pausing at Lucca, he ordered Antipope VICTOR IV's tomb to be broken open and his remains thrown out of the church. On 10 Dec. he reached Pisa, hoping to reconcile it with its rival Genoa so that both seaports could cooperate with the crusade, but fell ill and died on 17 Dec. He had been making for Rome, for decades hostile to the papacy, but death came too soon, and he was buried in the Duomo at Pisa.

PL 202, 1537–64; *LP* 2, 349; 451; JW 2, 528–35; Watterich 2, 683–92; G. Kleemann, *Papst Gregor VIII* (Bonn, 1913); P. Kehr, 'Gregor VIII als Ordensgründer', *Miscell. F. Ehrle* 2, 248–75 (*ST* 38, 1924); W. Holtzmann, 'Die Dekretalen Gregors VIII', *MIÖG* 58 (1950), 113–23; K. Wenck,

'Die römischen Päpste zwischen Alexander III und Innocenz III', in A. Brackmann (ed.), *Papstum und Kaisertum* (Festschrift P. Kehr, Munich, 1926), 415–74; Mann 10, 312–40; *PRE* 7, 1164 (C. Mirbt); Seppelt 3, 301–4.

CLEMENT III (19 Dec. 1187–late Mar. 1191). Two days after the death of GREGORY VIII the cardinals at Pisa, after their first choice, Teobaldo of Ostia, had declined office, elected Paolo Scolari, cardinal bishop of Praeneste (now Palestrina). A wealthy Roman, related to influential families in the city, he had been brought up in Sta Maria Maggiore, later becoming its archpriest. Weak in health, without experience of political missions, he was nevertheless able, though at a heavy price, both to arrange the return of the papacy to Rome, from which hostility to the commune in control there had kept it exiled for six years, and to complete the reconciliation between church and empire which Gregory had successfully started. In achieving these ends he was helped by Leone de Monumento, a confidant of Emperor Frederick I (1152–90) as well as a Roman senator, who was present, and may have had influence, at his election.

After discussions with the commune he was triumphantly received in the city in mid-Feb. 1188 and thenceforth resided in the Lateran, in which neither of his predecessors had set foot. Under a compact signed on 31 May the senators recognized the pope's sovereignty, agreed to swear allegiance, and restored the papal revenues and right to coinage; but in return he had to make substantial payments, annual and on special occasions, leave the administration largely to them, and abandon their hated neighbour Tusculum to their tender mercies. The accord he reached with the empire was sealed by the treaty of Strasbourg of 3 Apr. 1189. A vexatious dispute over the see of Trier was solved by discarding the rival candidates and accepting the emperor's proposal of a fresh election. The papal state, occupied by Frederick's son Henry (Emperor Henry VI:

1191-7) in 1186 as a reprisal against URBAN III, was restored to the holy see, the empire, however, expressly reserving proprietary rights over it. In return Clement undertook to give the imperial crown to Henry. It is not known what, if any, agreement was reached about the *Matildine lands; it is likely that they remained in the emperor's hands without any formal decision about ownership.

Both settlements entailed the surrender of vital positions by the holy see, which in part accepted them because of its desperate financial straits; it is significant that, once established in Rome, Clement instituted an exacting financial regimen, appointing Cencio Savelli (later HONORIUS III) as treasurer. An even more compelling motive was the Third Crusade (1189-91), announced by Gregory and now getting under way, for its success depended on an understanding with the empire. Its organization and leadership lay with the secular princes, above all with Frederick, but Clement devoted all his efforts to promoting it. One of his first acts was to complete the negotiations begun by Gregory VIII for restoring peace between Pisa and Genoa, whose co-operation as sea-powers was necessary. Following Gregory, too, he sent legates throughout Europe, not only to preach the crusade but also to foster the harmony between nations which he considered indispensable to 'the Christian republic' in the hour of crisis. As a result, despite its weakness *vis-à-vis* the empire, he made the papacy a centre of unification and co-ordination.

In the interests of general peace Clement found a compromise solution for a double election to the Scottish see of St Andrews, disputed since 1178, and in 1188 released the Scottish church from the jurisdiction of York, making it directly dependent on Rome. But a new danger, foreseen by the curia when Frederick's son Henry and Constance of Sicily became engaged in LUCIUS III's time and married in Jan. 1186, loomed with the death of William II of Sicily (1166-89) without male heir on 18 Nov.

1189. Constance was now heir to his realms and Henry, acting as regent for his father now serving on the crusade, was resolved to claim the inheritance when free from present preoccupations in Germany. In Sicily there was nationalistic repugnance to a foreign ruler, and support converged on Count Tancred of Lecce, a grandson of King Roger II (1130-54), who was elected king by an assembly of magnates in Jan. 1190. Clement gave his assent to his coronation at Palermo, but refrained from investing him. This ambiguous stance was evidence, not so much of weakness, as of the quandary in which he was placed, anxious both to maintain good relations with the empire and to avert the dreaded union between it and southern Italy. It was not until Jan. 1191 that Henry, now sole ruler since Frederick's death in Anatolia on 10 Jun. 1190, marched into Italy to receive the imperial crown and then move south to Sicily; but when he reached Anguillara, on the south shore of Lake Bracciano, he learned that the pope was dead. The exact date of his death is not known.

PL 204, 1275-506; JW 2, 535-76; Watterich 2, 693-707; Haller 3, 265-73; K. Wenck, 'Die römischen Päpste zwischen Alexander III und Innocenz III', in A. Brackmann (ed.), *Papstum und Kaisertum* (Festschrift P. Kehr, Munich, 1926), 432-44; H. Kauffmann, *Die italienische Politik Kaiser Frederichs I nach dem Frieden von Constanz (1183-1189)* (Greifswald, 1933), 131-47; P. Zerbi, *Papato, impero e 'respublica christiana' dal 1187 al 1198* (Milan, 1955), 11-62; DHGE 12, 1096-109 (R. Foreville); NCE 3, 928 (J. R. Sommerfeldt); Seppelt 3, 304-9; Mann 10, 341-82.

CELESTINE III (Mar./Apr. 1191-8 Jan. 1198). Successor to CLEMENT III, the cardinal deacon Giacinto Bobo, of the aristocratic Boboni (later Orsini) family, was eighty-five when he was elected; he accepted reluctantly so as to avert a schism. Born *c.*1105, he was a student under Abelard (1079-1142) in Paris, and as a subdeacon serving the curia defended him, to Bernard of Clairvaux's annoyance, at the council of Sens in 1140. Created cardinal by CELESTINE II, once his fellow-student, in

1144, he proved a successful conciliator, mollifying Frederick I's (1152–90) anger with HADRIAN IV after the diet of *Besançon, urging moderation on his friend Thomas Becket (1118–70), and being charged by ALEXANDER III with the task of releasing Frederick from the sentence of excommunication. Loyal to Alexander, he also had the full confidence of Frederick, who put him on the commission for deciding controverted territorial issues after the peace of *Venice. Becket judged him one of the only two incorruptible cardinals. The date of his election is uncertain, but he was ordained priest and consecrated on 13 and 14 Apr. (Easter), taking the name of his old friend and patron Celestine II.

His reign was dominated by his relations with the formidable young Hohenstaufen king Henry VI (1191–7), already waiting outside Rome to receive the imperial crown before moving south to claim the kingdom of Sicily. Henry had inherited this through his consort Constance, although Tancred of Lecce (d. Feb. 1194) had been crowned its king in Jan. 1190 with Clement III's consent. With some misgivings Celestine crowned Henry on 15 Apr. without raising this delicate issue, although, to gratify the Romans who wished to destroy it, he induced him to evacuate their hated rival Tusculum. Henry marched south, in spite of a warning from Celestine, but his expedition collapsed before Naples and he retreated to Germany. Although faced with growing opposition there, he threw out fresh challenges to the pope, nominating bishops arbitrarily, rejecting Albert of Brabant, elected bishop of Liège and confirmed by Celestine, and then condoning his murder, and imprisoning Richard I Cœur de Lion (1189–99) although under papal protection as a returning crusader. Celestine's reaction was ambiguous. Whenever possible, he assisted Henry's opponents in Germany, placed the pro-imperial abbey of Monte Cassino under an interdict, invested Tancred with Sicily, and concluded the advantageous concordat of Gravina with him (May and July 1192). But

he took no direct action against the emperor, not even in the *causes célèbres* of Albert and Richard, but preferred cautious temporizing.

In spring 1194 his fortunes at home improved and, Tancred dead (20 Feb.), Henry made a second, swiftly successful, campaign to acquire the Norman kingdom, and at Christmas was crowned at Palermo. There was no question of swearing allegiance to the pope, whose power to intervene in church affairs in Sicily he took steps to curtail. Although breaking off relations, Celestine again refrained from drastic measures. But for Henry, dreaming now of permanent union between Sicily and the empire as a hereditary monarchy, and wanting his recently born son Frederick to be baptized by the pope, co-operation with him was essential. To win him over he proposed a crusade. Celestine took up the project with misgivings, but had the crusade successfully preached in England and other countries as well as Germany. Henry came to Italy in June 1196 eager for a settlement, but Celestine used delaying tactics, complaining about encroachments on papal territories and the imprisonment of bishops in Sicily. Henry persisted, and in negotiations between 20 Oct. and 17 Nov. offered the church, if it agreed to renounce all disputed territories, a permanent fixed income provided by all the major cathedrals. The financial attractions were considerable, but the church would lose its independence. Again Celestine postponed a decision, aware perhaps that the plan for a hereditary monarchy was losing support in Germany. In the event serious disturbances broke out in Sicily, not without the pope's connivance; after savagely repressing them, Henry died at Messina on 28 Sept. and was buried at Palermo.

Celestine's relations with other countries were inevitably secondary. His attempts to mediate in the Anglo-French conflict, which broke out when Philip II Augustus (1180–1223) began threatening English possessions in France, were ineffective; when he annulled Philip's divorce from his

Danish wife Ingeborg (May 1195), this did not deter the king from remarrying. In England the unpopularity of his legate, William of Ely, worked against him. He had a special concern for the Iberian peninsula, where he strove, with mixed success, to unite the rival Christian princes against Islam for the Reconquista (i.e. the campaigns to recover Spanish territory from the Muslims). In Rome, however, he strengthened the central administration, showed himself a sharp-sighted jurist, and was able to introduce order into the church's finances with the help of his outstanding chamberlain, Cardinal Cencio Savelli (later HONORIUS III), who in 1192 completed in the *Liber censuum* a comprehensive survey of all properties depending on the holy see and owing it dues.

On Henry's death the holy see took immediate steps to recover its lost territories in central Italy and concluded an alliance with the anti-imperial Tuscan league. But it is doubtful whether Celestine was personally involved in this. Illness and age were taking their toll, and at Christmas 1197 he expressed his wish to abdicate provided the cardinals agreed to elect his close collaborator, Cardinal Giovanni of Sta Prisca. They rejected the suggestion, and he died a few weeks later. His temporizing policy towards Henry VI was the result of moderation and patience rather than the weakness of an old man.

PL 206, 864–1240; JW 2, 577–644; 727; 771 f.; Watterich 2, 708–48; LP 2, 405 f.; 423; 439; 443; 451; P. Fabre, L. Duchesne and G. Mollat, *Le Liber censuum de l'église romaine* (Paris, 1889–1910; 1952); K. Wenck, 'Die römischen Päpste zwischen Alexander III und Innocenz III', in A. Brackmann (ed.), *Papstum und Kaisertum* (Festschrift P. Kehr, Munich, 1926), 441–56; 'Die innere Verwaltung der Kirche unter Papst Coelestin III', *Archiv für Diplomatik* 18 (1972), 342–98; Haller 3, 273–99; 522–53; Mann 10, 383–441; DHGE 12, 62–77 (R. Mols); DBI 23, 392–8 (V. Pfaff); LThK 2, 1254 f. (P. Zerbi); Seppelt 3, 317–24.

INNOCENT III (8 Jan. 1198–16 July 1216). On the day of CELESTINE III's death the cardinals, at the second ballot, unanimously elected Lotario, cardinal deacon of SS. Sergio and Bacco. Ordained priest on 21 Feb., he was consecrated on 22 Feb. (the feast of St Peter's Chair). Only thirty-seven, he was born in 1160/1 at Anagni, son of Trasimondo, count of Segni, and Claricia, of the patrician Scotti family. As a young man he studied theology at Paris under Peter of Corbeil and canon law at Bologna with the celebrated decretist (i.e. student of ecclesiastical decrees) Huguccio of Pisa (d. 1210). His uncle CLEMENT III nominated him cardinal in 1190, but Celestine III kept him in the background because his own family and the Scotti were enemies. This gave Lotario leisure to compose several mystical and dogmatic essays, notably *The Wretchedness of Man's Lot* and *The Mysteries of the Mass*, all learned but stilted and unoriginal. They gave no inkling of the brilliant and commanding role their author was to play as pope.

A man born to rule, uniting exceptional gifts of intellect and character with determination, flexibility, rare skill in handling men, and also humaneness, Innocent had an exalted conception of his position as Vicar of Christ (a title he made current), 'set midway between God and man, below God but above man', given 'not only the universal church but the whole world to govern'. But this theocratic doctrine represented for him an ideal rather than an actuality; the pope's 'plenitude of power' was for him spiritual, and he disclaimed the right to intervene in temporal affairs except where (as in the papal or vassal states) he was owed allegiance, where moral or spiritual issues were involved, or where there was no superior arbiter.

With characteristic resolution he at once established his authority in Rome, replacing officials of the empire and the commune with men who paid him homage. There were years of bitter struggles, however, including an enforced withdrawal to Praeneste (now Palestrina), before he finally mastered (1205) the in-fighting of rival families. Meanwhile he not only reasserted control over the papal states, virtually lost through Hohenstaufen policies, but, developing an initiative of Celestine III, added to them the duchy of Spoleto and the March of Ancona on the strength of so far unfulfilled promises of Pepin III (751–68) and Charlemagne (768–814). Although he failed to get possession of Romagna and the *Matildine lands, the territory he now ruled effectively sundered northern Italy and the kingdom of Sicily. Empress Constance, left regent of Sicily on Henry VI's death in 1197, acknowledged him as overlord, surrendering to him the state's traditional rights over the church, and on her death (?8 Nov. 1198) arranged for him to be regent and guardian of her infant son Frederick II (emperor 1220–50).

Innocent next had to deal with the crisis in Germany, where rival candidates, Philip of Swabia (1198–1208) and Otto of Brunswick (1198–1218), were elected in 1198 to succeed Henry VI as king. At first he remained neutral, but when both applied to him for the imperial crown he indicated, in the decretal *Venerabilem* (1202), that the pope had a right to intervene because he alone could bestow it and must choose the man best suited to defend the church. What decided him in favour of Otto, whom he eventually crowned on 4 Oct. 1209, was his promise to recognize the enlarged papal states and to renounce the much disputed right to the *spoils (i.e. the personal estates of deceased bishops and other ecclesiastics) in Germany. When Otto IV invaded southern Italy and Sicily, however, the pope excommunicated and deposed him (18 Nov. 1210) and, Philip being dead, transferred his support to Frederick of Sicily, who in the Golden Bull of Eger (12 July 1213) repeated Otto's assurances and also promised to leave Sicily independent. The German question occupied Innocent for years; he intervened in other countries, too, on the ground that princes were subject to the pope's judgement on sin. Thus he first (1209) excommunicated King John of England (1199–1216) for refusing to recognize Stephen Langton (d. 1228) as archbishop of

Canterbury; then (1213), when John made full submission and made his Anglo-Irish domains a papal fief, he declared Magna Carta void as improperly extorted from the king by the barons without papal consent. He several times tried to mediate in the constant strife between France and England, but in 1203 had to confirm that Philip II of France (1179–1223) was not bound, in dealing with his vassals, to heed the pope's admonitions; for years he put pressure on Philip to reinstate his divorced wife, but when the king took her back he did so for purely political reasons. Other kingdoms, like Aragón, Portugal, and Poland, became fiefs of the holy see, while in 1204 he recognized Joannitza as king of Bulgaria (1197–1207), sending him the royal crown.

Though a master of politics, Innocent's overriding concerns were the crusade, reform, and the combating of heresy. To achieve the first, he corresponded with Emperor Alexius III Angelus (1195–1203) about reunion and imposed a special tax on the clergy. Through the intrigues of Venice the Fourth Crusade (1202–4) was against his will diverted to Constantinople, but when the city fell (12 Apr. 1204) he accepted the *fait accompli* in the mistaken belief that the establishment of a Latin patriarchate there would assist reunion of the churches. Undiscouraged, he appealed in 1213 for a fresh crusade against Islam, and at the fourth Lateran council fixed it for 1217. As a reformer he began with the curia, simplifying living standards and promoting honest business practices. He restored the balance between episcopal and papal administration by limiting appeals to Rome and encouraging provincial and national councils; but he took care to reserve weightier matters to himself and insisted that bishops visit Rome every four years. He took steps to improve the quality and moral behaviour of the clergy and to restore the observance of their rules by religious houses. Sympathetic to the evangelical poverty preached by certain heretical groups, he was able to win back some of them (e.g. the Humiliati of Lombardy), and encouraged the realization of their ideals within the church, notably by authorizing the itinerant preaching of the first Franciscans. Against heresy itself he took energetic measures, declaring it (25 Mar. 1199) high treason against God; but he urged bishops to look for its causes and remedies and commissioned the austere Spaniard Dominic Guzmán (1170–1221), later founder of the Friars Preachers, to counter the *Albigenses of the Midi with their own weapon of public disputation. It was only after the murder in 1208 of his legate, who had been sent to convert them, that he ordered a crusade against the Albigenses in southern France which resulted in bloodshed and devastation and cast a shadow over the second half of his reign.

Innocent's legislative output was enormous; many of his more than 6,000 extant letters were decretals which canonists began collecting in his lifetime. In 1209/10 he himself issued a collection (the *Compilatio tertia*) and sent it to the university of Bologna. The fourth Lateran (Twelfth General) council, which he held in Nov. 1215 and which more than twelve hundred prelates attended, both summed up his previous reform activity and prepared the ground for the new crusade he contemplated. Its seventy decrees included a definition of the eucharist in terms of transubstantiation, the condemnation of all heresies and a summons to the secular power to assist in their repression, a ban on the founding of new religious orders, and the requirements that Catholics should make a yearly confession, that Jews and Muslims should wear a distinctive dress, and that Christian rulers should observe a four-year truce so that the crusade could be launched.

In summer 1216 Innocent travelled north in order, in the interest of the crusade, to settle personally differences between the seaports of Pisa and Genoa, and suddenly died at Perugia from one of the bouts of fever to which he was subject. A great and influential pope whose reign marked the climax of the medieval papacy, he was buried in Perugia, but LEO XIII (a former bishop of Perugia) had his remains transferred to the right-hand transept of St John Lateran, where his tomb by G. Lucchetti (1891) can be seen.

PL 214–17 (works, letters, etc.); F. Kempf (ed.), *Regestum Innocentii III papae super negotio Romani imperii* (Rome, 1947); C. R. Cheney and W. H. Semple, *Selected Letters of Pope Innocent III concerning England 1198–1216* (London, 1953); O. Hageneder and A. Haidacher, *Die Register Innocenz' III* (Graz etc., 1965–); M. Maccarone, crit. edn. of *De miseria humanae conditionis* (Lugano, 1955); F. Kempf, *Papstum und Kaisertum bei Innocenz III* (Rome, 1954); J. A. Watt, *The Theory of Papal Monarchy in the Thirteenth Century* (London, 1965); L. E. Binns, *Innocent III* (London, 1931); J. Clayton, *Pope Innocent III and His Times* (Milwaukee, 1941); Mann 11 and 12; *EB* (15th edn.) 9, 604–6 (G. B. Ladner); *NCE* 7, 521–4 (W. Ullmann); Seppelt 3, 317–92.

HONORIUS III (18 July 1216–18 Mar. 1227).

Two days after INNOCENT III's death at Perugia the cardinals met in that city and, having delegated the choice to two of their number, unanimously elected Cencio Savelli as his successor. Elderly and frail in health, he was a Roman aristocrat who had been canon of Sta Maria Maggiore, in 1188 became papal chamberlain, and was promoted cardinal deacon (1193) and later cardinal priest by Innocent III. In 1197 he became tutor to the future Emperor Frederick II. Mild and peace-loving, he was an efficient administrator who had helped to bring order into the church's finances by compiling (1192) the *Liber censuum* listing, by provinces and dioceses, the spiritual and secular institutions dependent on and owing dues to the holy see.

The overriding concern of his pontificate was the crusade which Innocent III had called for at the *fourth Lateran council in Nov. 1215. To achieve the necessary political unity he arbitrated between Philip II of France (1179–1223) and James I of Aragón (1213–76), put pressure on France to abandon its invasion of England, and helped King John's (d. Oct. 1216) son Henry III

(1216-72), still a minor, to obtain the English crown. Even so, the Fifth Crusade (1217-21), its strength frittered away in isolated operations, ended in failure. For this his legate on the spot, the obstinate and ambitious Cardinal Pelagius, was primarily responsible, but Frederick II, king of Germany and then emperor (1220-50), was also to blame. Although he had undertaken at Aachen in 1215 to go on crusade, he again and again postponed setting out. To Honorius his participation seemed indispensable, and to ensure it he crowned him emperor in St Peter's on 22 Nov. 1220 notwithstanding his having had his son Henry, in contravention of promises to the curia, elected German king earlier in the year. Frederick, who had arranged for the pope's return to Rome after a year's enforced absence owing to disturbances there, now swore to set out and join the crusade by Aug. 1221, but instead turned south to settle affairs in Sicily. Honorius had to acquiesce in further postponements, at Veroli in Apr. 1222 and at Ferentino in Mar. 1223, until Frederick finally agreed, under the treaty of S. Germano (July 1225), to accept excommunication if he failed to depart by summer 1227.

Frederick's consistent aim in these years was to ensure the union of his Sicilian kingdom and the empire and to restore the imperial power in Italy. This ran counter both to papal policy and to his own solemn promises to Innocent III, but whenever Honorius raised objections he hastened to reassure him. Thus in Sept. 1219 he reiterated the far-reaching assurances given to Innocent III in the *Golden Bull of Eger (1213), and before his coronation in 1220 he confirmed the constitutional separation of the empire and the kingdom of Sicily. The pope and curia, however, reacted sharply to his attempts to control church appointments in Sicily and to recover the March of Ancona and the duchy of Spoleto incorporated by Innocent III in the papal states. When in 1226 a revived Lombard league frustrated Frederick's plans for the reorganization of northern Italy, he trapped

Honorius into performing the invidious task of mediating between himself and the league.

Outmanoeuvred politically by the emperor, Honorius made his mark in other fields. To assist the crusade he crowned Peter of Courtenay, doomed to perish ignominiously c.1219 before claiming his throne, as Latin emperor of Constantinople on 9 Apr. 1217. He energetically supported missionary enterprise in the Baltic countries, and in 1218 undertook a crusade against the Moors in Spain. He intensified the crusade begun by Innocent III against the *Albigenses, calling upon Louis VIII (1223-6) of France to direct it; with his approval Frederick in 1220 and Louis in 1226 published ordinances, of great significance for the development of the Inquisition, imposing severe penalties on heretics. He sanctioned the Dominican order on 22 Dec. 1216, endorsing its name and preaching mission on 17 Jan. 1217, and on 29 Dec. 1223 approved the definitive rule of the Franciscans, on 30 Jan. 1226 that of the Carmelites; he also fostered the growth of the lay tertiaries associated with these orders. He authorized a collection of his decretals, the so-called *Compilatio quinta*, and circulated it to universities; it is regarded as the first official book of canon law, and illustrates his great administrative knowledge.

C. A. Horoy, *Honorii III opera* (5 vols., Paris, 1879-83); *MG*Epsaec XIII, I, 1-260; P. Pressutti, *Regesta Honorii III* (Rome, 1888-95); P. Fabre and L. Duchesne (eds.), *Liber censuum Romanae ecclesiae* (Paris, 1889-1910): vol. 3, ed. G. Mollat, Paris, 1952; J. Clausen, *Papst Honorius III (1216-1227)* (Bonn, 1895); Mann 13, 1-164; Haller 4, 1-46; *EC* 9, 141-3 (G. Mollat); *LThK* 5, 476 f. (P. Mikat); *NCE* 7, 126 f. (S. Williams); Seppelt 3, 390-411.

GREGORY IX (19 Mar. 1227-22 Aug. 1241). On HONORIUS III's death the cardinals delegated the decision about a successor to three of their number, who as their second choice proposed Ugo or Ugolino, a nephew of INNOCENT III and son of a count of Segni. Born at Anagni c.1155, he excelled in canon law and theology at Paris and Bologna, was promoted cardinal deacon by his uncle in 1198 and cardinal bishop of Ostia in 1206, and between 1199 and 1218 gave proof of his great political skills as papal legate in southern Italy, Germany, Lombardy, and Tuscany. In 1220 he gave the cross to Frederick II (1220–50) at his imperial coronation, and himself preached the crusade in central and north Italy in 1221. In contrast to his mild predecessor, he was masterful, unyielding, exceptionally energetic, but also intensely religious, in touch with contemporary spiritual movements, the friend of Dominic (1170–1221) and, above all, Francis of Assisi (1181/2–1226). As protector of the Franciscan order, he was influential in shaping its definitive rule in 1223, and he fostered the growth of the Poor Clares.

At the beginning and end of his reign he was involved in a dramatic struggle with Frederick II, with whom he had earlier been friendly. The first phase (1227–30) was sparked off by Frederick's apparent abandonment of the crusade (the Sixth: 1227–9) he had launched from Brindisi in Aug. 1227. In fact he had fallen seriously ill, but Gregory, recalling his procrastination in Honorius III's time, rejected his explanations and excommunicated him on 29 Sept. In June 1228 Frederick, recovered, set out again and, in spite of the obstacles put in his way by the pope, successfully negotiated the surrender of Jerusalem. Even so Gregory, outraged that an excommunicate should lead a crusade, maintained the ban. In addition he sought to set up an anti-king in Germany, released Frederick's Sicilian subjects from their allegiance, and raised an army to attack imperial forces violating the papal domains and to invade Sicily. Returning in June 1230, Frederick had no difficulty in crushing the pope's mercenaries, but took care to respect the frontiers of the papal patrimony. He wanted a reconciliation, and effected one by the treaty of Ceprano in July 1230, under which he made substantial concessions in Sicily and agreed not to infringe the papal territories, while

Gregory lifted his sentence of excommunication.

During nine years' uneasy truce pope and emperor collaborated to their mutual benefit. Thus Frederick helped Gregory, in 1232 and again in 1234 when he was forced to flee the city, in his sharp clashes with the citizens of Rome. In return Gregory tried to mediate between the emperor and the Lombard cities, and in 1234 excommunicated Frederick's rebel son Henry. Meanwhile he continued to favour the mendicant orders, canonizing Francis in 1228 and Dominic in 1234. In 1234 he published the *Liber extra*, the first complete, authoritative collection of papal decretals, which the Spanish canonist Raymond of Peñafort (d. 1275) compiled at his request and which remained the fundamental source of canon law until PIUS X and BENEDICT XV. His envoys conferred about reunion with representatives of the eastern church at Nicaea in Jan. 1234, but without reaching any agreement. He extended existing legislation against heretics, in Feb. 1231 making them liable to the death penalty at the hands of the civil power and, without abolishing the rights of bishops, instituted the papal as distinct from the episcopal Inquisition, entrusting its operation to the Dominicans. Himself a former student, he re-established the university of Paris in 1231 after two years' closure, granting it in the bull *Parens scientiarum* (13 Apr.) the right to regulate its own constitution; at the same time, by significantly modifying the ban on the study of Aristotle's philosophical writings at Paris, he opened the door to their constructive study by theologians. He also founded (1233) a university at Toulouse enjoying the same liberties as that of Paris.

In 1238 his conflict with the emperor resumed with redoubled ferocity. In 1231 he had vainly attempted to restrain him from promulgating his Constitutions of Melfi for the reorganization of Sicily as a centralized state subject to his will; they contained laws against heretics, including the penalty of burning, but Gregory saw danger to the church in the absolutism claimed. Relations deteriorated in 1236 when Frederick, campaigning against the Lombard cities, requested the pope to excommunicate them; Gregory retorted (23 Oct. 1236) by complaining about his oppression of the Sicilian church, and sternly reminded him that earthly sovereigns were subject to the successor of PETER. By 1238, however, it was clear that Frederick, victorious over the Lombard army at Cortenuova (Nov. 1237), aimed at nothing less than sovereignty over the whole of Italy, Rome itself included. In Oct. 1238 he sent his natural son Enzio to Sardinia, a papal fief, arranging a marriage between him and a Sardinian princess and designating him as king of the island; and in early Mar. 1239 he astutely tried to drive a wedge between curia and pope. On 20 Mar. 1239 Gregory, who intercepted his correspondence with the cardinals and who had meanwhile mustered an alliance of anti-imperial cities and restored his own authority in Rome, renewed Frederick's excommunication. The struggle now became an all-out one, with Frederick publicly calling for a general council to judge the pope, and Gregory branding him as a blasphemer, the forerunner of Antichrist. With Frederick invading the papal state and encircling Rome, Gregory summoned a general council to meet there at Easter 1241; but the emperor frustrated this by capturing most of the non-Italian participants, who were travelling by sea since he had closed the land routes, after a naval battle near Elba on 3 May. In early Apr. his forces closed on Rome, but the threatened assault never took place; in the burning August heat the aged pontiff, awaiting his fate with unshakeable courage, died. Frederick, who all along had insisted that his quarrel was not with the church but with the pope, withdrew to Sicily to await events.

G. Levi (ed.), *Registri dei cardinali Ugolino d'Ostia e Ottaviano degli Ubaldini* (Rome, 1890), 3–154; L. Auvray (ed.), *Les Registres de Grégoire IX* (4 vols., Paris, 1890–1955); P. Fabre and L. Duchesne (eds.), *Liber censuum* 2, 18–36 (Paris, 1910: contemporary life, probably by John of Ferentino); *Vita e curia* and *Vita* by Bernard Guidonis, Muratori III, 575–87; Potthast 1, 680–939; J. Felten, *Papst Gregor IX* (Freiburg, 1886); J. M. Powell, 'Frederick II and the Church: a Revisional View', *CHR* 48 (1963), 485–97; *EB* (15th edn.) 8, 419 f. (J. M. Powell); *NCE* 6, 775–7 (G. Mollat); Mann 13, 165–441; Seppelt 3, 411–52.

CELESTINE IV (25 Oct.–10 Nov. 1241). Successor to GREGORY IX, Goffredo da Castiglione was a Milanese of aristocratic family who first appears as canon and chancellor of Milan in the 1220s. Reports that he was a nephew of URBAN III and for a time was a Cistercian monk at Hautecombe, in Savoy, lack confirmation. A proficient theologian, he was created cardinal priest of S. Marco in Sept. 1227 by Gregory IX, by whom he was charged with both political and anti-heretical missions in Tuscany and Lombardy in 1228/9. Probably because of their disappointing results, he remained at the curia performing routine duties from 1229 to 1238, but in the latter year was promoted cardinal bishop of Sabina.

In the crisis following Gregory IX's death (22 Aug. 1241) the cardinals were reduced to twelve, of whom two were held prisoner by Emperor Frederick II (1220–50). The remaining ten were deeply divided, some favouring and others deploring the late pope's implacable hostility to the emperor. To compel them to reach a decision the senator Matteo Rosso Orsini, who was effectively dictator of Rome, following a procedure frequently adopted in the north Italian communes and certain religious orders, had them shut up, but in deliberately cruel and squalid conditions, in the crumbling palace known as the Septizonium. At the first ballot Goffredo, the candidate of the emperor's ally Cardinal John Colonna, obtained more votes than the anti-imperial candidate, but not the two-thirds majority required by the *third Lateran council (1179). They then resolved to elect someone outside their own ranks, but Orsini deterred them from doing so by brutal threats. Worn out by harsh treatment, illness, and the death of one of their colleagues, they at last, on 25 Oct., after some sixty days of enforced confinement, elected Goffredo, who took the style of Celestine IV; his age and wretched state of health probably suggested that his reign would be short and that they would later be able to proceed to a free election under less straitened conditions. So in fact it proved, for two days later Celestine fell seriously ill and died on 10 Nov. Although one chronicler reports that he was crowned on 28 Oct. and presided at mass on All Souls' Day, the more likely account is that he died before being consecrated and without performing any official act.

Potthast 1, 938; 940 f.; K. Hampe, 'Ein ungedruckter Bericht über das Konklave von 241', *SBHeid* 4 (1913), 1–31; K. Wenck, 'Das erste Konklave der Papstgeschichte', *QFIAB* 18 (1926), 101–70; *DHGE* 12, 77–9 (R. Mols); *DBI* 23, 398–402 (A. Paravicini Bagliani); Seppelt 3, 449–51.

INNOCENT IV (25 June 1243–7 Dec. 1254). The death of CELESTINE IV was followed by an eighteen months' vacancy, while the cardinals negotiated with Emperor Frederick II (1220–50) for the release of two whom he had held prisoner since May 1241, and Frederick, excommunicated by GREGORY IX, did everything he could to obtain a sympathetic pope. The man eventually chosen at Anagni was Sinibaldo Fieschi, a Genoese, son of Count Hugo of Lavagna, a brilliant canon lawyer who had studied and later taught at Bologna. Appointed a curia judge in 1226, he rose rapidly in the service of Gregory IX, being promoted cardinal priest and vice-chancellor in 1227; he was governor of the March of Ancona 1235–40. A born ruler like Gregory, but lacking both his intemperate vehemence and his mystical piety, he was as unscrupulous in choosing means as resolute in achieving ends. Typically, he indulged in nepotism on an unprecedented scale to create a network of political support everywhere. Like INNOCENT III, he held that as Christ's Vicar the pope was supreme over earthly princes, but recognized that he

possessed this supremacy *de jure*, not *de facto*.

Under him the conflict between the papacy and the Hohenstaufen house reached its climax. Believing him well disposed, Frederick rejoiced at his election and started negotiations for the removal of his excommunication. A draft treaty providing for this in return for the evacuation of the papal states and other far-reaching concessions was agreed on 31 Mar. 1244. It was never ratified, however, partly because, to the dismay of the Lombards, it bypassed the crucial issue of the rights claimed by the empire in Lombardy, but even more because of Innocent's distrust of the emperor. Resolved to bring matters once for all to a head with him, Innocent now took the drastic step of fleeing secretly (28 June 1244) by sea to Genoa and then (Dec. 1244) settling at Lyons, where he could develop his plans in safety. The vigorous activity of the curia while he remained there demonstrated that the papacy could function efficiently away from Rome.

Here between 26 June and 17 July 1245 he held the first council of Lyons, i.e. the general council (the Thirteenth) which Gregory IX had planned but Frederick had frustrated; its agenda covered reform, help for the Holy Land and, in particular, the liberation of the Holy Sepulchre, the Mongol invasions, and 'the business between church and emperor'. Frederick, who was cited but did not appear, was charged with perjury, breach of peace, sacrilege, and heresy. Ably defended by his justiciar Thaddeus of Suessa, he was nevertheless pronounced guilty and deposed, his subjects were released from their allegiance, and the German princes were invited to elect a new king. In public manifestos Frederick challenged the pope's competence to depose an emperor; Innocent retorted that Christ had invested PETER and his successors with absolute temporal as well as spiritual sovereignty. In Germany he supported successive anti-kings elected by the princes, and used the mendicant orders to preach a crusade against Frederick; he even connived at a plot to murder him; but in spite of attempts by Louis IX of France (1226–70) to mediate, the conflict was still unresolved when Frederick died on 13 Dec. 1250. Returning triumphantly to Italy in 1251, Innocent continued the struggle with Conrad IV, Frederick's second son and designated successor on the German throne (1237–54), being determined to wrest the kingdom of Sicily from the Hohenstaufen and restore it as a papal fief. In turn he offered its crown to Richard of Cornwall, Charles of Anjou, and Henry III of England (1216–72), who accepted it for his eight-year-old son Edmund; but when Conrad died (21 May 1254) and Manfred (c. 1232–66), the bastard son whom Frederick had appointed regent for the kingdom, acknowledged the pope as overlord, Innocent annexed it to the papal states on 24 Oct. 1254 and took up residence in Naples. He seemed to have attained his objective; but in early Nov. Manfred revolted and routed the papal troops near Foggia. The news reached Innocent as he lay dying and hastened his end.

Innocent lowered the prestige of the papacy because he used his spiritual powers constantly to raise money, buy friends, and injure foes; he treated the endowments of the church as papal revenues, and his exploitation of the system of papal provisions to benefices (i.e. the pope's right to nominate to vacant benefices over the head of the ordinary patron) aroused scandal. In 1252 he established the Inquisition as a permanent institution in Italy, combining all earlier papal and imperial enactments in the bull *Ad extirpanda* (15 May), which sanctioned the use of torture to extract confessions. With his encouragement Louis IX of France set out in 1248 on the ill-starred Seventh Crusade (1248–54). Neither his daring idea of sending missionaries in 1245–7 to convert the Grand Khan of the Mongols, nor the reunion discussions involving unprecedented concessions on both sides which he held in 1253/4 with Emperor John III Vatatzes of Nicaea (1222–

54), came to anything; but he had greater success in organizing, through his legate William of Modena, the recently converted provinces of Prussia into four dioceses. One of the great jurist popes, he published not only three official collections of his own constitutions and decretals, but also a comprehensive commentary (the *Apparatus in quinque libros decretalium*) on the decretals of Gregory IX.

His tomb, originally in the basilica of Sta Restituta at Naples but now in the late 13th-cent. cathedral which incorporates it, proudly proclaims that 'he laid low Christ's enemy, the dragon Frederick'.

T. T. Haluščynskyi and M. M. Wojnar (eds.), *Acta Innocentii PP.IV 1243–1254* (Rome, 1962); E. Berger (ed.), *Les Registres d'Innocent IV* (4 vols., Paris, 1884–1919); Potthast 2, 943–1286; *Apparatus in quinque libros decretalium* (Frankfurt, 1570; Venice, 1575); G. von Puttkamer, *Papst Innocenz IV* (Münster i.W., 1930); M. Pacaut, 'L'Autorité pontificale selon Innocent IV', *MA* 66 (1960), 85–119; J. A. Watt, *The Theory of Papal Monarchy in the Thirteenth Century: the Contribution of the Canonists* (London, 1965); J. A. Cantini, 'De autonomia judicis saecularis et de Romani pontificis plenitudine potestatis in temporalibus secundum Innocentem IV', *Salesianum* 23 (1961), 407–80; J. M. Powell, 'Frederick II and the Church: a Revisionist View', *CHR* 48 (1963), 487–97; *DTC* 7, 1981–95 (É. Amann); *EB* (15th edn.) 9, 606–8 (F. Guerello); *NCE* 7, 524 f. (J. M. Muldoon); Mann 14.

ALEXANDER IV (12 Dec. 1254–25 May 1261). On the death of INNOCENT IV at Naples the cardinals wished to return to Rome, but the mayor forced them to proceed to an election there and then by bolting the city gates. They then concurred in the election of Rinaldo, count of Segni, a nephew of GREGORY IX, who made him cardinal deacon in 1227 and cardinal bishop of Ostia in 1231. Born in the closing years of the 12th cent., gentle, indecisive, and undistinguished, he was given relatively minor responsibilities under Gregory IX, and under Innocent IV remained in the background, preoccupied with the problems of the Franciscan order, of which he was cardinal protector. The curia, a section of which was critical of Innocent IV's implacable hostility to the Hohenstaufen, may have hoped that, having earlier enjoyed excellent relations with Emperor Frederick II (1220–50), he would adopt a more conciliatory line.

In the event Alexander was too weak, or had no wish, to modify his predecessor's policies. The most urgent problem was Sicily, which the curia wished restored to the holy see but which Frederick II's bastard son Manfred (c.1232–66) controlled as regent on behalf of Conradin (d. 1268), infant son of Frederick's heir Conrad IV (d. 1254). After abortive negotiations Alexander excommunicated Manfred in Mar. 1255. Although Conradin was a ward of the holy see and the pope had promised to protect his rights, which included the dukedom of Swabia and the kingdom of Sicily, he now called on the nobles of Swabia to recognize the claims of Alfonso X of Castile (1252–84) instead, and on 9 Apr. 1255 enfeoffed Edmund (1245–96), second son of Henry III of England (1216–72), with Sicily. He cancelled the arrangement, however, in 1258 because Henry could not meet the exorbitant military and financial conditions laid down, but had no alternative solution. Meanwhile a campaign to reassert papal authority in Sicily ended in defeat; by 1258 the entire kingdom was firmly in Manfred's hands and on 10 Aug., on a rumour that Conradin was dead, he had himself proclaimed king at Palermo. Alexander's fulminations were treated with contempt, and before long most of the papal state, the March of Ancona, Spoleto, and Romagna came into Manfred's power; he dominated northern Italy, too, through a league of cities under his leadership. Even in Rome, a city so racked by power struggles that Alexander resided mainly at Viterbo, the Ghibellines, or Hohenstaufen party, contrived to get Manfred elected senator in spring 1261.

In the interregnum in Germany following Conrad IV's death in 1254, Alexander supported the anti-king William of Holland elected after Innocent IV's deposition of

Frederick II, but on William's death in 1256 he characteristically could not make up his mind between Richard of Cornwall (1209–72) and Alfonso of Castile when both were elected; his main concern was that Conradin should not be chosen. If he lacked political insight, however, and even failed to nominate any cardinals, he was more at home in strictly church affairs. Thus he took steps to reverse the exploitation of the system of papal *provisions to benefices which Innocent IV had practised. He reopened (1256) with Emperor Theodore II Lascaris of Nicaea (1254–8) the reunion discussions started by Innocent IV, but without result; and he sought to organize a crusade against the Mongols. Devoted to the mendicant orders, he revoked the restrictions imposed by Innocent IV on their pastoral and preaching activities; he himself founded the Augustinian Hermits in 1256 by banding together several Italian congregations of hermits under the rule of St Augustine. He canonized Clare of Assisi (1194–1253), foundress of the Poor Clares, in 1255. In 1256 he decided in favour of the friars at the university of Paris when the secular clergy challenged their teaching. But these modest interventions were overshadowed by the humiliation in which, when he died at Viterbo, his reign ended.

C. Bourel de la Roncière and others (eds.), *Les Registres d'Alexandre IV* (Paris, 1902–59); Potthast 2, 1286–473, 2124–9; Haluščynskyi-Wojnar (ed.), *Acta Alexandri PP.IV* (Rome, 1966); F. Tenckhoff, *Papst Alexander IV* (Paderborn, 1907); G. Barraclough, 'The Constitution "Execrabilis" of Alexander IV', *EHR* 49 (1934), 193–218; D. L. Douie, *The Conflict between the Seculars and the Mendicants at the University of Paris in the XIIIth Century* (London, 1954); *DBI* 2, 189–93 (R. Manselli); Mann 15, 1–129; Seppelt 3, 488–501.

URBAN IV (29 Aug. 1261–2 Oct. 1264). As ALEXANDER IV failed to create any, there were only eight cardinals when he died, and the meagre conclave meeting at Viterbo debated vainly for three months. Eventually they elected an outsider, Jacques Pantaléon, patriarch of Jerusalem, who was visiting the curia on business of the Holy Land. Born son of a shoemaker *c.* 1200 at Troyes, he studied at Paris and *c.* 1245 became canon of Laon and then archdeacon of Liège, and as such attended the first council of Lyons in 1245. INNOCENT IV, who noticed him there, sent him in 1247 as legate to Poland, Prussia, and Pomerania. In 1252 he became bishop of Verdun, and in 1255 Alexander IV named him patriarch of Jerusalem and legate in the Latin kingdom. A diplomat of wide experience, vigorous in word and action, he knew what he wanted and worked for it with the independence which came from being a Frenchman free from the entanglements of Italian politics.

Urban saw clearly that, if Innocent IV's victory over the empire was to be consolidated, a sovereign dependent on the holy see must be set up in place of Manfred (*c.* 1232–66), Emperor Frederick II's (1220–50) bastard son, in the kingdom of Sicily and the power of the Hohenstaufen dynasty removed once for all from Italy. First, however, he reinforced the depleted sacred college by naming fourteen cardinals, six of them Frenchmen of remarkable ability. Although he was never able, because of civil strife, to reside in Rome as pope, he struggled to get a government which acknowledged his suzerainty precariously established there. In a few months he recovered most of the papal state, control of which Alexander IV had lost. By putting pressure on the bankers and merchants of Tuscany he was able not only to revive a Guelph, or pro-papal, party there, but also to assure himself of the finance needed for his projects. By opposing Pallavicini, Manfred's deputy in Lombardy, and promoting his enemies, the Este and Visconti families, he began rebuilding papal prestige in the north.

Urban's solution for Sicily was the fateful one of offering its crown, Louis IX of France (1226–70) having refused it, to his able and ambitious brother Charles, count of Anjou (1226–85). The claims of Edmund of England (1245–96), whom Alexander IV had invested with the kingdom, were amicably liquidated, Louis IX's scruples were

overcome, and negotiations were started with Charles. For some months they were held up because Manfred professed himself ready to recognize the pope's suzerainty and pay tribute, and was backed by the fugitive Latin emperor Baldwin II of Constantinople (1237–61), who hoped that he would lead a crusade to win back the Latin empire. The profound suspicion, however, in which the curia held the Hohenstaufen proved too much, and on 17 June 1263 a treaty was drawn up under which Charles would be enfeoffed with the kingdom of southern Italy and Sicily in return for a lump sum of 50,000 marks sterling and the promise of an annual tribute of 10,000 ounces of gold, freedom for the church in the kingdom, and military aid as required; he was not to accept any offer of the German or the imperial crown, nor to exercise rule in imperial provinces in Italy or the papal state; he was also to possess himself of his fief within one year. When Manfred heard what was being planned, he reopened hostilities in Tuscany, Campania, and the papal patrimony later in the summer. Urban had to take refuge in Orvieto, where he was forced to accept certain modifications of the draft treaty requested by Charles, and even to recognize his election, in violation of its terms, as senator of Rome. When Orvieto was threatened, he retreated to Perugia, where he died; but by then the treaty had been signed, and Angevin domination was now assured not only for the kingdom of Sicily but, as events were to prove, for Italy itself.

Apart from banning the election of Frederick II's grandson Conradin (d. 1268), the last of the Hohenstaufen line, Urban did nothing to solve the interregnum problem in Germany. Once the two rival candidates, Richard, earl of Cornwall (1227–72), and Alfonso X, king of Castile (1252–84), had acknowledged his right to arbitrate between them, he postponed a decision indefinitely. He was more concerned for the east, where Constantinople fell to Emperor Michael VIII Palaeologus of Nicaea (1259–82) in August 1261, and campaigned vigorously for the restoration of the Latin empire. In summer 1262 Michael, who wished to discourage any plans for a crusade against Constantinople, wrote to him proposing an end to the schism, and in 1263/4 Urban held far-reaching discussions with the emperor, who was prepared to recognize the Roman primacy and make other concessions; but he died before any agreement could be reached. In 1264, impressed by the miracle of Bolsena (1263), according to which a priest saying mass there had seen blood issuing from the consecrated elements, he extended the feast of Corpus Christi, with which he had been familiar at Liège, to the whole church, and commissioned the Dominican philosopher and theologian Thomas Aquinas (c.1225–74) to prepare an office for it.

J. Guiraud and S. Clémencet, *Les Registres d'Urbain IV* (4 vols., Paris, 1901–58); Potthast 2, 1474–542; W. Sievert, 'Das Vorleben des Papstes Urban IV', *RQ* 10 (1896), 451–505; 12 (1898), 127–61; K. Hampe, *Urban IV und Manfred 1261–64* (Heidelberg, 1905); Mann 15, 131–206; *DTC* 15, 2288–95 (É. Amann); *LThK* 10, 544 f. (H. Schmidinger); *NCE* 14, 478 f. (H. Wieruszowski); Seppelt 3, 501–12.

CLEMENT IV (5 Feb. 1265–29 Nov. 1268). On URBAN IV's death the cardinals at Perugia were so sharply divided that they took four months to elect a successor. He was another Frenchman, Guy Foulques, son of a successful judge, born c.1195 at Saint-Gilles-sur-Rhône. After studying law at Paris, he became legal consultant to King Louis IX (1226–70). He married and had two daughters, but after his wife's death took orders and served as archdeacon of Le Puy. His promotion was rapid: bishop of Le Puy in 1257, archbishop of Narbonne in 1259, Urban IV created him cardinal bishop of Sabina in Dec. 1261 and in Nov. 1263 sent him as legate to England to support Henry III (1216–72) against the barons. Elected in absence while travelling home, he had to come to Perugia disguised as a monk because of hostile conditions in north Italy. As pope he resided, again because of

the hostile atmosphere in Rome, first at Perugia and then at Viterbo.

A legalist, more timid than Urban IV, he completed Urban's policy of excluding the Hohenstaufen dynasty from Italy and installing Charles, count of Anjou (1226–85), as king of Sicily and Naples in place of Manfred (c.1232–66), Emperor Frederick II's bastard son. Fearing that Manfred would seize Rome, he put pressure on Charles, who reached the city in May 1265, where on 28 June five cardinals commissioned by the pope invested him with the southern kingdom. With much heart-searching Clement now helped him to borrow vast sums, secured by a thirty-year tithe on the French church, from Tuscan bankers to finance the Sicilian campaign he was pledged to undertake. A crusade had been preached against Manfred in France, and a powerful French army moved to the frontier of the kingdom. The decisive battle was fought at Benevento on 26 Feb. 1266 and resulted in Manfred's defeat and death. His new realms now lay open to Charles, but two years later, on the crest of a reaction against the excesses of his rule, the last of the Hohenstaufen, the youthful Conradin, duke of Swabia and king of Jerusalem, marched to Italy to win back his imperial heritage. In the interregnum in Germany Clement had forbidden his election as king, and now tried to halt his advance by excommunicating him and his adherents, and deposing him from the throne of Jerusalem. Conradin was rapturously received in Rome in July 1268, but on 23 Aug. was defeated by Charles at Tagliacozzo (prov. of L'Aquila) and himself captured and, after trial, beheaded. Clement did nothing to prevent this unworthy act; he had deliberately appointed Charles imperial vicar in Tuscany on 17 Apr., an office which gave him legal power to execute the young prince as a disturber of the peace.

The papacy had gained its objectives, but its triumph was mixed with disillusion. Whereas its aim had been that the new lord of Sicily should be confined to his kingdom, Clement had to acquiesce in the predominance Charles had acquired for himself in central and north Italy and in the papal state itself; when the threat of Conradin loomed, he even found himself appointing his young vassal to positions of immense authority in Italy undreamed of in the original treaty. He had got rid of the Hohenstaufen, only to find that the Angevin house was as great a threat to the independence of the holy see.

In 1267 and 1268 Clement was in correspondence with the Byzantine emperor Michael VIII Palaeologus (1259–82), who in 1261 had liberated Constantinople from the Latins and who now wished the pope to prevent the expedition King Charles was planning for the recovery of the city; at the same time the emperor indicated his eagerness for church union. Clement, who had approved Charles's project, sent (4 Mar. 1267) a peremptory reply demanding full submission on the part of the Greeks. The exchanges continued but came to nothing. His bull *Licet ecclesiarum* (27 Aug. 1265), which reserved to the holy see the appointment to benefices which fell vacant when the incumbent was visiting the curia, was a landmark in the centralization of the western church; its preamble accepted it as a principle that the appointment to all benefices belonged to the pope. He died at Viterbo, and was buried in the Dominican convent of Sta Maria in Gradi outside the walls.

E. Jordan, *Les Registres de Clément IV* (Paris, 1904); Potthast 2, 1542–650; J. Heidemann, *Papst Clemens IV: Das Vorleben des Papstes und sein Legationsregister* (Münster, 1903); E. Jordan, *Les Origines de la domination angevienne en Italie* (Paris, 1910); A. Nitschke, 'Der Prozess gegen Konradin', *ZSavRGKan* 42 (1956), 25–54 (cf. H. M. Schaller, *QFIAB* 37 (1957), 311–27; A. Nitschke, *QFIAB* 38 (1958), 268–77); Mann 15, 207–345; *DHGE* 12, 1109–15 (G. Mollat); *DBI* 26, 192–202 (N. Kamp); Seppelt 3, 512–19; 521–3.

GREGORY X, BL. (1 Sept. 1271–10 Jan. 1276). Following the death of CLEMENT IV, the cardinals at Viterbo, divided as much by human rivalries as by divergent attitudes to

Charles I, count of Anjou, now king of Sicily (1266–85) but rivalling the Hohenstaufen in his hold on central and north Italy, wrangled for almost three years about a successor. As public indignation mounted, the civic authorities, to speed a decision, first locked them in the papal palace, then removed its roof and threatened a starvation diet. At last, having delegated the choice to a committee of six, they elected Tedaldo Visconti, archdeacon of Liège, then on a crusade with the future Edward I of England. Nobly born *c.*1210 at Piacenza, he served for years with Cardinal James of Praeneste, helped to organize the first council of Lyons in 1245, in 1265 accompanied Cardinal Ottobono on his mission to England, and was the confidant of the French and English royal families. Between 1248 and 1252 he studied at Paris, meeting the great theologians Thomas Aquinas (*c.*1225–74) and Bonaventura (*c.*1217–74). Learning of his election at Acre (Akko, in Israel), he reached Viterbo on 10 Feb. 1272; he then went to Rome, in which neither of his two predecessors had set foot, and, after being ordained priest, was consecrated in St Peter's on 27 Mar.

When leaving Palestine, Gregory vowed never to forget Jerusalem; a crusader at heart, he made the liberation of the holy places the theme of his short reign. As early as 13 Apr. 1272 he issued invitations to a general council with a threefold agenda: a new crusade, reunion with the Greek church, and clerical reform. Meanwhile, to create the conditions necessary for a crusade, he struggled to settle the internecine strife between Guelphs (i.e. the pro-papal party) and Ghibellines (i.e. the pro-imperial party) in the cities of Tuscany and Lombardy and, the way being opened by the death of one of the rival claimants, Richard of Cornwall (1209–72), encouraged the election of a German king. As well as uniting Europe for the crusade, this would provide a counterpoise to the Angevin domination in Italy. When the other claimant, Alfonso X of Castile (1252–84), sought recognition, Gregory referred him to the electors, to Charles's annoyance gave no support to his favoured candidate, Philip III of France (1270–85), and eventually approved the election on 1 Oct. 1273 of Rudolf, count of Habsburg and landgrave of Alsace (1218–91); on 24 Oct. he was crowned king of the Romans at Aachen. Next, at the council of Lyons, Rudolf's representatives fulfilled the curia's hopes by renouncing in his name all rights over the papal territories and recognizing the permanent separation of Sicily from the empire. He confirmed these promises at a meeting with Gregory at Lausanne in Oct. 1275.

While still in Palestine, the pope-elect informed the Byzantine emperor, Michael VIII Palaeologus (1259–82), of his longing for church union; both in fact desired it, Gregory because it would assist the crusade, Michael as a means of checking the ambitious plans being made by Charles of Sicily for the recovery of Constantinople for the west. Despite scornful opposition from Charles and the French section of the curia, Gregory pressed ahead, sending envoys to Constantinople in Oct. 1272, and on their return inviting Michael to send delegates to the forthcoming council, to be reckoned the Fourteenth Ecumenical gathering. This opened at Lyons, which Gregory chose so as to exclude pressure from Charles, on 7 May 1274, and the Greek delegates arrived on 24 June; they had been reluctantly granted a safe conduct by the king. In agreement with the understanding already reached, they assented to the Roman creed, including the *double procession of the Holy Spirit, and the primacy of the holy see, and at the fourth session (6 July) the pope formally ratified the union.

Even more important in his eyes were the plans made at the council for the crusade, to be financed by a tithe on ecclesiastical incomes. The kings of England, France, Aragón, and Sicily agreed in principle to take part, as did Michael Palaeologus provided that the west would make a lasting peace with him, restraining King Charles

and his ally Baldwin II, exiled Latin emperor of Constantinople (1237–61). Among reforms carried through was the famous constitution *Ubi periculum* (16 July), designed to prevent protracted vacancies in the holy see by providing that the cardinals must assemble not more than ten days from the pope's death at the place where he died, must stay together without contact with the outside world, and must be subjected to progressively austerer conditions the longer the electoral process took. Other decrees attacked various abuses, such as unduly long vacancies of benefices, pluralism, and absenteeism, and placed severe restrictions on religious orders with the exception of the Franciscans and the Dominicans.

Returning from Lyons to Rome, Gregory met Rudolf at Lausanne in Oct. 1275; he had been crowned king at Aachen two years before, and arrangements were now made for his coronation as emperor on 2 Feb. 1276. Gregory then crossed the Alps, visited several north Italian cities to settle disputes, but was struck down by fever and died at Arezzo on 10 Jan. 1276. A brilliant pope of wide-ranging abilities, he was buried in the Duomo, and at Arezzo and other places associated with him a cult soon developed; BENEDICT XIV added his name to the Roman Martyrology. Feast 10 Jan., but since 1963 9 Jan. His untimely death spelled the ending of Rudolf's hopes for the imperial crown as of the prospects of the crusade, and the union with the Greek church proved ephemeral.

J. Guiraud, *Les Registres de Grégoire X* (Paris, 1892–1906; new edn. 1960); Potthast 2, 1651–703; *Vita* in Muratori 3.1, 587 f.; 3.2, 424–6; G. Pachymeres, *De Michaele Palaeologo* (PG 143, 822–54); L. Gatto, *Il pontificato di Gregorio X* (Rome, 1959); D. J. Geanakoplos, *Emperor Michael Palaeologus and the West, 1258–1282* (Cambridge, Mass., 1959); BSS 7, 379–87 (F. Molinari); NCE 6, 777 (M. François); Mann 15, 347–561; Seppelt 3, 521–38.

INNOCENT V, BL. (21 Jan.–22 June 1276). Following the conclave procedure GREGORY X had himself prescribed, on the eleventh day after his death the cardinals available mct at Arezzo and elected Pierre of Tarentaise, in the upper Val d'Isère (Savoy). Born c.1224, he joined the Dominican house at Lyons c.1240, studied at Paris and in June 1259 graduated master in theology, and held the so-called 'chair of the French' 1259–64. In 1259 he collaborated with Albertus Magnus (c.1200–80) and Thomas Aquinas (c.1225–74) in drafting a rule of studies for Dominicans. His important commentary on Peter Lombard's (c.1100–60) theological treatise known as The Sentences, which had been denounced as unsound in the late 12th cent. but had been rehabilitated by the fourth Lateran council in 1215, illustrates the transition from the older Augustinian to the new Aristotelian concepts; he also wrote on practical ethics and expounded scripture. Twice provincial of France (1264–7; 1269–72), he preached the crusade under CLEMENT IV, while Gregory X named him archbishop of Lyons in 1272 and cardinal bishop of Ostia in 1273. He helped to prepare, and took a prominent part at, the second council of Lyons (1274), and, having been appointed general penitentiary, accompanied Gregory X on his journey in 1275/6 from Lyons to Italy. In 1274 he had preached the funeral sermon at Lyons over the great Franciscan theologian Bonaventura (c.1217–74).

The first Dominican to become pope, the friend of Bonaventura (c.1217–74), Innocent was a man of learning and austere piety rather than political initiative. His election signalled a switch by the curia from Gregory X's policy of seeking to counterbalance the domination in Italy of Charles of Anjou, king of Sicily (1266–85), by making Rudolf I of Habsburg (1218–91) emperor. He immediately (2 Mar.) confirmed Charles in his functions as senator of Rome and imperial vicar in Tuscany, and requested (9 and 17 Mar.) Rudolf, whom Gregory had invited to Rome for his coronation, to postpone coming until his differences with the curia and King Charles were resolved and the question of imperial rights in Romagna settled; meanwhile he should declare void

the oaths of allegiance his officials had exacted there. He certainly followed Gregory in placing a new crusade and the peace necessary to its launching in the forefront of his programme, and was successful in reconciling Genoa with King Charles and ending hostilities between Ghibelline (i.e. pro-imperial) Pisa and the Guelph (i.e. pro-papal) Tuscan league. But in resuming Gregory's negotiations with the Byzantine emperor Michael VIII Palaeologus (1259–82) for his participation in the crusade and implementing the church union agreed at the second council of Lyons, he weakened under Charles's continuous pressure. As a result, when informing Michael of Charles's plans to recapture Constantinople by force, he emphasized that it had been violently wrested from the Latins, and on the issue of union demanded that the Greek clergy should take personal oaths in a prescribed form accepting the *Filioque and the primacy of the pope. He died, however, just as the envoys carrying these stiff requirements were boarding ship at Ancona.

Charles showed his gratitude to this devout, sensitive, but weak pontiff by commissioning a porphyry tomb (now lost) for him in the Lateran basilica. In 1898 LEO XIII beatified him. Feast 22 June.

T. Turco and G. B. de Marinis, Innocentii V in quattuor libros sententiarum commentaria (4 vols., Toulouse, 1649–52); Potthast 2, 1704–10; M. H. Laurent, 'Le Bienheureux Innocent V et son temps', ST 129, 1947; Beatus Innocentius PP. V (Petrus de Tarantasia OP), Studia et documenta, Rome, 1943; BSS 7, 844–6 (N. Del Re); DTC 7, 1996 f. (J. Forget); EC 7, 14–16 (A. P. Frutaz); NCE 7, 525 (W. H. Principe); Seppelt 3, 535–8.

HADRIAN V (11 July–18 Aug. 1276). As senator of Rome and actually residing in the city Charles of Anjou, king of Sicily (1266–85), had oversight, under the *conclave constitution approved by the second council of Lyons (1274), of the meetings of cardinals in St John Lateran to elect a successor to INNOCENT V. As their deliberations dragged on, he applied the rules rigorously, cutting down their rations and confining them so strictly that several were prostrated by the sweltering heat. Eventually, through the influence of the king, whose partisan he was, Cardinal Ottobono Fieschi was chosen. Born c. 1205 in Genoa, of the family of the counts of Lavagna, he was a nephew of INNOCENT IV who, after he had held offices at Rheims, Paris, and Parma, in 1251 named him cardinal deacon of S. Adriano. In 1265 CLEMENT IV sent him as legate to England with wide powers in order to preach a crusade, organize church affairs, and resolve the conflict between Henry III (1216–72) and his barons. His mission crowned with success, he returned to the curia in June 1268 and worked to promote Angevin policies in Italy, becoming one of the most respected and influential members of the sacred college.

On the day following his election Hadrian assembled the cardinals in the Lateran and, because of its 'many intolerable and obscure provisions', suspended GREGORY X's conclave decree, promising to propose a fresh one. This was his sole recorded administrative act, for a few days later he left Rome, with its oppressive summer heat, and settled, seriously ill, at Viterbo. Here he died, without being ordained priest, consecrated, or crowned, on 18 Aug. Dante later accused him (*Purg.* 19, 88–145) of the sin of avarice. His tomb in S. Francesco is a sumptuous masterpiece by a Florentine contemporary, Arnolfo di Cambio (c. 1245–1302).

Potthast 2, 1709 f.; R. Graham, 'Letters of Cardinal Ottobono', *EHR* 15 (1900), 87–120; *LP* 2, 457; N. Schöpp, *Papst Hadrian V (Kardinal Ottobuono Fieschi)* (Heidelberg, 1916); *DBI* 1, 335–7 (L. Gatto).

JOHN XXI (8 Sept. 1276–20 May 1277). There was uproar and violence in Viterbo when, ten days after HADRIAN V's death there, the mayor proposed sealing off the electoral conclave, only to be informed that the late pope had suspended GREGORY X's *conclave constitution. When the excitement this provoked had been quelled, the cardinals, on the suggestion of Cardinal Orsini (later NICHOLAS III) once he realized

that he stood no chance himself, elected Cardinal Pedro Julião (better known as Peter of Spain). A Portuguese from Lisbon, born son of a doctor in 1210/20, he was a dedicated scholar who graduated in arts at Paris c. 1240, and then (1247–50) taught medicine at the new university of Siena. After being dean of Lisbon and archdeacon of Braga, through his friend Cardinal Ottobono (Hadrian V) he got to know Gregory X, who made him his personal physician and promoted him archbishop of Braga (1272: not confirmed) and cardinal bishop of Tusculum (1273). He took part in the second council of Lyons (1274), but his principal achievements were as a prolific writer on scientific and philosophical subjects. His best-known work was a widely used logic textbook, *Summulae logicales* (c. 1250), which some have seen as the source of the 14th-cent. emphasis on probable arguments; but he also wrote a treatise on *The Soul*, commentaries on Aristotle and the mystical theologian Pseudo-Dionysius (c. 500), a study in ophthalmology called *The Eye*, a popular manual on curing illnesses entitled *The Poor Man's Treasury*, and a host of other essays.

His adoption of the style John XXI, there having been no John XX, was probably the result of confusion in the enumeration of the several popes called John in the 10th and 11th cents. Although accepting election, he had no intention of forsaking scholarly pursuits, and in fact possessed little experience of curial business. He retired to a cell he had constructed in the rear of his palace at Viterbo and left most decision-making to Cardinal Orsini. It is not surprising, therefore, that his reign marked a return to the policies of Gregory X. His first acts were to renew Hadrian V's suspension of the conclave decree and to root out and punish those responsible for the recent disorders in Viterbo; Orsini was a champion of free papal elections. Then when Charles of Anjou did homage as king of Sicily (1266–85), he pointedly refrained from confirming him as senator of Rome and imperial vicar in Tuscany, but sought to reconcile him with King Rudolf I of Habsburg (1273–91) so as to prepare the way for Rudolf's coronation as emperor. With a crusade in view he made every effort to restore peace between Alfonso X of Castile (1252–84) and Philip III of France (1270–85), collected tithes to provide the money required, and even treated with the Tatars for a joint campaign against the Muslims. Under him the negotiations with the Greeks interrupted by INNOCENT V's death were restarted and identical demands dispatched to the Byzantine court. While the Greek church as a whole remained unmoved, Emperor Michael VIII Palaeologus (1259–82) was hoping that the pope would thwart King Charles's projected campaign to recapture Constantinople for the west, and so with his heir Andronicus and Patriarch John Beccus (d. 1297) he made full submission to the Roman requirements. It was as a result of John's bull *Relatio nimis implacida* (18 Jan. 1277) that Stephen Tempier, bishop of Paris, condemned 219 Averroist (i.e. heterodox Aristotelian) propositions, among them 19 of Thomas Aquinas (c. 1225–74).

For a man in good health with medical qualifications, death came suddenly to John: the ceiling of his hastily built study collapsed on him, and he died of the injuries received a few days later. Placed by Dante (*Par.* 12, 134 f.) among theologians in 'the heaven of the Sun' in Paradise, he was criticized by contemporaries for moral instability and dislike for the religious orders. His recumbent effigy (late 13th-cent.), formerly covering his tomb, can be seen in the Duomo at Viterbo.

E. Cadier, *Le Registre de Jean XXI* (Paris, 1898); Potthast 2, 1710–18; M. A. Alonso, *Obras filosóficas* (Madrid, 1961); J. P. Mullally, *The Summulae logicales of Peter of Spain* (Notre Dame, 1945); M. Grabmann, 'Handschriftliche Forschungen und Funde zu den philosophischen Schriften des Petrus Hispanus, des späteren Papstes Johannes XXI', *SAM* (1936), Heft 9; 'Die Lehre vom Intellectus possibilis und Intellectus agens im Liber *De anima* des Petrus Hispanus', *Archiv d'hist. doct. et litt. du moyen âge* 11 (1937/8), 167–208; M. H. da Rocha Pereira, *Obras médicas de*

Pedro Hispano (Coimbra, 1973); J. M. Da Cruz Pontes, *A Obra filosófica de Pedro Hispano Portugalense* (Coimbra, 1972); F. Copleston, *A History of Philosophy* 3, 51–3 (London, 1953); *EC* 6, 590–2 (G. B. Picotti); *NCE* 7, 1013 f. (J. Ferreira); Seppelt 3, 539–42; 550 f.

NICHOLAS III (25 Nov. 1277–22 Aug. 1280). After JOHN XXI's unexpected death the seven cardinals took six months to choose a successor. The most obvious candidate was Cardinal Giovanni Gaetano, born in Rome 1210/20 as son of Matteo Rossi and Perna Gaetani, of the noble Orsini family, for more than thirty years a member of the sacred college, able, statesmanlike and widely experienced, the power behind John XXI's moves to curb the Angevin king Charles of Sicily's (1266–85) predominance in Italy. For this reason, while three cardinals backed him, he was fiercely opposed by three partisans of Charles. When the deadlock was at last broken and Orsini elected, he adopted the name Nicholas because he had been cardinal deacon of S. Niccolò in Carcere.

As pope he made it his objective, like GREGORY X but in reaction to INNOCENT V, to restore the political independence of the holy see in Italy *vis-à-vis* the house of Anjou. In Rome he persuaded Charles of Sicily, when his office as senator expired in Sept. 1278, not to seek reappointment, decreed (11 July) that no outside prince should henceforth hold it without special leave, and then had himself elected to it for life, thereby creating the papal *signoria* over Rome. He also sought to limit Charles's influence in central Italy, getting him to resign as imperial vicar in Tuscany and pacifying, with mixed success, the warring city factions which gave him an excuse to interfere. Meanwhile he was negotiating with King Rudolf I of Habsburg (1273–91), Gregory X's emperor-designate, who not only confirmed the privileges and donations granted by previous emperors, but formally renounced (14 Feb. 1279) all imperial claims to Romagna. As the territory had been disputed for generations, Nicholas thus effectively enlarged the papal state and rounded off its frontiers as they were to remain until 1860. Finally, aiming at a long-term understanding between the houses of Anjou and Habsburg which would ensure papal supremacy in Italy, he deployed all his diplomatic skill in arranging an alliance between them, to be sealed by the marriage of Rudolf's daughter Clementia and Charles's grandson Charles Martell (1271–95), under which each swore to respect and defend the other's realms unless either attacked the church. The complex project, which included Clementia's receiving Burgundy as her dowry, seems also (the proposal is disputed) to have envisaged the eventual partition of the empire into the four kingdoms of Germany, Burgundy, Lombardy, and Tuscany, with Germany as a hereditary, no longer an elective, monarchy, and the emperor overlord of all four.

In the interests of the crusade agreed at the second council of Lyons (1274) Nicholas continued John XXI's efforts, but without result, to arbitrate between Alfonso X of Castile (1252–84) and Philip III of France (1270–85), each claiming the kingdom of Navarre, and pressed on with the collection of the subsidy voted by the council. He disappointed the Byzantine emperor Michael VIII Palaeologus (1259–82) by refusing to excommunicate Charles's Latin allies in Epirus and Thessaly, but effectively blocked the king's plans for launching an attack on Constantinople by inviting Byzantine envoys to discuss peace terms and getting Charles, in spite of unconcealed reluctance, to grant them a safe-conduct. The terms he sent Michael for the implementation of the union of the churches were even stiffer than those of Innocent V and included the acceptance of a permanent papal legate at Constantinople. He had no wish, however, to imperil the fragile union, and empowered his envoys to be accommodating where they deemed it desirable. Nearer home he reformed procedure in the papal chancery and improved the quality of the sacred college by several distinguished appointments. A friend of the Franciscans, whose protector he had been as cardinal, and of the Dominicans, he promoted members of both orders to diplomatic posts and bishoprics. By his bull *Exiit qui seminat* (14 Aug. 1279) he temporarily settled the interpretation of absolute poverty for the Franciscans on the basis of a distinction, derived from the Franciscan theologian Bonaventura (*c.*1217–74), between total lack of possessions, declared meritorious, and the 'moderate use' of things necessary to life and the fulfilment of one's vocation. Among other works, he carried out a radical restoration of St Peter's, of which as cardinal he had been archpriest, and (the first pope to do so) made the Vatican palace his residence, enlarging and remodelling it and purchasing plots to form its gardens.

In the midst of his ceaseless activities he suffered a stroke and died at his new summer residence at Soriano, near Viterbo, before completing his negotiations with Charles and Rudolf of Habsburg. A man of impressive bearing and commanding personality, he was consigned to hell by Dante (*Inferno* 19, 61 ff.) because of his nepotism and avariciousness; a contemporary chronicler remarked that 'he would not have had his like upon the earth if only he had had no relatives to whom to show excessive favours'. He was buried in the chapel of St Nicholas which he had constructed in St Peter's.

Potthast 2, 1719–56; 2132; J. Gay and S. Vitte, *Les Registres de Nicholas III* (Paris, 1898–1938); A. Demski, *Papst Nikolaus III* (Munich, 1903); R. Sternfeld, *Der Kardinal Johann Gaetan Orsini (Papst Nikolaus III, 1244–77)* (Berlin, 1905); E. Dupré-Theseides, *Roma dal comune di popolo alla signoria pontificia* (Bologna, 1952); G. Barraclough, 'The Chancery Ordinance of Nicholas III', *QFIAB* 25 (1933–4), 192–250; D. P. Waley, *The Papal State in the 13th Century* (New York, 1961); *DTC* 11, 532–6 (É. Amann); Mann 16, 57–166; *NCE* 10, 442 f. (J. M. Muldoon); Seppelt 3, 539–58.

MARTIN IV (22 Feb. 1281–28 Mar. 1285). On NICHOLAS III's death the cardinals assembled at Viterbo, but as GREGORY X's *conclave constitution was in abeyance they haggled in an atmosphere of intrigue and partisan animosities for six months. Even then it was only the violence of a new mayor of Angevin sympathies, who imprisoned two cardinals of the Orsini family and prevented Matteo Orsini, leader of the late pope's faction, from participating, which forced an election. The man chosen, as a result of powerful pressure from the Angevin king Charles of Sicily (1266–85), was Simon de Brie, or Brion, born 1210/20 at Brie (Seine-et-Marne), a mild, indecisive Frenchman who, after being archdeacon and chancellor of Rouen and then treasurer of St Martin's, Tours, became (1260) king Louis IX's (1226–70) chancellor and keeper of the seal. Named cardinal priest of Sta Cecilia by URBAN IV, he played an important role in the transfer of power in Italy to Charles of Anjou (1264/5), and under both CLEMENT IV and Gregory X served as legate in France. He now borrowed the name of France's patron saint, calling himself Martin IV because Marinus I and II were incorrectly given as Martin II and III in 13th-cent. official lists; in fact he was the second pope of that name. Since the Romans refused him entry to the city, he was crowned at Orvieto, and mostly resided there.

The most French of 13th-cent. popes, he completely reversed his predecessor's policies. Eager to make every concession to Charles, when the Romans elected Martin senator for life, he transferred the office to the king, effectively handing over the papal state as well by appointing his officials as rectors, i.e. governors. In Romagna he replaced Nicholas III's nephew as rector by a Frenchman from Charles's retinue, and appointed the French canonist, William Durandus (c. 1230–96), as vicar general. He accepted Sicilian garrisons in the papal state, which led in Romagna to fighting with the Ghibellines, or imperial party, in which the papal troops were worsted in May 1282. With King Rudolf I of Habsburg (1273–91), as a result of Nicholas III's efforts to

reconcile him with Charles, his relations were correct, and while there was no talk about his future coronation the pope raised no objections when Rudolf sent his chancellor to Tuscany in spring 1281 to watch over his interests. On the other hand, he gave full backing to Charles's project of recovering Constantinople for the west by force of arms, sanctioning (July 1281) a naval alliance between him and Venice. It came as no surprise, therefore, when on 18 Nov. 1281 he excommunicated Emperor Michael VIII Palaeologus (1259–82) as a schismatic, in spite of his having done all in his power to comply with papal demands, and so precipitated the annulling in 1283 of the union of churches agreed at the second council of Lyons (1274) by Emperor Andronicus II Palaeologus (1282–1328). Charles's campaign, to which Martin compliantly gave the character of a crusade, was to be launched in Apr. 1283, but the plan was frustrated by the rising of Sicily against the French, for which the tolling of bells for vespers on 30 Mar. 1282 gave the signal (the Sicilian Vespers). His lack of political judgement and blind dependence on Charles were exposed when the victorious rebels offered the island in vassalage to the holy see: he spurned the offer, called on them to submit to Charles, promised him every assistance in recovering it, and excommunicated and deposed (21 Mar. 1283) King Peter III the Great of Aragón (1276–85) when he was offered, and accepted, the Sicilian crown.

A friend and protector of the mendicant orders, by his bull *Ad fructus uberes* (13 Dec. 1281) Martin granted their members enhanced rights of preaching and hearing confessions which exasperated the secular clergy and stimulated controversial debates in the universities. A dangerous intrusion on the pastoral rights and duties of parochial clergy, it had to be modified in 1300 by BONIFACE VIII. A pope criticized by German contemporaries for his unconcealed pro-French stance and notorious for his procrastination in business, he died at Perugia a few weeks after his friend and patron Charles I of Sicily (7 Jan. 1285).

F. Olivier-Martin and others, *Les Registres de Martin IV* (Paris, 1901–35); Potthast 2, 1756–95; *LP* 2, 459–65; M. Backes, *Kardinal Simon de Brion* (Breslau, 1910); R. Sternfeld, 'Das Konklave von 1280 und die Wahl Martins IV', *MIÖG* 31 (1910), 1–53; J. R. Strayer, 'The Crusade against Aragon', *Speculum* 28 (1953), 102–13; R. Kay, 'Martin IV and the Fugitive Bishop of Bayeux', *Speculum* 40 (1965), 460–83; A. Fábrega Grau, 'Actitud de Pedro III el Grande de Aragón ante la propria deposición fulminada por Martín IV', *MiscHistPont* 18 (Rome, 1954); Mann 16, 167–356; *NCE* 9, 301 (H. Wieruszowski); Seppelt 3, 555–65.

HONORIUS IV (2 Apr. 1285–3 Apr. 1287). To exclude outside pressures the cardinals at Perugia acted swiftly on MARTIN IV's death in that city, and four days later unanimously elected Giacomo Savelli, cardinal deacon of Sta Maria in Cosmedin, to succeed him. Born in 1210 of aristocratic Roman lineage, once a student at Paris, created a cardinal by URBAN IV in 1261, he was a grand-nephew of HONORIUS III, whose name he adopted. Although his choice indicated the desire to loosen the Angevin connection, he and his family had enjoyed excellent relations with Charles of Anjou, king of Sicily (1266–85), and he had been a member of the commission which in 1265 invested him with the Sicilian throne. In Rome his election was enthusiastically received, and he was crowned there (a privilege denied to Martin IV) on 20 May. Elected senator for life, he used as his deputy his brother Pandulf, who re-established order in the city with a strong hand. Through Honorius's firmly conciliatory methods peaceful conditions were quickly restored in the papal territories, especially Romagna, and he was able, elderly as he was and racked with arthritis, to reside undisturbed in Rome, first in the Vatican and then in a new palace he built on the Aventine.

The most urgent political task facing Honorius was Sicily; here he decided, following the wishes of the French majority of cardinals, to continue Martin IV's policy of trying to retrieve it for the Angevins. He therefore gave financial and moral backing to Philip III of France (1270–85) in his so-called crusade to take possession of Aragón, from which Martin had purported to depose King Peter III (1276–85) on his acceptance of the crown of Sicily, and rejected the attempts of Edward I of England (1272–1307) to mediate. The crusade proved a disaster, and in late autumn 1285 Philip III and Peter III both died. In the new situation Peter's eldest son succeeded to the throne of Aragón as Alfonso III (1285–91), while his younger son James became king of Sicily (1285–95). It was expected that Honorius would now release Alfonso from excommunication, especially since he had ratified the armistice between France and Aragón arranged by Edward I, but he refused to do so. He insisted that Sicily belonged to the house of Anjou, and excommunicated James when he had himself crowned at Palermo on 2 Feb. 1286. He was furious when Charles of Anjou's heir, Charles II of Salerno (1285–1309), who had been taken prisoner by Peter III of Aragón, renounced his title to Sicily in favour of James in order to obtain his freedom, and he refused to accept the treaty of Barcelona (Feb. 1287) under which he agreed to do so.

Despite all the curia's efforts, Sicily was lost to the Angevins. Honorius had to be content, Charles of Anjou being dead and his heir a prisoner of war, with taking steps to re-establish, as overlord, orderly government in the mainland portion of the kingdom after the oppressive rule of the French. This he achieved by issuing two bulls on 17 Sept. 1285, the one regulating the rights and privileges of the clergy, the other the civil administration in all its aspects. Meanwhile, reverting to the policy of GREGORY X, he resumed contact with his emperor-designate, Rudolf I of Habsburg (1273–91). His coronation was fixed for 2 Feb. 1287, but here again Honorius met with disappointment, and because Rudolf could not make the journey to Rome in time had to agree to a postponement. At the diet of

Würzburg (16–18 Mar. 1287) the legate he sent to make alternative arrangements, John of Tusculum (the only cardinal he created), met with a rebuff from the German prelates and princes who, in their fear that their freedom of election might be curtailed, bluntly rejected all requests for financial contributions. The embassy had to leave Germany in disarray, and Rudolf's coronation was again postponed; it was in fact never to take place.

Honorius condemned in 1286 the so-called 'Apostolics', a sect with extreme views on evangelical poverty founded at Parma in 1260; but in general he was a keen supporter of the religious orders. From the start he confirmed and extended the privileges of the Dominicans and the Franciscans, advancing their members to bishoprics on occasion and entrusting them exclusively with the Inquisition. He also promoted the study of Oriental languages at Paris as a help towards the reunion of the churches. During his reign interest in the crusade announced by Gregory X at the second council of Lyons (1274) languished, and the funds raised to finance it were frittered away on the curia's political objectives, such as the war with Aragón and the recovery of Sicily for the Angevins, which were designated 'crusades'.

Potthast 2, 1795–825; M. Prou, *Les Registres d'Honorius IV* (Paris, 1888); B. Pawlicki, *Papst Honorius IV* (Münster, 1896); G von Gaisberg-Schockingen, *Das Konzil und der Reichstag von Würzburg 1287* (Marburg, 1928); *PRE* 8, 324–7 (H. Schulz); *NCE* 7, 127 f. (J. M. Muldoon); Mann 16, 357–450; Seppelt 3, 555 f.; 565–74.

NICHOLAS IV (22 Feb. 1288–4 Apr. 1292).

The vacancy after HONORIUS IV's death dragged on for almost eleven months. The conclave was hopelessly divided, and when six cardinals died in the intense summer heat and most of the others fell sick it suspended its meetings. Only a Franciscan friar, Girolamo Masci, stayed on in Rome, and when the cardinals reassembled in Feb. 1288 they unanimously elected him as a compromise on 15 Feb.; they quashed his

initial refusal by electing him again on 22 Feb. Born on 30 Sept. 1227 at Lisciano, near Ascoli Piceno, son of a clerk, he early joined the Franciscans, became provincial of their Dalmatian province in 1272, and in 1274 succeeded the theologian and mystic Bonaventura (*c.*1217–74) as general of the order. In 1272 he was one of the envoys sent by GREGORY X to Constantinople to negotiate the presence of Greek delegates at the projected second council of Lyons (1274). When he was on a peace-making mission to France in 1278, NICHOLAS III named him cardinal priest of Sta Pudenziana, and sought his advice when preparing his bull on poverty (*Exiit qui seminat*: 14 Aug. 1279); MARTIN IV created him cardinal bishop of Palestrina.

The first Franciscan to become pope, Nicholas was, like his predecessor, elected senator of Rome for life, but was prevented by intermittent disorders from residing there continuously. He was himself partly to blame for the in-fighting of aristocratic houses, for in contrast to his predecessors he singled out the Colonna family, with which he had earlier had ties, for favour in an effort to buttress the position of the papacy. One of its members he created cardinal, others he appointed to administrative positions in the papal state, while in 1290 he arranged for the energetic Giovanni Colonna to be elected sole senator. So marked was his subservience to the Colonna that he was popularly lampooned as enclosed in a pillar (their family emblem) with only his tiara-crowned head emerging. Yet these jibes did not deter him from making Rome the home of famous artists like Arnolfo di Gambio, Pietro Cavallini, and Giacomo Torriti, or from using their talents to remodel and embellish St John Lateran and Sta Maria Maggiore; close to the latter he constructed a palace which he made his principal residence when in Rome.

Nicholas carried out the curia's policies in regard to both Rudolf I of Habsburg (1273–91), emperor-designate, and Sicily. He corresponded with Rudolf about the date of his much-delayed coronation, but nothing came of the exchanges, and the king died without the imperial diadem in 1291. He spent time and effort trying to compel Aragón to restore Sicily to the house of Anjou, which had lost it after the *Sicilian Vespers (30 Mar. 1282). He organized an alliance of Castile with France against Aragón, annulled the treaty of Champfranc (28 Oct. 1288) which confirmed James of Aragón as king of Sicily (1285–95), and on 29 May 1289 crowned Charles II of Salerno (1285–1309), Charles of Anjou's (1265–85) heir, as king of Naples and Sicily at Rieti, first however making him do homage to himself as his overlord and promise not to accept any office in Rome or the papal state without his approval. When James successfully attacked the south Italian mainland, he authorized tithes to finance Charles's resistance, but in Aug. 1289 had to accept an armistice arranged by Edward I of England (1272–1307). He released Alfonso III of Aragón (1285–91) from his excommunication when he undertook, in a treaty with Charles II and Philip IV of France (1285–1314), not to assist his brother James of Sicily. But Sicily had not been isolated as he hoped; Alfonso died on 18 June 1291, James became king of Aragón as well as Sicily, and he appointed his brother Frederick as vicegerent of the island.

Nicholas felt more concern for a crusade than either of his predecessors, and after the sack of Tripoli (Lebanon) in Apr. 1289 issued a summons to one, himself dispatching a small fleet. The fall (May 1291) of Acre (Akko, Israel), the last Christian outpost in the Holy Land, caused him to make fresh appeals, but nothing came of them. The outcome might have been different if he and the European monarchs had formed an alliance against the Muslims with Il-Khan Arghun of Iran, who sent them urgent requests for joint action; but they only responded with promises. Nicholas, however, earned the title of missionary pope by sending (1289) Giovanni di Monte Corvino (d. c.1330), a Franciscan friar, to the court of the Great Kubla Khan (1260–94);

this mission led to the first establishment of the Catholic church in China, where previously only Nestorians had been influential, and Giovanni was in 1307 appointed first archbishop of Peking by CLEMENT V. Nicholas also sent missionaries, mostly Franciscans, to the Balkans and the near east. A constitutional measure of far-reaching importance was his bull *Coelestis altitudo* (18 June 1289) by which, in some degree consolidating existing 13th-cent. practice, he assigned one half of the revenues of the holy see to the college of cardinals, granting it also a share in their administration (under the control of the cardinal chamberlain), and making appointments to rectorates and other offices in the papal state contingent on its agreement.

Nicholas was buried in his beloved Sta Maria Maggiore, where a 16th-cent. monument by Domenico Fontana and others covers his tomb.

E. Langlois, *Les Registres de Nicolas IV* (Paris, 1886–1905); *LP* 2, 466 f.; Potthast 2, 1826–915; O. Schiff, *Studien zur Geschichte Papst Nikolaus IV* (Berlin, 1897; Vaduz, 1965); R. Röhricht, 'Der Untergang des Königsreichs Jerusalem', *MIÖG* 15 (1894), 1–58; J. R. Strayer, 'The Crusade against Aragón', *Speculum* 28 (1953), 102–13; S. Runciman, *The Sicilian Vespers* (Cambridge, 1958); J. Richard, 'Le début des relations entre la papauté et les Mongols de Perse', *Journal Asiatique* 237 (1949), 291–7; Mann 17, 1–253; *NCE* 10, 443 (J. M. Muldoon); Seppelt 3, 572–80.

CELESTINE V, ST PETER (5 July–13 Dec. 1294: d. 19 May 1296).

After NICHOLAS IV's death the papal throne remained vacant for twenty-seven months, with the twelve cardinals, split by family and personal rather than political animosities, unable to reach the required two-thirds majority. Twice several of them abandoned turbulent Rome and its unhealthy heat; in 1293 the cardinals of the Colonna family who stayed behind made a fruitless attempt to carry through an election on their own. In Oct. 1293, however, the conclave reassembled at Perugia, and an election became more urgent when Charles II, king of Sicily and Naples (1285–1309), arrived there in Mar. 1294, eager to have ratified a secret treaty he had made in 1293 at La Junquera with James II of Aragón (1291–1327) for the evacuation of Sicily by his brother Frederick. The cardinals declined, but he sought to speed up the election by producing a short list of four names for them. This had no effect, but after his departure pressures mounted—disorders in May and June at Rome, fighting in the Orvieto region, the tragic death of the youthful brother of Cardinal Napoleone. When they met in a tense atmosphere on 5 July, Cardinal Latino Malabrança revealed that a devout hermit had written prophesying divine retribution if they left the church without a head any longer. Questioned, he disclosed that the hermit was none other than the renowned Pietro del Morrone. As dean of the college he then gave his vote for him, and by stages the two-thirds majority and eventually unanimous accord were reached.

Pietro was then eighty-five, having been born in 1209 or early 1210 in the county of Molise, the eleventh child of simple peasants named Angelerio and Maria. When still in his teens he entered the Benedictine house of Sta Maria di Faifula (near Montagano), but c.1231 was drawn to the solitary life in the wild Abruzzi. Ordained priest in Rome, he lived for several years in a cave on Mount Morrone, above Sulmona, but withdrew c.1245 to the more inaccessible heights of the Maiella to escape public curiosity. All the time he was attracting like-minded disciples, and these (later to be called Celestines) URBAN IV incorporated in June 1263 in the Benedictine order; the local bishop had allowed Pietro to build a church (Sta Maria) at the foot of Morrone in 1259. His brotherhood had links with the radical Franciscans, or *'Spirituals', and to ensure its independence from episcopal intervention he travelled on foot to Lyons in 1274, arriving just after the second council, and obtained from GREGORY X a solemn privilege confirming both its incorporation in the Benedictine order and its properties. Returning from Lyons, he held at S. Spirito,

Maiella, its first general chapter, which recognized the rule of St Benedict (c.480–c.550) as binding and published liturgical and disciplinary guidelines. His activities were at their height in the following decade; in 1276 he became abbot of Sta Maria di Faifula as well as prior of S. Spirito, Maiella, and he made contact with Charles I of Anjou, king of Sicily (1266–85), who in 1278 took Sta Maria under royal protection. His fame as an ascetic, miraculous healer, and monastic leader spread beyond the Abruzzi, and his was a familiar name in the curia and the court of Naples. In 1293 he moved from the Maiella back to Mount Morrone, where he had built the monastery of S. Spirito (now a prison), and settled in a tiny grotto 637 m. up the mountain (S. Onofrio), relinquishing the direction of the community to others.

Various factors contributed to the cardinals' astonishing choice: weariness with the stalemate, hope that a bold stroke might rejuvenate the papacy, the 13th-cent. dream of an 'angel pope' who would usher in the age of the Spirit, but it is unlikely that the hand of Charles II was behind it. The election, however, which Pietro himself accepted only under extreme protest, was widely acclaimed, and in radical spiritual circles he was hailed as in truth the hoped for 'angel pope'. Astride a donkey he was escorted by Charles II and his son Charles Martell to L'Aquila, where he was consecrated as Celestine V in his own church of Sta Maria di Colmaggio on 29 Aug. The cardinals wanted the ceremony at Perugia or Rieti, but Charles insisted on a town in his own domains. He also saw to it that the new pope took up residence (5 Nov.), not at Rome, as the curia demanded, but at Naples in the Castel Nuovo. Celestine was in fact a puppet manipulated by Charles, appointing his creatures to key positions in the curia and the papal state and, when he created twelve cardinals (18 Sept.), meekly accepting Charles's nominees (including seven Frenchmen). At Charles's request he ratified the treaty of La Junquera (1 Oct.), including a clause requiring James II to restore Sicily to the church within three years, and reintroduced Gregory X's rules for the *conclave, making the king its guardian for the next occasion. Naïve and incompetent, so ill educated that Italian had to be used in consistory instead of Latin, he let the day-to-day administration of the church fall into confusion, even assigning the same benefice to more than one applicant. Where he showed initiative was in showering privileges on his own congregation, even taking steps to incorporate in it great Benedictine abbeys like Monte Cassino, and protecting the Franciscan Spirituals.

As Advent approached, he considered handing over the government of the church to three cardinals while he fasted and prayed, but the plan was sharply opposed. In his agony of soul he was already pondering abdication, and consulted Cardinal Benedetto Caetani, a noted canonist, on the possibility of voluntary resignation. Benedetto having assured him (incorrectly) that there were precedents, he first had a statement of his reasons for abdicating drafted, then on 10 Dec. published a bull declaring that Gregory X's conclave procedure was operative in the case of an abdication, and finally, on 13 Dec., in full consistory read out a formula of abdication prepared by Benedetto and, stripping off the papal insignia, became once more 'brother Pietro'. In a last appeal he begged the cardinals to proceed swiftly to a fresh election for the good of the church.

It was Pietro's earnest desire to return to his retreat on Mount Morrone, but his successor BONIFACE VIII (none other than Benedetto Caetani) could not permit this; pliable in clever hands, Pietro could easily have been made the rallying-point of a schism. He was therefore kept under guard and, although he managed to escape and be at large for several months, was eventually captured and strictly confined in the tower of Castel Fumone, east of Ferentino. There is no proof that he was treated with undue harshness. When he died of an infection caused by an abscess on 19 May 1296, his remains were first interred at Ferentino but in 1317 transferred to Sta Maria di Colmaggio, where he was crowned pope. Under pressure from Philip IV of France, pursuing his vendetta against Boniface VIII, CLEMENT V canonized him on 5 May 1313 as a confessor, not as a martyr as Philip had proposed. Feast (no longer observed universally) 19 May.

AASS May 4, 418–537; A. M. Frugoni, *Celestiniana* (Rome, 1954); F. X. Seppelt, *Monumenta Coelestiniana* (Paderborn, 1921); F. Baethgen, *Der Engelpapst* (Leipzig, 1943); *Beiträge zur Geschichte Cölestins V* (Halle, 1934); P. Herde, *Papst Cölestin V (Peter vom Morrone)* (Stuttgart, 1981); *DBI* 23, 402–15 (P. Herde); *DHGE* 12, 79–101 (R. Mols); Mann 17, 247–341; Seppelt 3, 555; 582–7.

BONIFACE VIII (24 Dec. 1294–11 Oct. 1303). CELESTINE V having re-enacted GREGORY X's *conclave regulations, the cardinals met in Castel Nuovo, Naples, ten days after his abdication and next day, on the third scrutiny, elected Cardinal Benedetto Caetani. Born *c.*1235 at Anagni, of a modestly aristocratic family of the Campagna, he studied law at Bologna, in 1264 and 1265–8 accompanied legates to France and England respectively, and in the late seventies became papal notary. MARTIN IV made him cardinal deacon in 1281, NICHOLAS IV cardinal priest in 1291; on both occasions he was allowed to retain his numerous benefices and used their revenues to aggrandize his family. His abrasive manner and diplomatic skill were displayed in France in 1290–1, when he brilliantly championed the rights of the mendicant orders at Paris, and then succeeded in mediating the treaty of Tarascon (Feb. 1291) with Aragón and in preventing the outbreak of war with England. It was he, an acknowledged authority on canon law, who advised Celestine V on his abdication, a role which earned him the hatred of the Franciscan Spirituals (who, as opposed to the main body of Franciscans, called for the literal observance of St Francis's rule and testament, especially as regards poverty). Once elected, he annulled (27 Dec.) most of the privileges recklessly granted by Celestine, dismissed the curial officials imposed by the Angevin Charles II of Sicily and Naples (1285–1309), and moved his court from Naples to Rome, where he was consecrated and crowned as Boniface VIII on 23 Jan. 1295.

Masterful, conscious of his intellectual superiority, Boniface constantly intervened on the international plane, but his policies all too often misfired because they were impulsively conceived, even more because his conception of the pope as universal arbiter was no longer palatable to the new political order. Thus after apparent success in 1295, his long struggle to restore Sicily to Charles II of Naples ended in 1302 with his reluctant acceptance (peace of Caltabellotta) of the independence of the island under Frederick of Aragón (1296–1337). His efforts to mediate, in the interests of a crusade, between Venice and Genoa (1295), to uphold Scotland's independence against England (1299), and to secure the crown of Hungary for Charles II's grandson Charles I Robert, or Carobert (1288–1342), came to nothing. He had greater success in bringing Erik VI Menved of Denmark (1286–1319), who had imprisoned the archbishop of Lund in 1294, to heel; and while originally hostile to Albert I of Austria (1298–1308), elected German king in 1298, he found it prudent in Apr. 1303, in return for valuable concessions, to recognize him as emperor-designate. His attempts to halt hostilities between France and England over the English king's fiefs of Guienne and Gascony opened a fateful quarrel between him and Philip IV of France (1285–1314). Both countries raised money for the war by taxing their clergy, a practice canonically forbidden without the consent of the pope; but when Boniface sought to ban it with the bull Clericis laicos (25 Feb. 1296), Philip retaliated by prohibiting the export of money and valuables and by expelling foreign merchants. This was a shrewd blow at the pope, whose budget relied on revenue from France, and after blustering he had to climb down, empowering the king in July 1297 to tax the clergy in case of need without consulting Rome. The peace thus temporarily restored was sealed by his canonization (11 Aug. 1297) of Philip's revered grandfather Louis IX (1214–70).

He might not have yielded to Philip so easily had he not been faced with a revolt of the powerful Colonna family. Although clashing with him over property in the Campagna, they had supported his election, but had become disenchanted with his high-handed style, opposed his Sicilian policy, and joined the Franciscan Spirituals in questioning the validity of Celestine V's abdication and so his own election. They thus started a conspiracy of calumny against him, and when they hijacked a convoy of papal treasure in May 1297 he struck at them with extreme harshness, deposing and excommunicating their two cardinals. They reacted with a solemn memorial calling for a general council to adjudicate his legitimacy as pope and investigate his alleged murder of Celestine, but in reply he organized a holy war against them, razed their fortresses, seized their lands and exploited them to enrich himself. By Oct. 1298 the Colonna, who had circulated European princes with a dossier of his supposed crimes but in the present détente could not get the expected help from France, had to submit; but the two Colonna cardinals took refuge in Philip's court, there to continue their propaganda. Meanwhile Boniface's triumph seemed complete, and he could proclaim 1300 a year of jubilee (the first holy year), with plenary indulgences for pilgrims to the Apostles' shrines. His self-confidence was now at its height and he occasionally dressed up in imperial insignia, boasting that he was emperor no less than pope.

In autumn 1301 the conflict with Philip flared up afresh with fatal violence. The king had summarily imprisoned a contumacious bishop of Pamiers and demanded his degradation, but Boniface perceived that the whole issue of royal or papal control of the clergy was at stake. Without examining the case he condemned (Ausculta fili: 5 Dec. 1301) the violation of the church's freedom, withdrew the exemptions earlier granted, and summoned the French higher clergy to a synod in Rome in Nov. 1302 to discuss his grievances; papal supremacy over the secular power was emphasized. There ensued a propaganda war, with the court caricaturing the bull and arguing that the king was subject to no one in secular matters, the pope contending that he claimed no suzerainty over France but could take the king to task when he erred. After the Roman synod, which thirty-nine French bishops dared to attend, Boniface published his widely discussed bull *Unam sanctam* (18 Nov. 1302), an extreme but by no means novel statement of the supremacy of the spiritual over the temporal power; its closing sentence affirmed that it was necessary to salvation that every creature should be subject to the Roman pontiff. Boniface proposed conditions for a reconciliation, but Philip, influenced by his new adviser Guillaume de Nogaret (*c.*1260–1313), now switched to all-out personal attack. A list of charges against the pope, based on the Colonna memorials and extending from illegitimacy through sexual misconduct to heresy, was made public, and an insistent demand raised for a general council to depose him. At Anagni Boniface repudiated the accusations and prepared the bull *Super Petri solio* excommunicating Philip, intending to publish it on 8 Sept. 1303. On the previous day, however, Nogaret, who had gone to Italy with authority to arrest him, arrived at Anagni with Sciarra, head of the Colonna family, and a band of mercenaries, stormed the papal palace, and demanded that Boniface should resign. When he refused, they seized him, planning to take him to France to be judged by a council, but the mood of the city changed; he was rescued by the citizens, and his captors were driven off. After a rest, he returned to Rome under the protection of the Orsini family on 25 Sept., but on 12 Oct. died at the Vatican, broken in body and spirit.

Largely unsuccessful in his political activities, Boniface made a lasting contribution by the publication, in 1298, of the *Liber sextus*, continuing the five books of GREGORY IX's **Liber extra* (1234) and forming the third part of the *Corpus of Canon Law*, which attests his acumen as a jurist. He also introduced much-needed order into the curial administrative system, catalogued the papal library and reorganized the Vatican archives, and by his bull *Super cathedram* (18 Feb. 1301) drastically limited the mendicant orders' right to preach and hear confessions so as to reduce friction with the secular clergy. He was a patron of learning, founding a university at Rome in 1303 and planning one for Avignon, and of artists (including Giotto and Arnolfo di Cambio); he commissioned or permitted the erection of so many statues of himself that hostile tongues accused him of encouraging idolatry. These were the achievements of a man who, although the charges brought against him and to be fiercely pressed after his death were mostly fabrications or distortions, was singularly unsympathetic, combining exceptional ability with arrogance and cruelty, insatiable acquisitiveness for his family, and insensitive contempt for his fellow-men; feared and hated, he could not keep a friend.

G. A. L. Digard and others, *Les Registres de Boniface VIII* (Paris, 1884–1939); H. Denifle, 'Die Denkschriften der Colonna gegen Bonifaz VIII', *ALKGMA* 5 (1889), 493–529; T. S. R. Boase, *Boniface VIII* (London, 1933); F. M. Powicke, 'Pope Boniface VIII', *History* 18 (1934), 307–29; G. A. L. Digard, *Philippe le Bel et le saint siège de 1295 à 1304* (Paris, 1936); H. Finke, *Aus den Tagen Bonifaz VIII* (Münster, 1902); C. T. Wood, *Philip the Fair and Boniface VIII* (2nd edn. London, 1971); *EB* (15th edn.) 3, 32–4 (G. B. Ladner); *NCE* 2, 671–3 (B. Tierney); *DBI* 12, 146–70 (E. Dupré-Theseider); Mann 18, 1–420; Seppelt 4, 9–61.

BENEDICT XI, BL. (22 Oct. 1303–7 July 1304). In the uproar in Rome following BONIFACE's unexpected death the cardinals, having excluded Giacomo and Pietro Colonna under protest as excommunicate, unanimously elected Niccolò Boccasino, cardinal bishop of Ostia. Born at Treviso in 1240, son of a notary of humble family, he joined the Dominican order in his teens, lectured in theology for more than a decade and wrote commentaries on the Psalms, Job, St Matthew, and Revelation, and was elected Dominican provincial for Lombardy in 1286, master-general in 1296. In this capacity he vigorously upheld the legitimacy of Boniface VIII, contested by the Colonna cardinals and the Franciscan *Spirituals. In recognition of his loyalty Boniface named him cardinal in 1298, having already found him useful in 1297 in negotiating peace between France and England, and in 1301 sent him as legate to Hungary to back the claims of Charles I Robert, or Carobert (1288–1342), grandson of Charles II of Naples (1285–1309), to the throne. Unsuccessful though it was, Charles's gratitude for this service helped him to be chosen pope, for the king occupied Rome during the conclave. The Bonifacian cardinals supported him as a champion of the late pontiff who, although never identified with his anti-French policies, had stood courageously by him when he was brutally attacked at Anagni. He called himself Benedict after Boniface's original name Benedetto.

Weak, peace-loving, and scholarly (he felt at ease only with Dominicans), Benedict did what he could to promote conciliation at a time of acute crisis. He first dealt with the two Colonna cardinals who, excluded from his election, were now denouncing it as invalid. Torn between conflicting advice, he on 23 Dec. 1303 absolved them and their relatives from Boniface's sentence of excommunication, without however restoring to them either their rank or their confiscated properties. While this compromise fell far short of their hopes, it exasperated their Bonifacian enemies; the resulting factional strife unleashed such tumults in Rome that he judged it safer to move to Perugia in Apr. 1304. He showed greater firmness towards Frederick III of Sicily (1296–1337), reluctantly recognized by Boniface in 1303 but now taking advantage of the embarrassment of the holy see, and in 1304 obliged him to renew his allegiance

and payment of dues. His efforts, however, to restore peace in faction-ridden Florence and Tuscany ended unsuccessfully. The most delicate problem, however, was Philip IV of France (1285–1314), Boniface's deadly foe, who was demanding a general council to condemn the dead pope posthumously. Benedict wanted peace, but without loss of principle or insult to his predecessor, and since he regarded Philip as effectively excommunicate he did not at first notify him formally of his election. In Mar. 1304, however, when the king's envoys arrived in Rome authorized to congratulate him and to 'accept' any absolution that might be necessary, he published a bull (25 Mar.) releasing Philip and his family from any censures incurred. This unconditional absolution did nothing to abate the French campaign for a general council, and in Apr. and May Benedict revoked all Boniface's punitive measures affecting either France or the king, his advisers, and officials; pardon was assured to all Frenchmen who had been involved in the outrage against Boniface at Anagni except its ringleader, the king's minister Guillaume de Nogaret (c. 1260–1313). Boniface's bull *Clericis laicos (1296) prohibiting princes from taxing their clergy without Rome's consent was almost completely withdrawn, and Philip was granted tithes for two years. All these concessions were evidence of Benedict's precarious position, but, France having been thus appeased and the threat of a general council having for the moment receded, he felt able on 7 June to denounce Nogaret and his Italian accomplices as guilty of sacrilege by their crimes at Anagni, ordering them to appear before him, on pain of excommunication, before 29 June.

The grievous sickness of the pope prevented the execution of his threat; on 7 July Benedict died at Perugia, the victim of acute dysentery and not, as was widely alleged, of poisoning. Unlike his high-handed predecessor, he could do nothing without the cardinals. The three he himself created were Dominicans; his zeal for his order led him also to annul Boniface's bull

Super cathedram (18 Feb. 1301) restricting the right of the mendicants to preach and hear confessions. He also harassed the Franciscan Spirituals, and when threateningly admonished by Arnold of Villanova, Boniface's Catalan physician and himself an ardent Spiritual, imprisoned him without trial. He was buried in S. Domenico, and miraculous cures were soon being reported at his tomb. He was beatified by CLEMENT XII in 1736. Feast 7 July.

C. Grandjean, *Les Registres de Benoît XI* (Paris, 1883–1905); B. Guido, *Vitae pontif. Rom.* (Muratori 3.1, 672 f.); P. Funke, *Papst Benedikt XI* (Münster, 1891); A. M. Ferrero, *Benedetto XI papa domenicano* (Rome, 1934); *DHGE* 8, 106–16 (L. Jadin); Mann 18, 421–86; *DBI* 8, 370–8 (I. Walter); Seppelt 4, 56–60.

CLEMENT V (5 June 1305–20 Apr. 1314). On BENEDICT XI's death the cardinals at Perugia were almost equally divided between an anti-French faction demanding vengeance for the attack on BONIFACE VIII at Anagni (7 Sept. 1303) and a pro-French group seeking the rehabilitation of the Colonna cardinals disgraced by Boniface and *rapprochement* with Philip IV of France (1285–1314). After eleven months' bitter debate and intrigue they failed to agree on one of themselves and, the Bonifacians having been cleverly split, elected Bertrand de Got, since 1299 archbishop of Bordeaux, by an exact two-thirds majority. It was a victory for the pro-French minority, for although Bertrand could be trusted to respect Boniface VIII's memory, he had long enjoyed special favour with the French court. Born *c.* 1260 at Villandraut, Gironde, of an influential Gascon family, he studied canon and civil law at Orléans and then Bologna. After holding canonries at Bordeaux and elsewhere, he became vicar-general to his brother Bérard, archbishop of Lyons. In 1294 he served on a diplomatic mission to England, and in Mar. 1295 was appointed bishop of Comminges. It is significant that as such he attended Boniface VIII's Roman synod of Nov. 1302 without incurring Philip IV's displeasure.

Intelligent, but indecisive and weak, racked by internal cancer which forced him to withdraw for months from public view, Clement was under constant pressure from the coldly calculating French king. Thus his first plan was to be crowned at Vienne, where he hoped in the interests of a crusade to establish definitive peace between the English and French kings, but he cancelled this to meet Philip's wishes and was crowned on 15 Nov. at Lyons. When he created ten cardinals in Dec. 1305, nine of them (including four nephews) were French; further creations in 1310 and 1312 reinforced French domination of the college. Both at the start of his reign and later he seriously intended moving to Rome, but after wandering about Provence and Gascony for several years he finally yielded to Philip's request and in Mar. 1309 settled with the curia at Avignon, inaugurating the seventy years 'Babylonian captivity' of the papacy. He chose Avignon because it belonged, not to the French crown, but to his vassals the Angevin kings of Naples, forming an enclave in the papal county of Venaissin and offering easy access to the sea. Even so, his residence there had a provisional air: while in the city, he occupied the Dominican priory, but spent even more time outside in the surrounding country, and he transferred from Rome only the immediately necessary papal archives.

Clement's dependence was painfully exposed by Philip's exploitation of him in his vendetta against Boniface VIII. For six full years the king kept pressing for a general council to condemn (a prospect horrifying to the curia) the dead pope for heresy and other odious crimes. Although Clement resisted and played for time, he eventually agreed to the case being opened at Candlemas 1309. Political events, however, caused delays, and in Apr. 1311 the king suspended proceedings. But the price Clement had to pay was humiliating: the rehabilitation of the Colonna cardinals and full compensation for the family, the annulment of all Boniface's acts prejudicial to French interests, the absolution of the king's minister Guillaume de Nogaret, ringleader of the assault on Boniface, the bull *Rex gloriae* (27 Apr. 1311) praising Philip for his zeal in attacking the dead pope, and the canonization (5 May 1313) of CELESTINE V (but as a confessor, not as a martyr by Boniface's hand, as Philip wished). But even more humiliating was his collaboration with the king in his suppression of the Knights Templars. Returned from the Holy Land, they were now large-scale bankers and property-owners, and rumours (now largely discounted) circulated about their heretical ideas, blasphemous rites, and immoral practices. Philip, who probably coveted their wealth, had all the Templars in France arrested on 13 Oct. 1307; the confessions extracted from them under torture were handed to the pope, and the condemnation of the order was demanded. Initially hesitant, Clement's will was broken by a barrage of threats, and he agreed to hold a general council (reckoned the Fifteenth) at Vienne (Oct. 1311-May 1312); he had probably come to accept the Templars' general guilt. As the mood of the council favoured them, Clement was induced, by the king's personal intervention and, probably, by threats to reopen the process against Boniface VIII, to dissolve the order by an administrative ordinance (*Vox clamantis*) in private consistory on 22 Mar. 1312; the council had to hear his sentence in silence on 3 Apr. He ruled that its French property should be assigned to the Hospitallers (Knights of St John of Jerusalem); in practice Philip held it till his death.

Clement was capable of independent policies when free from French pressures. In 1305/6 he released Edward I of England (1272-1307) from his vows to his barons and, at his remonstrances, suspended Robert of Winchelsea (d. 1313) as archbishop of Canterbury, restoring him in 1308 at Edward II's (1307-27) request. In 1306 he excommunicated Robert I the Bruce of Scotland (1306-29) for the murder of his old enemy and possible rival John ('the Red') Comyn in a church and deposed two

bishops who had supported the Scottish rebels. His ruling in favour of Charles I Robert, or Carobert (d. 1342), as king of Hungary (1307) settled fifteen years' disastrous dissension. He waged a harsh but successful war against Venice in order to recover papal rights over Ferrara. When the German king, Albert I of Habsburg, was assassinated in 1308, he managed effectively to evade recommending Philip IV's brother, Charles of Valois, and accorded recognition to Henry IV of Luxembourg (1308-13), who was crowned as emperor Henry VII by three cardinals in the Lateran (St Peter's was held by the troops of Robert of Naples: 1309-43) on 29 June 1312. When Henry, however, came into conflict with Robert of Naples and so with French interests, Clement succumbed to influence from Philip IV and demanded an armistice of the emperor on pain of excommunication. After Henry's early death on 24 Aug. 1313, he published his famous bull *Pastoralis cura* in which, carrying even further Boniface VIII's theocratic ideas, he asserted the superiority of the papacy over the empire, with the right to name imperial vicars during a vacancy. He then nominated Robert of Naples imperial vicar in Italy.

Implementing decrees of the council of Vienne, Clement sought to settle (*Exivi de paradiso*: 6 May 1312), on a stricter basis than the order proposed but less strictly than the radicals wished, the chronic dispute between the Franciscans and the *Spirituals on the nature of evangelical poverty, and in the interests of missionary work ordered the establishment of chairs of Oriental languages at Paris, Oxford, Bologna, and Salamanca. He founded universities at Orléans and Perugia. Under him the centralization of church government greatly increased: new types of benefice were reserved to papal nomination, which also became the most frequent method of appointment to bishoprics. A trained jurist, he promulgated (21 Mar. 1314), together with the decrees of the council of Vienne, the collection of decretals by himself and his two predecessors known as the *Clementines*. As a man he was devout, easygoing, kindly; but his nepotism was extreme even for his age (five of his family were promoted cardinals alone), while he bequeathed such vast legacies from the papal treasury that not only was it exhausted but an embarrassing lawsuit was started under his successor. He died at Roquemaure, near Carpentras, and was buried at Uzeste, 5 km. from his birthplace in the parish church he had recently built.

Regestum Clementis papae V ex Vaticanis archetypis (Rome, 1885–92); R. Fawtier and Y. Lanhers, *Tables des registres de Clément V* (Paris, 1948–57); Baluze-Mollat 1, 1–106; 2, 31–175; 3, 1–234; G. Lizerand, *Clément V et Philippe le Bel* (Paris, 1910); G. Mollat, *The Popes at Avignon* (ET, London, 1963); G. Lizerand, *Le dossier de l'affaire des Templiers* (Paris, 1923); H. G. Richardson, 'Clement V and the See of Canterbury', *EHR* 56 (1941), 96–103; J. Bernard, 'Le Népotisme de Clément V et ses complaisances pour la Gascogne', *Annales du Midi* 61 (1949), 369–411; *DHGE* 12, 1115–29 (G. Mollat); *DBI* 26, 202–15 (A. Paravicini Bagliani); *NCE* 3, 929 f. (E. R. Labande); Seppelt 4, 60–91.

JOHN XXII (7 Aug. 1316–4 Dec. 1334). The cardinals took over two years to find a successor to CLEMENT V. Meeting first at Carpentras, they dispersed because of violence, and only reassembled at Lyons, under pressure from Philip, count of Poitiers (soon to be Philip V of France: 1316–22), in Mar. 1316. Divisions along national lines (Gascon, Italian, etc.) aroused passionate feelings, but they at last agreed on a compromise candidate, Jacques Duèse, who had the backing of both Philip and King Robert of Naples (1309–43). Born at Cahors *c.*1244 of rich bourgeois stock, trained in law at Montpellier, he became bishop of Fréjus in 1300, from 1308 to 1310 was chancellor to Charles II (1285–1309) and then Robert of Naples, and was made bishop of Avignon in 1310, cardinal priest of S. Vitale in 1312, cardinal bishop of Porto in 1313. Second of the Avignon popes, he consolidated the stay of the papacy there in spite of early statements

that he wished to move to Rome. He lived first in the Dominican priory, later in the episcopal palace.

Elderly, feeble in health, diminutive and wisp-like, John was immensely energetic as well as administratively experienced, and did much to restore the efficient working of the curia and its financial viability, both badly run down by his predecessor. Authoritarian by nature, he greatly extended direct papal *provision, or nomination, to benefices, enlarged the pool available by forbidding (*Execrabilis*: 19 Nov. 1317) the holding of more than two, and virtually removed the election of bishops from chapters. To increase efficiency he split up excessively large dioceses and redrew the boundaries of others; and he created a new fiscal system, extending to all countries the payment to the holy see of annates, i.e. the first year's revenue of a benefice, reserving (1319) all minor benefices for three years to the papacy, and levying special subsidies. He compiled a new tax book fixing fees for documents issued by his chancery, and augmented and partly reorganized the curia. Their authority being uncertain, he officially published Clement V's decretals (the *Clementines*) in 1317, while his own decretals (the *Extravagantes*) long remained the basis of ecclesiastical jurisprudence.

Early in his reign John took sharp action, at the instance of Michael of Cesena, general of the Franciscans (1316–29), against the *Spirituals, banning their abbreviated habit and ordering them to obey their superiors, and accept the legitimacy of laying up stores of provisions (1317); those who proved obstinate were handed over to the Inquisition, and four were burned at the stake (1318). He soon came to blows, however, with the order itself when its general chapter at Perugia, directed by Michael of Cesena, pronounced (June 1322), in defiance of a decision of the Inquisition, that it was orthodox teaching that Christ and the Apostles owned nothing as their own. John's reaction was, first, to renounce ownership of the order's property, titularly vested in the holy see, and then to denounce the Perugia declaration as heresy (12 Nov. 1323). The entire order was outraged, and some members branded John as a heretic himself, and although the majority submitted in summer 1325 a large minority went into schism. This included Michael of Cesena, who escaped in May 1328 from detention at Avignon and fled, with William of Occam (*c.* 1285–1347) and Bonagratia of Bergamo, to the court of Louis IV the Bavarian (1314–47). John excommunicated them in Apr. 1329, and on 16 Nov. issued a bull (*Quia vir reprobus*) declaring that the right to hold property pre-dated the Fall, and that scripture depicted the Apostles as owning personal possessions.

The renegade Franciscans soon became allies of John's enemy Louis IV. At his accession John had invited Louis and Frederick the Fair of Austria (1308–30), both elected German king in Oct. 1314, to settle their dispute amicably; then, acting on the theocratic doctrine that when the empire was vacant its administration reverted to the holy see, he dismissed the officers of the former emperor, Henry VII (1308–13), confirmed Clement V's nomination of Robert of Naples as imperial vicar in Italy, and exerted himself to assert papal authority there. When Louis defeated his rival in Sept. 1322, appointed his own imperial vicar and began claiming royal rights in Italy, and supported the pope's enemies in Milan and elsewhere, the conflict became increasingly furious, with John denouncing him and uttering dire warnings, Louis repudiating the pope's claims, John finally excommunicating him (23 Mar. 1324), and Louis appealing to a general council and branding John as heretical because of his attitude to the Franciscan Spirituals' doctrine of poverty. Louis was helped not only by the schismatic Franciscans, but by Marsilius of Padua (*c.* 1275–1342), the exponent of the theory of the lay state, whose *Defensor Pacis* (1324) had been condemned by John, along with its author, in 1327. Accompanied by Marsilius,

Louis entered Rome in Jan. 1328, had himself crowned emperor by the aged Sciarra Colonna, captain of the people, on 17 Jan., and on 18 Apr. published a decree declaring 'Jacques of Cahors' deposed on grounds of heresy; a straw effigy of him, in pontifical robes, was solemnly burned. In his place Louis had a Franciscan Spiritual, Pietro Rainalducci, elected pope by representatives of the Roman clergy under the name of NICHOLAS V; he installed him himself. But the charade was short-lived. His position there becoming untenable, Louis left Rome early in 1329 and after six months at Pisa returned to Germany, while John continued to fulminate against him and to demand his abdication. Abandoned by his patron, the antipope went into hiding, but soon made his submission at Avignon, where John pardoned him and kept him in honourable captivity.

John actively promoted missions in Asia, establishing bishoprics in Anatolia, Armenia, and India, and in Iran the archbishopric of Sultanieh, with six suffragan sees (1318), entrusting it to the Dominicans. He started the papal library at Avignon and founded a university at Cahors. Whereas he condemned in Mar. 1329 twenty-eight sentences of Meister Eckhart (*c.* 1260–1327), the great German mystic, his own last years were clouded by renewed charges of heresy, provoked by four sermons he delivered in winter 1331–2. While traditional doctrine held that the souls of the saints are in paradise already enjoying the full vision of God, John taught that this would be delayed for them until after the final judgement; until then they would contemplate only the humanity of Christ. These views, put forward as personal opinions, were sharply condemned by the university of Paris in 1333 and by the majority of theologians he consulted. His enemies, especially William of Occam, exploited the scandal to the full, and Louis IV the Bavarian intrigued with Cardinal Napoleone Orsini for his condemnation and deposition by a general council. John fell ill, and on his deathbed, in the presence of the cardinals, made a modified retraction, confessing that the souls of the blessed see the divine essence face to face *as clearly as their condition allows*.

An able if impetuous ruler of the church, astute at reading men's characters and aims, John consolidated French influence in the college of cardinals, all his creations with the exception of one Spaniard and four Romans being Frenchmen. Personally extremely frugal and simple in life-style, he accumulated a considerable fortune, although contemporary gossip grossly exaggerated it. His worst fault was the unbounded nepotism with which he showered money and material gifts on his relatives and Gascon compatriots and promoted them by preference when offices, often the highest in the church, had to be filled.

G. Mollat (ed.), *Lettres communes de Jean XXII* (Paris, 1904–47); A. Coulon and S. Clémencet, *Lettres secrètes et curiales du pape Jean XXII* (Paris, 1900–65); Baluze-Mollat 1, 107–94; G. Mollat, *The Popes at Avignon* (ET, London, 1963); N. Valois, 'Jacques Duèse, pape sous le nom de Jean XXII', *Hist. litt. de la France* 34 (1915), 391–630; H. Otto, 'Zur Italienischen Politik Johanns XXII', *QFIAB* 14 (1911), 140–265; D. L. Douie, 'John XXII and the Beatific Vision', *Dominican Studies* 3 (1950), 154–74; *CE* 8, 431–4 (J. P. Kirsch); *DTC* 8, 633–41 (G. Mollat); *NCE* 7, 1014 f. (D. L. Douie); *EB* (15th edn.) 10, 233 f. (J. Cogley); Seppelt 4, 89–121; 124–7; 132–4; and see index.

NICHOLAS (V) (antipope 12 May 1328– 25 July 1330: d. 16 Oct. 1333). Originally Pietro Rainalducci, he was born in humble circumstances at Corvaro, in the Abruzzi, in the third quarter of the 13th cent. After five years of marriage he left his wife Giovanna Mattei, joined the Franciscans in 1310, and for several years lived at their house at Sta Maria in Aracoeli, Rome. Represented by some contemporaries as a saintly ascetic, by others as a hypocrite of doubtful reputation, he seems to have been a harmless person of little importance. When Emperor Louis IV the Bavarian (1314–47) purported to depose JOHN XXII, pope at Avignon, on 18 Apr. 1328, he had Pietro elected in his place by a committee of thirteen chosen from the

Roman clergy on 12 May. Taking the style Nicholas V, he was crowned by Louis on 15 May, and on 22 May named six cardinals and then set about forming a curia. In all he created nine cardinals and about a score of bishops, picked in the main from Augustinian friars and Franciscans who were upset by John XXII's policies. The schism spread from Rome to Milan, wherever the German party was in the ascendant, and owed much to the fierce propaganda of malcontent religious belonging to the two orders. William of Occam (c.1285–1347), a relentless critic of John XXII, and Michael of Cesena (c.1270– 1342), the Franciscan general he had deposed, backed Nicholas enthusiastically; while Sicily, weary of the papal interdict which had long rested on it, came over to his obedience, receiving from him a new archbishop of Monreale (18 May 1328) in the person of Jacopo Alberti, one of his cardinals.

When Louis left Rome on 4 Aug. 1328, pursued by the jeers and hisses of the crowd, he took his 'idol' (as contemporaries mockingly called Nicholas) with him. The antipope's influence, confined as it was to parts of Italy, was rapidly waning, but he spent some months moving about the papal states, finding time to pillage the church of S. Fortunato, Todi, of all its treasures. On 2 or 3 Jan. 1329 he rejoined the emperor at Pisa, and was accorded a sumptuous welcome. Michael of Cesena, William of Occam, and other leaders of the disaffected Franciscans were in the city, and fortified by their support Nicholas presided on 19 Feb. at a bizarre ceremony in the cathedral at which a straw puppet representing John XXII and dressed in pontifical robes was formally condemned, degraded, and handed over to the secular arm. But when the defection of Azzone Visconti forced Louis to move to north Italy on 11 Apr., Nicholas did not this time accompany him. According to his own account, he had decided to break with his protector, and since Michael of Cesena, William of Occam, and all his cardinals save one now abandoned him, this is probably correct. He found temporary refuge with Count Bonifacio of Doronatico, who hid him for three months in his castle of Burgaro. Alarmed by the approach of a Florentine army, the count then took him back secretly to Pisa. Alerted of his presence there, John XXII, who had excommunicated him, requested (10 May) the count to hand him over. Negotiations were opened, and the pope undertook to spare his life and grant him pardon and a pension of 3,000 florins. Nicholas humbly accepted, on 25 July renounced his office before the archbishop of Pisa and the bishop of Lucca, set sail on 4 Aug., and on 6 Aug. landed at Nice. Arriving at Avignon on 24 Aug., he appeared, once more Pietro of Corvaro, next morning in the papal consistory clad in a Franciscan habit, with a halter round his neck. After he had repeated his abjuration at great length and avowed himself a 'schismatic pope', John pardoned him and treated him as leniently as he had promised. For the three remaining years of his life he was detained in honourable confinement in the papal residence. He died on 16 Oct. 1333 and was interred in the church of the Franciscans, Avignon.

Baluze-Mollat 1, 143–51; 2, 196–210; 3, 433–50; K. Eubel, 'Der Registerband des Gegenpapstes Nikolaus V', *Archiv. Zeitschrift* NS 4 (1893), 123–212; A. Mercati, 'Supplementi al registro dell'antipapa Nicolò V', *ST* 134 (1947), 59–76; K. Eubel, 'Der Gegenpapst Nikolaus V und seine Hierarchie', *HJ* 12 (1891), 277–308; G. Mollat, *The Popes at Avignon* (ET, London, 1963); *EC* 10, 505 f. (A. Pietro Frutaz).

BENEDICT XII (20 Dec. 1334–25 Apr. 1342). Born *c.* 1280–5 of humble parentage at Saverdun, near Toulouse, Jacques Fournier joined the Cistercian house at Boulbonne, Haute-Garonne, as a lad, studied at Paris and graduated as master of theology, and in 1311 succeeded his uncle as abbot of Fontfroide, near Narbonne. As bishop of Pamiers (1317) and then Mirepoix (1326), he proved an indefatigable inquisitor, skilful at extracting confessions from suspected heretics but sending only a handful to the stake. JOHN XXII,

who placed entire confidence in him, twice congratulated him on extirpating heresy from his dioceses, and in Dec. 1327 promoted him cardinal priest of Sta Prisca. A deeply learned theologian, he not only advised John on doctrinal issues but wrote several tracts to refute current errors. There is a story that on John's death the most obvious candidate, Cardinal John de Comminges, was passed over because he refused to promise not to restore the holy see to Rome. Accurate or not, it throws light on what was evidently a burning issue facing the conclave. Its speedy choice of Jacques, who as Benedict XII became the third of the Avignon popes, is said to have caused surprise, not least to himself; it may have been that the cardinals felt the need of a theological specialist after an amateur like John XXII.

A contrast to his predecessor in appearance as in method, Benedict was tall, portly and loud-voiced, and more interested in the reform of abuses than in politics. Shortly after his coronation all clerical hangers-on at Avignon who had no sound reason for staying were sent back to their benefices, and he remained a stickler for clerical residence. He reorganized the various departments of the curia, and had a drastic review made of the gratuities expected by functionaries of every class. Petitions which had been granted had to be properly registered so as to exclude the possibility of illicit charges being made for them. The field of action of the Sacred Penitentiary, which issued indulgences and dispensations, was strictly defined (*In agro dominico*: 8 Apr. 1338); and the first recorded decisions of the tribunal known as the *Rota date from this reign. Benedict abruptly revoked the 'expectancies', i.e. the conferments of benefices in anticipation of vacancies, granted by his predecessors, and except in the case of cardinals and patriarchs forbade the system of holding benefices *in commendam*, under which the holder (who might be a layman) drew the revenues during a vacancy. He also discouraged pluralities, and insisted on such a careful scrutiny of candidates for positions that many were left vacant for long periods, giving rise to rumours that he was himself drawing their income. To curtail the greed of ecclesiastics he limited the fees for documents issued by his officials, and made episcopal and other visitations less burdensome by fixing the charges imposed. A monk himself, he made special efforts to bring the religious orders back to primitive standards of strictness. Vagabond monks who had left their houses were ordered to return, and mendicants were forbidden to join orders from which they might be appointed to benefices. New and severe constitutions were prescribed for the Cistercians, Franciscans, and Benedictines, regulating their temporal powers, providing for regular chapters and visitations of monasteries, and setting up houses of study and improved training for novices.

Well intentioned though they were, these measures were made largely ineffective by the brevity of his reign, the weakness of his successor and, in the case of his monastic legislation, the excessive minuteness and insufficient regard for the tradition and needs of the order with which they were drafted. The bull *Summi magistri* (20 June 1336), however, remained in force for the Benedictine order until the council of Trent (1545–63). In the theological field he lost no time in settling the controverted question of the degree of vision of God enjoyed by the blessed after death which had troubled John XXII's closing years. In *Benedictus deus* (29 Jan. 1336) he ruled that such souls have 'an intuitive, face-to-face vision of the divine essence'. He moved less confidently in the diplomatic domain, where his pacific intentions were often frustrated by French interests. His efforts to prevent the outbreak of the Hundred Years War (1337–1453) between France and England, and once it had started to halt hostilities, came to nothing; but the war destroyed any hopes he had of a crusade. His subservience to French policy was in fact even greater than John XXII's and caused resentment in England. In Italy he failed to continue John

XXII's military measures to assert the freedom and independence of the papacy; as a result the temporal authority of the church in Romagna, the March of Ancona, and even in Bologna until June 1340, practically ceased to exist. At the beginning of his reign prospects for a settlement with Emperor Louis IV the Bavarian (1314–47) seemed bright, and discussions were opened on conditions for raising the interdict imposed by John XXII. Louis was prepared to be accommodating, but when a reconciliation seemed near it was opposed by Philip VI of France (1328–50) and the king of Naples, to whom a *rapprochement* was anathema. Further opposition came from Germany itself, where opinion was alienated by the delaying tactics of the curia. As a result the first diet of Frankfurt promulgated in May 1338 the celebrated manifesto *Fidem Catholicam* proclaiming the doctrine that the imperial authority derives directly from God, not from the pope. Then in Aug. 1338 Louis himself at the second diet of Frankfurt published the imperial law *Licet iuris*, which declared that the imperial rank and power, which depend on God alone, lawfully belong to him who has been duly chosen by the electors; the confirmation or consent of the holy see is not required. Even Louis's *rapprochement* with France in 1341 did not bring a settlement with the pope nearer.

At his accession Benedict, pressed by envoys from Rome to restore the papacy to the city, seems to have seriously contemplated the prospect, envisaging a provisional installation at Bologna. As early as 1335 he started the restoration and re-roofing of St Peter's, and between 1335 and 1341 spent large sums on it and on the Lateran. Not only the French king, however, but the majority of the cardinals were against such a move; the anarchical situation in Italy and the papal state provided them with seemingly plausible arguments. He was thus led to take steps which fixed the curia even more firmly at Avignon. Thus at his only creation (18 Dec. 1338) he named five French cardinals and only one Italian.

Again, he arranged for the transport of the entire papal archives from Assisi to Avignon. Most momentous of all, in the first months of his reign he began the construction of a permanent palace there, planning it as an impregnable fortress as well as a residence for the pope and his court; the austere Palais Vieux is his work.

Just but legalistic and hard, an unimaginative reformer, Benedict drew much contemporary criticism to himself; Petrarch even described him as an unfit and drunken helmsman of the church. Most of these strictures, however, emanated from critics upset by his reforms, while Petrarch had a grudge against him because of his dependence on the French and his construction of the palace. In fact his life-style was unpretentious, and he normally wore his monk's habit. In an age when nepotism was unbridled he was completely innocent of it.

J. M. Vidal (ed.), *Benoît XII: Lettres communes* (Paris, 1902–11); *Benoît XII: Lettres closes et patentes interessant les pays autres que la France* (Paris, 1913–50); C. Daumet (ed.), *Lettres closes, patentes et curiales se rapportant à la France* (Paris, 1899–1920); Baluze-Mollat 1, 193–240; 576–80; 3, 483–7; J. M. Vidal, 'Notice sur les œuvres de Benoît XII', *RHE* 6 (1905), 557–65; 785–810; A. L. Tàutu, *Acta Benedicti PP.XII* (Rome, 1958); J. Duvernoy (ed.), *Le Registre de l'Inquisition de Jacques Fournier, évêque de Pamiers (1318–1325)* (Toulouse, 1965); B. Guillemain, *La Politique bénéficiale du pape Benoît XII* (Paris, 1952); *La Cour pontificale d'Avignon 1309–1376* (Paris, 1962); G. Mollat, *The Popes at Avignon* (ET, London, 1963); *DHGE* 8, 116–35 (L. Jadin); *NCE* 2, 275f. (G. Mollat); Seppelt 4, 119–34; *DBI* 8, 378–84 (B. Guillemain).

CLEMENT VI (7 May 1342–6 Dec. 1352). Born in 1291 at Maumont, Limousin, as Pierre, second son of the Guillaume Roger who bought the lordship of Rosier d'Egleton (Corrèze) in 1333, he was entered as a lad of ten at the Benedictine house of La Chaise-Dieu (Haute-Loire). After a thorough education at Paris, where he learned to love books, he was granted a doctorate in theology by JOHN XXII in May 1323, and became abbot of

Fécamp in 1326, bishop of Arras in 1328, archbishop of Sens in 1329, and finally archbishop of Rouen in 1330. He was already chancellor of France, having been helped in his career by his high repute as an orator and a diplomat, and stood well with both Philip VI of France (1328–50) and John XXII. He was entrusted with important missions by the government, was nominated in 1333 to preach the crusade then in preparation, and was created cardinal in Dec. 1338. Philip VI was so keen for him to succeed BENEDICT XII that he sent his son to Avignon to influence the election, but before he arrived the conclave had unanimously chosen Pierre. Weary of Benedict's austere and rigid rule, the cardinals were attracted by his easygoing, more accommodating character and his manners of a *grand seigneur*.

Fourth of the Avignon popes, Clement in Jan. 1343 received a Roman deputation which, having conferred on him the rank of senator, begged him to restore the papacy to Rome and, in view of the brevity of life, to reduce the interval between jubilee years celebrated there from one hundred years, fixed by BENEDICT VIII, to fifty. He granted the latter plea, and 1350 was duly observed as a jubilee, to the great economic benefit of the impoverished city; his bull announcing it (*Unigenitus*: 27 Jan. 1343) has importance as defining the 'treasury of merits', viz. of Christ and the saints, at the church's disposal as the basis of indulgences. But so far from promising the return of the curia to Rome, he took steps to ensure its continued stay at Avignon, purchasing the city and the county of Venaissin from Queen Joanna I of Naples (1343–82) in 1348, substantially enlarging the palace, and appointing mostly Frenchmen to the sacred college; he proved in fact a French pope even more than his Avignon predecessors. He actively concerned himself, however, with the political situation in Rome, at first supporting Cola di Rienzo (c.1313–54), the messianic tribune of the people who in May 1347 carried out a bloodless coup in the city, and then abandoning him. Visiting Avignon in

1343 on a mission to persuade him to settle in Rome, Cola had fascinated the pope by his denunciations of the misrule of the Roman nobles, but his proclamation as dictator in summer 1347 of a sovereign Roman people independent of pope and emperor alarmed the curia, and in Dec. Clement's legate declared him stripped of his offices and excommunicate. In Dec. 1351 Clement again confirmed a populist leader, Giovanni Cerroni, as senator and captain, but his rule proved equally short-lived.

Despite his diplomatic skill and personal friendship for the kings of both countries, Clement was unable to end the Hundred Years War (1337–1453) between England and France; he played a decisive role, however, in bringing about the truce of Malestroit in 1343. His sympathies lay with France, which he actively supported by loans and subsidies. In seeking to reassert papal authority in Italy he returned to the energetic policies of John XXII, but with inadequate resources and results. A campaign conducted by a papal army in Romagna in 1350–1 failed miserably, and he was forced to grant Bologna in fief for twelve years to his cunning adversary Giovanni Visconti, archbishop and lord of Milan. The league which he formed with Venice, Cyprus, and the Knights of St John against the Turks had slightly greater success, leading to the temporary occupation of Smyrna (Izmir) in Oct. 1344 and to a naval victory at Imbros (1347). He subsequently engaged in negotiations with the Armenians and with the Byzantine emperor John VI Cantacuzenus (c. 1292–1383) with a view to church union, but they proved fruitless.

Always a determined opponent of Emperor Louis IV the Bavarian (1314–47), Clement had the satisfaction of bringing to a conclusion the struggle between him and the papacy which had dragged on from John XXII's reign. He renewed John's anathemas in Aug. 1342, and in Apr. 1343, after some months of ineffectual negotiations, brought fresh charges against him and called on him to lay down the imperial office within three months. Louis was

prepared to make substantial submission, but Clement was now working for his deposition and the election of Charles, king of Bohemia (1346–78), in his place. On 13 Apr. 1346 he solemnly pronounced Louis excommunicate and deposed, and on 11 July Charles was elected king of the Germans by part of the electoral college at Rense. Charles had already sworn to Clement to respect the domains of the church and never to enter Italy without leave of the holy see or set foot in Rome except for the day of his coronation, and accepted other undertakings which caused him to be labelled 'the priests' king'. Louis refused to recognize his election, but before hostilities could get going was killed at a boar-hunt on 11 Oct. 1347. His death resulted in the general recognition of Charles, who was crowned at Bonn on 26 Nov.; it also obliged the philosopher–theologian William of Occam (c. 1285–1347) and the schismatical Franciscans whom he had protected to make their submission to the holy see.

Clement's luxurious court and gorgeous retinue were those of a secular prince, not a prince of the church. He delighted in banquets and colourful festivities; his predecessors, he declared, had not known how to live as popes. An open-handed patron of artists and scholars, he was instinctively generous and held that no petitioner should go away unsatisfied. He was also an unblushing nepotist who lavished offices and gifts on relatives and countrymen. The enormous expenditure incurred not only by these indulgences but by huge loans to France, the purchase of Avignon (80,000 gold florins) and construction of the sumptuous Palais Neuf, and the campaigns in Italy and against the Turks, rapidly exhausted the vast funds which John XXII and Benedict XII had accumulated. Fresh taxes had to be imposed, and he steadily increased the number of appointments to sees and benefices reserved to himself. This provoked resistance, especially in Germany and England; in the latter the First Statute of Provisors (1351) and that of Praemunire (1353) were enacted to outlaw papal presentations to benefices and appeals to the Roman courts. The charges brought by contemporaries against his sexual life cannot be explained away, but he was personally devout, a protector of the poor and needy who showed charity and courage when the Black Death appeared at Avignon in 1348–9, and defended the Jews when they were blamed for it. He died after a short illness and was buried at La Chaise-Dieu; his grave was desecrated and his remains burned by Huguenots in 1562.

E. Déprez and others (eds.), *Clément VI (1342–52): Lettres closes, patentes et curiales se rapportant à la France* (Paris, 1901–59); E. Déprez–G. Mollat (eds.), *Clément VI (1342–52): Lettres closes, patentes et curiales interessant les pays autres que la France* (Paris, 1960–1); Baluze-Mollat 1, 241–308; 2, 335–433; A. Pélissier, *Clément VI le magnifique* (Paris, 1951); P. Fournier, 'Pierre Roger (Clément VI)', *Hist. litt. de la France* 37 (1938), 209–38; P. Schmitz, 'Les Sermons et discours de Clément VI O.S.B.', *RBén* 41 (1929), 15–34; G. Mollat, 'Le Saint-Siège et la France sous le pontificat de Clément VI (1342–1352)', *RHE* 55 (1960), 5–24; *The Popes at Avignon* (ET, London, 1963); Y. Renouard, *The Avignon Papacy 1305-1403* (ET, London, 1970), esp. 42–9; *DHGE* 12, 1129–62 (G. Mollat); *DBI* 26, 215–22 (B. Guillemain).

INNOCENT VI (18 Dec. 1352–12 Sept. 1362). Although it only lasted two days, the conclave at Avignon following CLEMENT VI's death made a determined attempt to restrict the pope's autocracy and augment the influence of the sacred college. All twenty-five cardinals present swore, several with reservations, that the pope should not create cardinals until the total fell below sixteen, that there should not be more than twenty, and that the choice of new cardinals should require the consent of at least two-thirds of the existing ones. Such consent should also be necessary for proceedings against a cardinal or for the alienation of any part of the papal state; half the revenues of the holy see, as allotted by NICHOLAS IV in 1289, should be guaranteed to the college. These and other provisions having been agreed, the conclave, anxious to preclude

interference by the French king, speedily elected Étienne Aubert, a Limousin born in 1282 at Monts, near Pompadour, a distinguished jurist who had been professor of law at Toulouse and later chief judge of the city. After taking orders, he rose to become bishop of Noyon (1338) and then of Clermont (1340). His fellow-countryman Clement VI named him cardinal priest in 1342, cardinal bishop of Ostia in 1352, and appointed him grand penitentiary and administrator of the see of Avignon in the absence of a bishop.

Fifth of the Avignon popes, Innocent was prematurely old, shaky in health and sometimes indecisive, but showed his independence by soon (6 July 1353) declaring the compact or capitulation agreed by the conclave, to which he himself had assented subject to its being lawful, null as violating the rule restricting business during a conclave to the election and as infringing the plenitude of power inherent in the papal office. Meanwhile, reviving the spirit of BENEDICT XII, he set about reforming the curia and eradicating abuses. The papal household was reduced and its life-style simplified (changes which in any case his parlous finances made necessary); clergy were obliged to reside in their benefices and pluralities were discouraged; aspirants to offices had to produce evidence of their fitness; to ensure impartiality the auditors, i.e. judges, of the *Rota were assigned fixed stipends. His reforming zeal embraced the orders too: he gave strong support to the grand master of the Dominicans in restoring discipline, and took severe measures with the Knights of St John. He was particularly harsh on the *Spiritual Franciscans, and on his orders the Inquisition sent several of them to prison or the stake. Because of his sternness the saintly Bridget of Sweden (d. 1373), who was then in Rome and had hailed his election with enthusiasm, turned against him and denounced him as a persecutor of Christ's sheep. Nevertheless, while listening in consistory in 1357 to the attacks of Archbishop FitzRalph of Armagh (1347–60) on the privileges of the mendicants, he refrained from publicly endorsing them.

Envisaging as he did the return of the papacy to Rome, Innocent was constantly preoccupied with the pacification of the papal state, dominated by petty tyrants, and its restoration to allegiance to the holy see. He was able to achieve this through the brilliant campaigns of the Spanish cardinal Gil de Albornoz (c. 1295–1367), who as his legate in Italy subdued most of the territories by mid-1357 and modernized their administration. Taken in by the intrigues of the Visconti of Milan, to whom Albornoz would not cede Bologna, Innocent weakly replaced him in 1357, but had to reappoint him in Sept. 1358, when he recovered Bologna for the holy see. In response to appeals from Rome Innocent also decided to use Cola di Rienzo (c. 1313–54), the visionary populist tribune whom Clement VI had excommunicated but who had recently been acquitted after trial at Avignon, to assist Albornoz in re-establishing papal authority in Rome itself; he hoped that he would win over the masses and lead the opposition to the nobles. He therefore released Cola, who on 1 Aug. 1354 entered Rome in triumph with the title of senator which the pope had granted him. But the move proved a failure; Cola's reinstatement was brief, and he died ingloriously in a riot on 8 Oct. 1354. With Charles IV of Bohemia (1346–78), who had been elected king of the Romans in 1346, Innocent's relations were friendly. With his consent, as stipulated in undertakings made to Clement VI, the king crossed the Alps in autumn 1354, was crowned king of Lombardy on 6 Jan. 1355, and on Easter Sunday (5 Apr.) received the imperial crown, by the pope's mandate, from the cardinal bishop of Ostia at Rome. Again as laid down in his undertakings to Clement VI, Charles left Rome for Germany that very evening. His hasty visit caused mocking comment, but the following year, after consultations at the diets of Nürnberg and Metz, he published the so-called Golden Bull, which regulated definitively the election of German kings

but made no mention of the pope's right to approve the man elected and by implication excluded his right to act as vicar of the realms during a vacancy. It is significant that Innocent raised no objection to it, and did not allow it to alter his warm relations with Charles.

In other fields Innocent met with repeated disappointments. Negotiations at Avignon in 1354 between English and French plenipotentiaries failed to prevent the resumption of the Hundred Years War in 1355; and when King John II of France (1350–64) was captured by the Black Prince at Poitiers in Sept. 1356, he was unable to prevail upon Charles IV, to whom France's weakness offered advantages, to use his influence to secure his release. He at least had the satisfaction of arranging the treaty of Brétigny (1360), which halted the conflict for a decade. Time and again, but always in vain, he imposed ecclesiastical penalties on Peter I of Castile (1350–69), who repudiated his wife, while the efforts of the curia to mediate peace between Castile and Aragón proved equally fruitless. Nothing came of his plans for a crusade or of his negotiations for reunion with the Greeks, which he made conditional on total subjection to the papacy. He also had financial worries, for the wars in Italy consumed vast sums, and by Nov. 1358 he was reduced to selling papal treasures. On top of everything Avignon was becoming a dangerous city, exposed to plundering raids by companies of mercenary troops set free from the wars by the truces of Bordeaux and, still more, Brétigny (1357 and 1360). For protection strong walls and extensive fortifications were constructed from 1357, but even so one of the so-called free companies seized Pont-Saint-Esprit in late Dec. 1360, cutting the communications of Avignon with the outside world, and Innocent had to buy the marauders off. When he died two years later, he had had his fill of anxieties and blighted hopes, and had been disappointed in his frequently expressed wish to return to Rome.

A. L. Tàutu (ed.), *Acta Innocentii PP.VI* (Rome, 1961); E. Déprez (ed.), *Innocent VI: Lettres closes, patentes et curiales se rapportant à la France* (Paris, 1909); P. Gasnault and others (eds.), *Innocent VI: Lettres secrètes et curiales* (Paris, 1959–76); *LP* 2, 492 f.; Baluze-Mollat, 1, 309–48; 2, 433–91; W. Scheffler, *Karl IV und Innocenz VI 1355–60* (Berlin, 1911); A. Pélissier, *Innocent VI le réformateur* (Tulle, 1961); G. Mollat, *The Popes at Avignon* (ET, London, 1963), 44–51; 119–42; 152–4; B. Guillemain, *La Cour pontificale d'Avignon (1309–1376)* (Paris, 1962), esp. 140 f.; Y. Renouard, *The Avignon Papacy* (ET, London, 1970), esp. 49–53; *DTC* 7, 1997–2001 (G. Mollat); *LThK* 5, 690 f. (G. Schwaiger); *NCE* 7, 525 f. (W. R. Bonniwell); Seppelt 4, 147–57.

URBAN V, BL. (28 Sept. 1362–19 Dec. 1370). The sixth of the Avignon popes and the first to restore the curia to Rome, Guillaume de Grimoard was born of noble parentage at the castle of Grisac (Lozère) in 1310. After studying at Montpellier and Toulouse, he made his profession as a Benedictine at St Victor, Marseilles, and, having obtained his doctorate in 1342, lectured in canon law at Montpellier and Avignon. After serving as vicar-general at Clermont and at Uzès, he became abbot of St Germain, Auxerre, in 1352, then of St Victor, Marseilles, in 1362. In 1352, 1354, 1360, and 1362 he acquired a thorough knowledge of political issues as papal legate in Italy. After INNOCENT VI's death the cardinals' first choice of a successor, a brother of CLEMENT VI, declined office, and as they could not agree on one of themselves they unanimously elected Guillaume, then on a mission to Naples. Landing at Marseilles on 27 Oct., he was enthroned and crowned at Avignon, characteristically without the customary pomp, on 31 Oct. and 6 Nov.

Austere, deeply religious, unworldly, Urban as pope lived as a Benedictine, retaining his black habit and giving time to prayer and study as well as administration. Never a cardinal, he was often insecure *vis-à-vis* the college or powerful magnates. He continued Innocent VI's reforms, reducing the luxury of his court, curbing the greed of officials, checking pluralism. He halved the rate of tithes, encouraged the holding of provincial councils, but extended the Avignon popes' centralizing policies, in 1363 reserving the filling of all patriarchal and episcopal sees and of major monasteries to the holy see. A scholar himself, he supported hundreds of poor students with bursaries, endowed colleges at Montpellier, reformed the statutes of several universities, and founded new ones at Orange, Kraków, and Vienna. All this, with his patronage of the arts and a generous building programme, won him plaudits but exhausted his treasury.

Urban's wider policies were slanted towards the east, with reunion with the Byzantine church as a prime aim. Stirred by Pierre de Lusignan, king of Cyprus (1359–69), fresh from successes against the Turks in Cilicia, he proclaimed a new crusade against them in Apr. 1363, placing King John II of France (1350–64) at its head. In the event it had meagre success: Urban failed to muster the wide support necessary, John died in 1364, and although Pierre captured Alexandria in Oct. 1365 he could not hold it. Again, Urban made a humiliating peace in Feb. 1364 with Bernabò Visconti of Milan (1323–85), the church's aggressive enemy in north Italy, against whom his legate Cardinal Gil de Albornoz (*c.* 1295–1367) was conducting a successful campaign and whom he had initially placed under a ban. What caused this switch of tactics, which entailed paying vast sums to Bernabò for evacuating Bologna, was his conviction that peace was necessary for his crusade, and his naïve belief that the mercenary companies thus set free, instead of ravaging the countryside, could be mobilized against the Turks.

As early as 23 May 1363 Urban had informed the Romans of his sincere desire to transfer his court to Rome once certain grave obstacles were out of the way. One such obstacle, Bernabò Visconti, was, for the moment, removed by the peace of Feb. 1364; and Albornoz's brilliant campaigns had reduced the papal state to obedience. Other obstacles, however, remained, not least the ruinous condition of Rome, where the Vatican was uninhabitable. It had become increasingly clear to Urban that only with Rome as his base could he realize his great objectives—the destruction of the marauding companies of mercenaries against whom he vainly tried to organize a league, his cherished crusade, and reunion with the eastern church. This last point weighed heavily with him, for only at old Rome could the pope negotiate appropriately with new Rome. Emperor Charles IV (1355–78), who had a lively interest in detaching the papacy from French influence, visited Avignon in May 1366, added his powerful persuasions, and offered to be his escort. At last, showing real courage and resisting the violent objections of the French cardinals as well as the reasoned pleas of the French court, he took the decision and on 30 Apr. 1367 left Avignon with the reluctant curia. Landing at Corneto (now Tarquinia), in the papal state, on 3 June, he was received by Cardinal Albornoz, whose military and administrative achievements had alone made the return possible. After a short but disturbed stay at Viterbo, he entered Rome with a strong military escort on 16 Oct. and, as the Lateran was uninhabitable, took up residence in the Vatican, the restoration of which he had ordered when still at Avignon. Here he stayed for almost three years, moving during the summer heats to Viterbo and Montefiascone.

Urban had left a large administrative bureaucracy at Avignon, and this continued to manage the financial affairs of the church. In Rome he busied himself with the repair and decoration of dilapidated churches and other buildings; in particular, he began the complete rebuilding of St John Lateran, which had been burnt down in 1360. He also took steps to reform the civic administration. But when he created eight cardinals in Sept. 1368, his choice of six Frenchmen and only one Roman showed that his heart was still in France. The two great events of his stay were the arrival of Emperor Charles IV in Oct. 1368 and of the

Byzantine emperor, John V Palaeologus (1354–91), in June 1369. During Charles's visit Urban crowned his queen as empress, and held long discussions with him about affairs in north and central Italy. Emperor John's object, the result of negotiations going back to 1364, was to recruit western aid against the Turkish threat to Constantinople, and to obtain this he was prepared to submit personally to the holy see. This he solemnly did, abjuring the Orthodox faith before the pope on the steps of St Peter's and becoming a Latin Catholic. No Byzantine clergy, however, were present, and no reunion of the churches was accomplished. The eastern church leaders wanted an ecumenical council, but Urban set his face against the suggestion, preferring to organize a Latin church within the Greek empire and to dispatch friars to the east as missionaries.

Even before 1370 a disillusioned Urban was beginning to think of returning to Avignon. He was subject to constant pressure from the French cardinals to do so, and the situation in Italy was increasingly disquieting. Perugia revolted, and had to be placed under an interdict; in spring 1370 the Romans joined forces with it, and Urban had to seek refuge in Viterbo and then Montefiascone. Mercenaries hired by Bernabò Visconti were again threatening the frontiers of the patrimony. A further motive was supplied by the flaring up again of the Hundred Years War in 1369; peace between England and France was essential for his crusade, and he could negotiate this more effectively at Avignon. By now he was convinced that the Holy Spirit, which had guided him to Rome, was beckoning him back. Turning a deaf ear to the appeals of the Romans, the pleadings of Petrarch, and the dire warnings of the saintly Bridget of Sweden (c. 1303–73), who prophesied his early death, he left Montefiascone on 26 Aug., embarked at Corneto on 5 Sept., and reached Marseilles on 16 Sept. He made his state entry into Avignon on 27 Sept. He fell gravely ill, however, in Nov. and died on 19 Dec. Interred in the cathedral at Avignon, his remains were transferred by his brother Cardinal Anglico to the abbey of St Victor, Marseilles, on 5 June 1372. His tomb soon became the centre of a cult, but it was only in 1870 that he was beatified by PIUS IX. Feast 19 Dec.

A. Fierens and C. Tihon (eds.), *Lettres d'Urbain V (1362–1370)* (Rome, 1928–32); P. Lecacheux and G. Mollat (eds.), *Lettres secrètes et curiales du pape Urbain V (1362–70) se rapportant à la France* (Paris, 1902–55); M. H. Laurent (ed.), *Urbain V: Lettres communes* (Paris, 1954–8); M. Dubruelle (ed.), *Les Registres d'Urbain V* (Paris, 1928); A. L. Tàutu (ed.), *Acta Urbani PP. V (1362–70)* (Rome, 1964); T. Leccisotti, *Documenti Vaticani di Urbano V* (Monte Cassino, 1952); Baluze-Mollat, 349–414; E. de Lanouvel, *Urbain V* (Paris, 1929); J. P. Kirsch, *Die Rückkehr der Päpste Urban V und Gregor XI von Avignon nach Rom* (Paderborn, 1898); G. Mollat, *The Popes at Avignon* (ET, London, 1963), esp. 52–60; 143–6; 154–61; 315–18; Y. Renouard, *The Avignon Papacy* (ET, London, 1970), esp. 55–63; W. P. de Vries, 'Die Päpste von Avignon und der christliche Osten', *OChP* 30 (1964), 85–128; *DTC* 15, 2295–302 (G. Mollat); *EC* 12, 908 f. (G. Tabacco); Seppelt 4, 157–64.

GREGORY XI (30 Dec. 1370–27 Mar. 1378). The seventeen cardinals meeting at Avignon to choose URBAN V's successor took only two days to agree unanimously on Cardinal Pierre Roger de Beaufort. Forty-two years old, he was born in 1329 at the château of Maumont, near Limoges, son of Guillaume de Beaufort and Marie du Chambon. Canon of Rodez and of Paris when only eleven, at nineteen his uncle CLEMENT VI named him cardinal deacon and then sent him to Perugia university, where he received a thorough training in law under Pietro Baldo degli Ubaldi. Respected for his learning and knowledge of Italian politics, he soon became prominent in the sacred college; while at Rome (1367–70) Urban V entrusted him with important responsibilities. Last of the authentic Avignon popes, he suffered from poor health, was deeply religious with a strongly mystical bent, and combined a sensitive and modest bearing with a determination which could be relentless.

Gregory often declared his conviction that the proper seat for the pope was Rome. Only there could he exercise authority over the papal state, recently pacified and reorganized by Cardinal Gil de Albornoz (*c.*1295–1367). He also cherished hopes of a crusade and of reunion with the eastern church, and for both Rome was the appropriate centre. But if he made his intention to move there clear from the start, several years elapsed before he was able to do so. First, his treasury was empty, and pending the arrival of subsidies requested from the episcopate he was reduced to borrowing. Secondly, peace between England and France in the Hundred Years War, an essential pre-condition of a crusade, could be more effectively negotiated from Avignon. So legates passed to and fro and conferences which came to nothing were repeatedly held in the early 1370s. Thirdly, the dangerous situation in north Italy, where the expansionist policies of the Visconti of Milan threatened Romagna and Piedmont, had to be cleared up. Resolved to settle accounts once for all, Gregory formed a league against the Visconti in Aug. 1371, a new legate was sent to Lombardy, and Amadeus VI of Savoy (1343–83) took command of the papal troops; an interdict was laid on the Visconti in early 1373 and then a crusade preached against them. By spring 1375 preparations were under way for Gregory to set out for Italy to complete their destruction, but nothing came of them: in June the curia, weakened by the defection of allies and its exhausted finances, had to make peace with Milan. At this point the kings of England and France, and also Louis I, duke of Anjou (1360–84), and Peter IV of Aragón (1336–87), had recourse to Gregory for his arbitration. Once again, therefore, departure for Italy was put off until spring 1376.

News of this further postponement caused discontent in Rome and Italy generally, and this was cleverly exploited by Florence, usually an ally of the holy see but exasperated by its withholding of food supplies from Romagna during the dearth of

1374–5. She was able to rouse virtually the entire papal state to revolt, and in a few months Bologna itself joined in. Gregory replied by laying an interdict on Florence, her allies, and the rebel cities, paralysing her banking and commercial life, and dispatching to Italy a powerful army of mercenaries commanded by Cardinal Robert of Geneva (later Antipope CLEMENT VII), which swiftly reconquered the papal state. Finally, resisting the pathetic appeals of his relations, the cardinals, and the French court, but confirmed in his resolve by the saintly Catherine of Siena (1347–80), who from mid-June spent three months at Avignon, he himself left the city for good on 13 Sept. 1376. Although the fleet conveying him left Marseilles on 2 Oct. 1376, its voyage was so stormy that it did not reach Corneto (now Tarquinia), in the papal state, until 6 Dec., and it was only on 17 Jan. 1377 that he made his solemn entry into Rome and took up residence in the Vatican.

Although affairs in Italy claimed most of his attention, Gregory devoted time and thought to the reform of the religious orders. Thus he supported the grand master of the Knights of St John in getting rid of laxity and restoring discipline, and in 1373 he carried through important constitutional changes for the Dominicans, including the institution of a cardinal protector. He was particularly active in repressing heresy in Provence, Germany, and Spain; in France he used the Inquisition ruthlessly, and called on the help of King Charles V (1364–80) so effectively that the prisons were soon too full to receive those who escaped the stake. On 22 May 1377 he addressed five bulls to Edward III of England (1327–77), the archbishop of Canterbury and the bishop of London, and the university of Oxford, condemning nineteen propositions from the reformer John Wycliffe's (c. 1330–84) earlier writings, calling for his teaching to be investigated, and threatening the university if it did not act more promptly to stamp on error. Although his plans for helping eastern Christians against the Turks by a crusade proved fruitless, he came to the

rescue of the Dominican missions in the east which had been decimated by pestilence. His relations with the Holy Roman empire were friendly, but the holy see had to accept a diplomatic setback when Emperor Charles IV (1355–78) had his fifteen-year-old son Wenceslas elected and crowned king of the Romans in June–July 1376 without consulting it, and only subsequently, in a letter fictitiously dated before the election, went through the motions of seeking the pope's approval.

Gregory's stay in Italy was disillusioning, and also unexpectedly short. Peace negotiations started by Florence broke down because of the severe terms on which he insisted. The atmosphere worsened because of the appalling blood-bath which his legate Robert of Geneva ordered at Cesena in Feb. 1377, and hostility at Rome became so marked that he retired to Anagni. The return of Bologna to its allegiance and the defection of the Florentine commander-in-chief provided some consolation, but the struggle between him and Florence still dragged on; Catherine of Siena bitterly blamed him for his intransigence. But both sides were weary, and a peace conference under the chairmanship of Bernabò Visconti (1323–85) met at Sarzana in Mar. 1378. But Gregory was dead before it completed its work, exhausted by his labours and filled with gloomy forebodings of the dissensions and possible schism which he could discern ahead. Last of the French popes, who so loved France that the cardinals he created were almost exclusively Frenchmen, but who brought the papacy back to Rome, he was buried in Sta Francesca Romana in the Forum.

L. Mirot and others (eds.), *Lettres secrètes et curiales relatives à la France* (Paris, 1935–57); G. Mollat (ed.), *Lettres secrètes et curiales interessant les pays autres que la France* (Paris, 1962–5); C. Tihon (ed.), *Lettres de Grégoire XI* (Brussels, 1953–62); A. L. Tàutu (ed.), *Acta Gregorii XI* (Rome, 1966); Baluze-Mollat 1, 415–67; A. Pélissier, *Grégoire XI ramène la papauté à Rome* (Tulle, 1962); J. P. Kirsch, *Die Rückkehr der Päpste Urban V und Gregor XI von Avignon nach Rom* (Paderborn,

1898); G. Mollat, *The Popes at Avignon* (ET, London, 1963), esp. 59–63; 161–73; Y. Renouard, *The Avignon Papacy* (ET, London, 1970), esp. 61–6; *NEC* 6, 778 (E. R. Labande); Seppelt 4, 164–71.

URBAN VI (8 Apr. 1378–15 Oct. 1389). The conclave in the Vatican following GREGORY XI's death (the first to meet in Rome since 1303) was held amid scenes of unprecedented uproar. Dreading the election of a Frenchman and the return of the papacy to Avignon, excited crowds demonstrated in the streets and even invaded the palace, clamouring for 'a Roman, at any rate an Italian', as pope. The heads of the city regions called in the evening to warn the sixteen cardinals (Gregory had left six at Avignon) of the danger of disappointing the popular will. Next morning rioting broke out afresh, and at a panic-stricken session all but one cast their votes for Bartolomeo Prignano, archbishop of Bari. Before his consent could be obtained the mob burst in, but the terrified cardinals placated it by an injudicious piece of play-acting, pretending that an elderly Roman cardinal had been elected, and then dispersed. Next day, however, twelve returned and confirmed the election of Bartolomeo. Close on sixty, he had been born at Naples c.1318, was an expert in canon law, had been archbishop of Acerenza (1363) and then of Bari (1377), for twenty years was a leading figure in the curia at Avignon, and since Gregory XI's move to Rome in 1376 had been regent of the papal chancery. As an official and a prelate, he was admired for his austerity, efficiency, and scrupulous conscientiousness; what he had not so far revealed was his intransigent obstinacy, violent temper, and determination to assert his rights even beyond what was practicable.

The cardinals duly enthroned Bartolomeo as Urban VI on 18 Apr. (Easter), notified his accession to the cardinals still at Avignon, to Emperor Charles IV (1355–78), and to Christian sovereigns, and for some weeks tried to collaborate with him, apparently having no reservations about his election. From the very first, however, Urban subjected them to violent abuse and uncontrollable tirades. He planned reform, including a radical simplification of the cardinals' life-style and the freeing of the church from dependence on states, but he went about it with a humiliating truculence and a paranoid sense of his authority. Laymen like Otto of Brunswick, the envoys of Queen Joanna I of Naples (1343–82), and the duke of Fondi were no less blisteringly rebuffed. The suggestion that the curia should return to Avignon was met with a furious threat to create enough Italian cardinals to swamp the French majority. His unexpected elevation seems to have upset the balance of his mind, and the conviction grew that he was deranged and incapable. One by one the French cardinals withdrew to Anagni, there to debate the next move. The more radical wanted to seize his person, others hoped he would accept a system of coadjutors, but Urban rejected any accommodation. On 2 Aug., therefore, they published a declaration that the April election was invalid 'as having been made, not freely, but under fear' of mob violence, and invited him to abdicate. On 9 Aug. they informed the Christian world that he had been deposed as an intruder. Moving then to Fondi, where they were protected by Queen Joanna, they elected Cardinal Robert of Geneva as pope on 20 Sept. His coronation as CLEMENT VII on 31 Oct. inaugurated the Great Schism of the west (1378–1417).

Europe had now to decide between Urban and Clement, both of whom dispatched letters and embassies to sovereigns, universities, and cities claiming to be the true pope. While France after a short neutrality, with Burgundy, Savoy, Naples, and Scotland, adhered to Clement, England and Germany, with most of Italy and the countries of central Europe, declared for Urban; national interest was usually the determining factor. Urban also had a passionate advocate in the visionary Catherine of Siena (1347–80). Spain for a while stayed neutral. Meanwhile the two rivals, each excommunicating the other, faced each other in Italy with armed forces, but the victory of Urban's mercenaries near Marino in Apr. 1379 and his capture of Castel Sant'Angelo both secured him full control of Rome and forced Clement to retreat to Naples, and then to Avignon (June 1379). Urban had already organized a new curia, since his original one had gone over to Clement, by naming twenty-nine cardinals, wisely selected from different nationalities, on 17 Sept. 1378.

After this Urban had no direct contact with his rival; an expedition which Clement promoted to occupy part of the papal state ended disastrously in 1384. Never questioning his legitimacy, Urban showed little interest in solutions for the schism being canvassed in courts and universities; in 1386, for example, he repulsed the suggestion of a general council put forward by certain German princes. His main preoccupation was a petty, endlessly shifting struggle, punctuated by explosions indicative of his mental instability, over the kingdom of Naples, which he wished to secure for a worthless nephew. First, he excommunicated and deposed Queen Joanna (in 1380) for recognizing and helping Clement, and replaced her with her cousin Charles of Durazzo (1381–6), whom he crowned in Rome in 1381. He then quarrelled with Charles over his nephew's claims, and in 1384 began interfering in the affairs of the kingdom. Meanwhile Charles, in concert with certain cardinals, plotted to place him, because of incapacity, under a council of regency. Hearing of this, the outraged pontiff imprisoned and brutally tortured six cardinals, while Charles replied by besieging him at Nocera. Urban escaped and fled to Genoa, where five of the cardinals mysteriously disappeared. On Charles's death in Hungary (Feb. 1386) he refused to be reconciled with his widow, moved to Lucca (Dec. 1386), and then to Pisa (Oct. 1387) where he recruited soldiers for a campaign against Naples, now in the hands of the Clementines, but lack of money prevented him from carrying this through.

In Oct. 1388, having fallen out with his mercenaries, he went back to Rome, where his refractory temperament alienated the population. He died there a year later, perhaps as the result of poisoning. He had been deserted by several of his cardinals and left the papal state in anarchy, his treasury empty, and his own reputation at its lowest ebb. He carried out few, if any, memorable ecclesiastical acts beyond the decision to observe every thirty-third year (the life span of the Saviour) as a holy year, and the extension of the feast of the Visitation of the Blessed Virgin, hitherto observed by the Franciscans, to the entire church. His tomb remains in the crypt of St Peter's.

K. Krofta (ed.), *Acta Urbani VI* (Prague, 1903); H. V. Sauerland, 'Aktenstücke zur Geschichte des Papstes Urban VI', *HJ* 14 (1893), 820–32; Dietrich of Niem, *De schismate* (ed. G. Erler, Leipzig, 1890); L. Macfarlane, 'An English Account of the Election of Urban VI, 1378', *BullInstHistRes* 26 (1953), 75–83; T. Lindner, 'Papst Urban VI', *ZKG* 3 (1879), 409–28; 534–46; M. Seidlmayer, *Die Anfänge des grossen abendländischen Schismas* (Münster, 1940); W. Ullmann, *The Origins of the Great Schism* (London, 1948); O. Přerovský, *L'elezione di Urbano VI e l'insorgere dello scismo d'Occidente* (Rome, 1960); *DTC* 15, 2302–5 (G. Mollat); *NCE* 14, 480 (G. Mollat); Seppelt 4, 188–206.

CLEMENT (VII) (antipope 20 Sept. 1378–16 Sept. 1394). Born at Geneva in 1342 as Robert, son of Count Amadeus III and Marie de Boulogne (a cousin of the French king), he was chancellor of Amiens and canon of Paris as a young man, became bishop of Thérouanne in 1361 and of Cambrai in 1368, and was created cardinal by GREGORY XI in May 1371. As Gregory's legate in Italy in command of an army of Breton mercenaries, he was responsible for frightful massacres in the war against Florence, especially at Cesena in Feb. 1377. In the tumultuous election following Gregory's death he gave his vote for URBAN VI, was the first to do homage to and seek favours from him, and on 14 Apr. 1378 wrote to Emperor Charles IV (1355–78) notifying him of the election. Nevertheless, towards the end of May, disgusted by the pope's insulting behaviour, he began organizing a revolt against him. When the French cardinals withdrew to Anagni and, convinced that Urban was deranged and incapable, declared his election void as having been carried through under threats of violence and then purported to depose him (2 and 9 Aug.), Robert was one of the leading spirits among them. On 20 Sept., meeting in the cathedral at Fondi (in the kingdom of Naples), they elected him pope at the first ballot; the fact that he was neither French nor Italian may have counted in his favour. The three Italian cardinals did not vote but concurred by their presence. His election, followed by his proclamation on 21 Sept. and his coronation on 31 Oct., inaugurated the Great Schism of the west (1378-1417), of which he was the first antipope.

At first fortune smiled on Clement, an accomplished politician. Virtually the entire curia went over to him, and he had powerful military support as well as the friendship of Queen Joanna of Naples (1343-82). But his troops were crushed by Urban's mercenaries at Marino in Apr. 1379. Since the Clementine garrison in Castel Sant'-Angelo had surrendered to Urban earlier in the month, he then retired to Naples but found that, while Queen Joanna supported him, the population was hostile, and on 22 May he left Italy for Avignon for good. Meanwhile the rival popes, as well as excommunicating each other, were endeavouring, by letters and embassies, to persuade the Christian world of their legitimacy. After a brief neutrality Charles V of France (1364-80) sided with Clement (Nov. 1379), as did Burgundy, Savoy, Naples, and France's ally Scotland. Clement also made strenuous efforts to secure recognition in the empire, but his success there was only sporadic. In general the empire and the German king Wenceslas (1378-1400) adhered to Urban, as did the eastern and nordic countries, Hungary, and England. But Castile and Aragón, after considerable delay, were induced to come out for Clement, as did Latin enclaves in the east like Cyprus and Morea.

At Avignon Clement quickly organized an administrative machine complete in every department, and established a court rivalling those of kings in brilliance and luxury. But the great object of his policy was to wrest Rome from his rival. As early as Apr. 1379 he had encouraged Louis I of Anjou (1360-84), son of the French king, with the offer of a kingdom of Adria to be carved out of the papal state, to take up arms on his behalf. An expedition to recover Naples from Charles of Durazzo (1381-6), to whom Urban had assigned it after deposing Joanna, was brilliantly started, but ground to a halt with Louis's death in Sept. 1384. After Charles's murder in Feb. 1386 it was victoriously resumed by Louis II of Anjou (1384-1417), who was acclaimed king by the people of Naples in July 1386. Strengthened by these and other successes in southern Italy, and by the influence he had acquired in Lombardy through the marriage of Louis of Touraine, future duke of Orléans, with a Visconti, Clement had just begun negotiations with Florence and Bologna when the death of Urban (15 Oct. 1389), now profoundly unpopular, robbed him of his trump card. He had already welcomed to his sacred college two Roman cardinals whom Urban's truculence and cruelty had disillusioned. A grave situation seemed to threaten Urban's successor, BONIFACE IX, when the new French king, Charles VI (1380-1422), flattered Clement with the prospect of personally conducting him to Rome (Mar. 1391), and France revived (1392-3) the project of a kingdom of Adria in fief to the pope. But nothing came of the former suggestion, and by this time Clement was too wary to encourage the latter, although he did offer to invest the duke of Orléans with extensive territories belonging to the holy see. In 1400 he sustained a serious blow when the young king Ladislas of Sicily (1386-1414) ousted Louis II of Anjou from Naples and restored the kingdom to the obedience of Boniface IX.

Throughout his reign Clement was plagued with crippling financial difficulties. Patronage, the extravagance of his court, the diplomatic missions he dispatched in every direction, and his campaigns in south Italy all cost money and drained his treasury. He was obliged to resort to constant borrowing and to impose heavy taxes, but was fortunate that one of the countries he could tax was France, the most prosperous and populous in the west. He was driven to demand subsidies even from religious institutions which had hitherto been exempted, and did not allow himself to be over-worried by the complaints of a desperately overtaxed clergy. Not the least expensive of his vexations were the marauding incursions of Raymond of Turenne, a nephew of Gregory XI who owned important properties in Provence, notably Les Baux, and whose mercenaries from 1386 to 1392 were in the habit of seizing castles and villages and harrying travellers, and had to be bought off with huge indemnities.

Politically adroit, Clement showed discernment in selecting his cardinals. One of his first was the sixteen-year-old Peter of Luxemburg (beatified in 1527), whom he named bishop of Metz and cardinal in 1384 and whose extraordinary asceticism and charity he astutely hoped would add lustre to his pontificate. He never doubted the validity either of his own election or of the deposition of his rival; indeed, at Urban's death he cherished the vain hope that the Roman conclave would solve its problem by recognizing him. Both then and in the years preceding his own death there was strong pressure on him to abdicate; public opinion in France, led by the university of Paris, was converging on the view that the only way to end the schism was 'the way of cession', i.e. the voluntary resignation of both popes. Clement, however, just like his rival, remained deaf to such suggestions; the most he was willing to do, to appease the widespread unease, was to order the celebration of a mass 'for the removal of the schism' (29 Oct. 1393), the recital of prayers, and the holding of processions. He

died of apoplexy on the morning of 16 Sept. 1394.

E. Göller (ed.), *Repertorium Germanicum* I: *Clemens VII von Avignon* (Berlin, 1916); Baluze-Mollat 1, 469–539; Dietrich of Niem, *De schismate* (ed. G. Erler, Leipzig, 1890); N. Valois, *La France et le grand schisme d'Occident* (Paris, 1896–1902); W. Ullmann, *The Origins of the Great Schism* (London, 1948); O. Přerovský, *L'elezione di Urbano VI* (Rome, 1960); Y. Renouard, *The Avignon Papacy* (ET, London, 1970), esp. 69–73; Seppelt 4, 198–209; *DHGE* 12, 1162–75 (G. Mollat); *NCE* 3, 932 (G. Mollat).

BONIFACE IX (2 Nov. 1389–1 Oct. 1404). As successor to URBAN VI the fourteen Roman cardinals elected, as a compromise choice, Pietro Tomacelli, who had been born *c.*1350 at Naples of aristocratic family. Little is known about his earlier career except that Urban VI, like him a Neapolitan, promoted him cardinal deacon of S. Giorgio in 1381, cardinal priest of Sta Anastasia in 1385. A complete contrast to his predecessor, he was deficient in education and experience of office, but made up for this by his outgoing personality, practical realism, skill in managing people, and persuasive eloquence. With him the Great Schism (1378–1417) continued; the cardinals had not seriously considered postponing an election in the interest of a compromise. Excommunicated by the Avignon pope CLEMENT VII, he promptly excommunicated him, denounced (1391) as sinful proposals to settle the schism by a general council, and soon had the satisfaction of welcoming back several cardinals who had gone over to Clement out of disillusionment with Urban.

An adroit and capable ruler, Boniface exerted himself to reassert papal authority in the confused Italian scene. He at once broke with Urban's nepotist policies for the kingdom of Naples, of which Clement VII had recently made Louis II of Anjou king (1384–1417), gave full backing to Ladislas (1386–1414), Charles of Durazzo's son, and after he had sworn fealty had him crowned king at Gaeta (29 May 1390). The struggle dragged on for a decade, but with

mercenaries and money supplied by Boniface Ladislas was able to defeat the
Clementine forces, enter Naples in July
1400, and restore the kingdom to obedience
to Rome. In north Italy Boniface extended
his influence through tactful mediation. In
the papal state, left by Urban in anarchy, he
gradually regained control of the chief
strongholds, militarily assisted by his two
brothers, whom he set over Spoleto and
Ancona respectively, and following a policy
of leaving power with the dominant local
families provided they did him homage and
paid tribute. With Rome his relations were
at first excellent, helped by the profitable
jubilee (decreed by Urban in Apr. 1389)
over which he presided in 1390, and with
the city's support he campaigned successfully against rebellious Viterbo in Mar.
1392. Relations rapidly worsened, however,
and that summer he had to move to Perugia
and then to Assisi. It was not long before he
was back on his own terms, for the Romans
feared that he would withdraw the papacy
from their city. In summer 1398 he took
advantage of the discovery of a plot against
him to make himself undisputed master of
Rome, abolishing its republican independence and entrusting the administration to
senators nominated by himself. The common people and even the bourgeoisie were
well content with his benevolent despotism,
a token of which was his reconstruction of
the ruined Castel Sant'Angelo and his forti-
fication of the Capitol.

Boniface took no serious steps to eliminate the schism. Convinced that as pope of
Rome he was the true pope, he worked hard
to retain the loyalty of Germany and England, the leading nations of his obedience,
and paid no attention to the proposals being
widely canvassed for ending the division.
To avoid suspicion of prolonging it, he
promised Clement VII in 1390 that, if he
abdicated, he would allow him and his cardinals to retain the purple and would nominate him as legate for France and Spain. In
1392 he made friendly overtures to Charles
VI of France (1380–1422), and in June
1393 undertook to convince him of the

validity of Urban VI's election; his adhesion,
he claimed, would certainly bring about that
of the antipope too. On Clement VII's death
he resisted attempts by the new antipope,
BENEDICT XIII, to open direct negotiations
with him, and had nothing to fear from him
during the period (1398–1403) in which
France withdrew its recognition of Avignon.
Meanwhile he was unable to enlarge his
sphere of influence in Europe; Sicily and
Genoa actually fell away from him. To
prevent the spread of Clementine support
in Germany he showered favours on the
German king Wenceslas (1378–1400),
authorizing him to raise tithes on church
property and urging him to come to Rome to
receive the imperial crown. When
Wenceslas was deposed and Rupert, elector
palatine (d. 1410), elected in Aug. 1400, he
was wary of possible repercussions and
delayed giving the formal approval
requested by the electors. When he at last
gave it on 1 Oct. 1404, the bull he published
travestied the facts by claiming that
Wenceslas had been deposed by his
authority.

Admired by contemporaries as a skilled
manipulator of men and affairs, Boniface
had the worst possible reputation for nepotism and financial unscrupulousness. If he
was personally free from the cupidity and
avarice of which he was accused, his
desperate need for money drove him to raise
it by means which were scandalous even by
the standards of the day. Under him the
papal conferring of benefices, in any case
vastly extended, became a matter of barefaced marketing, with *provisions, expecta-
tives (i.e. mandates from the pope granting
the succession to benefices), and offices
sold for cash down to the highest bidder. He
so increased church taxes that 'Boniface's
*annates' became a byword. Similarly the
commercial possibilities of indulgences
were exploited to the full, the privileges of
jubilees, for example, being extended to
cities far beyond Rome and being made
obtainable by paying the cost of the journey
there plus the amount the pilgrim might
have offered at the Roman shrines. He was

BENEDICT (XIII) (antipope 1394–1417)

assisted in his financial business by Baldassare Cossa (later Antipope JOHN XXIII), whom he promoted cardinal in 1402. On 22 Sept. 1404 Boniface received an embassy from Antipope Benedict XIII, who proposed that the two rivals or their plenipotentiaries should meet to discuss the settlement of the schism; the possibility of abdication should be on the agenda. The pope, who was seriously ill with the stone, objected that he was not fit enough for a meeting; in fact, he had no intention of treating with the antipope on equal terms. At a further meeting on 29 Sept. there were violent exchanges. Boniface's health deteriorated rapidly and he died within days. The Romans held the envoys responsible, and they were flung into gaol and only released on payment of an enormous ransom. During his reign Boniface created six cardinals and canonized (7 Oct. 1391) Bridget of Sweden (1302/3–73).

Muratori 3.2, 830–2; 1115; *LP* 2, 507; 530 f.; 549–51; Dietrich of Niem, *De schismate* (ed. G. Erler, Leipzig, 1890); O. Raynaldus, *Annales ecclesiastici* (for 1390–1404) (ed. J. D. Mansi, Lucca, 1747–56); L. Zanuto, *Il pontificato di Bonifacio IX* (Udine, 1904); *DHGE* 9, 909–22 (E. Vansteenberghe); *EC* 2, 1875f. (P. Paschini); *NCE* 2, 673 f. (E. J. Smyth); Seppelt 4, 206–13; 215; 220 f.; P 1.

BENEDICT (XIII) (antipope 28 Sept. 1394–26 July 1417: d. 23 May 1423). When Antipope CLEMENT VII died, there were hopes that the Great Schism (1378–1417) might be ended if the Avignon cardinals refrained from electing a successor. When they met in conclave on 26 Sept. 1394 they were handed letters from King Charles VI of France (1380–1422) urging them to postpone an election, but they left them unopened. All twenty-one, however, swore to work for the elimination of the schism, each undertaking, if elected, to abdicate if and when the majority judged it proper. They then unanimously chose Pedro de Luna, cardinal deacon of Sta Maria in Cosmedin, who had opposed the oath and only taken it with reluctance. Born c.1328 of noble parents at Illueca, Aragón, he had

studied, obtained his doctorate, and lectured in canon law at Montpellier before being named cardinal by GREGORY XI in 1375. A man of irreproachable conduct and inflexible resolve, he took part in the tumultuous election of URBAN VI with complete sang-froid, and was one of the last to abandon him, but once convinced that his election was invalid became a determined supporter of Clement VII. In Dec. 1378 he went to the Iberian peninsula for eleven years as his legate, and by his diplomacy swung Aragón, Castile, Navarre, and Portugal to his obedience. He also reformed the university of Salamanca, and presided over several reforming synods. Appointed plenipotentiary legate to France and other countries in 1393, he posed in Paris as a partisan of ending the schism by the abdication of both popes, declaring that he would follow this course if he were pontiff.

Although apparent readiness to step down helped him to get elected, he was in fact to contribute more than anyone, by his adroitness, obstinacy, and unshakeable belief in his legitimacy, to the tragic prolongation of the schism, in spite of pressure from the French court, hierarchy, and university world. The first phase opened in May 1395 with the arrival at Avignon of a powerful deputation from Charles VI of France urging him to abdicate in accordance with his oath. Benedict countered this with endless evasive objections, arguing that negotiation offered a better way. Charles mustered support for the policy of abdication from other princes, but an Anglo-French mission in June 1397 and a German one in May 1398 were unable to move Benedict; to the latter he denounced the abdication of a lawful pope as sinful. Meanwhile, pursuing his preferred 'way of discussion', he tried to negotiate between Dec. 1395 and autumn 1396 with his Roman rival BONIFACE IX, but without result. All this hedging exasperated the French court, but only in July 1398 did the government, as advised by a widely representative national synod, formally withdraw France from its obedience to

Benedict, thereby effectively depriving him of his revenues from the French church. Not only did most of his cardinals now desert him, but Navarre, Castile, and other regions also withdrew their obedience.

The next phase began with a reaction in Benedict's favour, in part caused by his resolute conduct. First besieged in his palace, then imprisoned there for years, he escaped in disguise to Provence in Mar. 1403. His cardinals now (29 Mar.) returned to submission, and before long France, thanks largely to the efforts of Louis, duke of Orléans, and Castile restored their obedience. He had had to undertake, however, to abdicate in the event of the death, resignation, or deposition of his Roman rival, and to work constructively for the termination of the schism; but his preferred method was direct negotiation. In Sept. 1404 he sent an embassy to Rome proposing a meeting of both pontiffs or their plenipotentiaries, with the possibility of resignations on the agenda, but it foundered on the intransigence of Boniface IX. No progress towards union was achieved in INNOCENT VII's brief reign, but prospects looked brighter when GREGORY XII, pledged to a specific programme of conciliation, was chosen as his successor. By the treaty of Marseilles (21 Apr. 1407) the two popes agreed to meet at Savona, near Genoa, on 29 Sept. or by 1 Nov. at the latest. Through Gregory's procrastination and eventual refusal, however, the meeting, from which the world expected much, never took place, although the claimants, Benedict at Portovenere and Gregory at Lucca, carried on sterile exchanges for many months. The breakdown in these negotiations caused widespread disappointment and indignation, and in May 1408 the French government, defying Benedict's threat of a ban and interdict, again withdrew from his obedience and declared its neutrality; it even ordered his arrest.

Benedict made his escape unhindered from Italy to Perpignan, which now became the seat of his court. His cardinals, however, now deserted him, joined forces with

Gregory XII's, and with them summoned (29 June 1408) a general council to meet in March 1409 at Pisa. Invited to attend, Benedict, like Gregory, refused, and called a council of his own to meet at Perpignan on 1 Nov. When the council of Pisa met, he, with Gregory, was condemned and deposed at the 15th session (5 June 1409); on 26 June a new pope, ALEXANDER V, was elected with its approval. Full of energy, and also illusions, Benedict fiercely continued the struggle, although his obedience was now reduced to Spain, Portugal, and Scotland, and launched from Barcelona (1 Dec.) excommunications on his detractors and the new pontiff; he also composed polemical tracts in his own defence. During the council of Constance (1414–17) Sigismund, German king and later emperor (1433–7), went to Perpignan to persuade him to abdicate honourably, but his overtures were obstinately rebuffed. He now (1415) took refuge in the impregnable castle of Peñiscola, on a promontory of the coast of Valencia, claiming to envoys of the council that this was now the true church, the ark of Noah. On 26 July 1417, at the 37th session of the council, he was again deposed and extruded from the church. He still had many supporters in Castile, and on 27 Nov. 1422 he created four more cardinals. An indomitable nonagenarian still breathing defiance, he died at Peñiscola on 23 May 1423 and is still remembered there as 'Papa Luna'. His crozier and chalice are displayed in the parish church, but his remains were transferred in 1429 to his native castle at Illueca, where they were desecrated and (except for his skull) cast to the winds by French troops in 1811.

Pedro de Luna, *Libro de las consolaciones de la vida humana* (ed. P. de Gayangos, Madrid, 1860); Baluze-Mollat 1, 423–542; 597 f.; Dietrich of Niem, *De schismate* (ed. G. Erler, Leipzig, 1890); M. de Alpartil, *Chronica actitatorum temporibus domini B.XIII*, *QFGG* 12 (1906); S. Puig y Puig, *Pedro de Luna* (Barcelona, 1920); N. Valois, *La France et le grand schisme d'Occident* (Paris, 1896–1902); A. Glasfurd, *The Antipope (Peter de Luna, 1342–1423)* (London, 1965); *DTC* 12, 2020–9

INNOCENT VII (1404–6)

(É. Amann); *DHGE* 8, 135–63 (F. Baix and L. Jadin); *NCE* 2, 277 (G. Mollat); Seppelt 4, 213–55.

INNOCENT VII (17 Oct. 1404–6 Nov. 1406). Third of the Roman popes during the Great Schism (1378–1417), Cosimo Gentile de' Migliorati was born of bourgeois parentage *c.* 1336 at Sulmona, in the Abruzzi, studied law at Bologna under the celebrated jurist Lignano, himself became professor at Perugia and at Padua, and was taken into the curia by URBAN VI, whom he served as papal collector (of taxes or tithes) in England for ten years. Archbishop of Ravenna in 1387, he was transferred to Bologna in 1389. In the same year BONIFACE IX named him cardinal priest of Sta Croce in Gerusalemme and sent him as legate to Tuscany and Lombardy to restore peace between the Visconti of Milan and the cities of Florence and Bologna. Influential and respected, he was elected to succeed Boniface IX by the eight cardinals available, in spite of pleas from Antipope BENEDICT XIII's envoys, then present in Rome, that the conclave should postpone an election.

At the conclave Innocent, like the other cardinals, had vowed, if elected, to do everything in his power to end the schism, if necessary abdicating. In spite of this he rejected Benedict XIII's proposals for a personal meeting of the two pontiffs, but towards the end of 1404, yielding to strong pressure from Rupert, elected German king in Aug. 1400, he summoned a council of his own obedience, to meet on 1 Nov. 1405. When Benedict XIII landed at Genoa in May 1405 and requested a safe-conduct for envoys he proposed to send to Rome, he received a refusal which questioned his bona fides. That the projected council had to be twice postponed and then abandoned was scarcely Innocent's fault. His election had aroused considerable opposition in Rome, and he had to call upon Ladislas, king of Naples (1386–1414), to suppress the revolt and negotiate a treaty ensuring civic liberties for the population (24 Oct. 1404). In return he was obliged to swear not to enter into any arrangement with the Avignon pope which did not recognize Ladislas's title to the kingdom of Naples (a promise likely to restrict his freedom of action in any negotiations to end the schism). Some months later the Romans, dissatisfied with the concessions granted them, attempted to extract more from him, first by discussions, and then by armed force. In the course of these exchanges a worthless nephew of his, Ludovico Migliorati, seeking to help his harassed uncle, had eleven leading citizens murdered, with the result that the infuriated mob stormed the Vatican; Innocent and his cardinals were lucky to escape alive to Viterbo. Exploiting the situation, Ladislas consolidated his hold on Rome and its environs and seized Castel Sant'Angelo. Since the people preferred Innocent's rule to Ladislas's and realized that he had no share in Ludovico's nefarious deeds, he was able to return to Rome at their behest in early Mar. 1406. He had to excommunicate Ladislas before he would withdraw his troops from the castle, but once he had made his submission Innocent named him defender and standard-bearer of the church (1 Sept. 1406).

Although admired for his strict life and legal expertise, Innocent proved easygoing and ineffective. He was so indulgent to his nephew that he not only let him off with a merely spiritual penalty for his murderous conduct, but made him lord of Ancona and Fermo. He was a patron of learning, however, and on 1 Sept. 1406 announced the reorganization of the university of Rome and the establishment of faculties of medicine, philosophy, logic, and rhetoric, and of a chair of Greek.

LP 2, 508–10; 531–3; 552–4; Muratori 3.2, 832–7; O. Raynaldus, *Annales ecclesiastici* (for 1404–6) (ed. J. D. Mansi, Lucca, 1747–56); Dietrich of Niem, *De schismate* 2 (ed. G. Erler, Leipzig, 1890); N. Valois, *La France et le grand schisme d'Occident* (Paris, 1896–1902); *PRE* 9, 135–7 (Zoepfel-Beurath); *EC* 7, 17 f. (P. Brezzi); Seppelt 4, 224 f.

GREGORY XII (30 Nov. 1406–4 July 1415: d. 18 Oct. 1417). Successor of INNO-

CENT VII, Angelo Correr was born of noble family at Venice c. 1325, and was successively bishop of Castello (1380), Latin patriarch of Constantinople (1390), cardinal priest of S. Marco (1405), and papal secretary. In their eagerness to see the end of the Great Schism (1378–1417), each of the fourteen Roman cardinals at the conclave following Innocent VII's death swore that, if elected, he would abdicate provided Antipope BENEDICT XIII did the same or should die; also that he would not create new cardinals except to maintain parity of numbers with the Avignon cardinals, and that within three months he would enter into negotiations with his rival about a place of meeting. A learned and widely read octogenarian, of exemplary austerity but vacillating character, Angelo owed his elevation primarily to the keen concern he had hitherto shown for the restoration of unity.

At first it seemed that the hopes everywhere aroused by his election would be speedily fulfilled. Gregory immediately announced to the Christian world his readiness in appropriate circumstances to renounce his title, and sent a delegation (led by an inexperienced and unsuitable nephew) to Benedict XIII at Marseilles to agree a place where the two might confer. After stormy discussions it was decided (21 Apr. 1407) that, each accompanied by his cardinals and with security guaranteed, they should meet at Savona, a city belonging then to the Avignon obedience, by 1 Nov. at latest. From this point, however, Gregory's attitude altered; personal doubts and fears, combined with pressures from quarters apprehensive of what might ensue if he had to resign (King Ladislas of Naples (1386–1414), the kings of Hungary and Bohemia, even the nephews who basked in his indulgence), made him postpone, and eventually refuse, the planned meeting. For months the two popes, Gregory at Lucca and Benedict at Portovenere, engaged in sterile negotiations; it was evident that, for all his protestations, Benedict had no intention of stepping down, while Gregory had good reasons to fear his hostile designs. As

the negotiations dragged on, Gregory's cardinals became increasingly restive. An open break became inevitable when Gregory, suspicious of their loyalty, broke his preelection promise and on 4 May announced the creation of four new cardinals (including two of his nephews). All but three of his original college now left him and fled to Pisa; from there, in a letter addressed to him, they appealed over his head to Christ and a general council, and circulated a letter to Christian princes declaring their zeal for union. They then joined forces with four of Benedict's cardinals at Livorno, made a solemn agreement with them to establish the peace of the church by a general council, and in early July sent out with them a united summons for such a council to meet at Pisa in March 1409.

Both popes were invited to attend the forthcoming council, but both naturally refused, Gregory very indignantly, and summoned councils of their own. The council of Pisa duly met, under the presidency of the united college of cardinals, in the Duomo on 25 Mar. Charges of bad faith, and even of collusion, were laid in great detail against both popes; it was recalled that, after his propitious start, Gregory had come to denounce the 'way of abdication' as heretical, had imprisoned advocates of it, and had declared that he intended to die as pope. A memorial protesting against the council and supporting Gregory was presented by envoys of Rupert, elected German king in 1400, on 15 Apr., but in vain; an attempt by his protector Carlo Malatesta to mediate between him and the council a few days later proved equally fruitless. At the 15th session, on 5 June, Gregory and Benedict were both formally deposed as schismatics, obdurate heretics, and perjurors, and the holy see was declared vacant. On 26 June the cardinals elected a new pope, ALEXANDER V.

Despite the council's apparent success, it had not resolved the schism. Although their respective followings were much diminished, Gregory and Benedict XIII were still figures to be reckoned with and tenaciously upheld their claims. Gregory opened his council at Cividale, near Aquileia, on 6 June 1409. It was sparsely attended, and after eight or nine sessions he abandoned it on 6 Sept., but not before excommunicating Benedict and Alexander V. As the archbishop of Aquileia was hostile, he fled in disguise to Gaeta under the protection of King Ladislas of Naples; he still had the support of Naples, Hungary, Bavaria, and the German king Rupert. When JOHN XXIII, elected as council pope to succeed Alexander V in 1410, concluded a treaty with the treacherous Ladislas, Gregory was banished from Naples on 31 Oct. 1411 and had to take refuge with Carlo Malatesta, lord of Rimini. When the council of Constance (reckoned in part or whole the Sixteenth General, 1414–17), originally summoned by John XXIII at the instigation of the German king Sigismund, later emperor (1433–7), to produce a final settlement, had deposed John, it entered into negotiations with Gregory, who conveyed to it his willingness to abdicate provided he was allowed formally to convoke the assembled prelates and dignitaries afresh as a general council; as pope he could not recognize one called by John. This procedure was accepted, and at the 14th solemn session, on 4 July 1415, his cardinal John Dominici read out his bull convoking the council, whereupon Carlo Malatesta announced his resignation. The two colleges of cardinals were united, Gregory's acts in his pontificate were ratified, and he himself was appointed cardinal bishop of Porto and legate of the March of Ancona for life; he was declared ineligible for election as pope, but was to rank next in precedence to the new pontiff. He died, however, at Recanati, not far from Ancona, on 18 Oct. 1417 three weeks before the election of MARTIN V.

LP 2, 510 f.; 533–6; 554 f.; Muratori 3.2, 837–42; A. Finke (ed.), *Acta concilii Constanciensis* (II–IV) (Münster, 1923–8); N. Valois, *La France et le grand schisme d'Occident* (Paris, 1896–1902); A. Mercati, 'La biblioteca privata e gli arredi della capella di Gregorio XII', *ST* 42 (1924), 128–65; MC 1,
199–256; 2, 59; P 1; Seppelt 4, 228–48; *EC* 6, 1141–3 (R. Ciasca); *NCE* 6, 778 f. (J. Muldoon).

ALEXANDER V (antipope 26 June 1409–3 May 1410). After the council of Pisa (Mar.–Aug. 1409), in an attempt to end the Great Schism (1378–1417), had deposed GREGORY XII and Antipope BENEDICT XIII on 5 June 1409, a joint conclave of their cardinals unanimously elected Pietro Philarghi (Peter of Candia) as pope. A Greek from northern Crete (then Venetian), humbly born and orphaned in infancy, he was sheltered and taught by a friar minor, joined the Franciscans himself c.1357, and studied at Padua, Norwich, and Oxford, where he graduated bachelor of theology. After teaching in Franciscan houses in Russia, Bohemia, and Poland, he lectured (1378–80) on the *Sentences* of Peter Lombard (c.1100–60) at Paris, obtaining his doctorate in 1381. In 1386 he held a chair of theology at Pavia, where his reputation as a humanist commended him to Gian Galeazzo Visconti, later to be duke of Milan (1395–1402). With his backing he became successively bishop of Piacenza (1386), Vicenza (1388), and Novara (1389), and archbishop of Milan (1402). During these years he carried out important diplomatic missions for his patron, in 1395 procuring the title of duke for him from the German king Wenceslas (1378–1400). His career altered in 1405, when INNOCENT VII named him cardinal priest of SS. Apostoli and legate for Lombardy. He was among the cardinals who, impatient at Gregory XII's dilatoriness in ending the schism, broke with him in May 1408 and collaborated with Baldassare Cossa (later Antipope JOHN XXIII) in arranging the council of Pisa. He took a prominent part at it, delivering the keynote address and presiding over the theologians who pronounced Gregory XII and Benedict XIII heretics. He owed his election to the suggestion of Cardinal Baldassare, who had been first thought of, and like all the cardinals had taken an oath that, if elected, he would not disperse the council until he had reformed the church.

Although he was a shrewd and experienced administrator, Alexander scarcely fulfilled the hopes placed on him. Not only was his reign unexpectedly short, but it was already apparent that the schism was far from over. Although France, England, Bohemia, Prussia, and northern and central Italy rallied to Alexander, Gregory XII and Benedict XIII retained each his diminished allegiance; there were thus three popes instead of two. Nor did the eagerly awaited reforms materialize. His first act was to make a lavish distribution of bishoprics and other favours to friends and clients, and then (1 July) to publish decrees ratifying everything the cardinals had done since May 1408 and uniting the two colleges into one. On 7 Aug. further decrees were promulgated, securing in their benefices and possessions all who adhered to the council, confirming their acts, and announcing a fresh council to be held in three years. He then dissolved the council, deferring reforms to the future one. A more pressing need than reform was the reconquest of the papal state; Umbria and Rome itself were occupied by King Ladislas of Naples (1386–1414) in the name of Gregory XII. To weaken Gregory Alexander excommunicated Ladislas, invested Louis II of Anjou (d. 1417) with his kingdom, and dispatched an army commanded by Louis and Baldassare Cossa against Rome. The expedition had initial success, but captured the city only after a lengthy siege in Jan. 1410. Alexander, who had condemned the teachings of the reformer John Wycliffe (c. 1330–84) on 12 Dec. 1409, did not take up residence there, but under pressure from Baldassare settled in Bologna. Here he received on 2 Feb. a deputation of Romans offering him homage and begging him to come to their city. He delayed, and died suddenly on 3 May 1410 at Bologna; there were mischievous, but probably false, rumours that Baldassare had poisoned him.

A devoted Franciscan (he was buried, appropriately, in the church of S. Francesco at Bologna), he provoked a storm of criticism by a bull (12 Oct. 1409) extending, to the detriment of the secular clergy, the rights of the mendicants to preach and hear confessions. He was also an admired scholar and teacher whose *Principia* and commentary on the *Sentences*, markedly nominalistic in their tone, have been increasingly recognized as throwing important light on the development of medieval thought. Usually classified as an antipope, his claim to be an authentic pope is still debated, and some historians give him the compromise description of 'council pope'.

F. Ehrle, *Der Sentenzenkommentar Peters von Candia* (Münster, 1925); A. Emmen, *Petri de Candia Tractatus quattuor de immaculata conceptione; Tractatus de immaculata Deiparae conceptione* (Florence, 1954 and 1955); Muratori 3.2, 842A; *LP* 2, 511 f.; 531; B. Platina, *De vita Christi ac omnium pontificum* 212 (207) (ed. G. Gaida, 1913); A. B. Emden, *A Biographical Register of the University of Oxford to AD 1500* (Oxford, 1957–9) 1, 345 f.; MC 1; N. Valois, *La France et le grand schisme d'Occident* (Paris, 1896–1902); P 1; *DBI* 2, 193–6 (A. Petrucci); *EC* 1, 794 f. (P. Paschini); *NCE* 11, 213 (F. J. Gray).

JOHN (XXIII) (antipope 17 May 1410–29 May 1415: d. 22 Nov. 1419). A Neapolitan of noble but impoverished family, Baldassare Cossa began his career as a piratical adventurer in the naval war between Louis II of Anjou (d. 1417) and Ladislas of Naples (1386–1414). After studying law and graduating doctor at Bologna, he was appointed archdeacon of the city by his compatriot BONIFACE IX who, noticing his administrative as well as soldierly abilities, later made him papal treasurer. An unscrupulous, grasping and ambitious man as well as an unblushing libertine, he assisted the pope in his dubious money-raising policies, and in Feb. 1402 Boniface created him cardinal deacon of S. Eustachio and sent him as legate to Romagna and Bologna. Here he continued his profligate habits (gossip had it that he seduced two hundred women during his legation), but by his ruthless severity restored Bologna to the papal state. When the Great Schism (1378–1417) reached its climax, he was one of the cardinals who, impatient at GREGORY XII's dilatoriness in reaching a solution, broke with him in May 1408 and joined forces with the cardinals of BENEDICT XIII who had abandoned him. Along with Cardinal Pietro Philarghi he took the lead in arranging the council of Pisa (Mar.–Aug. 1409), and after it had deposed Gregory XII and Benedict XIII engineered the election of Pietro as Pope ALEXANDER V. His was the paramount influence on Alexander during his short reign, and when he died suddenly at Bologna Baldassare was accused, libellously, of having poisoned him. Meeting at Bologna, the Pisan cardinals unanimously elected him as Alexander's successor. The factors influencing their choice, simony apart, included pressure from Louis II of Anjou, fear of the menacing armed forces at Baldassare's disposal, and their own appreciation that a pope of military experience was indispensable if Rome was to be recovered from Ladislas of Naples, Gregory XII's chief protector.

While there were still three claimants to the papacy, John commanded much the widest support, with France, England, and several Italian and German states recognizing him. With the help of Louis of Anjou, who defeated Ladislas at Roccasecca on 19 May 1411, he was able to establish himself in Rome. He had already, in conformity with the Pisan decisions, summoned a reform council to meet there on 1 Apr. 1412. It duly met, but was so poorly attended that all it accomplished was the condemnation (10 Feb. 1413) of all the English reformer John Wycliffe's writings; John had had John Huss, the Bohemian reformer (c.1369–1415), banned in Feb. 1411, and in Aug. 1412 imposed on him major excommunication (which included being cut off from all intercourse with other Christians) for denouncing his crusade against Ladislas. Louis having failed to exploit his victory, John came to terms with Ladislas, and in return for being enfeoffed with the kingdom of Naples Ladislas was persuaded to abandon Gregory XII. In summer 1413, however, Ladislas turned

against John; he was forced to flee from Rome precipitately and seek shelter outside the gates of Florence. In his desperate straits he appealed for help to Sigismund, German king and later emperor (1433–7), who was convinced that only a general council could resolve the schism and now demanded the holding of one at Constance as the price of his support. Although he would have preferred a council on ground of his own choosing, John had no option but to agree, and on 9 Dec. 1413 issued a bull convoking a council to meet at Constance in Nov. 1414.

After the sudden death of Ladislas on 6 Aug. 1414, John's first instinct was to devote himself to winning back the papal state, but under strong pressure from his cardinals (his own creations included several outstanding personalities) he went to Constance and on 5 Nov. solemnly opened the council (reckoned, in part or whole, the Sixteenth General Council). At the start of this impressively attended gathering the numerous Italian party accompanying John pressed for confirmation of the acts of the council of Pisa, which would have eliminated Gregory XII and Benedict XIII while leaving John secure, but, after it had been agreed that voting should be by 'nations', Germany, France, and England argued on 15 Feb. 1415 for the common abdication of all three claimants. John finally yielded to the pressure, but haggled for a week about the terms of his abdication. Then during the night of 20/21 May he fled the city disguised as a groom and sought refuge at Freiburg. By his flight he hoped to disrupt the council, but it provoked the assembly, at its fourth and fifth sessions (30 Mar. and 6 Apr. 1415), to publish revolutionary decrees proclaiming the superiority of the council over the pope, then to suspend him (he had been brought back as a prisoner) from his functions as pope on 14 May, and finally, after a trial at which he was accused of simony, perjury, and the grossest misconduct, to declare him deposed at the twelfth session (29 May). Now a broken man, John admitted the wrong he had done by his flight, acquiesced in the judgement of the council and declared it infallible, and of his own accord ratified its (canonically irregular) sentences of suspension and deposition, renouncing any right he might have to the papacy. John kept his word never to appeal against his condemnation. For three years he was held in strict confinement in Germany in the custody of the elector Ludwig III of Bavaria, but in 1419 purchased his liberty from him for a huge sum. He then went to Florence and made his submission to the recently elected pope. MARTIN V appointed him cardinal bishop of Tusculum (Frascati), but he held this office for only a few months. His magnificent tomb with his sombre effigy and the papal insignia, the work of Bartolomeo di Michelozzo and Donatello, can be seen in the baptistery at Florence.

LP 2, 512 f.; 536 f.; Muratori 3.2, 854 f.; B. Platina, De vita Christi ac omnium pontificum 213 (208) (ed. G. Gaida, 1913); Dietrich of Niem, De schismate 3 (ed. G. Erler, Leipzig, 1890); Acta concilii Constanciensis (ed. H. Finke and others, Münster, 1896–1928); J. Blumenthal, 'Johann XXIII: seine Wahl und seine Persönlichkeit', ZKG 21 (1901), 488–516; E. J. Kitts, Pope John the Twenty-third and Master John Hus of Bohemia (London, 1910); MC 1; PRE 9, 271 f. (B. Bess); DTC 8, 641–4 (G. Mollat); EC 4, 708 f. (P. Paschini); EB (1961 edn.) 13, 87 (C. H. Lawrence); Seppelt 4, 241–53.

MARTIN V (11 Nov. 1417–20 Feb. 1431). After the council of Constance (1414–18), called to end the Great Schism (1378–1417) and reform the church, had deposed JOHN XXIII and BENEDICT XIII and received the abdication of GREGORY XII, there were lengthy discussions on electoral procedure; and then a unique conclave of twenty-two cardinals and thirty representatives of the five 'nations' present in only three days elected Cardinal Oddo Colonna. Sole member of that powerful family to become pope, he was born at Gennazano in 1368, studied law at Perugia, and under URBAN VI became protonotary. INNOCENT VII created him cardinal deacon of S.

Giorgio in Velabro, but in summer 1408 he broke with Gregory XII and was active in preparing the council of Pisa (1409). At Constance he remained loyal to John XXIII until his precipitate flight. Unassuming but an authoritarian of iron will, he styled himself Martin after the saint of the day of his election.

His election effectively ended the schism, for John XXIII accepted his own deposition, and although Benedict XIII and then CLEMENT VIII held out as antipopes until 1429 they had only minute followings. But if the council expected him to promote reform 'in head and members', it was disappointed. Out of respect for public opinion Martin carried out some limited reforms, but he was resolved to reassert, not lessen, papal authority, and he could not afford serious loss of revenue. He at once reconstructed the curia as the council stipulated, drawing on curial officials of both the Roman and Avignon obediences, but his regulations (26 Feb. 1418) for his chancery failed to remove abuses and retained the pope's rights in collating benefices. On 20 Mar. 1418 he published seven reforms dealing mainly with papal taxation and abuses of papal provisions, e.g. relinquishing the pope's claim to the revenues of vacant sees, and then negotiated separate concordats with Germany, France, Italy, Spain, and England. If these curtailed the papal prerogative, they were restricted, save in England's case, to five years, after which he returned to the old policy of papal reservations so far as particular governments allowed. Thus he had considerable success, both in northern (1425) and southern (1426) France, in recovering privileges lost during the schism; but he failed in his repeated efforts to get the English Statutes of *Provisors (checking papal nomination to vacant benefices) revoked. He closed the council on 22 Apr. 1418, and in a constitution of 10 May, which was not published, forbade any appeal from the pope to a future council.

Martin at once set about rescuing the papal state from the chaos into which it had fallen during the schism. Although pressed

CLEMENT (VIII) (antipope 1423–9)

to reside in either Germany or Avignon, he left Constance on 16 May 1418 and, after lengthy stays at Mantua and Florence, entered Rome on 28 Sept. 1420. Through concessions to Queen Joanna II of Naples (1414–35) he had secured the removal of the occupying Neapolitan troops. His chief obstacle now was the formidable *condottiere* Braccione di Montone, who dominated central Italy. Martin first contained him by recognizing him as lord of Perugia and other cities, and then defeated him in battle at L'Aquila (2 June 1424); a revolt by Bologna which involved the whole of north Italy he crushed by force of arms in 1429. His reorganization of the papal state enabled him not only to recoup his treasury but to enrich his Colonna relatives with vast estates in papal territories.

Martin advanced the prestige of his office in Europe, sending numerous embassies on peace missions, notably to England and France, still locked in the Hundred Years War (1337–1453). He maintained contact with Constantinople and agreed in principle to the holding of a reunion council there, but because of the political situation and the Byzantine emperor's far-reaching demands nothing for the moment came of this. He was also unsuccessful with the crusades he declared against the adherents of the reformer John Huss (*c.* 1369–1415) in Bohemia. He showed unusual moderation towards the Jews, denouncing (1422 and 1429) violent anti-Jewish preaching and forbidding compulsory baptism of Jewish children under twelve; and in 1427 he received the Franciscan reformer Bernardino of Siena (1380–1444) and approved the cult of the Holy Name propagated by him. In Rome he carried out a vast programme of reconstruction of ruined churches and public buildings, enlisting the services of celebrated artists. His appointments to the sacred college were exceptionally distinguished, but he kept a tight rein on his cardinals and did not brook their interference.

Averse though he was to councils and the theory that popes were subject to them, he obeyed the decree *Frequens* (5 Oct. 1417) of Constance requiring councils to be held at regular intervals, and summoned one to meet at Pavia in five years (22 Sept. 1423). He did not attend it himself, and because of an outbreak of plague his legates transferred it to Siena. Since anti-papal tendencies, as at Constance, soon manifested themselves, he made the sparse attendance a pretext for dissolving it in March 1424, announcing a further council to be held in Basle in 1431. Meanwhile he judged it wise to publish a reform constitution of his own (16 May 1425), concerned mainly with the life-style of the curia and the residence of prelates.

By the end of 1430 public pressure for the council to be held at Basle was mounting, and Martin reluctantly yielded to it. On 1 Feb. 1431 he nominated Cardinal Cesarini, whom he had recently sent as legate to Germany, as its president, with authority to suspend or dissolve it as he saw fit. Hardly three weeks later he died suddenly of apoplexy. He was buried in St John Lateran, where his recumbent effigy in brass can be seen.

Muratori 3.2, 857–68; B. Platina, *De vita Christi ac omnium pontificum* 214 (207) (ed. G. Gaida, 1913); E. von Ottenthal, 'Die Bullenregister Martin V und Eugen IV', *MIÖG*: Ergänzungsband 1 (1885), 401–589; K. A. Fink, 'Martin V und Bologna'; 'Die altesten Breven und Brevenregister'; 'Die politische Korrespondenz Martins V nach den Brevenregistern' *QFIAB* 23 (1931/2), 182–217; 25 (1933/4), 292–307; 26 (1935/6), 292–307; P. Partner, *The Papal State under Martin V* (London, 1958); MC 2; *DTC* 10, 197–202 (G. Mollat); *NCE* 9, 301 f. (K. A. Fink); Seppelt 4, esp. 258–76; J. Haller, 'England und Rom unter Martin V', *QFIAB* 8 (1905), 249–304.

CLEMENT (VIII) (antipope 10 June 1423–26 July 1429: d. 28 Dec. 1446). Before his death BENEDICT XIII, last of the Avignon popes in the Great Schism (1378–1417), made his four cardinals swear to elect a successor, and on 10 June 1423, at Peñiscola on the Spanish Mediterranean coast, the three who were available chose Gil Sanchez Muñoz. Born at Teruel *c.* 1360, he had an uncle of the same name who had played a notable role in the events leading to the success in the west of the schism resulting from the double election of URBAN VI and CLEMENT VII in 1378. His nephew shared the same ideas and, on his uncle's death in 1389, replaced him in the entourage of Cardinal Pedro de Luna, becoming a close associate after his election as Benedict XIII. At the time of Benedict's death he was provost of Valencia as well as archpriest of Teruel. He took the style Clement VIII out of respect for Robert of Geneva (Antipope Clement VII).

Although censured by Queen Maria of Aragón (acting as regent for Alfonso V (1416–58), absent in Italy) and for a while blockaded by royal forces in the impregnable promontory of Peñiscola, Clement presided over a papal court in miniature, creating two cardinals and surrounding himself with an appropriate circle of dignitaries. Among other acts he excommunicated Jean Carrier, the cardinal who had been absent during his election and who, judging it invalid because of simony, had nominated on his own another antipope, BENEDICT XIV; he also stripped him of his cardinalate. At Rome MARTIN V, hearing of Clement's election, instructed the archbishop of Tarragona and the bishops of Tortosa and Barcelona to acquit the misguided prelates involved provided they returned to their senses. But the comedy of Peñiscola could not last. Alfonso V of Aragón, although never regarding Clement as true pope, certainly found him useful for putting pressure on Martin V, and in Aug. 1423 suspended the measures taken by Queen Maria against him. When he eventually settled his outstanding difficulties with the pope, he sent a delegation headed by his private secretary Alfonso de Borgia (later CALLISTUS III) to Peñiscola to counsel the antipope and his curia to abdicate voluntarily. Clement complied with good grace, and at a dignified ceremony on 26 July 1429 revoked the condemnations passed by him and his predecessors on the lawful pope, renounced his rank and removed his pon-

tifical dress, and in conclave with his cardinals went through the motions of electing 'Oddo Colonna' (Martin V) as pope. Three weeks later (14 Aug.) the papal legate formally reconciled him, and he took an oath of allegiance to the pope. Martin V bore him no rancour, and on 26 Aug. 1429 nominated him bishop of Majorca. He held this office until his death on 28 Dec. 1446; his splendid tomb is in the chapter house of the cathedral at Palma.

M. de Alpartils, *Chronica actitatorum temporibus domini Benedicti XIII* (ed. Ehrle, Paderborn, 1906); Mansi XXIII, 1117–24; S. Puig y Puig, *Pedro de Luna* (Barcelona, 1920), 363–453; 606–17; M. Garcia Miralles, *La personalidad de Gil Sanchez Muñoz y la solución del cisma de Occidente* (Teruel, 1954); *EC* 10, 1749 f. (A. Amore); *DHGE* 12, 1245–9 (R. Mols).

BENEDICT (XIV) (antipope 12 Nov. 1425–?: d.?). While the three of Antipope BENEDICT XIII's cardinals who were at Peñiscola, on the Spanish coast north of Valencia, when he died elected Gil Sanchez Muñoz as CLEMENT VIII (10 June 1423), the fourth, Jean Carrier, was far away in the county of Armagnac, acting as Benedict's vicar-general. Rejoining his colleagues on 12 Dec. 1423, he decided, after a prolonged examination, that their election of Sanchez Muñoz was invalid because of simony and other irregularities. On 12 Nov. 1425 he therefore took it upon himself to nominate as pope a certain Bernard Garnier, a sacrist of Rodez, and consecrated him. Out of respect for Benedict XIII this suddenly elevated pontiff adopted his name, but from that moment he disappeared into oblivion. Nothing is known of his earlier or subsequent career, or of the date of his death; but in 1467, in the region of Armagnac, some fanatics were still awaiting the vindication of Benedict XIV.

A. Degert, 'La fin du Schisme d'Occident', *Mélanges Léon Couture* (1902), 223–42; *DHGE* 12, 1247 (R. Mols); Seppelt 4, 273.

EUGENE IV (3 Mar. 1431–23 Feb. 1447). On MARTIN V's death the cardinals, resentful of his harsh yoke, all undertook that whoever should be elected would not only devote himself to reform at the impending council at Basle, but would accept the full collaboration of the sacred college in the government of the church and the papal state. Their choice fell on Gabriele Condulmaro, who was born of wealthy bourgeois parents at Venice *c.* 1383, who as a young man settled as a monk with some friends at an Augustinian house in the lagoon, and whom his relative GREGORY XII promoted bishop of Siena in 1407 and then cardinal at his controversial creation of 12 May 1408. After Gregory's abdication (4 July 1415) he took part in the council of Constance (1414–18), and Martin V appointed him governor of the March of Ancona and of Bologna. Once elected, he published a bull confirming the electoral pact, although he was to pay little heed to it during his stormy pontificate.

Eugene first moved against the Colonna family, forcing them to disgorge vast territories which Martin V had granted to his nephews; his violent measures produced lasting troubles in all parts of the papal state, and made the Colonna his lifelong enemies. But the continuous shadow over his reign was the reform council of Basle, which Martin V had summoned, for which he himself confirmed Cardinal Giuliano Cesarini (d. 1444) as president, and which was opened in Cesarini's absence by papal representatives on 23 July 1431. The initial attendance was sparse and this, combined with profound mistrust of its intentions, caused Eugene to dissolve it on 18 Dec. 1431, promising a new council to be presided over by himself in eighteen months' time. His precipitate action created consternation at Basle, shocked Cesarini, and alienated opinion generally. The council refused to disperse, on 15 Feb. 1432 appealed to the teaching of the council of Constance that a general council is superior to a pope, and on 18 Dec. 1432 issued an ultimatum to him. As only six of the twenty-one cardinals were on his side, schism seemed inevitable, but it was averted largely through the mediation of the German king Sigismund (1410–37), whom Eugene crowned emperor at Rome in May 1433. But he had to withdraw his bull of dissolution (15 Dec. 1433) and acknowledge the council's legitimacy and unbroken continuance in humiliating terms.

At home Eugene faced a chaotic situation, with the *condottiere* F. Sforza occupying the papal state, and a revolution fomented by the vengeful Colonna breaking out in Rome in May 1434. Disguised but still pelted by the crowd, he fled to Florence, where he mainly resided until 1443; it was a stay which brought him and the curia into touch with the artistic and intellectual aspirations of the Renaissance. Meanwhile his concessions to the council had only whetted its appetite for radical solutions. While carrying through some much needed reforms, it decreed (9 June 1435) the suppression of *annates and other papal dues, and set about cutting both papacy and curia down to size. Eugene denounced its pretensions in a memorandum circulated in June 1436 to Christian princes, but it was over union with the eastern church, an item on the council's agenda to which both he and it attached importance, that the final rupture came. While the great majority of the council proposed Basle itself or Avignon or Savoy for the negotiations, Eugene preferred a city in Italy. Having won over the Greeks, he transferred the council on 18 Sept. 1437 to Ferrara. He opened it there through his legate Cardinal Albergati on 8 Jan. 1438, but moved it because of an alleged danger of plague (really for financial reasons) to Florence in Jan. 1439. Here an act of union between the two churches, destined to be ephemeral but forced on the Byzantine emperor John VIII Palaeologus (1425–48) by the imminence of a Turkish invasion, was promulgated in the decree *Laetentur coeli* on 6 July 1439. Later Eugene signed agreements, on the basis of orthodoxy, with the nominally *monophysite Armenians in 1439, with the Copts or Jacobites of Egypt in 1443, and with certain hitherto dissident Nestorian groups in Mesopotamia in 1444 and in Cyprus in

1445; but a crusade he financed in 1443 ended disastrously at Varna, in Bulgaria (10 Nov. 1444).

The union, with its recognition by the Greeks of the pope's primacy and their acceptance of agreed statements on Purgatory, the eucharist, and the *Filioque*, as well as the fact that most of the fathers abandoned Basle for Ferrara–Florence, greatly strengthened Eugene's authority. The rump left at Basle suspended him on 24 Jan. 1438, deposed him on 25 June 1439, and on 5 Nov. 1439 elected FELIX V as antipope. Eugene riposted (4 Sept. 1439) by challenging the earlier phases of the council of Constance and condemning that of Basle. The council was encouraged by the declared neutrality of France and Germany, and by the incorporation by France of twenty-three of its reform decrees restricting the pope's authority in the Pragmatic Sanction of Bourges, which the French clergy issued on 7 July 1438 and which upheld the right of the French church to administer its temporal property independently of the holy see and disallowed papal nominations to vacant benefices. But its puppet pope had little following, and Eugene's recognition in spring 1443 of the claims of Alfonso V of Aragón (1416–58) to the crown of Naples deprived it of its most substantial support, since the king withdrew his bishops from it. It also enabled Eugene to return to Rome in Sept. 1443 after a nine years' absence. Here he strove to counter the effects of the schism. Antipope Felix V's ablest adviser, Enea Silvio Piccolomini (later PIUS II), had made peace with Eugene in 1442, and in Sept. 1445 helped to arrange an agreement between him and Frederick III, the new German king (1440–93). Eugene's protests against the Pragmatic Sanction of Bourges were ineffectual, but through the Concordat of the Princes, negotiated by Piccolomini with the German electors in Feb. 1447, the whole of Germany declared for him. Concessions were made by both sides, but Eugene safeguarded his position by publishing on his deathbed a bull declaring that he did not intend by these to derogate from the authority or privileges of the holy see.

Although Eugene's reign was a troubled one, it resulted in victory for the papacy over the council, and dealt a death-blow to the attempt to introduce democracy into the government of the church. But he himself, impulsive and lacking in political capacity, deeply pious but prone to blunders, was more at the mercy of events than their controller. As he lay dying, he is said to have bitterly regretted ever having left his monastery.

E. von Ottenthal, 'Die Bullenregister Martins V und Eugens IV', *MIÖG:* Ergänzungsband 1, 1885; J. Gill, *Eugenius IV: Pope of Christian Union* (Westminster, Maryland, 1961); F. P. Abert, *Papst Eugen der Vierte* (1884); P 1; MC 2; *DHGE* 15, 1355–9 (P. de Vooght); *EC* 5, 802–4 (P. Paschini); *NCE* 5, 626 f. (J. Gill); Seppelt 4, 274–306.

FELIX V (antipope 5 Nov. 1439–7 Apr. 1449: d. 7 Jan. 1451). After deposing EUGENE IV the council of Basle (1431–49) elected Amadeus VIII, duke of Savoy, in his place. The election was irregular, being carried out by one cardinal and thirty-two electors nominated by a commission, but it demonstrated the council's resolve to choose someone of wealth and international standing as well as holiness. Born at Chambéry on 4 Dec. 1383, Amadeus succeeded his father Count Amadeus VII in 1391, and by astute diplomacy so extended his realm that it eventually included Piedmont and stretched from Neuchâtel in the north to the Ligurian coast. In recognition of his power Sigismund, German king and later emperor (1433–7), raised Savoy to a duchy in 1416. In Oct. 1434, deeply affected by the deaths of his wife (1422) and eldest son (1431), he withdrew to the château of Ripaille, near Thonon on the Lake of Geneva, where he founded and governed an order of knights-hermits of St Maurice. He planned to keep the diplomatic business of Savoy in his own hands, while leaving day-to-day administration to his second son Ludovico.

A profoundly spiritual layman, he accepted his election only with great hesitation on 14 Dec. 1439, abdicating as duke on 6 Jan. 1440 and, after ordination and consecration, being crowned as Felix V at Basle on 24 June. He failed to secure recognition, however, beyond his own territories and a few smaller states; the greater powers held aloof or were hostile. He nominated several eminent men as cardinals, although some declined his invitation; for a time he employed Enea Silvio Piccolomini (later PIUS II) as his secretary. But his relations with the rump council, which should have been his chief support, were never happy; on 17 Nov. 1442, wearied by the fathers' studied insults, he retired to Lausanne and then Geneva. By 1445 he was beginning to look for release from an impasse as embarrassing to himself as it was becoming dangerous to his family. In 1449, through the mediation of Charles VII of France (1422–61), an accommodation was at last reached with the new Roman pope, NICHOLAS V, as a result of which Felix solemnly abdicated on 7 Apr., having first retracted all the censures pronounced on his adversaries. In return Nicholas appointed him (18 June) cardinal bishop of Sta Sabina, with a substantial pension, and also papal vicar and legate in Savoy and adjacent dioceses. The last of the antipopes, he did not long enjoy these dignities but died at Geneva on 7 Jan. 1451; he was buried at Ripaille.

His *Bullarium* (8 vols., unprinted) is in the Archivio di Stato of Turin. F. Cognasso, *Amadeo VIII* (Turin, 1930); *DBI* 2, 749–53 (F. Cognasso); *DHGE* 2, 1166–74 (G. Mollat); *EC* 5, 1136 f. (G. B. Picotti); MC 2; Seppelt 4, 295 f.; 299 f.; 302 f.

NICHOLAS V (6 Mar. 1447–24 Mar. 1455). A doctor's son, born at Sarzana, near La Spezia, on 15 Nov. 1397, Tommaso Parentucelli was a student at Bologna; to earn his keep he for a time tutored wealthy Florentine families, being thus introduced to leading figures in art and culture. After completing his doctorate in theology he served Bishop Niccolò Albergati of Bologna

for twenty years, moving with him in 1426 to Rome and so joining the curia. On Niccolò's death EUGENE IV, to whose notice he came during the discussions with the Greeks at Florence (1439), named him bishop of Bologna in 1447, an appointment he could not take up because the city was in revolt. In autumn 1446 he went as papal legate to the diet of Frankfurt, and with his colleagues succeeded in swinging it round to the recognition of Eugene IV. For this service he was created cardinal in Dec. 1446. At the conclave following Eugene's death he emerged as a compromise candidate because the favourite, a Colonna, was blocked by family jealousies. He took the name Nicholas out of regard for his old patron.

More patient and politically adroit than Eugene, Nicholas proved the constructive conciliator the church needed. Enjoying good relations with the Roman families, he had considerable success in restoring order in the city, while in the papal state he got rid of the mercenary troops, won or bought back cities, and recognized petty princelings as his vicars. He granted virtual independence to unruly Bologna, and prudently stood aside from the power struggle that ensued on the death of Filippo Maria Visconti, duke of Milan, content that the *condottiere* Francesco Sforza eventually succeeded and so left the March of Ancona in undisputed papal possession. He at once ratified the settlement Eugene had reached with the German church, and by the concordat of Vienna (Feb. 1448) obtained the recognition by Frederick III (1440–93) of papal rights to *annates and church appointments in Germany. A notable achievement was his peaceful liquidation of the schism with the rump council of Basle and its pope FELIX V. As early as 1447 he prevailed on Charles VII of France (1422–61) to mediate, and, by patience and tactful concessions, was able to persuade Felix to abdicate (7 Apr. 1449) in return for an honourable status and income, and the council, now at Lausanne since Frederick III had withdrawn its safe-conduct for

Basle, to dissolve itself (24 Apr.) after having gone through the motions of electing 'Tommaso of Sarzana' as pope. The mutual censures and processes were annulled, the possession of benefices was confirmed, and several of Felix's cardinals were admitted to the Roman college. In thanksgiving for unity restored he proclaimed 1450 a year of jubilee, and the thousands of pilgrims flocking to Rome not only confirmed it as the centre of Christendom but usefully replenished the papal finances. In the same year he canonized the Franciscan reformer Bernardino of Siena (1380–1444), and sent Cardinals Nicholas of Cusa and Capistrano to Germany and Cardinal d'Estouteville to France on missions of reform.

Although he himself failed to initiate any programme of reform, Nicholas deliberately brought the intellectual and artistic aspirations of the Renaissance into partnership with the church. A scholar and man of letters, he enjoyed the company of scholars and humanists, and arranged for the translation of numerous Greek authors, classical as well as patristic, into Latin. A compulsive bibliophile all his life, he spent vast sums on collecting manuscripts and having them copied; at his death he left some 1,200 Greek and Latin MSS, and was the real founder of the Vatican library. The impulse he gave to the Renaissance was equally strong in architecture and the decorative arts. He took in hand not only the rebuilding of countless churches, palaces, and bridges in Rome, but a planned strengthening of its fortifications; in the papal state he erected numerous strongholds. To adorn his buildings he employed outstanding artists, including Fra Angelico and his assistant Benozzo Gozzoli. In all these enterprises his aim was to advance the church by making it the leader of culture.

On 19 Mar. 1452 Nicholas crowned Frederick III emperor in St Peter's (the last imperial coronation to take place in Rome). Notwithstanding, dark clouds overshadowed his closing years. In early Jan. 1453 a plot against his life was brought to light. It was inspired by a republican dreamer, Stefano Porcaro, whom he had earlier treated leniently, and revealed the deceptiveness of Rome's outward calm. He had Stefano and his fellow-conspirators executed, but was worried and suspicious from then on. Then in June 1453 the news of the sack of Constantinople by the Turks (29 May) filled Europe with horror and dread. Nicholas tried to rally Christendom to a crusade (30 Sept. 1453), but to no effect. He also summoned a congress of Italian states to Rome to work out a peace settlement for Italy, but again in vain. Eventually secret negotiations between Venice and Milan led to the peace of Lodi (9 Apr. 1454), in which Florence soon joined. Although irked that he had been left out so far, Alfonso I, king of Naples and Sicily (1442–58), was persuaded by Nicholas to accept it too, and on 26 June 1455 a solemn peace covering all Italian powers except Genoa was established for twenty-five years.

When Nicholas died in Mar. 1455, enfeebled by gout, he felt disappointed and on the defensive. His dream of himself as the restorer of Rome, patron of men of letters, and assertor of the papacy as the leader of civilization had been dimmed by the harsh realities of the fall of Constantinople, the new responsibilities it placed on his shoulders, and his awareness of his own unfitness to undertake them. The first of the Renaissance popes, he was untouched by nepotism, but left the urgent problem of religious reform untackled.

Vespasiano da Bisticci, *Vite di uomini illustri* (ed. P. d'Ancona and E. Aeschlimann, Milan, 1951); B. Platina (ed. G. Gaida, in Muratori[2] 3.1, 328–39); G. Manetti in Muratori 3.2, 907–60; G. Sforza, *Ricerche su Niccolò V* (Lucca, 1884); K. Pleyer, *Die Politik Nikolaus V* (Stuttgart, 1927); P 2, 1–314; MC 3; *DTC* 11, 541–8 (G. Mollat); *NCE* 10, 443–5 (J. Gill); Seppelt 4, 307–26.

CALLISTUS III (8 Apr. 1455–6 Aug. 1458). Son of a small landowner, Alfonso de Borja or Borgia was born at Játiva, in Valencia, on 31 Dec. 1378. After studying and then teaching law at Lérida, he became a respected jurist at the court of Aragón and private secretary to King Alfonso V (1416–58). In 1429 he negotiated for him the abdication of Antipope CLEMENT VIII and was rewarded with the wealthy see of Valencia. He again showed diplomatic skill in 1443 by detaching the king from the council of Basle (1431–49) and reconciling him with EUGENE IV; for this he was created cardinal priest of SS. Quattro Coronati. He had no special prominence during his twelve years' cardinalate but lived an austere, retired life in his palace, reputedly averse from luxury and display. His surprise election as NICHOLAS V's successor resulted from a compromise, one of the two obvious candidates being unacceptable as a friend of the Colonna family, the other (the distinguished Greek theologian and humanist John Bessarion: 1403–72) as a Greek. His great age was taken to presage a caretaker pontificate.

Callistus at once flung himself, with an energy amazing in an old man crippled with gout, into organizing a crusade to reconquer Constantinople, captured in May 1453, from the Turks. This was his overriding preoccupation; he himself vowed to expend all his efforts, if need be his life, on the holy war. He dispatched preachers and legates armed with indulgences throughout Europe, imposed taxes, and fixed 1 Mar. 1456 for the departure of a combined fleet and army. In Rome he set about building galleys in the Tiber, raising funds by selling gold and silver works of art, even valuable book bindings. His enthusiasm, however, met with a lukewarm response from the Christian powers, immersed in their national concerns. As a result the sporadic military successes, such as the rout of the Turks before Belgrade (July 1456), the defeat of their fleet off Lesbos (Aug. 1457), and the relief of several Christian islands in the Aegean, though rapturously received, could not be exploited. Meanwhile Callistus's Turkish tithes created resentment in France, where the university of Paris called for a general council, and in Germany, where they fuelled the growing dissatisfac-tion with papal interference and exactions. It called for all the ingenious diplomacy of his new cardinal Enea Silvio Piccolomini (later PIUS II) to fend off German demands for the equivalent of the Gallican liberties of the French church. Nearer home he fell out with his old patron Alfonso, king of Aragón and Naples, infuriated by the king's diver-sion of a crusader fleet to attack Genoa and advance his own territorial aims instead of fighting the Turks. The quarrel continued, and on Alfonso's death Callistus schemed that a nephew of his own should become king of Naples instead of Ferrante, or Ferdinand I (1458–94), the king's natural son.

Austere, rigidly pious, charitable, Cal-listus was also obstinate and self-willed, and did not brook opposition from his cardinals. After Nicholas V, his disinterest in the arts disappointed humanists, but he was not positively hostile to them, as they suggested. If he halted Nicholas's grandiose plans for rebuilding Rome, his natural parsimony but still more the needs of the crusade were to blame. The favours he lavished on relatives and compatriots aroused great bitterness. To feel secure he garrisoned the fortresses of the papal state with Spanish comman-ders, while he appointed his nephew Pedro Luis, duke of Spoleto, as governor of Castel Sant'Angelo and prefect of Rome. Two other nephews he created cardinals in their early twenties; one of them, Rodrigo Borgia (later ALEXANDER VI), he promoted vice-chancellor of the curia. His Spanish nominees dominated the papal court, but the benefices he awarded them were mostly Spanish, not Italian.

Callistus reopened the case of Joan of Arc, burnt at the stake at Rouen on 30 May 1431 on charges including witchcraft and heresy, and on 16 June 1456 the original judgement passed on her was quashed and her innocence declared. In the same year he revived the harsh legislation, allowed to lapse by his predecessors, banning the social intercourse of Christians with Jews. Among the saints he canonized was (1 Jan. 1457) Osmund of Salisbury (d. 1099). To commemorate the victory over the Turks at Belgrade he ordered the feast of the Transfiguration to be universally observed on 6 Aug. His death on that day in 1458 was the signal for an outbreak of violence against the hated 'Catalans'.

Regesto Ibérico de Calixto III (ed. J. Rius Serra, Madrid, 1948 ff.); B. Platina, in Muratori[2] 3.1, 339–45; *LP* 2, 546–60; O. Raynaldus, *Annales ecclesiastici* (for 1455–8) (ed. J. D. Mansi, Lucca, 1747–56); M. E. Mallett, *The Borgias: The Rise and Fall of a Renaissance Dynasty* (London, 1969: see index); P. Brezzi, 'La política di Callisto III', *Studi Romani* 7 (1959), 31–51; MC 3; P 1; *PRE* 2, 642 f. (G. Voigt); *DHGE* 11, 438–44 (E. Vansteenberghe); *NCE* 2, 1081 f. (M. Batllori); *DBI* 16, 769–74 (M. E. Mallett), Seppelt 4, 326–31.

PIUS II (19 Aug. 1458–15 Aug. 1464). Born on 18 Oct. 1405 at Corsignano (he was to rename it Pienza), near Siena, son of noble but impoverished parents, Enea Silvio Piccolomini worked as a boy in the fields, then steeped himself in humanist culture for eight years as a student at Siena and Florence. From 1432 to 1435 he was at the council of Basle (1431–49) as secretary to Cardinal Domenico Capranica and then other prelates, and in 1435 travelled widely on diplomatic errands with or for Cardinal Niccolò Albergati. In 1436 he became an official of the council, being thus enabled to display his brilliance as an orator. A firm opponent then of EUGENE IV, he was appointed secretary to Antipope FELIX V (elected 5 Nov. 1439), and wrote dialogues defending the authority of the council. When Felix sent him to the diet of Frankfurt in 1442, King Frederick III of Germany (1440–93) noticed him and his astonishing literary flair, crowned him poet laureate, and invited him to exchange Felix's service for his. Enea accepted, and became close friends with Frederick's chancellor, Caspar Schlick. To this period belong his widely read novel, *Lucretia and Euryalus*, celebrating Schlick's amorous adventures, and his erotic comedy *Chrysis*. In 1445 he severed connection with Felix V and was formally reconciled with Eugene IV. In the same year, moved by a serious illness, he

abandoned his dissolute life (he had fathered several bastards), and on 4 Mar. 1446 was ordained priest. In the following years he was largely responsible for persuading Frederick III and the German electors to abandon their neutrality in the schism and recognize Eugene IV. For his services NICHOLAS V made him bishop of Trieste in 1447 and of Siena in 1450, while Frederick continued to use his diplomatic abilities until 1455. On 18 Dec. 1456 CALLISTUS III, as reward for successful negotiations with Alfonso V, king of Aragón and Naples (1416–58), raised him to the cardinalate which he had long coveted. To this period belongs his important *History of Emperor Frederick*. At a conclave marked by lobbying in which he himself took part Enea, only fifty-three but already prematurely old, was elected to succeed Callistus III; he chose the name Pius in reminiscence of Vergil's 'pius Aeneas'.

The election of a connoisseur and practitioner of letters was acclaimed by humanists, but although he continued a voluminous author (writing, for example, his memoirs) Pius proved a friendly critic of them rather than their patron. Having for years called for resistance to the Turkish advance into Europe, he now made it his overriding aim to organize a crusade to check it. So he at once (Oct. 1458) issued a crusade bull in impressive terms and summoned a congress of Christian rulers to meet at Mantua on 1 June 1459. Meanwhile, faced with a choice between René I, duke of Anjou (1436–80), and Ferrante, or Ferdinand I (1458–94), natural son of Alfonso V of Aragón, for the throne of Naples, he decided, in the interest of the balance of power in Italy, in favour of Ferrante. When the congress met after a slow start, his proposals for raising troops and money at once ran into opposition. France would do nothing, angry because of his rejection of Duke René. The Germans eventually promised an army, but although a three years' war was agreed upon, the congress was a failure. Convinced that the decline of papal influence was due to the inflated prestige of councils, Pius published a bull (*Execrabilis*: 18 Jan. 1460) condemning, in defiance of his own earlier views, all appeal from the pope to a future council.

Hastening back from Mantua, Pius found himself faced with war between the French and Spanish in southern Italy and a rising of the barons in the Campagna. He dealt with these troubles without difficulty, but at the cost of still further alienating the French, from whom he was seeking the withdrawal of the *Pragmatic Sanction of Bourges. When Louis XI (1461–83) came to the throne in 1461, he announced that he had abolished it, but this was a manoeuvre to induce the pope to change his mind over Naples; when Pius continued to support Ferrante, Louis yielded to French opinion and reintroduced the traditional liberties of the French church by decree. In Germany, where there were powerful anti-papal currents, Pius excommunicated Duke Sigismund of Tirol for his hostility to the reform programme Nicholas of Cusa wanted to introduce in Brixen, and the duke appealed to a general council. At the same time Pius became embroiled with Diether von Isenburg, archbishop of Mainz, who sided with George of Podebrady, king of Bohemia (1458–71), in his efforts to replace Frederick III as king of the Romans. Diether, too, appealed to a general council, and Pius declared him deposed. He also crossed swords with George of Podebrady, who, angered by the pope's refusal to accept the Compacts of Basle agreed (1437) between Catholics and conservative Hussites, openly challenged his direction of the crusade and traditional position as arbiter of Christianity. All these difficulties, as well as the claims of the crusade, prevented Pius, who was more thoroughly aware than anyone of the grievances throughout Europe against the curia, from carrying out the programme for general and curial reform on which he had been working since his election.

The crusade was never far from Pius's thoughts, and in 1460–1, deserted by the European princes, he prepared his remark-

able, still problematical, 'Letter to Sultan Mehmet II', containing a detailed refutation of the Koran, an exposition of Christian faith, and an appeal to Mehmet to abandon Islam, be baptized, and accept the crown of the eastern empire. The letter was never sent, but throws light on the pope's personality and utopian aspirations. In Oct. 1463, encouraged by the agreement of Venice and Hungary to join forces, he again called for a crusade, making Ancona the rendezvous for the following summer; to shame Christian rulers into action, he would personally lead it. While there was some popular support, the rulers held back. Nevertheless he held fast to his great project, took the cross in St Peter's in June 1464 and then, although seriously ill, made for Ancona. There he found, to his disappointment, only a handful of crusaders; but when at last the Venetian galleys came in sight, he died, and the enterprise came to nothing. His heart was interred at Ancona, while his body was taken to Rome. With his brilliant gifts, unrivalled experience, and literary accomplishment, he stood out among the popes of his epoch. If his favouritism for relatives and Sienese compatriots was a serious fault, his often criticized transfers of allegiance did him credit. Although ambition and opportunism played their part, he was genuinely disillusioned with the council of Basle, and was sincere when he challenged critics, in his 'bull of retractation' (26 Apr. 1463), to 'reject Aeneas, listen to Pius'. His moral conversion, too, was profound and lasting, and he had a vision of a united Christian Europe which was original and refreshing.

Opera quae extant omnia (ed. M. Hopperus, Basle, 1551); *Orationes politicae et ecclesiasticae* (ed. J. D. Mansi, Lucca, 1755–9); *Opera inedita* (ed. J. Cugnoni, Rome, 1883); *Epistolae* (ed. R. Wolkan, Vienna, 1909–18). For lives by G. A. Campano and B. Platina, see G. C. Zimolo, *Raccolta degli storici Italiani* iii, 2 (Bologna, 1964). For his *Commentarii*, or memoirs, see L. C. Gabel, *Memoirs of a Renaissance Pope* (London, 1960). C. M. Ady, *Pius II* (London, 1913); R. J. Mitchell, *The Laurels and the Tiara: Pope Pius II* (New York, 1963); G. Paparelli, *Enea Silvio Piccolomini: L'umanesimo sul soglio di Pietro* (2nd edn., Ravenna, 1978); J. G. Rowe, 'The Tragedy of Aeneas Silvius Piccolomini (Pope Pius II)', *ChHist* 30 (1961), 288–313; MC 3, P 3; *DTC* 12, 1613–32 (E. Vansteenberghe); *NCE* 11, 393 f. (J. G. Rowe); Seppelt 4, 331–48; 350–52; 361 f.

PAUL II (30 Aug. 1464–26 July 1471). Born at Venice on 23 Feb. 1417, Pietro Barbo belonged to a rich merchant family and was originally intended for a business career, but took orders when his maternal uncle became pope as EUGENE IV. Through him he rapidly became archdeacon of Bologna, bishop of Cervia and then of Vicenza, protonotary of the Roman church, and (in 1440 when just twenty-three) cardinal deacon. He was influential under NICHOLAS V, who named him cardinal priest of the *title church of S. Marco, and CALLISTUS III, but less so under PIUS II, whose successor he was unexpectedly elected at the first ballot. Dissatisfied with Pius's independent style and nepotism, the conclave had sworn an 18-point electoral pact defining the future pontiff's conduct and relations to his cardinals and requiring the calling of a general council within three years, but Paul immediately declared that he accepted these rules only as guide-lines. He forced a modified version of them on the sacred college, thus losing its full trust. Had he fully implemented the reform prescriptions, the excesses of the so-called Renaissance papacy might have been checked in advance.

Handsome, vain (he toyed with adopting the name Formosus II), without intellectual distinction, Paul loved display and delighted the people by sports and entertainments. He was a great promoter of carnivals, to the expense of which Jews were obliged to contribute. His decree of 19 Apr. 1470 that, beginning with 1475, holy years should be held every twenty-five years was characteristic. His taste for magnificence is illustrated by the Palazzo S. Marco (now the Palazzo di Venezia), which he began building as cardinal in 1455 and made his chief residence in Rome from 1466. His abolition of the college of abbreviators, or papal draughtsmen, who were often scholars or literary men, in 1466, and his imprisonment and torture of the historian Bartolomeo Platina (1421–81) when he protested, made him hated in humanist circles. So did his suppression of the Roman academy (1468), which he suspected of cultivating pagan rituals and ideas, and his ban on the study of pagan poets by Roman children. But, far from being hostile to culture or humanism, he surrounded himself with scholars, restored ancient monuments, and eagerly collected artistic objects; he installed the first printing-press in Rome. Beginning in 1469, with the citizens' consent, he revised the statutes of Rome; and he frowned on the acceptance of presents by officials in the papal state. He also, in 1470, imposed on corporations owning benefices a tax payable every fifteen years known as *quindemia*.

The continuation of the war against the Turks, and the use of the great alum mines discovered near Tolfa to finance it, were items in the electoral pact which Paul accepted. He at once began collecting funds and gave support, financial if not military, to sorely pressed Hungary and the heroic Albanian leader George Skanderberg (d. 1468). To create the peaceful conditions necessary he sought in 1469 to intervene in north Italy, where the death of Francesco Sforza of Milan in 1466 had brought dangerous instability. It was unfortunate that the prince best qualified to lead a campaign against the Turks, George of Podebrady, king of Bohemia (1458–71), was under suspicion of Hussite heresy at Rome. When Paul came to the throne, efforts were made to settle the affair amicably, but in Dec. 1466 the pope felt obliged to excommunicate the king, and even call for a crusade against him. When Negroponte (Evvia) in Greece, the last outpost of Venice in the Levant, fell to Sultan Mehmet II (conqueror of Constantinople in 1453) in 1470, Paul issued a general summons to a crusade against the Turks and convened the Italian powers to a congress at Rome, but all he could obtain was a defensive alliance concluded on 22 Dec. 1470.

His diplomacy was more successful in the Middle East, where he made an alliance against the Turks with the Iranian prince Uzun-Hassan.

Paul had excellent relations with Emperor Frederick III (1440–93), who paid him a private visit in 1468 but failed to persuade him to organize a general council at Constance. The prospect of a general council was constantly held over him as a threat in his difficult, in the end unsuccessful, negotiations with Louis XI of France (1461–83) for the removal of the 'liberties' claimed by the French church under the *Pragmatic Sanction of Bourges. In his closing months Paul was planning to reconcile the Russian church with Rome by arranging a marriage between Ivan III of Russia (1462–1505) and the daughter, now Catholic, of Thomas Palaeologus, exiled despot of Morea (d. 1465), but before the negotiations were completed he died suddenly of a stroke. The papal biographer Platina, as Vatican librarian (1475), took his revenge on him by painting his portrait in the blackest colours.

J. Ammanati, *Epistolae et commentarii* (Milan, 1506); Michael Canensius and Caspar da Verona in Muratori 3.2, 994–1022; 1025–50; B. Platina in Muratori² 3.1, 363–98; O. Raynaldus, *Annales ecclesiastici* (for 1465–71) (ed. J. D. Mansi, Lucca, 1747–56); R. Weiss, *Un umanista Veneziano: papa Paolo II* (Rome, 1958); P 4; MC 4; *PRE* 15, 28–31 (C. Beurath); *DTC* 12, 3–9 (É. Amann); NCE 11, 12 f. (M. François); Seppelt 4, 342 f.; 348–53.

SIXTUS IV (9 Aug. 1471–12 Aug. 1484). Born at Celle, near Savona, of impoverished parents on 21 July 1414, Francesco della Rovere was educated by the Franciscans, early joined the order, and, after studying at Bologna and Padua, lectured at several universities. A sought-after preacher, he was also an acute theologian who wrote treatises on issues dividing the Franciscans and the Dominicans. After serving as provincial of Liguria, he was elected general of his order on 19 May 1464; on 18 Sept. 1467 he was promoted cardinal of S. Pietro in Vincoli on the recommendation of the Greek John Bessarion, who admired his

scholarship. In the indecision following PAUL II's sudden death he emerged as the unexpected favourite of the conclave. His election was assisted by lavish gifts to the duke of Milan, who strongly backed it, and by the preferments promised by his nephew Pietro Riario, who acted as his attendant, to leading cardinals. Strict in his personal life but ruthlessly determined and unscrupulous about means, he inaugurated a line of pontiffs who systematically secularized the papacy.

Initially he was enthusiastic for a crusade against the Turks and spent lavishly on equipping a fleet, but in spite of his appeals the European powers hung back, and his fleet only achieved modest successes in the Aegean, taking part, e.g., in landings at Smyrna (Izmir) in 1472. He proclaimed another crusade in 1481, when Otranto on the Italian mainland fell to the Turks (11 Aug. 1480), but its recovery in Sept. 1482 owed more to the sudden death of Sultan Mehmet II (3 May) than to the papal galleys. His relations were strained with Louis XI of France (1461–83), who firmly upheld the *Pragmatic Sanction of Bourges (1438) and whose ordinance (8 Jan. 1475) requiring royal approval for the publication of papal decrees in France he denounced. He continued (1474 and 1476) Paul II's negotiations with Ivan III of Russia (1462–1505) for the reunion of the Russian church with Rome, and also for Russian support against the Turks, but to no avail. A loyal Franciscan, he greatly increased the privileges of the mendicant orders, approved (1476) the feast of the Immaculate Conception with its own mass and office, and canonized (1482) the Franciscan theologian Bonaventura (d. 1274). On 1 Nov. 1478, at the request of the Catholic kings, he set up the Spanish Inquisition, in 1482–3 sought to check its abuses, and in 1483 confirmed Tomás de Torquemada (1420–98) as grand inquisitor. In 1478 he annulled the decrees of the council of Constance (1414–17).

To Sixtus, however, the routine business of the holy see took second place to the aggrandizement of the papal state and of his own family. Soon after his election, flouting his election oath, he made two youthful nephews, Pietro Riario and Giuliano della Rovere (later JULIUS II), cardinals, loading them with lucrative preferments. A swarm of other relatives were enriched and advanced on a completely unprecedented scale. When Pietro succumbed to his dissipations in 1474, his place of sinister influence was taken by his brother Girolamo, now a count and married to a daughter of Duke Galeazzo Sforza of Milan (1447-76). Men of demonic energy, he and Giuliano involved the pope, often feigning to protest, in the disputes and turmoils of Italian politics. The most disreputable affair into which Girolamo dragged Sixtus was the Pazzi conspiracy of 1478, in which the murder of Lorenzo and Giuliano de' Medici was planned and of which the pope, even if he did not give his consent to the bloodshed, was fully cognizant. Lorenzo escaped wounded, but Giuliano was killed. As a consequence Sixtus entered into a fruitless and inglorious war with Florence (1478-80), and then, at the prompting of Girolamo, incited the Venetians to attack Ferrara; in 1483 he changed sides and turned against Venice, imposing spiritual penalties on it. The peace of Bagnolo of 1484 did not bring the territorial gains in Romagna he and his nephew were hoping for, but instead dangerous risings in Rome and Latium. What with his costly military and building operations as well as the demands of his greedy relatives, papal expenditure increased enormously during his reign, and in spite of creating new, highly dubious sources of revenue and exploiting the granting of indulgences he left a huge deficit to his successor. The widespread disquiet at the abuses of the papal court found an outlet in Mar. 1482 when a reform-minded archbishop, the Croatian Andrea Zamometič, in earlier days Sixtus's friend, made an abortive attempt to reconvene the council of Basle (1431-49) and have him suspended until it had passed judgement on him. Sixtus responded in 1483 with a renewed ban on appeals to

general councils. His death next year was said to have been hastened by vexation at having peace forced on him by the princes and cities of Italy.

Most of the thirty-four cardinals he created (six of them nephews) were men of little worth. A more attractive aspect of his chosen role as a Renaissance prince was his munificence as a founder and restorer of useful institutions and as a patron of letters and art. He transformed Rome from a medieval into a Renaissance city, opening up new streets and widening and paving old ones, building the Ponte Sisto, erecting churches—Sta Maria del Popolo (his family burial place), Sta Maria della Pace, the Sistine Chapel with its walls painted by Umbrian masters—and restoring the Ospedale di S. Spirito. He drew to Rome the greatest painters and sculptors, improved church music and founded the Sistine choir, established the Vatican archives, and was the second founder of the Vatican library. His tomb, in the Vatican Grottoes, is a masterpiece in bronze by Antonio del Pollaiuolo.

B. Platina, *Vita*, Muratori[2] 3.1, 1053-68; Infessura, *Diario della città di Roma* (ed. O. Tommasini, Rome, 1890); *Diario di Roma di Notajo*, Muratori 3.2, 1071-108; V. Pacifici, *Un carme biografico di Sisto IV del 1477* (Tivoli, 1924); *AFrH* 28 (1935), 198-234; 477-99; C. Bauer, 'Studi per la storia delle finanze papali durante il pontificato di Sisto IV', *Arch. Rom. Soc. Storia Patria* 1 (1927), 314 404; *DTC* 14, 2199-217 (A. Teetaert); MC 4; P 4; *LThK* 9, 810 f. (G. Schwaiger); *NCE* 13, 272 f. (E. G. Gleeson); *EC* 11, 780-2 (P. Paschini); Seppelt 4, 353-70.

INNOCENT VIII (29 Aug. 1484-25 July 1492). The conclave following SIXTUS IV's death was a hotbed of intrigue, with his nephew Giuliano della Rovere (JULIUS II), aware that he himself stood no chance, lobbying for the election of someone he could dominate. The man chosen, after endorsing the petitions of several cardinals for favours in his cell the night before, was the easygoing but ineffective Giovanni Battista Cibò. The son of a Roman senator, he was born at Genoa in 1432, spent his youth at the court of Naples and then studied at Padua and Rome, took orders and, through the favour of Cardinal Calandrini, was made bishop of Savona in 1467 and then Molfetta in 1472, and was created a cardinal by Sixtus IV in 1473. He had little experience of politics, and, having fathered several illegitimate children before ordination, he now provided for them by marriage into princely houses.

Irresolute, lax, chronically ill, but personally affable as he was, there could be no question of church reform in Innocent's reign. His court, like Sixtus IV's, was as colourful and loose as any Italian prince's, and his cardinals, mostly Sixtus's creations, were worldly *grands seigneurs*. He inherited vast debts from Sixtus, and the financial state of the curia continued to get worse. To alleviate it he resorted to the expedient of creating countless unneeded curial and other offices and then selling them to the highest bidder. His insolvency was not helped by his siding in 1485, persuaded by Giuliano, with the rebellious Neapolitan barons against Ferdinand I of Naples (1458-94), who refused to pay the papal dues. The results were disastrous for Rome and the papal state, and he had to accept a disadvantageous peace in Aug. 1486. Freed for a time from Giuliano's influence, he now made an alliance with Lorenzo de' Medici, to whose daughter he married his undeserving son Franceschetto, and whose thirteen-year-old son he raised to the cardinalate. Hostilities with Naples, however, broke out afresh in 1489, since Ferdinand failed to fulfil his side of the peace, and in Sept. Innocent excommunicated and deposed him. A reconciliation was patched up in Jan. 1492, but the papacy lost L'Aquila and most of its political prestige.

The attempts Innocent made to rally action to meet the Turkish menace proved abortive. The fact that he was the first pope to enter into relations with the Ottoman empire may have contributed to this. In 1489 he agreed an arrangement with the Ottoman sultan Bayezid II (1481-1512) whereby, in return for 40,000 ducats yearly

and the gift of the Holy Lance (supposed to have pierced Christ's side at his crucifixion), he detained his fugitive brother and potential rival Jem in close confinement at Rome. To escape from Bayezid Jem had fled to Rhodes, and the grand master of the Knights of St John, in return for a cardinal's hat, handed him over to the pope, who was glad to have such an important hostage for the sultan's good behaviour.

In 1486 Innocent formally recognized Henry VII as rightful king of England on the threefold ground of conquest, inheritance, and national choice. He is also remembered both for his bull *Summis desiderantes* (5 Dec. 1484) ordering the Inquisition in Germany to proceed with the utmost severity against supposed witches, which gave a powerful stimulus to the persecution of witchcraft, and for his ban (1486) on the discussion and study of the theses of Pico della Mirandola (1463-94), the exponent of Renaissance Platonism. As his ineffective reign drew to its close, he and Rome were filled with jubilation by the news of the expulsion of the Moors from Granada (2 Jan. 1492), but the triumph was due to Ferdinand V and Isabella of Castile (1474-1504), not to the holy see; in recognition of this he awarded Ferdinand and his successors the title of 'Catholic Kings'. As pope he was incapable of exercising firm control over Rome and left the papal states in anarchy, and his death was the signal for an outbreak of unprecedented violence and disorder.

Diarium Romanae urbis ab anno 1481 ad 1492 and Infessura, *Diarium* (Muratori 3.2, 1070-108 and 1189-243); J. Burckard, *Liber notarum ab anno 1483 usque ad annum 1506* (Muratori² 23.1.2); J. da Volterra, *Diarium Romanum (1479-1484)* (Muratori² 23.3); *PRE* 9, 137-9 (Zöpffel-Beurath); MC 4; P 5; *NCE* 7, 526 f. (W. R. Bonniwell); *EC* 7, 18 f. (P. Brezzi); Seppelt 4, 369-76.

ALEXANDER VI (11 Aug. 1492-18 Aug. 1503). Rodrigo de Borja y Borja (Borgia in Italian) was born on 1 Jan. 1431 at Játiva, near Valencia. His maternal uncle, then bishop of Valencia but after 1455 CALLISTUS III, loaded the youth with benefices, sent him to study at Bologna, and in Feb. 1456 named him cardinal deacon. As well as holding a string of bishoprics and abbeys, Rodrigo became vice-chancellor of the holy see in 1457, a lucrative office he held under the next four popes, amassing such vast wealth that he was reckoned the second richest cardinal. At the same time he lived an openly licentious life, fathering several children; he was fondest of those born to the aristocratic Roman Vannozza Catanei— Juan, Cesare, Lucrezia, Goffredo. In 1460 his scandalous behaviour earned him a sharp but unheeded rebuke from PIUS II. Possessed of ambition, energy, and versatile talents, he worked hard but unsuccessfully for election as successor to SIXTUS IV. At the conclave (6–11 Aug.) following INNO-CENT VIII's death, however, although as a Spaniard not at first regarded as a serious candidate, he eventually emerged as victor. He had swung several cardinals over to his cause by barefaced bribery and promises of rich preferments.

An experienced administrator, Alex-ander made a favourable start, restoring order in Rome, dispensing justice vigorously, and promising reform of the curia and a united effort against the Turkish menace. It was soon evident, however, that his consuming passion, gold and women apart, was the aggrandizement of his rela-tives, especially Vannozza's children. Thus he soon named Cesare, still only eighteen, bishop of several sees, including the wealthy one of Valencia, and a year later, along with Alessandro Farnese (brother of Giulia, his current mistress), a cardinal. Cesare's brother Juan, duke of Gandía, he married to a Spanish princess, and in 1497 enfeoffed him with the duchy of Benevento, which he carved out of the papal state. For Lucrezia he arranged one magnificent marriage after the other; in his absence from Rome he sometimes left her as virtual regent in charge of official business. In June 1497 he was momentarily shattered by the murder of Juan, his special favourite, with suspicion falling on Cesare. Grief-stricken, he vowed to devote himself henceforth to church reform, and had a bull full of admirable proposals drafted; but it remained a draft. He lacked the resolution to abjure sensu-ality; he soon resumed his pleasures and family machinations, with Cesare now increasingly his evil genius.

Family interest conditioned the shifts of Alexander's Italian policy. Initially at odds with Ferdinand I of Naples (1458–94), he supported him against the claims of Charles VIII of France (1483–98) after the marriage of his son Goffredo in 1493 to the king's grand-daughter (whose dowry was the rich principality of Squillace). On Ferdinand's death (25 Jan. 1494), he recognized and crowned his son Alfonso II as king (1494–5). At this Charles, incited by Alexander's deadly enemy, Cardinal della Rovere (later JULIUS II), invaded Italy, breathing threats of a council to depose the pope, who in his difficult straits did not hesitate to seek help from the Turkish sultan Bayezid II (1481–1512). He could not defend Rome and had to come to terms with Charles, who easily conquered Naples; but Alexander refused, in spite of strong pressure, to invest him with it. Eventually, by allying himself in a 'holy league' (31 Mar. 1493) with other powers which threatened Charles's rear, he forced him to withdraw from Italy, and in June 1497 sent Cesare as legate to Naples to crown Frederick of Aragón (1496–1501). From 1498, however, under the influence of Cesare, whom he released from the car-dinalate, he moved closer to France, annul-ling the marriage of the new king, Louis XII. He sent Cesare as envoy to France, where a grateful Louis created him duke of Valentinois and gave him a princess as his bride. Alexander's volte-face was so com-plete that in 1501 he ratified the partition of Naples between France and Spain. Mean-while Cesare proceeded, with French aid, to subdue Romagna, being created duke of this largest province of the papal state in 1501. But the ambitions of Cesare and Alexander, now wholly under his sway, envisaged the appropriation of the entire papal state and central Italy by the Borgia family, and this project, with the systematic crushing of the great Roman families, filled the rest of the reign. The enormous sums required for its realization were raised by assassinations, followed by seizures of property, and by the cynical creation of cardinals who had to pay dearly for their elevation.

In 1493, at the instance of the Castilian sovereigns, Alexander drew a line of demarcation a hundred leagues west of the Azores between Spanish and Portuguese zones of exploration in the new world; as it favoured Spain, it was modified by the Treaty of Tordesillas of 7 June 1494. He also granted the monarchs control of the church in the lands they colonized. In 1495 he began his long duel with the preacher and reformer Girolamo Savonarola (1452–98) which, started with patience, ended in May 1498 with the excommunication, examination under torture, and execution of the Florentine friar; Alexander found his opposition to Florence's joining the anti-French coalition as inconvenient as his denunciations of papal corruption and his calls for a council to reform the church and depose the pope. Devout and a stickler for orthodoxy in spite of personal profligacy, he celebrated the holy year of 1500 with suitable pomp, using the vast sums accruing from indulgences to finance Cesare's expeditions. In general his concern for the needs of the church—e.g. for the reform of monasteries, for the religious orders, and for missions in the new world—took a markedly second place to more worldly goals. He had a genuine love, however, for art and, although a less lavish patron than Sixtus IV or Julius II, richly restored Castel Sant'Angelo, embellished the Vatican with the Borgia apartments decorated by Pinturicchio, and persuaded Michelangelo to draw plans for the rebuilding of St Peter's. Involved in political and family scheming till the end, he and Cesare were suddenly taken ill in Aug. 1503, and while the younger man survived with difficulty, Alexander died. His death is usually explained as due to malaria, but there are strong grounds for believing that father and son were victims of poison

intended for a cardinal who was their host at dinner which was mistakenly given to themselves.

O. Raynaldus, *Annales ecclesiastici* (for 1492–1503) (ed. J. D. Mansi, Lucca, 1747–56),208–416; J. Burckard, *Liber notarum* (Muratori[2] 32.1); P. de Roo, *Materials for a History of Pope Alexander VI, his Relations and his Times* (Bruges, 1924); G. Parker, *At the Court of the Borgia* (Folio Society, London, 1963); G. Pepe, *La politica dei Borgia* (Naples, 1945); G. Soranzo, *Studi intorno a papa Alessandro VI* (Milan, 1950); O. Ferrara, *The Borgia Pope* (ET, London, 1942); J. Schnitzer, *Der Tod Alexanders VI* (Münster, 1929); 'Um den Tod Alexanders VI', *HJ* 50 (1930), 256–60; P 5 and 6; MC 4 and 5; *DBI* 2, 196–205 (G. B. Picotti); *EC* 1, 795–801 (G. M. Pou y Marti); *NCE* 1, 290–2 (M. Batllori); *ED* (15th edn.) 1, 467 f. (F. X. Murphy); Seppelt 4, 396–94.

PIUS III (22 Sept.–18 Oct. 1503). Born at Siena in 1439, Francesco Todeschini was, through his mother, a nephew of PIUS II, who allowed him to assume his family name (Piccolomini) and arms, took him into his household, and arranged for his legal studies at Perugia. After he had obtained his doctorate, his uncle made him archbishop of Siena (he was only twenty-one, and a deacon), and a few weeks later (5 Mar. 1460) cardinal deacon of S. Eustachio. Pius II then sent him as legate to the March of Ancona, and in 1464 left him in charge of Rome and the papal state when he himself went to Ancona to lead the crusade. For many years cardinal protector of England and Germany, he became the trusted friend of both nations. PAUL II appointed him legate in Germany, where his fluency in German helped him to defend the interests of the church with the emperor and before the diet of Regensburg (1471). Although he continued influential under ALEXANDER VI, who sent him on an abortive mission to Charles VIII of France in Nov. 1494, he kept his distance from him; he had angrily refused to be bribed to vote for him at the conclave of Aug. 1492, and in June 1497 he protested, alone of the sacred college, against his proposed transfer of substantial papal territories to his son Juan, duke of

Gandía. A man of culture as well as integrity, he founded the Libreria Piccolomini at Siena to house his uncle's library, entrusting the decoration to Pinturicchio (1502).

Francesco owed his election at the conclave (16–22 Sept. 1503) following Alexander VI's death less to his intrinsic merits (he had been considered seriously more than once before) than to the need to find a neutral candidate to break the deadlock caused by competing national interests and the threat of interference by Cesare Borgia. His fragile health (he was racked with gout) and premature old age also stood in his favour, for a short pontificate which would provide a breathing-space was desired. In the event his reign proved even briefer than expected. His health was so weak that several of the customary ceremonies had to be omitted at his coronation on 8 Oct. 1503, and ten days later he died. His death was regarded by contemporaries as a misfortune, for there were signs that, had he lived, he would have summoned a general council within two years and promoted the serious reform measures that were desperately needed.

E. Piccolomini, 'La famiglia di Pio III', *ASRomana* 26 (1903), 146–64; 'Il pontificato di Pio III', *AstIt* 32 (1903), 102–38; J. Schlecht, *Pius III und die deutsche Nation* (Münster, 1914); *PRE* 15, 435 f. (Zöpffel-Beurath); P 6; *DTC* 12, 1632 f. (É. Amann); *EC* 9, 1496 (G. B. Picotti); *NCE* 11, 394 f. (D. R. Campbell); Seppelt 4, 394 f.

JULIUS II (1 Nov. 1503–21 Feb. 1513). Born on 5 Dec. 1453 of poor parents at Albissola, near Savona, and originally intended for commerce, Giuliano della Rovere was educated, through his uncle Francesco's influence, by the Franciscans at Perugia, and took orders. When his uncle became Sixtus IV (1471), he named Giuliano bishop of Carpentras and (16 Dec. 1471) cardinal priest of S. Pietro in Vincoli; he soon acquired other bishoprics, abbacies and benefices, including the cardinal bishopric of Sta Sabina. As legate in France in 1480–2 he successfully mediated

between Louis XI (1461–83) and Maximilian I of Austria (1486–1519) over the latter's Burgundian inheritance. He was prominent under INNOCENT VIII, whose election he managed, but an enemy of ALEXANDER VI. Fearing assassination, he fled in 1494 to France, where he encouraged Charles VIII (1483–98) to undertake the conquest of Naples. He accompanied the king on his campaign (1494–5), but his efforts to get his backing for a council to depose Alexander for simony were foiled by the wily pope. Although he negotiated Cesare Borgia's marriage with a French princess in 1499, he was lucky to escape Alexander's plots and remained in hiding until his death. At the ensuing conclave he was not chosen, but PIUS III reigned only twenty-six days; on his death Giuliano at last attained his ambition, and with the help of lavish promises and bribes was unanimously elected pope at a conclave lasting a single day.

A forceful ruler, ruthless and violent, Julius eschewed family aggrandizement and strove, with all diplomatic and military means available, to restore and extend the papal state, which the Borgias had alienated, and to establish a strong, independent papacy in an Italy free from foreign domination. First, having dexterously got rid of the still dangerous Cesare Borgia (d. 1507) by making Italy too hot for him, he vainly urged Venice to evacuate those parts of Romagna she had occupied earlier in 1503. Then, having allied himself with France and Germany, he won back all Romagna from her except Rimini and Faenza in 1504. In 1506, in a brilliant campaign led by himself in full armour, he wrested Perugia and Bologna from their petty tyrants. In Mar. 1509 he joined the League of Cambrai formed in 1508 between France, Germany, and Spain, excommunicated Venice on 27 Apr., and in May defeated her so disastrously that she was forced to surrender Rimini and Faenza and also the control of church appointments and taxation rights that she had usurped. He had no wish, however, unduly to weaken

Venice, indispensable in any war with the Turks, and now decided that France, powerfully established in the north, was the real danger to Italy and must be driven out. He therefore made peace with Venice and, to win the support of Spain, enfeoffed Ferdinand II of Aragón (1476–1516) with Naples (3 July 1510) in disregard of France's claims.

Julius first attacked Ferrara, an ally of France and the only vassal state still unsubdued. His troops seized Modena in 1510 and captured Mirandola in Jan. 1511, with himself at their head. He failed, however, to win Ferrara, and had to see Bologna fall temporarily to the French; he himself narrowly escaped capture. Meanwhile Louis XII of France (1498–1515) counterattacked by holding a synod at Tours (Sept. 1510) which renewed the *Pragmatic Sanction of Bourges, and by calling, in the name of a group of rebel cardinals, for a council to meet at Pisa on 1 Sept. 1511 to depose the pope. It assembled on 1 Oct., held several sessions, and decreed the suspension of Julius. To meet the threat, especially as Emperor Maximilian I favoured the Pisan council, Julius now summoned the fifth Lateran council to meet in Rome in 1512. On the political plane he formed (Oct. 1511) the Holy League with Venice and Spain for the defence of the papacy; Henry VIII of England (1509–47) joined it later in the year. The League's armies were severely defeated at Ravenna (11 Apr. 1512), but its fortunes changed with the arrival of Swiss troops, and before the end of 1512 the French had to quit Italian soil. Parma, Piacenza, and Reggio Emilia were added to the papal state, of which Julius could claim to be the re-founder.

Politics and wars dominated Julius's reign; Erasmus in his *Praise of Folly* (1509) caricatured his military ardour, and the Florentine historian Guicciardini remarked that there was nothing of the priest about him except the dress and the name. His strictly church activities were largely routine: in 1503, for instance, he issued the dispensation which enabled Henry VIII

later to marry his brother's widow, Catherine of Aragón. Nevertheless, he published a bull (dated 14 Jan. 1505) declaring papal elections nullified by simony, and founded the first bishoprics in South America. He opened on 3 May 1512 the fifth Lateran (Eighteenth General) council (1512–17), being gratified at the third session by the adhesion of Emperor Maximilian; but the five sessions held in his lifetime were concerned mainly with condemning the schismatic Pisan council (1511–12) and the Pragmatic Sanction of Bourges. His most enduring achievement was as the patron and inspirer of artists, notably Michelangelo, the youthful Raphael, and Bramante. The last he commissioned to prepare plans for the new St Peter's, assisting at the laying of the foundation stone on 18 Apr. 1506, and arranging for the cost to be defrayed by the sale of indulgences (later to be bitterly criticized by the Protestant reformers). In spite of expensive wars and building projects he was a frugal administrator who, having inherited an empty treasury, left it more than full. As a man he was headstrong, irascible, sensual (as cardinal he fathered three daughters), and was nicknamed 'Il terribile'; as pope he had policies which were at least disinterested and intelligible even if they aimed no higher than making the papal state the first power in Italy. When he died of fever, he was mourned as the liberator of Italy from foreign domination, and has subsequently been saluted as the promoter of its unification.

J. Burckard, *Liber notarum* (index), Muratori[2] 32.1; O. Raynaldus, *Annales ecclesiastici* (for 1503–13) (ed. J. D. Mansi, Lucca, 1747–56); M. Brosch, *Papst Julius II und die Gründung des Kirchenstaates* (Gotha, 1878); E. Rodocanachi, *Le pontificat de Jules II* (Paris, 1928); F. Seneca, *Venezia e Papa Giulio II* (Padua, 1962); P 6; MC 5; DTC 8, 1918–20 (G. Mollat); NCE 8, 52–4 (D. R. Campbell); EB (15th edn.) 10, 333–5 (H. Kühner); Seppelt 4, 394–408.

LEO X (11 Mar. 1513–1 Dec. 1521). The conclave of Mar. 1513 elected, swiftly and without simony (owing to JULIUS II's stern ban), the thirty-seven-year-old cardinal Giovanni de' Medici. Second son of Lorenzo the Magnificent, he was born at Florence on 11 Dec. 1475 and was early destined for the church, being tonsured when still seven and named cardinal deacon at thirteen. Leading humanists tutored him as a boy, and he was a student of theology and canon law at Pisa from 1489 to 1491. At seventeen he joined the sacred college at Rome, but soon returned to Florence on his father's death later in 1492. He left it when his family was exiled in 1494, and travelled (1494-1500) in France, Holland (meeting Erasmus), and Germany. Returning to Rome in May 1500, he immersed himself in literature, the arts, the theatre, and music, but after ALEXANDER VI's death began acquiring political influence. Appointed legate of Bologna in 1511, with charge of the papal army, he was taken prisoner at Ravenna in Apr. 1512, but escaped. In 1512 he was able to re-establish Medici control of Florence, of which he remained effective ruler until the conclave, and indeed during his pontificate.

A polished Renaissance prince, Leo was also a devious and double-tongued politician and an inveterate nepotist. His aim was to keep Italy and his own Florence free from foreign domination and to advance his family outside Florence. In 1513, faced with a French attempt, in alliance with Venice, to recover Milan and Naples, he reluctantly joined the League of Mechlin (5 Apr.) with Emperor Maximilian I (1493-1519), Spain, and England. After the defeat of France at Novara (6 June), he reached an understanding with Louis XII (1498-1515) under which France withdrew support from the schismatic council of Pisa (1511-12). When Louis's successor Francis I (1515-47) revived France's claims and defeated the allies at Marignano (13/14 Sept. 1515), recovering Milan for France, Leo switched policies and, against the cardinals' advice, meeting the king at Bologna, agreed a settlement with him. The holy see had to surrender Parma and Piacenza, but he was able to maintain Florence intact for the

Medici and, more important, to arrange a concordat with France which, though accepted with difficulty by the curia, remained operative until the French Revolution. Although this involved unprecedented concessions, allowing the crown to nominate to all higher church offices and reserving only lesser benefices to the pope, it finally removed the *Pragmatic Sanction of Bourges. Less creditable was the war he waged in 1516 to replace Francesco della Rovere as duke of Urbino by his own nephew Lorenzo, son of his brother Piero de' Medici; it resulted in political and financial disaster. In 1517 he turned the tables on some disaffected cardinals who plotted to poison him by executing the leader (Alfonso Petrucci), imprisoning several others, and packing the sacred college by creating (1 July) thirty-one new cardinals. The problem of the imperial succession in 1519 showed his diplomacy at its most tortuous; at first he seemed to favour Francis I of France, at times worked for the Elector Frederick of Saxony (d. 1525), and only when it became inevitable accepted the Habsburg Charles I of Spain (Charles V, 1519-56), in May 1521 concluding an alliance against France with him.

In his electoral oath Leo had undertaken to continue the fifth Lateran council (1512-17), and as constructive proposals for reform were in the air great hopes were placed on the lead he would give. He duly opened the sixth session on 27 Apr. 1513, and at the eighth and ninth sessions (19 Dec. 1513 and 5 Mar. 1514) received respectively the disavowal of the anti-papal second council of Pisa (1511-12) by Louis XII and the adhesion of the French episcopate; the eighth session also ratified a dogmatic definition on the individuality of the human soul. The council later ratified the abolition of the Pragmatic Sanction and Leo's concordat with Francis I. The remaining sessions touched on reform, revealing an awareness of the principal abuses crying out for removal; but while a reform commission was set up and reform decrees published, these in the main tightened up existing legislation without providing the means for its enforcement. When Leo closed the council on 16 Mar. 1517, after decreeing a crusade against the Turks and a three-year tax on benefices to finance it, it was evident that there had been no sense of the urgency of the situation and no real direction from the pontiff.

Easygoing and pleasure-loving, the patron of artists and re-founder (Nov. 1513) of Rome university, Leo was recklessly extravagant, so desperate for money that he pawned his palace furniture and plate. In addition to his pleasures, he had to pay for his wars, the projected crusade, and not least the construction of St Peter's; to raise money he borrowed extensively and sold offices, even cardinals' hats. For St Peter's he renewed the indulgence authorized by Julius II, and by a lucrative but simoniacal deal with Albrecht of Brandenburg, archbishop of Magdeburg and Mainz (1490–1548), arranged for the indulgence to be promoted by preachers in his dioceses. When the Dominican John Tetzel (c. 1465–1519) began preaching it in Jan. 1517, the Augustinian monk Martin Luther (1483–1546) reacted by posting his ninety-five theses of protest on the church door at Wittenberg. When a summary of Luther's ideas reached Rome early in 1518, Leo instructed the general of his order to silence him. He then tried to win over Luther's protector, the Elector Frederick of Saxony, but had no success. After debates between the theologian John Eck (1486–1543) and Luther at Leipzig in 1519, Leo published the bull *Exsurge Domine* (15 June 1520) condemning Luther on forty-one counts; then on 3 Jan. 1521, Luther having publicly burned the bull, he excommunicated him in the bull *Decet Romanum pontificem*. On 11 Oct. 1521 he bestowed the title 'Defender of the Faith' on Henry VIII of England in recognition of his book defending the seven sacraments against Luther. The hesitations and delays in his dealings with the reformer are partly explained by his preoccupation with political and family manoeuvres, but even more by the complete

failure of himself and the curia to appreciate the significance of the revolution taking place in the church. When he died suddenly of malaria he left Italy in political turmoil, northern Europe in growing religious disaffection, and the papal treasury deeply in debt.

P. Bembo, *Libri xvi epistolarum Leonis P.M. nomine scriptarum* (Venice, 1535–6; Basle, 1539); P. Giovio, *Vita Leonis* (Florence, 1548); P. de Grassis, *Il diario di Leone X* (ed. D. Delicati and M. Armellini, Rome, 1884); J. Hergenröther, *Regesta Leonis X* (Freiburg i.B., 1884–91); W. Roscoe, *The Life and Pontificate of Leo the Tenth* (London, 1853); E. Rodocanachi, *Le pontificat de Léon X* (Paris, 1931); F. Nitti, *Leone X e la sua politica* (Florence, 1892); P 7 and 8; MC 6; *DTC* 9, 329–32 (G. Mollat); *LThK* 6, 950–2 (G. Schwaiger); *NCE* 8, 643–5 (J. G. Gallaher); Seppelt 4, 408–30.

HADRIAN VI (9 Jan. 1522–14 Sept. 1523). Deeply divided between powerful contenders (who included the English lord chancellor, Thomas Wolsey) as well as by political rivalries, the conclave after LEO X's death eventually elected a cardinal then absent in Spain. A carpenter's son born at Utrecht on 2 Mar. 1459, Adrian Florensz Dedal was educated by his widowed mother with the Brethren of the Common Life and, entering Louvain university at seventeen, became a professor of note, twice rector, and finally (1497) chancellor. His lecture notes on *The Sentences* of Peter Lombard (d. 1160) and his twelve *Quodlibeta* reveal him as a late scholastic with a canonical and moral bias. In 1507 Emperor Maximilian I (1493–1519) appointed him tutor to his grandson Charles V (1519–56), and in 1515, now a counsellor of Margaret, regent of the Netherlands, he went to Spain to ensure his charge's succession to the throne. On the death of King Ferdinand of Aragón in 1516 Adrian acted as regent along with the humanist Cardinal Ximénes (1436–1517) until Charles took over in 1517. Named bishop of Tortosa and inquisitor for Aragón and Navarre in 1516, inquisitor for Castile and León also in 1518, he was created cardinal of Utrecht in 1517 at Charles's special request. During

Charles's absence in 1520–2 for his coronation he served as viceroy and dealt, though incompetently, with a serious revolt. The confidence of Charles, now emperor, as well as his own high moral standing contributed to his election.

Ascetic and devout, but always a professor, Hadrian (he retained his baptismal name) saw his principal tasks as checking the Reformation by reform of the central administration and uniting Christian Europe against the Turks, who under Sultan Süleyman I the Magnificent (1520–66) had stormed (1521) Belgrade and were threatening Hungary and besieging Rhodes. This programme he expounded at his first consistory on 1 Sept. 1522, having travelled to Rome by sea so as to underline his independence of both France and the empire. His reception by the Roman people, who were disgusted by the choice of a northern 'barbarian', was hostile, and was made more so both by the drastic economies forced on him by Leo X's crippling debts and by his evident disinterest in Renaissance art. The cardinals were consternated by his reluctance to distribute lucrative benefices in the traditional way and by his determination to purge the secularized curia. Instead of collaborating with him they hampered his efforts to introduce improvements, and he became increasingly isolated from them and dependent on a few Spanish or Flemish intimates.

In dealing with the Lutheran revolt in Germany Hadrian did not appreciate the gravity of the situation. At the diet of Nuremberg (Dec. 1522) he was represented by Francesco Chieregati, whose instruction contained the frank admission that blame for the disorder in the church lay primarily with the curia itself—an admission aptly described as the first step towards the Counter-Reformation. He was strongly opposed, however, to doctrinal change and demanded that Martin Luther (1483–1546), whose opinions he had condemned as inquisitor in Spain, should be punished for heresy and that the edict of Worms (8 May 1521) banning his teachings should be

carried out. At the same time his attempts to mobilize a European front against the Turks were marked by diplomatic gaucherie and ended in failure. First, he alienated Charles V, who expected him to join his league against Francis I of France (1515–47), by his endeavour to be strictly neutral. Then, when Rhodes fell to the Turks (21 Dec. 1522), he sought to impose a three-year truce on Christendom on pain of the severest ecclesiastical penalties. This, and his arrest of Cardinal Soderini, who was discovered secretly plotting with Francis I, provoked the king to open rupture; he stopped the transfer of money from France to Rome, and prepared to invade Lombardy. Hadrian had no option but to make a defensive alliance with the empire, England, Austria, Milan, and other Italian cities, on 3 Aug. 1523. Shortly afterwards, disillusioned, worn out by his exertions and the summer heat, he fell seriously ill and sank to his death after a reign full of good intentions but too short to be effective.

M. von Domarus and P. Kalkoff, *HJ* 16 (1895), 70–91; 39 (1918), 31–72 (on sources for his life); A. Mercati, 'Diarii di concistori del pontificato di Adriano VI', *ST* 157 (1951), 83–113; E. H. J. Reusens, *Analecta historica de Adriano VI* (Louvain, 1862); *Syntagma doctrinae theologicae Adriani VI* (Louvain, 1862); E. Hocks, *Der letzte deutsche Papst, Adrian VI* (Freiburg i.B., 1939); J. Posner, *Der deutsche Papst Adrian VI* (Recklinghausen, 1962); P 9; MC 6; *LThK* 4, 1309 (R. R. Post); *NCE* 1, 147 f. (K. M. Sanu); Seppelt 4, 426–38.

CLEMENT VII (19 Nov. 1523–25 Sept. 1534). The fifty-day conclave following HADRIAN VI's death resulted in the election of the cardinal favoured by Emperor Charles V (1519–56), Giulio de' Medici. Bastard son of Giuliano de' Medici by his mistress Fioretta, he was born at Florence on 26 May 1479 shortly after his father's murder and was brought up by his grandfather, Lorenzo the Magnificent. In 1513 his cousin LEO X, brushing aside the impediment of illegitimacy, made him archbishop of Florence and cardinal, and as vice-chancellor from Mar. 1517 he was largely responsible for Leo's policies, including his measures against the German reformer Luther (1483–1546). From May 1519 he governed Florence, and in 1521 took the lead in arranging an alliance between the pope and Charles V. Under Hadrian VI he again became powerful in the curia, contributing to the defensive alliance between the holy see and the empire. His election was widely acclaimed, but it soon became evident that, excellent as second-in-command, he lacked the character and capacity for supreme office at a time of crisis. Cultivated, experienced, and hardworking, but also indecisive and easily discouraged, he was narrow in outlook and interests. Failing to comprehend the spiritual revolution going on in the church, he acted mainly as an Italian prince and a Medici, and even in secular affairs was too timid and vacillating to pursue consistent policies.

Caught in the struggle between Charles V and Francis I of France (1515–47) to dominate Italy, Clement worked for peace among Christian powers, ostensibly to meet the Turkish threat but also to secure Florence and the papal state. First, he disappointed Charles by declining to renew Hadrian VI's defensive alliance. Then, impressed by Francis's success in reconquering Milan (Oct. 1524), he made an alliance with him and Venice (Dec. 1524 and Jan. 1525) which infuriated Charles. Next year, however, the defeat of the French at Pavia and the capture of Francis forced him again to seek the emperor's protection. In May 1526 he changed sides again, joining the League of Cognac with France, Milan, Florence, and Venice to check Charles's growing power. The inevitable result was the imperial invasion of Italy and the sack of Rome (6 May 1527). Clement took refuge in Castel Sant'Angelo but had to surrender, and for six months was a prisoner of Charles's troops. By agreeing to the occupation of important cities in the papal state, promising neutrality, and paying a huge indemnity, he procured his release on 6 Dec. 1527, but until Oct. 1528 lived away from the devastated city at Orvieto and

then Viterbo. By now he saw that his interest lay with the emperor, and in June 1529 he and Charles agreed on common action against heresy in Germany and against the Turks, then advancing on Vienna; their reconciliation was sealed by Charles's coronation at Bologna (24 Feb. 1530: the last imperial coronation by a pope) and by the restoration of Medici rule in Florence. Clement had most of his temporal power restored, but had to remain subservient to the emperor. Even so, moved by family interests and fear of Charles's predominance in Italy, he made a fresh approach to France in 1531, travelling personally to Marseilles to marry his grandniece to Francis I's second son in Oct. 1533, and carrying out lengthy discussions with the king there.

This precarious relationship between pope and emperor prevented an effective rejoinder to Turkish successes in Hungary in 1526 and assisted the spread of the Reformation in Germany. In Jan. 1524 Clement sent Cardinal Lorenzo Campeggio (1472–1539) to the diet of Nuremberg to assure Charles of support for the edict of Worms (1521) outlawing Luther, but the fact that Charles was at war with the pope enabled the diet of Speyer (June 1526) to reject the edict and give the reformers a valuable breathing space. Clement's obliviousness to the needs of the times came out particularly in his refusal, despite pressure put on him by Charles and his own conditional promises, to summon the general council which, even at this stage, might have taken constructive action. In his handling of Henry VIII's divorce from Catherine of Aragón he displayed the same wavering and procrastination, at first appearing ready to accommodate the king, then under pressure from Catherine's nephew, Charles V, transferring the case to Rome (July 1529), and only on 11 July 1533 pronouncing Henry excommunicate (a deferred sentence) and his divorce and remarriage void. The English church now inevitably moved into schism. His efforts to prevent the adoption of Lutheranism in

Norway, Denmark, and Sweden, and to check Zwinglianism in Switzerland, proved unavailing; and he had no time for the movements of reform and renewal already at work within the church. It was small consolation that, while these losses were taking place in Europe, he was able to preside over the erection of new bishoprics in Mexico and the spread of Catholicism in South America.

A true Medici, Clement was a patron of men of letters, like the historian Francesco Guicciardini and the political theorist Niccolò Machiavelli, and of artists, like Cellini, Raphael, and Michelangelo. From the last he commissioned the monuments to members of his family in the Sagrestia Nuova of S. Lorenzo, Florence, and, just before his death, the 'Last Judgement' in the Sistine Chapel.

BullRom VI; H. M. Vaughan, The Medici Popes, Leo X and Clement VII (London, 1908); St. Ehses, 'Die Politik des Papstes Clemens VII bis zur Schlacht vom Pavia', HJ 6 (1885), 557-603; 7 (1886), 553-93; P 9 and 10; MC 5; DHGE 12, 1175-224 (R. Mols); DBI 26, 237-59 (A. Prosperi); Seppelt 4, 426 f.; 437-53.

PAUL III (13 Oct. 1534-10 Nov. 1549). Born at Canino on 29 Feb. 1468, descendant of a famous condottiere family with properties around Lake Bolsena and south of Viterbo, Alessandro Farnese received a polished humanist education at Rome and Florence, was a student at Pisa, and was made treasurer of the Roman church (1492) and cardinal deacon (1493) by ALEXANDER VI; his nickname was 'cardinal petticoat' because his sister Giulia was the pope's mistress. Although not ordained priest till 1519, he held many bishoprics and lucrative benefices, combined wide artistic and philosophical interests with diplomatic missions, and kept a noble Roman mistress who bore him three sons and a daughter. Named bishop of Parma by JULIUS II in 1509, he took his new responsibilities seriously, holding a diocesan synod and putting the reform decrees of the fifth Lateran council (1512-17) into effect.

Breaking off his liaison with his mistress in 1513, he reorganized his private life and, after ordination in June 1519, became identified with the reform party in the curia. On CLEMENT VII's death he was the oldest cardinal (67), dean of the sacred college, respected for his experience and shrewdness, and was unanimously elected after a two-day conclave.

A true Renaissance pope, Paul favoured artists, writers, and scholars. He restored Rome university, enriched the Vatican library, and exploited the talents of painters and architects, notably Michelangelo, whom he commissioned to complete the 'Last Judgement' in the Sistine Chapel and to supervise work on the new St Peter's. The Palazzo Farnese, which he began, attests his pride in his family. Under him the Vatican resounded with masked balls and brilliant feasts; in 1536 he revived the carnival. A determined nepotist, he provoked protests by naming two grandsons, boys of 14 and 16, cardinals in Dec. 1534 and then promoting them to key offices. Throughout he worked hard, often at the expense of the church's interests, to establish the Farnese family among the powerful houses of Italy. Yet despite these preoccupations his pontificate marked a fresh approach to the great issues agitating Christendom. Though not, as often claimed, the first pope of Catholic reform, Paul sensed the need to meet the challenge of Protestantism constructively, and took certain hesitant steps to encourage renewal within the church itself. He therefore placed a general council and reform in the forefront of his programme.

Although the council, announced for Mantua in 1537 and for Vicenza in 1538, had to be postponed because of objections from Francis I of France (1515-47) and Emperor Charles V (1519-56), he at once reduced the expense of the sacred college and revitalized it by a series of brilliant nominations, including Giovanni Carafa (later PAUL IV), Gasparo Contarini (1483-1542), Reginald Pole (1500-58), and Marcello Cervini (later MARCELLUS II). In 1536 he set up a commission to examine the state of the church; on 9 Mar. 1537 it submitted a plain-spoken, far-reaching report (*Consilium de emendenda ecclesia*) which, although leaked and misused, became the basis of the work of the council of Trent. He encouraged reforms in the religious orders and the development of new congregations—the Theatines, Barnabites, Somaschi, and Ursulines. Most noteworthy was his approval (by the bull *Regimini militantis ecclesiae*: 27 Sept. 1540) of the Society of Jesus, and his establishment (21 July 1542) of the Congregation of the Roman Inquisition or the Holy Office, with punitive powers of censorship, as the central authority for combating heresy. When the peace of Crépy (18 Sept. 1544) ended the war between France and the empire, he was able, after years of frustration, to hold his general council, which opened at Trent, a city recommended by the emperor, on 13 Dec. 1545; he himself was represented by three legates. It was not the uncommitted council of all Christians desired by the Protestants, nor did Paul yield to Charles V's wish that it should confine itself to discipline and reform. It was agreed that dogma and reform should be discussed concurrently, and in its first seven sessions it hammered out decrees on Scripture and tradition, original sin, justification, and the sacraments. There being renewed tension between pope and emperor, an outbreak of typhus was made the pretext for transferring the council to Bologna (11 Mar. 1547), which lay directly in the papal sphere of influence; but since Charles objected and refused to allow bishops subject to him to attend there, Paul was obliged to suspend the eighth session on 1 Feb. 1548 (suspension formally published on 14 Sept. 1549), without any further reform decrees being issued.

On 17 Dec. 1538 (the bull had been ready since Aug. 1535) Paul excommunicated Henry VIII (Clement VII's earlier sentence had been suspended) and placed England under an interdict, but he failed to persuade the continental powers to impose sanctions as he had hoped: the net result

was to alienate England still further. Throughout his reign he sought to observe neutrality between Charles V and Francis I, although regarding France as the natural counter-balance to the emperor's predominance in Italy; the persistent rivalry of these powers was the chief obstacle to effective action against the Ottoman Turks, who threatened the coasts of Italy as well as the Christian outposts in the east. He supported Charles in his war to crush the defensive alliance of German Protestants known as the Schmalkaldic League (1545-7), and encouraged Francis to persecute the Huguenots in France; but in the end his family ambitions brought him into conflict with the emperor. In 1545 he bestowed Parma and Piacenza, parts of the papal state, on his dissolute son Pierluigi, an enemy of Charles, but on Pierluigi's murder in 1549 Charles claimed the two duchies for his own son-in-law Ottavio, the pope's grandson. This set-back, and the bitterness of having his own family ranged against him, hastened Paul's death. As he lay dying, racked by violent fever, family affection reasserted itself in the nepotist pope; he forgave Ottavio, and ordered Parma to be ceded to him. The portrait by Titian, painted in 1543 when he was seventy-five, represents him in the full vigour of his pontificate.

BullRom VI; C. Capasso, *Paolo III, 1534–49* (Messina, 1923–4); L. Dorez, *La Cour du Pape Paul III* (Paris, 1932); W. H. Edwards, *Paul III oder die geistliche Gegenreformation* (Leipzig, 1932); P 11 and 12; *DTC* 12, 9–20 (L. Marchal); *EC* 9, 734–6 (H. Jedin); *LThK* 8, 198–200 (G. Schwaiger); *NCE* 11, 13 f. (C. L. Hohl, Jr.); *EB* 15th edn.) 13, 1087 f. (F. X. Murphy); Seppelt 5, 12–59.

JULIUS III (8 Feb. 1550–23 Mar. 1555). As a result of irreconcilable divisions between the pro-French and pro-imperial factions the conclave following PAUL III's death was a difficult one lasting ten weeks. The English Reginald Pole (1500–58) missed election by a single vote. Eventually a compromise between French and Farnese cardinals secured a majority, in spite of

Emperor Charles V's (1519–56) hostility, for Giovanni Maria Ciocchi del Monte. Born at Rome on 10 Sept. 1487, son of a well-known jurist, he studied law at Perugia and Siena and became chamberlain to JULIUS II (whose name he adopted). In 1511 he succeeded his uncle as archbishop of Siponto, became bishop of Pavia in 1520, and under CLEMENT VII served twice as governor of Rome. In 1534 Paul III made him vice-legate of Bologna, creating him cardinal priest in Dec. 1536 and cardinal bishop of Palestrina in Oct. 1543. As one of its co-presidents he opened the council of Trent on 13 Dec. 1545. It was as co-president that he exasperated Charles V by his responsibility for transferring the council to Bologna in 1547.

Although an outstanding canonist, Julius was a typical Renaissance pontiff, generous to relatives, pleasure-loving, devoted to banquets, the theatre, hunting. Essentially weak, he created scandal by his infatuation with a fifteen-year-old youth, Innocenzo, picked up in the streets of Parma, whom he made his brother adopt and named cardinal. Yet he was aware of his universal pastoral role, and also of the church's need for reform and for the resumption of the suspended council; he had bound himself to the last in the pre-election oath sworn by fourteen cardinals. After strenuous negotiations, therefore, with the emperor's gratified agreement, he called on it (*Cum ad tollenda*: 14 Nov. 1550) to reassemble at Trent on 1 May 1551. It duly met and held several sessions (nos. 11–16), with theologians representing German Protestant estates attending some. Henry II of France (1547–59), however, disregarding the threats of Julius and of the council, refused French participation, and the council fell victim to the Habsburg–Valois war which resulted from the pope's attempt to eject Ottavio Farnese, Paul III's grandson, from Parma, with which, in deference to his predecessor's dying wish and his own pre-election compact, he had originally enfeoffed him as a vassal of the holy see but which Charles claimed as belonging to the

empire. When the combined papal and imperial armies failed to defeat the French, and the revolt of German princes against Charles in spring 1552 forced him to leave his base at Innsbruck, Julius was obliged on 28 Apr., at its 16th session, to suspend the council indefinitely, and next day to make a disadvantageous truce with France which restored Parma to Ottavio.

Discouraged by the breakdown of his policies, Julius now spent most of his time at the luxurious Villa di Papa Giulio which he erected just outside the Porta del Popolo. Naturally indolent, he devoted himself here to pleasurable pursuits, with occasional bouts of more serious activity. Politically he endeavoured, though without success, to mediate peace between Henry II and Charles V; his neutrality inspired mistrust on all sides. With the help of a committee of cardinals he carried through piecemeal reforms, controlling pluralism, restoring monastic discipline, and modifying curial administration. He encouraged the recently (1534) founded Society of Jesus, confirming its constitution on 21 July 1550, and, prompted by Ignatius Loyola (1491–1556), established (31 Aug. 1552) the Collegium Germanicum for the training of German secular priests who would work to restore Catholicism in their native land. He was concerned for the extension of the faith in the Indies, the Far East, and the Americas. But the most striking success of his reign was the return, short-lived though it was to be, of England to obedience to the holy see. The accession of the Catholic Mary I (6 July 1553) was hailed with great joy in Rome, and Julius appointed Reginald Pole, a relative of the queen, as legate with far-reaching powers; on 30 Nov. Pole solemnly absolved the English nation from schism and presided over a synod of both convocations.

A generous patron of the arts and humanism, Julius appointed the scholar–bibliophile Marcello Cervini (later MARCELLUS II) librarian to the Vatican, Michelangelo chief architect of St Peter's, and the composer Palestrina choirmaster of the Cappella Giulia. He built S. Andrea della Via Flaminia to commemorate his escape from death when held a hostage by the emperor after the sack of Rome (May 1527). For years a victim of gout, he died shortly after sending Cardinal Morone, at the request of Charles V, to the diet of Augsburg (1555) in the vain hope of bringing Germany back to papal allegiance on the model of England.

A. Massarelli, *Diaria* v-vii (ed. S. Merkle, *Concilii Tridentini Diariorum* II, Freiburg i.B., 1911); H. Jedin, 'Analekten zur Reformtätigkeit der Päpste Julius III und Pauls IV', *RQ* 42 (1934) 305–32; 43 (1935), 87–156; L. Miran, 'Le dernier pape de la Renaissance, Jules III', *Revue des études historiques* 94 (1928), 247–60; P 13; *DTC* 8, 1920 f. (G. Mollat); *EC* 6, 758–60 (G. B. Picotti); *LThK* 5, 1205 f. (G. Schwaiger); *NCE* 8, 54 f. (E. D. McShane).

MARCELLUS II (9 Apr.–1 May 1555). After a short, contentious conclave in which the French and the imperialist factions were equally balanced, the reform party was able to push through the election of their candidate, Marcello Cervini, as successor to JULIUS III. Born at Montepulciano, near Siena, on 6 May 1501, son of an official in the Sacred *Penitentiary (the tribunal of the holy see which handles matters of conscience) skilled in chronology, he studied at Siena and then at Rome, where CLEMENT VII commissioned him to complete a revision of the calendar begun by his father. A cultivated scholar and bibliophile, when driven from Rome by plague in 1526 he translated Latin and Greek works into Italian and Latin, and made friends with leading humanists. Returning to Rome in 1531, he was taken up by Cardinal Farnese, who on becoming Pope PAUL III made him protonotary apostolic and tutor to his nephew Cardinal Alessandro. As Paul relied heavily on Alessandro, Marcellus's influence in affairs ecclesiastical and political grew, and in 1539, 1540, and 1544 he was appointed successively bishop of Nicastro, Reggio Emilia, and Gubbio; on 10 Dec. 1539 he was named cardinal priest of Sta Croce. Although largely an absentee, he cared conscientiously for his sees, energeti-

cally promoting reforms; he was also a devoted patron of the Servites and the Augustinian hermits. In these years he was much used on diplomatic missions to the French and imperial courts, being appointed legate to the latter in 1543. On 6 Feb. 1545 he was chosen one of the three co-presidents of the council of Trent, where his inflexible support for papal policies earned him the emperor's disapproval. In 1548 he was given the congenial task of reorganizing the Vatican library, and was made a member of Paul III's reform commission. Under Julius III he became its president, but his outspoken criticism of the pope's nepotism and indolent luxury made it necessary for him to retire to Gubbio.

Few elections have aroused such eager hopes as Marcellus's (exceptionally, he kept his baptismal name). Able and experienced, upright and zealous for reform, he seemed the chief pastor for whom the crisis-ridden church was crying out. He at once gave proof of his resolve to be guided by the strictest reforming principles. He cut the expense of his coronation to a minimum, reduced the size and cost of his court, deferred the examination of petitions for favours, and insisted that justice be impartially administered. To exclude nepotism he forbade his numerous relatives to come near Rome. He took steps to collect all reform documents prepared under Julius III with the aim of promulgating a comprehensive reform bull. Then after a reign of twenty-two days, worn out by restless activity and the burden of his responsibilities, his frail constitution gave in and he died of a stroke. The first real reform pope, he is commemorated by the 'Missa Papae Marcelli' which the great composer Palestrina, then a singer in the Sistine chapel, wrote in response to his complaint about the quality of the Good Friday liturgical chants.

P. Polidori, *De vita, gestis et moribus Marcelli II* (Rome, 1744); O. Raynaldus, *Annales ecclesiastici* (for 1555) (ed. J. D. Mansi, Lucca, 1747–56); G. B. Manucci, *Il conclave di papa Marcello* (Siena, 1921); S. Morison, 'Marcello Cervini . . . Bibliography's Patron Saint', *Italia mediev. e uman.* 5 (1962), 301–19; P 14; *EC* 8, 17–19 (R. Palmarocchi); *NCE* 9, 190 f. (E. D. McShane); Seppelt 5, 68–71.

PAUL IV (23 May 1555–18 Aug. 1559). Born near Benevento on 28 June 1476, scion of a Neapolitan baronial family, Giampietro Carafa was educated at Rome in the home of his uncle Oliviero Carafa, acquiring a thorough grounding in Greek and Hebrew. Through his uncle he rose rapidly in the church, being bishop of Chieti, or Theate, 1505–24, legate of LEO X to Henry VIII of England 1513–14, archbishop of Brindisi 1518, nuncio in Flanders and Spain 1515–20. Already reform-minded, he at this stage combined strict personal asceticism with humanist interests and corresponded with Erasmus; as a Neapolitan he nourished an aversion to Spain and Spanish ascendancy. Returning to Rome, he joined the Oratory of the Divine Love and worked to amend abuses in his dioceses. Chosen by HADRIAN VI to collaborate with his projected reform programme, he renounced his bishoprics in 1524 and with Gaetano di Thiene (Cajetan, 1480–1547) founded the Theatines, dedicated to strict poverty and to restoring the apostolic way of life and reforming abuses in the church, and became their first superior. From now on, whether at Venice after the sack of Rome (1527) or at Rome after his nomination as cardinal in Dec. 1536, he was an aggressive leader of the reform party, abandoning humanist sympathies in his hostility to reconciliation with the Lutherans. As head of the reactivated Inquisition he was described as showing inhuman severity. Appointed archbishop of Naples in Feb. 1549, he was dean of the sacred college from 1553. He was seventy-nine, a man admired but dreaded, when, against Emperor Charles V's wishes, he was elected to succeed MARCELLUS II.

Paul's election was hailed by partisans of reform, but their hopes were not fulfilled. Autocratic and passionate, inspired by a medieval conception of the papal

supremacy, he relinquished his predecessors' neutrality and, in his revulsion from Spanish rule in Italy, was led by his nephew Carlo Carafa to ally himself with France and make war on Spain. The papal forces were defeated by the duke of Alva as viceroy of Naples, the papal state was overrun, and he was forced to accept the, fortunately generous, peace of Cave (12 Sept. 1557). His other ventures into politics also lacked moderation. He denounced the peace of Augsburg (25 Sept. 1555), which recognized the coexistence of Catholics and Lutherans in Germany, as a pact with heresy, and refused to recognize the abdication of Emperor Charles V in 1556 or the election of Ferdinand I (1558–64) in 1558 on the ground that papal approval had not been obtained. His dislike of Spain made him quarrel with Mary I of England, and on her death (17 Nov. 1558) he made the ultimate victory of Protestantism in England easier by insisting on the restitution of confiscated church lands and requiring Elizabeth I to submit her claims to him.

As a reformer the ascetic, self-willed pope laboured with fanatical energy and zeal. For him it was out of the question to revive the suspended (28 Apr. 1552) council of Trent; violently anti-Protestant, he believed he could carry through the necessary reforms himself more swiftly and efficiently. In spring 1556 he instituted a special commission of some sixty prelates with the idea that it should replace the council and be itself expanded into a papal council by the accession of foreign bishops. This was never realized, and after the peace of Cave he devoted his energies to the Roman Inquisition, greatly increasing its jurisdiction and placing Michele Ghislieri (later PIUS V) at its head. He regularly attended its sessions, and such was his passion for orthodoxy that he had an innocent man like Cardinal Giovanni Morone (1509–80) imprisoned in Castel Sant' Angelo for heresy and deprived Reginald Pole (1500–58) of his legateship to England. A further instrument he created, through the Congregation of the Inquisition, was the Index of Forbidden Books (1557: revised edition published in Jan. 1559), of unprecedented and quite unrealistic severity. Suspecting Jews of somehow abetting Protestantism, he confined them strictly in ghettos in Rome and the papal state, and forced them to wear distinctive headgear. But although his reign did not bring the eagerly awaited renewal of the church, it prepared the ground for it. Thus he was scrupulous in his choice of cardinals, insisted on episcopal residence, forbade the presentation of secular clerks to monasteries, and ordered the arrest of monks who had left their houses. The irony was that, blinded by hatred for the Habsburgs and distrustful of strangers, he made his morally worthless nephew Carlo not only a cardinal but also his political adviser, and relied heavily on other relatives, promoting them to lucrative positions. When his eyes were opened to their unprincipled behaviour, he denounced them, stripped them of their offices, and expelled them from Rome (Jan. 1559); but the damage to his policies and reputation was obvious to more worldly eyes.

Paul appointed a commission to reform the missal and the Roman breviary. He took steps to improve the dignity of divine service at Rome and, through the governor, to repress public immorality and violence. But the narrow-mindedness and harshness of his measures, his own intolerance, and his blindness to his nephews' faults, made him personally unpopular and his reign a disappointment. On his death popular hatred for him and his family exploded, the rioting crowds destroyed the headquarters of the Inquisition and released its wretched prisoners, and his statue on the Capitol was toppled over and mutilated.

BullRom VI; Lives by A. Caracciolo (in *Collectanea de vita Pauli IV*, Cologne, 1642) and Bart. Carrara (Ravenna, 1748–53); G. M. Monti, *Ricerche su Paolo IV Carafa* (Benevento, 1925); R. Ancel, 'Paul IV et le concile', *RHE* 8 (1907), 716–41; 'L'activité reformatrice de Paul IV: le choix des cardinaux', *RevQuestHist* 86 (1909), 67–103; T. Torriani, *Una tragedia nel cinquecento romano:* *Paolo IV e i suoi nepoti* (Rome, 1951); P 14; *DTC* 12, 20–3 (G. Mollat); *EC* 9, 736–8 (H. Jedin); *LThK* 8, 200–2 (G. Schwaiger); Seppelt 5, 70–91.

PIUS IV (25 Dec. 1559–9 Dec. 1565). After a conclave of almost four months, with the French and Spanish factions deadlocked, Giovanni Angelo Medici, behind whom a third group led by Cardinal Carafa threw its weight, was chosen to succeed PAUL IV. A notary's son (no relation of the Florentine Medici), he was born at Milan on 31 Mar. 1499, studied first medicine and then jurisprudence, took his doctorate in law at Bologna in 1525, and under PAUL III gave proof of administrative ability as governor in the papal state, commissioner with the papal forces in Hungary and Transylvania (1542–3), and vice-legate to Bologna. The father of three natural children, his star rose when an elder brother married into the pope's family; on 14 Dec. 1545 he was made archbishop of Ragusa and on 8 Apr. 1549 a cardinal. Under JULIUS III he served on the tribunal known as *Signatura gratiae*, but fell into disfavour with Paul IV, with whose anti-Spanish attitude and fanaticism he had no sympathy, and in 1558 withdrew of his own accord from Rome. Admired as a jurist, he was not known as an advocate of reform.

In contrast to his despotic predecessor, Pius was affable and convivial, with a private life which intrigued gossips; but he was also politically astute. He at once reversed Paul's repressive measures, rehabilitating Cardinal Giovanni Morone (1509–80), unjustly suspected of heresy, abolishing the ban on vagrant monks, restricting the competence of the Inquisition, and starting the revision of the unworkable *Index of Forbidden Books of 1559. Discarding Paul's anti-Habsburg policies, he entered into friendly relations with Philip II of Spain (1556–98) and Emperor Ferdinand I (1558–64), and filled the vacant nunciatures to Vienna, Venice, and Florence. In response to popular hatred for Paul's nephews, he had two of them, Cardinal Carlo Carafa and Giovanni, duke of Palino, tried and executed (5 Mar. 1561) for instigating the war against Spain, murder, and other crimes. He himself, nevertheless, indulged freely in nepotism. But his nomination (31 Jan. 1560) of the youthful Carlo Borromeo (1538–84) as cardinal and archbishop of Milan proved a blessing for the church, and brought him a secretary who increasingly influenced his worldly uncle in favour of reform at the papal court.

Pius's historic achievement was to reconvene the council of Trent, suspended in 1552, and bring it to a successful conclusion. The credit for this rested with him and not, as was formerly held, with Borromeo. Its recall, to which Pius pledged himself in his pre-election oath, was precipitated by the advance of Calvinism in France, which posed a threat which only a general council could meet. The question was whether it should be a new council, as France and Emperor Ferdinand I wished (the latter because he still hoped for the reconciliation of the Lutherans), or a continuation of the old one, as Philip II demanded. Pius's bull of convocation (*Ad ecclesiae regimen*: 29 Nov. 1560) evaded the point, but when the council met at Trent on 18 Jan. 1562 it effectively resumed the interrupted agenda. It passed through several crises, notably over the issue of whether the pope could dispense bishops from the obligation of residence, and at one stage was brought near collapse through the great powers' threats to its autonomy; but Pius kept control of it and overcame all difficulties, largely through the advice and diplomatic skill of Cardinal Morone, whom he made president in spring 1563. The council was dissolved on 4 Dec. 1563 at its 25th session, and Pius confirmed its decrees orally on 26 Jan. 1564, publishing the formal bull *Benedictus Deus* on 30 June 1564.

Pius now worked, with mixed success, to get the council accepted in Catholic countries. Having reserved the authentic interpretation of its decrees to himself, he entrusted this, and their enforcement, to a congregation of cardinals on 2 Aug. 1564. He began the enforcement in Italy on 1

Mar., directing bishops present in Rome to take up residence in their dioceses. On 24 Mar. 1564 he published, in the bull *Dominici gregis*, the council's Index of Forbidden Books. The council having left the question of communion in both kinds to his discretion, he conceded the chalice, at the discretion of the bishops, to the laity of Germany, Austria, Hungary, and other regions in an effort to check Protestantism, but deferred the issue of married priests. On 13 Nov. 1564 he ordered bishops, superiors, and doctors to subscribe the new 'Profession of the Tridentine Faith'. Since in his view the reform of the administration lay outside the council's competence, he had already (1561 and 1562) published decrees reforming the Rota (the principal judicial tribunal of the holy see), the Sacred *Penitentiary, the Chancery, and the Camera; in carrying through these changes he was actively assisted by Cardinal Borromeo. He initiated, but did not live to complete, the compilation of the catechism and the reform of the missal and the breviary.

With Pius the papacy gained prestige for the vigorous lead it gave to Catholic reform, but he could not prevent the spread of Protestantism in Germany, France (where he gave financial subsidies to the crown for its wars with the Huguenots), or England (where he refrained from excommunicating Elizabeth I in the hope that the country would return to Catholic allegiance). His administration of the papal state, devastated as a result of Paul IV's Spanish war, was maladroit; he had to raise new taxes which occasioned widespread discontent, and in his last year sparked off an unsuccessful attempt on his life. Reviving the Renaissance tradition dropped by Paul IV, he was generous to artists and scholars, restoring and founding universities, setting up at Rome a press for printing Christian texts, strengthening the fortifications of the city, and adorning it with buildings like the Porta Pia, Sta Maria degli Angeli (in the Baths of Diocletian), and the Villa Pia in the Vatican gardens.

PIUS V (1566-72)

BullRom VI and VII; Onofrio Panvinio, *Vita Pii IV* (Bologna, 1599); J. Süsta (ed.), *Die römische Kurie und das Konzil von Trient unter Pius IV* (Vienna, 1904–14); G. Constant, *Concessions à l'Allemagne de la communion sous les deux espèces* (Paris, 1923); P. Paschini, *Venezia e l'Inquisizione romana da Giulio III a Pio IV* (Padua, 1959); P 15 and 16; *DTC* 12, 1633–47 (G. Constant); *EC* 9, 1496–8 (H. Jedin); *NCE* 11, 395 f. (H. H. Davis); Seppelt 5, 90–118.

PIUS V, ST (7 Jan. 1566–1 May 1572). At the nineteen-day conclave following PIUS IV's death the rigorist party led by Cardinal Carlo Borromeo (1538–84) achieved the surprise election of Michele Ghislieri. Born of poor parents on 17 Jan. 1504 at Bosco, near Alessandria, Antonio Ghislieri was a shepherd until he became a Dominican at fourteen, adopting the name Michele. After studying at Bologna, being ordained (1528), and lecturing for sixteen years at Pavia, he was made inquisitor for Como and Bergamo. His zeal brought him to the notice of Cardinal Giampietro Carafa, on whose recommendation JULIUS III appointed him commissary general of the Roman Inquisition in 1551. When Carafa became Pope PAUL IV, he named his protégé bishop of Nepi and Sutri (1556), cardinal (1557), and finally inquisitor general (1558). With Pius IV his intimacy with the Carafa family and severity as inquisitor brought him into disfavour, but as protector of the Barnabites and bishop of Mondovi (Piedmont: both since 1560) he devoted himself wholeheartedly to reform. His earnestness, asceticism, and evangelical poverty suggested even to the Spanish ambassador that he was the pope called for by the times.

Pius made it his avowed objective to put into effect, in every sphere, the decrees of the council of Trent. A man who always thought and acted from a spiritual viewpoint, he made no change in his mortified style of life, continuing to wear a monk's rough undergarments beneath his papal robes. He imposed the strictest standards on his greatly reduced court, and in a series of decrees sought to stamp out blasphemy, profanation of holy days, and public immorality in Rome. To contemporaries he seemed to want to turn the city into a monastery. Although prevailed on to make a grand-nephew, the Dominican Michele Bonelli, a cardinal and use him as secretary of state, he set his face against nepotism and gave his relatives the minimum support. He forbade (29 Mar. 1567) the reinvestiture of fiefs reverting to the holy see; any future alienation of land in the papal state was banned with the severest penalties. More positively, he enforced clerical residence, and conducted a systematic review of religious orders, abolishing some, like the Humiliati (1571), which had become degenerate. The cardinals he named were all conscientiously chosen, and he appointed a commission (3 May 1567) to examine episcopal appointments. In compliance with Trent he published the Roman catechism (1566), the revised Roman breviary (1568), and the Roman missal (1570); he also set up a commission (1569) to revise the Vulgate. He restricted the use of indulgences and dispensations, remodelled the penitential system, and in an effort to promote the Tridentine reforms in Italy personally visited the Roman basilicas, arranged for a commission to visit the parishes, and appointed apostolic visitors for the papal state and Naples. He also took steps to have the decrees of the council of Trent circulated throughout the world as far as Mexico, Goa, and the Congo.

In his eagerness to extirpate heresy Pius relied heavily on the Inquisition, building a new palace for it, sharpening its rules and practice, and personally attending its sessions. Under him the number of persons accused and sentenced, often men of culture and distinction, soared, and as a result he could congratulate himself on having kept Italy free from any trace of Protestantism. Even so, he blamed himself for his leniency. He was no less harsh on the Jews, permitting some for commercial reasons to live in ghettos in Rome and Ancona, but otherwise expelling them from the papal state. In Mar. 1571 he established the Congregation of the Index as a new administrative department with executive powers, with the result that hundreds of printers fled to Germany and Switzerland. In Oct. 1576 he condemned seventy-nine theses of Michael Baius (1513–89), the Flemish precursor of *Jansenism who had pessimistic views on the Fall and need for grace, but in the same year (11 Apr.) declared the great Dominican thinker Thomas Aquinas (c.1225–74) a doctor of the church and had a new edition of his writings published (1570).

Pius's interventions on the international stage often lacked political realism. His rehabilitation of the disgraced Carafa family and his uncompromising stand against state control of the church (expressed in his reissue in a stricter form in 1568 of the bull *In coena Domini*, read aloud on Maundy Thursday and listing ecclesiastical censures reserved to the pope) alienated the Catholic rulers whose support he needed. Even before his stiffening of its terms, and still more after, the bull was a constant irritant to secular sovereigns because of its exalted claims for the papacy. His excommunication and purported deposition of Elizabeth I of England (25 Feb. 1570), the last such sentence on a reigning monarch by a pope, was an ineffective anachronism and made matters worse for her Catholic subjects; it also antagonized Spain, France, and the empire. In France he assisted the regent Catherine de Médicis financially and militarily against the Huguenots, only to be disillusioned when they were granted freedom of religion by the peace of Saint-Germain (8 Aug. 1570). His relations with Maximilian II (1564–76), strained because of his equivocal stance towards Protestantism, reached breaking-point when Pius trespassed on the emperor's sphere by nominating Cosimo I as grand duke of Tuscany (5 Mar. 1570). With Philip II of Spain (1556–98), his most natural ally, he continually clashed because of the control exercised over the church by the crown in Spain; complete rupture was avoided only by the tireless efforts of his nuncio, Archbishop Giambattista Castagna (URBAN VII).

His most ambitious and successful enterprise was the formation, with Venice and Spain, of a holy league against the Turks; a combined naval force met the Turkish fleet in the Gulf of Corinth on 7 Oct. 1571 and inflicted on it at Lepanto a defeat which shattered Turkish superiority in the Mediterranean. Attributing the victory to the intercession of the BVM, he declared 7 Oct. the feast of Our Lady of Victory, later to be changed by Gregory XIII to the feast of the Rosary.

Single-minded, devout to the point of bigotry, relentless in his persecution of heresy, Pius did not long survive the victory. A great reform pope whose work was to bear fruit for decades and who left a distinctive Tridentine impress on the church, he was beatified on 1 May 1672 by CLEMENT X, canonized on 22 May 1712 by CLEMENT XI. Feast 30 Apr. (formerly 5 May).

AASS May I (1680), 617–714 (early lives included); *BullRom* VII; *Epistulae apostolicae* (ed. F. Goubau, Antwerp, 1640); W. E. Schwartz, *Der Briefwechsel Maximilians II mit Pius V* (Paderborn, 1889); F. van Ortroy, *AnB* 33 (1914), 187–215 (text of oldest, anonymous life); G. Alberigo, 'Studi e problemi relativi all'applicazione del Concilio di Trento in Italia', *RSTI* 62 (1958), 239–98; Ch. Hirschauer, *La politique de S. Pie V en France (1566–72)* (Paris, 1926); L. Browne-Olf, *The Sword of St Michael: St Pius V* (Milwaukee, 1943); G. Grente, *Le pape des grands combats: S. Pie V* (Paris, 1956); P 17 and 18; *DTC* 12, 1647–53 (R. Hedde and É. Amann); *EC* 9, 1498–1500 (H. Jedin); *LThK* 8, 531 f. (A. Franzen); Seppelt 5, 119–52.

GREGORY XIII (14 May 1572–10 Apr. 1585). Fourth son of a local merchant, Ugo Boncompagni was born at Bologna on 1 Jan. 1502, graduated as doctor of laws at the university there, and remained as professor of law for eight years (1531–9). At this stage he led a free life and had a natural son, Giacomo, whom he later made governor of Castel Sant'Angelo. In 1539 he went to Rome, was ordained when about forty, and under PAUL III became so highly regarded as a lawyer and administrator that he was given a succession of responsible judicial posts. PAUL IV sent him on diplomatic missions to France (1556) and Brussels (1557), and in July 1558 named him bishop of Vieste. From 1561 to 1563 he attended the council of Trent as an expert in canon law, and played a noteworthy part in drafting its decrees. In recognition of his services PIUS IV made him cardinal priest of S. Sisto on 12 Mar. 1565 and entrusted him with the important legation to Spain. Here he won the confidence of Philip II (1556–98), and the king's influence was largely responsible for securing his election at the exceptionally brief conclave following PIUS V's death.

More easygoing and readier to compromise than Pius V, Gregory proved no less resolute in promoting the Tridentine decrees and Catholic reform; influenced in part by Carlo Borromeo (1538–84), he had exchanged his earlier worldliness for religious earnestness. An independent worker, he allowed only a restricted role to his closest adviser, Tolomeo Galli, the first papal secretary of state in the modern sense. He appointed a commission of cardinals to ensure that the decrees were carried out, and was particularly concerned that bishops should be carefully chosen and the duty of residence observed. One of his achievements was to transform the nunciatures, hitherto primarily diplomatic agencies, into instruments of church reform. This led him to establish new ones at places like Lucerne (1579), Graz (1580), and Cologne (1584) where the critical situation demanded direct representation of the holy see. In full agreement with the Tridentine view that reform was impossible without a well-trained clergy, he established colleges in Rome and other cities at vast expense, entrusting them, in the main, to the Jesuits (whose privileges he increased). In Rome he reconstructed and richly endowed (1572) the Roman College (later named after him the Gregorian University), secured the future of the German College, and established the English College (1579). He also founded a Greek, a Maronite, and an Armenian college, and a Hungarian college (later amalgamated with the German College). These famous seminaries, especially the German and English Colleges, were soon to bear rich fruit in a continuous flow of professionally equipped priests to their Protestant homelands.

Fervently concerned for the maintenance and restoration of Catholicism, Gregory gave the Counter-Reformation a more militant slant. When news of the St Bartholomew's Day massacre in France of Huguenots (23/4 Aug. 1572) reached Rome, he celebrated it with Te Deums and thanksgiving services as a victory for the church over infidelity as well as the defeat of political treachery; and he actively subsidized the Catholic League against the Huguenots. Even so, his efforts to get the decrees of Trent accepted in Catholic France met with disappointment. He encouraged Philip II of Spain to turn his attention to the Netherlands and Ireland, from which he hoped that an attack might be launched on Elizabeth I of England. When his dreams of an Irish invasion of England collapsed (1578 and 1579), he gave his personal support to plots to have the queen assassinated. In the Netherlands he had the satisfaction of seeing the southern provinces joining for the defence of the Catholic faith in the Union of Arras (6 Jan. 1579), but his negotiations with John III of Sweden (1568–92), who demanded concessions like clerical marriage, suppression of the invocation of saints, and communion in both kinds, came to nothing and the country remained Lutheran. His attempts, too, to secure the union of the Russian church with Rome broke down. Poland, however, was won over definitively to the church, while in Germany the expansion of Protestantism was arrested and much territory was recovered for Catholicism. Here he was assisted from 1573 by the German Congregation, a special commission of cardinals charged with fostering Catholicism in Germany. It was typical of him that, in order to ensure Catholic property rights in northwest Germany, he allowed the worldly Ernst of Bavaria, youngest son of Duke Albrecht V (1550–79), to accumulate as many as five bishoprics in defiance of the Tridentine prohibition of pluralism.

Gregory supported the Jesuits not only in Europe but in missionary work as far afield as India, China, Japan, and Brazil. He approved (1575) the Congregation of the Oratory of Philip Neri (1515–95), and sanctioned (1580) the reform of the Discalced Carmelites by Teresa of Avila (1515–82). He organized the publication, as required by Trent, of an improved edition of the Corpus of Canon Law (1582), and was quick to recognize the importance for church history of the rediscovery (1578) of the Roman catacombs. Finally, his name remains associated with the reform of the Julian Calendar, projected under earlier popes but completed by a commission at the papal Villa Mondragone near Frascati on 24 Feb. 1582. The new calendar, involving the dropping of ten days (5–14 Oct. 1582) and a new rule for leap years, was adopted by Catholic states, but Protestant states did not follow suit for more than a century.

As well as fostering scholarship, Gregory was a considerable builder; he completed, for example, the Gesù, the mother church of the Jesuit order, and started a great palace on the Quirinal as a summer residence. His expenditure on such works, as well as on subsidies to Catholic princes and on his colleges and foundations, was crippling, and he was obliged to raise additional revenue from papal monopolies and customs. He also used his legal and administrative skills to obtain the reversion of papal lands whenever the title seemed defective. One of the results of this was widespread banditry caused by the dispossessed and disgruntled nobles, and in his latter years serious disorder and lawlessness came to prevail in the papal state and in Rome itself.

BullRom VIII; A. Ciappi, *Compendio delle attioni e vita di Gregorio XIII* (Rome, 1591); G. P. Maffei, *Annali di Gregorio XIII pontifice massimo* (Rome, 1742); I. Bompiano, *Historia pontificatus Gregorii XIII* (Rome, 1655); L. Karttunen, *Grégoire XIII comme politicien et souverain* (Helsinki, 1911); G. Levi della Vida, 'Documenti intorno alle relazioni delle chiese orientali con la S. Sede durante il pontificato di G. XIII', *ST* 143 (1948); P 19 and 20; *DTC* 6, 1809–15 (P. Moncelle); *EC* 6, 1143 (M. E. Viora); *LThK* 4, 1188–90 (G. Schwaiger); *NCE* 6, 779–81 (D. R. Campbell); Seppelt 5, 151–78.

SIXTUS V (24 Apr. 1585–27 Aug. 1590). A farm worker's son, Felice Peretti was born at Grottammare, in the March of Ancona, on 13 Dec. 1520. An uncle who was a Franciscan saw to his schooling, and at twelve he joined the order at nearby Montalto. After a brilliant student career he was ordained at Siena in 1547 and in 1548 graduated doctor of theology at Fermo. Already a striking preacher, he was taken to Rome in 1552 by Cardinal Carpi, protector of the Franciscans. Here his Lenten sermons brought him renown. In 1556 PAUL IV, who had noticed the ascetic friar, put him on his reform commissions, and next year made him inquisitor for Venice. His severity led to his recall, but PIUS IV reappointed him in 1560. In 1566 PIUS V, who as grand inquisitor had valued him, appointed him vicar-general of the Franciscans and bishop of Sant'Agata dei Goti (near Caserta), and in 1570 named him cardinal; he was bishop of Fermo 1571–7. Under GREGORY XIII, with whom he had clashed on a mission to Spain in 1565, Cardinal Montalto (as he had come to be called) was under a cloud, and spent the long reign at his villa on the Esquiline preparing a distinctly uneven edition of St Ambrose. These years of retirement, as well as his care to avoid giving offence, meant that he became virtually unknown except to a powerful circle of friends, to whom he owed his unanimous election as successor to Gregory at a conclave virtually free from great-power influence. He took the name Sixtus out of regard for Sixtus IV, a Franciscan like himself.

A man born to rule, energetic, violent, and inflexible, Sixtus at once set about restoring order to the papal state, which Gregory had left in the grip of uncontrollable banditry. He did so in two years, using ruthlessly repressive measures. Thousands of brigands were publicly executed, and the nobles they relied on for shelter were mercilessly punished. He then turned to economic and financial reforms. By regulating food prices, draining marshes, and encouraging agriculture and the wool and silk industries, he improved the lot of his subjects. His success in replenishing the papal treasury, left empty by Gregory, was spectacular. By cutting expenditure to the bone (his personal standards were Franciscan), raising new taxes, exploiting the sale of offices, and floating new loans, he accumulated in Castel Sant'Angelo, in spite of enormous expenditure on public works, a sum of over four million scudi, most of them in gold. This made him one of the richest princes in Europe, and assured him an unprecedented financial independence.

Sixtus's prestige as pope rests on his lasting reorganization of the church's central administration. On 3 Dec. 1586, by the constitution *Postquam verus*, he fixed the maximum number of cardinals at seventy, a total not exceeded until JOHN XXIII. His own nominations were in general responsible, although his appointment of his fifteen-year-old nephew Alessandro caused a shock. He also remodelled the secretariat of state, creating (22 Jan. 1588) fifteen permanent congregations of cardinals, six to oversee secular administration and the rest to supervise spiritual affairs. This arrangement, which remained broadly unchanged until the Second Vatican Council (1962–5), reduced the importance of the consistory and thereby the claims of the sacred college to co-rule with the pope. Sixtus used his new curial machinery to enforce effectively the decrees of the council of Trent, in particular its prohibition of simony and pluralism. A turning-point in the Catholic reformation was his re-enactment (20 Dec. 1585) of the rule that bishops should regularly visit the holy see and submit reports on the state of their dioceses. He also, in compliance with Trent, set up a commission to revise the Vulgate but, impatient with its progress, took the task into his own hands and published (2 May 1590) a version so full of blunders that it had to be withdrawn after his death. Cool towards the Jesuits, he was generous to the Franciscans, and declared the Franciscan theologian St Bonaventura (d. 1274) a doctor of the church.

In international affairs Sixtus's interests ranged widely. In visionary moments he dreamed of using his treasure to crush the Turks and create a Christian state around the Holy Sepulchre. More practically, he helped Kings Stephen Báthory (1576–86) and Sigismund III Vasa (1587–1632) to advance Catholicism in Poland, induced Charles Emmanuel, duke of Savoy (1580–1630), to attach Geneva to his realm, and promised Philip II of Spain (1556–98) huge subsidies for the invasion of England—but refused to pay them after the defeat of the Armada (July–Aug. 1588). Distrustful of Spanish domination, he sought to maintain a balance of Catholic powers, but felt obliged to assist Philip against the Huguenot Henry of Navarre (Henry IV of France, 1589–1610), whom he excommunicated in 1585. In his last months, however, the prospect of Henry's making good his claim to the French crown and being converted to Catholicism caused him to resist Philip's demands, even at the risk of open rupture. In the wider world he promoted missionary efforts in Japan, China, the Philippines, and South America.

Aptly called 'the iron pope', Sixtus was a splendid patron of building and scholarship in the spirit of the Catholic renewal. Largely through his constructions Rome became a magnificent baroque city; he also imaginatively remodelled its layout, opening up boulevards to link the seven pilgrimage churches, planting cross-crowned obelisks on key sites, and building aqueducts to provide a new water supply, the 'Acqua Felice'. He rebuilt the Lateran palace and completed the dome of St Peter's. He also constructed a new, more spacious Vatican library, and established the Vatican press, which in 1587 published an edition of the Septuagint. His end, brought on by successive attacks of malaria, was hastened by acrimonious confrontations, in his last weeks, with the Spanish ambassador over the French kingship. Generally reckoned a great pope, he was execrated by his subjects; on hearing of his death, the Roman mob tore down his statue on the Capitol.

BullRom VIII and IX; J. A. Santorio, 'Acta consistorialia Sixti V', *Analecta iuris pontificii* XI, 830–74 (Rome, Paris, Brussels, 1872); G. Cugnoni, 'Documenti chigiani concernenti Felice Peretti, Sisto V', *ASRomana* 5 (1882), 1–32; 210–304; 542–89; J. A. de Hübner, *Der eiserne Papst* (German trans., Berlin, 1932); L. M. Personé, *Sisto Quinto* (Florence, 1935); R. Canestrari, *Sisto V* (Turin, 1954); P 21 and 22; *DTC* 14, 2217–38 (A. Teetaert); *EC* 11, 780–7 (G. B. Picotti); *NCE* 13, 273–5 (D. R. Campbell); Seppelt 5, 175–209.

URBAN VII (15–27 Sept. 1590). Largely through Spanish influence, Giambattista Castagna was elected to succeed SIXTUS V. Born at Rome on 4 Aug. 1521, son of a Genoese nobleman and a Roman mother, he studied at Perugia and Padua, graduated doctor of laws at Bologna, and in 1551, when his uncle, Cardinal Girolamo Verallo, went to France as legate to Henry II (1547–59), served on his staff. Returning home, he became a high official in the Signatura, the supreme tribunal of the church, and in 1553 was named archbishop of Rossano, in Calabria. Having served briefly under PAUL IV as governor of the papal state, he took an active part in the final phase (1562–3) of the council of Trent. In 1564 PIUS IV commissioned him to accompany Cardinal Boncompagni (later GREGORY XIII) on his legation to Spain. He remained as nuncio there until 1572, and at a critical point in the relations between PIUS V and Philip II (1556–98) was responsible for preventing a complete rupture. Resigning the see of Rossano, he became nuncio to Venice in 1573, and then governor of Bologna. Gregory XIII appointed him a consultor (expert adviser) of the Holy Office, and on 12 Dec. 1583 promoted him cardinal priest. Sixtus V, whose election he had not supported, appreciated his abilities, confirmed him as governor of Bologna, and used his services on the Inquisition.

The election of such a moderate, earnest, and experienced prelate aroused high hopes, and such indications of future policy as he was able to give confirmed his generous and reforming aims. Although robust in health, however, he was struck down by malaria on the night following his election and died before his coronation could take place. He bequeathed his personal fortune, amounting to 30,000 scudi, to the provision of dowries for impoverished Roman girls.

L. Arrighi, *Vita Urbani VII* (Bologna, 1614); G. Moroni, *Dizionario di erudizione storico-ecclesiastico* (Venice, 1857), vol. 46, 36–41; P 22; *EC* 12, 910–12 (R. Ciasca), *NCE* 14, 480 f. (E. D. McShane).

GREGORY XIV (5 Dec. 1590–16 Oct. 1591). After a conclave of more than two months, notorious for factional intrigues and brutal intervention by the Spanish government, Cardinal Niccolò Sfondrati, the most generally acceptable on its list of seven, was elected successor to URBAN VII. Born at Somma, 49 km. from Milan, on 11 Feb. 1535, he was a student at Perugia and Padua, graduated doctor of laws at Pavia, and was then ordained. A decisive influence on his life was his friendship with (St) Charles Borromeo (1538–84). When just twenty-five, he was named bishop of Cremona by PIUS IV. Soon after, he attended the reconvened council of Trent (1562–3), where he argued against pluralism and for the obligation of bishops under divine law to reside in their dioceses. The council over, he devoted himself assiduously to his diocese, introducing religious to make up for the shortage of clergy, and putting the reform decrees of Trent into full operation. GREGORY XIII named him cardinal of Sta Cecilia on 12 Dec. 1583. As such he was given only modest curial responsibilities, but was admired for his reforming zeal and devotion to (St) Philip Neri (1515–95) and the Oratory.

Physically weak, weaker still in willpower, and often in pain, Gregory (he took his patron's name) was of exemplary, self-effacing piety, but almost wholly without

INNOCENT IX (1591)

curial or political experience. Awareness of this led him to make his self-seeking nephew, 29-year-old Paolo Emilio Sfondrati, a cardinal (19 Dec. 1590) and entrust him as secretary of state with the conduct of business. No more experienced than his uncle, Paolo at once began building a power-base for himself and placing his relatives in important positions in the papal state. All this, especially his handling of business properly appertaining to the pope and the new direction he gave to papal policy, aroused resentment and complaints in the sacred college. Inclined, as a Milanese, to defer to Spanish interests, Gregory abandoned Sixtus V's endeavour to maintain a balance and gave full backing to Spain's aspirations in France. He sent a substantial monthly subsidy to the city of Paris, threatened by the still Protestant Henry of Navarre (since Aug. 1589 Henry IV of France), supported the Spanish-backed Holy League, renewed (1 Mar. 1591) Sixtus's excommunication of Henry, declaring him ineligible for the French crown, and dispatched a papal army to France financed out of Sixtus's painfully accumulated treasure. These measures proved largely ineffective, except that they rallied moderate Catholics to Henry and hastened his conversion.

During his brief reign Gregory strove to mitigate the scourges of plague, food shortage, and brigandage which afflicted Rome, although the inefficiencies of his nephew contributed to the second. From his sick-bed he continued the work of reform, strictly enforcing episcopal residence, defining (15 May 1591) the qualifications of candidates for bishoprics, forbidding mass to be said in private houses, and arranging for the revision of Sixtus V's defective Vulgate. He also banned (21 Mar. 1591) all betting on papal elections, the length of a pontificate, or the creation of cardinals.

A. B. Ciaconius, *Vitae et res gestae summ. pontif. Romanorum* (Rome, 1601 and 1602); A. Cicarelli, *Gregorio XIV* (in continuations of B. Platina, e.g. Venice, 1685); M. Facini, *Il pontificato di Gregorio*

XIV (Rome, 1911); D. L. Càstano, *Gregorio XIV* (Turin, 1957); P 22; *EC* 6, 1144–6 (R. Ciasca); *NCE* 6, 781 f. (R. L. Foley); Seppelt 5, 210–12.

INNOCENT IX (29 Oct.–30 Dec. 1591). Cardinal Giovanni Antonio Fachinetti was elected to succeed GREGORY XIV. Spanish pressure on the conclave was kept in the background, but he was on the list of those acceptable to King Philip II (1556–98). Born on 20 July 1519 at Bologna, where his family had moved from Verona, he studied at the university there and graduated doctor of laws in 1544. Moving to Rome, he joined the staff of Cardinal Alessandro Farnese, who sent him as his representative to Avignon for four years and then entrusted him with his business at Parma. PIUS IV made him bishop of Nicastro, in Calabria, in 1560; two years later he took an active part in the final phase of the council of Trent. From 1566 to 1572, under PIUS V and GREGORY XIII, he was nuncio in Venice and negotiated the anti-Turkish league which resulted in the naval triumph at Lepanto (Oct. 1571). For health reasons he resigned his diocese in 1575 and returned to Rome, where Gregory XIII not only appointed him to responsible positions in the curia and the Inquisition, but named him patriarch of Jerusalem (12 Nov. 1576) and then cardinal (12 Dec. 1583). One of the leading prelates of the day, his election was no surprise, for he had been a serious candidate at previous conclaves. For the anti-Spanish party his age and fragile health presaged a short reign which would give them a breathing-space.

Like Gregory XIV, he followed, as expected, a pro-Spanish policy in France, supporting Philip II and the Holy League against the still Protestant Henry IV (1589–1610), but with characteristic thriftiness drastically reduced his financial subsidies. Even so, the successes of Henry compelled him, shortly before his death, to allocate 36,000 ducats to the papal army which was attempting to raise the siege of Rouen. Concerned to put the papal finances on a sound basis, he revealed in consistory (3 Nov. 1591) his plan to establish, like SIXTUS

274

V, a substantial reserve in Castel Sant'-Angelo for use in emergencies, and on 4 Nov. he renewed, in stricter terms, Pius V's ban on the alienation of church property. One of his first acts was to divide the work of the secretariat of state into three sections, one for France and Poland, one for Italy and Spain, and one for Germany. He took steps to repress banditry around Rome, to regulate the course of the Tiber, and to improve sanitary conditions in the Borgo. On 18 Dec. he fell ill, but insisted on making a pilgrimage to the seven churches; as a result he caught a chill and died within a few days. A scholarly man, he had written on Aristotle's *Politics* and other subjects; but these works have never been published.

A. Cicarelli, *Vita Innocentii IX* (in continuation of B. Platina); A. B. Ciaconius, *Vitae et res gestae summ. pontif. Romanorum* (Rome, 1601 and 1602); *BullRom* XIX; P 22; *EC* 7, 19 (P. Brezzi); *NCE* 7, 527 f. (R. L. Foley).

CLEMENT VIII (30 Jan. 1592–5 Mar. 1605). Born at Fano on 24 Feb. 1536, Ippolito Aldobrandini was son of a noted Florentine barrister whom hostility to the Medici had driven from Florence. The generosity of Cardinal Alessandro Farnese enabled him to study law at Padua, Perugia, and Bologna. He was then taken up by Pius V, the protector of his family, who appointed him consistorial advocate and later (1569) auditor of the *Rota or supreme tribunal. In 1571/2 he accompanied the pope's nephew, Cardinal Bonelli, on a diplomatic mission to Spain and France which, though unsuccessful, introduced him to the wider political world. Under Gregory XIII he was in the shade, but in late 1580 was ordained priest, probably through the influence of (St) Philip Neri (1515–95). His promotion was rapid under Sixtus V, who in 1585 made him datary, i.e. head of the department responsible for appointments reserved to the holy see (15 May), and then cardinal priest (18 Dec.). After serving as grand penitentiary in 1586, he earned diplomatic laurels as legate to Poland in 1588/9, when he satisfactorily

settled a dangerous dispute between King Sigismund III Vasa (1587–1632) and the house of Habsburg. He was seriously considered at the three conclaves of 1590/1, and although not the Spanish favourite had enough Spanish support to be elected to succeed Innocent IX.

As pope Clement VIII mirrored the ideals of Catholic reform. Not only was he a tireless worker, conscientiously attentive to detail even when confined to bed by gout, but his piety and austerity were transparent. He fasted, meditated, said mass, made his confession with exemplary frequency, and went on foot every month to the pilgrimage churches. Philip Neri was his intimate, and Cesare Baronius (1538–1607), the church historian and Oratorian, his confessor. Among the cardinals he promoted was the saintly Jesuit theologian Robert Bellarmine (1542–1621). Against this, he was indecisive, prone to put off business, and driven by painful illness to be forever changing his abode. This put a heavy burden on the papal finances (his household cost four times as much as Sixtus V's), as did his love for brilliant display and his excessive generosity to his family. Although as cardinal he had criticized nepotism, he promoted his nephews Cinzio and Pietro Aldobrandini to the purple in autumn 1593 and surrendered the conduct of affairs almost entirely to them. Other relations basked in his favour, and he so doted on a fourteen-year-old grand-nephew that he made him a cardinal.

Although the movement of renewal was beginning to flag, Clement continued the task of applying the decrees of the council of Trent. In a series of measures he promoted the reform of religious houses. In 1592 he published a corrected version (the 'Clementine edition') of Sixtus V's defective Vulgate (1590) which remained authoritative until the 20th cent. He then issued revised versions of the principal liturgical books: the pontifical (1596), the breviary (1602), and the missal (1604). A stricter, enlarged Index, including a ban on Jewish books, came out in 1596; but fear of possible political repercussions prevented him

LEO XI (1605)

from bringing out a collection of decretals supplementing that issued by CLEMENT V. He sharpened the severity of the Inquisition, which in his reign sent more than thirty heretics (including the ex-Dominican philosopher Giordano Bruno: 1548–1600) to the stake. Both his concern for orthodoxy and his indecision were attested by the attention he devoted, without reaching any solution, from 1595 to 1605 to the dispute between Jesuits and Dominicans over the theory of Luis de Molina (1535–1600) concerning grace, free will, and God's foreknowledge.

In the political sphere Clement took the momentous decision, with heart-searching and long hesitation, to recognize Henry IV, since 1593 a Catholic, as king of France (1589–1610) and to absolve him (17 Sept. 1595) from Sixtus V's excommunication. This entailed his reluctant acceptance of the Edict of Nantes (13 Apr. 1598) allowing the Huguenots religious freedom, civil equality, and other rights. The papacy, however, was freed from Spanish domination, and Clement was responsible for the peace of Vervins negotiated in 1598 between France and Spain. With Henry's help, moreover, he was able to secure in 1597, in the face of Spanish and imperial opposition, the reversion of the duchy of Ferrara to the holy see on the failure of the Este dynasty. On 23 Dec. 1595 he endorsed proposals, subsequently accepted by the synod of Brest-Litovsk (6–10 Oct. 1596), under which some millions of Orthodox Christians in Poland joined the Roman church with permission to retain their liturgy. His appointment of Francis de Sales (1567–1622) as co-adjutor bishop of Geneva in 1599 (bishop in 1602) gave a notable fillip to the Counter-Reformation in Switzerland. To offset these successes he failed, in spite of persistent efforts, to organize an effective coalition of Christian powers against the Turks threatening Hungary and Austria. In England he was involved (1598–1602) in controversy over the archpriest George Blackwell whom he had appointed in 1598; his hopes that

Britain would return to Catholicism, nourished by Machiavellian professions of interest by James VI and I, proved illusory. In Sweden, too, his dream of a Catholic restoration collapsed when the Catholic Sigismund III of Poland, who succeeded to the throne in 1593, was defeated by his Protestant uncle, Duke Charles of Södermanland (Charles IX: 1604–11) in 1598 and deposed.

Clement left the papacy stronger and more independent than he had inherited it. To reinforce its freedom of action he took steps to reduce Spanish influence, hitherto disproportionate, in the sacred college. The jubilee of 1600, which brought millions of pilgrims to Rome (80,000 witnessed his opening of the Holy Door, or *Porta santa*, at St Peter's on 31 Dec. 1599) bore brilliant testimony to the rejuvenated papacy of the Counter-Reformation.

BullRom IX, X, XI; P. van Isacker, 'Notes sur l'intervention militaire de Clément VIII en France à la fin du xvie siècle', *RHE* 12 (1911), 702–13; P 23 and 24; *DBI* 26, 259–82 (A. Borromeo); *DHGE* 12, 1249–97 (R. Mols); *EC* 3, 1827–30 (G. Soranzo); *NCE* 3, 933 f. (J. C. Willke); Seppelt 5, 213–43.

LEO XI (1–27 Apr. 1605). Born at Florence on 2 June 1535, Alessandro Ottaviano de' Medici belonged to a collateral branch of the ruling Florentine family and through his mother Francesca Salviati was a nephew of LEO X. Deflected from ordination by his mother while she was alive, he served for fifteen years as Grand Duke Cosimo I's ambassador in Rome, where he became the favourite disciple of (St) Philip Neri (1515–95). The impression he created was so favourable that GREGORY XIII created him bishop of Pistoia in 1573, archbishop of Florence in 1574, and cardinal in 1583. A deeply religious man who had close relations with the Dominicans of S. Marco, he was active in introducing the Tridentine reforms into his dioceses; he also spent lavishly on restoring Roman churches and, later, on acquiring the Villa Medici. He helped to persuade CLEMENT

276

VIII to absolve Henry IV of France (1589–1610) from excommunication, being himself appointed legate in France in Apr. 1596 and remaining there for two years. As legate he worked hard to restore church discipline, which had broken down during the religious wars, but was unable to get Henry to have the decrees of the council of Trent published in France as he had promised. He was in charge of the negotiations which led to the peace of Vervins between France and Spain (2 May 1598). In 1600 he became cardinal bishop of Albano, in 1602 of Palestrina. With strong support from France, but in the teeth of Spanish opposition, he was elected to succeed Clement VIII, and adopted his uncle's name.

While generally welcomed, the new pope was elderly and frail in health. He caught a chill while taking possession of the Lateran and died before the month was out. He had no time to initiate a policy, but it is known that he arranged to send generous aid to Emperor Rudolf II (1576–1612) in his war against the Turks, settled (10 Apr.) an awkward dispute between the clergy of Castile and León and the Jesuit order, appointed a commission to reform the system of voting in conclave, and gratified the Roman people by abolishing some onerous taxes.

BullRom XI; V. Martin, 'Le reprise des relations diplomatiques entre la France et le St-Siège en 1595', *RevSR* 2 (1922), 237–70; *DTC* 9, 332 f. (G. Mollat); *EC* 7, 1155 (G. B. Picotti); P 25; Seppelt 5, 22 f.; 241–3.

PAUL V (16 May 1605–28 Jan. 1621). Born at Rome on 17 Sept. 1552, Camillo Borghese came of Sienese stock, his father being a noted professor of law. After studying at Perugia and Padua and graduating doctor of laws, he held progressively important offices in the curia, and after a successful mission to Spain was created cardinal in 1596, vicar of Rome and inquisitor in 1603. His surprise election to succeed LEO XI, when only fifty-two and hardly known to the outside world, resulted from a compromise between rival factions.

The keynote of Paul's policy was neutrality between France and Spain, but he held views on the pope's supremacy which were outmoded in Catholic, not to say Protestant, countries. This brought him at once into collision with Italian states over the church's prerogatives. Savoy, Genoa, even Naples gave way, but Venice stood firm: having forbidden the erection of new churches and the acquisition of land by the church without permission, it was now bringing two clerics to trial in the secular courts. Paul protested (10 Dec. 1605 and 26 Mar. 1606) and, when the republic held its ground, excommunicated its senate and placed the city under an interdict (17 Apr. 1606). Venice declared the interdict invalid; most of the local clergy flouted it, while those who observed it, notably the Jesuits, were expelled. A vigorous pamphlet war ensued, with the Servite theologian Fra Paolo Sarpi (1552–1623) brilliantly arguing the republic's case, and Cardinals Bellarmine (1542–1621) and Baronius (1538–1607) the pope's. The defection of Venice to Protestantism, even a European war, became possibilities, but through the mediation of France a settlement was at last agreed and the city was absolved from ecclesiastical censures (21 Apr. 1607). The incident was a moral defeat for Paul, for although the imprisoned clergy were set free, he failed to obtain full satisfaction from the republic, much less its abandonment of the principle at stake. The Jesuits remained excluded from Venetian territory, and interdicts had been shown to be paper weapons.

After this sobering experience Paul was more cautious in his efforts to preserve for the church positions it held and to recover others it had lost. He wrote to James I of England urging him not to make Catholics suffer for the Gunpowder Plot (5 Nov. 1605); but when Parliament required of them an oath denying the pope's right to depose princes, he denounced it and forbade them to take it (1606 and 1607). This divided English Catholics, for their archpriest, George Blackwell, advised them to swear the oath; he was replaced in 1608. In

GREGORY XV (1621-3)

France Paul's condemnation of *Gallican-ism (1613) provoked the states-general in Oct. 1614 to declare that the king held his crown from God alone. Through his nuncios, however, he secured the withdrawal of the claim, as well as the dismissal of Edmond Richer, dean of the Sorbonne, who had written (1611) against papal pretensions. Although the states-general of 1614/15 refused to authorize the promulgation of the decrees of the council of Trent in France, Paul was greatly gratified when the French clergy, taking their courage in their hands, voted (7 July 1615) their publication in provincial councils. His reign saw the outbreak of the Thirty Years War (1618-48) in Germany, and while initially hesitant about supporting the Catholic League (a legalist, he did not wish to be suspected of violating the peace of Augsburg of 1555), he gave substantial subsidies to Emperor Ferdinand II and the League from 1620 onwards.

Religious reform was close to Paul's heart, and he renewed (19 Oct. 1605), without allowing any exceptions, the obligation of episcopal residence, published (20 June 1614) the revised *Rituale Romanum*, and tightened discipline in the religious orders. He approved (24 Feb. 1612) the Congregation of the Oratory founded by Philip Neri, and the French Oratory of Pierre de Bérulle (10 May 1613); he also canonized (1 Nov. 1610) Charles Borromeo (1538-84) and Frances of Rome (Francesca Romana: 1384-1440), and beatified Ignatius Loyola (1491-1556), Francis Xavier (1506-52), Philip Neri (1515-95), and Teresa of Avila (1515-82). He encouraged missions, approving (27 June 1615) the use of the vernacular in the liturgy in China. He indefinitely postponed (28 Aug. 1607) the debate on Molinism (i.e. the doctrine that the efficacy of grace has its foundation, not in the substance of the grace itself, but in the divine foreknowledge of human co-operation with it), which had preoccupied CLEMENT VIII, declaring it not ripe for a decision; on the other hand, he censured (5 Mar. 1616) Galileo Galilei

(1564-1642) for teaching the Copernican theory of the solar system, and suspended through the Congregation of the Index Copernicus's treatise 'until corrected'.

Paul had a lively concern for Rome and, as well as completing the nave, façade, and portico of St Peter's, restored the aqueduct of Trajan and, renaming it 'Acqua Paola', used it to supply water to numerous fountains throughout the city. He placed scholars in his debt by forming the collection of secret Vatican archives. He was unstinting in his solicitude for his relatives, and at his death the Borghese family rivalled the Orsini and the Colonna in wealth and influence. The vast income enjoyed by his nephew, Cardinal Scipioni, enabled him to build the Villa Borghese.

Paul suffered a stroke during the procession to celebrate the defeat of the elector Frederick V (1596-1632), the short-lived Calvinist king of Bohemia, in the battle of the White Mountain near Prague on 8 Nov. 1620, and died of a second one shortly after.

BullRom XI, XII; A. Bzowski, *Paulus V Papa* (Rome, 1626); C. P. Goujet, *Histoire du pontificat de Paul V* (Amsterdam, 1765); C. P. de Magistris, *Per la storia del componimento della contesa tra la Rep. Veneta e Paolo V, 1605-1607* (Turin, 1941); P 25 and 26; DTC 12, 23-37 (L. Marchal); EC 9, 738-41 (G. B. Picotti); NCE 11, 16 (T. F. Casey); Seppelt 5, 248-68.

GREGORY XV (9 Feb. 1621-8 July 1623). Son of Count Pompeio, Alessandro Ludovisi was born at Bologna on 9 Jan. 1554, studied liberal arts at the Roman College under the Jesuits (1569-71), and graduated doctor of laws at Bologna in 1575. He then took holy orders, and the curia was quick to use his talents. He was given a series of increasingly responsible judicial posts, and took part in delicate diplomatic missions, e.g. to Poland and to Benevento. Nominated archbishop of Bologna in 1612, he negotiated peace between Charles Emmanuel I of Savoy (1580-1630) and Philip III of Spain (1598-1621) in 1616, receiving a cardinal's hat in recognition (19 Sept.). Largely through lobbying by Cardinal Borghese, PAUL V's nephew, he was elected by acclaim as his successor. Already sixty-seven and frail in health, but beloved for his kindness, he needed an energetic collaborator and immediately found one in his 25-year-old nephew Ludovico Ludovisi, whom he made a cardinal. This brilliant, fastidious young man had all the necessary drive, imaginative versatility, and cool courage, and the chief credit for Gregory's achievements belongs to him. In return his uncle heaped honours and riches on him; the latter he used to aggrandize himself and to build churches, villas, and art galleries, as well as to promote charities.

The first Jesuit-trained pope, Gregory, and Ludovico equally, strove not only to continue the inner renewal of the church but to regain ground it had lost. Two of his measures in the strictly church sphere were of exceptional significance. First, to meet widespread criticism of papal elections and the influences brought to bear on them, he reorganized their procedure in minutest detail, decreeing (*Aeterni patris filius*: 15 Nov. 1621, and *Decet Romanum pontificem*: 12 Mar. 1622) that, while acclaim should not be excluded, elections should normally take place after the closure of the conclave, and that voting should be by secret written ballot. The revised system, although it took centuries to eliminate outside political pressures entirely, has remained virtually unaltered. Secondly, in order to provide the church with a supreme central authority covering the whole mission field, he founded (6 Jan. 1622) the Sacred Congregation for the Propagation of the Faith; on 22 June he signed the bull *Inscrutabili* instituting it. Thirteen cardinals were assigned to it; its guiding idea was that, as universal shepherd of souls, the pope had an overriding responsibility for propagating the faith. It was to be the organ for co-ordinating missionary enterprise not only in heathen lands, hitherto supervised by Catholic sovereigns (whose lively resistance it now encountered), but also in countries which had become Protestant and had lost

their hierarchies. It thus developed into the headquarters of the Counter-Reformation.

In the political world Gregory went over to the offensive: when sending Bishop Carlo Carafa as nuncio to the imperial court, he commissioned him to win over the emperor and the Catholic princes to active support of Catholic restoration. The objective of the papacy, as he saw it, was to promote and maintain unity among the Catholic powers. Thus to assist Emperor Ferdinand II (1619-37) and the Catholic League to exploit their victory over the Protestant elector Frederick V (1596-1632) near Prague on 8 Nov. 1620, he provided massive financial subsidies; while Carafa saw to it that Protestantism was crushed and Catholicism reimposed in Bohemia. Again through Carafa, aided by the Capuchin Hyacinth of Casale, he contrived that the dignity of Elector Palatine, vacated by Frederick V, was transferred (Feb. 1623) to Maximilian I of Bavaria (1573-1651). This he saw as a triumph for the church, for Catholicism now had a majority among the five Palatine electors. In return a grateful Maximilian presented him with the library of Heidelberg, with its precious manuscripts. Meanwhile he pressed Philip III of Spain to break the twelve years' truce in the Netherlands. In France he encouraged the anti-Calvinist policies of the government, and showed his satisfaction at its successes by erecting Paris (Oct. 1622) into a metropolitan see. In the strategic territory of the Valtellina, disputed between France and Spain, he got himself accepted as arbiter and occupied the territory with papal troops, thereby preventing war between the two powers and safeguarding the faith of the Catholic inhabitants. In England he was prepared to sanction a marriage (which in fact never took place) between Prince Charles, heir of James I and later Charles I, and the Infanta Maria of Spain in return for the promise of a substantial softening of the penal laws against James's Catholic subjects.

Gregory's short reign was of great significance for the Catholic revival. It was appropriate that, at a sumptuous ceremony on 12 Mar. 1622, he canonized several of its heroes: Teresa of Avila (1515–82), Ignatius Loyola (1491–1556), Philip Neri (1515–95), and Francis Xavier (1506–52), one of the greatest of Christian missionaries.

BullRom XII, XIII; G. Gabriele, 'Il conclave di Gregorio XV', ASRomana 50 (1927), 5–32; D. Albrecht, Die deutsche Politik Papst Gregors XV (Munich, 1956); DTC 6, 1815–22 (P. Moncelle); EC 6, 1146–8 (R. Ciasca); LThK 4, 1190 (D. Albrecht); NCE 6, 782 f. (M. L. Shay); P 27; Seppelt 5, 262–75.

URBAN VIII (6 Aug. 1623–29 July 1644). After a long (19 July–6 Aug.), sweltering, contentious conclave Maffeo Barberini was elected, by 50 out of 55 possible votes, to succeed GREGORY XV. Born at Florence in 1568 (baptized 5 Apr.), of a rich commercial family long established in the city, he went to school with the Jesuits there, was a student at Rome, graduated doctor of laws at Pisa (1589), and then, helped by an uncle who was protonotary apostolic, launched on a successful career in the curia. Sent to France as envoy extraordinary to Henry IV (1589–1610) in 1601, he was back there, now titular archbishop of Nazareth, as nuncio in 1604. For his services PAUL V appointed him cardinal in 1606, bishop of Spoleto in 1608, legate of Bologna in 1611, and prefect of the Signatura in 1617.

Authoritarian, keenly conscious of his position, Urban kept business in his own hands and rarely discussed it with his cardinals. Ambassadors commented on his diplomatic grasp and assurance. A literary connoisseur and owner of a fine library, he composed and published well-constructed, if florid, Latin verses. A reckless nepotist, he made a brother and two nephews cardinals, advanced other brothers, and enriched them all so exorbitantly that in old age he felt conscience-stricken and consulted theologians on his use of the papal revenues. He himself spent lavishly on beautifying Rome, and on 18 Nov. 1626 consecrated the new St Peter's. He was also concerned for the security of the city and the papal state, building Castelfranco on the northern frontier, fortifying the port of Civitavecchia, strengthening Castel Sant'-Angelo, and equipping it with cannon made of bronze ripped from the Pantheon. He chose Castel Gandolfo, some 25 km. southeast of Rome, for summer retreats, entertaining scholars there.

Urban's reign coincided with the Thirty Years War (1618–48), when Cardinal Richelieu (1585–1642) was aiming at French hegemony in Europe and the victories of Gustavus Adolphus of Sweden (1611–32) reinforced Protestantism in Germany. In spite of his unconcealed sympathy for France and antipathy to Spain, he struggled to maintain an uneasy neutrality between the contestants, conscious of his role as the common father of Christendom with the duty to intervene for the restoration of peace. Yet because of his profound fear of Habsburg domination in Italy, his policy was effectively pro-French. Thus he withheld until it was too late the subsidies his predecessor had given to Emperor Ferdinand II (1619–37), supported the French candidate in the war of the Mantuan succession, and, although working to prevent the alliance of France and Protestant Sweden in 1631, took no effective action against Richelieu until its consequences became apparent. When France's open entry into the war in 1635 compelled Ferdinand to make concessions to the Protestants in the peace of Prague (30 May 1635), he severely blamed the emperor, but merely admonished the cardinal to keep the peace; it was evident that, while posing as neutral, he was actually backing France. The news of Gustavus's death in battle (16 Nov. 1632) was the signal for thanksgiving masses in Rome, but the outcome of Urban's one-sided neutrality was to bring the Counter-Reformation in the empire to a close.

Although overshadowed by his political involvement, Urban's ecclesiastical activities deserve note. He took a personal part in revising the breviary (1631), rewriting many of the hymns himself. He settled (1625, confirmed 1634) the canonical procedures for canonization and beatification, and gave its final form to the bull *In coena Domini, prescribed for reading on Maundy Thursday and listing specified offenders subject to excommunication. He gave strong support to missions, founding (1627) the Collegio Urbano for training missionaries, setting up a polyglot printing press, and dispatching missionaries to the Far East. He sanctioned new religious orders such as the Visitation (1626) and the Lazarists (1632) of St Vincent de Paul (c. 1580–1660). To comply with the decrees of Trent he insisted (1634) that bishops, including cardinals, should reside in their dioceses. Under him Galileo Galilei (1564–1642), for years a personal friend, was condemned for the second time and under threat of torture forced (22 June 1633) to abjure the Copernican system, while in the bull *In eminenti* (1642: published June 1643) Cornelius Jansen's (1585–1638) *Augustinus* was censured in general terms. The debate thus sparked off by this famous synthesis of St Augustine's (354–430) extremer views on grace and predestination was to agitate the church for generations.

Although he was deeply concerned for the integrity of the papal state, Urban's sole success here was his incorporation in it of Urbino (1625–31) as a result of the last duke's renunciation of his title. In his closing years (1641–4), egged on by the greed of his nephews, he allowed himself to be involved in a war over the papal fief of Castro on the pretext that its holder, Odoardo Farnese, had defaulted on his debts. Odoardo found support in France and in a league comprising Venice, Tuscany, and Modena, and the outcome was the pope's humiliating defeat. The petty war, however, led to devastation and crippled finances for the papal state. It was little wonder that the Roman populace, already cruelly oppressed by his prodigal extravagance, broke into riotous jubilation at the news of his death.

BullRom XIII-XV; A. Nicoletti, *Vita di Papa Urbano VIII: Storia del suo pontificato* (MS in

Vatican Library, Coll. Barberini); W. N. Weech, *Urban VIII* (London, 1905); A. Leman, *Urbain VIII et la rivalité de la France et de la Maison de l'Autriche de 1631 à 1635* (Lille, 1920); A. Kraus, 'Das päpstliche Staatsekretariat unter Urban VIII', *RQ* Supplementheft 29, 1964; J. Grisar, *Päpstliche Finanzen, Nepotismus und Kirchenrecht unter Urban VIII* (Rome, 1943); P 28 and 29; *EC* 12, 912–16 (R. Ciasca); *NCE* 14, 482 f. (V. Ponko); Seppelt 5, 274–306.

INNOCENT X (15 Sept. 1644–1 Jan. 1655). Born in Rome on 7 May 1574, Giambattista Pamfili studied at the Roman College with help from an uncle, graduated doctor of laws, and entered on a legal career in the curia. After being a judge of the *Rota 1604–21, he served as nuncio in Naples, and in 1625 accompanied URBAN VIII's nephew Francesco Barberini on his legation to France and Spain. He clearly impressed Francesco, for Urban appointed him nuncio to Spain in 1626 and cardinal in Aug. 1627 (*in petto*: he announced the creation in Nov. 1629). His election, after a 37-day conclave, represented a reaction against Urban's pro-French tendencies; it was opposed by the French court, but Cardinal Jules Mazarin's (1602–61) veto arrived too late.

An old man, taciturn and mistrustful, slow in reaching decisions, Innocent at once turned on the Barberini, Urban VIII's hated relatives, setting up a commission to inquire into the riches they had amassed and meanwhile sequestering their possessions. Only the threats of Mazarin, the all-powerful French minister who took them under his protection, induced him to pardon them. Innocent himself, however, was not immune from nepotism, although none of the kinsmen he loaded with offices, wealth, and favours had the ability to fill the role of cardinal nephew (as the relative, usually a nephew, whom popes from PAUL III until the late 17th cent. tended to employ as their closest collaborator was designated). Much more powerful and sinister in his court was Donna Olimpia Maidalchini, a sister-in-law of insatiable ambition and rapacity. The suggestion that their relationship was immoral was mischievous gossip, but her dominance was such that Innocent took no important decision without consulting her. But he did not use her son, Cardinal Camillo Pamfili, as secretary of state. This post he gave to Cardinal Panciroli and then, after 1651, to Fabio Chigi (later ALEX-ANDER VII), who was the first of the recognized secretaries of state with whom nuncios and legates corresponded directly and who themselves signed letters and instructions.

Innocent confirmed Chigi as representative of the curia at the congress for ending the Thirty Years War (1618–48) meeting at Münster. Like Chigi, he bitterly opposed the far-reaching concessions to Protestantism which Emperor Ferdinand III (1637–57) and Elector Maximilian I of Bavaria (1623–51) deemed unavoidable and included in the peace of Westphalia (24 Oct. 1648), and denounced them in the brief Zelus domus Dei; although dating it 26 Nov. 1648, he delayed publication until 20 Aug. 1650 so as not to aggravate the position of Catholics in Germany. His protest was brushed aside and had no practical effect. In spite of the peace, war dragged on between France and Spain and Innocent tried to hold a balance between them, although predisposed in favour of Spain which he judged less of a threat to the church and Italy. Portugal having broken away from Spain in 1640, he declined formally to condemn the revolt, as Spain desired, but also refused (1648) to recognize John IV of Braganza (1640–56) as king, or to fill vacant sees with his nominees. Again, when Naples revolted against Spain in 1647 and the French ambassador urged him to seize the opportunity, as feudal lord, of incorporating the kingdom in the papal state, he preferred to temporize and see the restoration of Spanish rule; it was better to have a declining power like Spain installed in Naples than to let France gain a foothold. He granted financial aid to Venice and Poland in their struggle against the Turks, but had not enough money to assist Ferdinand III. Innocent gave strong backing to missions in non-Christian countries, strengthened the powers of the Congregation of Propaganda, founded a Maronite college at Ravenna, and raised the Dominican College at Manila, in the Philippines, to university status. He took a stand in the keen debate on the propriety of adapting certain traditional Chinese rituals in the mission field, approving a decree of the Propaganda (12 Sept. 1645) condemning the practice. Much the most momentous issue, however, on which he had to pronounce was Jansenism, the extremist presentation of St Augustine's teaching on grace and free will set out in Cornelius Jansen's *Augustinus (published 1640 at Louvain). In Apr. 1651 he appointed a special commission to examine five propositions extracted from this work, and himself took part in several of its sessions; on 31 May 1653 he published the bull Cum occasione unconditionally condemning the five propositions. Jansen's supporters, led by Antoine Arnauld (1612–94), reacted by accepting the condemnation of the propositions, but denying that they were to be found in Augustinus; they distinguished between the church's infallibility in matters of doctrine and its duty of silence before matters of fact (the distinction between 'droit' and 'fait'). Shortly before his death Innocent, whose anti-Jansenist line agreed with the French government's policy, explained that in the five propositions he had condemned Jansen's teaching as found in Augustinus.

A combination of straitened finances and thrift prevented Innocent from embellishing Rome on the scale of his predecessors, but under him the interior decoration of St Peter's was completed, the Piazza Navona was restored to its ancient form as a stadium and adorned with its fountains, and the sumptuous Villa Doria Pamfili was erected before the Porta San Pancrazio. He also reorganized the prisons of the papal state along more humane lines. A strangely perceptive portrait of him, by Velázquez (1650), can be seen in the Galleria Doria.

BullRom XV; A. Tauretto, Vita (Bologna, 1674); I.

Ciampi, *Innocenzo X Pamfili e la sua corte* (Imola, 1878); W. Friedensburg, 'Regesten zur deutschen Geschichte aus der Zeit des Pontifikats Innocenz' X', *QFIAB* 4 (1902), 236–85; 5 (1903), 60–124, 207–22; 6 (1904), 146–73; 7 (1905), 121–38; N. J. Abercrombie, *The Origins of Jansenism* (Oxford, 1936); H. Couville, *Étude sur Mazarin et ses démêlés avec le pape Innocent X 1644–1648* (Paris, 1914); P 30; *EC* 7, 19–22 (G. B. Picotti); *LThK* 5, 692 f. (B. Sutter); *NCE* 7, 528 f. (J. S. Brusher); Seppelt 5, 302–22.

ALEXANDER VII (7 Apr. 1655–22 May 1667). Born at Siena on 13 Feb. 1599, Fabio Chigi studied philosophy, law, and theology at the university there, began mixing in intellectual circles at Rome in Dec. 1626, and in 1628 entered the papal service. He served as vice-legate in Ferrara 1629–34, returning to Rome in the latter year and being ordained priest. Named bishop of Nardò (Puglia) in 1635, he was sent to Malta as inquisitor and apostolic delegate. His reputation, however, rested mainly on his service as nuncio in Cologne 1639–51; in this capacity he represented the pope at the negotiations leading to the peace of Westphalia (1648). Throughout he firmly refused to enter into discussions with heretics, and when the treaties were concluded protested vehemently against provisions he considered injurious to Catholicism. In 1651 INNOCENT X made him secretary of state, and in 1652 cardinal and bishop of Imola. A career diplomat with rich spiritual interests, he was chosen, after an eighty-day conclave and in spite of initial opposition (only grudgingly withdrawn) from the powerful French minister and cardinal Jules Mazarin (1602–61), as Innocent X's successor.

Alexander's personal weakness, and also the weakness of his position as pope, were soon made evident. It was hoped that he would eschew nepotism, and he began by forbidding his relatives even to visit Rome. But by 1656 he allowed himself to be persuaded by the curia itself that the pope's family should live in style and thus strengthen his position, and he began loading them with offices, palaces, and estates. The influence he allowed them, however, except in administering the papal state, was limited. Even more damaging was his inability, because of their personal hostility, to establish good relations with Cardinal Mazarin and, after his death, with Louis XIV of France (1643–1715). Because Rome sheltered Cardinal de Retz, his *bête noire* and rival who had escaped from France in 1654, Mazarin took his revenge by lending French support to claims of the Farnese and Este families on papal territories, and by excluding Alexander from any participation in the peace of the Pyrenees (7 Nov. 1659) between France and Spain. After Mazarin's death Louis XIV, on the pretext that the immunity of his embassy in Rome had been infringed and his ambassador's life endangered by Corsican troops in the papal service, withdrew his ambassador, expelled the nuncio in Paris, occupied the papal enclaves of Avignon and Venaissin, and threatened to invade the papal state. Since Alexander was without allies, he had no option but to proffer abject apologies and accept the humiliating conditions of the treaty of Pisa (12 Feb. 1664), including the requirement to set up a pyramid in Rome admitting the soldiers' guilt. He had to defer completely to the king's wishes on episcopal appointments. Not surprisingly, he got little or no help from Louis for the league of European powers he was trying to organize against the Turkish threat.

Alexander's relations with Venice were more satisfactory; he was able to persuade the city to permit the return of the Jesuits (Dec. 1656), expelled during its conflict with PAUL V. In return he provided modest financial and military aid against the Turks. On the death of Emperor Ferdinand III (Apr. 1657), he supported the candidature of Leopold I of Austria (emperor 1658–1705), who was elected in the teeth of Mazarin's opposition. On the other hand, Spain refused to receive his nuncio, and when (like Innocent X) he declined to recognize John IV of Portugal (1640–56) or to fill bishoprics with his nominees, the king left them unfilled, appropriated their incomes, and even thought of setting up a national church.

The conversion on 24 Dec. 1654 of Queen Christina of Sweden (1632–54), the Protestant Gustavus Adolphus's (1594–1632) daughter, following her abdication in June, and her formal reception into the church on 3 Nov. 1655, brought especial satisfaction to Alexander, although the ex-queen, who settled in Rome and made her palace an intellectual centre, proved a great burden to him personally and to his treasury. By a decree of 23 Mar. 1656 he accepted the viewpoint of Jesuit missionaries in China, permitting the performance of certain indigenous rites as being effectively civil ceremonies, and (9 Sept. 1659) relieved native Chinese clergy of the duty of reading the office in Latin. Since the debate over *Jansenism continued unabated, Alexander intervened (16 Oct. 1656) to pronounce that the five propositions condemned by Innocent X (31 May 1653) were in fact contained in Cornelius Jansen's *Augustinus* and had been condemned according to his meaning; on 15 Feb. 1665, in compliance with Louis XIV's wishes, he issued a constitution (*Regiminis apostolici*) requiring all clergy to subscribe a formulary accepting the pope's decisions and rejecting the five propositions without reserve. In these years Alexander was also involved in the controversy over Probabilism, i.e. the theory (supported by the Jesuits) that, where the propriety of an action is in doubt, it is lawful to follow a solidly probable opinion favouring it even when the case against it is more probable. He did not condemn Probabilism as such but, notwithstanding his partiality for Jesuits, formally condemned forty-five moral propositions savouring of laxity (24 Sept. 1665 and 18 Mar. 1666).

As pope Alexander found the administration of the papal state, in which he had revelled as cardinal, distasteful, and delegated most of it to the Congregation of State. He had sensitive literary interests, which in youth had found an outlet in such volumes of poems as *Philomathi Musae iuveniles*. He was also deeply spiritual, daily meditating on the writings of Francis de Sales (1567–1622), whom he beatified (1661) and canonized (1665), and presenting the main themes of Salesian piety in small anonymous devotional works. He delighted in the company of scholars and writers, enriched Rome university and the Vatican library, and was a splendid patron of art. It was he who, among other works, commissioned Bernini to enclose the piazza of St Peter's within two semicircular colonnades.

Philomathi Musae iuveniles (Cologne, 1645; Antwerp, 1654; etc.); *BullRom* XVI, XVII; V. Borg, 'Fabio Chigi, Apostolic Delegate in Malta' (official correspondence), *ST* 249 (1967); S. Pallavicini, *Della vita di Alessandro VII* (1839–40); P 31; N. J. Abercrombie, *The Origins of Jansenism* (Oxford, 1936); *DBI* 2, 205–15 (M. Rosa); *DHGE* 2, 230–44 (P. Richard); *EC* 1, 801–3 (G. I. della Rochetta); Seppelt 5, 305–8; 321–35.

CLEMENT IX (20 June 1667–9 Dec. 1669). Born at Pistoia on 27 Jan. 1600, of a noble family which derived its wealth from sheep-farming, Giulio Rospigliosi studied liberal arts at Rome with the Jesuits, and then theology and law at Pisa. With the patronage of the Barberini, who admired his artistic flair, and of URBAN VIII himself he rose steadily in the curia from 1624 to 1644, when he was appointed titular archbishop of Tarsus and given the responsible post of nuncio to Spain. Leaving Madrid in Jan. 1653, he was made governor of Rome after INNOCENT X's death, while the new pope, ALEXANDER VII, appointed him secretary of state and cardinal in 1657. In this capacity he managed, in spite of the hostility of the powerful minister Cardinal Mazarin (1602–61) and Louis XIV (1643–1715) to Alexander, to retain the esteem of the French court. On Alexander's death he therefore had strong French backing; since Spain also favoured him, and the cardinals wanted a pontiff capable of healing the rift between Paris and Rome, his election was assured. Assuming a name indicative of a policy of appeasement, he almost wholly broke with the traditional nepotism, and assigned his relatives only modest and moderately profitable offices.

Much of Clement's short reign was spent in resolving already existing tensions. Thus when Spain recognized (Feb. 1668) the independence of Portugal, he felt able to settle the confused ecclesiastical situation in that country by at last filling the numerous vacant sees. Much more important was the relaxation of relations with France. A humiliating inscription admitting the guilt of the papal soldiers which Louis XIV had forced Alexander VII to set up in Rome was removed; but Clement in return had to allow the French crown a free hand in church appointments. Again, while it flattered him to play a role in the negotiations which ended the War of Devolution (1667–8) between France and Spain, he was no match diplomatically for Hugues de Lionne (1611–71), Mazarin's brilliant successor as French foreign minister, and the peace of Aachen (2 May 1668) left in France's hands the fortified towns in Flanders it wanted. It was also de Lionne who was the true architect of the 'Clementine Peace' (Feb. 1669) which brought a temporary respite to the agitation over *Jansenism. A minority of Jansenists, including four bishops and the nuns of the Jansenist convent of Port-Royal south-west of Paris, still refused subscription to the formulary condemning five propositions from Cornelius Jansen's *Augustinus which Alexander VII imposed in Feb. 1665, but as a result of discussions between de Lionne and the papal nuncio Clement was prevailed on to accept (19 Jan. 1669) the recalcitrant bishops' subscription in spite of its being hedged around with qualifications to which he had to turn a blind eye. It was in fact a victory for Louis XIV, who considered the Jansenists a threat to the unity of his kingdom; and it soon became apparent at Rome that the 'Peace' was being interpreted as a sign of the church's weakness in the face of French pressure.

Close to Clement's heart was a project to assist Venice to recover Crete, almost wholly occupied by the Turks in the past two decades, and in spring 1668 and 1669 he succeeded in organizing, with the help of France, Spain, and the empire, two expeditions. In spite of naval superiority, divisions within the Christian forces, and eventually the withdrawal of the French, led to the collapse of the enterprise. On 6 Sept. 1669 the Venetians had to surrender their last stronghold on the island, the capital Candia (Iraklion), leaving the holy see to shoulder crippling debts to Venice and the other participants.

Clement's health deteriorated in autumn 1669 and he died of a stroke, his end being hastened by the bitter news from Crete. A connoisseur of letters, he was something of a poet and wrote religious dramas, based on Spanish models and set to music, which were successfully performed. He had the distinction of creating the comic opera as a dramatic form; the first example was *Chi soffre speri*, which had its première in the Palazzo Barberini on 27 Feb. 1639.

Lettere famigliari (MS *Vat. lat.* 13.362–13.367); *BullRom* XVII; C. Gérin, *Louis XIV et le S. Siège* (Paris, 1894), II, 179–390; N. J. Abercrombie, *The Origins of Jansenism* (Oxford, 1936); *DHGE* 12, 1297–313 (R. Mols); *DBI* 26, 282–93 (L. Osbat and R. Meloncelli); Seppelt 5, 334–43.

CLEMENT X (29 Apr. 1670–22 July 1676). As none of the factions could muster a majority, and as France and Spain vetoed certain candidates, the conclave after CLEMENT IX's death dragged on for almost five months before 79-year-old Emilio Altieri was elected. Born in Rome of a distinguished local family on 12 July 1590, he studied at the Roman College, took his doctorate in laws in 1611, worked as a barrister under Giambattista Pamfili (later INNOCENT X) when judge of the *Rota, and was ordained in Apr. 1624. After three years as an auditor in the Polish nunciature, he served as bishop of Camerino 1627–54, being sent by Innocent X as nuncio to Naples in 1644. His tenure of this difficult assignment did not satisfy Innocent, and he was recalled in 1652. His fortunes revived, however, under ALEXANDER VII, who in 1657 appointed him secretary of the Congregation of Bishops and Regulars and a consultor (expert adviser) of the Holy Office. A month before his death Clement IX named him cardinal. After election he adopted his patron's name.

Aware that at his age he needed assistance, Clement assigned the role of *cardinal nephew to Cardinal Paluzzi degli Albertoni, whose nephew had married Clement's niece (sole heiress of the Altieri), making him and his branch of the Paluzzi, as a token of relationship, adopt the name Altieri. The appointment was far from happy, for Paluzzi not only took complete control of affairs, reducing the secretaries of state to ciphers, but exploited the pope's kindness to accumulate offices and riches for himself and his family. The vast sums he spent extending the Palazzo Altieri so offended public opinion that Clement deemed it prudent never to visit it. Paluzzi could also be heavy-handed, as when in autumn 1674 he alienated the diplomatic corps by commuting their tax immunities, thereby provoking a crisis which necessitated an undignified climb-down.

Clement was much preoccupied by the threat of the Turks to Poland, itself weakened by internal disorders, and strove to form a defensive alliance against them, even appealing (without success) to the Protestant king Charles XI of Sweden (1660-97). Both Clement and Cardinal Odescalchi (later INNOCENT XI) gave financial aid to John Sobieski (1624-96), who not only decisively defeated the Turks at the Dniester (11 Nov. 1673) but, the Polish throne having fallen vacant, was elected king (May 1674). Louis XIV of France (1643-1715) stood aside from the formation of a common anti-Turkish front, since he was preparing a war of conquest against Holland. For a time he led Clement to believe that it was a holy war for the restoration of Catholicism, so that the pope frowned on the intervention of Spain and on the military aid given by Emperor Leopold I (1658-1705) to the Dutch. By summer

1674 Clement realized that he had been deceived, and in Oct. 1675 sent envoys to Paris, Vienna, and Madrid to prepare for peace negotiations, but Louis did all he could to frustrate his efforts, which came to nothing. Meanwhile relations between king and pope were rapidly worsening, for when Louis infringed church privileges, confiscating church property and requisitioning religious houses so as to divert their income to military preparations, Clement's complaints fell on deaf ears. Louis's claim, however, to the unrestricted right of regalia (i.e. appointments to ecclesiastical offices and the income of vacant sees and abbeys), asserted in 1673 and 1675, did not apparently provoke any response from the holy see; Clement's successor was to inherit the problem.

The aged pope had to face unprecedented pressure from the Catholic powers to appoint their nominees to the cardinalate; on a famous occasion in May 1675 the French ambassador threatened violence when requested to withdraw after an acrimonious audience. In the circumstances Clement had on occasion to yield to these demands. On 21 June 1670, reacting to a unilateral decree of the French government subjecting even members of exempt orders to episcopal jurisdiction, he ruled that religious must have the local bishop's permission for preaching or hearing confessions outside their own churches. His unusually numerous canonizations included Cajetan (1480-1547), founder of the Theatine order, the Jesuit Francis Borgia (1510-72), and Rose of Lima (1586-1617), South America's first saint; and he beatified PIUS V, the Spanish mystic John of the Cross (1542-91), and the martyrs of Gorcum in south Holland (put to death by Calvinists on 9 July 1572).

BullRom XVIII; C. Gerin, *Louis XIV et le S. Siège* (Paris, 1894), II, 391-646; M. Dubruel, 'La cour de Rome et l'extension de la régale', *Rev. hist. église de France* 9 (1923), 161-76; P 31; *DHGE* 12, 1313-26 (R. Mols); *DBI* 26, 293-302 (L. Osbat); Seppelt 5, 344-6.

INNOCENT XI, BL. (21 Sept. 1676–12 Aug. 1689). After a two-month conclave Benedetto Odescalchi was unanimously chosen to succeed CLEMENT X, Louis XIV of France (1643–1715) having agreed to withdraw his threatened veto. Born at Como on 19 May 1611, he came of a rich commercial family, and was himself apprenticed at fifteen to its bank at Genoa after studying with the Jesuits at Como. Influenced by a friendly cardinal, he then read law at Rome and Naples, taking his doctorate in 1639, entered the papal service under URBAN VIII, and became successively protonotary, president of the apostolic chamber, governor of Macerata, and financial commissary in the Marches. INNOCENT X made him cardinal in 1645, legate of Ferrara in 1648 at a time of acute famine, and bishop of Novara in 1650. In these offices he earned a reputation for conscientious, charitable administration as well as austere piety; as bishop he spent his income on the poor. Resigning his see in 1654 on grounds of ill health, he lived quietly in Rome, absorbed in curial business. Surprised and abashed by his election, he would only accept it when the cardinals agreed to subscribe a fourteen-point programme of reform which he had proposed during the conclave.

Frugal in his personal life, Innocent at once set himself to sweep away moral and administrative abuses. Entirely free from nepotism himself, he sought to persuade the cardinals to outlaw it, but in vain. By reducing offices and stipends and by drastic economies, he restored the papal finances. He called for evangelical preaching and catechizing, the strict observance of monastic vows, the rigorous selection of priests and bishops, and frequent communion. His measures to control public decency, e.g. his prohibition of carnivals, were largely ineffective and met with ridicule. With his moral earnestness he had *Jansenist leanings and was critical of the Jesuits; on 2 Mar. 1679, without naming the *probabilism prevalent in Jesuit circles, he condemned sixty-five laxist propositions

savouring of it. When the Jesuit Tirso González de Santalla, of Salamanca, turned against probabilism, Innocent endorsed (1680) his system of probabiliorism, i.e. the view that in cases of doubt about the licitness of an action the opinion which seems more probable should be followed, and in 1687 procured his election as general of the order. On the other hand, although previously sympathetic to the Spanish Quietist Miguel de Molinos (c. 1640–97), author of a *Spiritual Guide* which inculcated complete passivity and minimized human effort, he was manoeuvred by the Jesuit-dominated Holy Office into permitting his arrest in 1685 and then denouncing his extremer views in the bull *Coelestis pastor* on 19 Nov. 1687.

Innocent's inflexible resistance to encroachments on the church's rights led him into continuous conflict with Louis XIV's absolutist pretensions. Clement X had made no rejoinder to Louis's decrees of 1673 and 1675 extending the right of *regalia (i.e. the king's right to administer both the temporalities and the spiritualities of vacant sees) to his entire realm, and, construing his silence as acquiescence, almost all the French clergy submitted. When two bishops protested, Innocent rejected the extension; whereupon an assembly of French clergy, at Louis's instigation, adopted (19 Mar. 1682) the four so-called Gallican Articles denying the pope any authority in temporal affairs or over kings, asserting the superior authority of general councils, and reaffirming the ancient liberties of the Gallican church. In reply Innocent rejected the Articles (11 Apr. 1682) and refused to ratify the appointments of bishops who had subscribed them; by Jan. 1688 thirty-five bishoprics were vacant in France. Louis hoped that his attacks on the Huguenots, culminating in the revocation of the *Edict of Nantes on 18 Oct. 1685, would induce the pope to be co-operative, but while approving the revocation Innocent suspected the motives behind it and deplored the violent methods of the persecution unleashed on the Protestants. The deadlock was intensified in 1687 when Innocent, having ended the rights of asylum enjoyed, and abused, by embassies in Rome, refused to receive the new and defiant French ambassador; and again in 1688, when he rejected Louis's nominee for the archbishopric and electorship of Cologne and appointed Emperor Leopold I's (1658–1705). In Jan. 1688 he secretly informed Louis that he and his ministers were excommunicate; in Sept. the king occupied the papal territories of Avignon and Venaissin. Open schism was avoided only by the intervention of Fénelon (1651–1715), later archbishop of Cambrai, and the advent of William of Orange to the English throne.

Innocent's dearest aim, and greatest achievement, was to mobilize resistance to the Turks advancing into Europe. Although thwarted by Louis's expansionist policies, he brought about (31 Mar. 1683) the alliance between Emperor Leopold I and John III Sobieski of Poland (1674–96) which led to the relief of Vienna (12 Sept. 1683). To push the Turkish threat still further back he then formed the Holy League of the empire, Poland, Venice, and Russia; this triumphantly liberated Hungary (1686) and recovered Belgrade (1688). Throughout he gave substantial subsidies to the enterprise. In the meantime, while welcoming the accession of the Roman Catholic James II in England (1685), he was suspicious of his subservience to Louis XIV and disapproved of his ill-judged methods of restoring Roman Catholicism in the country. Not surprisingly, when James lost his throne and appealed for help, Innocent replied that he could do nothing, his energies being taken up with the struggle with Louis. But the allegation that he knew of, and privately supported, the designs of the Protestant William of Orange for displacing James is groundless.

Innocent was seventy-eight when he died. Historians of all schools recognize him as the outstanding 17th-cent. pope. Although the Romans found his austerity oppressive in his lifetime, they soon began

venerating him after his death. A process of canonization was started by CLEMENT XI in 1714, but was suspended in 1744 because of objections by the French court. It was resumed in the altered atmosphere of the 20th cent., and PIUS XII announced his beatification on 7 Oct. 1956. Feast 12 Aug.

AAS 48 (1956), 754–9; 762–78; M. Santi, *Bibliografia di papa I. XI 1676–1689 fino al 1927* (Como, 1957); *BullRom* XIX; F. de Bojani, *Innocent XI: Sa correspondance avec ses nonces 1676–84* (Rome, 1910–12); I. I. Berthier, *Innocentii P.P. XI epistolae ad Principes* (Rome, 1891–5); G. Papasogli, *Innocenzo XI* (Rome, 1956); J. Orcibal, *Louis XIV contre Innocent XI* (Paris, 1949); L. O'Brien, *Innocent XI and the Renunciation of the Edict of Nantes* (Berkeley, 1930); P 32; *DTC* 7, 2006–13 (J. Paquier); *NCE* 7, 529 f. (S. V. Ramge); Seppelt 5, 346–71.

ALEXANDER VIII (6 Oct. 1689–1 Feb. 1691). Scion of a recently ennobled family, Pietro Ottoboni was born at Venice on 22 Apr. 1610, proved a brilliant student at Padua, graduating doctor of laws at seventeen, and at twenty, helped by a compatriot who was dean of the *Rota, entered the curial service. After being governor in the papal state 1638–43, he was judge of the Rota 1643–52, becoming famous for his judicial decisions. Made cardinal in Feb. 1652, he served as bishop of Brescia from 1654, returning to Rome in 1664 to play a leading role in the curia. He was the trusted collaborator of INNOCENT XI, who appointed him grand inquisitor of Rome and secretary of the Holy Office. Although the empire and France were for the first time represented by ambassadors extraordinary at the conclave of 1689, the cardinals were already resolved, before ascertaining the monarchs' wishes, that his knowledge and experience, efficient dispatch of difficult business, and his character marked him out for election. Initially hostile because of his earlier attitude to the French question, Louis XIV of France (1643–1715) concurred when both Ottoboni and his nephew provided assurances that, if chosen, he would pursue conciliatory policies.

Alexander in fact made serious, partially successful, efforts to break the deadlock with France. Louis XIV, his position weakened since the English revolution of 1688, wanted improved relations with Rome, and both handed back Avignon and Venaissin (occupied in Sept. 1688) and acquiesced in Innocent XI's suppression of the extravagant rights of asylum and tax immunity claimed by embassies in Rome. In return Alexander pleased him by raising, in the face of protests from Emperor Leopold I (1657–1705), Bishop Toussaint de Forbin-Janson of Beauvais to the cardinalate, overlooking his participation in the Gallican assembly of 1682; he also accepted the French ambassador rejected by Innocent XI. On the main issue, however, he stood firm, refusing to ratify the appointment of bishops nominated by the king unless they repudiated the four *Gallican Articles of 1682. The quarrel then broke out afresh, and Alexander felt obliged to annul both Louis's extension of the right of *regalia to his entire realm and the four Articles in the constitution *Inter multiplices*. This he drafted on 4 Aug. 1690, but published only on his deathbed on 31 Jan. 1691 after a plan to influence the king through Madame de Maintenon, his secret wife since 1684, had come to nothing. His *rapprochement* with France, limited though it was, brought cool relations with the empire, while his failure to raise any of Leopold's nominees to the purple led to the withdrawal of the imperial ambassador. He also greatly reduced the subsidies Innocent XI had given Leopold for war against the Turks, preferring to give generous support, in money, troops, and galleys, to his beloved Venice.

With his experience of the Holy Office Alexander was a jealous guardian of the faith. On 24 Aug. 1690 he condemned two laxist propositions current among Jesuits, one denying the necessity of an explicit act of love for God after the attainment of reason, the other admitting the notion of 'philosophic sin', i.e. a sin involving no offence to God because committed without knowledge or thought of him. He then (7

Dec. 1690) condemned thirty-one *Jansenist propositions concerning penance, the Virgin, baptism, and the church's authority. He also punished with life imprisonment the surviving followers of the Spanish Quietist Miguel de *Molinos (c. 1640–92).

Aged seventy-nine when elected, Alexander was a complete contrast to his severe predecessor, and not only delighted the Romans by his lavish style but recklessly revived the nepotism Innocent had disdained. He is said to have declared that he had to work fast since the twenty-third hour had struck. He appointed his grandnephew Pietro, aged twenty, *cardinal nephew and his nephew Giambattista secretary of state, investing them and other relatives with lucrative benefices. He was popular in the papal state, where he reduced taxes, increased cheap food imports, and introduced other improvements; but his recruitment of troops for the assistance of Venice against the Turks met with angry resistance. A connoisseur of letters, he moved at ease in literary circles, and enriched the Vatican library by the purchase of the valuable manuscripts ('Reginenses') and other collections of Queen Christina of Sweden (1626–89), settled in Rome since her abdication and her public reception into the church in 1655.

BullRom XX; *Decisiones S. Rotae Romanae coram P. Ottobono* (Rome, 1657); G. A. Hanotaux, *Recueil des instructions données aux ambassadeurs et ministres de France* (Paris, 1888–1913); S. V. Bischoffshausen, *Papst A. VIII und der Wiener Hof* (Stuttgart, 1900); P 32; *DHGE* 2, 244–51 (P. Richard); *EC* 1, 803–5 (P. dalla Torre); *NCE* 1, 293 (S. V. Ramge); *LThK* 1, 318 f. (K. Repson); *DBI* 2, 215–19 (A. Petrucci); Seppelt 5, 370–4.

INNOCENT XII (12 July 1691–27 Sept. 1700). The conclave following ALEXANDER VIII's death lasted five months, with the opposing French and imperial factions divided also among themselves. As a compromise Antonio Pignatelli was at last elected when disturbances in Rome and the summer heat forced a decision. A Neapolitan aristocrat born near Spinazzola (Puglia) on 13 Mar. 1615, he was educated at the Jesuit college at Rome, joined the curia under URBAN VIII, and became successively vice-legate of Urbino, governor of Viterbo, and nuncio to Tuscany (1652), Poland (1660), and Vienna (1668). He fell into disfavour under CLEMENT X, who sent him to Lecce as bishop. Recalled to Rome in 1673 to become secretary of the Congregation of Bishops and Regulars, he was created cardinal by INNOCENT XI (1 Sept 1681), then bishop of Faenza, legate of Bologna, and finally archbishop of Naples (1687).

Devout and charitable, simple in his personal life, he adopted Innocent XI's name and took him as his model. He at once embarked on a programme of reform in Rome and the papal states, insisting on economical administration and completely impartial justice. He drastically reduced the sale of offices, compensating the treasury for the resulting loss by cutting court expenses to the bone, and also by enlarging the harbours of Civitavecchia and Nettuno to promote trade. He developed charitable institutions like the Hospital of S. Michele for poor youths, and opened the Lateran as a refuge for people incapacitated for work; the poor and needy, he claimed, were his nephews. To raise the level of the clergy he founded (1694) the Congregation for the Discipline and Reform of Regulars, and prohibited (1695) the practice, common in Germany, of electoral chapters nominating to bishoprics and monasteries. Most revolutionary of all, he struck at the roots of nepotism, decreeing (*Romanum decet pontificem*: 22 June 1692) that the pope should never grant estates, offices, or revenues to relatives; if they were poor, he should treat them like others in need. Further, only one relative should be eligible, if otherwise suitable, for the purple, and his income should have a modest ceiling. After resistance from several cardinals, he persuaded them all to sign the decree.

With Louis XIV of France (1643–1715), whose political situation after the formation of the Grand Alliance made a *rapprochement* with Rome desirable, Innocent reached a compromise which broke the fifty-year politico-religious deadlock between France and the holy see. First, he ratified the appointment of bishops nominated by the king since 1682 who had not taken part in the Assembly of the Clergy of that year. Louis then (14 Sept. 1693) promised to revoke the Declaration of the French Clergy which obliged French bishops to subscribe the four *Gallican Articles, and the bishops who had attended the 1682 assembly wrote retracting their signatures. Innocent now granted the bishops canonical institution, and by the end of 1693 the French hierarchy was restored. Against these apparent gains the pope had to accept Louis's extension of the right to the *regalia to his entire realm, and the king's concession left the Gallican Articles themselves intact; *Gallicanism was to govern church affairs in France until the Revolution and Napoleon. This accommodation, however, between France and Rome was viewed with suspicion in Vienna, and although Innocent at first gave liberal support to Emperor Leopold I (1688–1705) for defence against the Turks, tension between the two courts gradually increased, being greatly exacerbated by the arrogant conduct of the imperial ambassadors. A crisis came when the emperor, instigated by ambassador Count Martinitz, decreed that all who owed feudal allegiance to the empire in Italy should produce proof of tenure, and the pope felt obliged to annul the decrees so far as they affected the papal state as a gross intrusion on his sovereignty. The French ambassador was quick to take advantage of the resulting tension.

To prevent frivolous charges being brought against suspected *Jansenists in Belgium, Innocent forbade (6 Feb. 1694) the bishops to demand additions to ALEXANDER VII's constitution of 1665 condemning the five propositions extracted from Cornelius Jansen's *Augustinus in the sense the author had intended. As the Jansenists regarded this as a favourable signal, he issued another brief (25 Nov. 1696) declaring that nothing was further from his intention than to modify the teaching of his predecessor on the Jansenist heresy. Towards the end of his life he was called upon, much against his will but under strong pressure from Louis XIV, to pass judgement on the mystical doctrines taught by Madame de Guyon (1648–1717) and supported by Archbishop François Fénelon of Cambrai (1651–1715). On 12 Mar. 1699 he published the brief *Cum alias* denouncing twenty-three sentences from Fénelon's *Explications des maximes des saints*. He declined, however, to censure Celestino Sfondrati's book on predestination, which Bishop Jacques Bénigue Bossuct had accused of Quietism in 1697.

Although Innocent redoubled his efforts after 1696 to bring an end to the European war between France and the Grand Alliance, the holy see was not represented at the congress leading to the treaty of Ryswick (20 Sept. 1697). He was able, however, to secure the inclusion in its terms of an important clause requiring the Roman Catholic faith to be preserved intact in any places the treaty made subject to Protestant rule. The issue of the Spanish succession came before him at the close of his reign when the heir designate of the childless Charles II (1665–1700), the Bavarian electoral prince Joseph Ferdinand, suddenly died (6 Feb. 1699). Charles II was at first inclined to leave his inheritance to Archduke Charles of Austria (to be Emperor Charles VI: 1711–40), but the primate of Spain, Cardinal Portocarrero, and the council of state favoured Philip, duke of Anjou, Louis XIV's grandson. When consulted by Charles, Innocent on the advice of a commission of cardinals took the fateful decision to recommend Philip, and the king made a final will leaving his Spanish dominions to him; as Philip V he was king of Spain 1700–46. The pope's death on 27 Sept. 1700 was followed by Charles's on 1 Nov.

BullRom XX; P 32; *DTC* 7, 2013–15 (J. Paquier); *LThK* 5, 695 (G. Schwaiger); *EC* 7, 25–7 (R. Palmarocchi); *NCE* 7, 530 f. (J. Calicchio); Seppelt 5, 374–83.

CLEMENT XI (23 Nov. 1700–19 Mar. 1721). Of aristocratic Umbrian stock, Giovanni Francesco Albani was born at Urbino on 23 July 1649, and received a thorough classical education at Rome, where the former Queen Christina of Sweden (1626–89) welcomed him to her academy. After studying philosophy and law, he entered the curial service in 1677, first holding governorships in the papal states, being promoted secretary of briefs in 1687, and in Feb. 1690 being created cardinal. His influence was a determining one under ALEXANDER VIII and INNOCENT XII; it was he who drafted the latter's bull outlawing nepotism. He was only ordained priest in Sept. 1700. At the 46-day conclave of that autumn neither the French nor the imperial faction could win the day, and Albani was elected as the candidate of the *zelanti*, i.e. the cardinals who wanted a non-political pope with the church's interest at heart. Only fifty-one, devout, austere, but lacking political flair, he accepted with genuine reluctance after several days' anxious reflection, although his elevation was enthusiastically received even in Protestant countries.

The War of the Spanish Succession (1701–14), which filled much of his reign, soon exposed his and the papacy's ineffectiveness. Having initially come out in favour of the Bourbon Philip of Anjou (Philip V of Spain: 1700–46) as heir to the Spanish inheritance, he tried to be neutral as war approached. His offers to mediate fell on deaf ears, as did his protest (Apr. 1701) against the assumption without papal consent of the title of king of Prussia by the Elector Frederick III of Brandenburg. He soon found himself caught between two fires, for both Philip V and Emperor Leopold I (1658–1705), who backed the Habsburg duke Charles (Emperor Charles VI: 1711–40) for the Spanish throne, demanded to be invested with Naples and Sicily. Leopold, too, with good reason suspected him of being a partisan of France; nor could he prevent Italy from becoming a theatre of war. In Jan. 1709, when the troops of Leopold's successor Joseph I (1705–11) had invaded the papal states, conquered Naples, and threatened Rome, Clement had to accept the new emperor's harsh terms, which included his abandonment of Philip V and recognition of Archduke Charles as Spanish king. This led at once to rupture with Spain. In the treaty of Utrecht (1713) Clement found himself ignored, and Sardinia and Sicily, Parma and Piacenza were disposed of with cynical disregard of the pope's overlordship. Sicily was assigned to Duke Victor Amadeus II of Savoy (1675–1730) along with control of the church there (the *'Sicilian monarchy'); when Clement protested and published a bull (20 Feb. 1715) rescinding the 'monarchy', Victor paid not the least attention. When the Turks declared war on Venice in 1714, Clement dreamed of emulating PIUS V, but his efforts to form an alliance against them could not prevent the entire Peloponnese from falling into their hands; while in 1717, in spite of guarantees he had given the emperor, he had the mortification of seeing a Spanish fleet he had equipped to fight the Turks diverted by Cardinal Giulio Alberoni to wrest Sardinia from the empire.

Clement played a decisive role, largely at the instigation of Louis XIV of France (1643–1715), in the repression of *Jansenism. On 15 July 1705 he condemned (Vineam Domini Sabaoth) the suggestion, approved by the Sorbonne, that one could safely reject the five Jansenist propositions denounced by INNOCENT X while maintaining 'respectful silence' as to whether they actually occurred in Cornelius Jansen's works. On 13 July 1708 he condemned, as based on a corrupt text of the New Testament and as infected with Jansenist error, the Réflexions morales of Pasquier Quesnel (1634–1719), the learned Oratorian who was now leader of the Jansenist party. Finally, he published on 8 Sept. 1713 the famous bull Unigenitus Dei Filius condemning 101 allegedly Jansenist propositions extracted from Quesnel's work. The bull evoked intense opposition, and after Louis

XIV's death in 1715 the leaders of the Jansenist movement appealed to a general council. Clement, however, stood firm, and excommunicated (28 Aug. 1718) the 'appellants'—without, however, their taking any notice. Eventually the French government (4 Dec. 1720) forced the parlement to register the bull, although with a reservation safeguarding the traditional liberties of the Gallican church.

Clement was keenly interested in missionary work, and not only founded missionary colleges but promoted missions overseas, notably in India, the Philippines, and China. It fell to him to decide on the propriety, disputed between Dominicans and Jesuits, of adapting in the mission field pagan beliefs and ceremonies to Christian practice. On 20 Nov. 1704, approving a sentence of the Holy Office, he ruled against the use by missionaries of Chinese rites, especially the cult of Confucius and ancestors, on the pretext that they were primarily civic acts; he reiterated the ruling in the constitution Ex illa die (19 Mar. 1715). Jesuit missionaries, in contrast to the Dominicans, favoured the Chinese rites, and ALEXANDER VII had sanctioned them in 1656; their prohibition by Clement led to the persecution of Chinese Christians and the closure of missions, and was only finally lifted by PIUS XII in 1939.

In 1708 he declared the feast of the Immaculate Conception of the BVM obligatory throughout Christendom. A busy, if painstaking and indecisive, administrator, Clement appointed seventy cardinals in his long reign. He was a generous patron of the arts and scholarship, being particularly interested in archaeology. A great benefactor of the Vatican library, he appointed J. S. Assemani (1687–1768) its librarian and sent him to the east to collect manuscripts for it.

Opera omnia, including Bullarium (ed. by Cardinal Albani, Rome, 1722–4); BullRom XXI; P. Polidori, De vita et rebus gestis Clementis XI (Urbino, 1727); A. Aldobrandini, La guerra di successione di Spagna negli stati dell'Alta Italia dal 1701 al 1705 e la politica di Clemente XI (Rome,

1931); F. Pometti, 'Studi sul pontificato di Clemente XI', *ASRomana* 21 (1898), 279–457; 22 (1899), 109–79; 23 (1900), 239–76, 449–515; P 33; *DHGE* 12, 1326–61 (R. Mols); *LThK* 2, 1227 f. (A. Cornaro); *DBI* 26, 302–20 (S. Andretta); Seppelt 5, 382–413.

INNOCENT XIII (8 May 1721–7 Mar. 1724). After a long, contentious conclave at which Cardinal Althan, on behalf of the emperor, vetoed the initially favoured candidate, CLEMENT XI's secretary of state Fabrizio Paolucci, Michelangelo dei Conti was unanimously elected. Son of the duke of Poli, near Palestrina, he was born there on 13 May 1655, was a student at Ancona and then with the Jesuits at Rome, and early entered the service of the curia. After holding governorships in the papal states, he was nuncio in Switzerland 1695–8, and then in Portugal 1698–1709. Promoted cardinal by Clement XI on 7 June 1706, he was successively bishop of Osimo (1709–12) and Viterbo (1712–19), resigning the latter see for reasons of health. When elected, he adopted the name of INNOCENT III, from whose family he was descended.

Possessing both diplomatic skill and a desire for a quiet life, Innocent set about resolving the tensions with the great powers which had troubled his predecessor's reign. Thus he invested (9 June 1722) Emperor Charles VI (1711–40) with Naples and Sicily, which Clement XI had refused to do since he had not been consulted about their transfer to the empire in 1720, and in July 1721 he gratified the regent of France (Philip II of Orléans: 1715–23) by raising his powerful but corrupt minister Guillaume Dubois (1656–1723) to the purple. On the other hand, he was unable to prevent Charles VI from claiming supreme authority over the Sicilian church, in spite of Clement XI's having abolished the *'Sicilian monarchy' in 1715, or from investing the Spanish prince Don Carlos with Parma and Piacenza, duchies traditionally fiefs of the papacy. Further, his negotiations with the emperor for the withdrawal of the occupying force left in Comacchio, between Ravenna and Ferrara, in

1709 dragged on inconclusively. Like his predecessors, he recognized the Old Pretender ('James III') as king of England and Scotland, not only paying him an income but promising him 10,000 ducats on his re-establishing Roman Catholicism in Britain.

Innocent had a deep aversion to the Jesuits, dating from his time as nuncio in Portugal, and was minded to suppress the order when he learned that its missionaries were not complying with Clement XI's ban on *Chinese rites. Instead he forbade it to receive novices unless within three years he had satisfactory proof of its obedience. His antipathy to the Jesuits, as well as the fact that he had protested as cardinal against Clement XI's failure to consult the sacred college before publishing the bull *Unigenitus outlawing *Jansenism, raised hopes in Jansenist circles that he would adopt a friendlier attitude to them. In fact, on becoming pope, he confirmed the bull, and when seven French bishops wrote to him in June 1721 asking him to withdraw it, he had their petition censured by the Holy Office. In a letter to the French king he declared his complete agreement with Clement XI's constitution, and requested him to take active measures against the bishops.

Innocent created his brother Bernard a cardinal, but any fears that he was succumbing to nepotism were groundless; he limited Bernard's income to the sum stipulated by INNOCENT XI in his ban on nepotism. In the papal states he was concerned for economic and cultural development, but his short reign was overshadowed by constant illness.

BullRom XXI; A. Ciaconius, *Vitae et res gestae Pontificum Romanorum* (Rome, 1751) 6, 381–408; M. von Mayer, *Die Papstwahl Innocenz' XIII* (Vienna, 1874); E. Michaud, 'La fin de Clément XI et le commencement du pontificat d'Innocent XIII', *RevIntTheol* 5 (1897), 42–60, 304–31; P 34; *DTC* 7, 2015 f. (J. Paquier); *EC* 7, 27 (F. Fonzi); Seppelt 5, 413–15.

BENEDICT XIII (29 May 1724–21 Feb. 1730). Eldest son of the duke of Gravina (Puglia) and born there on 2 Feb. 1649,

Pietro Francesco Orsini came of a family which had produced CELESTINE III and NICHOLAS III. As a youth, despite opposition from relatives, he renounced his inheritance and joined the Dominicans, making his profession at Rome on 9 Feb. 1669 and taking the name in religion of Vincenzo Maria. After lecturing in philosophy at Brescia, he was named a cardinal, much against his will, in Feb. 1672 by CLEMENT X, whose niece had married his brother. Archbishop of Manfredonia (1675), bishop of Cesena (1680), and archbishop of Benevento (1686), he lived as a simple friar, wholly devoted to his pastoral duties; he held several provincial and diocesan synods, and yet found leisure to publish works of (mainly) ascetical and practical theology. After nine weeks of frustrated wrangling the conclave of 1724, with the French, Spanish, and Habsburg factions concurring, unanimously elected him as a pope whose lack of political experience might ensure his neutrality. He only accepted on the bidding of the general of his order, taking the style of Benedict XIV, but altering it to Benedict XIII since the previous bearer of that name (Pedro de Luna) had been an antipope.

As pope he made no change in his monkish life-style, shunning the Vatican's splendid apartments; he also remained archbishop of his beloved Benevento, carrying out weeks-long visitations in 1727 and 1729. At Rome he concentrated on his diocese, taking particular delight in consecrating churches and altars, visiting the sick, administering sacraments, and giving religious instruction. Concerned for clerical discipline, he inveighed against the extravagances of cardinals, and against the wearing of wigs and fashionably trimmed beards; he also banned the popular and profitable public lottery in the papal states. In spring 1725, a year of jubilee, he personally conducted a provincial synod in the Lateran and had its decisions immediately circulated in print; it was his fond hope that it would set an example to bishops everywhere and that the pastoral ideals it inculcated would be eagerly implemented. With his primarily religious absorption he needed reliable collaborators for the business of the church at large; unfortunately, while retaining Fabrizio Paolucci as secretary of state, he placed implicit trust in an unscrupulous scoundrel, Niccolò Coscia, whom he had found useful at Benevento, and allowed him a free hand. Coscia, promoted cardinal in 1725 in the face of protests from the sacred college, appointed like-minded self-seekers from Benevento to influential positions, and on Paolucci's death had a creature of his, Niccolò Maria Lercari, made the new secretary of state. His policy was to isolate his master from the cardinals, and systematiclly enrich himself and his coterie by selling offices and accepting bribes; in the end the pope was advised exclusively by this corrupt and unscrupulous inner circle.

The weakness of Benedict's external policies, and the collapse of the finances of the papal states, were largely due to Coscia's interventions. They explain, for example, the ease with which Victor Amadeus II of Savoy (1675–1730) obtained (1725) both the recognition of his royal title, assumed in 1713 in the face of papal disapproval, and the right to present to all bishoprics in Sardinia. The king won even more concessions in the concordat of 1727, and suitably rewarded the venal papal negotiators. By similar methods, in spite of CLEMENT XI's rescission of the *'Sicilian monarchy' in 1715, Emperor Charles VI's (1711–40) agents extracted a bull (30 Aug. 1728) from Benedict which, without actually recognizing the 'monarchy', granted the ruler of Sicily effective control of church affairs. It is significant that, when Benedict resisted demands from John V of Portugal (1706–50) to make the nuncio to Lisbon a cardinal, thereby risking a schism, he was not under Coscia's influence but stiffened by the sacred college.

Any hopes the *Jansenists in France drew from the election of a Dominican as pope were soon shattered. To counter their claim that the bull *Unigenitus conflicted with the teaching of St Augustine and St Thomas Aquinas on grace and predestination, Benedict instructed (6 Nov. 1724) the Dominicans to hold fast, in spite of misrepresentations, to the doctrine of those masters; while at the Lateran synod of 1725 he called for unconditional submission to *Unigenitus*. In the bull *Pretiosus* (28 June 1727) he declared that the teaching of St Thomas and the Thomist school had nothing to do with the errors of Cornelius Jansen (1585–1638) and Pasquier Quesnel (1634–1719). From now onwards he played a secondary role in the Jansenist debate, and it was the curia which, after lengthy negotiations, secured the submission (11 Oct. 1728) of Cardinal de Noailles, archbishop of Paris, who had opposed it from the start, to *Unigenitus*.

Consistently with his religious outlook, Benedict canonized many saints, including John of the Cross (1542–91) and Aloysius Gonzaga (1568–91). His extension of the feast of Pope ST GREGORY VII to the whole church provoked a crisis in the holy see's international relations, for several governments found provocative the passages in the office provided referring to Gregory's deposition of Emperor Henry IV (1056–1106), and banned the liturgical text. For all his pastoral goodness Benedict was unpopular with the Roman people, partly because of his maladministration of the finances of the papal states, but much more because of their hatred of Coscia and his creatures who were to blame for it. On the pope's death they vented their fury on the guilty Beneventans, who were lucky to escape with their lives.

Opere tutte Latine ed Italiane (Ravenna, 1728–34); *BullRom* XXII; G. B. Pittoni, *Vita* (Venice, 1730); A. Borgia, *Vita* (Rome, 1752); G. Vignato, *Storia di Benedetto XIII* (Milan, 1953); G. Cardillo, 'Benedetto XIII e il giansenismo', *Memorie Domenicane* 58 (1941), 217–22; 59 (1942), 38–43; P 34; *DHGE* 7, 163 f. (J. Carreyre); *EC* 2, 1279–82 (C. Castiglioni); *DBI* 8, 384–93 (G. De Caro); Seppelt 5, 415–24.

CLEMENT XII (12 July 1730–6 Feb. 1740). The four-month conclave of 1730 was exceptionally contentious, with half the cardinals present being proposed at one stage or another. Eventually the Florentine Lorenzo Corsini was unanimously chosen. Born on 7 Apr. 1652, eldest son of a noble family enriched by commerce, he had his schooling at Florence, and then studied at the Roman College and at Pisa, graduating doctor of laws in 1675. On his father's death in 1685 he decided on an ecclesiastical career, renounced his inheritance, and entered the curial service, in which he had the help of relatives. His wealth enabled him to purchase useful positions, and in Apr. 1690 ALEXANDER VIII named him titular archbishop of Nicomedia. The following year he was designated nuncio to Vienna, but the emperor, irritated that his nominees had not received the purple, declined to receive him. He therefore remained in Rome, gaining financial expertise as treasurer (1696) of the apostolic chamber. In May 1706 he was made cardinal by CLEMENT XI, and at several conclaves was among the principal *papabili*, or cardinals considered in the running for election. His new family home in the Palazzo Pamfili, on the Piazza Navona, was the centre of Rome's scholarly and artistic life. He took the name of his patron Clement XI.

Aged seventy-nine, often bedridden with gout, blind from 1732, Clement relied increasingly on his immediate circle, especially on his nephew Neri Corsini, whom he named cardinal but who had little capacity for state business. He first had Cardinal Niccolò Coscia, BENEDICT XIII's evil genius, and his coterie brought to trial; Coscia was sentenced to a huge fine and ten years' imprisonment in Castel Sant'Angelo. He then made strenuous efforts to remedy the débâcle into which the finances and administration of the papal states had fallen. Among the measures he adopted were the revival of state lotteries, which Benedict XIII had banned, the issue of paper money, the restriction of the export of valuables, and new taxes on imports. A free port was created at Ancona, and attempts made to stimulate trade and industry. His endeavours were hampered, however, by corrupt administration, reduced revenues from the Catholic powers, and the losses resulting from the invasion of the papal states. At his death the burden of debt was still increasing. In addition, numerous favours improperly granted by Benedict XIII out of excessive goodness were cancelled or at least modified.

The decline in the papacy's international standing, noticeable in preceding reigns, continued under Clement XII; the powers coerced or ignored it at will. In 1731 he had to look on helplessly while Emperor Charles VI (1711–40) asserted suzerainty over Parma and Piacenza, which traditionally owed feudal allegiance to the holy see, on behalf of Don Carlos of Spain (later Charles III: 1759–88). He was a helpless spectator, too, in the War of the Polish Succession (1733–8), ineffectually backing first one candidate and then another, and having finally to acquiesce in a shift of power in Italy arranged over his head under the treaties of Vienna (1735 and 1738). Meanwhile the papal states were overrun by Spanish armies, the Roman population revolted against the recruitment of troops by the Spaniards, and in May 1736 Spain, followed by Naples, broke off diplomatic relations with the holy see. To restore them Clement had to make substantial concessions to the Spanish government and invest Don Carlos (1738) unconditionally with the kingdom of the two Sicilies. He felt obliged, because of a hostile plebiscite, to disavow the annexation of San Marino to the papal state, proclaimed by his legate in Oct. 1739. A bull addressed in 1732 to the Protestants of Saxony, where the ruling house had become Catholic in 1697, assuring them of undisturbed possession of secularized church properties in the event of their conversion to the Catholic faith, produced no results and has been cited as an illustration of his political naïvety.

At first, because of the hostility of the powers to the holy see, Clement created no non-Italian cardinals, but later he did not feel strong enough to resist their pressing demands. By constitutions of 10 Jan. 1731 and 5 Oct. 1732 he restricted the rights of the cardinals, particularly in financial administration, during a vacancy. In the constitution *In eminenti* (28 Apr. 1738) he published the first papal condemnation of Freemasonry, attacking its naturalistic bias, demand for secret oaths, religious indifferentism, and possible threat to church and state. A keen supporter of missions, notably in the Far East, he renewed (26 Sept. 1735) Clement XI's prohibition of *Chinese rites, and started a fresh inquiry into the whole issue. He was in touch with the Uniat Maronites in Lebanon, founding a college for them in Rome in 1732 and sending J. S. Assemani, orientalist and custodian of the Vatican library, to preside in 1736 as papal legate over the synod of Mount Lebanon, which effected a complete change in Maronite liturgical and canonical life. In 1737 he canonized Vincent de Paul (c. 1580–1660), an uncompromising opponent of *Jansenism.

Helped by the wealth of his family, but also by the proceeds of his lotteries, Clement embellished Rome with remarkable buildings, notably the museum of antique sculptures on the Capitol, the principal façade of St John Lateran and the Andrea Corsini chapel inside the basilica; he put visitors to Rome in his debt by laying out the Piazza di Trevi and erecting the famous Fontana di Trevi. He enlarged the Vatican library, and presented it with valuable collections of manuscripts, medals and vases.

BullRom XXIII and XXIV; A. Fabroni, *De vita et rebus gestis Clementis XII commentarius* (Rome, 1760); L. P. Raybaud, *Papauté et pouvoir temporel sous les pontificats de Clément XII et Benoît XIV* (Paris, 1963); P 34; *DHGE* 12, 1361–81 (R. Mols); *NCE* 3, 936 f. (J. S. Brusher); *DBI* 26, 320–8 (A. Caracciolo); Seppelt 5, 422–8.

BENEDICT XIV (17 Aug. 1740–3 May 1758). Born at Bologna on 31 Mar. 1675, of noble but impoverished parentage, Prospero Lorenzo Lambertini studied at the

Collegio Clementino, Rome, taking his doctorate in theology and law in 1694. Outstanding in ability and juridical training, he rose rapidly in the curia, becoming secretary of the Congregation of the Council in 1720. As Promotor of the Faith 1708–27 he had charge of canonizations, and wrote a classic treatise on the subject (*De servorum Dei beatificatione et beatorum canonizatione*: 1734–8) marked by a fresh, historical approach; it remains an indispensable study. BENEDICT XIII, whose close adviser he was, promoted him titular bishop of Theodosia (1724), archbishop of Ancona (1727), and cardinal (1728). Translated to Bologna in 1731, he proved an efficient, greatly loved pastor, but found time to publish a pioneer study of diocesan synods as well as works on the feasts of Jesus Christ and of the BVM and on the mass. At the six-month conclave of 1740, the longest in modern times, he was not considered until the last moment, when he was elected as a compromise to everyone's surprise.

The choice was fortunate, for Benedict combined an unusually sympathetic personality with a high degree of political realism. Conciliatory by nature and conviction, he concluded concordats containing substantial concessions with Sardinia (1741), Naples (1741), Spain (1753), and Austria for Milan (1757). The one with Spain, which surrendered practically all church appointments to the crown, was the most far-reaching. In the same spirit he restored relations with Portugal, disrupted since Benedict XIII's time, granting King John V (1706–50) the title 'Most Faithful' and conceding his most exorbitant demands for control of church affairs. He was no less accommodating, in the interests of their Catholic subjects, with Protestant sovereigns. Thus he cultivated good relations with Frederick II of Prussia (1740–86), which through the conquest of Silesia had significantly increased its Catholic population, and acknowledged his title as king, denied him by previous popes. As a result of this *rapprochement* he was able to prevent the setting up of a Prussian state

church, with its own vicar-general and effectively independent of the holy see. His acceptance of these arrangements, often criticized as weakness, was proof of his awareness of what was possible in a world of absolutist states. His touch was less sure in dealing with the complex situation arising out of the death of Emperor Charles VI (20 Oct. 1740) and the War of the Austrian Succession (1740–8). First, he irritated Maria Theresa of Austria (1740–80) by belatedly (20 Dec. 1740) recognizing her hereditary right, and then deepened the estrangement by recognizing (Feb. 1742) Charles Albert of Bavaria as Emperor Charles VII (1742–5). As a result he had to witness the sequestration of all benefices in Austria, and the invasion of the papal states by warring troops. On Charles VII's death (Jan. 1745) he assumed a neutral stance and in Dec. 1745, in spite of pressure from France and Spain, recognized Francis I, consort of Maria Theresa, as emperor (1745–65). In the peace of Aachen (1748) Parma and Piacenza were disposed of without regard to the feudal rights of the holy see, Benedict's protest being merely noted as a dissenting view.

In spite of the burden of debt caused by the wars, Benedict did much to improve the finances of the papal states, reducing taxation and encouraging agriculture and freedom of trade. He drastically cut the papal military budget, but failed to carry out the thorough reform of the administration that was necessary. In the strictly church field, where his heart lay, his legislation was wide-ranging. More than once he impressed on bishops their duties of residence, of training their clergy, and of pastoral visitation, and he set up special commissions to select worthy bishops and to deal with their problems. In the decree *Matrimonia quae* (4 Nov. 1741), issued originally for Belgium and Holland but later extended to other countries, he exempted the marriages of non-Catholics and mixed marriages from the juridical form prescribed by the council of Trent. Concerned for the purity of the liturgy, he appointed a commission in 1741

CLEMENT XIII (1758–69)

to reform the breviary; in 1747, dissatisfied with its proposals, he took the work in hand himself, but was not able to complete it. Between 1748 and 1754 he reduced the number of holy days in Italy and several other countries. In a brief to the Portuguese bishops of South America (1741) he called for more humane treatment of the Indians. By the bull *Ex quo singulari* (11 July 1742) he finally suppressed the *Chinese rites favoured by Jesuit missionaries, following it with the bull *Omnium sollicitudinum* (12 Sept. 1744) extending the ban, in milder terms, to Malabar rites in India. He renewed (18 May 1751) CLEMENT XII's denunciation of Freemasonry, and condemned various writings of the Enlightenment, such as Montesquieu's *Esprit des lois* (13 Mar. 1752). His characteristic moderation, however, was revealed in his publication of an improved edition of the Index (1758), preceded by a constitution (1753) prescribing fairer and more scholarly standards for the inclusion of books in it, as also in a letter to the French bishops (16 Oct. 1756) stressing the authority of the bull *Unigenitus, but ruling that only brazen flouters of it should be refused the last rites. A month before his death, in view of attacks on the Jesuits, he instructed Cardinal Saldanha, patriarch of Portugal, to investigate the order in that country, with particular reference to charges that it was neglecting its rule and engaging in trade.

Approachable and witty, with a tongue which could be sarcastic and an openness which his confidants sometimes abused, Benedict kept up his scholarly interests till the end. A connoisseur himself of church history, he founded not only academies for literary discussion but chairs of higher mathematics, chemistry, and surgery. His wide sympathies won him the respect of Protestants, and even of the French *philosophes*; Voltaire dedicated his tragedy *Mahomet* to him, causing eyebrows to be raised in strict Catholic circles. A devout churchman but also a modern man, he was described by Horace Walpole as 'a priest without insolence or interest, a prince without favourites, a pope without nephews'.

Bullarium (Rome, 1746–57); *Benedicti XIV opera omnia* (ed. E. de Azevedo, Rome, 1747–51); *Opera* (more complete edn., with bulls: Prato, 1839–46); F. Heiner, *Benedicti XIV papae opera omnia inedita* (Freiburg i.B., 1904); E. de Heeckeren, *Correspondance* (Paris, 1912); E. Morelli (ed.), *Le lettere . . . al Cardinale de Tencin* (Rome, 1955–65); L. A. de Caraccioli, *Vita* (Paris, 1783); P 35 and 36; *DHGE* 8, 164–7 (J. Carreyre); *EC* 2, 1281–5 (L. Oliger); *DBI* 8, 393–408 (M. Rosa); *NCE* 2, 278 (M. L. Shay); Seppelt 5, 428–55.

CLEMENT XIII (6 July 1758–2 Feb. 1769). France having vetoed the first choice of the conclave of 1758, the cardinals, who wanted a pope both different from BENEDICT XIV and not anti-Jesuit, elected Carlo della Torre Rezzonico. Born at Venice on 7 Mar. 1693, of an extremely rich commercial family which had purchased its ennoblement in 1687, he studied under the Jesuits at Bologna, graduated doctor of laws at Padua (1713), and was trained in diplomacy at the *Accademia ecclesiastica* at Rome. Entering the curia in May 1716, he held a series of responsible posts, becoming judge of the *Rota for Venice in 1728; three volumes of his judicial decisions were published the year after his election as pope. In Dec. 1737 CLEMENT XII named him cardinal. Appointed bishop of Padua in 1743, he modelled his pastoral activity on St Charles Borromeo (1538–84), striving to improve clerical standards, reconstructing the seminary at his own expense, and spending lavishly on poor relief; but he also settled (1751) a long-standing dispute between Venice and the empire over the patriarchate of Aquileia. Venice was delighted by his election, and withdrew anti-papal legislation dating from 1754.

Mild and well intentioned, but indecisive and therefore dependent on his entourage, notably on the imperious pro-Jesuit Luigi Torrigiano, his secretary of state, Clement felt he must be uncompromising in upholding the rights of the holy see. He had at once to face an all-out offensive against the Society of Jesus which had been fore-

298

shadowed by Benedict XIV's request for an investigation of its conduct in Portugal, and which, pressed home by the concerted efforts of the Bourbon Catholic powers, was to dominate his reign. On charges of illegal trading, inciting revolts in Paraguay, and complicity in a plot to murder the king, the all-powerful minister Pombal, who stood for state absolutism and hated the Society, sequestered its assets in Portugal and her colonies, and deported its members to the papal states (1759). Clement protested in vain; his nuncio was expelled and diplomatic relations ruptured for a decade. Portugal was soon followed by France, where hostility to the Jesuits was deep-seated. Attempts at appeasement proved fruitless; Clement rejected proposals for a separate vicar-general for France with the words, 'Let them be as they are, or cease to be'. On 1 Dec. 1764 the Society was abolished by royal decree. On 7 Jan. 1765 Clement published a bull (*Apostolicum pascendi*) reaffirming support for the Society and applauding its achievements, but it had no effect; the attack only spread more widely. In Feb. 1767, in spite of his pleas, the Jesuits were expelled from Spain, and in Nov. 1767 from Naples and Sicily. Parma followed suit in Feb. 1768, infuriated by a monitory of Clement's annulling certain decrees violating the church's rights in the duchy and invoking the censures of the Maundy Thursday bull *In coena Domini* on their authors. The Bourbon courts united in protest against this, and when Clement refused to cancel his brief France occupied the papal enclaves of Avignon and Venaissin, Naples those of Benevento and Pontecorvo. The climax came in Jan. 1769, with the powers formally requesting the pope to dissolve the order. Clement, who had no intention of complying, summoned a special consistory for 3 Feb., but had a stroke and died the day before it met.

In 1764 Clement denounced Febronianism, a German counterpart to *Gallicanism in France and, like it, confining the pope's jurisdiction to purely spiritual matters, which J. N. von Hontheim (1701–90) was

propagating under the pen-name of Justinus Febronius. The pope requested the German bishops to outlaw the movement in their dioceses, but their response was slow and faint-hearted. Unsympathetic to the Enlightenment, he had Helvétius's *De l'Esprit* and the *Encyclopédie* placed on the Index in 1759, Rousseau's *Émile* in 1763. His own encyclical *Christianae reipublicae salus* (25 Nov. 1766) passed a general condemnation on all publications not in line with Catholic dogma. Among his canonizations was Jeanne de Chantal (1572–1641), the friend of St Francis de Sales; and in 1765 he authorized the mass and office of the Sacred Heart, a devotion dear to the Jesuits. He supported scholarship and the arts, but dismayed the artists of Rome by ordering the provocative nudities of statues and paintings, including the frescos in the Sistine Chapel, to be discreetly covered.

BullRomCon I–III; G. J. X. de Lacroix de Ravignon, *Clément XIII et Clément XIV* (Paris, 1854), vol. i; P. Dudon, 'De la suppression de la Compagnie de Jésus (1758–73)', *Revue des questions historiques* 132 (1938), 75–107; P 36 and 37; *DHGE* 12, 1381–410 (R. Mols); *DBI* 26, 328–43 (L. Cajani and A. Foa); *NCE* 3, 937–40 (E. D. McShane); Seppelt 5, 456–69.

CLEMENT XIV (19 May 1769–22 Sept. 1774). The stormy conclave of 1769 was dominated by political manoeuvring by the Catholic powers, more particularly by the Bourbon monarchs' demand to CLEMENT XIII for the suppression of the Society of Jesus, and by their threat to veto a pro-Jesuit candidate. The cardinals' eventual choice, Lorenzo (baptized Giovanni Vincenzo Antonio) Ganganelli, had apparently (the question has been much discussed) given no promise, but had agreed when sounded that suppression of the order was canonically possible and had certain advantages. Born at Sant'Arcangelo, near Rimini, on 31 Oct. 1705, son of the village doctor, he joined the Franciscans when seventeen, adopting his father's name. Graduating doctor of theology in 1731, he lectured for several years at Franciscan colleges, being appointed rector of St Boniface's, Rome, in

1740. He was already admired as an author, and in 1743 dedicated his *Diatriba theologica* to St Ignatius Loyola (1495–1556). He was named consultant of the Holy Office in 1746; and in both 1753 and 1756, ambitious probably for higher office, he declined the generalship of his order. On 24 Sept. 1759 Clement XIII created him cardinal. Hitherto regarded as a friend of the Jesuits, he now distanced himself from them, and also from Clement XIII's intransigent opposition to the Bourbons. An accomplished theologian, he loved music, poetry, and also riding. Outwardly reserved, he lacked inner self-confidence and, afraid of being influenced, preferred to work alone; as pope he allowed the cardinals little say in his decisions.

Clement took it for granted that his first task was to appease the Catholic powers, which soon reminded him (22 July 1769) that they expected nothing less than the abolition of the Society. As secretary of state he appointed Cardinal Pallavicini, a much liked former nuncio to Madrid, and under pressure from their ambassadors wrote to both Louis XV of France (1 Oct.) and Charles III of Spain (30 Nov.) promising the speedy liquidation of the Jesuit question. After ten years' break he restored relations with Portugal at the price of sending a complaisant nuncio, raising the brother of the Marquis of Pombal, the prime minister, to the purple, and confirming Pombal's nominees in bishoprics. On Maundy Thursday 1770 he won great plaudits by omitting (it was never revived) the reading of the bull *In coena Domini* with its controversial anathemas, the use of which by Clement XIII against Parma in 1768 had precipitated the Bourbons' ultimatum. For four years, however, he postponed definitive action, hoping that a compromise, such as the radical reform of the Jesuits or their gradual attrition by a ban on novices, would placate the powers. His will was finally broken in spring 1773 by warnings that the Bourbon states were prepared for a complete break with Rome, and by Empress Maria Theresa (1740–80),

hitherto pro-Jesuit, declaring her neutrality on the issue. The draft of a bull of abolition had already been worked out in consultation with the Spanish embassy, and on 16 Aug. 1773 Clement published it as the brief *Dominus ac Redemptor noster*. In this he decreed the complete dissolution of the order, citing precedents of orders dissolved, listing difficulties it had had with other orders and with temporal rulers, and emphasizing the need to restore peace in the church and the Society's present inability to fulfil the objectives for which it had been founded.

In the circumstances Clement had little option but to issue this momentous brief, which was hailed as a triumph for enlightenment, but which brought about the elimination, with varying degrees of harshness, of the Jesuits everywhere save in Prussia and Russia, whose sovereigns forbade its promulgation. The resulting damage to the Catholic school system in Europe and to missionary work overseas cannot be exaggerated. Clement had at least the satisfaction of seeing Avignon and Venaissin, occupied by France in protest against Clement XIII, returned to the holy see; Naples, too, restored Benevento and Pontecorvo, but belatedly and with humiliating conditions. His efforts to prevent the first partition of Poland came to nothing when Prussia, Russia, and Austria appropriated large sections of it in Feb. and Aug. 1772. He brought new hope to Catholics in England by hospitably receiving (1772–4) members of the British royal house at Rome, and by diminishing, if not abandoning, the traditional papal support for the exiled Stuarts. His plans for rehabilitating the finances of the papal states by developing industry and agriculture, though well intentioned, proved unsuccessful; but in Rome itself he enriched the papal collections and started the Museo Pio–Clementino. During his closing year he was afflicted by depression, morbidly afraid of assassination, and when he died the rapid decomposition of his body fuelled suspicions of poison; the medical report of his

PIUS VI (1775–99)

autopsy showed them to be unfounded. At his funeral the customary eulogies made no reference to his suppression of the Society of Jesus. His reign saw the prestige of the papacy sink to its lowest level for centuries.

BullRomCon IV; Lettere ed altre opere (Milan, 1831); Lettere, bolle e discorsi (ed. C. Frediani, Florence, 1845); Epistolae et brevia selectiora (ed. A. Theiner, Florence, 1854); A. von Reumont, Ganganelli, Papst Clemens XIV: seine Briefe und seine Zeit (Berlin, 1847); A. L. de Caraccioli, Vita (Florence, 1776); A. Theiner, Geschichte des Pontificats Clemens' XIV (Leipzig, 1853); P 38; DHGE 12, 1411–23 (E. Préclin); EC 3, 1836–41 (P. Paschini); NCE 3, 940–2 (E. D. McShane); DBI 26, 343–62 (M. Rosa); Seppelt 5, 469–84.

PIUS VI (15 Feb. 1775–29 Aug. 1799). Born at Cesena, in Emilia, on 25 Dec. 1717, of aristocratic, impoverished parentage, Giovanni Angelo Braschi graduated doctor of laws at Cesena (1735), studied at Ferrara, and became secretary to Cardinal Antonio Ruffo, then legate of Ferrara. He acted as Ruffo's aide at the six-month conclave of 1740, and when Ruffo became bishop of Ostia and Velletri administered his dioceses. His diplomatic adroitness commended him to BENEDICT XIV, who made him (1753) his private secretary. A prelate in 1758, he was appointed treasurer of the apostolic chamber by CLEMENT XIII in 1766; CLEMENT XIV named him cardinal in Apr. 1773. As he had stood aside from recent controversies, he was elected at the 134-day conclave of 1774–5 with the backing both of those who, thinking him pro-Jesuit, hoped for some alleviation of Clement XIV's brief dissolving the Society of Jesus, and of the anti-Jesuits, with whom he had a tacit understanding that he would implement Clement's policy.

Worthy but worldly, proud of his handsome appearance, Pius was concerned for ostentation and obsolete protocol, and proved unequal to the challenges of the age. He revived nepotism, assigning substantial allowances to his relatives and building the Palazzo Braschi for his nephew Luigi. Keen to be remembered as a patron of the arts, he spent lavishly on splendid buildings like the sacristy of St Peter's and the Museo Pio–Clementino, as well as on improving roads and streets. All these extravagances, not least his brave but unsuccessful attempt to drain the Pontine Marshes, bankrupted his treasury. Characteristically, he handed over the freehold of much of the reclaimed marshland to his nephews.

Politically Pius had to face a rising tide of secularism and atheism as well as the mounting claims of governments to control the church in their realms. It was fortunate for him that the sovereigns of France, Spain, and Portugal, while tenacious of traditional rights and watchful of his conduct towards the Jesuits, were relatively well disposed. Naples, however, stiffened its attitude, refusing (to his petty annoyance) feudal homage and claiming for its king the right to present to bishoprics; Pius found it more dignified to withhold canonical investiture. Developments were even more alarming in the empire, where Joseph II (1765–90), influenced by *Febronianism and the Enlightenment, was setting up a system ('Josephinism') involving complete religious toleration, the restriction of papal intervention to the spiritual sphere, and the subjection in all respects of church to state. His Toleration Edict of Oct. 1781 suppressed certain religious orders and transferred monasteries from the jurisdiction of the pope to that of the diocesan bishops. Pius even journeyed to Vienna in 1782 to dissuade him, but failed to obtain any concessions whatsoever. In 1781 the originator of Febronian ideas, J. N. von Hontheim (1701–90), was induced to make a formal, but in fact hollow, retractation, and the ideas flourished unchecked in south and west Germany. When Pius sought (1786) to establish a nunciature at Munich, he was defiantly informed (25 Aug.) by the German archbishops that the German church was controlled by its bishops and did not need papal intervention. Josephinism spread to Tuscany, where Joseph's brother, Grand Duke Leopold II (emperor 1790–2), planned to make the church independent of the pope. The synod of Pistoia (Sept. 1786),

301

presided over by Bishop Scipio de' Ricci, supported him, adopting the four *Gallican Articles of 1682 and exempting bishops from the pope's authority. Pius eventually exerted himself, forced de' Ricci to resign, and on 28 Aug. 1794 condemned eighty-five of the Pistoian articles in the bull *Auctorem fidei*. Meanwhile, in deference to the Bourbon courts, he tried to put pressure on Frederick II of Prussia (1740–86) and Catherine II of Russia (1762–96), in whose domains many Jesuits had found refuge, to apply Clement XIV's brief of suppression; but he failed to persuade Catherine, who set up a novitiate for Jesuits in 1780. In 1783–4 he gave his secret approval to the continued existence of Jesuits in Russia.

With the French Revolution a much more ominous chapter opened. Pius was cautious, at first taking no action about the Civil Constitution of the Clergy (12 July 1790), which reorganized the French church and made the clergy salaried officials. But when an oath of loyalty to the regime was demanded of them, he denounced (10 Mar. and 13 Apr. 1791) the Constitution as schismatical, declared the ordinations of the new state bishops sacrilegious, suspended priests and prelates who had taken the civil oath, and condemned the Declaration of the Rights of Man (1789). Diplomatic relations were at once broken off, France annexed the enclaves of Avignon and Venaissin, and the French church was completely split. Pius angered France by giving his support to the First Coalition against her and by hospitably receiving numerous royalist refugees. In 1795 he spurned Spanish offers of mediation, and when Napoleon Bonaparte occupied Milan in spring 1796 he rejected the French demand that he withdraw his condemnation of the Civil Constitution and of the Revolution. Napoleon then invaded the papal states, and Pius had to accept peace terms involving a vast indemnity, the handing over of valuable manuscripts and works of art, and the cession of substantial portions of his states (peace of Tolentino: 19 Feb. 1797); his brief *Pastoralis sollicitudo*

(5 July 1796), recognizing the Republic and ordering Catholics to obey it, did not satisfy the Directory.

The situation soon deteriorated, and when the French general L. Duphot was killed in a riot in Rome the Directory ordered the occupation of the papal states. On 15 Feb. 1798 General Louis Berthier entered Rome, proclaimed the Roman Republic and the deposition of Pius as head of state, and forced him to withdraw to Tuscany. For several months he lived at the charterhouse at Florence, cut off from almost all his advisers, but able to use the nuncio to Florence as secretary of state. The Directory planned to banish him to Sardinia, but his precarious health ruled that out. When war broke out afresh, fearful of attempts to rescue him, it had him conveyed from Florence (28 Mar. 1799) via Turin across the Alps to Briançon (30 Apr.) and then Valence (13 July). He died a prisoner in the citadel there, and was buried in the local cemetery; his body was transferred to St Peter's, Rome, in Feb. 1802. At his death, after one of the longest pontificates in history, many assumed that the destruction of the holy see had at last been accomplished, and the fortunes of the papacy had indeed reached their nadir under him; but Pius had left instructions (13 Jan. 1797 and 13 Nov. 1798) for the holding of the next conclave in emergency conditions.

BullRomCon V–X; J. M. Gendry, *Pie VI* (Paris, 1907); J. Flory, *Pie VI* (Paris, 1942); A. Latreille, *L'Église catholique et la Révolution française*, vol. 1 (Paris, 1946); P 39 and 40; *DTC* 12, 1653–69 (G. Bourgin); *NCE* 11, 398–400 (A. Latreille); *LThK* 8, 532 f. (H. Raab).

PIUS VII (14 Mar. 1800–20 July 1823). The conclave after PIUS VI's death, in agreement with his wish that the senior cardinal should convene it at the place of his choice, met in Venice under Austrian protection. A fourteen-week stalemate was broken by the compromise election of Luigi Barnabà Chiaramonte. Of noble parentage, born at Cesena, in Emilia, on 14 Apr. 1742, he joined the Benedictines at fourteen with the name Gregorio, studied at Padua and Rome, and was professor of theology at Parma 1766–75, at S. Anselmo, Rome, 1775–81. Pius VI made him bishop of Tivoli in 1782, translating him to the more important see of Imola and naming him cardinal in 1785. Always open to modern ideas, as bishop he proved a courageous leader in times of political change; he startled conservatives at Christmas 1797 by declaring in a sermon that there was no necessary conflict between Christianity and democracy. Once pope, he showed his independence by resisting pressure to remain on Austrian soil, moving to Rome as soon as it was practicable (3 July 1800). His secretary of state, whom he named a cardinal, was a man of genius, Ercole Consalvi (1757–1824).

Pius first persuaded the Austrians and Neapolitans (but not the French) to evacuate papal territories occupied in the previous reign, and then, with Consalvi's help, restarted their administration with a few modest reforms. Both he and Consalvi wanted to come to terms with revolutionary France so far as was consistent with Catholic principles and, responding to overtures from Napoleon Bonaparte, then First Consul, negotiated with him the concordat of 16 July 1801. This restored Catholicism in France, recognizing that it was the religion of the great majority of Frenchmen, and although a tough bargain was struck, the new arrangements brought distinct advantages to the church. These were reduced, however, by the Organic Articles appended by Napoleon unilaterally (6 Apr. 1802), which tightened the state's hold over the church and restricted papal intervention in France. In Sept. 1803 Pius agreed a similar, but more favourable, concordat with the Italian Republic, but could not arrange one for Germany after the secularization of church property (1803). In 1804, against the advice of the curia, he went to Paris to take part in Napoleon's coronation as emperor (2 Dec.), but his hopes that he would accept modifications in

the Organic Articles or restore papal territories still held by France proved fruitless. With the renewal of war in Europe his relations with the emperor rapidly worsened, for Napoleon expected his co-operation whereas he felt obliged to stay neutral. Although Napoleon secured Consalvi's resignation (17 June 1806), Pius's refusal to support the continental blockade of England led the emperor to occupy Rome (2 Feb. 1808) and annex what remained of the papal states (17 May 1809). Pius retorted by excommunicating (10 June) all 'robbers of Peter's patrimony', without, however, mentioning Napoleon by name. He was thereupon arrested (5 July) and interned at Savona, near Genoa, in virtual isolation. His reaction was to refuse investiture to bishops nominated by the emperor, but eventually, under extreme pressure, he agreed verbally (Sept. 1811) to their institution by their metropolitans. This did not satisfy Napoleon, who had him transferred (May–June 1812) to Fontainebleau. Here he forced him, exhausted and ill, to sign (25 Jan. 1813) a draft convention (the 'Concordat of Fontainebleau') in which he made far-reaching surrenders, including the implied renunciation of the papal states. In remorse Pius soon (24 Mar.) retracted his signature, but military reverses forced Napoleon to send him back to Savona in Jan. 1814 and to release him on 10 Mar. 1814. He re-entered Rome on 24 Mar., but had to seek refuge in Genoa in spring 1815 when Napoleon escaped from Elba. He finally returned to the Vatican on 7 June 1815.

The prestige of Pius personally, as of the papacy, was enhanced by his harsh captivity, which he bore with courage reinforced by his Benedictine training, and which aroused widespread sympathy. One of his first acts (7 May 1814) was to reinstate Consalvi, who at the Congress of Vienna (1814–15) negotiated the restitution of virtually all the holy see's temporal domains except Avignon and Venaissin. Pius refused to join the Holy Alliance of 1815 since it entailed subscribing a religious manifesto along with schismatics and heretics. Consalvi now took in hand a second reconstruction of the papal states, but his attempt to blend administrative, judicial, and financial reforms on the liberal French model with the antiquated papal system exasperated reactionaries and progressives alike, and led to serious revolts. Meanwhile Pius, still leaning heavily on him, set about restoring the organization of the church, everywhere in disarray as a result of the recent troubles, co-operating in France and Spain with the counter-revolution, while in non-Catholic countries with state churches he appealed to the new ideas of tolerance and liberty. Both the territorial changes effected by the Congress of Vienna and the more favourable climate enabled him to conclude concordats with several states, including Protestant Prussia (1821) and Orthodox Russia (1818). In France the concordat eventually accepted was that of 1801, Louis XVIII's proposal (1817) for one more favourable to the holy see having met with opposition. In 1817 Pius re-established the Sacred Congregation of Propaganda; and although initially opposed to the South American republics which had revolted against Spain, by 1822 he was affirming the neutrality of the holy see towards political changes in that continent.

But Pius's chief concerns were religious rather than administrative and political. It was typical of him that, soon after his return (31 July 1814), in face of opposition from the powers, he restored the Society of Jesus, having years earlier (1801 and 1804) regularized its existence in Russia and Naples. He regarded himself as the protector of sound doctrine, and condemned the Protestant Bible Societies (June 1816), the indifferentism encouraged by the Enlightenment, and Freemasonry (Sept. 1821). A gentle and courageous man, he gladly offered refuge in Rome to relatives of his fallen persecutor Napoleon. He encouraged artists like Canova, reopened the colleges the French had closed, and sought to make the city once more a centre of the arts. He made a real attempt to adapt the papacy, within limits, to the modern world, and when he died it enjoyed a respect which it had lacked when he entered on his office; it was beginning once more to be regarded as a supra-national authority.

BullRomCon XI–XV; *RaccCon* 1; A. F. Artaud de Montor, *Histoire de la vie et du pontificat du Pape Pie VII* (Paris, 1836); A. Latreille, *Napoléon et le Saint-Siège* (Paris, 1935); FM 20 (J. Leflon); J. Leflon, *Pie VII* I (to 1800), (Paris, 1958); Schmidlin 1, 16–366; *DTC* 12, 1670–83 (G. Bourgin); *EC* 9, 1504–8 (F. Cognasso); *LThK* 8, 533–5 (R. Aubert); *NCE* 11, 400–4 (J. Leflon).

LEO XII (28 Sept. 1823–10 Feb. 1829). Of noble parentage, Annibale Sermattei della Genga was born in the Castello della Genga, near Spoleto, on 22 Aug. 1760, was a student in Rome, and after ordination (1783) became private secretary to Pius VI, who in 1784 sent him as ambassador to Lucerne. Titular archbishop of Tyre in 1793, he was nuncio in Cologne and Bavaria 1794–1805, being chosen for several diplomatic missions. Pius VII sent him as envoy to the diet of Regensburg in 1805, and in 1806 entrusted him with concordat negotiations (in the event unsuccessful) with the courts of Bavaria, Baden, and Württemberg. In 1808 he was in Paris on business with Napoleon, but was coolly received and soon returned. During Pius VII's captivity he lived, effectively a state prisoner, at his abbey of Monticelli (near Piacenza), but on the pope's restoration in 1814, was sent as nuncio to Paris. Here he fell out with Cardinal Ercole Consalvi (1757–1824), secretary of state, who criticized his failure to negotiate the restitution of Avignon, and retired again to Monticelli. In 1816, however, Pius VII named him cardinal and bishop of Senigallia, which in 1818 he exchanged for Spoleto. In 1820 he became vicar-general of Rome and prefect of several congregations. At the hotly contested conclave of 1823 he was elected by the votes of the *zelanti, conservatives with a primarily religious interest who wished a break with the 'liberal' Consalvi and a return to more reactionary policies.

A simple, devout man, morally strong but lacking the flair of leadership, Leo shared the wish of the *zelanti* that his pontificate should have a less political, more religious orientation. He at once replaced Consalvi with a conservative as secretary of state, appointed a Congregation of State to advise on political and religious matters, and published (May 1825) measures condemning indifferentism, toleration, and Freemasonry, reinforcing the Index and the Holy Office, favouring the Jesuits, and (against the advice of the great powers) announcing a holy year for 1825. His reactionary approach was most evident in dealing with the papal states. Although some of Pius VII's reforms were left intact and useful, if unpopular, fiscal measures introduced, the feudal aristocracy was installed afresh in privileged positions, ecclesiastical courts of the pre-1800 pattern returned, the laicization of the administration was halted, new chairs were founded at universities but teaching was supervised in ways intended to stifle criticism, and Jews were again restricted to ghettos. The modern state which Consalvi had been tentatively fostering reverted to a police regime infested with spies and intent on stamping out, with penalties ranging from petty clerical surveillance of private life to execution, any possible flicker of revolution. The result was inevitably economic stagnation, the alienation of the middle classes, and hatred for the personally mild pontiff who was held to blame for making the papal state one of the most backward in Europe.

Leo's election revived fears in European courts that he would reverse Pius VII's conciliatory policies. His first actions seemed to bear out these fears, for he insisted on reviving a symbolic acknowledgement of the vassal status of Naples, and wrote to Louis XVIII of France (4 June 1824) deploring his failure to observe the concordat of 1817 and his tolerance of laws inspired by the Revolution. He soon came, however, to appreciate the value of good relations with the powers, startled the *zelanti* by seeking the advice of Consalvi and appointing him prefect of the Propaganda, and adopted a moderate, flexible attitude.

Thus he resumed Consalvi's policy of concordats, and negotiated agreements advantageous to the church with Hanover (1824) and the united Netherlands (1827). As a result of his intervention with the sultan of Turkey the emancipation of the Catholic Armenian communities was achieved in 1830. After initial hesitation, caused by fear of offending Ferdinand VII of Spain (1814–33), he declared in consistory (21 May 1827) that he would henceforth himself provide for vacant sees in the newly independent republics of Latin America, regardless of the king's continuing claim to patronage. For a short time he was influenced by the ideas of men like G. Ventura (1792–1861) and F. R. de Lamennais (1782–1854)—he cordially received the latter, and even thought of him as a possible cardinal—suggesting that the papacy as the spiritual leader of humanity should cease to rely on political action, but in general he favoured a policy of collaboration with the conservative sovereigns in the effort to hold back the rising tide of liberalism.

Although the Roman Catholic Relief Act was not passed (13 Apr. 1829) until just after his death, Leo seized every opportunity to promote the emancipation of Roman Catholicism in Great Britain; Consalvi had foretold that he would soon have the satisfaction of seeing this objective realized. His concern in this matter reflected the guiding theme of his pontificate: not politics, but religious renewal and unceasing warfare against errors which seemed to threaten the faith. To him the whole point of the holy year of 1825, in which in spite of sickness he played an exhausting part, was to restore contact between the pope and Christian people, and thus to promote a general return to the faith. Hence, too, his attempts to align the monasteries with the apostolic efforts of the church, to raise the standards of clerical life and education, and to awaken a religious spirit in the masses. All too frequently, however, his endeavours were hampered by a narrowly clerical outlook and an approach based neither on

PIUS VIII (1829–30)

insight nor on understanding of the world developing around him. When he died he was profoundly unpopular.

BullRomCon XVI–XVII; *RaccCon* 1, 402–5; 689–722; A. F. Artaud de Montor, *Histoire du Pape Léon XII* (Paris, 1843); N. Wiseman, *Recollections of the Last Four Popes* (London, 1858); R. Colapietra, *La Chiesa tra Lamennais e Metternich: il pontificato di Leone XII* (Brescia, 1963); Schmidlin 1, 367–474; *EC* 7, 1156–8 (F. Fonzi); *NCE* 8, 646 f. (T. F. Casey).

PIUS VIII (31 Mar. 1829–30 Nov. 1830). Born at Cingoli, near Ancona, on 20 Nov. 1761, of noble parentage, Francesco Saverio Castiglione was educated at Osimo, later studying canon law at Bologna and Rome. Having become an expert in the subject, he served the commission investigating the synod of *Pistoia (1786) as secretary, was vicar-general to a series of able bishops and then provost of Cingoli, and was himself appointed bishop of Montalto in 1800. He was imprisoned 1808–14 for refusing to swear allegiance to the Napoleonic regime in Italy. PIUS VII created him cardinal and bishop of Cesena, in Emilia, in 1816, and in 1821 called him to Rome to be bishop of Frascati and Grand Penitentiary. The pope, who greatly valued him, hoped he would succeed him, and in fact he just missed being elected in 1823. At the five-week conclave of 1829 he was the candidate of the moderates, and in spite of serious ill health was elected with the backing of both France and Austria.

Pius aimed at reviving the tradition of Pius VII, whose name he adopted. Not greatly interested in politics, he had a keen concern for pastoral and doctrinal issues. He used his first (and only) encyclical (*Traditi humilitati nostrae*: 24 May 1829) to trace the breakdown of religion and the social and political order to indifferentism in matters of faith, the activities of the Protestant Bible Societies, attacks on the sacredness of marriage and church dogmas, and secret societies. In a brief of 25 Mar. 1830 he condemned both the influence of Freemasonry in education and the loose morals of the rising generation. Yet while

inflexibly upholding traditional positions, he could on occasion be accommodating. Thus he greatly mitigated the harsh police regime which LEO XII had imposed on the papal states, and introduced a number of intelligent changes in the economic and social spheres. Again, in dealing with the problem of mixed marriages which had arisen in Prussia as a result of its acquisition of the Catholic Rhineland and Westphalia in 1815, he reaffirmed that such marriages could only receive the church's blessing if guarantees of the children's education in the Catholic faith were provided, but if they were not he was prepared to permit the priest to be present in a passive role. The government, which supported the German rule that the father's wishes should prevail, was not satisfied, and the conflict was to break out afresh in the following pontificate.

Pius delegated foreign affairs in the main to the openly pro-Austrian cardinal Giuseppe Albani, who had brought about his election and whom he at once appointed secretary of state. As a result his policy towards the dioceses of Latin America formerly subject to the Spanish crown was less progressive than that of Leo XII and reactionary compared with that of his successor. Under Albani the curia adopted a hostile attitude to the movements of national emancipation which broke out in Belgium, Ireland, and Poland in 1830; Albani stigmatized the alliance of Catholics and liberals in Belgium against King William I (1815–40) as 'monstrous'. On the other hand, against the advice of the curia and his own nuncio, Pius soon accepted the July Revolution (1830) in Paris which deposed the unpopular King Charles X (1824–30) in favour of Louis-Philippe, king of the French (1830–48). When some legitimist bishops and priests fled from France, he showed his disapproval by refusing them admission to the papal states. In view of the new regime's promise to respect the *concordat of 1801, he called on the French clergy to rally to it, and insisted on bestowing the traditional title of 'Most Christian King' on Louis-Philippe.

Although he had no hand in promoting it, Pius witnessed the passing of the Roman Catholic Relief Act in Great Britain (13 Apr. 1829). With the sultan of Turkey he negotiated civil and religious rights for the Armenian Catholics, and he established (16 July 1830) an archbishopric of the Armenian rite at Constantinople. In the USA the bishops held their first Provincial Council at Baltimore in Oct. 1829; its decrees, which resulted in a strengthening of the ties of the US church with Rome, were approved by Pius in 1830.

BullRomCon XVIII; A. F. Artaud de Montor, Histoire du Pape Pie VIII (Paris, 1844); N. Wiseman, Recollections of the Last Four Popes (London, 1858); E. Vercesi, Tre Pontificati (Turin, 1936); Schmidlin 1, 474–510; P. de Leturia, 'Pio VIII y la independencia de Hispanoamérica', MischHist-Pont 21 (1959), 387–400; EC 9, 1508–10 (F. Fonzi); LThK 8, 535 f. (R. Aubert); NCE 11, 404 f. (T. F. Casey).

GREGORY XVI (2 Feb. 1831–1 June 1846). Born at Belluno, Venetia, on 18 Sept. 1765, son of an aristocratic lawyer, Bartolomeo Alberto Cappellari entered at eighteen the Camaldolese (i.e. strict Benedictine) monastery of S. Michele at Murano, Venice, taking the name Mauro, and after ordination in 1787 became (1790) professor of science and philosophy. Coming to Rome in 1795, he published in 1799, during Pius VI's imprisonment by the French Directory, *The Triumph of the Holy See and the Church against the Attacks of Innovators*, upholding papal infallibility and the temporal sovereignty of the holy see, and denouncing all claims to subject it to state control. In 1805 he was made abbot of S. Gregorio al Celio, and in 1807 procurator-general of the Camaldolese order. Forced to leave Rome after Pius VII's arrest by Napoleon, he taught at Murano and Padua, but returned in 1814. After being consultant to several congregations and examiner of prospective bishops, he was named vicar-general of the Camaldolese in 1823, and cardinal in 1826. As prefect of the Propaganda (1826) he gave a new impulse to missionary enterprise; he also assisted Leo XII and Pius VIII in important business. At the difficult, fifty-day conclave of 1830 he was eventually elected with the backing of the *zelanti* and of the Austrian statesman Klemens von Metternich (1773–1859), who wanted an absolutist-minded pope who would not give way to 'the political madness of the age'.

An austere, learned monk, hostile to modern trends (he banned railways in his domains, calling them 'chemins d'enfer') and to Italian nationalism in particular, Gregory was immediately faced with uprisings in the papal states and in Rome itself, and with calls for a federal republic. He had to seek military aid from Austria, which quickly crushed the revolts. The great powers then intervened (31 May 1831), demanding radical administrative, judicial, and constitutional reforms in the states. Gregory was prepared to concede limited changes, but not to grant elected assemblies or a council of state composed of laymen. As a result disorders broke out afresh, Austrian troops had to be recalled, France seized Ancona, and for seven years the papal states were under military occupation. Supported by reactionary secretaries of state, T. Bernetti and (from 1836) L. Lambruschini, Gregory had to deal with mounting discontent and simmering rebellion for his entire reign, while the cost of maintaining a repressive regime with hired soldiers drained his treasury.

Gregory was equally uncompromising in the realm of ideas, and in his encyclical *Mirari vos* (15 Aug. 1832) denounced the notions of freedom of conscience and of the press, and of separation of church and state, associated with F. R. de Lamennais (1782–1854), the champion of Catholic liberalism, and his newspaper *L'Avenir*. Although he had received Lamennais kindly in Nov. 1831, he condemned his reply to *Mirari vos* in June 1834. Convinced that modern liberalism had its roots in indifferentism, he branded this intellectual attitude, as well as the activities of the London Bible Society and the New York Christian Alliance, in *Inter praecipuas machinationes* (8 May 1844).

Among other teachings he censured were (26 Sept. 1835) the rationalism of Georg Hermes (1775–1831) and the fideism of the abbé L. E. M. Bautain (1796–1867), who placed an excessive emphasis on faith. In the political field he stood for the independence of the church and had a horror of revolution, and his reign was a continuous struggle in the service of conservative ideals. For years he was at odds with Portugal and Spain, whose governments were embarking on unacceptable anticlerical legislation, and with Switzerland, where the Articles of Baden (21 Jan. 1834) sought to eliminate papal authority over Swiss Catholics. He protested (1845) with some success against Nicholas I's persecution of Catholics in Russia, but when the Poles revolted against the tsar in 1830–1, he addressed an encyclical (9 June 1832) to their bishops condemning revolutionary movements. The same respect for constituted authority led him, in a private letter from the Propaganda (15 Oct. 1844), to discourage the Irish clergy from political action. Yet he could on occasion be accommodating, and in response to government pressure acquiesced in the temporary withdrawal of the Jesuits from France in 1845. In Prussia, which insisted that children of mixed marriages should follow their father's religion, he took a strong line, recalling (27 Mar. 1832 and 12 Sept. 1834) Pius VIII's ruling and protesting (12 Dec. 1837) against the imprisonment of an archbishop who had followed it. With the accession of Frederick William IV (June 1840), however, his diplomacy was able to reach an advantageous arrangement (1841) under which Prussia gave up the right to interfere in mixed marriages; in addition the freedom of episcopal elections was guaranteed and a special department for Catholic affairs was set up in the ministry of religion.

Gregory's pontificate saw the reorganization of the hierarchy, the reform of the existing orders, and the founding of new ones. Doctrinally he promoted the Immaculate Conception of the BVM, without, however, defining it as a dogma of faith. But most noteworthy were the efforts which he, a former prefect of the Propaganda, devoted to the church outside Europe. The 19th-cent. revival of missions dates from his reign, and in reorganizing them he brought them firmly under papal control. Through him some seventy dioceses and vicariates apostolic were established, and almost two hundred missionary bishops were appointed. In the bull *Sollicitudo ecclesiarum* (7 Aug. 1831) he made clear his policy of negotiating, where there was a change of regime, with the *de facto* government, and was thus able to settle once for all the vexed issue of appointments to sees in Latin America and India, notwithstanding protests from Spain and Portugal. In the brief *In supremo* (3 Dec. 1839) he denounced slavery and the slave-trade as unworthy of Christians, and on 12 Nov. 1845 approved an instruction of the Propaganda encouraging a native clergy and hierarchy in mission territories. Gregory's concern extended also to Canada and the USA; he created four dioceses in the former in 1834–43 as well as reorganizing the see of Quebec (1844), and established ten dioceses in the latter and reorganized the see of Baltimore.

Gregory had a real interest in art and scholarship, and not only encouraged research in the Roman forum and the catacombs, but founded the Etruscan and Egyptian museums in the Vatican and the Christian museum in the Lateran. Brought up as a monk, good-hearted but obstinate and narrow, with little comprehension of the contemporary world, he left his successor a grievous legacy both in the church and in the papal states.

Mauro Cappellari, *Il trionfo della Santa Sede* (Venice, 1799); *Acta Gregorii papae XVI* (ed. A. Bernasconi, Rome, 1901–4: defective); Mercati, *RaccCon* 1, 724–50; *BullRomCon* XIX–XX; *Gregorio XVI: Miscellanea commemorativa* (2 vols., Rome, 1948); Schmidlin 1, 511–687; P. de Leturia, *Relaciones entre la Santa Sede y Hispanoamérica* (*AnGreg*, Rome, 1959–60); J. Schmidlin, 'Gregor XVI als Missionspapst', *Zeitschrift für Missionswissenschaft und Religionswissenschaft* 21 (1931), 209–28; A. Ventrone, *L'amministrazione dello Stato Pontificale 1814–70*

(Rome, 1942); *DTC* 6, 1822-36 (É. Amann); *EC* 6, 1148-56 (P. dalla Torre); *LThK* 4, 1190-2 (G. Schwaiger); *NCE* 6, 783-8 (A. Simon).

PIUS IX (16 June 1846-7 Feb. 1878). Fourth son of a count, Giovanni Maria Mastai-Ferretti was born at Senigallia, in the March of Ancona, on 13 May 1792 and studied at Viterbo and Rome. A victim of epilepsy in youth but now cured, he was ordained priest in 1819, served 1823-5 with a papal mission to Chile, took charge 1825-7 of the Hospice of S. Michele, Rome, and was archbishop of Spoleto 1827-32, bishop of Imola 1832-40. An indefatigable pastor, he was reputed a liberal because he advocated administrative changes in the papal states and sympathized emotionally with Italian national aspirations. He was named cardinal in 1840, and at the two-day conclave of 1846 was elected, as a moderate progressive, against the reactionary L. Lambruschini.

Pius at once (16 July) declared a political amnesty, granted some practical reforms in the papal states, and in 1847 set up city and state councils; he made gestures of support to Italian nationalism. The resulting outburst of popularity, however, along with his liberal reputation, subsided when he made it clear that, believing the temporal sovereignty of the holy see indispensable to its spiritual independence, he had no intention of establishing a constitutional state. In Mar. 1848 he was forced to concede a bicameral assembly, but when he firmly refused (29 Apr. 1848) to join in the war to expel Austria from Italy his neutrality seemed a betrayal. In a crisis made worse by economic breakdown his prime minister, Count Rossi, was murdered on 15 Nov. 1848, and Pius himself fled in disguise to Gaeta, south of Naples, on 24 Nov. On 9 Feb. 1849 a Roman republic was proclaimed. From Gaeta Pius appealed to the Catholic powers and, French troops having restored papal rule on 15 July, re-entered Rome with their help on 12 Apr. 1850. His liberal stance was now discarded, and with Giacomo Antonelli as secretary of state

(1848-76) he set up a paternalistic regime in the papal states which alienated the educated and frowned on national aspirations. Count Camillo Cavour, chief minister of Piedmont since 1852, skilfully exploited the situation in the interests of Italian unification, and by Sept. 1860, after the defeat of his newly raised army at Castelfidardo, Pius saw all his dominions, with the exception of Rome and its immediate environs, annexed to the new kingdom of Italy. For a decade he was protected by a French garrison, but the outbreak of the Franco-Prussian War necessitated its withdrawal, and on 20 Sept. 1870 Italian forces occupied Rome itself; in Oct. it was incorporated by a plebiscite in the Italian state. In the Law of Guarantees (13 May 1871) the government assured the pope of personal inviolability, the tenure of the Vatican and other buildings, and certain important immunities; but Pius refused to accept the *fait accompli* at the price of abandoning the sacred legacy of his predecessors. Henceforth he never set foot outside the Vatican, regarding himself as a prisoner. He had already, in the decree of 29 Feb. 1868 opening with the words *Non expedit* ('It is not expedient'), forbidden Catholics to take part in political life in the 'usurping' kingdom of Italy.

Politically Pius's pontificate, the longest in history, might seem to have been a disaster, but viewed ecclesiastically it was full of positive achievements. In the old and new worlds he founded over two hundred new dioceses and vicariates apostolic, notably in the USA and the British colonies; and he re-established the hierarchies in England (1850) and the Netherlands (1853). He restored the Latin patriarchate in Jerusalem (1847). He concluded concordats with numerous states, such as Russia (1847), Spain (1851), Austria (1855), and Latin American republics (1852-62), and gave strong support to the Catholic Union in Germany and the Central Party in Prussia (1852). A feature of the reign was an increasing centralization of authority, facilitated by modern means of transport but encouraged by the bishops' loss of political power and their consequent need to work closely with the pope; it helped to eliminate the last vestiges of *Gallicanism and *Josephinism. Pius carried out an unprecedented number of canonizations and beatifications, and consecrated (16 June 1875) the Catholic world to the Sacred Heart of Jesus (the feast of which he had extended to the entire church in 1856). But three events stand out as particularly significant. The first was his definition of the Immaculate Conception of the BVM, i.e. of her freedom from original sin, on 8 Dec. 1854. Made without mention of episcopal approbation, this gave a powerful stimulus to Marian devotion, and opened fresh possibilities of theological development. Secondly, after repeated condemnations of teaching deemed unsound and calls for a return to that of St Thomas Aquinas (d. 1274), he published (8 Dec. 1864) the encyclical *Quanta cura*, with the 'Syllabus of Errors' attached, which denounced 'the principal errors of our times', including the view that the pope 'can or should reconcile himself to, or agree with, progress, liberalism, and modern civilization'. This dealt a fatal blow to liberal Catholicism, and affirmed the autonomy of the church in relation to the religiously neutral modern state. Thirdly, he summoned the First Vatican (Twentieth General) Council (1869–70), which, in the constitution *Pastor aeternus* (18 July 1870), declared the definitions of the pope in faith and morals to be infallible in their own right, not as a result of the consent of the church, thereby completing the doctrinal development of centuries and removing all conciliarist interpretations of the role of the papacy. This owed much to Pius's personal intervention; but the Council's constitution on faith (*Dei filius*: 24 Apr. 1870), deploring contemporary pantheism, materialism, and atheism, defining the spheres of reason and faith, and basing positive Catholic doctrine firmly on revelation, was no less representative of his programme.

Pius was the first pope to identify himself wholeheartedly with ultramontanism, i.e.

the tendency to centralize authority in church government and doctrine in the holy see, but its triumph at Vatican I led not only to the Old Catholic schism in Holland and other countries, but to an outbreak of anticlericalism in Europe generally, culminating in the abrogation (1874) of the concordat by Austria and Bismarck's repressive attack on the church in Germany (the *Kulturkampf*), which Pius denounced in the encyclical *Quod nunquam* (5 Feb. 1875). Yet when he died, he had effectively created the modern papacy, stripped (as he never ceased to deplore) of its temporal dominion, but armed with vastly enhanced spiritual authority in compensation. His own mind being closed to modern political and intellectual trends, he left the church ill-equipped to respond to their challenges, but he also left it profoundly changed and strengthened in its inner life. Whether at the level of the clergy or of the great body of the faithful, his reign witnessed a vigorous spiritual regeneration. This could be traced directly to his persistent efforts to deepen the religious life, but also to his resolve to be above all a priest and pastor of souls, setting an example to his flock. A factor not to be overlooked is the extraordinary devotion that 'Pio Nono', with his winning personality, kindly wit, and patience in adversity, inspired, which caused even political adversaries to respect him, and which found enthusiastic expression at the celebration of his jubilees as priest (1869), pope (1871 and 1876), and bishop (1873). This affection, however, did not prevent the anticlerical Roman mob, on 13 July 1881, from holding up the procession accompanying his body from its provisional resting-place in St Peter's to S. Lorenzo fuori le Mura, and attempting to fling it into the Tiber. The first step towards possible canonization was taken in 1985 with the official recognition of his 'heroic virtue'.

Acta Pii IX Papae (9 vols., Rome, 1854–78); R. Aubert, *Le pontificat de Pie IX* (FM 21, 2nd edn. 1964); F. Hayward, *Pie IX et son temps* (Paris, 1948); E. E. Y. Hales, *Pio Nono* (London, 2nd edn. 1956); E. Vercesi, *Pio IX* (Milan, 1930); G.

Mollat, *La Question romaine de Pie VI à Pie IX* (Paris, 1932); Schmidlin 2, 1–330; *LThK* 8, 536–8 (R. Aubert); *EC* 9, 1510–23 (P. Pirri); *NCE* 11, 405–8 (R. Aubert); *EB* (15th edn.) 14, 482–6 (R. Aubert).

LEO XIII (20 Feb. 1878–20 July 1903). Sixth child in a family of the lesser nobility, Gioacchino Vincenzo Pecci was born at Carpineto, in the hills south of Rome, on 2 Mar. 1810. A brilliant boy with a flair for Latin which he retained through life, he studied at Viterbo (1818–24), the Roman College (1824–32), and the Academy of Noble Ecclesiastics (1832–7). Ordained in 1837, he immediately joined the papal service and was made governor, first, of Benevento (1838–41), and then of Perugia (1841–3), proving in both a firm and capable administrator. GREGORY XVI then sent him as nuncio to Belgium (1843–6), first appointing him titular archbishop of Damietta. This, with short visits to Cologne, London, and Paris, was his first contact with industrialized, parliamentary Europe, but his ill-judged support of the episcopate against the government in an educational controversy led King Leopold I (1831–65) to request his recall. He was then bishop of Perugia 1846–78, being named cardinal in 1853 but kept from Rome and curial responsibilities because he was suspect to Cardinal Antonelli, PIUS IX's secretary of state. As bishop he protested against the annexation of Perugia by Sardinia in 1860 and the secularizing legislation that followed. He also modernized the curriculum of his seminary, promoted a revival of Thomism and founded (1859) the Academy of St Thomas Aquinas, and began (as his pastoral letters of 1874–7 reveal) to argue for a *rapprochement* between Catholicism and contemporary culture. After Antonelli's death Pius IX recalled him (1877) to Rome as *camerlengo*, i.e. the official who administers the church in a vacancy. At the conclave of Feb. 1878, the first since the loss by the holy see of its temporal power, he was elected as an intelligent moderate at the third ballot. He had to

be crowned in the seclusion of the Sistine Chapel because the government feared demonstrations in his favour if he blessed the Roman crowd from the loggia of St Peter's. Almost sixty-eight, fragile in health, he seemed a stop-gap appointment, but ruled the church with masterly flair for over twenty-five years.

Leo's main achievement was his attempt, within the framework of traditional teaching, to bring the church to terms with the modern age. At the same time he made no sharp break with Pius IX, whose policies he continued in several fields. For example, his attacks on socialism, communism, and nihilism in *Quod apostolici muneris* (28 Dec. 1878), or on Freemasonry in *Humanum genus* (20 Apr. 1884), as his treatment of marriage in *Arcanum illud* (10 Feb. 1880), could have come from Pius's pen. Far from halting centralization, as progressives hoped, he increased it by intervening with national episcopates, strengthening the position of nuncios, and concentrating orders and congregations in Rome. But his distinctive contribution was the opening up of dialogue between the church and society in a striking series of pronouncements. In the intellectual field he directed Catholics (*Aeterna Patris*: 4 Aug. 1879) to the philosophy of St Thomas Aquinas (d. 1274), and founded an academy at Rome to study it. He also fostered the study of astronomy and natural sciences at the Vatican, called on Catholic historians to write objectively, and opened (18 Aug. 1883) the Vatican archives to scholars regardless of creed. To meet the challenge of new critical methods he laid down guidelines for biblical research in *Providentissimus Deus* (18 Nov. 1893). He devoted several encyclicals to the socio-political order, defining, e.g., the spheres of temporal and spiritual power in *Immortale Dei* (1 Nov. 1885), giving a grudging recognition to democracy in *Diuturnum illud* (29 June 1881), and arguing in *Libertas praestantissimum* (20 June 1888) for the church as the custodian of liberty as properly understood. In these (especially *Immortale Dei*) he was at pains to affirm the legitimacy of any form of government, even republicanism, provided it ensured the general welfare. His most famous manifesto, *Rerum novarum* (15 May 1891), upheld private property, but also the just wage, workers' rights, and trade unions; its advocacy of social justice earned him the title of 'the workers' pope'.

Like Pius IX, Leo was obsessed with the recovery of the papal states and the temporal power of the holy see, but by renewing Pius's ban on participation by Catholics in elections sacrificed the church's influence in the new Italy. In contrast to Pius, he was a political pope, replacing his predecessor's intransigence with flexible and skilful diplomacy, and scored several successes. The most noteworthy were the revision by Germany in 1886/7 of its anticlerical laws (the *Kulturkampf*), and his mediation in 1885 in the dispute between Germany and Spain over the possession of the Caroline Islands in the Pacific. He also reached accommodations with Belgium in 1884 and with Russia in 1894. His hope that support for Britain against rebellious Irish Catholics (1888) would lead to formal diplomatic exchanges was disappointed. But preoccupation with the recovery of temporal sovereignty dominated his foreign policy. When the concessions he had made to Germany failed to bring her support against Italy, and Germany and Austria renewed the Triple Alliance with Italy in 1887, he followed the advice of his new secretary of state, Mariano Rampolla (secretary 1887–1903), and sought to make France his ally. But his efforts to rally French Catholics to the Third Republic proved a failure. Royalist Catholics were outraged, the government maintained the *concordat of 1801 but intensified its anti-Catholic legislation, and Leo received no help from it on the *Roman question.

Leo gave a lead to the vast 19th-cent. expansion of Catholicism outside Europe, establishing 248 sees, 48 vicariates or prefectures, and 2 patriarchates. These included regular hierarchies for Scotland (1878), North Africa (1884), India (1886), and Japan (1891), as well as 28 new dioceses in the USA. He appointed the first Apostolic Delegate to the USA in 1892, and in Jan. 1899 censured 'Americanism', a movement seeking to adapt Catholicism to contemporary ideas and practices. His concern for reunion (he was the first to speak of 'separated brothers') was expressed in his letters *Praeclara* (1894) and *Satis cognitum* (1896), the one inviting both Orthodox and Protestants to return to Rome but avoiding any mention of schism, the other rejecting a federation of churches as falling far short of the true mystical body of Christ. His letter *Ad Anglos* (14 Apr. 1895) revealed special anxiety for the conversion of England, and he appointed a commission (1895) to investigate the validity of Anglican orders; in view of its negative report he pronounced them invalid in *Apostolicae curae* (13 Sept. 1896). In 1879 he made John Henry Newman (1801–90) a cardinal.

Notwithstanding his sensitive awareness of contemporary trends, Leo remained a man of deep, conservative piety, and devoted eleven encyclicals to the BVM and the Rosary, and two to the redemptive work of Christ and the eucharist respectively. He instituted (1893) a feast of the Holy Family, and, extending an initiative of Pius IX, consecrated the entire human race to the Sacred Heart of Jesus in the jubilee year 1900. Towards the close of his reign his attitudes hardened perceptibly, as was illustrated by his setting up a permanent Biblical Commission (30 Oct. 1902), his publication of new norms for censorship (1897) and a new Index (17 Sept. 1900), and the denial of real political significance to Christian Democracy in Italy (*Graves de communi*: 18 Jan. 1901). But after its political and spiritual isolation under Pius IX he transformed the international prestige of the papacy, and won it a recognition it had lacked for centuries. It was thus a bitter disappointment to him that, through the intervention of the Italian government, the holy see was excluded from the first Hague International Peace Conference (May–July

1899), summoned at the instance of Tsar Nicholas II of Russia (1895–1917) to discuss the limitation of armaments.

ASS 11–35 (Rome, 1878–1903); *Leonis Pont. Max. Acta* (23 vols., Rome, 1881–1905); *Epistolae encyclicae* (Freiburg i.B., 1878–1904); J. Bach (ed.), *Carmina, inscriptiones, numismata* (Cologne, 1903); C. de T'Serclaes, *Le Pape Léon XIII* (Paris and Bruges, 1894–1906); E. Soderini, *Il pontificato di Leone XIII* (Milan, 1932–3); F. Hayward, *Léon XIII* (Paris, 1937); Lillian P. Wallace, *Leo XIII* (Durham, N.C., 1966); G. Jarlot, 'L'Enseignement social de Léon XIII, Pie X et Benoît XV', *Studia Socialia* IX (1964), 17–257; Schmidlin 2, 331–589; *LThK* 6, 953–6 (R. Aubert); *EB* (15th edn.) 10, 807 f. (R. Aubert).

PIUS X, ST (4 Aug. 1903–20 Aug. 1914). Born at Riese, Upper Venetia, on 2 June 1835, son of the village postman and a seamstress, Giuseppe Melchiorre Sarto went to school at nearby Castelfranco, studied 1850–8 at the seminary at Padua, and, after ordination (18 Sept. 1858), spent nine years as a country curate, eight as parish priest of Salzano. After serving 1875–84 as chancellor of Treviso and spiritual director of its seminary, he became bishop of Mantua, a run-down diocese which he speedily revitalized. In June 1893 LEO XIII appointed him patriarch of Venice and cardinal, and for a decade he proved a hard-working pastor, absorbed in his clergy and flock, collaborating discreetly with the Italian government, and in local politics advocating an alliance of Catholics and moderate liberals against socialism. At the conclave following Leo XIII's death Cardinal Rampolla, his secretary of state, seemed at first the favourite, but on 2 Aug. the veto of Emperor Franz Joseph of Austria was announced. This did not prove decisive, however, for the cardinals (including Rampolla) protested energetically against the intervention and continued voting. It soon became apparent that a powerful body of opinion favoured a pope of a different style from Leo, and at the seventh ballot the choice fell on Sarto. He called himself Pius X out of regard for recent popes of that name who had bravely resisted persecution.

Adopting as his motto 'to restore all things in Christ' (Eph. 1: 10), Pius made clear from the start his intention of being a religious rather than a political pope. He regarded Leo XIII's policy of appeasing secular governments as a failure, and set himself, with his secretary of state, the Spaniard Rafael Merry del Val (1865–1930), to insist unyieldingly on the church's rights. This soon led to a diplomatic break with France (30 July 1904), where the situation was ripe for it, with the annulment by the ministry of Émile Combes (1902–5) of the 1801 *concordat, and the transfer of the church's property to lay associations (9 Dec. 1905). Pius denounced (11 Feb. 1906) the Law of Separation and, against the advice of most of the bishops, prohibited (10 Aug. 1906) any compromise settlement, thereby securing the church's independence at the price of material ruin. He protested equally forcibly against the separation of church and state in Portugal (1911), while his support of Catholic minorities in Poland and Ireland angered the Russian and British governments. Public opinion in the USA was offended (1910) by his refusal to receive ex-President Theodore Roosevelt after he had been lecturing in the Methodist church in Rome. In Italy, however, while standing firm on the Roman question, as the conflict between church and state in Italy since 1870 had come to be called, he introduced a gradual *détente* between the Vatican and the government; moved partly by fear of socialism, he permitted bishops (11 June 1905) to relax at their discretion his predecessors' ban (the *Non expedit*) on the participation of Catholics in elections.

Pius was no less intransigent in the theological and social fields. While at Venice he had viewed the liberalizing movement known as Modernism with alarm. After repeated warnings and placing suspect writings on the Index, he branded it as a 'synthesis of all heresies' in the decree *Lamentabili* (3 July 1907), which condemned sixty-five modernist propositions, and in the encyclical *Pascendi* (8 Sept. 1907); the suppression was completed by a *motu proprio* (*Sacrorum antistitum*: 1 Sept. 1910) imposing on clergy an oath disavowing Modernism. There ensued a widespread, often embarrassing, harassment of scholars which widened the breach between the church and the intelligentsia. Although favouring the Catholic movement in Italy, he sought to detach it from close political involvement and to subject it to the hierarchy. Paternalistic in his approach, he emphasized in *Il fermo proposito* (11 June 1905) that the chief objective of social groups should be 'to replace Jesus Christ in the family, the school, the community in general'. He therefore suspended (28 June 1904) the *Opera dei congressi*, which coordinated Catholic associations in Italy, condemned (25 Aug. 1910) Marc Sangier's *Le Sillon* movement in France, which aimed at reconciling Catholicism with left-wing political ideas, and set his face against interconfessional trade unions. By contrast he was tolerant almost to the last of the right-wing, monarchist *Action Française*.

If these measures were largely defensive, Pius was also responsible for a constructive renovation of the internal life of the church. First, he reorganized the curia, redefining its congregations and tribunals, eliminating obsolete offices, and streamlining the central administration (*Sapienti consilio*: 29 June 1908). Secondly, assisted by a special commission and the advice of Catholic universities, he thoroughly revised and codified the canon law; publication of the new code had to be held back until 1917, but work on it was virtually complete at his death. Significantly, his legislation included a prohibition of the veto traditionally exercised by Catholic powers at papal elections which had recently caused offence at his own (*Commissum nobis*: 20 Jan. 1904). Thirdly, a pastor himself before everything else, he took steps to improve the spiritual and moral level of the clergy and their pastoral effectiveness. This he achieved by reforming seminaries and their curricula, reorganizing catechetical instruction, and

instigating the preparation of a new catechism. He also became a forerunner of *Catholic Action by seeking to enlist layfolk, under the hierarchy, for collaboration in the apostolic tasks of the church. Fourthly, he gave a lasting stimulus to the spiritual life of Catholics generally (*a*) by numerous decrees enjoining frequent, even daily, communion, the admission of children to communion at the age of reason, and the easing of communion of the sick; and (*b*) by his reform of church music (22 Nov. 1903) and restoration of the Gregorian chant as the model, his recasting of the breviary (*Divino afflatu*: 1 Nov. 1911), and his initiation (1914) of a revision of the missal. These initiatives were so far-reaching that he has been hailed as a pioneer of the modern liturgical movement.

In many ways deeply conservative, and so regarded by contemporaries, Pius was also one of the most constructive reforming popes. A man of transparent goodness and humility as well as resolution and organizing ability, he was spoken of as a saint and credited with miracles in his lifetime. The process of his canonization was begun in 1923; he was beatified on 3 June 1951, and canonized on 29 May 1954. Feast 21 Aug.

ASS 36–41 (1903–8); *AAS* 1–6 (1909–14); N. Vian (ed.), *Lettere* (Rome, 1954); R. Bazin, *Pie X* (Paris, 1928); E. Vercesi, *Il pontificato di Pio X* (Milan, 1935); R. Merry del Val, *Memories of Pope Pius X* (ET, London, 1939); C. Ledré, *Pie X* (Paris, 1952); Schmidlin 3, 1–177; *DTC* 12, 1716–40 (É. Amann); *EC* 9, 1523–30 (G. Urbani); *LThK* 8, 538–40 (R. Aubert); *NCE* 11, 408–11 (C. Ledré).

BENEDICT XV (3 Sept. 1914–22 Jan. 1922). Born at Genoa on 21 Nov. 1854, of an old patrician family, Giacomo Della Chiesa graduated doctor of civil law at Genoa University in 1875, then studied at the Capranica College and the Gregorian University, Rome. After ordination on 21 Dec. 1878, he trained (1878–82) for the papal diplomatic service at the Academy of Noble Ecclesiastics. From 1883 to 1887 he was secretary to Mariano Rampolla, then nuncio to Spain, assisting him not only in diplomatic business like the papal mediation between Germany and Spain on the *Caroline Islands (1885), but also in organizing relief during a cholera epidemic. When Rampolla became secretary of state and cardinal in 1887, Della Chiesa remained with him, being promoted undersecretary of state in 1901 and continuing as such when Rampolla was succeeded by Rafael Merry del Val in 1903. He had hoped to become nuncio to Spain, but Pius X, who suspected him of being a disciple of Rampolla, appointed him archbishop of Bologna in 1907. Only in May 1914 did Pius name him cardinal, and three months later he was elected pope. Pius's death coincided with the outbreak of the First World War, and the surprise choice of Della Chiesa was due to the recognition that in the crisis the church needed an experienced diplomat at its head.

Benedict's reign was inevitably overshadowed by the war and its aftermath, but the diplomatic isolation of the holy see as a result of the unresolved *Roman question reduced any role he could play to one on the sidelines. While protesting against inhuman methods of warfare, he maintained strict neutrality and abstained from condemning any of the belligerents, with the result that each side accused him of favouring the other. In the early years he concentrated on alleviating suffering, opening a bureau at the Vatican for reuniting prisoners-of-war with their families and persuading Switzerland to receive soldiers of whatever country suffering from tuberculosis. On 1 Aug. 1917, however, he dispatched to the Allies and the Central Powers a seven-point plan proposing a peace based on justice rather than military triumph, but it was stillborn. France and Britain, regarding it as biased against them (as it was, in the current military situation), ignored it, while after an initial welcome Germany cooled towards it when the collapse of Russia made victory again seem possible. Benedict was undoubtedly attracted by Germany's offer to give Rome back to the holy see after defeating Italy, and dreaded Orthodox Rus-

sian expansionism in the event of an Allied victory. He was allowed no part in the peace settlement of 1919, the Allies having secretly (treaty of London: Apr. 1915) agreed with Italy that the Vatican should be excluded; in any case, he considered it a vengeful diktat.

After the war Benedict pleaded for international reconciliation (*Pacem Dei munus*: 23 May 1920) and, although critical of some of its aspects, gave general support to the League of Nations. He worked to reconstruct church–state relations in the new states which had emerged, and sent Achille Ratti (later Pius XI) as apostolic visitor to Poland and Lithuania in 1919; in 1920 he sent Eugenio Pacelli (later Pius XII) as nuncio to Germany. He was concerned for the new concordats which the freshly drawn map of Europe made desirable, and devoted his last consistorial allocution (21 Nov. 1921) to this problem. His reign saw a notable rise, from fourteen in 1914 to twenty-seven in 1922, in countries diplomatically represented at the holy see; they included Britain, which in 1915 sent a chargé d'affaires to the Vatican, the first since the 17th cent. Relations with France, breached since 1905, were resumed and an ambassador extraordinary appointed in 1921; a helpful factor was Benedict's canonization of Joan of Arc (1412–31) on 9 May 1920. Although he himself found no solution to the *Roman question, he prepared the ground for one. He put out feelers, through secretary of state Pietro Gasparri on 28 June 1915 and Cardinal Bonaventura Cerretti in Paris in June 1919, which signalled the Vatican's readiness for an honourable settlement, gave his blessing to the Popular Party founded by Dom Luigi Sturzo in Jan. 1919, thereby effectively abolishing the *Non expedit, and lifted (May 1920) the Vatican's ban on official visits to the Quirinal (once the summer residence of the pope, but since 1870 official residence of the king of Italy) by heads of Catholic states.

On 28 June 1917 Benedict promulgated the new code of canon law in large part completed by Pius X; in Sept. he appointed a commission to interpret it. Starting with his first encyclical *Ad beatissimi* (1 Nov. 1914), he successfully called a halt to the bitter animosity between diehard traditionalists and modernists, a legacy of Pius X's suppression of *Modernism. Like other popes, he dreamed of reunion with the separated churches of the east, and the outbreak of the Russian Revolution made him think that the moment for this had arrived. To assist the process he established (1 May 1917) the Congregation for the Oriental Church, and set up (15 Oct. 1917) the Pontifical Oriental Institute in Rome; on 5 Oct. 1920 he declared St Ephraem, the Syrian exegete and theologian (*c.*306–73), a doctor of the church. The war created a host of problems in the mission field, and Benedict came to be called 'the pope of missions', partly because of his constructive interest in them but also because of his letter *Maximum illud* (30 Nov. 1919), in which he urged missionary bishops to push forward with the formation of a native clergy, and to seek the welfare of the people among whom they worked, not the imperialist interest of their own country of origin.

Benedict died unexpectedly early, at the age of 67, of influenza which developed into pneumonia. Two years before, the Turks had erected a statue of him (by Canarica) in Istanbul which saluted him as 'the great pope of the world tragedy . . . the benefactor of all people, irrespective of nationality or religion'.

AAS 6–14; H. E. G. Rope, *Benedict XV: the Pope of Peace* (London, 1941); F. Hayward, *Un Pape méconnu: Benoît XV* (Tournai, 1955); W. H. Peters, *The Life of Benedict XV* (Milwaukee, 1959); P. Piffl, 'The Conclaves of Benedict XV and Pius XI', *Tablet* 217 (1963), 1004–6; 1028 f.; 1059–61; Schmidlin 3, 179–339; *DHGE* 8, 167–72 (E. de Moreau); *DBI* 8, 408–17 (G. de Rosa); *EC* 2, 1285–94 (G. Della Torre); *NCE* 2, 279 f. (W. H. Peters).

PIUS XI (6 Feb. 1922–10 Feb. 1939). Born 31 May 1857 at Desio, near Milan, son of a silk-factory manager, Ambrogio Damiano Achille Ratti was ordained 27 Dec. 1879 in the Lateran, obtained three doctorates at the Gregorian University, Rome, was professor 1882–8 at the seminary at Padua, and worked 1888–1911 at the Ambrosian Library, Milan. An expert palaeographer, he edited the Ambrosian missal and published other works; in his spare time he was a keen mountaineer. Moving to the Vatican Library in 1911, he became its prefect in 1914. In Apr. 1918 BENEDICT XV, recognizing his flair for languages, sent him as apostolic visitor to Poland, promoting him nuncio and archbishop of Lepanto in Oct. 1919. He carried out his difficult mission with skill and credit, refusing to leave Warsaw in Aug. 1920 when a Bolshevik attack threatened. In Nov. 1920, however, when papal delegate to the interallied plebiscite commission for Upper Silesia, he became, through no fault of his own, the target for Polish nationalist resentment. Benedict XV rescued him from an untenable situation by appointing him (13 June 1921) archbishop of Milan and cardinal. Next year, at the conclave of 2–6 Feb., he was elected as a compromise at the fourteenth ballot. His first public act was to give the blessing *Urbi et Orbi* from the external loggia of St Peter's, a gesture of peace to the *Quirinal not made since 1870.

Pius took as his motto 'Christ's peace in Christ's kingdom', interpreting it as meaning that the church and Christianity should be active in, and not insulated from, society. Hence his inauguration in his first encyclical (*Ubi arcano*: 23 Dec. 1922) of Catholic Action, i.e. the collaboration of layfolk with the hierarchy in the church's mission, his introduction of Catholic Action to numerous countries, and his encouragement of specialized groupings such as the Jocists, a Christian youth organization for workers. Hence, too, his institution of the feast of Christ the King (*Quas primas*: 11 Dec. 1925) as a counter to contemporary secularism, and his use for this purpose of the jubilee years 1925, 1929, and 1933, as well as of biennial eucharistic congresses. The same theme, with different emphases, reappears in encyclicals like *Divini illius magistri* (31 Dec. 1929), on Christian education; *Casti connubii* (30 Dec. 1930), defining Christian marriage and condemning contraception; *Quadragesimo anno* (15 May 1931), reaffirming but going beyond LEO XIII's social teaching, and its supplement *Nova impendet* (2 Oct. 1931), prompted by contemporary unemployment and the arms race; and *Caritate Christi* (3 May 1932), called forth by the world economic crisis. His numerous canonizations were also intended to promote the same religious ends. They included John Fisher (1469–1535), Thomas More (1478–1535), John Bosco (1815–88), and Teresa of Lisieux (1873–97); while he declared Albertus Magnus (*c.*1200–80), Peter Canisius (1521–97), John of the Cross (1542–91), and Robert Bellarmine (1542–1621) doctors of the church.

In dealing with political issues after the First World War Pius was assisted by able secretaries of state, Pietro Gasparri (1922–30) and Eugenio Pacelli (1930–9: later PIUS XII). To regularize the position and rights of the church he concluded concordats or other agreements with some twenty states. In France he brought about a substantial improvement in church–state relations, confirming in *Maximam gravissimamque* (18 Jan. 1924) a practical accommodation on the difficult issues arising out of the Law of Separation of 1905. His most significant diplomatic achievement was the Lateran Treaty (11 Feb. 1929) which he negotiated with Benito Mussolini, Italian prime minister since 1922, and which established the Vatican City as an independent, neutral state. For the first time since 1870 the holy see recognized Italy as a kingdom with Rome as its capital, while Italy indemnified it for the loss of the papal states and accepted Catholicism as the official religion. As time went on Pius was increasingly preoccupied with the new totalitarian states. His repeated efforts to check Soviet anti-Christian persecution had no effect, and in *Divini Redemptoris* (19 Mar. 1937) he sharply condemned atheistic communism.

Trusting Adolf Hitler's assurances, but also moved by fear of communism, he negotiated (20 July 1933) a concordat with National Socialist Germany which temporarily enhanced the prestige of the regime and curbed Catholic opposition to it, but for which he was heavily criticized. In 1933–6, however, because of its progressive oppression of the church, he had to address thirty-four notes of protest to the Nazi government. The break came in 1937 when he ordered the encyclical *Mit brennender Sorge* (14 Mar.), denouncing repeated violations of the concordat and branding Nazism as fundamentally anti-Christian, to be read from all pulpits. In the twenties and thirties he protested several times against the fierce persecution of the church in Mexico, urging Mexican Catholics in Apr. 1937, when the situation had eased, to organize peacefully and promote *Catholic Action. On 3 June 1933 (*Dilectissima nobis*) he denounced the harsh separation between church and state carried through in Spain by the republican government, and supported General Francisco Franco in the civil war which broke out in July 1936. His attitude towards Italian fascism, shaken in 1931 when Mussolini dissolved Catholic youth movements, dramatically hardened in 1938, when the regime adopted Hitler's racial doctrines.

Ardently involved in overseas missions, Pius required every religious order to engage in missionary work, with the result that he saw the number of missionaries doubled in his reign. Following Benedict XV, he pressed on with developing an indigenous Catholicism, personally consecrating (in the face of opposition) the first six Chinese bishops on 28 Oct. 1926. There followed consecrations of a native Japanese bishop (1927), and native priests for India, south-east Asia, and China (1933); the total of native priests rose in his reign from under 3,000 to over 7,000. He founded a faculty of missiology at the Gregorian University, and a missionary and ethnological museum in the Lateran. His calls for reunion between Rome and Orthodoxy met with little response, but he lavished attention on the

Uniat churches of the east (i.e. eastern-rite churches in full communion with Rome). He at first allowed, later approved, the conversations held between Roman Catholics and Anglicans at Malines in 1921–6. He was wholly negative, however, towards the growing pan-Protestant ecumenical movement, and caused dismay by declaring (*Mortalium animos*: 6 Jan. 1928) that Christ's church could never be a federation of independent bodies holding differing doctrines, and by forbidding Roman Catholics to take part in conferences with non-Romans.

The first scholar–pope since BENEDICT XIV, Pius quietly eased the tensions arising from the *Modernist debate, rehabilitating some leading figures who had been demoted. He considered the advancement of science and serious scholarship as a personal challenge, and among other measures he modernized and enlarged the reading room of the Vatican Library, raised three of its most scholarly prefects to the purple, founded (Dec. 1925) the Pontifical Institute of Christian Archaeology, erected the Pinacoteca for the Vatican collection of pictures, and removed the Vatican observatory (equipped with modern instruments) to Castel Gandolfo. He instructed the Italian bishops to take proper care of their archives, and radically reformed (*Deus scientiarum*: 24 May 1931) the training of the clergy. Well informed about scientific research, he founded the Pontifical Academy of Sciences in 1936, admitting to membership scientists of distinction from many countries. Armed with a strong sense of personal authority, he preferred to delegate as little as possible, and greatly reduced the role of the sacred college. He installed (1931) a radio station in the Vatican City, and was the first pontiff to use radio for pastoral purposes.

A. Ratti (Pio XI), *Scritti storici* (selection) (Florence, 1932); *AAS* 14–31 (1922–39); E. Pacelli, *Discorsi panegirici* (Milan, 2nd edn., 1939); D. Bertetto, *Discorsi di Pio XI* (Turin, 1961); *RaccCon* 11 (Rome, 1954); D. A. Binchy, *Church and State in Fascist Italy* (London, 1941); W. M.

Harrigan, 'Nazi Germany and the Holy See', *Catholic Historical Review* 47 (1961–2), 164–98; P. Hughes, *Pope Pius the Eleventh* (London, 1937); Schmidlin 4, *LThK* 8, 540–2 (G. Schwaiger); *EC* 9, 1531–43 (A. Frutaz); *NCE* 11, 411–14 (G. Schwaiger).

PIUS XII (2 Mar. 1939–9 Oct. 1958). A lawyer's son and descended from a family of jurists, Eugenio Maria Giuseppe Giovanni Pacelli was born in Rome on 2 Mar. 1876, attended a state secondary school, and studied at the Gregorian University, the Capranica College, and the S. Apollinare Institute, Rome. Ordained priest in Apr. 1899, he entered the papal service in 1901, and from 1904 to 1916 was Cardinal Gasparri's right-hand assistant in codifying the canon law; for several years he also taught international law at the Academy of Noble Ecclesiastics. In Apr. 1917 BENEDICT XV appointed him nuncio in Munich and titular archbishop of Sardes, and in June 1920 named him nuncio to the new German republic. These were busy years, for during the First World War he had to negotiate with the imperial government about Benedict XV's abortive peace plan (1917), while after the war he agreed a favourable concordat with Bavaria (1924) and a less advantageous one with Prussia (1929). Named cardinal on 16 Dec. 1929, he succeeded Gasparri as secretary of state on 7 Feb. 1930, and as such was responsible for concordats with Austria (June 1933) and National Socialist Germany (July 1933). Although Berlin took the initiative in the latter, Adolf Hitler's repeated violations of it and the deteriorating position of the church in Germany led to increasing difficulties for the holy see. Meanwhile Pacelli, an accomplished linguist who had earlier travelled to Britain, paid official visits to Argentina (1934), France (1935 and 1937), and Hungary (1938), and an extensive private one to the USA (1936). With the Second World War threatening, he was elected at a one-day conclave at the third ballot, obtaining 48 out of 53 votes. No secretary of state had been chosen since CLEMENT IX, but he was the best-known of the cardinals, and possessed the gifts and experience that seemed called for.

Pius saw himself as the pope of peace, and until 1 Sept. 1939 strove to avert war by diplomatic moves, on 3 May calling for an international conference to settle differences peacefully, and on 24 Aug. making a radio appeal to the world to abstain from resort to war; until the Italian prime minister Benito Mussolini's entry into the war on 10 June 1940, he worked to keep Italy out of it. He achieved neither aim, but through his efforts and presence Rome was treated as an open city. Faithful to the *Lateran Treaty (art. 24) as well as to his conception of the church's role, he remained strictly neutral ('impartial', he preferred to call it), but repeatedly called for a just and lasting peace on the basis of natural law. In his allocution for Christmas 1939 he laid down the five principles essential for one; they included general disarmament, recognition of minority rights, and the right of every nation to independence. Although convinced that communism was even more dangerous than Nazism, he did not endorse Hitler's attack on Russia, and he deplored the Allies' demand at Casablanca (Jan. 1943) for unconditional surrender. Throughout the war he supervised, through the Pontifical Aid Commission, a vast programme for the relief of war victims, especially prisoners of war; and when Hitler occupied Rome on 10 Sept. 1943, Pius made the Vatican City an asylum for countless refugees, including numerous Jews. He has been criticized, however, for failing to speak out sufficiently firmly against Nazi atrocities, especially the persecution of the Jews. His defenders have pointed (a) to unmistakable denunciations, albeit in general terms, of extermination on grounds of race (esp. 24 Dec. 1942 and 2 June 1943); (b) to his conviction, expressed more than once, that more explicit protests would only stimulate barbaric reprisals; and (c) to the assistance he personally gave, or connived at the giving of, to vast numbers of individual Jews. What remains clear is that the veiled or generalized language traditional to the curia was not a suitable instrument for dealing with cynically planned world domination and genocide.

Unaffected in his teaching office by the war, Pius published two major encyclicals while it was still raging. In *Mystici corporis Christi* (29 June 1943) he expounded the nature of the church in terms of Christ's mystical body, while in *Divino afflante Spiritu* (30 Sept. 1943) he permitted the use of modern historical methods by exegetes of Scripture. Closely linked with the former was *Mediator Dei* (20 Nov. 1947), which called for the intelligent participation of the laity in the mass. In 1951 and later he reformed the entire Holy Week liturgy, while in *Christus dominus* (16 Jan. 1953) and *Sacram communionem* (19 Mar. 1957) he standardized relaxations of the eucharistic fast and the holding of evening masses which wartime conditions had made necessary. Always Marian in his piety, he defined the dogma of the bodily Assumption of the BVM into heaven in *Munificentissimus Deus* (1 Nov. 1950), and devoted *Ad coeli reginam* (11 Oct. 1954) to her royal dignity, leaving open, however, the question of her mediation and co-redemptive role. He was the first to appreciate the Marian importance of Fátima. A conservative note was sounded in *Humani generis* (12 Aug. 1950), which warned against the accommodation of Catholic theology to current intellectual trends. Politically he inveighed against communism, threatening (e.g. 1 July 1949 and 28 July 1950) members of the party and its promoters with excommunication, and concluded accords advantageous to the church with Dr Salazar's Portugal (18 July 1950) and General Franco's Spain (27 Aug. 1955). In the moral field he condemned, with Germany in view, the conception of collective guilt (24 Dec. 1944; 20 Feb. 1946), and also any kind of artificial insemination (29 Sept. 1949). In *Miranda prorsus* (8 Sept. 1957) he sought to lay down guidelines for the audio-visual media.

Pius canonized 33 persons, including PIUS X. He created an unprecedentedly large number of cardinals, 32 in 1946 and 24 in 1953, drawing them from many countries and reducing the Italian element to one-third. Although the church suffered severe restrictions and losses in his reign, it also made striking advances, the number of dioceses rising from 1,696 in 1939 to 2,048 in 1958, and hierarchies being set up in China (1946), Burma (1955), and several African countries. He promoted important excavations (1939–49) under St Peter's aimed at identifying the Apostle's tomb. He sought to encourage relations with the Uniat and Orthodox churches of the east, and somewhat relaxed his predecessor's negative attitude to the ecumenical movement, formally recognizing it on 20 Dec. 1949 (after the formation of the World Council of Churches in 1948), and permitting Roman Catholics to engage in discussions with non-Romans on matters of faith. Tall, slender, ascetic in appearance but friendly in manner, he made a profound impression on the millions who flocked to Rome for the Holy Year of 1950 and the Marian Year of 1954, and on the thousands who attended his innumerable audiences. He was the first pope to become widely known by radio and television. Authoritarian in style, he acted himself as secretary of state from 1944, and increasingly diminished the role of the cardinals. In his latter years, however, when he was frequently prostrated with serious illness, this solitary bent placed undue power in the hands of the narrow, not always scrupulous, circle on which he was forced to depend. This brought a shadow over his pontificate, and when he died at Castel Gandolfo his moral authority probably stood higher in non-Roman than Roman circles.

E. Pacelli, *La personalità e la territorialità delle leggi specialmente nel diritto canonico* (Rome, 1912); *AAS* 33–50 (1939–58); *Discorsi e radiomessagi di S.S. Pio XII* (20 vols., Vatican City, 1939–58); P. Blet and others (eds.), *Actes et documents du S. Siège relatifs à la seconde grande guerre mondiale* (Rome, 1965 ff.: ET, 1968 ff.); S. Friedländer, *Pius XII and the Third Reich* (ET, London, 1966); I. Giordani, *Pio XII, Un grande papa* (Turin, 1961); L. Chaigne, *Portrait et vie de Pie XII* (Paris, 1966); M. O'Carroll, *Pius XII: Greatness Dishonoured* (Co. Dublin, 1980); R. Leiber, 'Pius XII as I knew him', *Catholic Mind* 57 (1959), 292–304; *LThK* 8, 542 f. (R. Leiber); *NCE* 11, 414–18 (R. Leiber); *ODCC* 1098 f.

JOHN XXIII (28 Oct. 1958–3 June 1963). Third of thirteen children in a family of frugal peasant farmers, Angelo Giuseppe Roncalli was born on 25 Nov. 1881 at Sotto il Monte, 12 km. from Bergamo. After attending the village school and the two seminaries at Bergamo, he went with a scholarship to the S. Apollinare Institute, Rome, in 1901, graduating doctor of theology in 1904. Secretary 1905–14 to Bishop Radini-Tedeschi of Bergamo, he also lectured in church history at the diocesan seminary. Conscripted in the First World War, he served first as a hospital orderly, then as a chaplain. In 1921 BENEDICT XV promoted him national director of the Congregation for the Propagation of the Faith. In his spare time he wrote monographs on diocesan history and on St Charles Borromeo (1538–84), his researches in the Ambrosian Library, Milan, bringing him into contact with Achille Ratti. It was Ratti who, as PIUS XI, launched him on a diplomatic career, appointing him titular archbishop of Areopolis and apostolic visitor (from 1931 apostolic delegate) to Bulgaria in Mar. 1925, and apostolic delegate to Turkey and Greece in 1934. Busy but lonely in the former post, he enjoyed the latter, establishing friendly relations with members of the Turkish government and leaders of the Orthodox churches. During the German occupation of Greece (1941–4) he worked to relieve distress and prevent the deportation of Jews. Appointed nuncio to France on 22 Dec. 1944, he dealt tactfully but firmly with the problem of the many bishops accused of collaborating with the Vichy regime, negotiated with the government over the financing of church schools and the nomination of bishops, and arranged for German prisoners-of-war who were ordinands to follow courses in theology at Chartres. He also looked favourably on experiments with worker priests, and from

1952 was permanent observer for the holy see at UNESCO. On 12 June 1953 he was named cardinal, and on 15 June patriarch of Venice, where he was noted for his pastoral zeal, informality, and firm resistance to communist manoeuvres. In 1958 he completed the fifth and last volume of his studies on St Charles Borromeo. At the conclave of 25–28 Oct. 1958 he was elected at the twelfth ballot; he was crowned on 4 Nov., the feast of his revered Charles Borromeo. Almost seventy-seven, many regarded his appointment as a caretaker one, but it proved a decisive turning-point.

At his coronation mass John announced his desire to be above all things a good shepherd, and this was the hallmark of his pontificate. At his first consistory he abolished the rule, dating from SIXTUS V, fixing 70 as the maximum number of cardinals, and by 1962 he increased the college to 87, making it larger and more international than ever before. On 25 Jan. 1959 he proposed three major projects: a diocesan synod for Rome, an ecumenical council, and the revision of the canon law. He held the synod, the first in Rome's history, in St John Lateran from 24 to 31 Jan. 1960; an overture to the council, its aim was to reinvigorate church life in Rome itself. His outstanding achievement, however, was the Second Vatican Council, the calling of which he attributed to a sudden inspiration of the Holy Spirit. Its objective, he later explained, was to be a new Pentecost, a means of regeneration for the church, bringing its teaching, discipline, and organization up to date, and opening a way towards the reunion of the separated brethren of east and west. He set up preparatory commissions and secretariats on 5 June 1960, and opened the council itself in St Peter's on 11 Oct. 1962. Official observers from eighteen non-Roman churches were present by invitation, and in his address he urged the fathers to expound truth positively without relying on anathemas. Although he did not attend the deliberations himself, he intervened decisively on 21 Nov. 1962 to rule that the

conservative schema on revelation, which had been rejected by more than half but not the necessary two-thirds of the fathers, should be redrafted by a mixed commission. On 8 Dec. 1962 he closed the first session, adjourning the council for nine months. Already stricken with illness, he did not live to see its resumption.

John set in motion his projected revision of canon law by creating a pontifical commission to deal with it (28 Mar. 1962); he had earlier (22 Feb. 1959) established a new papal commission for cinema, radio, and television. His concern for the liturgy was shown in his approval of new rubrics for the breviary and the missal (25 July 1960), his insertion of the name of St Joseph in the canon of the mass (13 Nov. 1962), and his permission for the use of the vernacular by certain Uniat churches. In his teaching a retreat from PIUS XII's emphasis on Mariology was perceptible; but some of his pronouncements, such as advice (20 June 1961) to New Testament exegetes to observe caution, and a warning (30 June 1962) against dangers in Teilhard de Chardin's work, sounded a reactionary note. His encyclicals and other utterances were more pastoral than dogmatic. His major encyclicals were *Ad cathedram Petri* (29 June 1959), in which he pleaded that truth, unity, and peace should be promoted in the spirit of love, and greeted non-Catholics as 'separated brethren and sons'; *Mater et magistra* (15 May 1961), which reinforced and brought up to date the social teaching of LEO XIII and PIUS XI and called on richer nations to help the poorer ones; and *Pacem in terris* (11 Apr. 1963), which, addressed to all mankind, set out the recognition of human rights and duties as the foundation of world peace and, distinguishing between Marxist ideology and the aspirations of communist regimes, pressed for peaceful coexistence between the West and the communist East. This last created a widespread impression, not least in the Soviet bloc, and led to his receiving Nikita Khrushchev's son-in-law in spring 1963. It also marked an important step in the inauguration by the Vatican of a more open eastern policy. During the Cuban missile crisis of 1962 John publicly urged both the USA and the USSR to exercise caution, winning the respect of Premier Khrushchev as well as of President John F. Kennedy. Next year the International Balzan Foundation awarded him its Peace Prize.

More than any pope, John wanted dialogue with the world, irrespective of creed. His concern for Christian unity was expressed in his establishment (5 June 1960) of the Secretariat for Christian Unity, with Cardinal Augustin Bea as its president. Other significant gestures were his dispatch of personal envoys to Istanbul to greet Ecumenical Patriarch Athenagoras I (1948-72) on 27 June 1961, and his reception of Archbishop Geoffrey Fisher of Canterbury on 20 Dec. 1960 (the first Anglican archbishop to be so received). He also exchanged greetings with Patriarch Alexis of Moscow. In Nov. 1961, with his approval, five official Roman Catholic observers attended the World Council of Churches in New Delhi. He removed words offensive to Jews from the Good Friday liturgy, and on one occasion introduced himself to Jewish visitors with the words, 'I am Joseph, your brother'.

Warm-hearted and unaffectedly simple in spite of his erudition and command of many languages, attached to his humble origins and always retaining a peasant's shrewdness and jovial humour, John brought a wind of change to his office, relaxing its hieratic stiffness and, after decades of growing centralization, giving the episcopate a new awareness of its importance. Typically, at Christmas 1958 he revived the custom, which had lapsed in 1870, of visiting the Regina Coeli prison and one of the local hospitals. When he died, after a prolonged and painful illness, *The Times* commented that few pontificates had so captured the imagination of the world.

A. G. Roncalli, *Gli atti della visita apostolica di s. Carlo Borromeo a Bergamo* (Florence, 1936); *Mons. G. M. Radini-Tedeschi, vescovo di Bergamo* (3rd edn., Rome, 1963); *Souvenirs d'un nonce: cahiers de France 1944-53* (Rome, 1963); *Il giornale dell'anima, e altri scritti di pietà* (Rome, 1964; ET by D. Whale, London, 1965); *Letters to his Family* (ET by D. Whale, London, 1969); *AAS* 50-5 (1958-63); E. E. Y. Hales, *Pope John and his Revolution* (London, 1965); M. Trevor, *Pope John* (London, 1967); P. B. Johnson, *Pope John XXIII* (London, 1975); P. Hebblethwaite, *John XXIII: Pope of the Council* (London, 1985).

PAUL VI (21 June 1963-6 Aug. 1978). Son of a prosperous lawyer who was also a political editor and parliamentary deputy, and of a pious mother to whom he was devoted, Giovanni Battista Montini was born at Concesio, near Brescia, on 26 Sept. 1897. Shy and of precarious health, but with an appetite for books, he attended the diocesan seminary from home, was ordained on 29 May 1920, and then pursued graduate studies in Rome. From 1922 he worked in the papal secretariat of state, a brief spell (May-Nov. 1923) in the Warsaw nunciature being broken off for health reasons. Continuing in the secretariat, he became deeply involved (1924-33) in the Catholic student movement, and from 1931 also taught diplomatic history at the papal academy for diplomats. On 8 July 1931 he was made a domestic prelate to the holy see, and on 13 Dec. 1937 assistant to Cardinal Eugenio Pacelli, then secretary of state. When Pacelli became PIUS XII in 1939, Montini continued to work closely with him, being assigned charge of internal church affairs in 1944. Promoted pro-secretary of state in Nov. 1952, he declined a cardinal's hat in Dec. 1953, and on 1 Nov. 1954 was appointed archbishop of Milan, an enormous diocese teeming with social problems; the nomination has been interpreted as a sign of papal disfavour. Styling himself 'the workers' archbishop', but accompanied by his now legendary ninety crates of books, he threw himself with immense energy into the task of restoring his war-battered diocese and winning over the disaffected industrial masses; for three weeks in Nov. 1957 he carried out an intensive mission aimed at reaching every parish in the city. If his efforts as a missioner and diocesan were not as successful as he had hoped, he found time for experiments in Christian unity, holding discussions, for instance, with a group of Anglicans in 1956. On 5 Dec. 1958 JOHN XXIII named him a cardinal, a customary promotion withheld under Pius XII in spite of repeated appeals from the Milanese, and as John's confidant he played a noteworthy part in the preparations for the Second Vatican Council (1962–5); his attitude to the first session (11 Oct.–8 Dec. 1962), at which he only spoke twice, was cool, not to say critical. During these years he travelled widely, visiting Hungary (1938), the USA (1951 and 1960), Dublin (1961), and Africa (1962). At the conclave of June 1963, attended by eighty cardinals and the largest so far in history, he was elected as John's successor at the fifth ballot. He chose a name which suggested an outward-looking approach.

Greatly under the spell of his predecessor, Paul immediately (22 June) promised to continue Vatican Council II, interrupted by John's death; he would also revise canon law, promote justice in civil, social, and international life, and work for peace and the unity of Christendom (a theme to become increasingly close to his heart). He opened the second session of the Council on 29 Sept. 1963, introducing important procedural reforms (e.g. the admission of laymen as auditors, the appointment of four moderators, and the relaxation of confidentiality), and closed it on 4 Dec. 1963, promulgating the *Constitution on the Liturgy* and the *Decree on Mass Media*. On 4–6 Jan. 1964 he made an unprecedented pilgrimage by air to the Holy Land, meeting Ecumenical Patriarch Athenagoras I in Jerusalem. Having on 6 Sept. announced the admission of women, religious and lay, as auditors to the council, he opened the third session on 14 Sept. 1964 and closed it on 21 Nov. 1964, promulgating the *Constitution on the Church* (with a note attached explaining the collegiality of bishops, i.e. the doctrine that the bishops form a college which, acting in concert with and not independently of its

head, the pope, has supreme authority in the church), the *Decree on Ecumenism* (modifying several passages on his own authority), and the *Decree on the Eastern Catholic Churches*; he also proclaimed, notwithstanding the fathers' reluctance, the BVM 'Mother of the Church'. During the recess he flew (2–5 Dec. 1964) to Bombay for the International Eucharistic Congress. At the fourth and last session (14 Sept.–8 Dec. 1965), during which he flew to New York (4 Oct.) to plead for peace at the United Nations, he undertook to establish a permanent synod of bishops, with deliberative as well as consultative powers. Before mass on 7 Dec. a joint declaration by himself and Patriarch Athenagoras I was read out deploring the mutual anathemas pronounced by representatives of the western and eastern churches at Constantinople in 1054 and the schism which resulted. Next day he solemnly confirmed all the decrees of the Council, and proclaimed an extraordinary jubilee (1 Jan.–29 May 1966) for reflection and renewal in the light of the Council's teachings.

Paul now began implementing the Council's decisions with great courage as well as an acutely felt sense of the difficulties; it was to his credit that he was able to steer the church through a period of revolutionary change without schism. He set up several important post-conciliar commissions (e.g. for the revision of the breviary, the lectionary, the order of mass, sacred music, and canon law), and carried through the substitution of the vernacular in the liturgy with unflinching determination. He reorganized the curia and the Vatican finances (in both administration and investments), and confirmed the permanent secretariats for the Promotion of Christian Unity, for Non-Christian Religions, and for Non-Believers. In pursuit of ecumenism he held meetings with the archbishop of Canterbury (Michael Ramsey) in Rome (24 Mar. 1966), and with Ecumenical Patriarch Athenagoras I at Istanbul (25 July 1967) and Rome (26 Oct. 1967). In May 1974 he flew to the shrine of the BVM at Fátima, Portugal (at her personal bidding, he claimed), to pray for peace. His public pronouncements included *Mysterium fidei* (3 Sept. 1965), paving the way for liturgical reform and reasserting traditional eucharistic doctrine; *Populorum progressio* (26 Mar. 1967), a pointed plea for social justice; *Sacerdotalis coelibatus* (24 June 1967), insisting on the necessity of priestly celibacy; *Humanae vitae* (25 July 1968), condemning artificial methods of birth control; and *Matrimonia mixta* (31 Mar. 1970). While the last permitted modest relaxations in the regulations for mixed marriages which scarcely satisfied non-Roman Catholics, *Humanae vitae* disappointed many in the church, not least because the majority of the pontifical commission appointed in 1963 to examine the subject had reported in favour of contraception in certain circumstances. On 6 Aug. 1968 the Lambeth Conference of Anglican Bishops rejected the encyclical; and while Paul remained confident of the rightness of his decision, he was profoundly shaken by the critical international reaction to it.

After 1968 some detected a deepening shadow over the pontificate. Paul seemed to withdraw into himself, worried by such trends as international terrorism and by tensions within the church (e.g. growing demands for the marriage of the clergy, the defiant resistance of Mgr Marcel Lefebvre and others to the liturgical reforms, the struggles between traditionalists and progressives, the signs of the emergence of a new modernism). There were rumours of his possible resignation in 1974; but real though it was, his inner malaise could be exaggerated. These years saw some of the 'pilgrim pope's' most striking international journeys: to Geneva to address the International Labour Organization and the World Council of Churches and to Uganda to honour its martyrs in June and July 1969; to Sardinia to celebrate Our Lady of Bonaria in Apr. 1970; and to the Far East (where he narrowly escaped assassination in Manila) in Nov.–Dec. 1970. On 25 Oct. 1970 he canonized, notwithstanding earlier Anglican protests, forty English and Welsh

Roman Catholic martyrs of the 16th and 17th cents.; he also proclaimed St Teresa of Avila (1515–82) and St Catherine of Siena (1347–80) doctors of the church, the first women to be so entitled. In the same year he fixed the retirement age for priests and bishops (75), and decreed that cardinals over 80 should not participate in curial business. In furtherance of *collegiality (which he supported so long as it did not impinge on the pope's primacy) he convened international episcopal synods in 1971 (on the priesthood), 1974 (on evangelization), and in 1977 (on catechesis). In Apr. 1972 he and the archbishop of Canterbury (Donald Coggan) issued a Common Declaration which pledged united work towards reunion, but made no mention of the intercommunion for which the archbishop had called. But perhaps his most important legacy to the church, brought to completion in this closing phase, was his steady enlargement and internationalization of the sacred college. When he was elected it had some 80 members, but by 1976 he had raised the total to 138; moreover, its Italian members were a small minority, and it included many representatives of the third world.

Although not a man with the common touch, Paul had a flair for the dramatic gesture; yet he tended to leave an ambiguous impression. John XXIII had described him as 'a little like Hamlet'. He was always torn between his forward-looking vision and his suspicion of any innovation which might undermine the integrity and authority of the church's teaching. He consistently emphasized the mystery and otherworldliness of the faith, and dreaded anything suggestive of scientific naturalism. Characteristically, he reduced the pomp and circumstance of the papacy, and sold the tiara presented to him at his election for the benefit of the poor. In his last year he was profoundly disturbed by the kidnap and eventual murder (c.9 May 1978) of his lifelong friend Aldo Moro, the Christian Democrat statesman, and his last public appearance was to preside at his funeral in

St John Lateran. Not long after he was stricken with arthritis, and after suffering a heart attack while mass was being said by his bed, he died at Castel Gandolfo on 6 Aug.

AAS 55–70; N. Vian, *Anni e opere di Paolo VI* (Rome, 1978); *Insegnamento di Paolo VI* (15 vols., Vatican City, 1963–77); *Paulus PP. Elenchus bibliographicus* (2nd edn., Brescia, 1981); E. Noel, *The Montini Story: Portrait of Pope Paul VI* (London, 1968); F. Bea, *Vocabor Paulus* (Turin, 1963); J. M. P. Guitton, *The Pope Speaks: Dialogues of Paul VI with J. Guitton* (ET, London, 1968); P. Ambrogiani, *Paul VI, le pape pèlerin* (Paris, 1971); P. Poupard, 'De Paul VI à Jean-Paul II', *Communio* 1979, n. 1, 71–6; Daniel-Ange, *Paul VI: un regard prophétique* (Paris, 1979); *NCE* 11 (1967), 16–23 (R. Tusco); *EB* (15th edn.) 13, 1088–90 (E. L. Heston); *DSp* 12 (1983), 522–36 (A. Boland); *La Documentation catholique*, no. 1748 (3–17 Sept. 1978).

JOHN PAUL I (26 Aug.–28 Sept. 1978). Born on 17 Oct. 1912 at Forno di Canale (since 1964 Canale d'Agordo), an upland village near Belluno, Albino Luciani came of poor, working-class parents; his father frequently went to Switzerland as a migrant worker, and his family were known as outspoken socialists. After training at local seminaries and doing his military service, he was ordained priest on 7 July 1935. After doctoral studies at the Gregorian University, Rome, and service as a curate in his native parish, he became vice-rector of the seminary at Belluno in autumn 1937. For ten years he taught general subjects, being also appointed vicar-general to the bishop of Belluno. In 1949 he was put in charge of catechetics for the Belluno eucharistic congress, recording his experiences in a book *Crumbs from the Catechism* (*Catechesi in Briciole*). At this time he had a good working relationship with local communists. In Dec. 1958 JOHN XXIII appointed him bishop of Vittorio Veneto, where he exercised a markedly pastoral, grass-roots ministry, playing a background role at Vatican Council II (1962–5), but becoming known in the Italian Conference of Bishops as an active member of its doctrinal commission. On 15 Dec. 1969, largely in response to

local demand, he was named patriarch of Venice. During his nine years there he hosted five ecumenical conferences, including the meeting of the Anglican–Roman Catholic International Commission which produced an agreed statement on authority in 1976; moved unobtrusively to the right politically, declaring publicly (at the election of June 1975) that communism was incompatible with Christianity; and published *Illustrissimi*, a series of whimsical but pointed letters to authors or characters in history or fiction (Pinocchio, Figaro, etc.), which revealed (among other things) a fondness for Dickens and for Mr Pickwick. He was said once to have remarked that, had he not become a priest, he might well have taken up a career as a journalist. From 1972 to 1975 he was vice-president of the Italian Conference of Bishops, and on 5 Mar. 1973 was made a cardinal. While conservative in theology and a defender of **Humanae vitae* (but also of the rights of conscience), he had no use for ecclesiastical display, encouraged parish priests to sell precious vessels and other church valuables for the benefit of the poor, and in 1971 proposed that the wealthy churches of the west should give one per cent of their income to the impoverished churches of the third world.

Although almost unknown outside Italy, he was elected at the third ballot on the first day of the conclave of Aug. 1978 following Paul VI's death. His candidature moved into the foreground once it became clear that the majority of cardinals wanted a completely new style of pope, without connections with the curial establishment, and after the election the prevailing mood of the electors was one of unrestrained joy; the man they had chosen was 'God's candidate'. His choice of name was said to express his desire to combine the progressive and the traditional qualities of John XXIII and Paul VI, and on 27 Aug. he announced to the cardinals (he was reading from an officially prepared text) his intention of continuing to implement Vatican Council II, at the same time preserving intact 'the great discipline of the church in the life of priests and of the faithful'. A more spontaneous act was to hold a press conference, during which he held the thousand journalists present spellbound. Always impatient of pomp and outward trappings, and transparently humble-minded, he dispensed with the traditional papal coronation, and at his inauguration (3 Sept.) in St Peter's Square was simply invested with the *pallium in token of his pastoral office. Three weeks later, about 11 p.m. on Thursday 28 Sept., he died of a heart attack while lying in bed reading some papers containing personal notes. His light was still on when he was found dead about 5.30 a.m. next day. Rumours of foul play, fanned by the lack of an autopsy, were later (1984) blown up into the claim that he was poisoned because he planned to clean up the Vatican Bank, demote important curial figures, and revise *Humanae Vitae*; but the evidence produced was a tissue of improbabilities. The first pope of demonstrably working-class origins, a man of practical common sense who captivated people with his friendly smile, it is impossible to guess what kind of policies he would have pursued had he lived.

Albino Luciani, *Catechesis in Easy Stages* (ET, London, 1949); *Illustrissimi* (ET, London, 1978); *Il magistero di Albino Luciani: scritti e discorsi* (ed. A. Cattabiani, Padua, 1979); *AAS* 70 (1978), 677–776; 797–903; *The Times*, no. 60420 (30 Sept. 1978), p. 16; P. Hebblethwaite, *The Year of Three Popes* (London, 1978); D. Yallop, *In God's Name* (London, 1984).

JOHN PAUL II (16 Oct. 1978–). The first Slav pope and the first non-Italian one since HADRIAN VI, Karol Wojtyła was born on 18 May 1920 at Wadowice, an industrial town 50 km. south-west of Kraków, Poland. His family was modest, his father being a retired army lieutenant living on his pension; Karol became especially close to him since his mother died when he was still a small boy. Joining the local primary school at seven, he went at eleven to the state high school, where he proved both an outstanding pupil and a fine sportsman, keen on football, swimming, and canoeing (he was later to take up skiing); he also loved poetry, and showed a particular flair for acting. In 1938 father and son moved to Kraków, where Karol entered the Jagiellonian University to study Polish language and literature; as a student he was prominent in amateur dramatics, and was admired for his poems. When the Germans occupied Poland in Sept. 1938, the university was forcibly closed down, although an underground network of studies was maintained (as well as an underground theatrical club which Karol and a friend organized). Thus Karol continued to study incognito, and also to write poetry; for a time he had an attachment to a girl. In winter 1940 he was given a labourer's job in a limestone quarry at Zakrówek, outside Kraków, and in 1941 was transferred to the water-purification department of the Solway factory in Borek Fałęcki; these experiences were to inspire some of the more memorable of his later poems. In 1942, after his father's death and after recovering from two near-fatal accidents, he felt the call to the priesthood, began studying theology clandestinely, but after the liberation of Poland by the Russian forces in Jan. 1945 was able to rejoin the Jagiellonian University openly. Graduating with distinction in theology in Aug. 1946, he was ordained priest by Cardinal Adam Sapieha, archbishop of Kraków, on 1 Nov. In Mar. of that year his first collection of poems, *Song of the Hidden God*, had been published. Sent by Sapieha to the Pontifical University (the Angelicum) in Rome, he obtained his doctorate in June 1948 for a dissertation on the concept of faith in St John of the Cross. After serving from 1948 to 1951 as a parish priest (at Niegowice, and then at St Florian's, Kraków), he returned to the Jagiellonian to study philosophy (Martin Buber, Gabriel Marcel, and above all Max Scheler, on whom he published his thesis in 1960). During these years (1952–8) he also lectured on social ethics at Kraków seminary, and in 1956 was appointed professor of ethics at Lublin, becoming acknowledged as one of Poland's foremost ethical thinkers. On 4 July 1958, while on a canoeing holiday with students, he was nominated titular bishop of Ombi and auxiliary to the see of Kraków by PIUS XII. On 30 Dec. 1963 PAUL VI named him archbishop of Kraków, a role in which he revealed himself as a politically astute and formidable adversary of the repressive communist government, and on 26 June 1967 created him a cardinal. He had already published *Love and Responsibility* (ET, 1981), a pastoral treatise on sexuality, in 1960, and at Vatican Council II (1962–5) became a prominent figure internationally. A member of the Preparatory Commission, he attended all four sessions and made an influential contribution to the debate on religious freedom, contending that the church must grant to others the liberty of thought, action, and speech that she claimed for herself. After the council he was active in implementing its decisions, in Rome as well as Poland, and attended four out of the five general episcopal synods set up by it; at the 1971 synod he was elected a member of its steering committee. He was also a member of several of the Vatican congregations, or ministries. In the 1960s and 1970s he was becoming a familiar figure on the world stage, repeatedly visiting North America (e.g. attending the eucharistic congress at Philadelphia in 1976), and travelling to the Middle East, Africa, south and east Asia, and Australia. In Poland he co-operated with his primate, Cardinal Stefan Wyszyński, in a struggle, broadly successful, to secure from the regime some kind of tolerable legal status for the church. In 1976, at the invitation of Paul VI (who had read his *Love and Responsibility* and used it in drafting *Humanae vitae*), he delivered the traditional course of Lenten addresses to the pope and the papal household (published in English in 1979 as *Sign of Contradiction*). He was thus a well-known and widely respected personality when at the conclave of Oct. 1978, no consensus having been found for any Italian candidate, the cardinals looked further afield and, apparently at the eighth ballot, elected him

at the relatively youthful age of fifty-eight by an overwhelming majority (103 out of 109 votes). As with JOHN PAUL I, whose name he adopted, there was no coronation; the inauguration of his ministry as 'universal pastor of the church' (a characteristic new title) took place in St Peter's Square on 21 Oct.

Addressing the cardinals on 17 Oct., the new pope pledged himself unreservedly 'to promoting, with prudent but encouraging action', the exact fulfilment of Vatican Council II. On 18 Oct. he told the ambassadors that, as he saw it, his role was to be 'the witness of a universal love'; politically the holy see sought nothing for itself but only that believers might be allowed true freedom of worship. His first encyclical, *Redemptor hominis* (Mar. 1979), was an eloquent statement of Christian humanism: true freedom is found, and human dignity best preserved, in the church. His second, *Dives in misericordia* (Dec. 1980), developed the same theme, calling on men to show mercy to one another in an increasingly threatened world. On 13 May 1981, while being driven in a jeep in St Peter's Square, he was shot and seriously wounded by a young Turk, Mehmet Ali Agca, underwent major surgery, and was convalescent until Oct. 1981. In his third encyclical, *Laborem exercens* (Sept. 1981), which he revised while recovering and which commemorated the anniversary of LEO XIII's *Rerum novarum*, he called for a new economic order, neither capitalist nor Marxist, but based on the rights of workers and the dignity of labour; he insisted on the primacy of man over things. A fourth, *Slavorum apostoli* (July 1985), appealed to the peoples of communist eastern Europe to resolve divisions on the basis of a common culture and religion. But John Paul's favourite, immensely successful, method of impressing his message on the world has been to make spectacular, skilfully organized journeys by air to countries near and far. In Jan. 1979 he went to South America to open the Latin American episcopal conference at Puebla, Mexico, and from 2 to 10 June he returned to

Poland, taking part in the ninth centenary of its patron St Stanislaus. Since then each year of his pontificate has been highlighted by several such pilgrimages, which have placed an immense strain on the Vatican administration but have emphasized the global mission of the papacy and enabled it to display *collegiality in action. Among the numerous journeys undertaken since becoming pope (he had made twenty-seven by August 1985) may be mentioned those to Turkey in 1979, during which he and the ecumenical patriarch attended each other's liturgies, without however sharing communion; to Britain in 1982, the first visit ever paid to it by a pope; to Fátima, Portugal, in 1982, to give thanks to the BVM for deliverance from assassination (he later presented her with the bullet); to Central America in 1983, when he pleaded for non-violent solutions to social problems; to the Far East, including South Korea, Papua New Guinea, and Thailand, in 1984; to Holland, where he received a cool, sometimes hostile, reception from progressive Catholics, in May 1985; and to seven states in Africa in August 1985. These visits followed a common pattern, with the pope kissing the ground on arrival, saying mass in front of enormous crowds, preaching sermons carefully attuned to the local situation, and giving full rein to his skills as an actor and to his outgoing personality.

In Feb. 1984 John Paul concluded with the Italian government a revision of the *Lateran Treaty (1929); this revision formalized the separation of church and state in Italy and, among other concessions, provided that Rome should no longer be recognized as a 'sacred city'. In Jan. 1982 he saw the UK representative to the holy see raised, for the first time, from the rank of minister to that of ambassador. At consistories on 2 Feb. 1983 and 25 May 1985 he created forty-six new cardinals; as well as continuing Paul VI's policy of making the sacred college more international, he endeavoured by his promotions to streng-

then the church in countries with Marxist regimes. Few popes have had such wide-ranging intellectual equipment as John Paul, and none has had such a far-reaching impact. His distinctive approach in politics, theology, and ethics has been conservative. Thus from the Puebla conference in 1979 to the discussion between Leonardo Boff, the Brazilian theologian, and Cardinal Josef Ratzinger in Sept. 1984 he has been resolutely opposed to 'liberation theology', which accepts the idea of class struggle and calls on the church to ally itself with the oppressed, as involving it too closely in political action. As early as Dec. 1979 the Dutch professor, Edward Schillebeeckx, was summoned to Rome to explain heterodox views on Christology, while with the pope's express approval the German bishops in 1980 withdrew the licence of Hans Küng, of Tübingen, to teach Catholic theology. Other warnings against dangerous trends in theology have been frequent, and he has reminded believers from time to time of the reality of heaven and hell, and of the centrality in Christian devotion of the eucharist and of the BVM. He has taken energetic steps to restore the morale and effectiveness of the Society of Jesus. In Chicago in 1980 he confirmed the church's traditional teaching on marriage, contraception, abortion, and homosexuality, and pointedly endorsed Paul VI's *Humanae vitae*. He has consistently maintained this posture throughout his reign, and has set his face against proposals to relax the rule of priestly celibacy. While his stance has disappointed progressives, others regard him as having restored to the church the sense of direction it seemed in danger of losing in the latter years of Paul VI's pontificate.

AAS 70, 906– ; P. Hebblethwaite, *The Year of Three Popes* (London, 1978); *Introducing John Paul II* (London, 1982); Lord Longford, *Pope John Paul II: an Authorized Biography* (London, 1982); P. Johnson, *Pope John Paul II* (London, 1982); John Paul II, *Collected Poems* (ET by J. Peterkiewicz, London, 1982).

APPENDIX
Pope Joan

From the mid-13th to the 17th cent. the tradition that there had been a female pope, commonly but not invariably named Joan, at some date in the 9th, 10th, or 11th cent., was almost universally accepted; it was still furnishing ammunition to attackers of the papacy and the Roman church in the late 19th cent. The story first appears, between 1240 and 1250, in the *Universal Chronicle of Metz* attributed to the Dominican Jean de Mailly, according to which Victor III (d. 1087) was succeeded by a talented woman who, disguised as a man, had worked her way up in the curia as a notary, and had eventually been promoted cardinal. She was betrayed when, mounting her horse, she gave birth to a child, and was ignominiously tied to the horse's tail, dragged round the city, and then stoned to death. The Dominican Stephen de Bourbon (d. *c.*1262) and the Franciscan of Erfurt who wrote (*c.*1265) the *Chronicon minor* give broadly similar accounts of the affair of the 'popess', the one placing it *c.*1100 and the other *c.*915. The tale was given definitive form, however, and very wide diffusion by the later editions of the immensely popular and influential *Chronicle of Popes and Emperors* by the Polish Dominican Martin of Troppau (d. 1297). According to these, Leo IV (d. 855) was succeeded by one John Anglicus, who reigned two years, seven months, and four days, but was in fact a woman. A native of Mainz, she went as a girl, dressed in a man's clothes but escorted by her lover, to Athens, had a brilliant student career there, and then settled in Rome, where her lectures attracted such distinguished audiences and her life was so edifying that she was unanimously elected pope. Her imposture was finally exposed when, riding in procession from St Peter's to the Lateran, she gave birth to a child in a narrow street between

the Colosseum and S. Clemente. She died on the spot and was buried there; because of the shameful episode, popes thereafter studiously avoided traversing the street. While Martin gives her name as John (i.e. Joan or Joanna in the feminine), other accounts call her Agnes, Gilberta, or Jutta, or leave her nameless.

The story, often embellished with fantastic details, was accepted without question in Catholic circles for centuries. It was taken up by humanists like Petrarch (d. 1374) and Boccaccio (d. 1375), and influenced iconography; Joan figures among the busts of popes placed *c.*1400 in Siena cathedral. Critics of the papal claims (e.g. John Hus at the council of Constance in 1415) were able to exploit the story without being contradicted. One enthusiastic writer, Mario Equicola of Alvito (near Caserta: d. 1525), even argued that Providence had used Joan's elevation to demonstrate the equality of women with men. Catholic criticism of the legend became increasingly vocal from the middle of the 16th cent., but it was a French Protestant, David Blondel (1590–1655), who effectively demolished it in treatises published at Amsterdam in 1647 and 1657. It scarcely needs painstaking refutation today, for not only is there no contemporary evidence for a female pope at any of the dates suggested for her reign, but the known facts of the respective periods make it impossible to fit one in. The origin of the story, however, has never been satisfactorily explained. Its kernel is generally taken to be an ancient Roman folk-tale which was blown up by a number of circumstances needlessly taken to be suspicious—e.g. the deliberate avoidance of a certain street by papal processions (probably because of its narrowness), the discovery in it of an enig-

POPE JOAN

matic statue taken to represent a woman suckling a child and of a puzzling inscription near by which could be twisted to support the legend, and the popular belief (from the late 13th cent.) that after his election a pope had to undergo tests that he was really of the male sex. It is likely, too, that the recollection that in the 10th cent. the papacy had been dominated by unscrupulous women like Theodora the Elder, Marozia, and the younger Theodora, helped to give it currency.

MGSS 22, 428 (Martin of Troppau); 24, 184 (*Chron. minor*); 514 (Jean de Mailly); J. J. I. von Döllinger, *Die Papstfabeln des Mittelalters* (2nd edn., Stuttgart, 1890); É. Vacandard, *Études de critique et d'histoire religieuse* (Paris, 1909–23), 4, 13–39; *EC* 6, 482–5 (F. Antonelli).

INDEX

(names of antipopes in italics)

331

INDEX

Aquileia, synod of (381), 35
Aquinas, Thomas, *see* Thomas Aquinas
archives, papal, 33 f., 56, 57, 107, 212, 219;
    see also Vatican archives
Argrinus of Langres, 117
Arians, Arianism, *28*, 29, 30, 31, 32, 33, 45,
    48, 50, 51, 58, 59
Aribert of Milan, 143
Aristotle, 190, 200, 275
Arius 28, 29
Arles, first council of, 27, 28; vicariate of,
    38, 40, 61, 67; primatial rights of, 51,
    164
Armenian Catholics, 242, 270, 282, 305,
    307
Arnauld, Antoine, 282
Arnold of Brescia, 173, 174
Arnoul of Rheims, 133, 134, 135, 137
Arnulf, 113, 114, 115, 117
Arsenius, 105, 106
Asclepiodotus, 13
Askidas, 61
Assemani, J. S., 292, 296
Assumption of BVM, 105, 319
Athalaric, 55, 58
Athanasius of Alexandria, 29, 30, 31, 32
Athanasius of Naples, 112, 118
Athenagoras I, 322, 323
Attila, 44
Aubert, Étienne, Innocent VI, 221
Augsburg, diet of, 264; peace of, 265, 278
Augustine, St, 24, 25, 29, 37, 38, 40, 41,
    42, 54, 55, 62, 67, 281, 282, 295
Augustine of Canterbury, 67
Augustinus, C. Jansen's, *281*, 282, 284, 285,
    290
Augustus, 16
Aurelian, 23
Austrian Succession, War of, 297
Auxentius, 33
Auxilius, 118, 119
Avignon, 212, 214, 215, 216, 217, 218, 219,
    220, 221, 222, 223, 224, 225, 226, 227,
    228, 229, 230, 231, 232, 234, 235, 239,
    240, 242, 274; Palais Neuf, 220; Palais
    Vieux, 219
Avignon and Venaissin, enclaves of, 212,
    283, 288, 289, 299, 300, 302, 303, 304
Avitus, 54

Baden, Articles of, 308
Baius, Michael, 269
Baldwin, count, 149
Baldwin II, 195, 198
Bamberg, 138, 139, 140, 143, 145, 146, 179

Bandinelli, Orlando, Alexander III, 176
baptism by heretics, *20*, 21
Barberini, Maffeo, Urban VIII, 280
Barbo, Pietro, Paul II, 249
Barnabites, 262, 268
Baronius, Cesare, 75, 100, 125, 275, 277
Basil the Great, 22, 33
Basil I, 109, 111, 112, 113
Basil II, 142
Basiliscus, 46
Basilius (praetorian prefect), 46, 51
Basle, council of, 240, 242, 243, 244, 246,
    247, 248, 251; Compacts of, 248
Bayezid II, 252, 253
Bea, Augustin, 322
Beatific vision, 215, 216, 218
Beaufort, Pierre Roger de, Gregory XI, 225
Becket, Thomas, *see* Thomas Becket
Bede, Venerable, 11
Belisarius, 60
Bellarmine, Robert, 275, 277, 317
Benedict, St, 67, 117, 124, 132, 157, 207
Benedictines, Benedictine order, 207, 218,
    223, 303, 307
benefices, reserved, 197, 213, 220, 223,
    239, 243
Benevento, treaty of, *175*, 180
Beorhtweald, 83, 84
Berengar I, 118, 120, 121, 122
Berengar II, 126, 127
Berengar of Tours, *147*, 152, 156, 159
Bernard of Clairvaux, 166, 167, 168, 169,
    170, 171, 172, 173, 180, 184
Bernardino of Siena, 240, 245
Bertrada, 95
Besançon, diet of, *175*, 176, 185
Bessarion, John, 246, 250
Bible Societies, 304, 306, 307
Biblical Commission, 312
Birinus, 70
Biscop, Benedict, 76
Bismarck, Otto von, 310
Blackwell, George, 276, 277
Blondel, David, 329
Bobbio, 69, 70, 136
Bobo, Giacinto, Celestine III, 184
Boccaccio, 329
Boccapecci, Teobaldo, Celestine (II), 167
Boccasino, Niccolò, Benedict XI, 210
Boethius, 54, 55
Boff, Leonardo, 328
Bohemond I, 161
Bolsena, miracle of, 196
Bonaventura, 197, 199, 202, 205, 250, 272
Boncompagni, Ugo, Gregory XIII, 269

332

INDEX

INDEX

Mamertus, 45
Mammolo, privilege of Ponte, *161*, 170
Manfred, 193, 194, 195, 196
Manichaeans, Manichees, 43, 51
Mantua, synod of, 153, 154
Manuel I Comnenus, 176
Marcel, Gabriel, 326
Marcellus of Ancyra, 29, 30
Marcia, 12, 13
Marcian of Arles, 20
Marcion, 10
Maria of Aragón, 241
Maria Theresa, 297, 300
Maronites, 270, 282, 296
Marozia, 120, 122, 123, 124, 330
marriage, clerical, 140, 150, 152, 155, 157,
    159, 267, 270
marriage, doctrine of, 150, 297, 306, 311,
    317, 328
marriages, mixed, 297, 306, 308, 324
Marscilles, treaty of, 233
Marsilius of Padua, 215
Martial of Limoges, 142
Martin of Troppau, 329
Martyrology of Ado, 10, 12, 39, 43, 87, 89
Martyrology of St Jerome, 15, 19, 25, 31,
    39
Marxism, 321, 327
Mary I, 263, 265
Masci, Girolamo, Nicholas IV, 205
mass, canon of, 7, 8, 9, 22, 37, 321
Mastai-Ferretti, Giovanni Maria, Pius IX,
    309
Mater et magistra, 321
Matilda (empress), 161, 171
Matilda of Tuscany, Matildine estates, 149,
    158, *168*, 180, 181, 184, 187
Maurice, 66, 67, 68
Maxentius, 25, 26
Maximilian I (Bavaria), 279, 282
Maximilian I (emperor), 255, 256, 257, 258
Maximilian II (emperor), 269
Maximinus Thrax, 15, 16
Maximus of Alexandria, 23
Maximus the Confessor, 73, 76
Maximus (usurper), 35
mayor of the palace, 88, *90*
Mazarin, Jules, 281, 283, 284, 285
Medici, Alessandro Ottaviano de', Leo XI,
    276
Medici, Giovanni Angelo, Pius IV, 266
Medici, Giovanni de', Leo X, 256
Medici, Giulio de', Clement VII, 259
Medici family, 257, 259, 260, 261, 266,
    275, 276

Meerssen, treaty of, 109
Mehmet II, 248, 249, 250
Meletius, 33
Melfi, synod of (1059), 152; (1089), 159
Mellitus, 67, 69, 70
'Memorial of the Apostles', 6
Menas, 59, 61
mendicant orders, 192, 194, 203, 208, 210,
    212, 218, 222, 237, 250
Mercury, John II, 58
Merry del Val, R., 313, 315
Methodius, 110, 111, 113
Metternich, Klemens von, 307
Michael II, 101
Michael III, 108
Michael VII, 153, 156
Michael VIII Palaeologus, 195, 196, 197,
    198, 199, 201, 202, 203
Michael of Cesena, 214, 215, 216
Mieszko I, 133
Migliorati, Cosimo Gentile de', Innocent
    VII, 234
Migniano, treaty of, *168*, 171
Milan, convention of, 26
Milan, council of, 30
Mincius, John, *Benedict X*, 150
Mirandola, Pico della, 252
Misenus, 48, 49
missal, revision of, 266, 267, 268, 275, 314,
    321
missions, missionary policy, 254, 261, 263,
    271, 272, 278, 279, 280, 281, 282, 292,
    293, 296, 298, 300, 307, 308, 312, 316,
    317
Mit brennender Sorge, 317
modalism, *13*, 14
Modernism, *313*, 314, 316, 318, 324
Molina, Luis de; Molinism, 276, 278
Molinos, Miguel de, *287*, 289
monarchical episcopate, 6, 7, 8, 9, 10
Mongols, 192, 193, 194
Mongos, Peter, 46, 47, 49
Monumento, Leone de, 183
monophysitism, monophysites, *44*, 45, 46,
    47, 49, 53, 54, 56, 58, 59, 62, 71, 73, 77,
    242
monothelitism, monothelites, *71*, 72, 73, 74,
    75, 76, 77, 78, 79, 80, 86
Montanism, Montanus, *11*, 13, 18
Monte, Giovanni Maria Ciocchi del, Julius
    III, 262
Monte Cassino, 87, 117, 125, 143, 149,
    150, 151, 155, 157, 158, 163, 164, 166,
    171, 173, 185, 208
Montesquieu, Charles de, 298

341

INDEX

Romanus I, 123
Romanus of Tusculum, John XIX, 141
Rome, sack of (410), 38; (455), 44, 45;
 (546), 62; (1527), 260, 264, 265;
 occupation of (1808), 303; (1870), 309;
 (1943), 319
Romulus Augustulus, 45
Roncaglia, diet of, 175
Roncalli, Angelo Giuseppe, John XXIII, 320
Roosevelt, Theodore, 313
Rospigliosi, Giulio, Clement IX, 284
Rose of Lima, 286
Rota, 217, 221, 267, 275, 281, 285, 288,
 298
Rotfield, 102
Rousseau, J.-J., 299
Rovere, Francesco della, Sixtus IV, 250
Rovere, Giuliano della, Julius II, 255
Rudolf I of Habsburg, 198, 199, 201, 202,
 203, 204, 205, 206
Rudolf II (emperor), 277
Rudolf Glaber, 142
Rufinus, 21, 36
Rufus of Thessalonica, 37, 40, 41
Rupert III, 231, 234, 235, 236
Russian Revolution, 316
Ryswick, treaty of, 291

Sabellius, Sabellianism, 13, 29, 33
Sacred Heart of Jesus, 299, 310, 312
Saint-Basle, synod of, 133, 134, 137
S. Clemente, 8, 38, 58, 105, 160, 329
S. Germano, treaty of, 189
Sta Maria Maggiore, 31, 33, 34, 41, 45, 50,
 52, 75, 78, 91, 106, 151, 183, 188, 205,
 206
St Paul's basilica, 28, 35, 36, 46, 47, 83, 93,
 104, 106, 110, 124, 125, 130, 139, 154
St Peter's, 28, 44, 45, 46, 49, 50, 51, 52,
 54, 55, 56, 57, 58, 59, 62, 63, 64, 65, 67,
 68, 71, 72, 75, 77, 80, 81, 83, 85, 88, 89,
 93, 94, 96, 97, 98, 99, 100, 103, 104,
 105, 106, 108, 110, 113, 115, 116, 120,
 121, 126, 127, 128, 132, 133, 134, 138,
 140, 142, 148, 158, 160, 161, 163, 164,
 168, 173, 175, 176, 179, 189, 197, 202,
 213, 218, 224, 228, 245, 248, 254, 256,
 258, 261, 263, 272, 276, 278, 280, 282,
 284, 301, 302, 310, 311, 316, 320, 321,
 326, 327, 329; excavations under, 6, 11,
 320
S. Sebastiano, 6, 43
Saladin, 183
Salazar, A. de Oliveira, 319
Sancho V, 153

Sangier, Marc, 314
Saracens, 103, 104, 109, 110, 111, 112,
 113, 118, 121, 141, 158
Sardinia, 15, 16, 17, 70, 80, 140, 191, 292,
 294, 302, 311, 324
Sarpi, Paolo, 277
Sarto, Giuseppe Melchiorre, Pius X, 313
Savelli, Cencio, Honorius III, 188
Savelli, Giacomo, Honorius IV, 204
Savonarola, Girolamo, 254
Sayings of the Elders, 63, 64
Scheler, Max, 326
Schillebeeckx, Edward, 328
Schmalkaldic League, 262
Scolari, Paolo, Clement III, 183
Scottish church, 184, 312
Scythian monks, 53, 54, 56
Sebastian, Passion of St, 24
secretary of state, papal, 147, 267, 268, 270,
 274, 282, 283, 284, 286, 289, 294, 298,
 300, 301, 302, 303, 304, 305, 306, 307,
 309, 311, 312, 313, 315, 317, 318, 320,
 322
Seligenstadt, synod of, 141
Semi-Pelagianism, 41, 54, 55
Sentences, Peter Lombard's, 199, 236, 237,
 258
Sentences of Sextus, The, 21
Serdica, council of, 29, 30, 39, 40
Sergius I, 71, 72
Sergius II, 139
Sergius of Damascus, 132
Severus of Antioch, 59
Sfondrati, Celestino, 291
Sfondrati, Niccolò, Gregory XIV, 273
Sforza, Francesco, 242, 244, 249
Sicco, John, John XVII, 138
Sicco of Spoleto, 130, 131
Sicilian monarchy, 159, 292, 293, 294
Sicilian Vespers, 203, 206
Sigismund (emperor), 233, 236, 238, 242,
 243
Sigismund III Vasa, 272, 275, 276
Signatura, 266, 273, 280
Simeon of Bulgaria, 122
simony, 63, 101, 104, 132, 137, 140, 144,
 145, 146, 147, 149, 150, 152, 153, 154,
 155, 157, 159, 162, 238, 241, 255, 256,
 258, 272
Simplician, 36
Sinuessa, pseudo-council of, 24
Sirmium, First Creed of, 31
Sistine chapel, 251, 261, 264, 299, 311
Skanderberg, George, 249
slavery, slave-trade, 308

345

INDEX